Software Architecture wi

Second Edition

Designing robust C++ systems with modern architectural practices

Andrey Gavrilin
Adrian Ostrowski
Piotr Gaczkowski

Software Architecture with C++

Second Edition

Portfolio Director: Kunal Chaudhari
Relationship Lead: Denim Pinto
Project Manager: K. Loganathan
Content Engineer: Richa Singh
Technical Editor: Aditya Bharadwaj
Copy Editor: Safis Editing
Indexer: Rekha Nair
Proofreader: Richa Singh
Production Designer: Ganesh Bhadwalkar
Growth Lead: Vinishka Kalra

First published: April 2021

Second edition: December 2025

Production reference: 1161225

Published by Packt Publishing Ltd.

Grosvenor House

11 St Paul's Square

Birmingham

B3 1RB, UK.

ISBN 978-1-80324-301-6

`www.packtpub.com`

I hate the way you require semicolons,
I hate the way templates confuse my mind,
I hate the way memory leaks quietly,
But most of all, I love that you let me hack reality,
With nothing but text, logic, and caffeine.

– Andrey Gavrilin

Contributors

About the authors

Andrey Gavrilin is a seasoned software engineer whose eagerness for computer games led him to explore C++, Pascal, and assembly language. He holds an MSc degree in engineering (industrial automation) and has worked across several domains, which allowed him to understand the importance of quality software architecture. His interests include system programming, embedded development, game programming, and electronics. An enthusiast of retro gaming and vintage computing, he enjoys studying how older technologies inform modern system design. These hobbies complement his professional work, providing creative inspiration and a fresh perspective on the IT evolution.

Adrian Ostrowski is a modern C++ enthusiast interested in the development of both the C++ language itself and the high-quality code written in it. A lifelong learner with over a decade of experience in the IT industry and in C++ specifically, he's always eager to share his knowledge. His past projects range from parallel computing, through fiber networking, to working on a commodity exchange's trading system.

In his spare time, Adrian used to promote music bands together with Piotr and has learned how to fly a glider. He likes riding his bicycle, going to music events, and browsing memes.

Piotr Gaczkowski has more than 10 years of experience in programming and practicing DevOps and uses his skills to improve people's lives. He likes building simple solutions to human problems, organizing cultural events, and teaching fellow professionals. Piotr is keen on automating boring activities and using his experience to share knowledge by conducting courses and writing articles about personal growth and remote work.

He has worked in the IT industry both in full-time positions and as a freelancer, but his true passion is music. When not making his skills useful at work, you can find him building communities.

About the reviewers

Deák Ferenc began his fearless journey into the realm of software development at a time when coding meant deciphering cryptic mnemonics from the pages of a magazine and manually keying them into a real ICE Felix HC-91 computer (a clone of the famous Sinclair ZX Spectrum). From these modest origins, he progressed through the rapidly shifting tides of technology, joyfully upgrading to a 386 with an EGA display. Those 16 colors left an indelible impression, binding him forever to the fascinating world of software creation.

Over the years, he has grown into a security- and safety-focused software developer with more than two decades of experience. Specializing in low-level system programming, optimization, and application safety analysis, he considers himself quite proficient in C and C++, but also skilled in Go, Java, Python, and various web technologies. His favorite areas of development include security, compilers, graphics, and networking, though he's always ready to explore new challenges as they arise. His goal is to tackle demanding software design and engineering problems while continually broadening his expertise and contributing to the ever-growing landscape of open source software. In his spare time, he channels his enthusiasm for technology into writing technical articles for various programming magazines.

When not bound to a keyboard, he is usually found in his second-most-favored spot in the world, next to a kitchen bench, where he hopefully cooks delicious meals following traditional recipes from the hills, mountains, and forests of Transylvania.

I'd like to extend my sincere thanks to the Packt community for reaching out and inviting me to be part of this exciting journey once again. I'm also deeply grateful to the authors for introducing me to numerous tips and technologies I wasn't familiar with, many of which have broadened my perspective and inspired me to explore new directions in my own work.

Alexei Kondratiev is a mission-critical software and embedded systems engineer with 20+ years of experience in medical, automotive, Advanced Driver Assistance Systems (ADAS), and aerospace domains, specializing in low-latency and high-throughput concurrent and asynchronous C++ software development. He has a solid background in network programming and protocols, distributed systems, system and embedded programming, troubleshooting, integration with open source projects, performance analysis, and optimization.

He is currently a C++ software developer at LTA Research, an aerospace research and development company that builds experimental and certified manned airships. At LTA, he is the owner of the Soft Real-Time Embedded Linux Airship Helium Gas Cells Volume Monitoring System, Soft Real-Time Hardware Simulation System, and Soft Real-Time Dynon Avionics SkyView HDX Emulator for the Glass Cockpit Electronic Flight Instrument System R&D C++ projects.

Join us on Discord!

Read this book alongside other users, developers, experts, and the author himself.

Ask questions, provide solutions to other readers, chat with the authors via Ask Me Anything sessions, and much more. Scan the QR or visit the link to join the community.

`https://packt.link/deep-engineering-cpp`

Table of Contents

Chapter 2: Architectural Styles 33

Chapter 3: Functional and Non-Functional Requirements 57

Part 2: The Design and Development of C++ Software 95

Chapter 4: Architectural and System Design Patterns 97

Chapter 6: Design Patterns and C++ Idioms 187

Chapter 7: Building and Packaging 235

Chapter 8: Package Management 269

Chapter 9: The Future of C++ Code Reuse: Using Modules 283

Part 3: Architectural Quality Attributes 299

Chapter 10: Writing Testable Code 301

Chapter 11: Continuous Integration and Continuous Deployment 331

Chapter 12: Security in Code and Deployment 363

Chapter 13: Performance 397

Chapter 15: Interservice Communication 495

Chapter 16: Containers 557

Chapter 17: Observability 595

Chapter 18: Cloud-Native Design 617

Chapter 16: Containers 557

Chapter 17: Observability 595

Chapter 18: Cloud-Native Design 617

Preface

Modern C++ allows you to write high-performing applications in a high-level language without sacrificing readability and maintainability. There's more to software architecture than just language, though. We're going to show you how to design and build applications that are robust and scalable and that perform well.

Complete with step-by-step explanations of essential concepts, practical examples, and self-assessment questions, you will begin by understanding the importance of architecture, looking at examples that help illustrate the key ideas.

You'll learn how to use established design patterns at the level of a single application, exploring how to make your applications robust, secure, performant, and maintainable. You'll then learn how to design and build higher-level services that connect multiple applications using patterns such as service-oriented architecture, microservices, containers, and serverless technology.

By the end of this book, you will understand how to build distributed services using modern C++ and associated tools to deliver solutions that your clients will recommend.

Are you interested in becoming a software architect or looking to learn more about modern trends in architecture? If so, this book should help you!

Who this book is for

Developers working with modern C++ will be able to put their knowledge to work with this practical guide to software architecture. The book takes a hands-on approach to implementation and associated methodologies that will have you up and running and productive in no time.

What this book covers

Chapter 1, Importance of Software Architecture and Principles of Great Design, looks at why we design software in the first place.

Chapter 2, Architectural Styles, covers the different approaches you can take in terms of architecture.

Chapter 3, Functional and Nonfunctional Requirements, explores understanding the needs of clients.

Chapter 4, Architectural and System Design Patterns, is all about creating effective software solutions.

Chapter 5, Leveraging C++ Language Features, gets you speaking native C++.

Chapter 6, Design Patterns and C++ Idioms, focuses on modern C++ idioms and useful code constructs.

Chapter 7, Building and Packaging, is about getting code to production.

Chapter 8, Package Management, is about Conan, a decentralized multi-platform package manager for C and C++.

Chapter 9, The Future of C++ Code Reuse: Using Modules, explains what C++ modules are.

Chapter 10, Writing Testable Code, teaches you how to find bugs before clients do.

Chapter 11, Continuous Integration and Continuous Deployment, introduces the modern way of automating software releases.

Chapter 12, Security in Code and Deployment, is where you will learn how to ensure that your systems are difficult to compromise.

Chapter 13, Performance, looks at performance (of course!). C++ should be fast—can it be even faster?

Chapter 14, Architecture of Distributed Systems, dives into various aspects of distributed systems.

Chapter 15, Interservice Communication, refers to the mechanisms and techniques used by services for communication and data sharing.

Chapter 16, Containers, gives you a unified interface to build, package, and run applications.

Chapter 17, Observability, provides powerful insights into services and systems with logging, monitoring, and tracing tools.

Chapter 18, Cloud-Native Design, goes beyond traditional infrastructure to explore cloud-native design.

To get the most out of this book

The code examples in this book are mostly written for GCC 14+. They should work with Clang 19+ or Microsoft Visual C++ 19.40+ as well, though certain features of C++20 and C++23 may be missing in older versions of the compilers.

The examples were compiled and run on Linux (GCC, Clang/Ubuntu, Manjaro), macOS (Clang), and Windows (MSVC), but the chapters on Docker, Podman, and Kubernetes require Linux cross-compilation to build and run containers. Recommendations to prepare a development environment are in the GitHub repository at `https://github.com/PacktPublishing/Software-Architecture-with-Cpp-2E/tree/main/devenv_readme`.

The examples in this edition are based on the Drogon framework, a high-speed web framework also used in game development and embedded programming. The first edition of this book used Microsoft's C++ REST SDK, but that project is no longer recommended in new projects because it is in maintenance mode.

According to TechEmpower's benchmarks (`https://www.techempower.com/benchmarks`), high-speed alternatives to this framework include Lithium, userver, Cutelyst, ffead-cpp, and cinatra. If high speed is not the main criterion, it makes sense to consider cpp-httplib, Poco, Seastar, Oat+, Boost, Crow, Pistache, Qt, Restbed, Wt, TreeFrog, and Restinio. You might also explore CppMicroServices, Nui, webpp, or cppcms.

Drogon provides a fully asynchronous programming mode and flexible routing. It supports cookies and built-in sessions, filter chains, middleware, plugins, file downloads and uploads, pipelining, Gzip and Brotli compression transmission, JSON requests and responses, **aspect-oriented programming** (**AOP**), and C++ coroutines. The main program, controllers, and views can be completely decoupled.

Drogon also includes a built-in database read/write engine compatible with PostgreSQL, MySQL/MariaDB, SQLite, and Redis, as well as an **object-relational mapping** (**ORM**) layer. The `drogon_ctl` command reads database tables to generate corresponding models, and can optionally create projects, controllers, filters, views, models, and stress-testing scaffolding.

Drogon's server-side rendering is handled by **C++ Server Pages** (**CSP**), similar to JSP, ASP, PHP, Jinja, or Go templates. The framework is based on a non-blocking I/O network library—Trantor—and supports HTTPS (OpenSSL) and WebSocket communication (server and client).

Drogon is cross-platform and compiles on Linux, macOS, FreeBSD, OpenBSD, HaikuOS, and Windows, supporting both x86-64 and ARM processor architectures.

If you are using the digital version of this book, we advise you to type the code yourself or access the code via the GitHub repository (link available in the next section). Doing so will help you avoid any potential errors related to the copying and pasting of code.

Download the example code files

The code bundle for the book is hosted on GitHub at `https://github.com/PacktPublishing/Software-Architecture-with-Cpp-2E`. We also have other code bundles from our rich catalog of books and videos available at `https://github.com/PacktPublishing`. Check them out!

Download the color images

We also provide a PDF file that has color images of the screenshots/diagrams used in this book. You can download it here: `https://packt.link/gbp/9781803243016`.

Conventions used

There are a number of text conventions used throughout this book.

`CodeInText`: Indicates code words in text, database table names, folder names, filenames, file extensions, pathnames, dummy URLs, user input, and Twitter handles. For example: "The implicitly created temporary `Array` object will be shallow-copied."

A block of code is set as follows:

```
Array<int> array{};
array = {1, 2, 3, 4, 5};
Array copy_array{array};
```

Any command-line input or output is written as follows:

```
Resource acquired
the door into summer
```

```
ABCDEFGHIJKLMNOPQRST
abcdefghijklmnopqrst
Resource released
```

Bold: Indicates a new term, an important word, or words that you see on the screen. For instance, words in menus or dialog boxes appear in the text like this. For example: "**Enterprise architecture** deals with the whole company or even a group of companies."

Warnings or important notes appear like this.

Tips and tricks appear like this.

> *Quotes appear like this.*

Get in touch

Feedback from our readers is always welcome.

General feedback: If you have questions about any aspect of this book or have any general feedback, please email us at `customercare@packt.com` and mention the book's title in the subject of your message.

Errata: Although we have taken every care to ensure the accuracy of our content, mistakes do happen. If you have found a mistake in this book, we would be grateful if you reported this to us. Please visit `http://www.packt.com/submit-errata`, click **Submit Errata**, and fill in the form.

Piracy: If you come across any illegal copies of our works in any form on the internet, we would be grateful if you would provide us with the location address or website name. Please contact us at `copyright@packt.com` with a link to the material.

If you are interested in becoming an author: If there is a topic that you have expertise in and you are interested in either writing or contributing to a book, please visit `http://authors.packt.com/`.

Share your thoughts

Once you've read *Software Architecture with C++*, we'd love to hear your thoughts! Scan the QR code below to go straight to the Amazon review page for this book and share your feedback.

https://packt.link/r/1803243015

Your review is important to us and the tech community and will help us make sure we're delivering excellent quality content.

Part 1

Concepts and Components of Software Architecture

This part introduces you to the basics of software architecture, demonstrating effective approaches to its design and documentation.

This part contains the following chapters:

- *Chapter 1, Importance of Software Architecture and Principles of Great Design*
- *Chapter 2, Architectural Styles*
- *Chapter 3, Functional and Nonfunctional Requirements*

1

Importance of Software Architecture and Principles of Great Design

The purpose of this introductory chapter is to show what role software architecture plays in software development. It will focus on the key aspects to keep in mind when designing the architecture of a C++ solution. We'll discuss how to design efficient code with convenient and functional interfaces. We'll also show how the domain-driven approach complements Agile principles and guides both code and architecture.

In this chapter, we'll cover the following topics:

- Understanding software architecture
- The importance of proper architecture
- The fundamentals of good architecture
- Developing architecture using Agile principles
- The philosophy of C++
- Following the SOLID and DRY principles
- Coupling and cohesion

Getting the most out of this book – get to know your free benefits

Unlock exclusive **free** benefits that come with your purchase, thoughtfully crafted to supercharge your learning journey and help you learn without limits.

Here's a quick overview of what you get with this book:

Next-gen reader

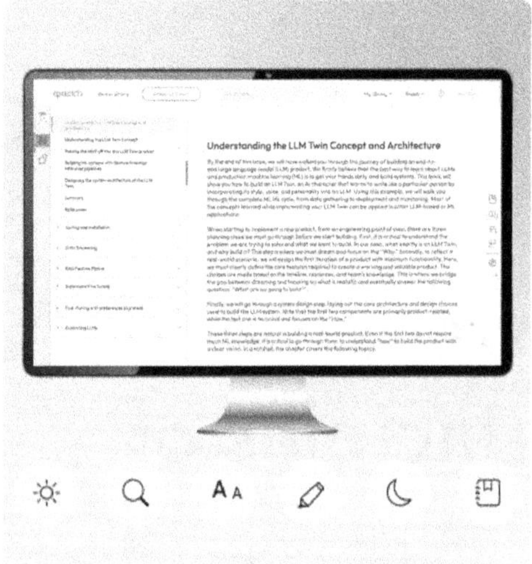

Figure 1.1: Illustration of the next-gen Packt Reader's features

Our web-based reader, designed to help you learn effectively, comes with the following features:

- Multi-device progress sync: Learn from any device with seamless progress sync.
- Highlighting and notetaking: Turn your reading into lasting knowledge.
- Bookmarking: Revisit your most important learnings anytime.
- Dark mode: Focus with minimal eye strain by switching to dark or sepia mode.

Interactive AI assistant (beta)

Figure 1.2: Illustration of Packt's AI assistant

Our interactive AI assistant has been trained on the content of this book, to maximize your learning experience. It comes with the following features:

- Summarize it: Summarize key sections or an entire chapter.
- AI code explainers: In the next-gen Packt Reader, click the Explain button above each code block for AI-powered code explanations.

Note: The AI assistant is part of next-gen Packt Reader and is still in beta.

DRM-free PDF or ePub version

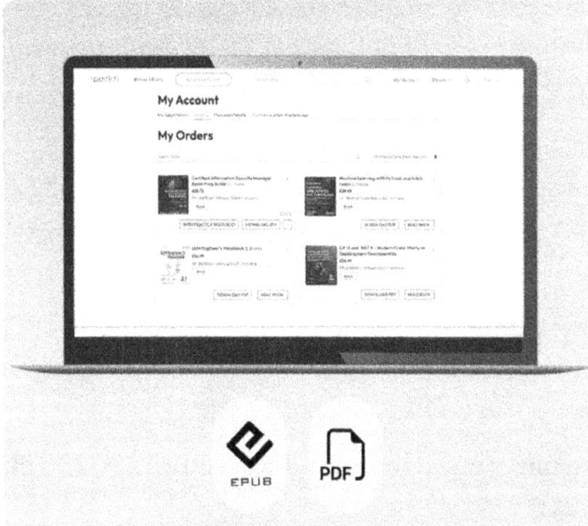

Figure 1.3: Free PDF and ePub

Learn without limits with the following perks included with your purchase:

- Learn from anywhere with a DRM-free PDF copy of this book.
- Use your favorite e-reader to learn using a DRM-free ePub version of this book.

Technical requirements

To play with the code from this chapter, you'll need the following:

- A Git client for checking out the book's repository
- A C++23-compliant compiler
- The GitHub link for code snippets: `https://github.com/PacktPublishing/Software-Architecture-with-Cpp-2E/tree/main/Chapter01`

Understanding software architecture

Let's begin by defining what software architecture is. When you create an application, library, or any software component, you need to think about how the elements you write will look and how they will interact with each other. This arrangement of elements and their interactions defines software architecture. In other words, you're designing different elements and their relationships with their surroundings.

Just like with urban architecture, it's important to think about the bigger picture so as not to end up in a haphazard state. Thus, the architecture of a software system is a metaphor similar to the architecture of a building; it is a set of important decisions about the organization of a software system. On a small scale, every single building may look okay, but they may not fit together well. Similarly, while software architecture aims to create a well-structured system, software development might progress in unexpected ways.

Keep in mind that whether you put thought into it or not, when writing software, you are creating an architecture. Therefore, avoid **accidental architectures**—those that arise without a clear strategy—as this can disrupt your IT systems.

On the other hand, **emerging architectures**—those that emerge gradually from the multitude of design decisions—are inevitable as systems grow. Over time, they become explicitly identified and are implemented intentionally after proving themselves.

So, what exactly should you be creating if you want to mindfully define the architecture of your solution? The Software Engineering Institute has this to say:

> *The software architecture of a system is the set of structures needed to reason about the system, which comprise software elements, relations among them, and properties of both.*

In the following section, we will discuss different types of architectures and explore how software architecture fits within a broader context. A clear understanding of the architecture type helps in correctly identifying the elements involved and defining the scope of work instead of just hopping into writing code.

Different ways to look at architecture

There are several ways to look at architecture, each with a different scope:

- **Enterprise architecture** deals with the whole company or even a group of companies. It takes a holistic approach and is concerned about the strategy of whole enterprises. When thinking about enterprise architecture, you should be looking at how all the systems in a company behave and cooperate with each other. It's concerned with the alignment between business and IT.
- **Solution architecture** is less abstract than its enterprise counterpart. It stands somewhere in the middle between enterprise and software architecture. Usually, solution architecture is concerned with one specific system and the way it interacts with its surroundings. A solution architect needs to come up with a way to fulfill a specific business need, usually by designing a whole software system or modifying existing ones.
- **Software architecture** is even more concrete than solution architecture. It concentrates on a specific project, the technologies it uses, and how it interacts with other projects. A software architect is interested in the internals of the project's components.
- **Infrastructure architecture** is, as the name suggests, concerned with the infrastructure that the software will use. It defines the deployment environment and strategy, how the application will scale, failover handling, site reliability, and other infrastructure-oriented aspects.

Solution architecture is based on both software and infrastructure architectures to satisfy the business requirements. Later in this chapter, we will talk about key principles of software architecture to prepare you for both small- and large-scale architecture design. Let's now discuss another critical aspect of understanding software architecture.

Communication and culture

The focus of this book is software architecture. Why would we want to mention communication and culture in a book around software, then? If you think about it, all software is written *by* people *for* people. The human aspect is prevalent, and yet we often fail to admit it.

As an architect, your role won't be just about figuring out the best approach to solving a given problem. You'll also have to communicate your proposed solution to your team members. Often, the choices you make will result from previous discussions.

These are the reasons communication and team culture also play a role in software architecture.

Conway's Law states that the architecture of the software system reflects the organization that's working on it. This means that building great products requires building great teams and understanding that social interaction impacts the success or failure of projects.

Development culture can be compared to an ecosystem. It is a daily task and cannot be introduced by decree. The culture can become destructive if you don't take care of it. Poor management can degrade even a well-established team culture within an organization.

Thus, if you want to be a great architect, developing people skills may be as important as developing technical ones.

Now that we have looked at both the technical and social aspects of software architecture, let's answer one fundamental question: why is architecture important?

The importance of proper architecture

A better question would be: why is caring about your architecture important? As we mentioned earlier, regardless of whether you put conscious effort into building it or not, your software will end up with some kind of architecture. If, after several months or even years of development, you still want your software to retain its qualities, you need to take some steps earlier in the process. If you won't think about your architecture, chances are it won't ever present the required qualities.

So, in order for your product to meet the business requirements (formal descriptions of business-related objectives and expectations) and attributes such as performance, maintainability, and scalability, you need to take care of its architecture, and it is best if you do it as early as you can in the process. Failing to do so could result in the issues discussed in the following two subsections.

Technical debt

Even after you have done the initial work and have a specific architecture in mind, you need to continuously monitor how the system evolves and whether it still aligns with its users' needs, as those may also change during the development and lifetime of your software.

Technical debt (sometimes also called software decay, software erosion, or software rot) occurs when the implementation decisions don't correspond to the **intentional architecture**. It is a metaphor describing the trade-offs between short-term gain and long-term stability of software development.

Technical debt could result from a variety of factors, such as unclear project requirements, poorly written or hastily written code, hardcoded values, lack of documentation, outdated documentation, lack of testing, insufficient testing, lack of code reviews, deprecated libraries or frameworks, deferred upgrades, or accumulated bug debt.

Accidental architecture

Failing to track whether the development adheres to the chosen architecture or failing to intentionally plan how the architecture should look will often result in a so-called accidental architecture, and it can happen regardless of applying best practices in other areas, such as testing, or having any specific development culture.

There are architectural anti-patterns and smells that suggest your architecture is accidental. Code resembling the big ball of mud or spaghetti code, an architectural anti-pattern that suggests a lack of structure, is the most obvious example. Having a god object, where one entity is responsible for everything at once, is another important sign of this. Altogether, if your software is getting tightly coupled with strong dependencies between software components—perhaps with circular dependencies, which occur when two or more components depend on each other—it's an important signal to put more conscious effort into how the architecture looks.

Let's now describe what an architect must understand to deliver a viable solution.

The fundamentals of good architecture

It's important to know how to recognize a good architecture from a bad one, but it's not an easy task. Recognizing anti-patterns is an important aspect of it, but for an architecture to be good, primarily, it must support delivering what's expected from the software, which involves meeting functional requirements, addressing attributes of the solution, or dealing with the constraints coming from various places. Many of these aspects can be easily derived from the architecture context.

Architecture context

The context is what an architect takes into account when designing a solid solution. It comprises requirements, assumptions, and constraints, which can come from the stakeholders, as well as the business and technical environments. It also influences the stakeholders and environments, for example, by allowing the company to enter a new market segment.

Stakeholders

Stakeholders are all the people who are somehow involved with the product. Those can be your customers, the users of your system, or the management. Communication is a key skill for every architect, and properly managing your stakeholders' needs is key to delivering what they expect and in a way they want.

Different things are important to different groups of stakeholders, so try to gather input from all those groups.

Your customers will probably care about the cost of writing and running the software, the functionality it delivers, its lifetime, its time to market, and the quality of your solution.

The users of your system can be divided into two groups: end users and administrators. The end users usually care about things such as usability, user experience, and the performance of the software. For administrators, more important aspects are user management, system configuration, security, backups, and recovery.

Finally, things that could matter for stakeholders working in management are keeping the development costs low, achieving business goals, being on track with the development schedule, and maintaining product quality.

Business and technical environments

Architecture can be influenced by the business side of the company. Important related aspects are the time to market, the rollout schedule, the organizational structure, the utilization of the workforce, and investment in existing assets.

By technical environment, we mean the technologies already used in a company or those that are, for any reason, required to be part of the solution. Other systems that we need to integrate with are also a vital part of the technical environment. The technical expertise of the available software engineers is of importance here, too: the technological decisions an architect makes can impact staffing the project, and the ratio of junior to senior developers can influence how a project should be governed. Good architecture should take all of that into account.

Equipped with all this knowledge, let's now discuss a somewhat controversial topic that you'll most probably encounter as an architect in your daily work, as it relates to a very common development methodology.

Developing architecture using Agile principles

Agile principles are concepts that encourage adaptability and efficiency in software development. The Agile Manifesto lists 12 guiding principles. You can refer to the link provided in the *Further reading* section to read about the principles. Seemingly, architecture and Agile development methodologies are in an adversarial relationship, as there are many myths around Agile methodology; these are also mentioned in a resource linked at the end of the chapter. There are a few simple principles that you should follow in order to develop your product in an Agile way while still caring about its architecture.

Agile, by nature, is iterative and incremental. This means preparing a big, upfront design is not an option in an Agile approach to architecture. Instead, a small but still reasonable upfront design should be proposed. It's best if it comes with a log of decisions with the rationale for each of them. This way, if the product vision changes, the architecture can evolve with it. To support frequent release delivery, the upfront design should then be updated incrementally. Architecture developed this way is called **evolutionary architecture**.

Thus, managing architecture doesn't require extensive documentation. In fact, documentation should cover only what's essential, as this way, it's easier to keep it up to date. It should be simple and cover only the relevant views of the system.

Also, the architect should not be considered as the single source of truth and the ultimate decision-maker. In Agile environments, it's the teams that make decisions. Having said that, it's crucial that the stakeholders are contributing to the decision-making process—after all, their points of view shape how the solution should look.

Nevertheless, an architect should remain part of the development team, as they often bring strong technical expertise and years of experience to the table. They should also take part in making estimations, resolving conflicts over software architecture, and planning the architecture changes needed before each iteration.

In order for your team to remain Agile, you should think of ways to work efficiently and only on what's important. A good idea to embrace to achieve those goals is domain-driven design.

Domain-driven design

Domain-driven design (DDD) is a term introduced by Eric Evans in his book of the same title. In essence, it's about improving communication between business and engineering by bringing the developers' attention to the domain model that primarily consists of entities and their relationships. Aligning the implementation of the software with this model often leads to designs that are easier to understand and evolve together with the model changes.

What has DDD got to do with Agile? Let's recall a part of the Agile Manifesto (2001):

> **Individuals and interactions** *over processes and tools*
>
> **Working software** *over comprehensive documentation*
>
> **Customer collaboration** *over contract negotiation*
>
> **Responding to change** *over following a plan*

So, how do DDD and Agile intersect? They have similar principles that create the basis for their integration:

- **Active stakeholder engagement:** A ubiquitous language in DDD facilitates effective communication. Similarly, Agile focuses on collaboration.
- **Flexibility and adaptability:** Agile embraces and implements changes, while DDD evolves the models to understand and represent domain specifics. Thus, both support dynamic environments.
- **Iterative development:** Agile focuses on small incremental steps of software development, and DDD refines the models as they evolve. Thus, DDD aligns with the iterative nature of Agile as well as its tendency to avoid excessive documentation.

DDD and Agile complement each other and can provide better alignment with business requirements.

In order to make the proper design decisions, you must understand the domain first. To do so, you'll need to talk to people a lot and encourage your developer teams to narrow the gap between them and businesspeople. The concepts in the code should be named after entities that are part of the ubiquitous language. It's basically the common part of business experts' jargon and technical experts' jargon. Countless misunderstandings can be caused by each of these groups using terms that the other understands differently, leading to flaws in business logic implementations and often subtle bugs. Naming things with care and using terms agreed upon by both groups can improve the clarity of the project. Having a business analyst or other business domain experts as part of the team can help a lot here.

If you're modeling a bigger system, it might be hard to make all the terms mean the same to different teams. This is because each of those teams really operates in a different context. DDD proposes the use of bounded contexts to deal with this. If you're modeling, say, an e-commerce system, you might want to think of the terms just in terms of a shopping context, but upon a closer look, you may discover that the inventory, delivery, and accounting teams actually all have their own models and terms.

Each of those bounded contexts is a different subdomain of your e-commerce domain. Ideally, each subdomain can be mapped to its own bounded context managed by a dedicated team—a part of your system with its own vocabulary. Structuring teams around specific domains is consistent with Conway's Law. It's important to set clear boundaries for such contexts when splitting your solution into smaller modules. When the boundaries are crossed, the domain models and terms may not remain relevant or acquire new meanings. Just like its context, each module has clear responsibilities, its own database schema, and its own code base. To help communicate between the teams in larger systems, you might want to introduce a context map, such as the one shown in *Figure 1.4*, which will show how the terms from different contexts relate to each other:

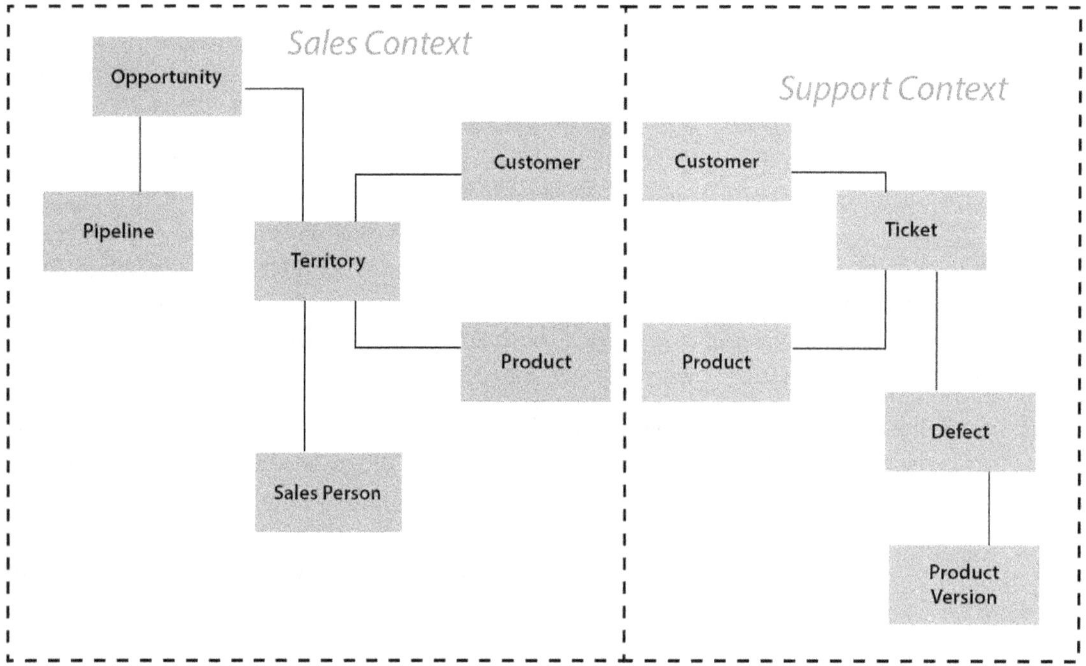

Figure 1.4: Two bounded contexts with the matching terms mapped between them (adapted from one of Martin Fowler's articles on DDD: https://martinfowler.com/bliki/BoundedContext.html)

As you now understand some of the important project-management topics, we can switch to a few more technical ones.

The philosophy of C++

Let's now move closer to the programming language we'll be using throughout this book. C++ is a multi-paradigm language that has been around for a few decades now. It has changed a lot since its inception. When C++11 came out, Bjarne Stroustrup, the creator of the language, said that it felt like a completely new language. The release of C++20 marked another milestone in the evolution of this beast, bringing a similar revolution to how we write code. C++23 is also a great addition to the language that expands on C++20 and brings new features. One thing has stayed the same during all those years, however: the language's philosophy. It can be summarized by the following key philosophies:

- You don't pay for what you don't use
- The language ensures backward compatibility across C++ standards
- It supports portability, interoperability, and cross-platform development
- What you do use is just as efficient as what you could reasonably write by hand

Not paying for what you don't use means that, for example, if you want to have your data member created on the stack, you can. Many languages allocate their objects on the heap, but it's not necessary for C++. Allocating on the heap has some cost to it—your allocator will probably have to lock a mutex for this, which can be a big burden in some types of applications. The good part is that you can easily allocate variables without dynamically allocating memory each time.

Backward compatibility in C++ is so important because there are systems that have been working for decades. If you take an old C++ project, it will most likely compile with a modern compiler, perhaps with some modifications.

Moreover, C++ was originally designed to be portable across different operating systems and processor architectures. Beyond that, C++ can interoperate with other programming languages: directly with C and through language bindings with Python, JavaScript (Node.js), Rust, Swift, Go, Java (JNI), and C#. Cross-platform development with C++ for different platforms is based on conditional compilation by applying preprocessor directives and operations.

Further, high-level abstractions are what differentiate C++ from lower-level languages such as C or assembly. They allow ideas and intent to be expressed directly in the source code, which works well with the language's type safety. Consider the following code snippet using fundamental number types for storing units of measurement:

```
struct Duration {
    int millis_;
};

void example() {
    auto d = Duration{};
    d.millis_ = 100;

    auto timeout = 1; // one second
    d.millis_ = timeout; // error: we meant 1000 milliseconds but assigned just
1
}
```

A much better idea would be to utilize the type-safety features, such as user-defined literals offered by the language, to avoid such conversion errors:

```
#include <chrono>

struct Duration {
    std::chrono::milliseconds millis_;
};
```

```
void example() {
    using namespace std::literals::chrono_literals;
    auto d = Duration{};
    // d.millis_ = 100; // compilation error, as 100 could mean anything
    d.millis_ = 100ms; // okay
    auto timeout = 1s; // or std::chrono::seconds(1);
    d.millis_ =
        timeout; // okay, converted automatically to milliseconds
}
```

The preceding abstraction can save us from mistakes and doesn't cost us anything while doing so. That's why it's called a zero-cost abstraction. Sometimes, C++ allows us to use abstractions that result in better code than if they were not used. One example of a language feature that could often result in such benefit is the `concepts` feature from C++20, covered in *Chapter 5, Leveraging C++ Language Features*.

Another great set of abstractions is the **Standard Template Library** (STL) and Boost libraries, which consist of different data structures and algorithms. Which of the following code snippets do you think is easier to read and easier to prove to be bug-free? Which expresses the intent better?

`std::string_view`, unlike `const char*`, is not a trivial type, but a class with a set of fields and methods. `const char*` is a null-terminated C string that requires either calculating the length of a string or storing the length separately from the string type.

In addition, when using modern C++ abstractions such as `std::string_view`, you do not need to reimplement algorithms such as `std::count` but can simply import them from the STL:

```
// Approach #1
int count_dots(const char *str, std::size_t len) {
    int count = 0;
    for (std::size_t i = 0; i < len; ++i) {
        if (str[i] == '.') count++;
    }
    return count;
}

// Approach #2
#include <algorithm>
#include <string_view>

int count_dots(std::string_view str) {
    return std::count(str.begin(), str.end(), '.');
}
```

Okay, the second function has a different interface, but even if it were to stay the same, we could just create a `std::string_view` object from the pointer and the length. Since `std::string_view` is such a lightweight type, your compiler should optimize it away by simply storing it in a processor register instead of memory.

Thus, using higher-level abstractions leads to simpler, more maintainable code. The C++ language has strived to provide zero-cost abstractions since its inception, so it's advisable to build upon that instead of redesigning the wheel using lower levels of abstraction.

To use these abstractions efficiently, it's important to understand how copying affects performance in C++.

Lightweight types or cheap-to-copy types, such as `std::string_view` in C++17, `std::span` in C++20, and `std::function_ref` in C++26, are designed to be passed by value. In contrast, heavier or expensive-to-copy types (in particular, `std::string` and `std::vector`) are preferred to be passed by reference because copying objects of expensive-to-copy types for passing by value can lead to a large memory footprint and a performance penalty. Therefore, passing constant references is an optimization that avoids copying while still preventing modification of the original object; however, for lightweight types, passing by value remains more efficient and literally cheap to copy.

By default, in C++, function arguments are passed by value, which means that an object passed to the function is copied and destroyed on return, but the original object should never be modified. It is easy to overlook that copy constructors are implicitly called when copying class objects, which can lead to object slicing if a subclass object is copied into a super class object that has neither the subclass member variables nor functions, leading to hard-to-detect bugs. If your class does not need copy or move constructors, delete them explicitly.

Building on the idea of writing simple and maintainable code, the next section introduces some rules and heuristics that are invaluable on the path to writing such code.

Following the SOLID and DRY principles

There are many principles to keep in mind when writing code. Regardless of whether you are writing C++ in a mostly object-oriented programming manner or not, you should keep in mind the SOLID and DRY principles.

SOLID principles

SOLID is a set of practices that can help you write cleaner and less bug-prone software. It's an acronym made from the first letters of the five concepts behind it:

- Single responsibility principle
- Open–closed principle
- Liskov substitution principle
- Interface segregation
- Dependency Inversion

Single responsibility principle

In short, the **single responsibility principle** (SRP) means each code unit should have exactly one responsibility. This means writing functions that do one thing only, creating types that are responsible for a single thing, and creating higher-level components that are focused on one aspect only.

For instance, our class manages some type of resources, such as file handles, and parses strings to find numbers:

```
class FileManagerAndParser {
public:
    int read(char* s, std::streamsize n) { return 0; }

    void write(const char* s, std::streamsize n) {}

    std::vector<int> parse(const std::string &s);
};
```

When maintaining this class and inheriting from it, you will need to track the changes of both functionalities instead of doing it separately. Moreover, some derived classes may simply not need additional functionality. Therefore, it is better to split the class into two classes, each with one responsibility:

```
class FileManager {
public:
    int read(char* s, std::streamsize n) { return 0; }

    void write(const char* s, std::streamsize n) {}
};

class Parser {
    std::vector<int> parse(const std::string &s);
};
```

Often, if you see a function with *and* in its name, it's violating the SRP and should be refactored. Another sign is when a function has comments indicating what each code block of the function does. Each such block would probably be better off as a distinct function.

The most well-known anti-pattern violating the SRP is the use of god objects that *know too much* or *do too much*. Following the SRP means decomposing complex classes that do many things at once into simple, specialized ones. This principle is intended to simplify further modifications and maintenance by reducing complexity, but excessive decomposition can be harmful as it introduces more complexity or makes maintenance more difficult.

A related topic is the **principle of least knowledge**, also known as the **Law of Demeter**. In its essence, it says that no object should know more than necessary about other objects, so it doesn't depend on any of their internals, and an object should only communicate with its immediate neighbors. Applying it leads to more maintainable code with fewer interdependencies between components. These recommendations are easy to remember:

- Each unit should only know about the units that are closely related to it
- Each unit should only talk to its immediate friends
- It shouldn't talk to strangers

The principle was proposed by Ian Holland at Northeastern University in 1987. It was named after the Demeter project, which was itself inspired by Demeter, the Greek goddess of agriculture.

Open–closed principle

The **open–closed principle** (**OCP**) states that software entities (such as functions, classes, and modules) are supposed to be both open for extension and closed for modification. *Open for extension* means that new functionalities can be added without changing the existing code. *Closed for modification* means existing software entities shouldn't be changed, as this can often cause bugs elsewhere in the system.

A great example of this principle in C++ is the `<<` operator in `std::ostream` closed for modification, but you can extend this class to support your custom class. All you need to do is overload the operator:

```
std::ostream &operator<<(std::ostream &stream, const MyPair<int, int> &mp)
{
    stream << mp.firstMember() << ", ";
    stream << mp.secondMember();
    return stream;
}
```

Note that our implementation of `operator<<` is a free (non-member) function. You should prefer those to member functions if possible, as it helps encapsulation. For more details on this, consult the article by Scott Meyers in the *Further reading* section at the end of this chapter. If you don't want to provide public access to some field that you wish to print to `ostream`, you can make `operator<<` a friend function, as shown here:

```
class MyPair {
    // ...
    friend std::ostream &operator<<(std::ostream &stream, const MyPair &mp);
};
std::ostream &operator<<(std::ostream &stream, const MyPair &mp) {
    stream << mp.first_ << ", ";
    stream << mp.second_ << ", ";
```

```
    stream << mp.secretThirdMember_;
    return stream;
}
```

Friend classes, methods, and functions in C++ are useful when a class and its friends have a special relationship and when protected and private members of the class must be hidden from other classes. In such cases, strong coupling is intentional, for example, as in the case of the << operator, or for testing private class members.

Note that this definition of OCP we discussed is slightly different from the more common one related to polymorphism. The latter is about creating base classes that can't be modified themselves but are open for others to inherit from them.

Speaking of polymorphism, let's move on to the next principle, which uses it correctly.

Liskov substitution principle

In essence, the **Liskov substitution principle** (**LSP**) states that if a function uses a pointer or reference to a base class, the function must be able to use the pointer or reference to objects of derived classes without knowing it. This rule is sometimes broken because the techniques we apply in source code do not always work in real-world abstractions.

A classic example is the relationship between squares and rectangles. Mathematically speaking, the former is a specialization of the latter, so there's an *is a* relationship between them. This tempts us to create a `Square` class that inherits from the `Rectangle` class. So, we could end up with code such as the following:

```
class Rectangle {
public:
    Rectangle(double width, double height) : width_(width), height_(height) {}
    virtual ~Rectangle() = default;
    virtual double area() { return width_ * height_; }
    virtual void setWidth(double width) { width_ = width; }
    virtual void setHeight(double height) { height_ = height; }

private:
    double width_;
    double height_;
};

class Square : public Rectangle {
public:
    Square(double side) : Rectangle(side, side) {}
    ~Square() override = default;
    double area() override { return Rectangle::area(); }
    void setWidth(double width) override {
```

```
        Rectangle::setWidth(width);
        Rectangle::setHeight(width);
    }
    void setHeight(double height) override { setWidth(height); }
};
```

Casting the derived `Square` class to its base class, `Rectangle`, results in a conceptual error:

```
Rectangle* s1 = new Rectangle(2, 3);
Rectangle* s2 = new Square(4);

s2->setWidth(5);
s2->setHeight(6);

std::cout << s1->area() << std::endl;  // 2*3=6 (expected)
std::cout << s2->area() << std::endl;  // 6*6=36, but 5*6=30
```

How should we implement the members of the `Square` class? If we want to follow the LSP and save the users of such classes from unexpected behavior, we can't: our square stops being a square if we set different values in `setWidth` and `setHeight` because the dimensions of a square are always equal. We can either stop having a square (not expressible using the preceding code) or modify the height as well, thus making the square look different than a rectangle. Therefore, the `Square` class has problematic `setWidth` and `setHeight` functions as a workaround. If the width changes, the height changes too, and vice versa, but we have the `Rectangle` base class and expect the sides to change independently.

If your code violates the LSP, it's likely that you're using an incorrect abstraction. In our case, `Square` shouldn't inherit from `Rectangle` after all. A better approach could be to make the two implement a `Shape` interface:

```
class Shape {
public:
    virtual double area() = 0;
    virtual ~Shape() = default;
};

class Rectangle : public Shape {
public:
    Rectangle(double width, double height) : width_(width), height_(height) {}
    ~Rectangle() override = default;
    double area() override { return width_ * height_; }
    virtual void setWidth(double width) { width_ = width; }
    virtual void setHeight(double height) { height_ = height; }

private:
```

```
    double width_;
    double height_;
};

class Square : public Shape {
public:
    Square(double side) : side_(side) {}
    ~Square() override = default;
    double area() override { return side_ * side_; }
    void setSide(double side) { side_ = side; }

private:
    double side_;
};
```

The conceptual error is resolved without loss of functionality since the Shape class is the base class of both classes:

```
Shape* s1 = new Rectangle(2, 3);
Square* s = new Square(4);
s->setSide(5);
Shape* s2 = s;

std::cout << s1->area() << std::endl;  // 2*3=6 (expected)
std::cout << s2->area() << std::endl;  // 5*5=25 (expected)
```

Since we are on the topic of interfaces, let's move on to the next item, which is also related to them.

Interface segregation principle

The **interface segregation principle** is just about what its name suggests. It is formulated as follows:

> *No client should be forced to depend on methods that it does not use.*
>
> *– Robert C. Martin, Agile Software Development: Principles, Patterns, and Practices, 2002*

That sounds pretty obvious, but it has some connotations that aren't that obvious. Firstly, you should prefer to have multiple smaller interfaces rather than a single big one. Secondly, when you're adding a derived class or extending the functionality of an existing one, you should think before you extend the interface that the class implements.

Let's show this with an example that violates this principle, starting with the following interface:

```
class IFoodProcessor {
public:
    virtual ~IFoodProcessor() = default;
    virtual void blend() = 0;
};
```

We could have a simple class that implements it:

```
class Blender : public IFoodProcessor {
public:
    void blend() override;
};
```

So far, so good. Now, say we want to model another, more advanced food processor, and we recklessly try to add more methods to our interface:

```
class IFoodProcessor {
public:
    virtual ~IFoodProcessor() = default;
    virtual void blend() = 0;
    virtual void slice() = 0;
    virtual void dice() = 0;
};

class AnotherFoodProcessor : public IFoodProcessor {
public:
    void blend() override;
    void slice() override;
    void dice() override;
};
```

Now, we have an issue with the `Blender` class as it doesn't support this new interface—there's no proper way to implement it. We could try to hack a workaround or throw `std::logic_error`, but a much better solution would be to just split the interface into two, each with a separate responsibility:

```
class IBlender {
public:
    virtual ~IBlender() = default;
    virtual void blend() = 0;
};

class ICutter {
public:
```

```
    virtual ~ICutter() = default;
    virtual void slice() = 0;
    virtual void dice() = 0;
};
```

Now, `AnotherFoodProcessor` can just implement both interfaces, and we don't need to change the implementation of our existing food processor.

We have one last SOLID principle left, so let's learn about it now.

Dependency inversion principle

Dependency inversion is a principle useful for decoupling by inverting the dependency relationship. In essence, it means that high-level modules should not depend on lower-level ones. Instead, both should depend on the same abstraction because classes should not rely on the implementation details of their dependencies.

C++ allows two ways to invert the dependencies between your classes. The first one is the regular polymorphic approach, and the second uses templates. Let's see how to apply both of them in practice.

Assume you're modeling a notification system that is supposed to have SMS and email channels. A simple approach would be to write it like so:

```
class SMSNotifier {
public:
    void sendSMS(const std::string &message) {
        std::cout << "SMS channel: " << message << std::endl;
    }
};

class EMailNotifier {
public:
    void sendEmail(const std::string &message) {
        std::cout << "Email channel: " << message << std::endl;
    }
};

class NotificationSystem {
public:
    void notify(const std::string &message) {
        sms_.sendSMS(message);
        email_.sendEmail(message);
    }

private:
```

```
    SMSNotifier sms_;
    EMailNotifier email_;
};
```

Each notifier is constructed by the `NotificationSystem` class. This approach is not ideal, though, since now the higher-level concept, `NotificationSystem`, depends on lower-level ones—modules for individual notifiers. Let's see how applying dependency inversion using polymorphism changes this. We can define our notifiers to depend on an interface as follows:

```
class Notifier {
public:
    virtual ~Notifier() = default;
    virtual void notify(const std::string &message) = 0;
};

class SMSNotifier : public Notifier {
public:
    void notify(const std::string &message) override { sendSMS(message); }

private:
    void sendSMS(const std::string &message) {
        std::cout << "SMS channel: " << message << std::endl;
    }
};

class EMailNotifier : public Notifier {
public:
    void notify(const std::string &message) override { sendEmail(message); }

private:
    void sendEmail(const std::string &message) {
        std::cout << "Email channel: " << message << std::endl;
    }
};
```

Now, the `NotificationSystem` class no longer has to know the implementations of the notifiers. Because of this, it has to accept them as constructor arguments:

```
class NotificationSystem {
public:
    using Notifiers = std::vector<std::unique_ptr<Notifier>>;

    explicit NotificationSystem(Notifiers notifiers)
```

```
      : notifiers_{std::move(notifiers)} {}

    void notify(const std::string &message) {
      for (const auto &notifier : notifiers_) {
        notifier->notify(message);
      }
    }

  private:
    Notifiers notifiers_;
};
```

In this approach, `NotificationSystem` is decoupled from the concrete implementations and instead depends only on the polymorphic interface named `Notifier`. The lower-level concrete classes also depend on this interface. This can help you shorten your build time and allows for much easier unit testing; now, you can easily pass mocks as arguments in your test code.

Using dependency inversion with virtual dispatch comes at a cost, however, as now we're dealing with memory allocations, and the dynamic dispatch has overhead on its own. Sometimes, C++ compilers can detect that only one implementation is being used for a given interface and will remove the overhead by performing devirtualization (often, you need to mark the function as `final` for this to work). Here, however, two implementations are used, so the performance cost of dynamic dispatch (commonly implemented as jumping through virtual method tables, or vtables for short) must be paid.

There is another way of inverting dependencies that doesn't have those drawbacks. Let's see how this can be done using a variadic template from C++11, a generic lambda from C++14, and variant, either from C++17 or a third-party library such as Abseil or Boost.

If you're not familiar with variant, it's just a class that can hold any of the types passed as template parameters. Because we're using a variadic template that can have any number of parameters, we can pass however many types we like. To call a function on the object stored in the variant, we can either extract it using `std::get` or use `std::visit` and a callable object—in our case, the generic lambda. It shows how duck-typing looks in practice.

First are the notifier classes:

```
class SMSNotifier {
public:
    void notify(const std::string &message) { sendSMS(message); }

private:
    void sendSMS(const std::string &message) {
        std::cout << "SMS channel: " << message << std::endl;
    }
};
```

```
class EMailNotifier {
public:
    void notify(const std::string &message) { sendEmail(message); }

private:
    void sendEmail(const std::string &message) {
        std::cout << "Email channel: " << message << std::endl;
    }
};
```

Now, we don't rely on an interface anymore, so no virtual dispatch will be done. The `NotificationSystem` class will still accept a vector of `Notifiers`:

```
template <typename... T>
class NotificationSystem {
public:
    using Notifiers = std::vector<std::variant<T...>>;

    explicit NotificationSystem(Notifiers notifiers)
        : notifiers_{std::move(notifiers)} {}

    void notify(const std::string &message) {
        for (auto &notifier : notifiers_) {
            std::visit([&](auto &n) { n.notify(message); }, notifier);
        }
    }

private:
    Notifiers notifiers_;
};
```

Since all our notifier classes implement the `notify` function, the code will compile and run. If your notifier classes had different methods, you could, for instance, create a function object that has overloads of `operator()` for different types.

Because `NotificationSystem` is now a template, we have to either specify the list of types each time we create it or provide a type alias. You can use the final class like so:

```
using MyNotificationSystem = NotificationSystem<SMSNotifier, EMailNotifier>;

auto sn = SMSNotifier{};
auto en = EMailNotifier{};
auto ns = MyNotificationSystem{{sn, en}};
ns.notify("Quinn, Wade, Arturo, Rembrandt");
```

This approach is guaranteed not to allocate separate memory for each notifier or use a virtual table. However, in some cases, this approach results in less extensibility, since once the variant is declared, you cannot add another type to it.

It's noteworthy that we used dependency injection in our examples. It is a software engineering technique to implement the dependency inversion principle. It's about injecting the dependencies from the outside through constructors or setters rather than creating them internally, which is beneficial to code testability (think about injecting mock objects, for example). There are frameworks for injecting dependencies across entire applications, such as [Boost].DI, Google Fruit, Hypodermic, Kangaru, and Wallaroo.

The DRY rule

DRY is short for **don't repeat yourself**. It means you should avoid code duplication and reuse it when possible. This means you should create a function or a function template if your code repeats similar operations a few times. Also, instead of creating several similar types, you should consider writing a template.

Let's look at an example where two functions implement the same functionality and see how we can eliminate the duplication using a template:

```
// two functions implement the same functionality to return minimal int and double values
int minimum(const int& x, const int& y) { return x < y ? x : y; }

double minimum(const double& x, const double& y) { return x < y ? x : y; }

// one template function replaces them to remove duplicated functionality
template <typename T>
T minimum(const T& x, const T& y) {
    return x < y ? x : y;
}

// the calls do not differ before and after applying the rule
cout << minimum(3, 5) << endl;
cout << minimum(3.0, 5.0) << endl;
```

It's also important not to reinvent the wheel when it's not necessary—that is, not to repeat others' work. Nowadays, there are dozens of well-written and mature libraries that can help you write high-quality software faster. We'd like to specifically mention a few of them: Boost, Folly, Abseil, Qt, EASTL, and BDE.

Sometimes duplicating code can have its benefits, however. One such scenario is developing microservices. Of course, it's always a good idea to follow the DRY rule inside a single microservice, but violating the DRY rule for code used in multiple services can actually be worth it. Whether we're talking about model entities or logic, it's easier to maintain multiple services when code duplication is allowed.

Imagine having multiple microservices reusing the same code for an entity. Suddenly, one of them needs to modify one field. All the other services now have to be modified as well. The same goes for dependencies of any common code. With dozens or more microservices that have to be modified because of changes unrelated to them, it's often easier for maintenance to just duplicate the code.

Since we're talking about dependencies and maintenance, let's proceed to the next section, which discusses a closely related topic.

Coupling and cohesion

Low cohesion and high coupling are usually associated with software that's difficult to test, reuse, maintain, or even understand, so it lacks many of the quality attributes usually desired to have in software.

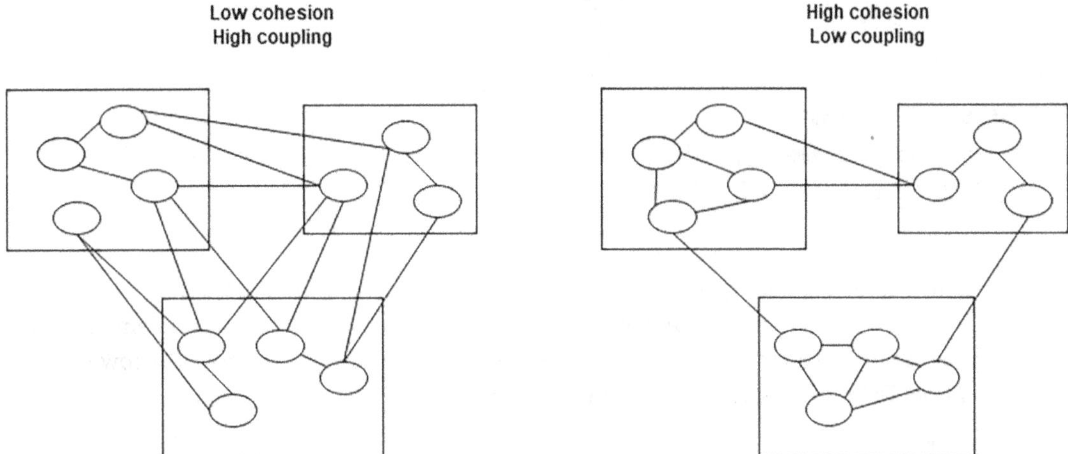

Figure 1.5: Coupling versus cohesion

Those terms often go together because one trait often influences the other, regardless of whether the unit we talk about is a function, class, module, library, service, or even a whole system. To give an example, usually, monoliths are highly coupled and have low cohesion, while distributed services tend to be at the other end of the spectrum.

Coupling

Coupling is a measure of how strongly one software unit depends on other units. A unit with high coupling relies on many other units. The lower the coupling, the better.

An example of tightly coupled classes is the first implementation of the `NotificationSystem` and notifier classes while discussing the dependency inversion topic. This principle reduces the degree of direct knowledge of modules about each other to reduce their coupling. Let's see what would happen if we were to add yet another notifier type:

```
class ChatNotifier {
public:
    void sendMessage(const std::string &message) {
```

```
        std::cout << "Chat channel: " << message << std::endl;
    }
};


class NotificationSystem {
public:
    void notify(const std::string &message) {
        sms_.sendSMS(message);
        email_.sendEmail(message);
        chat_.sendMessage(message);
    }

private:
    SMSNotifier sms_;
    EMailNotifier email_;
    ChatNotifier chat_;
};
```

It looks like instead of just adding the `ChatNotifier` class, we had to modify the `public` interface of the `NotificationSystem` class. This means they're tightly coupled, and that this implementation of the `NotificationSystem` class actually breaks the OCP. For comparison, let's now see how the same modification would be applied to the implementation using dependency inversion:

```
class ChatNotifier {
public:
    void notify(const std::string &message) { sendMessage(message);  }

private:
    void sendMessage(const std::string &message) {
        std::cout << "Chat channel: " << message << std::endl;
    }
};
```

No changes to the `NotificationSystem` class were required, so now the classes are loosely coupled. All we needed to do was add the `ChatNotifier` class. Structuring our code this way allows for smaller rebuilds, faster development, and easier testing, all with less code that's easier to maintain. To use our new class, we only need to modify the calling code:

```
using MyNotificationSystem =
    NotificationSystem<SMSNotifier, EMailNotifier, ChatNotifier>;

auto sn = SMSNotifier{};
```

```
auto en = EMailNotifier{};
auto cn = ChatNotifier{};
auto ns = MyNotificationSystem{{sn, en, cn}};
ns.notify("Azabeth Burns");
```

This shows coupling on a class level. On a larger scale, for instance, if you're having a microservice architecture, a common pattern is to have multiple services use a shared database and communicate via this database. This causes high coupling between those services, as you cannot freely modify the database schema without affecting all the microservices that use it. A better option is to have a database per service, wherein the low coupling can be achieved by introducing techniques such as message queueing, where services communicate by sending messages to a queue instead of calling each other. The services wouldn't then depend on each other directly, but just on the message format. However, having one database per service can be extremely expensive. The shared instance pattern is a compromise pattern that helps solve the issue. Here, services must request data from other services via the API or other techniques because services must access only their parts of the data to loosen coupling.

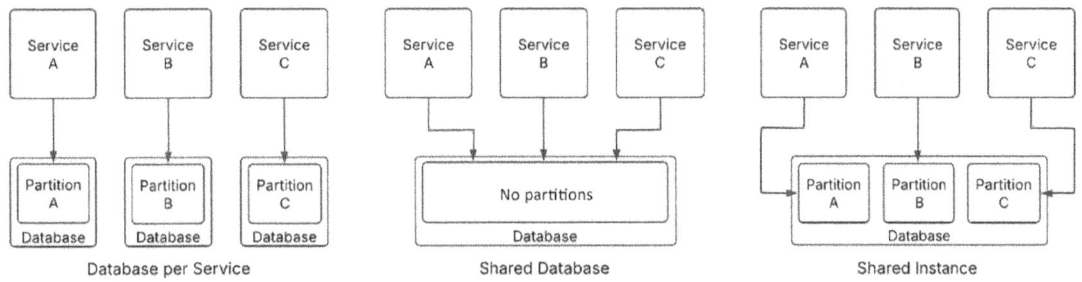

Figure 1.6: Microservices database design patterns

Let's now move on to cohesion.

Cohesion

Cohesion is a measure of how strongly software elements belong together. In a system, the functionality offered by components in a module should be strongly related to make it highly cohesive.

Consider the following example. It may seem trivial, but posting real-life scenarios, often hundreds if not thousands of lines long, would be impractical:

```
class CachingProcessor {
public:
    Result process(WorkItem work);
    Results processBatch(WorkBatch batch);
    void addListener(const Listener &listener);
    void removeListener(const Listener &listener);

private:
    void addToCache(const WorkItem &work, const Result &result);
```

```
    void findInCache(const WorkItem &work);
    void limitCacheSize(std::size_t size);
    void notifyListeners(const Result &result);
    // ...
};
```

We can see that our processor does three types of work and, therefore, violates SRP: the actual work, the caching of the results, and managing listeners. A common way to increase cohesion in such scenarios is to extract a class or even multiple classes:

```
class WorkResultsCache {
public:
    void addToCache(const WorkItem &work, const Result &result);
    void findInCache(const WorkItem &work);
    void limitCacheSize(std::size_t size);
private:
    // ...
};

class ResultNotifier {
public:
    void addListener(const Listener &listener);
    void removeListener(const Listener &listener);
    void notify(const Result &result);
private:
    // ...
};

class CachingProcessor {
public:
    explicit CachingProcessor(ResultNotifier &notifier);
    Result process(WorkItem work);
    Results processBatch(WorkBatch batch);
private:
    WorkResultsCache cache_;
    ResultNotifier notifier_;
    // ...
};
```

Now, each part is done by a separate, highly cohesive entity. Reusing them is now possible without much hassle. Even making them a template class should require little work. Last but not least, testing such classes should be easier as well.

Putting this on a component or system level is straightforward—each component, service, and system you design should be concise and focus on doing one thing and doing it right. This concludes our introductory chapter. Let's now summarize what we've learned.

Summary

In this chapter, we discussed what software architecture is and why it's worth caring about. We showed what happens when architecture is not updated along with the changing requirements and explored the fundamentals of good architecture. Then, we saw how to treat architecture in an Agile environment, before moving on to DDD. We also learned how C++ language features such as zero-cost abstractions, concepts, and the STL help express architectural decisions. Finally, we discussed the SOLID and DRY principles, and we defined the terms *coupling* and *cohesion*.

You should now be able to point out many design flaws in code reviews and refactor your solutions for greater maintainability, as well as be less error-prone as a developer.

In the next chapter, we will learn about the different architectural approaches or styles. We will also learn how and when we can use them to gain better results.

Questions

1. Why care about software architecture?
2. Should the architect be the ultimate decision-maker in an Agile team?
3. How is the SRP related to cohesion?
4. In what phases of a project's lifetime can it benefit from having an architect?
5. What's the benefit of following the SRP?

Further reading

- Agile Manifesto, *Manifesto for Agile Software Development*: `https://agilemanifesto.org/`
- Faizah Salami, *Top 10 Agile Myths and Facts for Software Testers*, Testsigma: `https://testsigma.com/blog/agile-myths/`
- Eric Evans, *Domain-Driven Design: Tackling Complexity in the Heart of Software*, Addison-Wesley Professional: `https://www.amazon.com/dp/0321125215`
- Scott Meyers, *How Non-member Functions Improve Encapsulation*: `https://www.aristeia.com/Papers/CUJ_Feb_2000.pdf`
- Dan Radigan, *Project Management Intro: Agile vs. waterfall Methodologies*, Atlassian: `https://www.atlassian.com/agile/project-management/project-management-intro`
- ISO/IEC, *Technical Report on C++ Performance*: `https://www.open-std.org/jtc1/sc22/wg21/docs/TR18015.pdf`
- Chris Richardson, *Pattern: Shared Database*, microservices.io: `https://microservices.io/patterns/data/shared-database.html`
- Chris Richardson, *Pattern: Database per Service*, microservices.io: `https://microservices.io/patterns/data/database-per-service.html`

- Nexus Software Systems, *SOLID Design Principles in C++: Enhancing Code Quality and Maintainability*: `https://nexwebsites.com/blog/solid-design-principles/`
- Catherine Mercer Bing, *Many Cultures, One Team: Build Your Cultural Repertoire*, Packt Publishing: `https://www.packtpub.com/en-ES/product/many-cultures-one-team-9781634620055`
- Domain-Driven Design, *Agile vs. Waterfall: Choosing the Right Methodology for Complex Projects*: `https://domaindrivendesign.org/agile-vs-waterfall-choosing-the-right-methodology-for-complex-projects/`
- Faraz Fallahi, *awesome-cpp: A Curated List of Awesome C++ (or C) Frameworks, Libraries, Resources, and Shiny Things*, GitHub: `https://github.com/fffaraz/awesome-cpp`

2

Architectural Styles

This chapter introduces the different architectural approaches or styles. Each section will discuss a different approach to designing software, along with its pros and cons, as well as describe when and how to apply it to reap its benefits. We'll begin this chapter by comparing stateful and stateless architectures. After that, we'll cover monolith systems, service-oriented design, and microservices. Then, we'll look at architectural styles from different angles by describing event-based architecture, event sourcing, layered systems, modular designs, and finally, hexagonal architecture.

Once you have completed this chapter, you'll be familiar with the following topics:

- Deciding between stateful and stateless approaches
- Understanding monoliths
- Understanding services and microservices
- Exploring event-based architecture
- Exploring event sourcing pattern
- Understanding layered architecture
- Learning module-based architecture
- Introducing hexagonal architecture

Technical requirements

You will need to know what a software service is. The code from this chapter can be found at the following GitHub page: `https://github.com/PacktPublishing/Software-Architecture-with-Cpp-2E/tree/main/Chapter02`.

Deciding between stateful and stateless approaches

Stateful and stateless are two opposite ways to implement APIs. Each has its pros and cons.

As the name suggests, stateful software's behavior depends on its internal state. Let's take a web service, for instance, as shown in *Figure 2.1*. If it remembers its state, the consumer of the service can send less data in each request, because the service remembers the context of those requests. However, saving on the request size and bandwidth has a hidden cost on the web service's side. If the user sends many requests at the same time, the service now has to synchronize its work. As multiple simultaneous requests can change the state, not having synchronization could lead to data races, which cause undefined or unpredictable behavior.

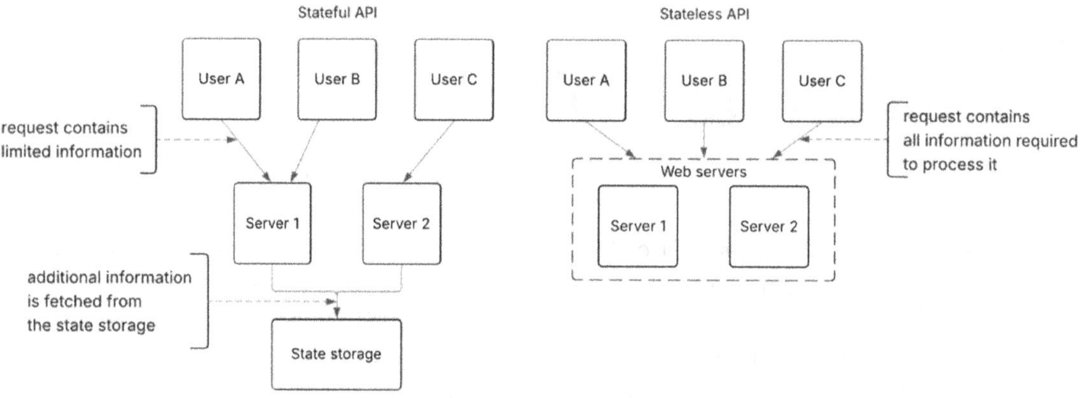

Figure 2.1: Stateful versus stateless APIs

Quick tip: Need to see a high-resolution version of this image? Open this book in the next-gen Packt Reader or view it in the PDF/ePub copy.

The next-gen Packt Reader and a **free PDF/ePub copy** of this book are included with your purchase. Scan the QR code OR visit `https://packtpub.com/unlock`, then use the search bar to find this book by name. Double-check the edition shown to make sure you get the right one.

If the service were stateless, however, then each request coming to it would need to contain all the data needed to process it successfully. This means that the requests would get bigger and use up more bandwidth, but on the other hand, it would allow for better performance and scaling of the service. If you're familiar with functional programming, you would probably find stateless services intuitive. Processing each request can be understood as a call to a pure function that returns the same output given the same input. In fact, many of the advantages that stateless programming provides stem from its functional programming roots. Mutable state is the enemy of concurrent code. Functional programming relies on immutable values, even if this means making copies instead of modifying existing objects. Thanks to this, each thread can work independently, and no data races are possible. We'll discuss functional programming in more detail in *Chapter 5, Leveraging C++ Language Features*.

Since there are no race conditions, no locks are required to protect a shared state from being accessed by multiple threads simultaneously. This can be an enormous boost in terms of performance because there is no overhead involved in maintaining and accessing session data. No locks also means that you will no longer need to deal with deadlocks, which occur when two threads sharing the same resource prevent each other from accessing the resource and stop functioning. Having pure functions means that your code will be easier to debug, too, since you don't have any side effects, which are changes in the state of the program or environment that are not reflected in the function output. Not having side effects, in turn, is also helpful for compilers, as optimizing code without side effects is a much easier task and can be performed more aggressively. This doesn't necessarily mean you should always go stateless, because the choice depends on many factors, including project requirements. If you need to support sessions and track user state, a stateful approach may be more appropriate. If performance and scalability are more important, a stateless approach would be better.

Take classes, for example. If you're modeling, say, a `Consultant` class, it makes sense that the class would contain fields such as the consultant's name, contact data, hourly rate, current and past projects, and whatnot. It is natural for it to be stateful. Now, imagine that you need to calculate the pay they receive for their work. Should you create a `PaymentCalculator` class? Should you add a member or a free function to calculate this?

If you go with the class approach, should you pass a `Consultant` instance as a constructor parameter or a method argument? Should the class have properties such as allowances?

Adding a member function to calculate the pay would break the **single responsibility principle** (**SRP**), as now the class would have two responsibilities: calculating the pay and storing the consultant's data (state). This means introducing a free function or a separate class for this purpose should be preferred to having such hybrid classes.

Another way of defining the SRP is as follows:

> *Gather together the things that change for the same reasons. Separate those things that change for different reasons.*
>
> *– Robert C. Martin, "The Single Responsibility Principle," The Clean Coder Blog, 2014*

That is, if we change the logic of an operation, we should change it in one place. In other words, the SRP not only requires *splitting while it can be split*, but also not to overdo it—*not splitting related things*. Do not unnecessarily complicate things.

Should there be a state in such a class in the first place? Let's discuss the different approaches to our `PaymentCalculator` class.

One approach would be to expose the properties required for calculation purposes:

```
class PaymentCalculator final {
public:
    double calculate() const { return hours_ * netHourlyRate_ * taxPercentage_;
```

```
}

    void setHours(double hours) { hours_ = hours; }
    void setHourlyRate(double rate) { netHourlyRate_ = rate; }
    void setTaxPercentage(double tax) { taxPercentage_ = tax; }
private:
    double hours_{};
    double netHourlyRate_{};
    double taxPercentage_{};
};
```

This approach has two cons. The first is that it's not thread-safe; a single instance of such a `PaymentCalculator` class cannot be used in multiple threads without locks. The second is that once our calculations become more complicated, the class will probably start duplicating more fields from our `Consultant` class.

To eliminate the duplication, we could rework our class to store a `Consultant` instance, like this:

```
class PaymentCalculator final {
public:
    double calculate() const { return {}; };

    void setConsultant(const Consultant &c) { consultant_ = c; };
    void setTaxPercentage(double tax) { taxPercentage_ = tax; };

private:
    std::reference_wrapper<const Consultant> consultant_;
    double taxPercentage_{};
};
```

This approach still has the disadvantage of not being thread-safe. Can we do any better? It turns out that we can make the class thread-safe by making it stateless:

```
class PaymentCalculator {
public:
    static double calculate(const Consultant &c, double taxPercentage) { return
{}; };
};
```

If there is no state to manage, it doesn't really matter if you decide to create free functions (perhaps in a distinct namespace) or group them as static functions of a class, as we did in the preceding snippet. In terms of classes, it's useful to distinguish between value (entity) types and operation types, as mixing them can lead to SRP violations.

Stateless and stateful services

The same principles that we discussed for classes can be mapped to higher-level concepts, for instance, microservices.

What does a stateful service look like? Let's take **File Transfer Protocol** (**FTP**) as an example. If it's not anonymous, it requires the user to pass a username and password to create a session. The server stores this data to identify the user as still connected, so it's constantly storing the state. Each time the user changes the working directory, the state gets updated. Each change done by the user is reflected as a change of state, even when they disconnect. Having a stateful service means that depending on the state, different results can be returned for two identically looking `GET` requests. If the server loses the state, your requests can even stop processing correctly.

Stateful services can also have issues with incomplete sessions or unfinished transactions and added complexity. How long should you keep the sessions open? How can you verify whether the client has crashed or disconnected? When should you roll back any changes made? While you can come up with answers to those questions, it's usually easier to rely on the consumers of your service communicating with it in a dynamic, *intelligent* way. Since they'll be maintaining some kind of state on their own, having a service that also maintains the state is not only unnecessary but often wasteful.

Stateless services take the opposite approach. Each request must contain all the data required in order for it to be successfully processed, so two identical idempotent requests (such as `GET`) will cause identical replies. This is assuming the data stored on the server doesn't change, but data is not necessarily the same thing as state. All that matters is that each request is self-contained.

Statelessness is fundamental in modern internet services. The **HyperText Transfer Protocol** (**HTTP**) is stateless, and many service APIs, for example, X's, are stateless as well. **Representational State Transfer** (**REST**), which X's API relies on, is designed to be functionally stateless. The whole concept behind REST is that all the state required for processing the request must be transferred within it. If this is not the case, then you can't say you have a RESTful service. There are, however, some exceptions to the rule, driven by practical needs.

If you're building an online store, you probably want to store information pertaining to your customers, such as their order history and shipping addresses. The client on the customer's side probably stores an authentication cookie or token, while the server will probably store some user data in a database.

In session-based authentication, a cookie is stored on the client side but points to a session that's managed on the server. This means both sides need to be involved. But in token-based authentication, the server creates a token that contains everything it needs to identify the user and sends it to the client. From then on, the client includes this token with each request. The server just verifies the token's validity without having to keep track of any session data in between, which makes things simpler.

Keeping sessions on the server side can be a limiting approach for services for several reasons: they add a lot of complexity that could be avoided, they make bugs harder to replicate, and, most importantly, they don't scale. If you wanted to distribute the load to another server, chances are you'd have trouble replicating the sessions with the load and synchronizing them between servers. Session-based authentication is best suited when you need real-time session control or centralized management, or when scalability is not a primary concern.

Unlike the cookie approach, the token approach has no session state on the server side, which only creates and verifies tokens identifying the users, allowing for more scalable solutions. *Figure 2.2* shows the difference between server-side session-based authentication and token-based authentication:

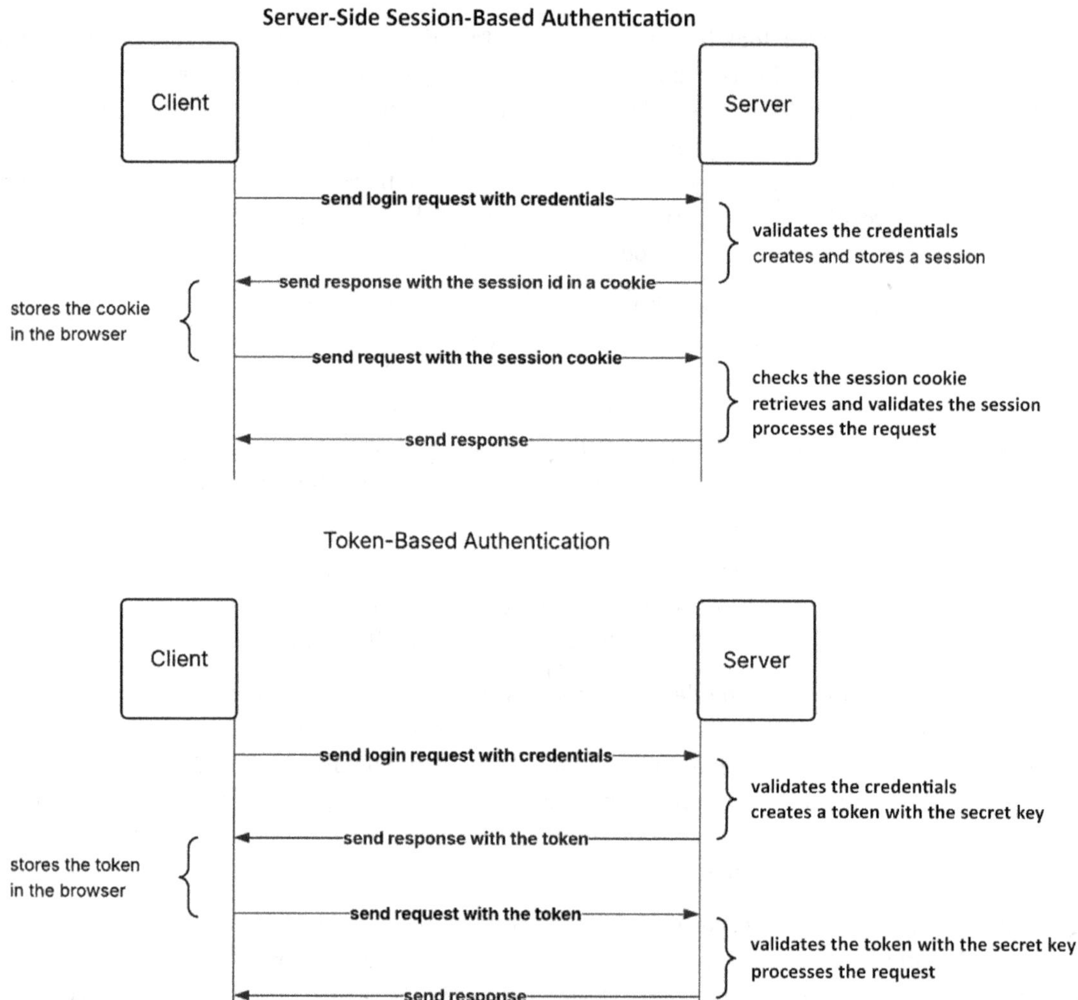

Figure 2.2: Server-side session-based authentication versus token-based authentication

This means that if you wish to have a stateful architecture, you need to have a good reason. Take the FTP protocol, for instance. It has to replicate the changes on both the client side and the server side. The user only authenticates to a single, specific server in order to perform single-state data transfers. Compare this with services such as Dropbox, where the data is often shared between users and the file access is abstracted away through an API, to understand why a stateless model would suit this case better.

Understanding monoliths

The simplest architectural style in which you can develop your application is a monolithic one. This is why many projects start by using this style. A monolithic application is just one big block, meaning that functionally distinguishable parts of the application, such as dealing with I/O, data processing, and the user interface, are all interwoven instead of being in separate architectural components. Monolithic applications have the following advantages:

- It can be easier to deploy a monolithic application than a multi-component one as there is just one thing that needs to be deployed
- They can also be easier to test, as end-to-end testing just requires that you launch a single component
- Integration between different parts of the system is usually easier
- Solutions can be scaled by just adding more instances behind a load balancer

With all those advantages, why wouldn't you use this architectural style? It turns out that there are also many drawbacks:

- It may take a lot longer to start a monolithic application than it would to start smaller, more integrated services. Note that startup time depends on the technologies used and the complexity of the system. Also, regardless of what you change in the application, you might not like that it forces you to rerun all the tests and redeploy the whole application at once. (We explore testing in more detail in *Chapter 10, Writing Testable Code*.) Now, imagine that one of your developers introduces a resource leak in the application. If the leaky code is executed over and over, that will not just bring down one part of the application, but the entire application.
- What's more, the longer you develop a monolithic application, the more problems you'll have in maintaining it. It's a challenge to keep the internals of such an application loosely coupled, as it's so easy to just add yet another dependency between its modules. As such an application grows, it becomes harder and harder to understand it, so the development process will most probably slow down over time because of the added complexity. It can also be hard to maintain design-driven development's bounded contexts when developing monoliths. But many companies, such as Instagram, manage to tame such applications. Instagram has a several-million-line monolithic Python application with strict rules for development culture.
- The scalability offered sounds nice in theory, but what if your application has modules with different resource requirements? How about needing to scale just one module from your application? The lack of modularity, an inherent property of monolithic systems, is the source of many flaws associated with this architecture.
- If you're a fan of using bleeding-edge technologies in your project, the monolithic style won't be what you're looking for. Since you now need to migrate your whole application at once, updating libraries or frameworks can become complex.

The preceding explanation suggests that a monolithic architecture is only good for simple and small applications, but that's not quite true. There are situations where it could certainly be a good idea to use it. If you care about performance, having a monolith can sometimes help you to squeeze more from your app in terms of latency or throughput when compared to microservices.

Inter-process communication will always incur some overhead, which monolithic applications don't need to pay. If you're interested in measurements, see the thesis titled *Performance Characteristics between Monolithic and Microservice-Based Systems* by Robin Flygare and Anthon Holmqvist.

Understanding services and microservices

Because of the drawbacks of monolithic architectures, other approaches have emerged. A common idea is to split your solution into multiple services that communicate with each other. You can then split the development between different teams, each taking care of a separate service. The boundaries of each team's work are clear, unlike in the monolithic architecture style.

Service-oriented architecture

A **service-oriented architecture**, or **SOA** for short, means that the business functions are modularized and presented as separate services for the consumer applications to use. Each service should have a self-describing interface and hide any implementation details, such as the internal architecture, technologies, or programming language used. This allows multiple teams to develop the services however they like, meaning that under the hood, each team can use what suits their needs best. If you have two teams of developers, one proficient in C# and one in C++, they can develop two services that can easily communicate with one another.

Advocates of SOA came up with a manifesto prioritizing the following:

- Business value over technical strategy
- Strategic goals over project-specific benefits
- Intrinsic interoperability over custom integration
- Shared services over purpose-specific implementations
- Flexibility over optimization
- Evolutionary refinement over pursuit of initial perfection

Even though this manifesto doesn't bind you to a specific tech stack, implementation, or type of service, the two most common types of services are **Simple Object Access Protocol** (**SOAP**) and REST. Aside from these, recently, a third one has been growing in popularity: **gRPC Remote Procedure Calls** (**gRPC**).

You need to consider the complexity of the implementation and the difficulty of testing the system before you choose SOA for your project. In addition, using this architecture may result in increased network load and delays in some services.

Microservices

As the name suggests, microservices is an architectural and organizational pattern where an application is split into a collection of loosely coupled services that communicate using network communication protocols. The microservices pattern is similar to the Unix philosophy, stating that a program should only have one purpose. According to the Unix philosophy, advanced problems are solved by composing such programs into Unix pipelines. Similarly, microservice-based systems are composed of many microservices and supporting services.

To achieve the desired quality attributes, microservices rely on established patterns, such as isolating faulty components to ensure fault tolerance; but in order to have an efficient architecture, you must decide on your approach to elements such as API gateways, service registries, load balancing, fault tolerance, monitoring, configuration management, and, of course, the technology stack to use.

Figure 2.3 presents schematic representations of monolithic, service-oriented, and microservices architectures to help differentiate between them:

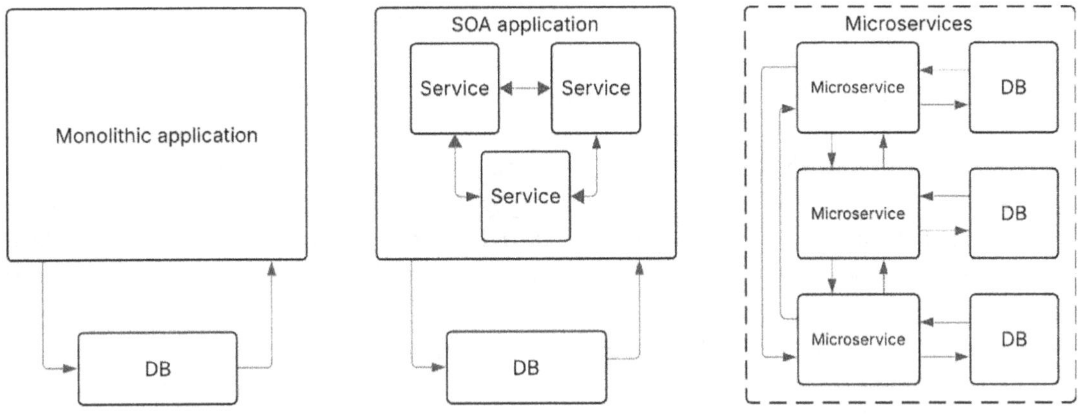

Figure 2.3: Comparison of monolithic, service-oriented, and microservices architectures

Let's start with an overview of the characteristics of this architectural style.

Characteristics of microservices

Since the microservices style is fairly recent, there is no single definition for it. Martin Fowler outlined several essential characteristics of microservices in his article titled *Microservices*, which we will describe here:

- Each service should be an independently replaceable and upgradeable component. This is connected to easier deployment and loose coupling between the services, as opposed to components being libraries in a monolithic application. In the latter case, when you replace one library, you often have to redeploy the whole application.
- Each service should be developed by a cross-functional team, focused on a specific business capability. Consider **Conway's Law**:

> *Any organization that designs a system (defined broadly) will produce a design whose structure is a copy of the organization's communication structure.*
>
> *– Melvyn Conway, How Do Committees Invent?, 1968*

If you don't have cross-functional teams, you end up with software silos. The lack of communication that comes with them will mean you will have to constantly jump through hurdles to successfully deliver.

- Each service should be a product that is owned by the development team throughout its lifetime. This is in contrast to the project mentality, where you develop software and just pass it on for someone to maintain.
- Services should have smart endpoints and use dumb pipes, not the other way around. This stands in contrast to traditional services, which often rely on the logic of an **enterprise service bus (ESB)**, which often manages the routing of messages and transforms them according to business rules. In microservices, you achieve cohesiveness by storing the logic in the service and avoid coupling with messaging components. Using message queues, such as ZeroMQ, can help with this goal.
- Services should be governed in a decentralized way. Monoliths are usually written using one specific technology stack. When they're being split into microservices, each one can choose whatever suits its specific needs best. Governing and assuring that each microservice runs 24/7 is done by a team responsible for this specific service instead of a central department. Companies such as Amazon and Netflix follow this approach and observe that making developers responsible for the flawless execution of their services in production helps to ensure high quality.
- Services should manage their data in a decentralized way. Instead of having one database for all of them, each microservice can choose a database that best matches its needs. Having decentralized data can lead to some challenges with handling updates, but it allows for better scaling. This is why microservices often coordinate in a transaction-free manner and offer eventual consistency, where temporary inconsistencies are allowed as long as all nodes in the distributed system reach the same state over time. In distributed systems, data may reside on different servers, often in different data centers. Therefore, this data may not be instantly synchronized across all nodes in the system.
- The infrastructure used by services should be managed automatically. To deal with dozens of microservices in an efficient manner, you need to have continuous integration and continuous delivery in place, as otherwise, deploying your services will be hell. Automated runs of all your tests will save you lots of time and trouble. Implementing continuous deployment on top of that will shorten the feedback loop and allow your customers to use your new features faster, too.
- Microservices should be prepared for the failure of other services that they depend on. In a distributed deployment environment with so many moving parts, it's normal for some of them to break from time to time. Your services should be able to handle such failures gracefully. Patterns such as Circuit Breaker and Bulkhead (described later in the book) can help to achieve this. To make your architecture resilient, it's also critical to be able to bring failing services back up efficiently or even to know ahead of time that they're going to crash. Real-time monitoring of latency, throughput, and resource usage is essential for this. Get to know chaos engineering tools, such as Chaos Mesh, Chaos Monkey, Gremlin, Harness Chaos Engineering, and LitmusChaos, as they are invaluable for creating a resilient architecture.
- Architectures based on microservices should be ready to constantly evolve. You should design microservices and the cooperation between them in a manner that allows for easy replacement of a single microservice, or sometimes even groups of them.

It's tricky to design the services properly, especially since some of the complexity that was once in the code of one bigger module can now be present as complex communication schemes between services. This means the experience and skill set of the architect plays a more important role than with traditional services or a monolithic approach.

On top of that, here are some other characteristics shared by many (but not all) microservices:

- Using separate processes that usually communicate over network protocols
- Using technology-agnostic protocols (such as HTTP, AMQP, gRPC, or MQTT)
- Keeping services small, granular, and independent with a low overhead from inter-process communication

Now, you should have a good understanding of what the characteristics of microservice-based systems are, so let's see how this approach compares with other architectural styles.

Benefits and disadvantages of microservices

The small size of services in a microservices architecture means that they're faster to develop, deploy, and understand. As the services are built independently of each other, the time necessary to compile their new versions can be drastically reduced. Thanks to this, it is easier to employ rapid prototyping and development when dealing with this architectural style. This, in turn, makes it possible to reduce the lead time, meaning that business requirements can be introduced and evaluated much more quickly.

Some other benefits of a microservice-based approach are the following:

- **Modularity**, which is inherent to this architectural style
- **Better testability**
- **Flexibility** when replacing system parts (such as single services, databases, message brokers, or cloud providers)
- **Integration with legacy systems:** It is not necessary to migrate an entire application, just the parts that currently require development
- **Enabling distributed development:** Independent development teams can work on multiple microservices in parallel
- **Scalability:** A microservice may be scaled independently of the others

On the other hand, here are some disadvantages of microservices:

- They require a mature DevOps approach and reliance on CI/CD automation
- They are harder to debug and require better monitoring and distributed tracing
- Additional overhead of inter-process communication (in terms of auxiliary services) may outweigh the benefits for smaller applications

Let's now explore one of the main reasons this architecture is widely favored—scalability.

Scaling microservices

Microservices scale differently from monolithic applications. In monoliths, the entire functionality is handled by a single process, and scaling is usually achieved by horizontal or vertical scaling. Horizontal scaling (duplication) means replicating the application across different machines to increase the capacity of a system, while vertical scaling means increasing resources such as processors, memory, disks, and so on for the same purpose. Scaling monoliths doesn't require considering which of the functionalities are heavily used and which do not require additional resources.

The scale cube model is effective for understanding microservices design principles. This model, as shown in *Figure 2.4*, covers three orthogonal ways to increase application performance: horizontal duplication (mirroring), functional decomposition (microservices), and data partitioning (sharding).

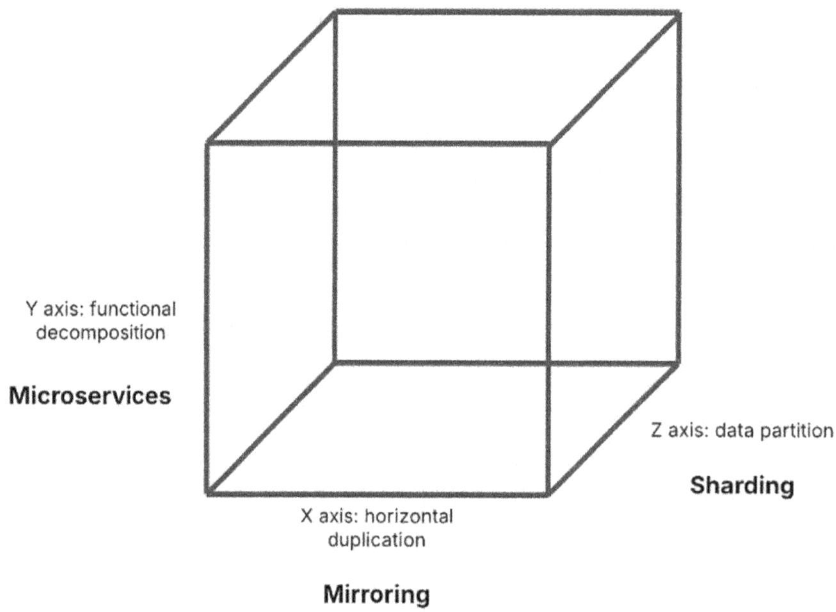

Figure 2.4: The scale cube

Horizontal duplication involves cloning services and distributing traffic between them to handle spikes in traffic. So, the system responds to requests within some expected timeframe.

Functional decomposition is the division of monolithic applications into smaller, focused, loosely coupled, highly cohesive, independently deployable, and more manageable microservices. With microservices, only the services facing heavy load can be replicated without affecting the entire application.

Data partitioning is commonly used to scale databases to improve their availability and performance, as each instance is responsible for a data subset. Partitioning splits data within a database into subsets, while sharding distributes data across various databases or servers. Don't confuse sharding with replication, where database instances are not parts of a shared store but are copies of each other.

Transitioning to microservices

Most companies have some kind of existing monolithic code that they don't want to immediately rewrite using microservices, but still want to transition to this kind of architecture. In such cases, it's possible to adapt microservices incrementally, by adding more and more services that interact with the monolith. You can create new functionalities as microservices or just cut out some parts of the monolith and create microservices out of them.

More details on migrating to microservices are available in *Chapter 14, Architecture of Distributed Systems*.

Exploring event-based architecture

Event-based systems revolve around processing events, which are defined as changes in the state of a system. There are components that generate events, the channels through which the events propagate, and the listeners who react to them, potentially triggering new events too. It's a style that promotes asynchrony and loose coupling, which increases performance, scalability, and ease of deployment.

With those advantages, there are also some challenges. One of them is the complexity of creating a system of this type. All the queues must be made fault-tolerant so that no events are lost in the middle of being processed. Processing transactions in a distributed way is also a challenge on its own. Using the correlation ID, a unique identifier attached to requests or messages, to track events between processes, along with monitoring techniques, can save you hours of debugging and scratching your head.

Examples of event-based systems include stream processors and data integrations, as well as systems aiming for low latency or high scalability.

Let's now discuss common topologies used in such systems. The two main topologies of event-driven architectures are broker-based and mediator-based. Those topologies differ in how the events flow through the system.

The mediator topology is best used when processing an event that requires multiple tasks or steps that can be performed independently. All events produced initially land in the mediator's event queue. The mediator knows what needs to be done in order to handle the event, but instead of performing the logic itself, it dispatches the event to appropriate event processors through each processor's event channel.

If this reminds you of how business processes flow, then you've got good intuition. You can implement this topology in **business process management** (**BPM**) or **business process execution language** (**BPEL**). However, you can also implement it using technologies such as Apache Camel or Mule ESB.

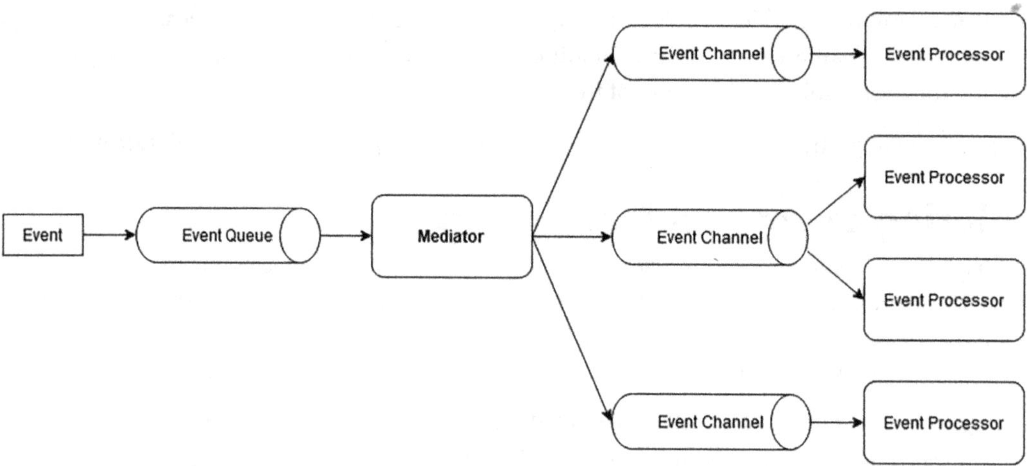

Figure 2.5: The mediator topology

A broker, on the other hand, is a lightweight component that contains all the queues and doesn't orchestrate the processing of an event. It can require that the recipients subscribe to specific kinds of events and then simply forwards all the ones that they are interested in. Many message queues rely on brokers, for example, ZeroMQ, which is written in C++ and aims for zero waste and low latency.

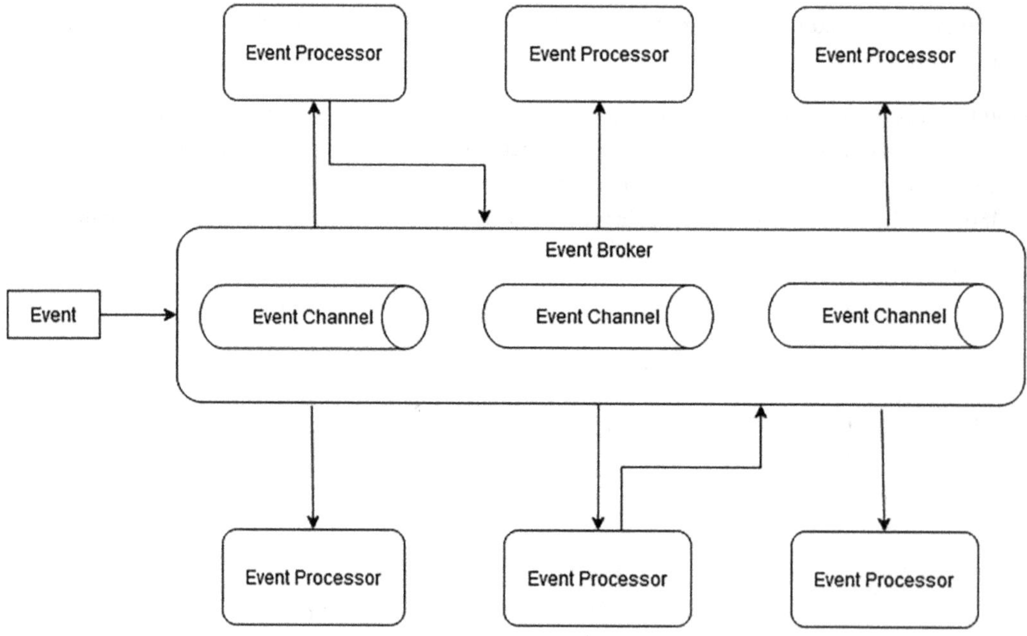

Figure 2.6: The broker topology

Now that you know the two common topologies used in event-based systems, let's learn about a powerful architectural pattern using events at its core.

Exploring the event sourcing pattern

You can think of events as notifications that contain additional data for the notified services to process. There is, however, another way to think of them: a change of state. Think how easy it would be to debug issues with your application logic if you were able to know the state in which it was when the bug occurred and what change was requested of it. That's one benefit of event sourcing. In essence, it captures all the changes that happen to the system by recording all the events in the sequence in which they happened.

Often, you'll find that the service no longer needs to persist its state in a database, as storing the events somewhere else in the system is enough. Even if it does, it can be done asynchronously. Another benefit that you derive from event sourcing is a complete audit log. *Figure 2.7* presents a schematic diagram of the architectural style:

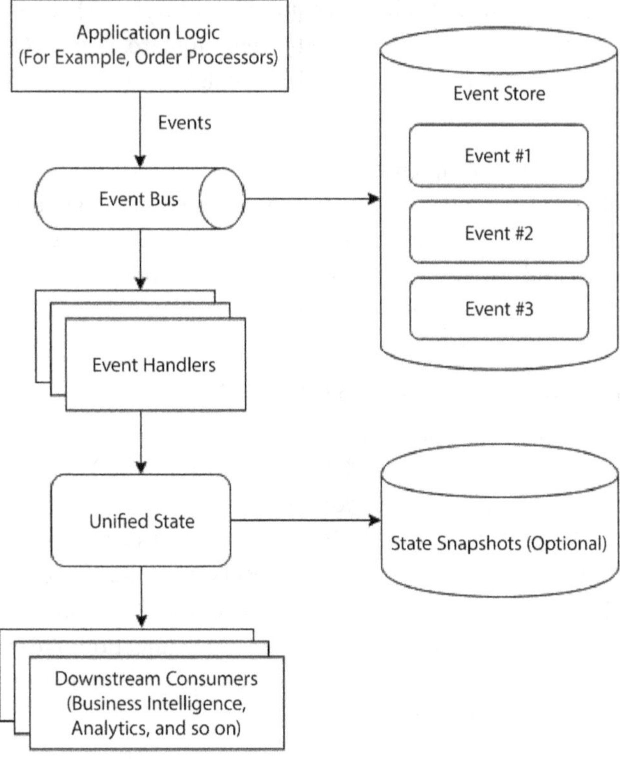

Figure 2.7: Event sourcing architecture

Event sourcing requires a lot of effort to model events because each event must contain all the information required to restore the full state of the system at a given point in time. Therefore, the events are immutable once they are stored; otherwise, the history and state may become corrupted or distorted. It's reminiscent of a version control system such as Git.

Periodic snapshots reduce the time it takes to replay all the events in case of a failure. Since replaying all the events to restore the current state can take a long time, snapshots allow the system to be restored from a saved point in time and replay events that occurred after that point in time. Snapshots can also help accommodate changes to the structure of events over time.

There is some delay between adding an event to the event store, publishing the event, and processing the event by consumers when further events may be arriving. Therefore, the system state is not updated immediately, but eventually becomes consistent.

This design pattern can be used in cases where coupling a message broker and database should be avoided, or where distributed transactions involving multiple resources are not supported, but the atomic change in the database and publishing to the message broker have to be consistent and synchronized to prevent errors.

Thanks to the reduced need for data synchronization, event-sourced systems, in combination with **command query responsibility segregation** (CQRS), which will be described in *Chapter 4, Architectural and System Design Patterns*, often offer low latency, which means they can respond to queries without much delay. This makes them a good fit for **high-frequency trading** (HFT) systems and activity trackers, among others. Unlike event-sourced systems, **create, read, update, delete** (CRUD) systems typically have a layered architecture, are synchronous, and block data operations during updates, which is much easier to implement.

There is no need to apply complex design patterns such as event sourcing to simple applications. This design pattern is suitable when it is necessary to reduce or completely eliminate conflicts of data update operations; record events that have occurred and replay them to restore a certain state of the system; roll back changes and save history; or capture the intent, purpose, or reason for creating/changing data. It is not for integrating data across a system.

Understanding layered architecture

If your architecture starts to look like spaghetti, or you want to prevent this, having your components structured in layers may help. Remember model-view-controller? Or maybe similar patterns, such as model-view-viewmodel or entity-control-boundary? These are all typical examples of a layered architecture (also called *N*-tier architecture if the layers are physically separated from each other). You can structure code in layers, create layers of microservices, or apply this pattern to other areas where you think it could bring its benefits. Layering provides abstraction and the separation of concerns, which simplifies development, testing, and dependency injection. This is the main reason why it's being introduced. Moreover, it can also help reduce complexity while improving the modularity, reusability, and maintainability of your solution.

A layered architecture is often pretty easy to implement since most developers already know the notion of layers—they simply need to develop several layers and stack them, as in the following diagram. The requests and responses move from level to level, passing through the layer directly to get to the next layer, where the components have only the business logic of that level:

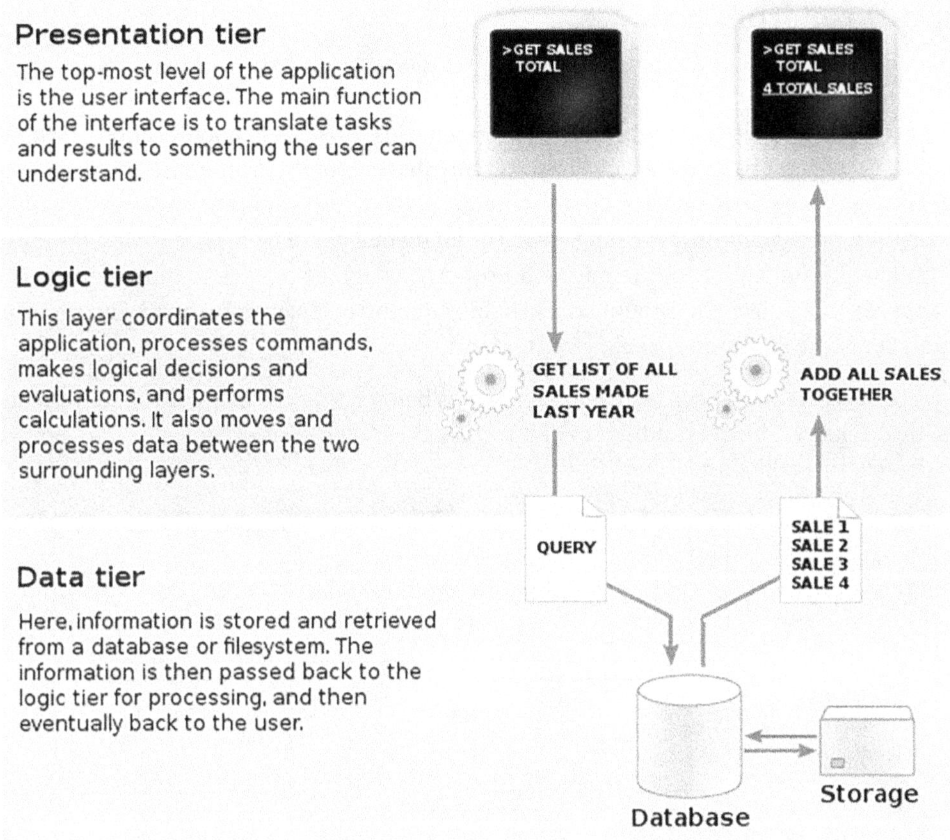

Presentation tier
The top-most level of the application is the user interface. The main function of the interface is to translate tasks and results to something the user can understand.
>GET SALES TOTAL
>GET SALES TOTAL
4 TOTAL SALES
Logic tier
This layer coordinates the application, processes commands, makes logical decisions and evaluations, and performs calculations. It also moves and processes data between the two surrounding layers.
GET LIST OF ALL SALES MADE LAST YEAR
ADD ALL SALES TOGETHER
QUERY
SALE 1
SALE 2
SALE 3
SALE 4
Data tier
Here, information is stored and retrieved from a database or filesystem. The information is then passed back to the logic tier for processing, and then eventually back to the user.
Database
Storage

Figure 2.8: An example of a three-tiered architecture using a textual interface in the presentation layer (image by Bartledan, public domain via Wikimedia Commons: https://commons.wikimedia.org/wiki/File:Overview_of_a_three-tier_application_vectorVersion.svg)

The challenge with creating an efficient layered architecture lies in specifying stable, well-defined interfaces between the layers. Often, you can have several layers on top of one. For instance, if you have a layer for domain logic, it can be a base for a presentation layer and a layer for providing APIs to other services. Most often, CRUD applications are based on this architecture.

Layered architecture isn't limited to a single application; the same design principle can also be extended to the system level—for example, in microservices. One way to do so is through the backends for frontends pattern.

Backends for frontends

It's not uncommon to see many frontends that rely on the same backend. Let's say you have a mobile application and a web application, both using the same backend. It may be a good design choice at first. However, once the requirements and usage scenarios of those two applications diverge, your backend will require more and more changes, serving just one of the frontends. This can lead to the backend having to support competing requirements, such as two separate ways to update the data store or different scenarios for providing data. Simultaneously, the frontends start to require more bandwidth to communicate with the backend properly, which also leads to more battery usage in mobile apps. At this point, you should consider introducing a separate backend for each frontend that handles only the interface-specific requirements.

This way, you can think of a user-facing application as being a single entity with two layers: the frontend and the backend. The backend can depend on another layer, consisting of downstream services. Refer to the following diagram:

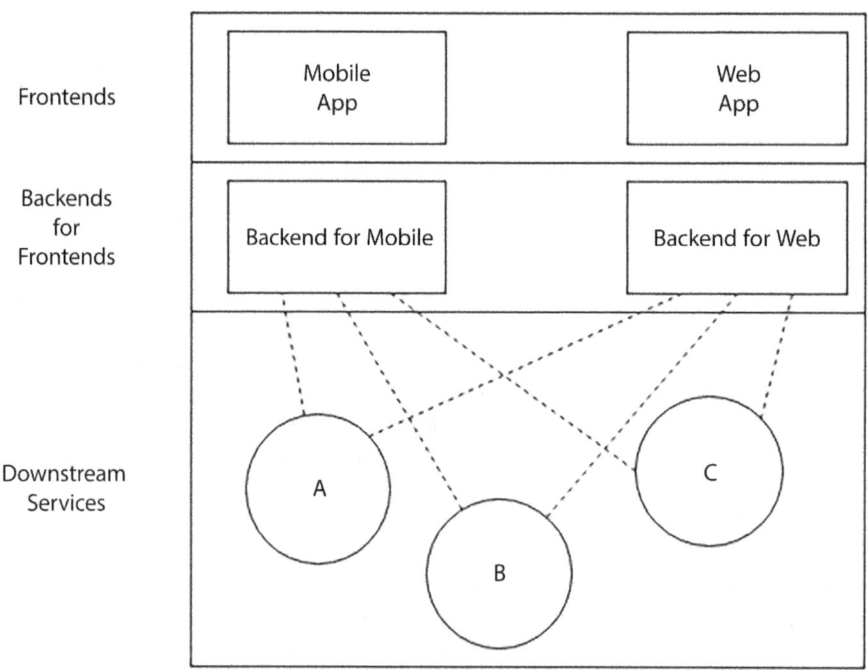

Figure 2.9: The Backends for frontends pattern

The drawback of using **backends for frontends** (**BFF**) is that some code must be duplicated to support different frontend clients. As long as this speeds up development and is not a burden in the long term, it's OK. But it also means that you should be on the lookout for possibilities to aggregate duplicated logic in a downstream service or reusable library. Sometimes, introducing a service just to aggregate similar calls can help solve duplication issues. Often, if you have many frontends, some can still share a backend and not cause it to have competing requirements. If you're creating mobile applications for iOS and Android, for instance, you could think of reusing the same backend for those and having separate ones for web and/or desktop applications.

Learning module-based architecture

In this section, by *modules*, we mean software components that can be loaded and unloaded at runtime, thereby enhancing a system's flexibility. This is different from C++20 modules, which are designed to resolve macro conflicts and double inclusion, improve compilation speed, and enhance encapsulation. For C++20's modules, refer to *Chapter 9, The Future of C++ Code Reuse: Using Modules*.

If you've ever needed to run a component with as little downtime as possible, but for any reason couldn't apply the usual fault-tolerance patterns, such as redundant copies of your service, making this component module-based can save the day. Or you may just be attracted by a vision of a modular system with versioning of all the modules, with an easy lookup of all the available services.

Other advantages could be decoupling, testability, and team collaboration. These benefits are the reason why OSGi modules were created in Java, inspired the SDK macchina.io EDGE, and were ported to C++ in a few frameworks: Apache Celix and C++ Micro Services. Examples of architectures using modules include IDEs such as Eclipse, **software-defined networking** (**SDN**) projects such as OpenDaylight, and home automation software such as openHAB.

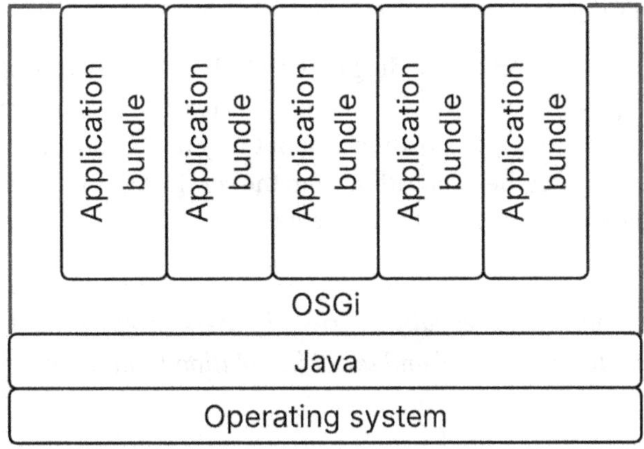

Figure 2.10: OSGi architecture

However, the cost of runtime flexibility is that most frameworks cannot be used with OSGi. Also, initialization of OSGi bundles is not trivial due to the dynamic startup order, and different versions of the services may not be detected by the framework. Moreover, the class loader needs to be aware of the resources that the framework needs at runtime beforehand. So, it is understandable why most projects choose other approaches.

OSGi also allows for automatic dependency management between modules, controlling their initialization and unloading, as well as controlling their discovery. Since it's service-oriented, you can think of using OSGi services as something akin to having tiny services in one "container." This is why one of the C++ implementations is named C++ Micro Services. To see them in action, refer to their *Getting Started* guide linked at the end of the chapter.

One interesting concept adopted by the C++ Micro Services framework, which stands out for its module-based architecture, is a new way to deal with singletons. The `GetInstance()` static function will, instead of just passing a static instance object, return a service reference obtained from the bundled context. At its core, this library dynamically registers services loaded from shared or static libraries called bundles. So effectively, singleton objects are emulated by non-singleton classes and get replaced by services that you can configure. It can also save you from the static deinitialization fiasco, where multiple singletons that depend on each other have to unload in a specific order.

The problem can also be resolved with Alexandrescu's Phoenix Singleton design pattern. It addresses the dead reference problem (where an object is accessed after it's been destroyed), by recreating destroyed objects at the same address by using the placement new operator.

Introducing hexagonal architecture

Hexagonal architecture is also called ports and adapters. Ports define the interfaces through which adapters interact with the application core, and any adapter can be replaced without affecting business logic. This makes it easy to change external technologies without affecting the core logic and even delay technological decisions.

This type of architecture helps in understanding how and why interfaces are utilized when designing an application. The main idea of hexagonal architecture is to structure an application in such a way that it can be developed and tested in isolation without relying on external tools and technologies, which separates the core logic of the application from the services it uses. This architecture adds the concept of ports and adapters to the layered architecture.

> *Allow an application to equally be driven by users, programs, automated test or batch scripts, and to be developed and tested in isolation from its eventual run-time devices and databases.*
>
> *– Alistair Cockburn, Hexagonal Architecture, 2005*

Figure 2.11 illustrates why this architectural style is referred to as hexagonal architecture. Here, external services tell the application what to do through driving (primary) ports, and the application uses driven (secondary) ports to do its job.

Driving (primary) adapters convert external inputs into formats understandable by the application's core logic, and driven (secondary) adapters convert internal outputs into formats understandable by external services. So, the adapters connect the application to the outside world.

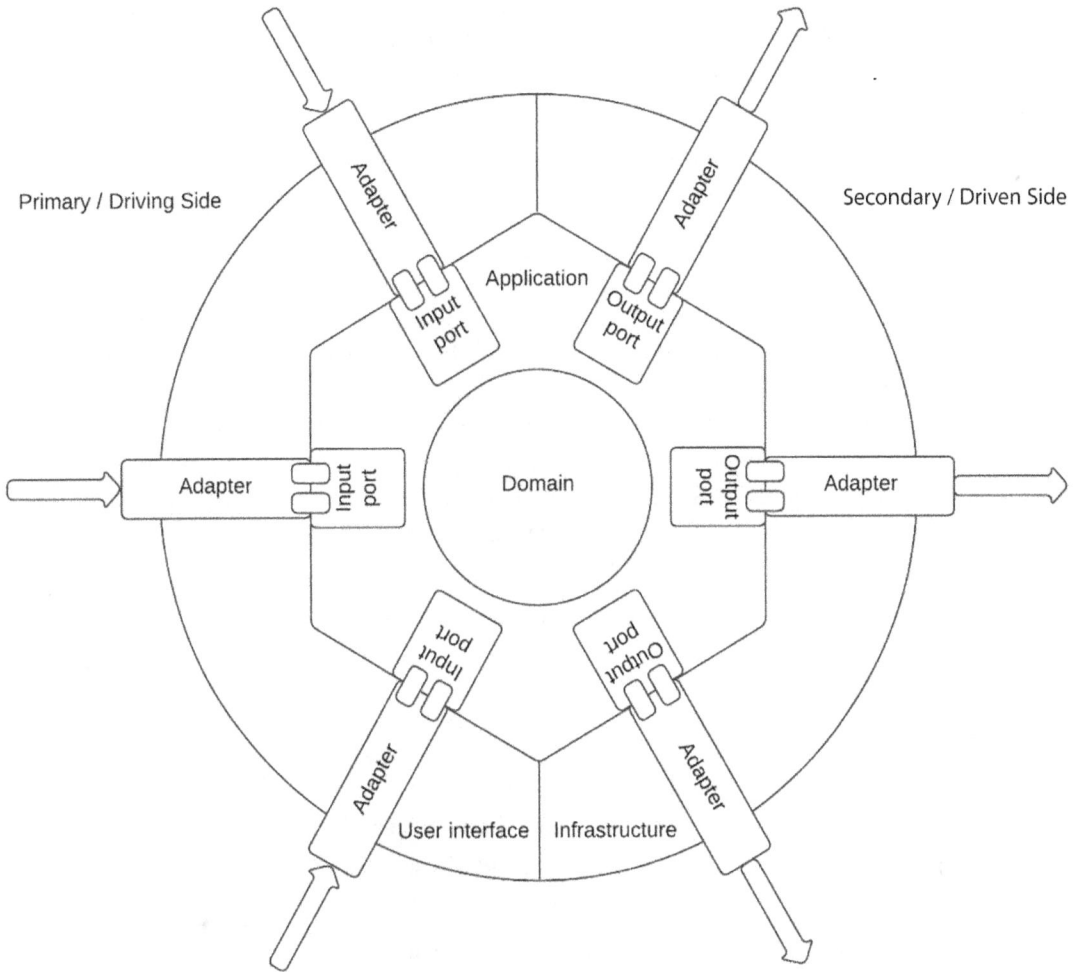

Figure 2.11: Hexagonal architecture

The principle of dependency inversion (commonly implemented using the dependency injection pattern) and the adapter pattern make driving and driven adapters independent of business logic. *Figure 2.12* shows how the principle is applied in the hexagonal architecture.

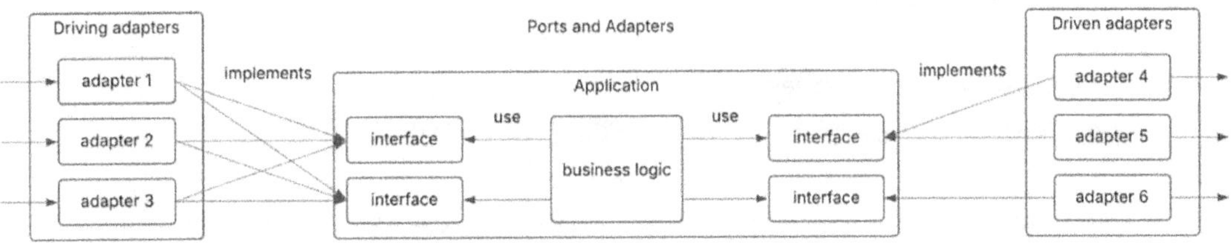

Figure 2.12: Dependency inversion principle and the adapter pattern in hexagonal architecture

However, hexagonal architecture has its drawbacks. It's unclear whether only primary adapters validate inputs or business logic is also involved. Ideally, these entities should be independent. Moreover, complex database requests may cause business logic to leak to adapters and transactions may require complex rollbacks.

This architecture is commonly used in banking applications to separate the logic of processing transactions, checking balances, and calculating fees from user interfaces and databases.

Summary

In this chapter, we've discussed the various architectural styles that you can encounter and apply to your software. We've discussed stateful and stateless services and monolithic architecture. We went through SOA, moved on to microservices, and discussed ways to scale applications, specifically using the scale cube model. Then, we discussed various other approaches to architecture, including an event-driven one and a runtime module-based one, and showed where layering can be spotted and why it could be useful. You now also understand how to implement event sourcing and recognize when to use BFF and hexagonal architecture. Moreover, you now know how architectural styles can help you achieve several quality attributes and what challenges they can bring.

In the next chapter, you'll learn how to know which of those attributes are important in a given system.

Questions

1. What are the traits of a RESTful service?
2. What toolkit can you use to aid you in creating a resilient distributed architecture?
3. Should you use centralized storage for your microservices? Why/why not?
4. When should you write a stateful service instead of a stateless one?
5. How does a broker differ from a mediator?
6. What is the difference between an *N*-tier and an *N*-layer architecture?
7. How should you approach replacing a monolith with a microservice-based architecture?

Further reading

- Robin Flygare and Anthon Holmqvist, *Performance Characteristics between Monolithic and Microservice-based Systems* (Dissertation): `http://urn.kb.se/resolve?urn=urn:nbn:se:bth-14888`
- SOA Manifesto: `https://soa-manifesto.org/default.html`
- Martin Fowler, *Microservices—A Definition of This New Architectural Term*: `https://martinfowler.com/articles/microservices.html#MicroservicesAndSoa`
- Lewis Coosner, *Microservices and the Scale Cube*, Incus Data Blog: `https://incusdata.com/blog/microservices-and-the-scale-cube`
- C++ Micro Services, *Getting Started* (C++ Micro Services Documentation): `http://docs.cppmicroservices.org/en/stable/doc/src/getting_started.html`
- Gaurav Gandhi, *Cookie vs Token Authentication*, Naukri Code 360: `https://www.naukri.com/code360/library/cookie-vs-token-authentication`

- Teniola Fatunmbi, *A Comparison of Cookies and Tokens for Secure Authentication*, Okta: `https://developer.okta.com/blog/2022/02/08/cookies-vs-tokens`
- Robert Engelen, *A Framework for Service-Oriented Computing with C and C++ Web Service Components*, ACM Transactions on Internet Technology, Volume 8, Issue 3: `https://doi.org/10.1145/1361186.1361188`
- Rahul Awati and James Denman, *Sharding*, TechTarget: `https://www.techtarget.com/searchoracle/definition/sharding`
- PlanetScale, *Sharding vs. Partitioning: What's the Difference?*: `https://planetscale.com/blog/sharding-vs-partitioning-whats-the-difference`
- Artem Polishchuk, *Scale Cube: A Guide to Scalability in System Architecture*, Bool.dev: `https://bool.dev/blog/detail/scale-cube-a-guide-to-scalability-in-system-architecture`
- Chris Richardson, *The Scale Cube*, microservices.io: `https://microservices.io/articles/scalecube.html`
- Robert C. Martin, *The Single Responsibility Principle*, The Clean Code Blog: `https://blog.cleancoder.com/uncle-bob/2014/05/08/SingleReponsibilityPrinciple.html`

3

Functional and Non-Functional Requirements

As an architect, it is important for you to recognize which requirements are significant for the architecture and why. This chapter will teach you about the functional and **non-functional requirements** (**NFRs**) of a solution. Functional requirements are those that tell you what your solution should do—its features, functions, and behaviors. On the other hand, non-functional ones are those that tell you how well the system performs its functions.

In this chapter, we'll cover the following topics:

- Understanding the types of requirements
- Recognizing **architecturally significant requirements** (**ASRs**)
- Gathering requirements from various sources
- Documenting requirements
- Documenting architecture
- Choosing the right views to document
- Generating automated documentation

By the end of this chapter, you will have learned how to recognize and categorize both types of requirements and how to create documentation that describes them in a clear manner.

Technical requirements

To replicate our steps to generate documentation from sources, you must have CMake, Doxygen, Sphinx, `sphinx_mdinclude`, and Breathe installed. We're using the Read the Docs Sphinx theme, so please install it as well. Feel free to use the latest versions of the tools mentioned.

You can find the related code at `https://github.com/PacktPublishing/Software-Architecture-with-Cpp-2E/tree/main/Chapter03`.

Understanding the types of requirements

While creating a software system, you should gather requirements as early as possible and constantly ask yourself whether what you're making is what your customers need. Many times, they won't even know what requirement fulfills their needs best. It's the role of a successful architect to discover the requirements of the product and to make sure they are being met. There are three distinct types of requirements that you need to consider: functional requirements, quality attributes, and constraints. Let's have a look at each of these.

Functional requirements

These requirements are the ones that define what your system should do, or what functionality it should offer. They may also specify what the system must not do.

Remember that functionality does not always influence architecture, so you'll have to keep an eye on which of those requirements will actually dictate what your solution will look like.

Often, if a functional requirement has some qualities that must be met, it can become architecturally significant. Consider an app for merchants and visitors of an event with music, various arts, and shops, happening in your city. A few examples of functional requirements for it could be the following:

- As a shopkeeper, I want to filter orders that contain a specific product
- As a shopkeeper, I want to manage the store's newsletter so that customers can subscribe to it and receive the latest updates

The first of those requirements tells us we'll have to have a component for tracking orders and products with search capabilities.

The second example is even more straightforward; now we know we need to have a service for subscribing and sending notifications. This is definitely an architecturally significant functional requirement.

By the way, the requirements are actually given as user stories. User stories are requirements given in the following format, known as the Connextra template: *As a <role>, I can/want to <capability>, so that <benefit>*. A user story in Agile software development is a tool to capture software features from the user's perspective. This is a common way to phrase requirements and can help stakeholders and developers find common ground and communicate better.

Depending on how exactly the UI should appear and what scale our app should be, we could just add a simple page to our app, or it could require more performant and scalable features such as Lucene or Elasticsearch for filtering orders. This means that we could be looking at an ASR—one that directly drives and justifies an architectural design—involving both functional requirements, such as filtering orders, and NFRs, such as performance and scalability. Let's now look at some NFRs describing operation capabilities and constraints that can also be ASRs.

Non-functional requirements

Instead of focusing on what functionality your system should have, NFRs focus on how well and under which conditions the system should perform said functionality. This group consists of two main subgroups: quality attributes and constraints.

Quality attributes

Quality attributes are the traits of your solution, such as performance, maintainability, and user-friendliness. There are dozens, if not hundreds, of different qualities your software can have. Try to focus just on the important ones instead of listing all that come to your mind when choosing which ones your software should have.

Examples of quality attribute requirements include the following:

- The system will respond in under 500 ms for 99.9% of all requests under usual load (don't forget to specify what the usual load is or will be)
- The website will not store customer credit card data used in the payment process (an example of confidentiality)
- When updating the system, if updating any component fails, the system will be rolled back to a state prior to the update (survivability)
- The system will be accessible from Windows, macOS, and Android (portability; try to understand whether it's needed to support platforms such as desktop, mobile, and/or web)

While catching functional requirements in a product backlog (a prioritized list of tasks) is pretty straightforward, we cannot say the same regarding quality attribute requirements. Fortunately, there are a few ways you could approach this:

- Some of them can be expressed in the **definition of done** or **acceptance criteria** for your tasks, stories, and releases
- Others can be expressed directly as user stories, as shown previously
- You can also check them as part of design and code reviews and create automated tests where applicable

Attribute-driven design (ADD) is a useful methodology focused on quality attributes and ways to achieve them to create adaptable, maintainable, and scalable systems. This method includes steps to create documentation and analyze the created architecture. The advantage of this method is detailed step-by-step instructions on the tasks that need to be performed in the design iteration, which lowers the entry threshold for an architect. To know more about ADD, refer to the related article linked in the *Further reading* section.

Constraints

Constraints are the non-negotiable decisions that you must follow while delivering the project. Those can be design decisions, technological ones, or even political (regarding people or organizational matters). Two other common constraints are time and budget. Examples of constraints could be as follows:

- The team will never grow beyond four developers, one QA engineer, and one sysadmin

- Since our company leverages Oracle DB in all its current products, the new product must use it too, so that we can make the most of our expertise

Constraints, along with the environment your application will run in, can significantly impact your architecture. For example, embedded apps need to be designed in a different way from those running in the cloud, and apps being developed by less-experienced developers should probably use a simple and safe framework instead of using one with a steep learning curve or developing their own.

NFRs are always going to influence your architecture. It's essential not to over-specify them, as having false positives will be a constant burden during product development. It's equally important not to under-specify them, as this can later come out in missed sales opportunities or failing to comply with regulatory bodies' requirements.

In the next section, you will learn how to strike a balance between those two extremes and to focus on just those requirements that really matter in your specific case.

Recognizing architecturally significant requirements (ASRs)

When designing a software system, it's common to deal with dozens or hundreds of requirements. In order to make sense of them and come up with a good design, you need to know which of them are important and could be implemented regardless of your design decisions, and which could even be dismissed. You should learn how to recognize the most important ones so you can focus on them first and deliver the most value in the shortest possible time.

ASRs are those that have a significant impact on your system's architecture. They can be both functional and non-functional. How can you identify which ones are actually significant? If the absence of a specific requirement were to allow you to create a different architecture, you are looking at an ASR. Late discovery of such requirements will often cost you both time and money, as you'll need to redesign some part of your system, if not the whole solution. You can only hope it won't cost you other resources and your reputation, too.

There are different methodologies for prioritizing requirements. For instance, you could prioritize requirements using two metrics: the business value and the impact on architecture. Those that will be high on both scales are most important and should be dealt with as a matter of priority. If you come up with too many such requirements, you should revisit your prioritization scheme. If it doesn't help, it might be that the system just isn't achievable.

Another methodology to prioritize requirements is the iron triangle with three major constraints: budget, time, and scope (features). These constraints can directly shape your architecture by forcing technical trade-offs. For example, budget constraints may limit your choice of technology, a fast-paced timeline may require simpler solutions, and expanding scope may call for a flexible architecture. Moreover, changing one constraint inevitably affects the others. Balancing these project constraints can help you determine the project's quality. The features and functionalities in the scope impact the budget. The budget influences the pace of development. The time frame has an effect on the depth and complexity of the features in the scope. (Here, it must be noted that complex systems often require consideration of more factors that the three that the triangle captures.)

This method has been used since at least the 1950s and has evolved into other variations such as the **Project Diamond** and the **Project Management Body of Knowledge** (**PMBOK**). To learn more about PMBOK, you can read the book titled *Becoming a PMP® Certified Professional* by Ashley Hunt.

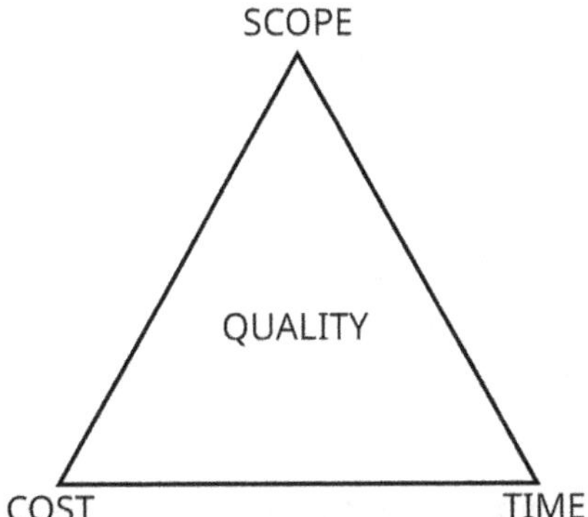

Figure 3.1: The project management triangle (image by Mapto, public domain via Wikimedia Commons: https://commons.wikimedia.org/wiki/File:Project-triangle-en.svg)

It is noteworthy that the two methodologies complement each other. The former helps guide technical and design decisions, while the latter offers a broader view for balancing overall project constraints related to time, scope, and budget. Using both perspectives together can help ensure that the architecture and the project remain aligned.

It's a common mistake to start by applying concrete technologies to your architecture from the very beginning of your architectural work. We strongly suggest that you first gather all the requirements, focus on the ones significant for the architecture, and only then decide what technologies and technology stacks to build your project on.

Since it's that important to recognize ASRs, let's talk about a few patterns that can help you with this.

Indicators of architectural significance

If you have a requirement to integrate with any external system, this is most likely going to influence your architecture. Let's go through some common indicators that a requirement is an ASR:

- **Needing to create a software component to handle it:** Examples include sending emails, pushing notifications, exchanging data with the company's **enterprise resource planning** (**ERP**) server, or using a specific data storage.
- **Having a significant impact on the system:** Core functionality often defines what your system should look like. Cross-cutting concerns, such as authorization, auditability, or having transactional behavior, are other good examples.
- **Being hard to achieve:** Having low latency is a great example; unless you think of it early in development, it can be a long battle to achieve it, especially if you suddenly realize you can't really afford to have garbage collections when you're on your hot path.

- **Forcing trade-offs when satisfying certain architectures:** Perhaps your design decision will even need to compromise some requirements in favor of other, more important ones if the cost is too high. It's a good practice to log such decisions somewhere and to notice that you're dealing with ASRs here. If any requirement constrains you or limits the product in any way, it's very likely significant for the architecture. If you want to come up with the best architecture given many trade-offs, then be sure to read about the **architecture trade-off analysis method (ATAM)**. A relevant resource is linked at the end of the chapter.

Hindrances in recognizing ASRs and how to deal with them

Contrary to intuition, many ASRs are difficult to spot at first glance. This is caused by two factors: they can be hard to define, and even if they're described, this can be done vaguely.

Your customers might not yet be clear about what they need, but you should still be proactive in asking questions to steer clear of any assumptions. For example, if your system is to send notifications, you must know whether those are in real time or whether a daily email will suffice, as the former could require you to create a publisher–subscriber architecture.

However, in most cases, you'll need to make some assumptions since not everything is known upfront. If you discover a requirement that challenges your assumptions, it might be an ASR. If you assume you can maintain your service between 3 a.m. and 4 a.m. and you realize your customers from a different time zone will still need to use it, it will challenge your assumption and likely change the product's architecture.

What's more, people often tend to treat quality attributes vaguely during the earlier phases of projects, especially less-experienced or less-technical individuals. On the other hand, that's the best moment to address such ASRs, as the cost of implementing them in the system is the lowest.

It's worth noting, however, that many people, when specifying requirements, like to use vague phrases without thorough thinking. If you were designing a service such as Uber, an example could be *When receiving a driver search request, the system must reply with an available drivers message fast, or the system must be available 24/7.*

Upon asking questions, it often turns out that 99.9% monthly availability is perfectly fine, and *fast* is actually a few seconds. Such phrases always require clarification, and it's often valuable to know the rationale behind them. Perhaps it is just someone's subjective opinion, not backed by any data or business needs. Also, note that in the request and response case, the quality attribute is hidden inside another requirement, making it even harder to catch.

Finally, requirements being architecturally significant for one system aren't necessarily of the same importance to another, even if those systems serve similar purposes. Some will become more important over time, once the system grows and starts to communicate with more and more other systems. Others may become important once the needs for the product change. This is why there's no silver bullet in telling which of your requirements will be ASRs and which won't.

Equipped with all this knowledge, you know how to distinguish the important requirements from the rest. Let's discuss a few techniques for gathering these requirements.

Gathering requirements

Regardless of a project's size, well-defined requirements are critically important because they define the purpose of any project. If these requirements are not clearly defined and agreed upon, they can lead to severe consequences at all stages of development, for example, the functionality does not meet user expectations, or the project encounters technical difficulties not foreseen at the initial stages. Therefore, it is necessary to pay attention to the process of gathering and analyzing requirements.

Knowing the context

When mining requirements, you should consider the broader context. You must identify what potential problems may have a negative impact on your product in the future. Those risks often come from the outside. Let's revisit our Uber-like service scenario. An example risk for your service could be a potential change in legislation: you should be aware that some countries may try to change the law to remove you from their market. Uber's way to mitigate those risks is to have local partners cope with regional limitations.

Future risks aside, you must also be aware of current issues, such as the lack of subject matter experts in the company or heavy competition on the market. Here's what you can do:

- Be aware of and note any assumptions being made. It's best to have a dedicated document for tracking those.
- Ask questions to clarify or eliminate your assumptions, if possible.
- You need to consider project dependencies, including external and internal, as they influence the development schedule. Other useful areas are the business rules that shape the day-to-day behavior of the company, as your product will likely need to adhere to and possibly enhance those.
- Moreover, if there's enough data relating to the users or the business, you should try to mine it to get insights and find patterns that can help with making decisions regarding the future product and its architecture. If you already have some users but are unable to mine data, it's useful to communicate with the domain specialists and also observe how the users behave.

You could anonymize readers by removing personally identifiable information and then record user activities when they perform their daily tasks using the currently deployed systems. This way, you could not only automate parts of their work but also change their workflow to a more efficient one based on concrete conclusions rather than abstract assumptions. However, asking for user consent is necessary if software telemetry is collected. Remember that users don't like changing their habits, so it's better to introduce changes gradually where possible.

Knowing existing documentation

Existing documents can be a great source of information, even though they can also have their issues. You should reserve some time to at least get familiar with all the existing documents related to your work. Chances are that there are some requirements hidden in them. On the other hand, keep in mind that the documentation is never perfect; it is highly likely that it will lack some significant information. You should also be prepared for it to be outdated.

There is never one source of truth when it comes to architecture, so aside from reading documents, you should have lots of discussions with the people involved. Nonetheless, reading documents can be a great way of preparing yourself for such discussions.

Knowing your stakeholders

To be a successful architect, you must learn to communicate with businesspeople as requirements come, directly or indirectly, from them. Whether they're from your company or a customer, you should get to know the context of their business. For instance, you must know the following:

- What drives the business?
- What goals does the company have?
- What specific objectives will your product help to achieve?

Once you are aware of this, it will be much easier to establish a common ground with many people coming from management or executives, as well as gathering more specific requirements regarding your software. If the company cares about the privacy of its users, for instance, it can have a requirement to store as little data about its users as possible and to encrypt it using a key stored only on a user's device. Often, if such requirements come from the company culture, it will be too obvious for some employees to even articulate them. Knowing the context of the business can help you to ask proper questions and help the company in return.

Having said that, remember that your stakeholders can, and will, have needs that aren't necessarily directly reflected in the company's objectives. They can have their own ideas for functionality to provide or metrics that the software should achieve. Perhaps a manager promised his employees a chance to learn a new technology or work with a specific one. If this project is important for their career, they can become a strong ally and even convince others of your decisions.

Another important group of stakeholders is the people responsible for deploying your software. They can come with their own subgroup of needs, called transition requirements. Examples of those include user and database migration, infrastructure transition, or data conversion, so don't forget to reach out to them to gather these as well.

Gathering requirements from stakeholders

At this point, you should have a list of stakeholders with their roles and contact information. Now, it's time to make use of it. Be sure to make time to talk with each stakeholder about what they need from the system and how they envision it. You can hold interviews such as 1:1 meetings or group ones. When talking with your stakeholders, help them to make informed decisions—show the potential outcomes of their answers on the end product.

It's common for stakeholders to say that all of their requirements are equally important. Try to persuade them to prioritize their requirements according to the value they bring to their business. Certainly, there will be some mission-critical requirements, but most probably, the project won't fail if a bunch of others won't be delivered, not to mention any nice-to-haves that will land on your requirements wish list.

Aside from interviews, you can also organize workshops for them, which could work like brainstorming sessions. In such workshops, once the common ground is established and everybody knows why they're taking part in such a venture, you can start asking everyone for as many usage scenarios as they can think of. Once these have been established, you can proceed with consolidating similar ones, after which you should prioritize, and, finally, refine all the stories. Workshops are not just about functional requirements; each usage scenario can have a quality attribute assigned as well. After refining, all the quality attributes should be measurable, testable, and usable for evaluating the quality of interest of the system. The final thing to note is this: you don't need to bring all stakeholders into such events, as they can sometimes take more than a day, depending on the size of the system.

Documenting requirements

Once you're done with the steps described previously, it's time to refine all the requirements you've gathered, but putting them in a single document is often impractical because they typically consist of many artifacts: architecture and workflow diagrams, wireframes, spreadsheets, checklists, and other forms of specialized documentation.

Requirements are produced and consumed by all stakeholders, and a broad set of them will need to read your document. This means that you should write it for the target audience so that it brings value for people of various technical skills, from customers, salespeople, and marketers, through designers and project managers, to software architects, developers, and testers.

Sometimes it makes sense to prepare two versions of the document, one for the people closest to the business side of the project and another, a more technical one, for the development team. However, usually, it's enough to just have one document written to be understandable by everyone, with sections (sometimes single paragraphs) or whole chapters meant to cover the more technical details.

Let's now take a tour of what sections could go into your requirements document.

Documenting the context

A requirements document should act as one of the entry points for people getting on board with your project: it should outline the purpose of your product, what business goals it is trying to accomplish, what key functionality it will deliver, who will use it, and how it can be used. Before design and development, the product team members should read it to have a clear idea of what they'll work on.

You can describe a few typical user personas, such as *John the CTO* or *Ann the driver*, to give the readers a better chance to think about the users of the system as real people and know what to expect from them.

All those things described in the *Knowing the context* section should also be summarized as part of this section, or sometimes even given separate sections in the document. The context should provide all the information required by most non-project stakeholders. It should be concise and precise.

The same goes for any open questions you may want to research and decide on later. For each decision you make, it's best to note the following:

- What the decision was
- Who made it and when
- What rationale stands behind it

Now that you know how to document the context of your project, let's learn how to properly describe its scope, too.

Documenting the scope

This section should define what's in the scope of the project, as well as what is beyond the scope. You should provide a rationale for why the scope is defined in a particular way, especially when writing about things that won't make the cut.

This section should also cover the high-level functional requirements and NFRs, but details should go into the subsequent sections of the document. If you're familiar with Agile practices, just describe epics and bigger user stories here.

If you or your stakeholders have any assumptions regarding the scope, you should mention those here. If the scope is subject to change due to any issues or risks, you should also write some words about it, and similarly for any trade-offs you had to make.

Documenting functional requirements

Each requirement should be precise and testable. Consider this example: *The system will have a ranking system for the drivers*. How would you create tests against it? It's better to create a section for the ranking system and specify the precise requirements for it there.

Consider this other example: *If there's a free driver close to the rider, they should be notified of the incoming ride request*. What if there's more than one driver available? What maximum distance can we still describe as being *close*? This requirement is both imprecise and lacking parts of the business logic. We can only hope that the case where there are no free drivers is covered by another requirement.

In 2009, Rolls-Royce developed its **Easy Approach to Requirements Syntax** (**EARS**) to help cope with this. In EARS, there are five basic types of requirements, which should be written in a different way and serve different purposes. They can be later combined to create more complex requirements. Those basic ones are as follows:

- **Ubiquitous requirement**: *The <system> shall <response>*. For example, *The application shall be developed in C++*.
- **Event-driven**: *When <trigger> <optional precondition>, the <system> shall <response>*. For example, *When an order arrives, the gateway shall produce a new order event*.
- **Unwanted behavior**: *If <trigger>, then the <system> shall <response>*. For example, *If the processing of the request takes longer than 1 second, the tool shall display a progress bar*.
- **State-driven**: *While <state>, the <system> shall <response>*. For example, *While a ride is taking place, the app shall display a map to help the driver navigate to the destination*.
- **Optional feature**: *Where <feature>, the <system> shall <response>*. For example, *Where A/C is present, the app shall let the user set the temperature through the mobile application*.

An example of a more complex requirement would be: *When using a dual-server setup, if the backup server doesn't hear from the primary one for 5 seconds, it should try to register itself as a new primary server*.

You don't need to use EARS, but it can help if you struggle with ambiguous, vague, overly complex, untestable, omissive, or otherwise badly worded requirements. Whatever way or wording you choose, be sure to use a concise model that is based on common syntax and uses predefined keywords.

It's also good practice to assign an identifier for each requirement you list, so you'll have an easy way to refer to them. For instance, the identifier *REQMI* can be used in place of *manage inventory*. This identifier can be used throughout the documentation instead of repeating the full requirement every time.

When it comes to more detailed requirements formats, it should have the following fields:

- **ID or Index:** This is used to easily identify a specific requirement.
- **Title:** You can use the EARS template here.
- **Detailed description:** You can put whatever information you find relevant here, for example, user stories.
- **Owner:** Who does this requirement serve? This can be the product owner, the sales team, legal, IT, and so on.
- **Priority:** This is pretty self-explanatory.
- **Deliver by:** If this requirement is needed for any key date, you can note it here.

Now that we know how to document functional requirements, let's discuss how you should approach documenting the non-functional ones.

Documenting NFRs

Each quality attribute, such as performance or scalability, should have its own section in your document, with specific, testable requirements listed. Most of the quality attributes are measurable, so having specific metrics can do a world of good to resolve future questions. You can also have a separate section about the constraints that your project has.

With regard to wording, you can use the same EARS template to document your NFRs. Alternatively, you can also specify them as user stories using the personas that you defined in the context of this chapter.

Managing the version history of your documentation

You can take one of the two following approaches: either create a version log inside the document or use an external versioning tool. Both have their pros and cons, but we recommend going with the latter approach. Just like you use a version control system for your code, you can use it for your documentation. We're not saying you must use a Markdown document stored in a Git repo, but that's a perfectly valid approach as long as you're also generating a *businesspeople-readable* version of it, be it a web page or a PDF file. Alternatively, you can just use online tools, such as Redmine wikis or Confluence pages, which allow you to put a meaningful comment describing what's been changed on each edit you publish and to view the differences between versions. If you decided to take a revision log approach, it's usually a table that includes the following fields:

- **Revision:** A number identifying which iteration of the document the changes were introduced in. You can also add tags for special revisions, such as *the first draft*, if you so wish.
- **Updated by:** Who made the change.

- **Reviewed by:** Who reviewed the change.
- **Change description:** A *commit message* for this revision. It states what changes have taken place.

Documentation should have owners because documents become stale and require more effort to maintain without owners.

Documenting requirements in Agile projects

Many proponents of Agile would claim that documenting all the requirements is simply a waste of time, as they will probably change anyway. However, a good approach is to treat them similarly to items in your backlog: the ones that will be developed in the upcoming sprints should be defined in more detail than the ones that you wish to implement later. Just like you won't split your epics into stories and stories into tasks before it's necessary, you can get away with having just roughly described, less granular requirements until you're certain that you need them implemented.

Note who or what was the source of a given requirement so that you'll know who can provide you with the necessary input for refining it in the future.

Let's take a trade fair, for example. Say in the next sprint, we'll be building the shop page for a visitor to view, and in the sprint after that one, we'll be adding a subscription mechanism. Our requirements could look like the following:

ID	Priority	Description	Stakeholders
DF-42	P1	The shop's page must show the shop's inventory, with a photo and price for each item.	Josh, Rick
DF-43	P2	The shop's page must feature a map with the shop's location.	Josh, Candice
DF-44	P2	Customers must be able to subscribe to shops.	Steven

As you can see, the first two items relate to the feature we'll be doing next, so they are described in more detail. Who knows, maybe before the next sprint, the requirement about subscriptions will be dropped, so it doesn't make sense to think about every detail of it.

There are cases, on the other hand, that would still require you to have a complete list of requirements. If you need to deal with external regulators or internal teams such as auditing, legal, or compliance, chances are they'll still require a well-written physical document from you. Sometimes, just handing them a document containing work items extracted from your backlog is OK. It's best to communicate with such stakeholders just like with any other ones: gather their expectations to know the minimum viable documentation that satisfies their needs.

What's important about documenting requirements is to have an understanding between you and the parties proposing specific requirements. How can this be achieved? Once you have a draft ready to go, you should show your documentation to them and gather feedback. This way, you'll know what was ambiguous, unclear, or missing. Even if it takes a few iterations, it will help you have a common ground with your stakeholders, so you'll gain more confidence that you're building the right thing.

Other sections

It's a good idea to have a *Links and resources* section in which you point to stuff such as the issue tracker boards, artifacts, CI, the source repo, and whatever else you'll find handy. Architectural, marketing, and other kinds of documents can also be listed here.

If needed, you can also include a glossary.

Now, you know how to document your requirements and related information. Let's say a few words about documenting the designed system.

Documenting architecture

Just as you should document your requirements, you should also document the emerging architecture. It's certainly not just for the sake of having documentation: it should help each person involved in the project to be more productive by making them better understand what's required from them and from the final product. Not all diagrams you'll make will be useful for everyone, but you should create them from the perspective of their future readers.

There's a multitude of frameworks to document your vision, and many of them serve specific fields, project types, or architectural scopes. If you're interested in documenting enterprise architecture, for instance, you could be interested in **TOGAF**. This is an acronym for **The Open Group Architecture Framework**. It relies on four domains, as follows:

- Business architecture (strategy, organization, key processes, and governance)
- Data architecture (logical and physical data management)
- Application architecture (blueprints for individual systems)
- Technical architecture (hardware, software, and network infrastructure)

Such grouping is useful if you document your software in the scope of the whole company or even broader ones. Other similar-scale frameworks include the **NATO Architecture Framework** (**NAF**; `https://eapad.dk/resource/nato-architecture-framework-naf-v-4/`), its American equivalent, the **Department of Defense Architecture Framework** (**DoDAF**; `https://dodcio.defense.gov/Library/DoD-Architecture-Framework/`), ArchiMate (`https://www.archimatetool.com/`), TOGAF (`https://www.opengroup.org/togaf`), **Business Process Model and Notation** (**BPMN**; `https://www.bpmn.org/`), and **Systems Modeling Language** (**SysML**; `https://sysml.org/`).

If you're not documenting enterprise architectures, and especially if you're just starting on your architectural self-development path, you'll probably be more interested in other frameworks, such as the 4+1 and C4 models.

Understanding the 4+1 model

The 4+1 view model was introduced by Philippe Kruchten in 1995 in his paper titled *Architectural Blueprints—The "4+1" View Model of Software Architecture*. The author claimed it is intended for "*describing the architecture of software-intensive systems, based on the use of multiple, concurrent views.*" Its name comes from the views it consists of.

This model is widely known since it has been on the market for so long and does its job. It's well suited for bigger projects, and while it can be used for small- and medium-sized ones as well, it can also turn out too complex for their needs (especially if they're written in an Agile way). If that's your case, you should try out the C4 model described in the next section.

A downside to the 4+1 model is that it does not enforce a formal notation or standard, and uses a fixed set of views, while a pragmatic approach to document architecture would be to choose views based on the specifics of your project (more on that later).

A nice upside, on the other hand, is how the views link together, especially when it comes to scenarios. At the same time, each stakeholder can easily get the parts of the model relevant to them. This brings us to how the model appears:

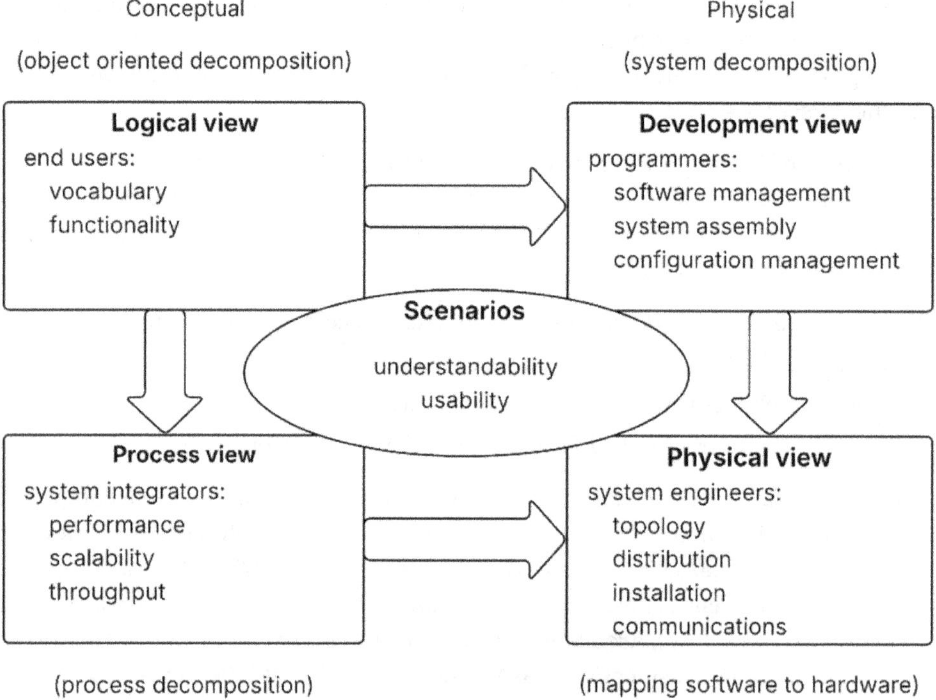

Figure 3.2: An overview of the 4+1 model

Actors in the preceding diagram are the ones most interested in their corresponding views. All the views can be represented using different kinds of **Unified Modeling Language** (**UML**) diagrams. Let's now discuss different components of the diagram:

- The **logical view** shows how functionality is provided to users. It shows the system's components (objects) and how they interact with each other. Most commonly, it consists of class, object, and composite structure diagrams. If you have thousands of classes or just want to better show the interactions between them, you should also have communication or sequence diagrams, both being parts of our next view:

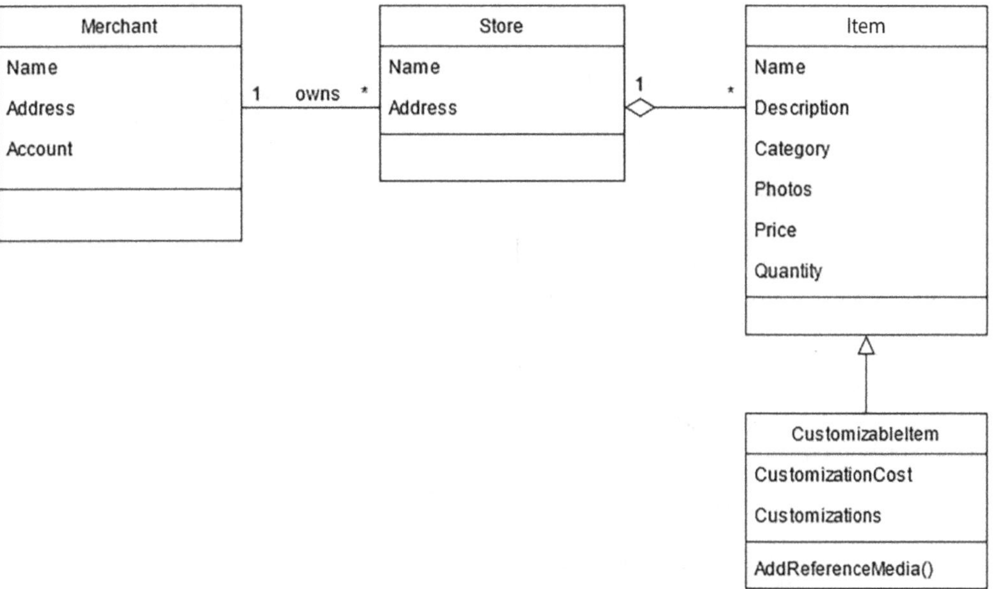

Figure 3.3: Class diagram illustrating the types we plan to have, along with their relations

- The **process view** revolves around the system's runtime behavior. It shows processes, the communication between them, and interactions with external systems. It's usually represented by sequence, communication, activity, state, interaction overview, and timing diagrams. This view addresses many NFRs, including concurrency, performance, availability, and scalability:

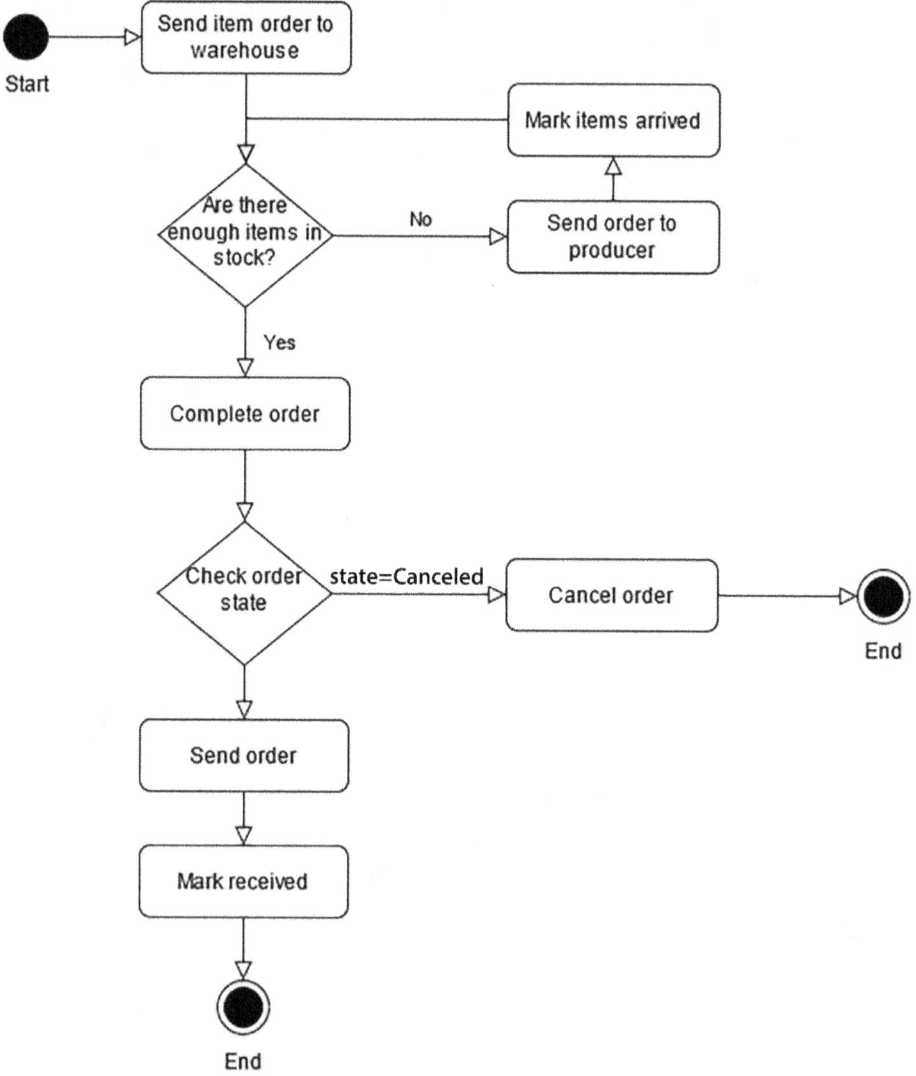

Figure 3.4: Activity diagram showing workflows and processes

- The **development view** is for decomposing into subsystems and revolves around software organization. Reuse, tooling constraints, layering, modularization, packaging, and execution environments—this view can represent them by showing a building block decomposition of the system. It does so by using components and packages, among others:

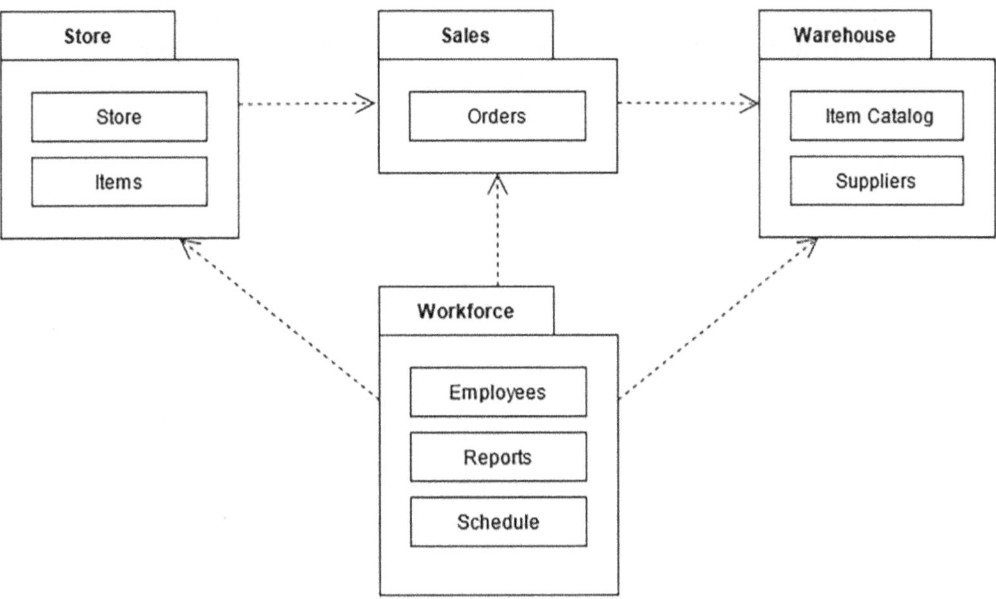

Figure 3.5: Package diagram providing a high-level view of the system and illustrating dependencies or relationships between specific packages

- The **physical view** is used to map software to hardware using deployment diagrams. Targeted at system engineers, it can cover a subset of NFRs concerned with the hardware, for example, communication:

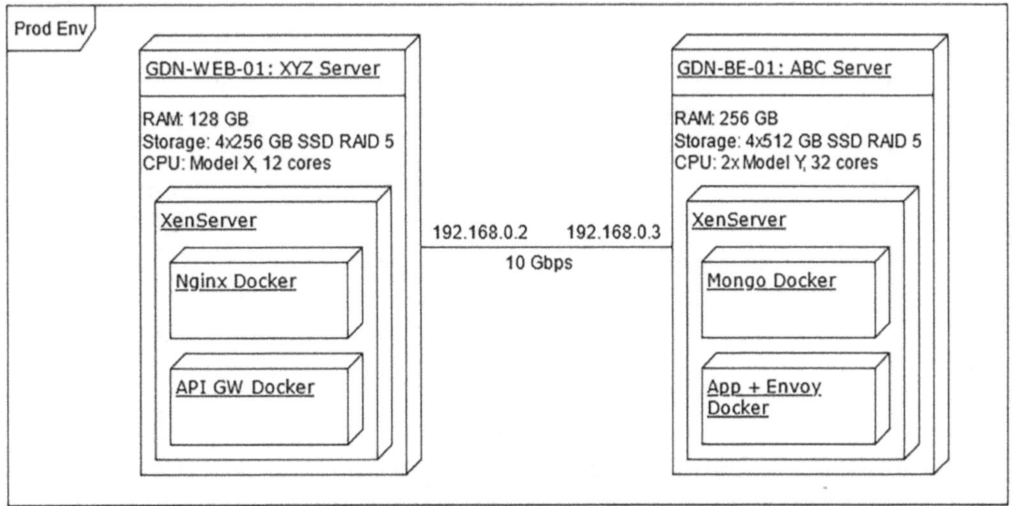

Figure 3.6: Deployment diagram demonstrating the hardware on which each software component will run, along with network-related information

- The **scenarios** are gluing all the other views together. Represented by use case diagrams, these can be useful for all stakeholders. This view shows whether the system does what it should and that it is consistent. When all the other views are finished, the scenario view can be redundant. However, they wouldn't be possible without usage scenarios. This view shows the system from a high level, while the other views go into the details:

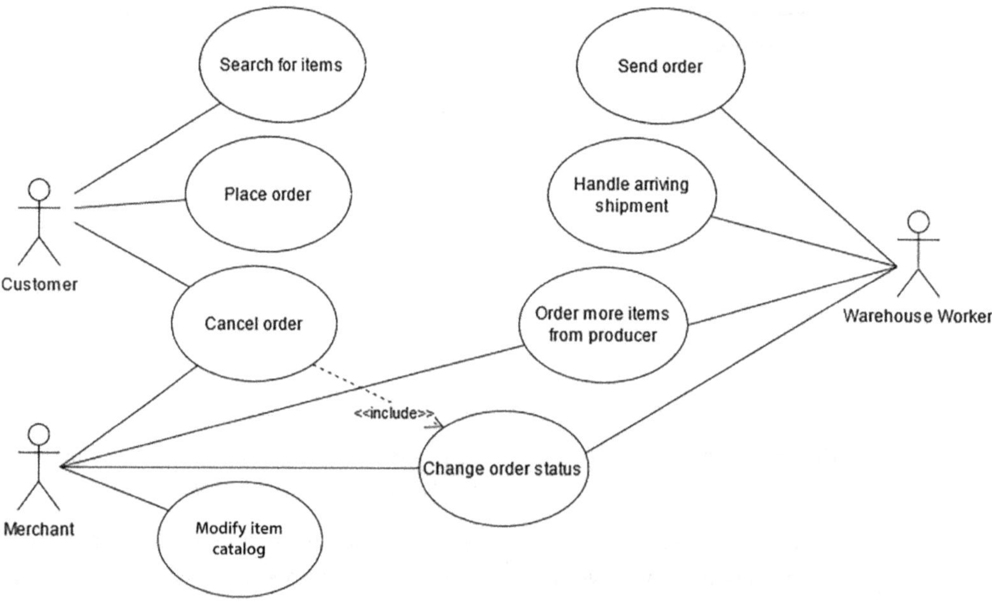

Figure 3.7: Use case diagram showing how specific actors interact with the system and how the interactions relate to each other

Each of those views is interconnected with the others, and often they must coexist to show the full picture. Let's think about expressing concurrency. It can't be done using only the logical view. As it's more expressive to map concurrency to tasks and processes, we need the process view. The processes, in turn, will be mapped to physical, often distributed, nodes, which brings the physical view into the picture. This means we'll need to effectively document such concerns in three views, each of which will be relevant for a specific group of stakeholders. Other connections between the views include the following:

- Both logical and process views are used in analysis and design to conceptualize the product
- Development and deployment in conjunction describe how the software is packaged and when each package will be deployed
- The logical and development views show how the functionality is reflected in the source code
- The process and deployment/physical views are meant to collectively describe NFRs

Now that you're familiar with the 4+1 model, let's discuss another one, which is simple yet extremely effective: the C4 model. We hope using it will be a blast (pun intended).

Understanding the C4 model

The C4 model is a great fit for small- to medium-sized projects. It's easy to apply, as it's quite simple and it doesn't rely on any predefined notation. If you want to start diagramming using it, you can try C4 shapes with the user-friendly drag-and-drop tools Draw.io, Mermaid, Miro, Lucidchart, or IcePanel.

In the C4 model, there are four main types of diagrams, as follows:

- System context
- Container
- Component
- Code

The other C4 models are system landscape, dynamic, and deployment.

Just like zooming in and out using a map, you can use those four types to show more details of a particular code region or *zoom out* to show more about the interactions and surroundings of either a specific module or even the whole system.

The system context is a great starting point for looking at the architecture, as it shows the system as a whole, surrounded by its users and other systems that it interacts with. You can take a look at an example C4 system context diagram here:

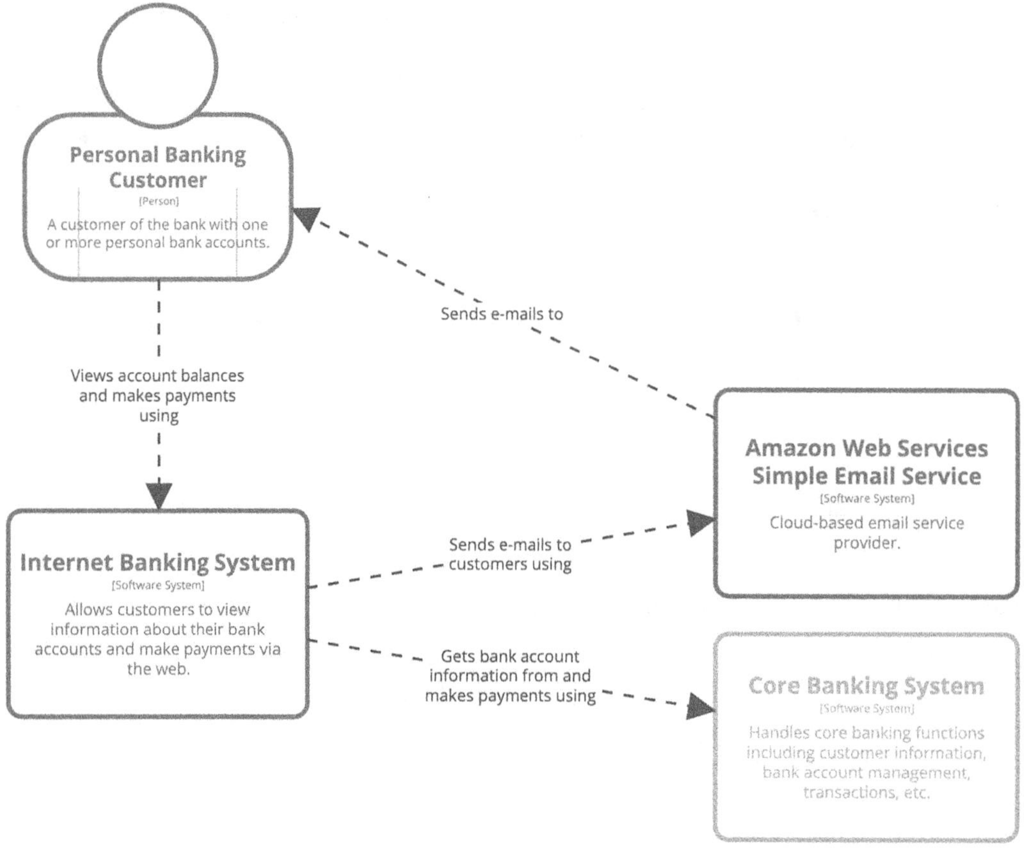

Figure 3.8: A C4 system context diagram (by Simon Brown, licensed under CC BY 4.0: https://c4model.com/diagrams/system-context)

As you can see, it shows the *big picture*, so it shouldn't focus on specific technologies or protocols. Instead, think of it as a diagram that could also be shown to non-technical stakeholders. Just by looking at the diagram, it should be clear that there's one actor involved (the human-shaped depiction of the customer), who interacts with one of the components of our solution, namely, the customer service system. This system, on the other hand, interacts with two more, with each of the interactions described along with the arrows.

The system context diagram we described is used to provide an overview of the system with a few details. Let's now look at the other diagrams one by one:

- **Container diagram:** This one is for showing the overview of the system internals. If your system uses a database, offers services, or just consists of certain applications, this diagram will show it. It can also show the major technology choices for the containers. Note that containers don't mean Docker containers, but applications or data stores; although each is a separately runnable and deployable unit, this diagram type is not about deployment scenarios. The container view is meant for technical people, but isn't limited to the development team only. Architects, as well as operations and support, are the intended audience, too.

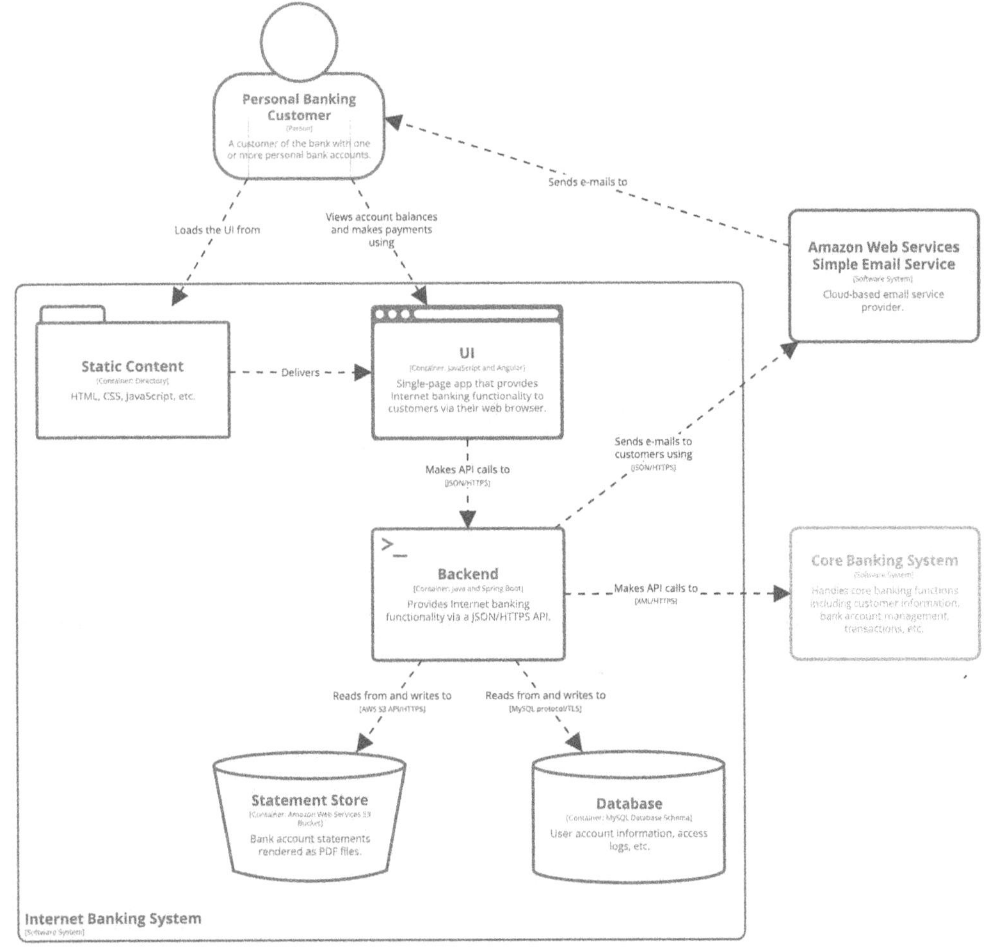

Figure 3.9: A C4 container diagram (by Simon Brown, licensed under CC BY 4.0: https://c4model.com/diagrams/container)

(This image is for visualization purpose only. Check the graphic bundle for a high-resolution version.)

- **Component diagram:** If you want more details about a specific container, this is where the component diagram comes into play. It shows how the components inside a selected container interact with each other, as well as with elements and actors outside the container. By looking at this diagram, you can learn about the responsibilities of each component and what technology it's built with. The intended audience for component diagrams is mostly focused on a specific container and consists of the development team and the architect.

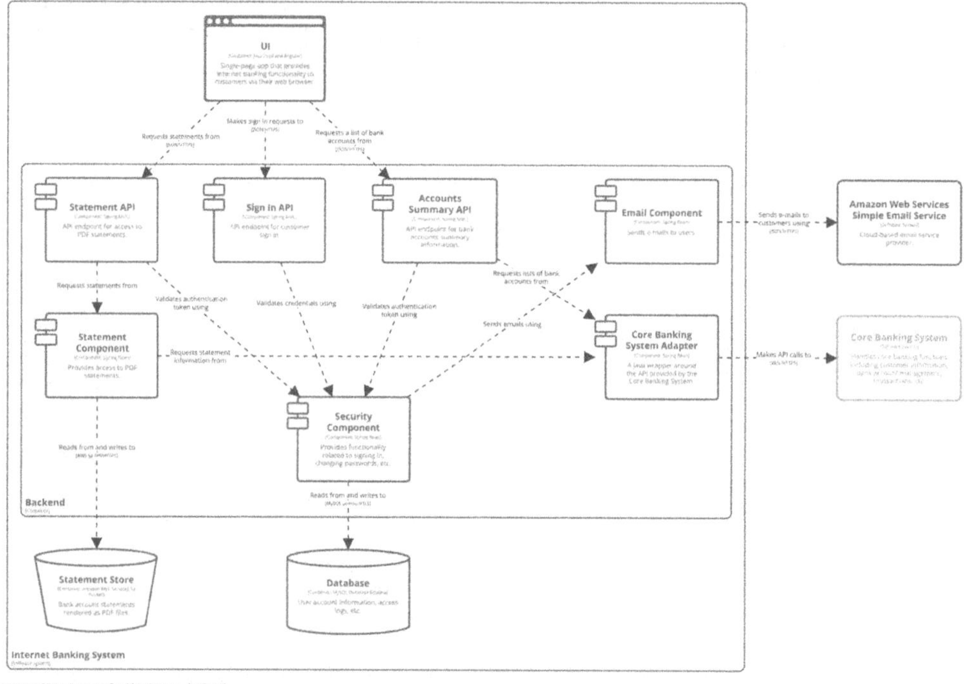

Figure 3.10: A C4 component diagram (by Simon Brown, licensed under CC BY 4.0: https://c4model.com/diagrams/component)

(This image is for visualization purpose only. Check the graphic bundle for a high-resolution version.)

- **Code diagrams:** We finally come to code diagrams, which emerge when you zoom in to a specific component. This view consists mostly of UML diagrams, including class, entity-relationship, and others, and ideally should be created automatically from source code by standalone tools and IDEs. You should definitely not make such diagrams for each component in your system; instead, focus on making them for the most important ones in a way that allows them to tell the reader what you had in mind. This means that less can be more in such diagrams, so you should omit unnecessary elements from code diagrams. In many systems, especially smaller ones, this class of diagram is omitted. The target audience is the same as in the case of component diagrams.

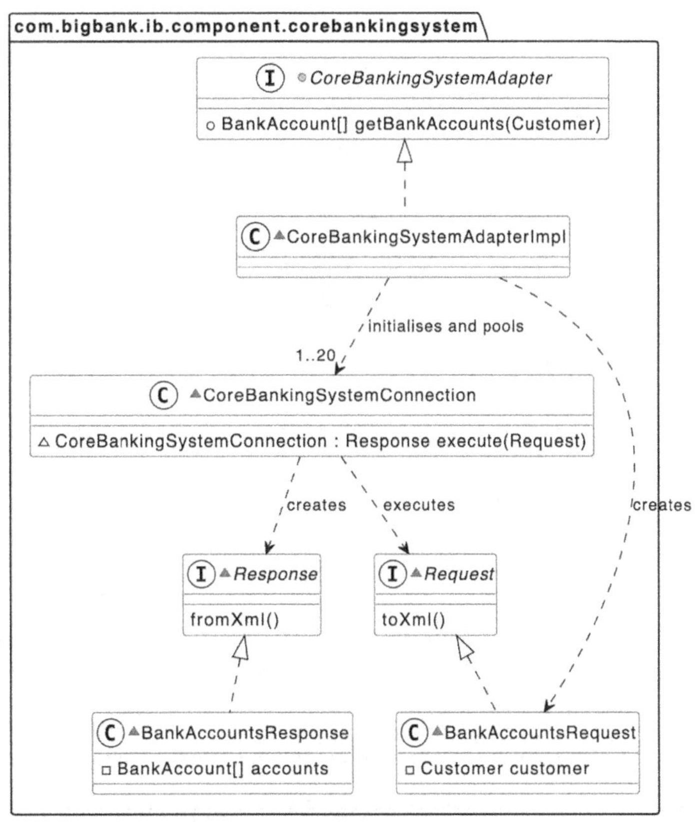

Code View: Internet Banking System - Backend - Core Banking System Adapter

Figure 3.11: A C4 code diagram (by Simon Brown, licensed under CC BY 4.0: https://c4model.com/diagrams/code)

You may find the C4 model lacking some specific views. If you're wondering how to demonstrate the deployment of your system, for instance, you might be interested to learn that aside from the main diagrams, there are also a few supplementary ones. One of them is the deployment diagram, which you can see next. It shows containers in your system mapped to nodes in your infrastructure. In general, it's a simpler version of UML's deployment diagram:

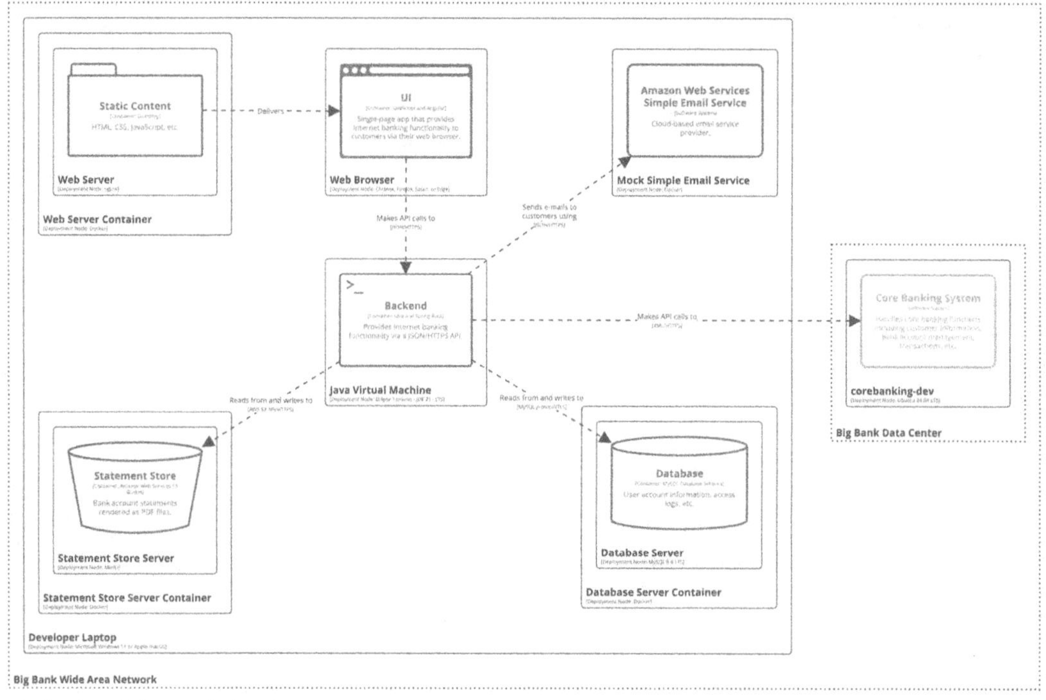

Figure 3.12: A C4 deployment diagram (by Simon Brown, licensed under CC BY 4.0: https://c4model.com/diagrams/deployment)

(This image is for visualization purpose only. Check the graphic bundle for a high-resolution version.)

Speaking of UML diagrams regarding the C4 model, you might also wonder why it puts so little effort into presenting the system's use cases. If that's your case, then you should think about supplementing the preceding models with either the use case diagram from UML or perhaps think about introducing some sequence diagrams.

When documenting architecture, it's more important what you document and what knowledge you share than to follow a specific hard set of rules. Choose whatever tools suit your needs the best.

Documenting architecture in Agile projects

In Agile environments, your approach to documenting architecture should be similar to the one about documenting requirements. First and foremost, consider who will be reading the materials you prepare to be sure you're describing the right things in the right way. Your documentation doesn't need to be a lengthy Word document. You can use presentations, wiki pages, single diagrams, or even recordings from meetings when someone describes the architecture.

What is important is to gather feedback on the documented architecture. Again, in the same way as with the documented requirements, it's important to reiterate the documents with your stakeholders to know where to improve them. Even though this may seem like you're wasting time, if done properly, it should save you some time in terms of delivering the product. Good enough documentation should help newcomers start being productive faster and guide more familiar stakeholders down the road. If you just discuss the architecture at some meetings, chances are, a quarter later, no one will remember why you made the decisions you made and whether they will remain valid in the ever-changing Agile landscape.

Reiteration is important when creating documentation because there will probably be some misunderstanding of an important detail or two. Other times, you or your stakeholders will gain more knowledge and decide to change things. Be prepared to go through the document at least a few times before it will be considered mature and done. Often, a few conversations over instant messaging, phone, or in-person will help you finish it quicker and address any follow-ups that could arise, so prefer those to emails or other asynchronous ways of communication.

Choosing the right views to document

Architecture is way too complex a topic to be described by a single big diagram. Imagine you're the architect of a building. To design the whole thing, you'd need separate diagrams for different aspects: one for plumbing, another one for electricity and other cables, and so on. Each of those diagrams would show a different view of the project. The same goes for software architecture: you need to present the software from different perspectives, aimed at different stakeholders.

Moreover, if you were building a smart house, chances are you would draw a plan of the devices you want to place around. Although not all projects will require such views, since it plays a role in your project, it may be worth adding it. The same approach is also valid for architecture: if you find a different view valuable to the document, you should do it. So, how do you know which views could be valuable? You can try to perform the following steps:

1. Start with the views from either the 4+1 model or the C4 model.
2. Ask your stakeholders what is essential for them to have documented, and think about modifying your set of views.
3. Choose views that will help you evaluate whether the architecture meets its objectives and that all the ASRs are satisfied. Read the first paragraph of each of the views from the next sections to check whether they suit your needs.

If you're still not sure which views to document, here's a set of tips: try picking the most important views, because when there are too many of them, the architecture will become too hard to follow. A good set of views should not only showcase the architecture but also expose the technical risks to the project.

There are different types of architectural views that you can include in your document. We'll describe them shortly here, but if you're interested, you should grab Nick Rozanski and Eoin Woods' book titled *Software Systems Architecture: Working with Stakeholders Using Viewpoints and Perspectives*.

Functional view

If your software is being developed as part of a bigger system, especially with teams that don't communicate on a daily basis, you should include a functional view (as in the 4+1 model).

One important and often overlooked aspect of documenting your architecture that gets covered in the functional view is the definition of the interfaces you provide, despite it being one of the most important things to describe. Whether it's an interface between two of your components or an entry point for the outside world, you should take the time to document it clearly, describing the semantics of objects and calls, as well as usage examples (which you can sometimes reuse as tests).

Another great benefit of including a functional view in your documentation is that it clarifies the responsibilities between the components of your system. Each team developing the system should understand where the boundaries are and who is responsible for developing which functionality. All requirements should be explicitly mapped to components to eliminate gaps and duplicated work.

An important thing to note here is to avoid overloading your functional view. If it gets messy, no one will want to read it. If you're starting to describe infrastructure on it, consider adding a deployment view. If you end up having a *god object* in your models, try to rethink the design and split it into smaller, more cohesive pieces.

One last important note about the functional view: try to keep each diagram you include on one level of abstraction. On the other hand, don't make it too vague by choosing an overly abstract level; ensure that every element is properly defined and understood by the interested parties.

Information view

If your system has non-straightforward needs with regard to information, its processing flow, management process, or storage, perhaps it's a good idea to include this kind of view.

Take the most important, data-rich entities and demonstrate how they flow through the system, who owns them, and who the producers and consumers are. It may be useful to mark how long certain data remains *fresh* and when it can be safely discarded, what the expected latency for it to arrive at certain points of the system is, or how to deal with identifiers if your system works in a distributed environment. If your system manages transactions, this process, along with any rollbacks, should also be clear to your stakeholders. Techniques for transforming, sending, and persisting data can also be important for some of them. If you are operating in the financial domain or have to deal with personal data, you most probably must obey some regulations, so describe how your system plans to tackle this.

The structure of your data can be diagrammed using UML class models. Remember to be clear about the format of your data, especially if it flows between two different systems. NASA lost the $125 million-worth Mars Climate Orbiter, which it co-developed with Lockheed Martin, because they used different units unknowingly, so keep an eye out for data inconsistencies between systems.

The processing flow of your data can use UML's activity model, and to show the life cycle of information, a state diagram can be used.

Concurrency view

If running many concurrent units of execution is an important aspect of your product, consider adding a concurrency view. It can show what issues and bottlenecks you may have (unless that sounds too detailed). Other good reasons to include are the reliance on interprocess communication, having a non-straightforward task structure, concurrent state management, synchronization, or task failure handling logic.

Use whatever notation you want for this view, as long as it captures the units of execution and their communication. Assign priorities to your processes and threads, if necessary, and then analyze any potential issues, such as deadlocks or contention. You can use state diagrams to show the possible states and their transitions for important units of execution (waiting for queries, executing a query, distributing results, and so on).

If you're not sure about the need to introduce concurrency to your system, a good rule of thumb is *don't*. And if you must, strive for a simple design. Debugging concurrency issues is never easy and always long, so if possible, try to optimize what you have first instead of just throwing more threads at the problem at hand.

If, by looking at your diagram, you're worried about resource contention, try to replace locks on big objects with more locks, but finer-grained; use lightweight synchronization (sometimes atomics are enough), introduce optimistic locking, or reduce what's shared (creating an additional copy of some data in a thread and processing it using techniques such as copy-on-write can be faster than sharing access to the only copy).

Development view

If you're building a big system with lots of modules, and you need to structure your code, have system-wide design constraints, or if you want to share some common aspects between parts of your system, presenting the solution from a development viewpoint should benefit you, along with software developers and testers.

A package diagram of the development view can be handy to show where different modules in your system are located, what their dependencies are, and other related modules (for example, residing in the same software layer). It doesn't need to be a UML diagram—even boxes and lines would do. If you plan for a module to be replaceable, this kind of diagram can show you what other software packages can be affected.

Tactics to increase reuse in your system, such as creating your own runtime framework for components, or tactics for increasing the coherence of your systems, such as a common approach to authentication, logging, internationalization, or other kinds of processing, are all part of the development view. If you see any common parts of the system, document them to be sure that all developers see them too.

A common approach to code organization, building, and configuration management should also go into this section of your documentation. If all this sounds like a lot to document, then focus on the most important parts and cover the rest just briefly, if at all.

Deployment and operational views

If you have a non-standard or complex deployment environment, such as specific needs with regard to hardware, third-party software, or networking requirements, consider documenting it in a separate deployment section, aimed at system administrators, developers, and testers.

If necessary, cover the following things:

- The amount of memory required
- The CPU thread count (with or without hyperthreading)
- Pinning and affinity regarding **non-uniform memory access** (NUMA) nodes
- Specialist networking equipment requirements, such as switches that mark packages to measure latency and throughput in a black-box manner
- The networking topology
- The estimated bandwidth required
- Storage requirements for your app
- Any third-party software that you plan to use

Once you have the requirements, you can map them to specific hardware and put them into a runtime platform model. You can use a UML deployment diagram with stereotypes if you desire formal modeling. This should show your processing nodes and client nodes, online and offline storage, network links, specialized hardware, such as firewalls or FPGA or ASIC devices, and a mapping between functional elements and the nodes they'll run on.

If you have non-straightforward networking needs, you can add another diagram showing the networking nodes and the connections between them.

If you depend on specific technologies (including specific versions of software), it's a good idea to list them to see whether there are any compatibility issues between the software you use. Sometimes, two third-party components will require the same dependency, but in different versions.

If you have a specific installation and upgrade plan, it might be a good idea to write a few words about it. Things such as A/B testing, blue-green deployments, or any particular container magic that your solution will rely on should be clear to everyone involved. Data migration plans should also be covered, if needed, including how long the migration can take and when it could be scheduled.

Any plans for configuration management, performance monitoring, operational monitoring, and control, as well as backup strategies, can all be things worth describing. You'll probably want to create a few groups, identify the dependencies of each, and define the approach for each such group. If you can think about any probable errors that may occur, have a plan to detect and recover from them.

A few notes to the support team can also go into this section: what support is required by which stakeholder group, what classes of incidents you plan to have, how to escalate, and what each level of support will be responsible for.

It's best to engage early with the operational staff and create diagrams specifically for them as a way to keep them engaged.

Now that we've discussed how to create documentation about your system and its requirements manually, let's switch to automating the documentation process.

Generating documentation

As engineers, we don't like manual labor. This is why, if something can be automated and save us work, it most likely will be. With all this effort to create good enough documentation, having the possibility to automate at least parts of the work can be bliss.

Generating requirements documentation

If you're creating a project from scratch, it can be hard to generate documentation out of thin air. However, sometimes it's possible to generate documentation if you have the requirements captured in an appropriate tool. If you're using Jira, for instance, a starting point would be to just export all items from an issue navigator view. You can use whatever filter you like and get printouts just for those items. If you don't like the default set of fields or just feel this is not what you're looking for, you can try out one of Jira's plugins for requirements management. They allow a whole lot more than just exporting requirements; for example, **Requirements for Jira** (**R4J**) allows you to create whole hierarchies of requirements, trace them, manage changes and propagate them through your whole project, perform impact analyses of any requirements changes, and, of course, export using user-defined templates. Many such tools will also aid you in creating test suites for your requirements, but none that we saw are free.

Generating diagrams from code

If you want to get to know your code structure without taking an initial deep dive into the sources, you might be interested in tools that generate diagrams from code.

One such tool is **CppDepend**, which enables you to create various dependency diagrams between different parts of your sources. What's more, it allows you to query and filter the code based on various parameters. Whether you want to just grasp how the code is structured, discover what the dependencies are between different software components and how tightly they're coupled, or quickly locate parts with the most technical debt, you might be interested in this tool. Although it is proprietary, it offers a fully functional trial and is free for non-commercial open source projects with a dedicated website and active community.

Some diagramming tools allow you to create code from class diagrams and class diagrams from code. **Enterprise Architect** enables you to take your class and interface diagrams and generate code in multiple languages. C++ is one of these and allows UML class diagrams to be generated directly from source code. Another tool that can do that is **Visual Paradigm.**

Generating (API) documentation from code

To help others navigate your existing code and use the APIs you provide, a good idea is to provide documentation generated from the comments in your code. There's no better place for such documentation than just right next to the functions and data types it describes, and this helps a lot in keeping them in sync.

A de facto standard tool for writing such documentation is **Doxygen**. Its positives are that it's fast (especially for big projects and HTML document generation), the generator has some built-in correctness checks (for example, for partially documented parameters in a function—a good marker to check whether the documentation is still up to date), and it allows the navigation of class and file hierarchies. Its disadvantages include not being able to do a full-text search, less-than-ideal PDF generation, and an interface some may find cumbersome.

Fortunately, the usability flaws can be remedied by using another popular tool for documentation. If you've ever read any Python documentation, you have probably stumbled upon Sphinx. It has a fresh-looking and usable interface and uses **reStructuredText** as a markup language. The good news is that there's a bridge between those two, so you can take XML generated from Doxygen and use it in Sphinx. This bridging software is called **Breathe**.

Let's now see how to set it up in your project. Let's assume we keep our sources in `src`, public headers in `include`, and documentation in doc. First, let's create a `CMakeLists.txt` file:

```
cmake_minimum_required(VERSION 3.10)

project("Breathe Demo" VERSION 0.0.1 LANGUAGES CXX)

list(APPEND CMAKE_MODULE_PATH "${CMAKE_CURRENT_LIST_DIR}/cmake")
add_subdirectory(src)
add_subdirectory(doc)
```

We've set the required CMake version for our project, specified its name, version, and the languages used (in our case, it's just C++), and added the `cmake` directory to the path under which CMake looks for its include files.

In the `cmake` subdirectory, we'll create one file, `FindSphinx.cmake`, which we'll use just as the name suggests, since Sphinx doesn't offer one already:

```
find_program(
  SPHINX_EXECUTABLE
  NAMES sphinx-build
  DOC "Path to sphinx-build executable")

# handle REQUIRED and QUIET arguments, set SPHINX_FOUND variable
include(FindPackageHandleStandardArgs)
find_package_handle_standard_args(
  Sphinx "Unable to locate sphinx-build executable" SPHINX_EXECUTABLE)
```

Now, CMake will look for our Sphinx build tool and, if found, will set appropriate CMake variables to mark the Sphinx package as found. Next, let's create our sources to generate the documentation. Let's have an `include/breathe_demo/demo.h` file:

```
#pragma once

// the @file annotation is needed for Doxygen to document the free
// functions in this file
/**
 * @file
 * @brief The main entry points of our demo
 */

/**
 * A unit of performable work
 */
struct Payload {
  /**
   * The actual amount of work to perform
   */
  int amount;
};

/**
   @brief Performs really important work
   @param payload the descriptor of work to be performed
 */
void perform_work(Payload payload);
```

Note the comment syntax. Doxygen recognizes it while parsing our header file so that it knows what to put in the generated documentation.

Now, let's add a corresponding `src/demo.cpp` implementation for our header:

```
#include "breathe_demo/demo.h"

#include <chrono>
#include <thread>

void perform_work(Payload payload) {
  std::this_thread::sleep_for(std::chrono::seconds(payload.amount));
}
```

No Doxygen comments here. We prefer to document our types and functions in the header files since they're the interface to our library. The source files are just implementations, and they don't add anything new to the interface.

Aside from the preceding files, we also need a simple `CMakeLists.txt` file in `src`:

```
add_library(BreatheDemo demo.cpp)
target_include_directories(BreatheDemo PUBLIC
  ${PROJECT_SOURCE_DIR}/include)
target_compile_features(BreatheDemo PUBLIC cxx_std_11)
```

Here, we specify the source files for our target, the directory with the header files for it, and the required C++ standard to compile against.

Now, let's move to the `doc` folder, where the magic happens. First, we have the `CMakeLists.txt` file, which starts with a check to establish whether Doxygen is available and skips document generation if it's not:

```
find_package(Doxygen)
if (NOT DOXYGEN_FOUND)
  return()
endif()
```

Note also the `return()` call, which will exit the current CMake list file, a not-that-widely-known but nevertheless useful trick.

Next, assuming Doxygen was found, we need to set some variables to steer the generation. We want just the XML output for Breathe, so let's set the following variables:

```
set(DOXYGEN_GENERATE_HTML NO)
set(DOXYGEN_GENERATE_XML YES)
```

To enforce the use of relative paths, use `set(DOXYGEN_STRIP_FROM_PATH ${PROJECT_SOURCE_DIR}/include)`. If you have any implementation details to hide, you can do this using `set(DOXYGEN_EXCLUDE_PATTERNS "*/detail/*")`. OK, since we have all the variables set, let's now generate:

```
# Note: Use doxygen_add_docs(doxygen-doc ALL ...) if you want your
documentation
# to be created by default each time you build. Without the # keyword you need
to
# explicitly invoke building of the 'doc' target.
doxygen_add_docs(doxygen-doc ${PROJECT_SOURCE_DIR}/include COMMENT
                 "Generating API documentation with Doxygen")
```

Here, we call a CMake function specifically written for using Doxygen. We define a target, `doxygen-doc`, which we'll need to explicitly invoke to generate our docs on demand, just like the comment says.

Now, we need to create a Breathe target to consume what we got from Doxygen. We can use our `FindSphinx` module to this end:

```
find_package(Sphinx REQUIRED)
configure_file(${CMAKE_CURRENT_SOURCE_DIR}/conf.py.in
               ${CMAKE_CURRENT_BINARY_DIR}/conf.py @ONLY)
add_custom_target(
  sphinx-doc ALL
  COMMAND ${SPHINX_EXECUTABLE} -b html -c ${CMAKE_CURRENT_BINARY_DIR}
          ${CMAKE_CURRENT_SOURCE_DIR} ${CMAKE_CURRENT_BINARY_DIR}
  WORKING_DIRECTORY ${CMAKE_CURRENT_BINARY_DIR}
  COMMENT "Generating API documentation with Sphinx"
  VERBATIM)
```

First, we invoke our module. Then, we fill in a Python configuration file with variables from our project for Sphinx to use. We create a `sphinx-doc` target that will generate HTML files as its output and will print a line in the build's output when doing so.

Finally, let's force CMake to call Doxygen each time we generate Sphinx docs, by adding the following dependency: `add_dependencies(sphinx-doc doxygen-doc)`.

If you wish to have more targets for documentation, it may be useful to introduce some CMake functions that will handle documentation-related targets for you.

Let's now see what lies inside our `conf.py.in` file, which is used to steer our feline tool. Let's create it and let it point Sphinx to Breathe:

```
extensions = [ "breathe", "sphinx_mdinclude" ]
breathe_projects = { "BreatheDemo": "@CMAKE_CURRENT_BINARY_DIR@/xml" }
breathe_default_project = "BreatheDemo"

project = "Breathe Demo"
author = "Breathe Demo Authors"
copyright = "2024, Breathe Demo Authors"
version = "@PROJECT_VERSION@"
release = "@PROJECT_VERSION@

html_theme = 'sphinx_rtd_theme'
```

As you can see from the preceding listing, we set the extensions for Sphinx to use, the name of the documented project, and a few other related variables. Note `@NOTATION@`, which is used by CMake to fill in the output file with the value of appropriate CMake variables. Finally, we tell Sphinx to use our ReadTheDocs theme (`sphinx_rtd_theme`).

The final pieces of the puzzle are reStructuredText files, which define what to include where in the docs. First, let's create an `index.rst` file, containing a table of contents and a few links:

```
Breathe Demo
============

Welcome to the Breathe Demo documentation!

.. toctree::
 :maxdepth: 2
 :caption: Contents:

Introduction <self>
 readme
 api_reference
```

The first link points to the current page, so we can get back to it from other pages. We'll display `Introduction` as the label. Other names point to other files with the `.rst` extension. Since we're including the `sphinx-mdinclude` extension, we can include our `README.md` file in the docs, which can save you some duplication. The contents of the `readme.rst` file are simply `.. mdinclude:: ../README.md`. Finally, we'll merge Doxygen's output in the `api_reference`.rst file using the following command:

```
API Reference
=============

.. doxygenindex::
```

So we just named the reference page as we liked and specified that the Doxygen-generated docs should be listed here, and that's all! Just build the `sphinx-doc` target and you'll get a page looking like this:

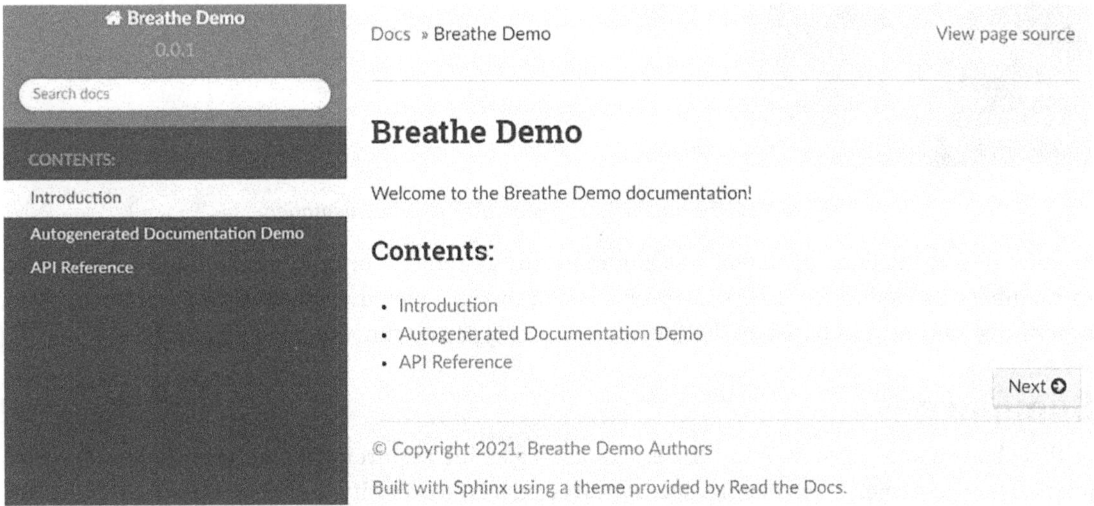

Figure 3.13: The main page of our documentation, consolidating both the generated and manually written parts

And when we look at the API docs page, it should look like this:

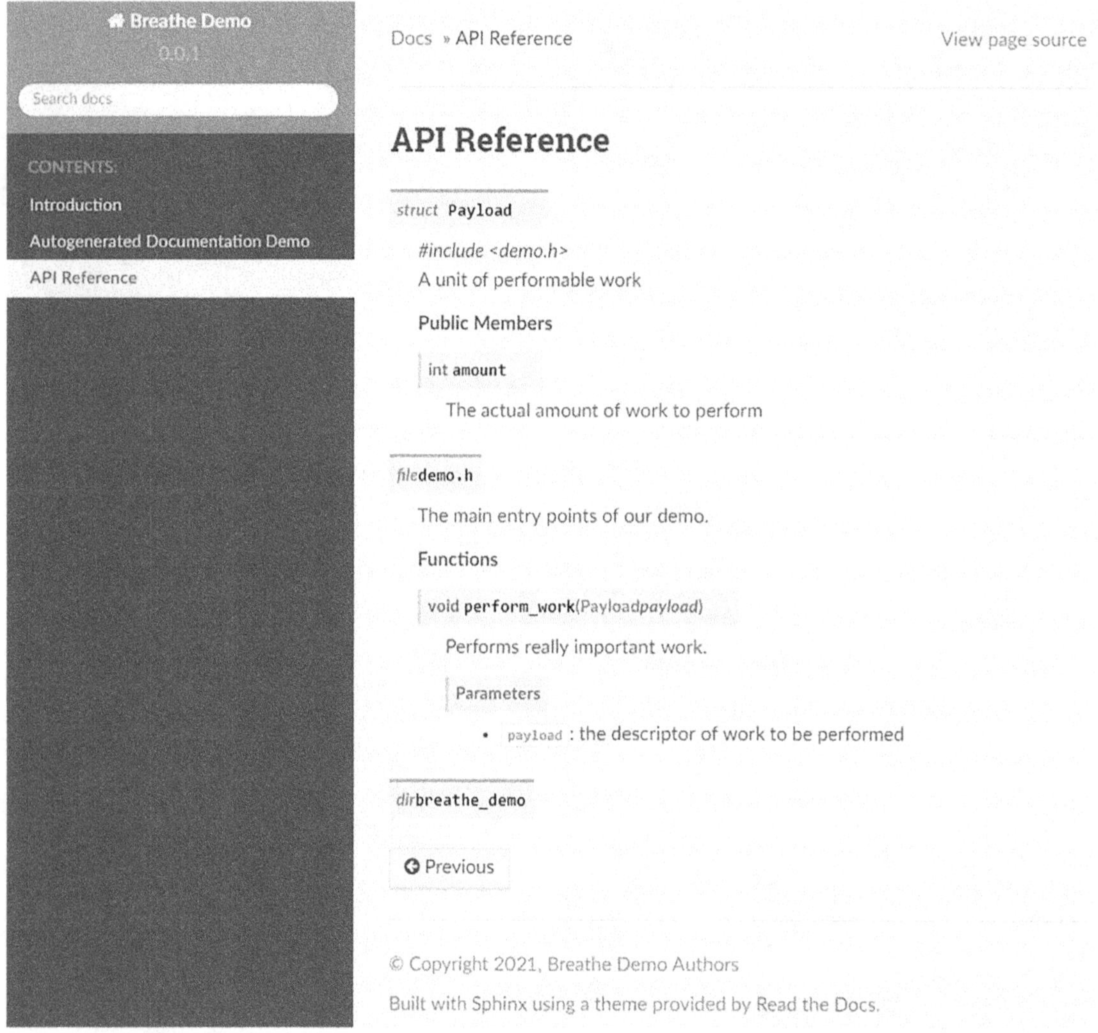

Figure 3.14: The automatically generated API documentation

As you can see, the documentation was automatically generated for our `Payload` type with each of its members, as well as for the free `perform_work` function, including each of its parameters. Also, everything was grouped based on the file in which the type and function are defined. Neat!

Summary

In this chapter, you got to know all the essentials regarding requirements and documentation. You learned how to gather requirements successfully and how to identify the most important ones. You can now prepare lean and useful documentation that shows only what's important in a view-oriented manner. You are able to distinguish between different types and styles of diagrams and use the one that suits your needs the best. Last, but not least, you are now able to automatically generate aesthetic documentation.

In the next chapter, you'll learn about useful architectural design patterns that will help you fulfill your system's requirements. We'll discuss various patterns and how to apply them to provide many important quality attributes, both on a single-component scale and across distributed systems.

Questions

1. What are quality attributes?
2. What sources should be used when gathering requirements?
3. How can you tell whether a requirement is architecturally significant?
4. How should you document graphically the functional requirements various parties may have regarding your system?
5. When is development view documentation useful?
6. How can you automatically check whether your code's API documentation is out of date?
7. How can you indicate on a diagram that a given process is handled by different components of the system?

Further reading

- Ashley Hunt, *Becoming a PMP® Certified Professional (PMBOK): A Study Guide to Mastering Project Management for the PMP® Exam*, Packt Publishing: `https://www.packtpub.com/en-us/product/becoming-a-pmp-certified-professional-9781838985912`
- JC Olamendy, *Evaluate the Software Architecture Using ATAM* (Blog), JC Olamendy's Thoughts: `https://johnolamendy.wordpress.com/2011/08/12/evaluate-the-software-architecture-using-atam/`
- Nick Rozanski and Eoin Woods, *Software Systems Architecture: Working with Stakeholders Using Viewpoints and Perspectives*, Second Edition, Addison-Wesley Professional : `https://www.amazon.com/dp/032171833X`
- John Terzakis, *EARS: The Easy Approach to Requirements Syntax* (Conference talk), Intel Corporation, ICCGI Conference: `https://www.iaria.org/conferences2013/filesICCGI13/ICCGI_2013_Tutorial_Terzakis.pdf`
- Philippe Kruchten, *Architectural Blueprints—The "4+1" View Model of Software Architecture*, Volume 12, Issue 6, IEEE Software: `https://www.cs.ubc.ca/~gregor/teaching/papers/4+1view-architecture.pdf`
- Henriette Baumann, Patrick Grassle, and Philippe Baumann, *UML 2.0 in Action: A Project-Based Tutorial: A Detailed and Practical Book and eBook Walk-Through Showing How to Apply UML to Real World Development Projects*, Packt Publishing: `https://www.packtpub.com/en-us/product/uml-20-in-action-a-project-based-tutorial-9781847190420`
- *The Unified Modeling Language (UML)*: `https://www.uml-diagrams.org/`
- C4 Model, *C4 Model Tools: Visual and Text-Based C4 Modelling and Diagramming Tools*: `https://c4model.tools/`
- C4 Model, *The C4 Model for Visualising Software Architecture*: `https://c4model.com/`

- Humberto Cervantes and Rick Kazman, *ADD 3.0: Rethinking Drivers and Decisions in the Design Process* (Presentation), Software Engineering Institute, Carnegie Mellon University: `https://insights.sei.cmu.edu/library/add-30-rethinking-drivers-and-decisions-in-the-design-process/`

Part 2

The Design and Development of C++ Software

This part presents techniques for creating effective software solutions with C++. It demonstrates techniques for solving common challenges and avoiding pitfalls when designing, developing, and building C++ code. The techniques come from the C++ language itself, as well as design patterns, tools, and build systems.

This part contains the following chapters:

4

Architectural and System Design Patterns

Patterns help us deal with complexity. At the level of a single software component, you can apply the well-known classic *Gang of Four* software patterns—those described in the book *Design Patterns: Elements of Reusable Object-Oriented Software* (1994). However, when we move higher up and start looking at the architecture between different components and examining how components interact and operate together, knowing when and how to apply architectural and system design patterns becomes crucial, and that's the focus of this chapter.

Although this chapter doesn't focus on C++ code directly, it addresses architectural and system design concerns that every experienced C++ developer eventually faces, especially when working on complex, distributed systems. The patterns discussed here are technology-agnostic, but are highly relevant to C++ projects that aim for scalability, fault tolerance, and production-readiness.

There are countless such patterns that are useful for different scenarios. In fact, to even get to know all of them, you would need to read more than just one book. That being said, we selected several patterns for this book, suited for achieving various architectural goals.

In this chapter, we'll introduce you to a few concepts and fallacies related to architectural design. We'll also show when to use the aforementioned patterns and how to design high-quality components that are easy to deploy.

The following topics will be covered in this chapter:

- Understanding the peculiarities of distributed systems
- Making your system fault-tolerant and available
- Integrating your system
- Achieving performance at scale
- Designing data storage
- Deploying your system
- Managing your APIs

By the end of this chapter, you'll know how to design your architecture to provide several important qualities, such as fault tolerance, scalability, and deployability.

Technical requirements

The code from this chapter requires the following tools to build and run: Docker and Docker Compose.

The source code snippets from the chapter can be found at `https://github.com/PacktPublishing/Software-Architecture-with-Cpp-2E/tree/main/Chapter04`.

Understanding the peculiarities of distributed systems

There are many types of software systems, each of them suited for different scenarios, built for different needs, and using different sets of assumptions. Generally, writing and deploying a classical, standalone desktop application is nothing like writing and deploying a microservice that needs to communicate with many others over a network.

In this section, we'll go through the various models that you can use to deploy your software, the common mistakes that people should avoid when creating distributed systems, and some of the trade-offs people make to create such systems successfully.

Different service models and when to use them

Let's first start with service models. When designing a complex distributed system, a service model defines how much of the infrastructure you will manage versus how much you can build upon existing building blocks. Sometimes, you might want to leverage existing software without the need to manually deploy an app or back up data, for example, by using Google Drive through its API as storage for your app. Other times, you can rely on an existing cloud platform such as Google's App Engine to deploy your solution without the need to worry about providing a language runtime, the software stack responsible for managing the execution of programs, or databases. If you can decide to deploy everything in your own way, you can either leverage an infrastructure from a cloud provider or use your company's one. The following diagram shows different service models:

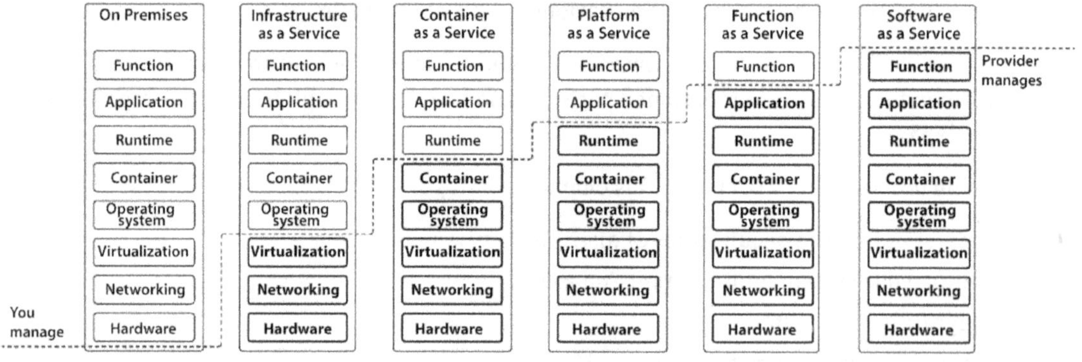

Figure 4.1: Service models

Let's discuss these different models and where each can be useful.

On-premises model

The classical way, and the only way available in the pre-cloud era, is to just deploy everything on your own premises. You need to buy all the hardware and software required and make sure it will provide enough capacity for your needs. If you're working for a start-up company, this may be a big upfront cost. Along with the growth of your user base, you need to buy and set up more resources so that your service can deal with even occasional spikes in load. All this means you need to predict the growth of your solution and act proactively, as there's no way you could just automatically scale depending on the current load.

Even in the cloud era, deploying on-premises is still useful and often spotted in the wild. Sometimes you're dealing with data that shouldn't, or even can't, leave your company's premises, either due to data privacy issues or compliance ones. Other times, you need to have as little network latency as possible, and you need your own geographically local data center to host the application. Sometimes you may calculate the costs and decide that, in your case, on-premises will be cheaper than a cloud solution. Last, but not least, your company might already have an existing data center that you can use.

Deploying on-premises doesn't mean you need to have a monolith system. Often, companies have their own private clouds deployed on-premises. This helps to cut costs by better utilization of the available infrastructure. You can also mix a private cloud solution with one of the other service models, which can be useful when you need that extra capacity from time to time. This is called a **hybrid deployment** and is offered by all major cloud providers, as well as provided by OpenStack's Omni project.

Hybrid clouds are a compromise between private and public clouds. Private clouds usually offer granular control over data security and privacy but come with higher costs and limited scalability, while public clouds are more scalable and cost-effective but often lack the same level of control.

Infrastructure as a Service model

Speaking of other models, the most basic cloud service model is called **Infrastructure as a Service** (**IaaS**). It's also the most similar to on-premises: you can think of IaaS as a way to have a virtual data center. As the name suggests, the cloud provider offers you a slice of the infrastructure they host, which consists of three types of resources:

- Compute, such as virtual machines, containers, or bare-metal machines (excluding operating systems)
- Networking, which, aside from the network itself, includes DNS servers, routing, and firewalls
- Storage, including backup and recovery capabilities

It's still up to you to provide all the software: operating systems, middleware, and your applications.

IaaS can be used in various scenarios such as hosting websites (might be cheaper than traditional web hosting), providing storage (for example, Amazon's S3 and Glacier services), and enabling high-performance computing and big data analysis (requires huge computing power). Some companies use it to quickly set up and purge test and development environments when needed.

Using IaaS instead of on-premises infrastructure can be a cost-effective way to test new ideas while saving you the time needed for configuration.

If your service observes spikes in usage, for example, during the weekends, you might want to leverage your cloud's automatic scaling capabilities: scale up when needed and scale back down later to save money.

IaaS solutions are offered by all the popular cloud service providers.

A similar concept, sometimes thought of as a subset or an extension of IaaS, is **Containers as a Service (CaaS)**. In CaaS, instead of bare-metal systems and virtual machines, the service provides you with containers and orchestration capabilities that you can use to build your own container clusters. DevOps engineers can interact with containers directly, configuring and scaling them as needed. CaaS offerings can be found with Google Cloud Platform and AWS, among others.

Platform as a Service model

If the infrastructure itself is not enough for your needs, you can use the **Platform as a Service (PaaS)** model instead. In this model, the cloud service provider manages not only the infrastructure (just like in IaaS), but also the operating systems, any required middleware, and the runtime—the platform that you will deploy your software on.

Often, a PaaS solution will provide you with app versioning capabilities, service monitoring and discovery, database management, business intelligence, and even development tools.

With PaaS, you're covered throughout the whole development pipeline: from building and testing to deploying, updating, and managing your service. However, PaaS solutions are more costly than IaaS offerings. On the other hand, with the whole platform provided, you can cut the costs and time to develop parts of your software and easily provide the same setup for development teams scattered around the globe.

All main cloud providers have their own offerings, for example, Google App Engine or Azure App Service. There are also independent ones, such as Heroku.

Aside from the more generic PaaS, there's also **Communications Platform as a Service (CPaaS)**, in which you're provided with the whole communications backend, including audio and video, which you can integrate into your solution. This technology allows you to easily provide video-enabled help desks or just integrate live chats into your apps.

Software as a Service model

Sometimes you might not want to develop a software component on your own and just want to use an existing one. **Software as a Service (SaaS)** basically gives you a hosted application. With SaaS, you don't need to worry about either the infrastructure or the platform built upon it, and not even about the software itself. The provider is responsible for installing, running, updating, and maintaining the whole software stack, as well as backups, licensing, and scaling.

There's quite a variety of software you can get in the SaaS model. Examples vary from office suites such as Microsoft 365 and Google Docs to messaging software such as Slack, through **customer relationship management** (**CRM**) systems, and span even to gaming solutions such as cloud gaming services, allowing you to play resource-hungry video games hosted on the cloud.

Usually, to access such services, all you need is a browser, so this can be a great step in providing remote work capabilities for your employees.

You can create your own SaaS applications and provide them to users either by deploying them however you like or through means such as AWS Marketplace.

On the other hand, this model has its trade-offs, as network outages and service interruptions result in loss of access to the provider's software and your data.

Moreover, the lack of direct control means that your provider is responsible for data security and privacy—not you. Also, your migration to another provider may be complicated and expensive due to dependency on the software stack, which is known as vendor lock-in.

Function as a Service model and serverless architecture

With the advent of cloud-native technologies, another model that is growing in popularity is **Function as a Service** (**FaaS**), a subset of the serverless architecture. With FaaS, you get a platform (similarly to PaaS) on which you can run short-lived applications or functions.

With PaaS, you typically always need to have at least one instance of your service running, while in FaaS, you can run them only when they're actually needed. This can increase the time to handle requests (measured in seconds) as you need to launch the function every time. However, some of those requests can be cached to reduce both the latency and costs. Speaking about costs, FaaS can get way more expensive than PaaS if you run the functions for a long time, so you must do the math when designing your system.

If used correctly, FaaS abstracts away the servers from the developers, can reduce your costs, and can provide you with better scalability, as it can be based on events, not resources. This model is commonly used for running prescheduled or manually triggered tasks, processing batches or streams of data, and handling incoming, not-so-urgent requests. A few popular providers of FaaS are AWS Lambda, Azure Functions, Genezio, Cloudflare Workers, Twilio Functions, IronFunctions, Netlify Functions, Vercel Functions, and Google Cloud Functions.

While related to cloud-native design, serverless architecture is a popular topic on its own. It gained a lot of popularity since the introduction of FaaS or CaaS products, such as AWS Lambda, AWS Fargate, Google Cloud Run, and Azure Functions.

Serverless is mostly an evolution of PaaS products such as Heroku. It abstracts away the underlying infrastructure so that developers can focus on the application and not on infrastructural choices.

An additional benefit of serverless over older PaaS solutions is that you don't have to pay for what you don't use. Rather than paying for a given service level, you typically pay for the actual execution time of the deployed workload with serverless. If you only want to run a given piece of code once a day, you don't need to pay a monthly fee for an underlying server.

While we didn't get into too much detail about serverless, it is important to note that it is rarely used with C++. When it comes to FaaS, only AWS Lambda and Google Cloud Functions currently support C++ as a possible language. Since containers are language-agnostic, you can use C++ applications and functions with CaaS products such as AWS Fargate, Azure Container Instances, or Google Cloud Run.

Serverless functions may still be relevant to you if you want to run non-C++ auxiliary code used along with your C++ application. Maintenance tasks and scheduled jobs are an excellent fit for serverless, and they usually don't require the performance or efficiency of C++ binaries.

C++ can also be compiled into **WebAssembly (Wasm)**, a portable binary-code format, which facilitates high-performance applications in modern web browsers. This format extends beyond the browser and moves to the cloud environments such as AWS Lambda, Azure Functions, Fermyon Cloud, wasmCloud, and Fastly Compute. Fermyon's SpinKube runs serverless apps (Spin Apps) on Kubernetes. Moreover, WasmEdge serves as a runtime for serverless apps, embedded functions, microservices, smart contracts, and IoT devices.

Now that we've covered on-premises and common cloud service models, let's discuss some of the wrong assumptions people make when designing distributed systems.

Avoiding the fallacies of distributed computing

When people new to distributed computing begin their journey with designing such systems, they tend to forget or ignore a few aspects of such systems. Although these issues were first noticed back in the 90s, they remain relevant even today.

The fallacies are discussed in the following subsections.

The network is reliable

Networking equipment is designed for long years of flawless operation. Despite that, many things can still cause packet loss, such as power outages, poor wireless networking signal, configuration errors, someone tripping over a cable, or even animals biting through wires. For instance, Google had to protect its underwater cables with Kevlar because they were being bitten by sharks (yes, really!). You should always assume that data can get lost somewhere over the network. Even if that doesn't happen, software issues can still occur on the other side of the wire.

To fend off such issues, be sure you have a policy for automatically retrying failed network requests and a way to handle common networking issues. When retrying, try not to overload the other party and not commit the same transaction multiple times. You can use a local application queue or a network-based message queue to store failed requests and retry sending them.

Patterns such as the circuit breaker pattern, which we'll show later in this chapter, can also help. Oh, and be sure to not just wait infinitely, hogging up resources with each failed request.

Latency is zero

Both the network and the services you're running must take some time to respond, even under normal conditions. Occasionally, they'll have to take longer, especially when under a bigger-than-average load. Sometimes, instead of a few milliseconds, your requests can take seconds to complete. For a useful reference on typical latency numbers, see `https://github.com/sirupsen/napkin-math#numbers`.

Figure 4.2, adapted from Jeff Dean's well-known talk *Numbers Everyone Should Know*, also provides an intuitive summary of typical latency numbers observed across different layers of systems:

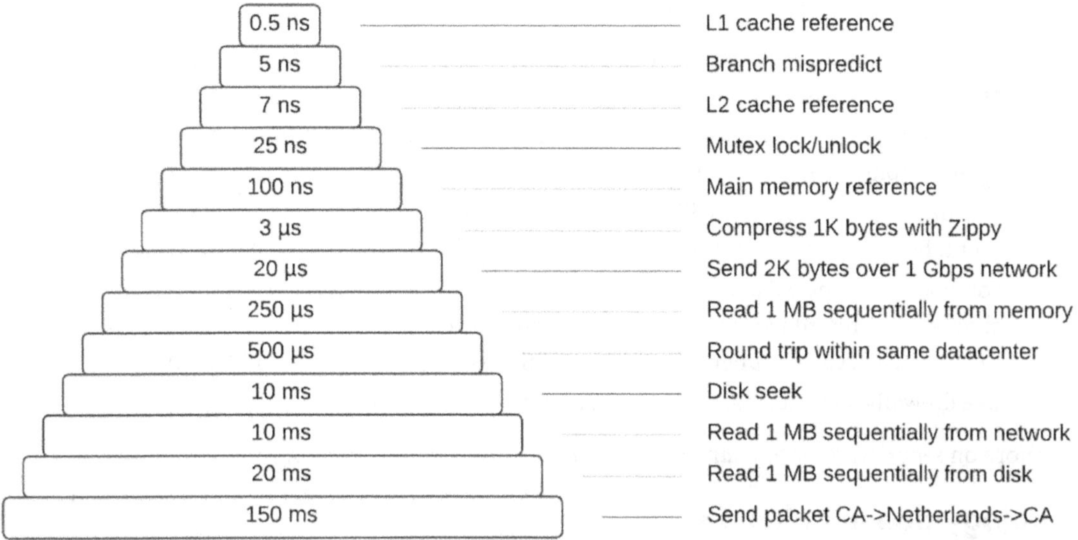

Figure 4.2: Numbers Everyone Should Know, from Jeff Dean (https://www.cs.cornell.edu/projects/ladis2009/talks/dean-keynote-ladis2009.pdf)

Try to design your system so it doesn't wait on too many fine-grained remote calls, as each such call can add to your total processing time. Even in a local network, 10,000 requests for 1 record will be much slower than 1 request for 10,000 records. To reduce network latency, consider sending and handling requests in bulk. You can also try to hide the cost of small calls by doing other processing tasks while waiting for their results.

Other ways to deal with latency are to introduce caches, push the data in a publisher–subscriber model instead of waiting for requests, or deploy closer to the customers, for example, by using **content delivery networks (CDNs)**, which are geographically distributed networks of proxy servers that help in content distribution to users by reducing network latencies.

Bandwidth is infinite

When adding a new service to your architecture, make sure you take note of how much traffic it's going to use. Sometimes you might want to reduce the bandwidth by compressing the data or by introducing a throttling policy.

This fallacy also has to do with mobile devices. If the signal is weak, often the network will become the bottleneck. This means the amount of data a mobile app uses should generally be kept low. Using the *backends for frontends* pattern described in *Chapter 2, Architectural Styles*, can often help save precious bandwidth.

If your backend needs to transfer lots of data between some components, try to make sure such components are close together: don't run them in separate data centers. With databases, this often boils down to better replication. Patterns such as CQRS (discussed later in this chapter) are also handy.

The network is secure

This is a dangerous fallacy. A chain is only as strong as its weakest link, and unfortunately, there are many links in distributed systems. Here are a few ways to make those links stronger:

- Be sure to always apply security patches to every component of your infrastructure, operating systems, and other components.
- Train your personnel and try to protect your system from the human factor; sometimes it's a rogue employee that compromises a system.
- If your system is online, it will get attacked, and it's possible that a breach will happen at one point. Be sure to have a written protection plan to react to such events.
- You might have heard about the **defense in depth** principle. It boils down to having different checks for different parts of your system (your infrastructure, your applications, and so on) so that when a breach happens, its range and the associated damage will be limited.
- Use firewalls, certificates, encryption, and proper authentication.

For more on security, refer to *Chapter 12, Security in Code and Deployment*.

Topology doesn't change

This fallacy became especially evident in the microservices era. Autoscaling and the emergence of the *cattle, not pets* approach (servers are like replaceable cattle rather than unique pets) to managing infrastructure mean that the topology will constantly change. This can affect latency and bandwidth, which implies that some of this fallacy's outcomes are the same as those caused by fallacies described earlier.

Figure 4.3 represents different types of network topology that can emerge in a constantly changing environment:

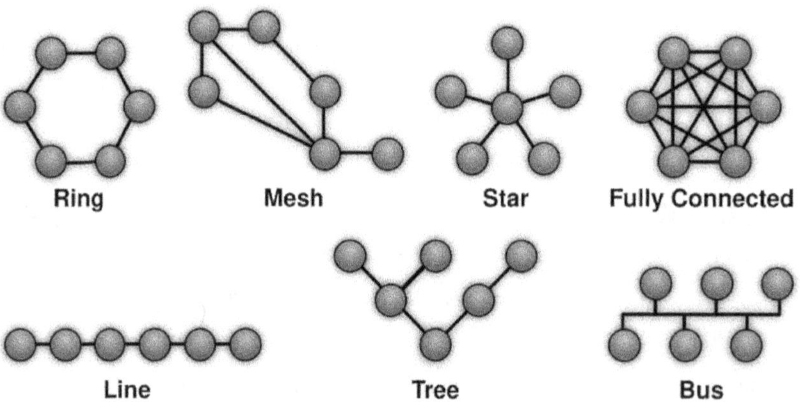

Figure 4.3: Network topology types

Fortunately, the mentioned approach also comes with guidelines on how to effectively manage your *herd* of servers. Relying on hostnames and DNS instead of hardcoding IP addresses, which can change, is a step in the right direction, and service discovery, described in *Chapter 18, Cloud-Native Design*, is another one.

A third, even bigger step is to always assume your instances can fail and automate reacting to such scenarios. Netflix's *Chaos Monkey* tool can also help you test your preparedness, as this tool randomly terminates virtual machines and containers, thereby simulating real-world chaos, to verify whether services are resilient to failures.

There is one administrator

The knowledge about distributed systems, due to their nature, is often distributed itself. Different people are responsible for the development, configuration, deployment, and administration of such systems and their infrastructure. Different components are often upgraded by different people, not necessarily in sync. There's also the so-called *bus factor*, which, in short, is the risk factor for a key project member being hit by a bus, resulting in loss of knowledge critical to maintain the project or system.

How do we deal with all of this? The answer consists of a few parts. One of them is the DevOps culture. By facilitating close collaboration between development and operations, people share the knowledge about the system, thus reducing the bus factor. Further, introducing continuous integration, delivery, and deployment can help with upgrading the project and keeping it always up. Continuous integration and continuous deployment are covered in *Chapter 11*.

You could also try to model your system to be loosely coupled and backward compatible, so upgrades of components don't require other components to be upgraded too. An easy way to decouple is by introducing messaging between them, so consider adding a queue or two. It will help you with downtime during upgrades as well.

Finally, try to monitor your system and gather logs in a centralized place. Decentralization of your system shouldn't mean you now need to manually look at logs on a dozen different machines. The **Elasticsearch, Logstash, Kibana** (**ELK**) stack is invaluable for this. Grafana, Prometheus, Loki, Jaeger, and the OpenTelemetry Collector are also very popular, especially with Kubernetes. If you're looking for something more lightweight than Logstash, consider Fluentd and Filebeat, especially if you're dealing with containers. These tools are covered in *Chapter 17*, *Observability*, and *Chapter 18*, *Cloud-Native Design*.

Transport cost is zero

This fallacy is important to consider while planning your project and its budget. Building and maintaining a network for a distributed system costs both time and money, regardless of whether you deploy on-premises or in the cloud—it's just a matter of when you pay the cost. Try to estimate the costs of the equipment, the data to be transferred (cloud providers charge for this), and the required manpower.

If you're relying on data compression, be wary that while this reduces networking costs, it can increase the price of your compute. In general, using binary APIs such as gRPC-based will be cheaper (and faster) than JSON-based ones, and those are still cheaper than XML because JSON and XML are text-based wordy formats while gRPC relies heavily on **Protocol Buffers** (**Protobuf**), an efficiently packed binary data. If you send images, audio, or video, it's a must to estimate how much this will cost you.

The network is homogeneous

Even if you plan what hardware to have and what software to run on your network, it's easy to end up with at least some heterogeneity. A slightly different configuration on some of the machines, a different communication protocol used by that legacy system that you need to integrate with, or different mobile phones sending requests to your system are just a few examples of this. Another one is extending your on-premises solution by using additional workers in the cloud.

Try to limit the number of communication protocols and formats used, strive to use standard ones because achieving interoperability is painful, and avoid vendor lock-in to ensure your system can still communicate properly in such heterogeneous environments.

Heterogeneity can also mean differences in resiliency. This follows from the fact that a homogeneous network is characterized by the use of identical network devices and protocols, including operating systems and applications, but a heterogeneous network is made up of different types of these components. Try to use the circuit breaker pattern along with retries to handle this, both of which we will discuss later in the chapter.

Now that we've discussed all the fallacies, let's discuss an important principle of distributed architectures—the **CAP theorem**—and the related concept of **eventual consistency**.

CAP theorem and eventual consistency

To design successful systems that spread across more than one node, you need to know and use certain principles. One of them is the CAP theorem. It's about one of the most important choices you need to make when designing a distributed system, and owes its name to the three properties a distributed system can have. They are as follows:

- **Consistency**: Every read would get you the data after the most recent write (or an error)
- **Availability**: Every request will get a non-error response (without the guarantee that you'll get the most recent data)
- **Partition tolerance**: Even if a network failure occurs between two nodes, the system as a whole will continue working

In essence, the theorem states that you can pick, at most, two of those three properties for a distributed system:

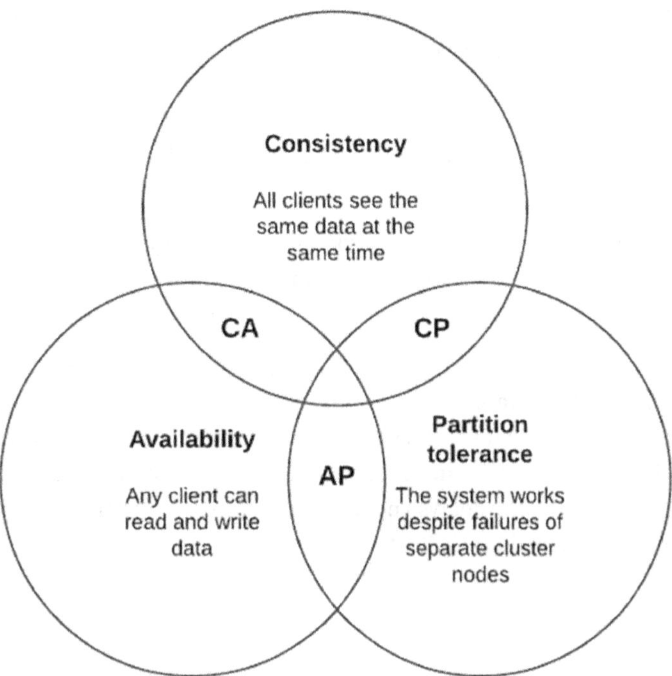

Figure 4.4: The CAP theorem, also known as Brewer's theorem

As long as the system operates properly, it looks like all three of the properties can be satisfied. However, as we know from looking at the fallacies, the network is unreliable, so partitions will occur. In such cases, a distributed system should still operate properly. This means the theorem makes you choose between delivering partition tolerance and consistency (that is, CP) or partition tolerance and availability (that is, AP). Usually, the latter is the better choice. If you want to choose CA, you must remove the other nodes entirely and be left with a single-node system.

If, under a partition, you decide to deliver consistency, you will have to either return an error or risk timeouts when waiting for the data to be consistent. If you choose availability over consistency, you risk returning stale data—the latest writes might be unable to propagate across the partition.

Both of those approaches are suited for different needs. If your system requires atomic reads and writes (*one at a time*), for instance, because a customer could lose their money, go with CP. If your system must continue operating under partitions, or you can allow eventual consistency, go with AP.

Okay, but what is eventual consistency? Let's discuss the different levels of consistency to understand this.

In a system offering strong consistency, each write is synchronously propagated. This means all reads will always see the latest writes, even at the cost of higher latency or lower availability. This is the type that **relational database management systems** (**RDBMSs**) offer (based on **ACID** guarantees, which stands for **atomicity, consistency, isolation, durability**) and is best suited for systems that require transactions.

In a system offering eventual consistency, on the other hand, you only guarantee that after a write, reads will eventually see the change. Usually, *eventually* means in a couple of milliseconds. This is due to the asynchronous nature of data replication in such systems, as opposed to the synchronous propagation from the previous paragraph. Instead of providing ACID guarantees, for example, using an RDBMS, here we have **BASE** semantics (meaning **basically available, soft state, eventual consistency**), often provided by NoSQL databases.

For a system to be asynchronous and eventually consistent (as AP systems often are), it needs to have a way to solve state conflicts. A common way to do so is to exchange updates between instances and choose either the first or the last write as the accepted one when synchronizing the updates.

The CAP theorem had been criticized for oversimplifying important concepts, which led to the introduction of BASE and the **PACELC theorem** as an extension of CAP. The PACELC theorem is formulated as *IF P -> (A or C), ELSE (L or C)*. That means if a network partition is present, then a system chooses consistency or availability, else the system chooses latency or consistency. This theorem regulates the need to find a trade-off between time delays and data consistency in distributed systems and classifies NoSQL databases more correctly than CAP.

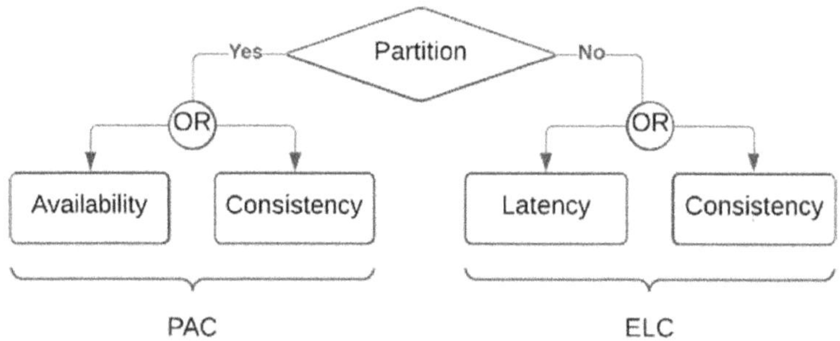

Figure 4.5: The PACELC theorem

Let's now discuss two related patterns that can help in achieving eventual consistency.

Saga and compensating transaction patterns

The saga pattern is useful when you need to perform distributed transactions.

Before the microservice era, if you had one host with one database, you could rely on the database engine to do the transaction for you. With multiple databases on one host, you could use **two-phase commits** (**2PCs**) to do so. With 2PCs, you would have a coordinator, who would first tell all the databases to prepare, and once they all report being ready, it would tell them all to commit the transaction.

Now, as each microservice likely has its own database (and it should if you want scalability), and they're spanned all over your infrastructure, you can no longer rely on simple transactions and 2PCs (losing this ability often means you no longer want an RDBMS, as NoSQL databases can be much faster).

Instead, you can use the saga pattern. Let's demonstrate it with an example.

Imagine you want to create an online warehouse that tracks how much supply it has and allows payment by credit card. To process an order, you need at least three services: one for processing the order, one for reserving the supplies, and one for charging the card.

Now, there are two ways the saga pattern can be implemented: choreography-based (also called event-based) and orchestration-based (also called command-based).

Choreography-based sagas

In the choreography approach, services exchange events without a centralized controller. In this case, the first part of the saga would be the order processing service sending an event to the supply service. This one would do its part and send another event to the payment service. The payment service would then send yet another event back to the order service. This would complete the transaction (the saga), and the order could now be happily shipped.

If the order service wanted to track the state of the transaction, it would simply need to listen to all those events as well.

Of course, sometimes the order would be impossible to complete, and a rollback would need to happen. In this case, each step of the saga would need to be rolled back separately and carefully, as other transactions could run in parallel, for example, modifying the supply state. Such rollbacks are called compensating transactions to undo all work done in previous stages of the operation. This approach is used in microservices because the division of the monolithic database into several databases makes ACID transactions impossible.

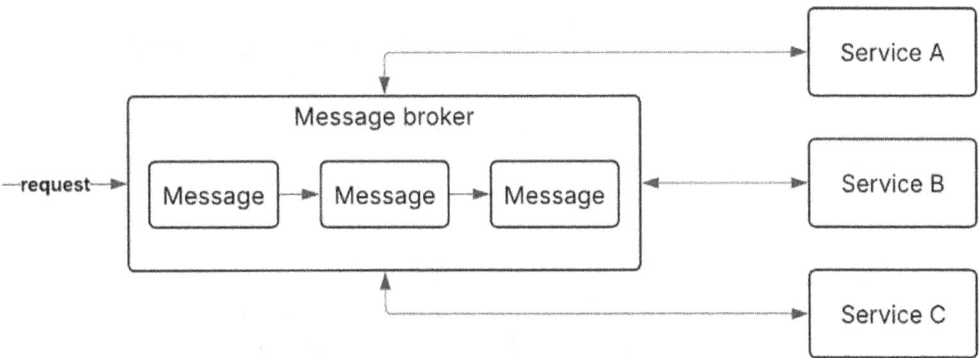

Figure 4.6: Choreography

This way of implementing the saga pattern is pretty straightforward, but if there any many dependencies between the involved services, it might be better to use the *orchestration* approach.

Orchestration-based sagas

In the orchestration approach, services depend on a centralized controller (orchestrator) that tells them which operations to perform based on events. In this case, we can use a message broker to handle communication between our services and an orchestrator that would coordinate the saga. Our order service would send a request to the orchestrator, which would then send commands to both the supply and payment services. Each of those would then do their part and send replies back to the orchestrator, through a reply channel available at the broker.

In this scenario, the orchestrator has all the logic needed to, well, orchestrate the transaction, and the services themselves don't need to be aware of any other services taking part in the saga.

If the orchestrator is sent a message that one of the services failed (for example, if the credit card has expired), it would then need to start the rollback. In our case, it would again use the broker to send an appropriate rollback command to specific services.

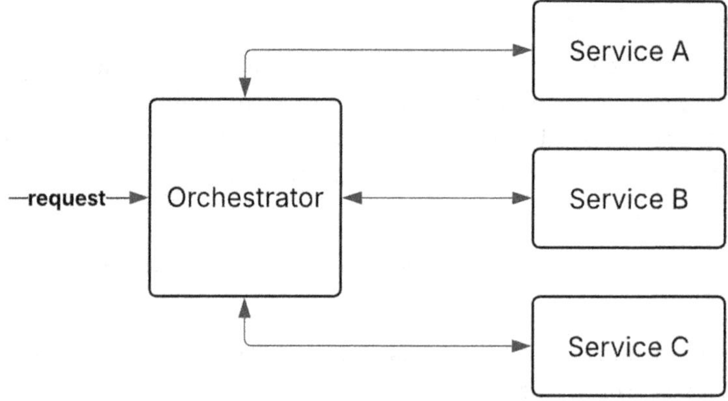

Figure 4.7: Orchestration

Okay, that's enough about eventual consistency for now. Let's now switch to other topics related to availability.

Making your system fault-tolerant and available

Availability and fault tolerance are software qualities that are at least somewhat important for every architecture. What's the point of creating a software system if the system can't be reached? In this section, we'll learn what exactly those terms mean and a few techniques to incorporate them into your solutions.

Calculating your system's availability

Availability is the percentage of the time that a system is up, functional, and reachable. Crashes, network failures, or extremely high load (for example, from a DDoS attack) that prevent the system from responding can all affect its availability.

Usually, it's a good idea to strive for as high a level of availability as possible. You may stumble upon the term *counting the nines*, as availability is often specified as 99% (two nines), 99.9% (three nines), and so on. Each additional nine is much harder to obtain, so be careful when making promises. Take a look at the following table to see how much downtime is acceptable per month at different availability levels:

Downtime/month	Uptime
7 hours 18 minutes	99% (two nines)
43 minutes 48 seconds	99.9% (three nines)

4 minutes 22.8 seconds	99.99% (four nines)
26.28 seconds	99.999% (five nines)
2.628 seconds	99.9999% (six nines)
262.8 ms	99.99999% (seven nines)
26.28 ms	99.999999% (eight nines)
.628 ms	99.9999999% (nine nines)

Table 4.1: Monthly downtime corresponding to different levels of availability

A common practice for cloud applications is to provide a **service-level agreement** (**SLA**), which specifies how much downtime can occur per a given period of time (for example, a year). An SLA for your cloud service will strongly depend on the SLAs of the cloud services you build upon.

To calculate a compound availability between two services that need to cooperate, you should just multiply their uptimes. This means if you have two services with 99.99% availability, their compound availability will be *99.99% * 99.99% = 99.98%*. To calculate the availability of redundant services (such as two independent regions), you should multiply their unavailability. For instance, if two regions have 99.99% availability, their total unavailability will be *(100% – 99.99%) * (100% – 99.99%) = 0.01% * 0.01% = 0.0001%*, so their compound availability is 99.9999%.

Unfortunately, it's impossible to provide 100% availability. Failures do occur from time to time, so let's learn how to make your system tolerate them.

Building fault-tolerant systems

Fault tolerance is a system's ability to detect such failures and to handle them gracefully. It's essential that your cloud-based services are resilient, as, due to the nature of the cloud, many different things can suddenly go south. Good fault tolerance can help your service's availability.

Different types of issues require different handling: from prevention, through detection, to minimizing the impact. Let's start with common ways to avoid having a single point of failure.

Redundancy patterns

One of the most basic preventions is introducing redundancy. Similar to how you can have a spare tire for your car, you can have a backup service that takes over when your primary server goes down. This stepping in is also known as a **failover**.

How does the backup server know when to step in? One way to implement this is by using the heartbeat mechanism described in the *Detecting faults* section.

To make the switch faster, you can send all the messages that are going into the primary server also to the backup one. This is called a **hot standby**, as opposed to a cold one—initializing from zero. A good idea in such a case is to stay one message behind, so if a *poisoned* message kills the primary server, the backup one can simply reject it.

The preceding mechanism is called an **active-passive** (or **master-slave**) failover, as the backup server doesn't handle incoming traffic. If it did, we would have an **active-active** (or **master-master**) failover. For more on active-active architectures, refer to the *Further reading* section.

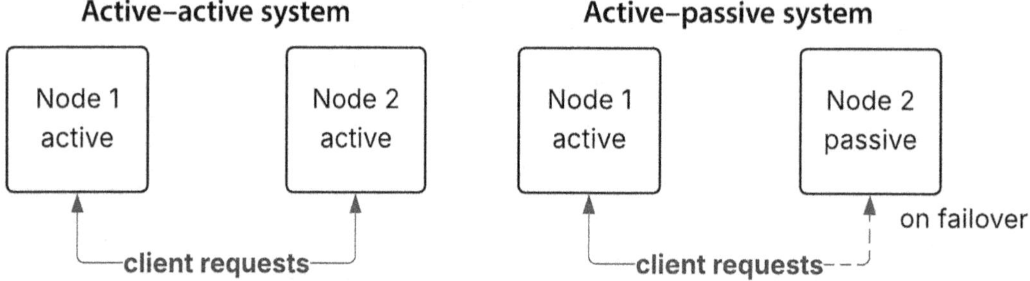

Figure 4.8: Active-active versus active-passive

Be sure you don't lose any data when the failover happens. Using a message queue with backing storage to resubmit messages for processing may help with this.

Leader election

It's also important for the servers to know which one is which—if more than one starts behaving as primary instances, this leads to desynchronization and data loss as one of the nodes is the organizer of a task distributed across the other nodes (computers). Choosing the primary server is called the leader election pattern. There are a few algorithms to do so, for example, by introducing a third-party arbiter, by racing to take exclusive ownership of a shared resource, by choosing the instance with the lowest rank, or by using algorithms such as bully election or token ring election.

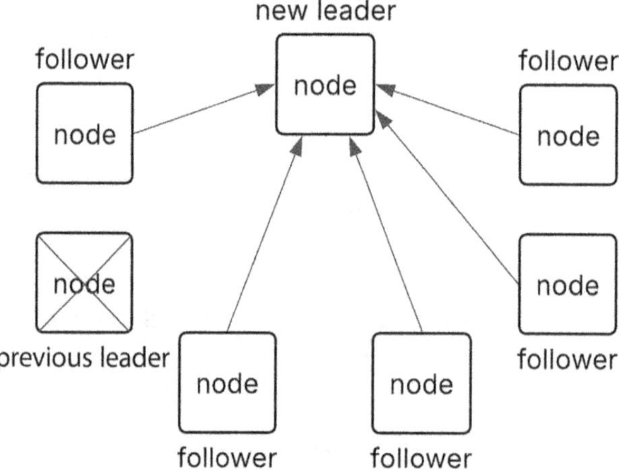

Figure 4.9: Leader election

Leader election is also an essential part of the next related concept: achieving consensus.

Consensus

If you want your system to operate even when network partitions happen or some instances of your service experience faults, you need a way for your instances to reach consensus. They must agree on what values to commit and often in what order. A simple approach is to allow each instance to vote on the correct state. However, in some cases, this is not enough to reach a consensus correctly or at all. Another approach would be to elect a leader and let it propagate its value. Because it's not easy to implement such algorithms by hand, we'd recommend using popular industry-proven consensus protocols such as Paxos and Raft. The latter is growing in popularity as it is simpler and easier to understand.

Let's now discuss another way for preventing system faults.

Replication patterns

This one is especially popular with databases, and it helps with scaling them, too. Replication means you will run a few instances of your service in parallel with duplicated data, all handling incoming traffic.

Don't confuse replication with sharding. The latter doesn't require any data redundancy but can often bring you great performance at scale. If you're using Postgres, we recommend you try out Citus (`https://www.citusdata.com/`), CockroachDB (`https://www.cockroachlabs.com/`), or YugabyteDB (`https://www.yugabyte.com/`).

In terms of databases, there are two ways you can replicate.

Master–slave replication

In this scenario, all the servers are able to perform read-only operations, but there's only one master server that can also write. The data is replicated from the master through the slaves, either in a one-to-many topology or using a tree topology. If the master fails, the system can still operate in read-only mode until this fault is remediated.

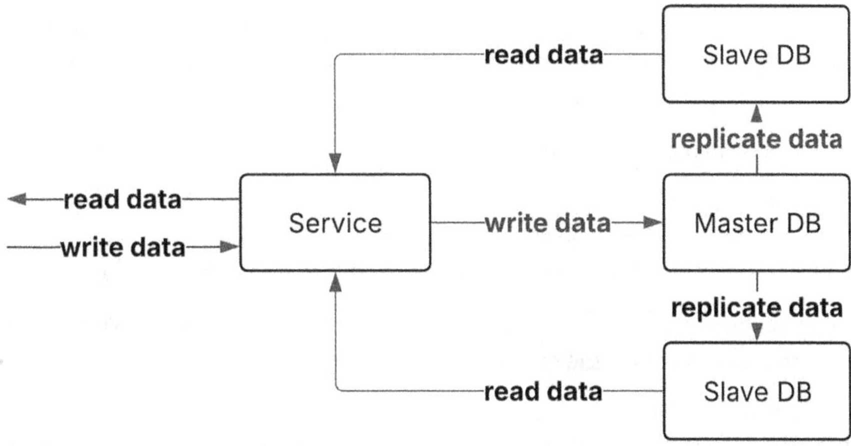

Figure 4.10: Master–slave replication

Multi-master replication

You can also have a system with multiple master servers. If there are two servers, you have a master–master replication scheme. If one of the servers dies, the others can still operate normally. However, now you either need to synchronize the writes or provide looser consistency guarantees. Also, you need to provide a router.

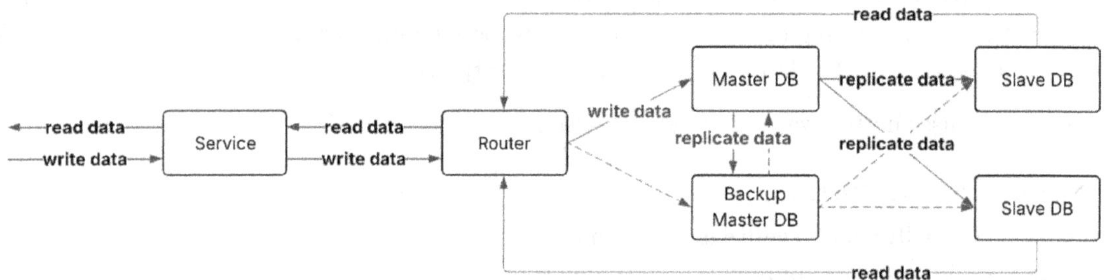

Figure 4.11: Multi-master replication

Examples of such replication include Microsoft's Active Directory, OpenLDAP, and Apache CouchDB.

Let's now discuss two ways to prevent faults caused by too high a load.

Queue-based load leveling pattern

This tactic is aimed at reducing the impact of sudden spikes in your system's load. Flooding a service with requests can cause performance degradation, reduced reliability, and even the loss of valid requests. Once again, queues are there to save the day.

To implement this pattern, we just need to introduce a queue for the incoming requests to be added asynchronously. You can use Amazon's SQS, Azure's Service Bus, Apache Kafka, ZeroMQ, RabbitMQ, EMQX, HiveMQ, or other queues to achieve that.

Now, instead of having spikes in incoming requests, the load will be averaged. Our service can grab the requests from the said queue and process them without even knowing that the load was increased. Simple as that.

If your queue is performant and your tasks can be parallelized, a side benefit of this pattern would be better scalability.

Also, if your service isn't available, the requests will still get added into the queue for said service to process when it recovers, so this may be a way to help with bumping the availability.

If the requests come infrequently, consider implementing your service as a serverless function that runs only when there are items in the queue to save costs.

Keep in mind that when using this pattern, the overall latency will increase due to the addition of the queue. Apache Kafka and ZeroMQ should yield low latency, but if that's a deal-breaker, there's yet another way to deal with increased load.

Back pressure pattern

If the load remains high, chances are you'll have more tasks than you're able to handle. This can cause cache misses and swapping if the requests can no longer fit into memory, as well as dropping requests and other nasty things. If you expect a heavy load, applying back pressure might be a great way to deal with it.

In essence, back pressure means that instead of putting more pressure on our service with each incoming request, we push back into the caller, so it needs to handle the situation. There are a few different ways to do so.

For instance, we can block our thread that receives network packets. The caller will then see that it is unable to push the request to our service—instead, we push the pressure upstream.

Another way is to recognize a greater load and simply return an error code, for example, `503`. You can model your architecture so that this is done for you by another service. One such service is the Envoy Proxy (`https://envoyproxy.io`), which can come in handy on many other occasions, too.

Envoy is a high-performance proxy server written in C++, designed for microservice architecture. It manages network communication between microservices and serves as an intermediate layer between clients and services. It provides efficient routing, load balancing, enhanced security, monitoring, and request tracing. In particular, Istio is a service mesh that employs Envoy to mediate all inbound and outbound traffic for services.

Envoy can apply back pressure based on predefined quotas, so your service will actually never get overloaded. It can also measure the time it takes to process requests and apply back pressure only if it goes above a certain threshold. There are many other cases for which a variety of error codes will be returned. Hopefully, the caller has a plan on what to do if the pressure goes back on them.

Note that we reference Envoy in this chapter not to prescribe its use, but as a way to demonstrate how discussed patterns are applied in real-world systems. Similar outcomes can be achieved using other tools as well.

Now that we know how to prevent faults, let's learn how to detect them once they occur.

Detecting faults

Proper and fast fault detection can save you a lot of trouble, and often money. There are many ways to detect faults tailored to different needs. Let's go over a selection of them.

Sidecar design pattern

Since we were discussing Envoy, it might be worth saying that it's an example of the sidecar design pattern. This pattern is useful in many more cases than just error prevention and detection, and Envoy is a great example of this.

In general, sidecars allow you to add a number of capabilities to your services without the need to write additional code. Similarly, as a physical sidecar can be attached to a motorcycle, a software sidecar can be attached to your service, in both cases extending the offered functionality.

How can a sidecar be helpful in detecting faults? First of all, by providing health checking capabilities. When it comes to passive health checking, Envoy can detect whether any instance in a service cluster has started behaving badly. This is called outlier detection. Envoy can look for consecutive `5XX` error codes, gateway failures, and so on. Aside from detecting such faulty instances, it can eject them so the overall cluster remains healthy.

Envoy also offers active health checking, meaning it can probe the service itself instead of just observing its reactions to incoming traffic.

Throughout this chapter, we'll show a few other usages for the sidecar pattern in general and Envoy in particular. Let's now discuss the next mechanism of fault detection.

Heartbeat mechanism pattern

One of the most common ways of fault detection is through the heartbeat mechanism. A heartbeat is a signal or a message that is sent at regular intervals (usually a few seconds) between two services.

If a few consecutive heartbeats are missing, the receiving service can consider the sending service *dead*. In the case of our primary-backup service pair from a few sections previously, this can cause a failover to happen.

When implementing a heartbeat mechanism, be sure that it's reliable. False alarms can be troublesome, as the services may get confused, for example, about which one should be the new master. A good idea is to provide a separate endpoint just for heartbeats, so it won't be as easily affected by the traffic on the regular endpoints, because the service must respond to the heartbeat request as soon as possible.

Leaky bucket counter pattern

Another way to detect faults is by adding a so-called leaky bucket counter. With each error, the counter would get incremented, and after a certain threshold is reached (the bucket is full), a fault would be signaled and handled. At regular time intervals, the counter would get decreased (hence, a leaky bucket). This way, the situation would only be considered a fault if many errors occurred in a short time period.

This pattern can be useful if, in your case, it's normal to sometimes have errors, for instance, if you're dealing with networking.

Now that we know how to detect faults, let's learn what to do once they happen.

Minimizing the impact of faults

It takes time to detect an ongoing fault, and it takes even more of this precious resource to resolve it. This is why you should strive to minimize the impact of faults. Here are a few ways that can help.

Retrying the call (retry pattern)

When your application calls another service, sometimes the call will fail. The simplest remedy for such a case is to just retry the call. If the fault was transient and you don't retry, that fault will likely get propagated through your system, causing more damage than it should. Implementing an automated way to retry such calls can save you a lot of hassle.

Remember our sidecar proxy, Envoy? Turns out it can perform the automatic retries on your behalf, saving you from making any changes to your sources.

For instance, see this example configuration of a retry policy that can be added to a route in Envoy:

```
retry_policy:
  retry_on: "5xx"
  num_retries: 3
  per_try_timeout: 2s
```

This will make Envoy retry calls if they return errors such as the `503` HTTP code or gRPC errors that map to `5XX` codes. There will be three retries, each considered failed if not finished within two seconds.

Avoiding cascading failures

We mentioned that without retries, the error will get propagated, causing a cascade of failures throughout the system. Let's now show more ways to prevent this from happening.

Circuit breaker pattern

The circuit breaker pattern is a very useful tool for this. It allows us to quickly notice that a service is unable to process requests, so the calls to it can be short-circuited. This can happen both close to the callee (Envoy provides such a capability) or on the caller side (with the additional benefit of shaving off time from the calls). In Envoy's case, it can be as simple as adding the following to your configuration:

```
circuit_breakers:
  thresholds:
    - priority: DEFAULT
      max_connections: 1000
      max_requests: 1000
      max_pending_requests: 1000
```

In both cases, the load caused by the calls to the service may drop, which, in some cases, can help the service return to normal operation.

How do we implement a circuit breaker on the caller side? Once you've made a few calls and, say, your leaky bucket overflows, you can just stop making new calls for a specified period of time (for example, until the bucket no longer overflows). Simple and effective.

Bulkhead pattern

Another way to limit the fault from spreading is taken straight from the stockyards. When building ships, you usually don't want the ship to get full of water if a hole breaks in the hull. To limit the damage of such holes, you would partition the hull into bulkheads, each of which would be easy to isolate. In this case, only the damaged bulkhead would get filled with water.

The same principle applies to limiting the fault impact in software architecture. You can partition your instances into groups, and you can assign the resources they use to groups as well. Setting quotas can also be considered an example of this pattern.

Separate bulkheads can be created for different groups of users, which can be useful if you need to prioritize them or provide a different level of service to your critical consumers.

Geodes pattern

The last approach we'll discuss for minimizing the impact of faults is called **geodes**. The name comes from geographical nodes. It can be used when your service is deployed in multiple regions.

If a fault occurs in one region, you can just redirect the traffic to other, unaffected regions. This will, of course, make the latency much higher than if you'd made calls to other nodes in the same data center, but usually, redirecting less critical users to remote regions is a much better choice than just failing their calls entirely.

Now that you know how to provide availability and fault tolerance through your system's architecture, let's discuss how to integrate its components together.

Integrating your system

A distributed system is not just a collection of isolated instances of your applications running unaware of the existing world. The instances constantly communicate with each other and have to be properly integrated to provide the most value.

Much has already been said on the topic of integration, so in this section, we'll try to showcase just a handful of patterns for effective integration of both entirely new systems, as well as new parts of the system that need to coexist with other existing parts, often legacy ones.

To not make this chapter a whole book on its own, let's start this section with a recommendation for further reading. If you're interested in integration patterns, especially focused on messaging, then Gregor Hohpe and Bobby Woolf's *Enterprise Integration Patterns* book is a must-read for you.

Now, let's take a brief look at two patterns covered in their book.

Pipes and filters pattern

The first integration pattern that we'll discuss is called pipes and filters. Its purpose is to decompose a big processing task into a series of smaller, independent ones (called filters), which you can then connect together (using pipes, such as message queues). This approach gives you scalability, performance, and reusability.

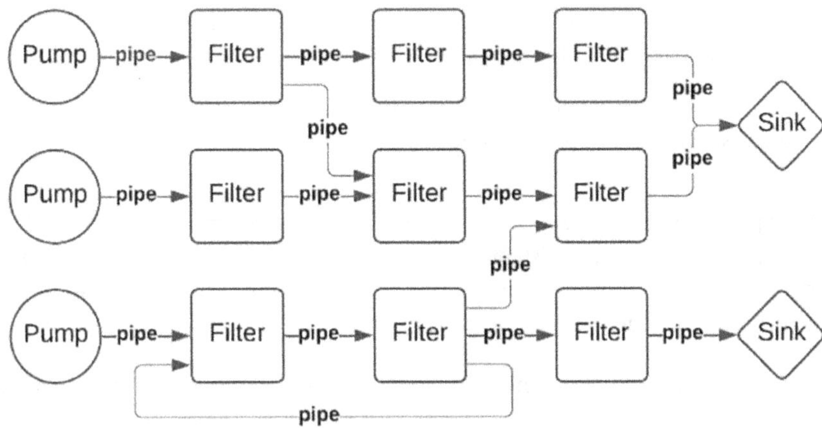

Figure 4.12: Pipes and filters

Assume you need to receive and process an incoming order. You can do it in one big module, so you don't need extra communication, but the different functions of such a module would be hard to test, and it would be harder to scale them well.

Instead, you can split the order processing into separate steps, each handled by a distinct component: one for decoding, one for validating, another one for the actual processing of the order, and then yet another one for storing it somewhere. With this approach, you can now independently perform each of those steps, easily replace or disable them if needed, and reuse them for processing different types of input messages.

If you want to process multiple orders at the same time, you can also pipeline your processing: while one thread validates a message, another thread decodes the next one, and so on.

The downside is that you need to use synchronized queues as your pipes, which introduces some overhead.

To scale one step of your processing, you might want to use this pattern along with the next one on our list.

Competing consumers pattern

The idea of competing consumers is simple: you have an input queue (or a messaging channel) and a few instances of consumers that fetch and process items from the queue concurrently. Each of the consumers can process the message, so they compete with each other to be the receiver.

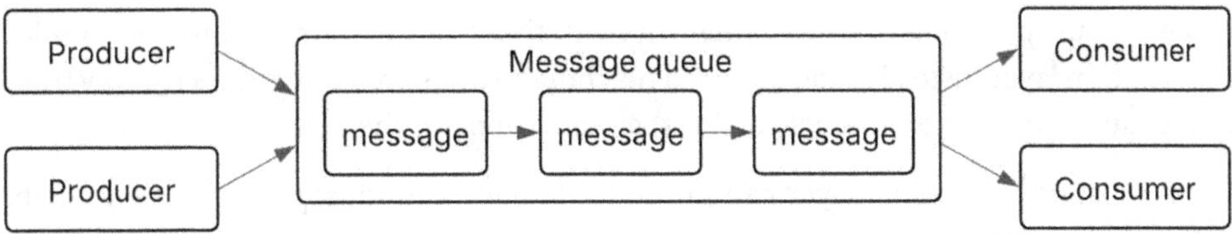

Figure 4.13: Competing consumers

This way, you get scalability, free load balancing, and resilience. With the addition of the queue, you now also have the queue-based load leveling pattern in place.

This pattern integrates effortlessly with priority queues if you need to shave latency from a request or just want a specific task submitted to your queue to be performed in a more urgent manner.

This pattern can get tricky to use if the ordering is important. The order in which your consumers receive and finish processing messages may vary, so make sure that either this doesn't impact your system, or you find a way to reorder the results later on. If you need to process messages in sequence, you might not be able to use this pattern.

Let's look at a few more patterns, this time to help us integrate new systems with existing systems.

Transitioning from legacy systems

Developing a system from scratch can be a blissful experience. Development instead of maintenance and a possibility to use a bleeding-edge technology stack—what's not to like? Unfortunately, that bliss often ends when integration with an existing legacy system starts. Fortunately, though, there are some ways to ease that pain.

Anti-corruption layer pattern

Introducing an anti-corruption layer can help your solution in painless integration with a legacy system that has different semantics. This additional layer is responsible for communication between those two sides.

Such a component allows your solution to be designed with more flexibility, without the need to compromise your technology stack or architectural decisions. To achieve that requires only a minimal set of changes in the legacy system (or none, if the legacy system doesn't need to make calls to the new system).

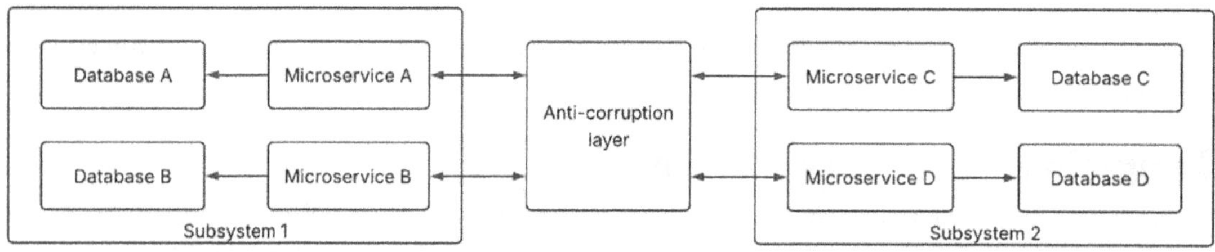

Figure 4.14: Anti-corruption layer

For instance, if your solution is based on microservices, the legacy system can just communicate with the anti-corruption layer instead of locating and reaching each microservice directly. Any translations (for example, due to outdated protocol versions) are also done in the additional layer.

Keep in mind that adding such a layer can introduce latency and must satisfy quality attributes for your solution, for example, scalability.

Strangler pattern

The strangler pattern allows the gradual migration from a legacy system to a new one. While the anti-corruption layer we just looked at is useful for communication between the two systems, the strangler pattern is meant for providing services from both to the outside world.

Early in the migration process, the strangler facade (a proxy or API gateway) will route most of the requests into the legacy system. During the migration, more and more calls can be forwarded to the new one, while *strangling* the legacy system more and more, limiting the functionality it offers. As the final step of the migration, the strangler, along with the legacy system, can be retired—the new system will now provide all the functionality:

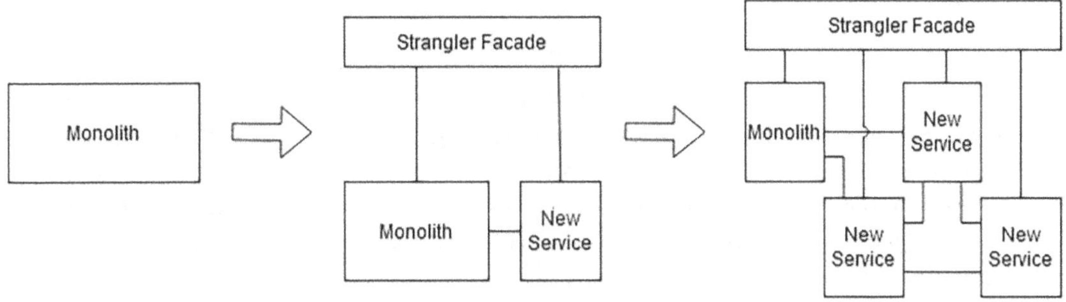

Figure 4.15: The strangling of a monolith. After the migration, the strangler can still be used as an entry point, or adapter, for legacy requests

This pattern can be overkill for small systems and can get tricky if the data store should be shared or is for event-sourced systems. When adding it to your solution, be sure to plan for achieving the proper performance and scalability.

Speaking of those two attributes, let's now discuss a few things that help achieve them.

Achieving performance at scale

When designing C++ applications, performance is usually a key factor. While using the language can go a long way in the scope of a single application, the proper high-level design is also essential to achieving optimal latency and throughput at scale. Let's discuss a few crucial patterns and aspects that help with this.

CQRS and event-sourcing patterns

There are many ways to scale compute, but scaling data access can be tricky. However, it's often necessary when your user base grows. **Command query responsibility segregation** (CQRS) is a pattern that can help here.

CQRS

In traditional **create, read, update, delete** (**CRUD**) systems, both reads and writes are performed using the same data model, and the data flows in the same way. The titular segregation basically means to treat queries (reads) and commands (writes) in two separate ways.

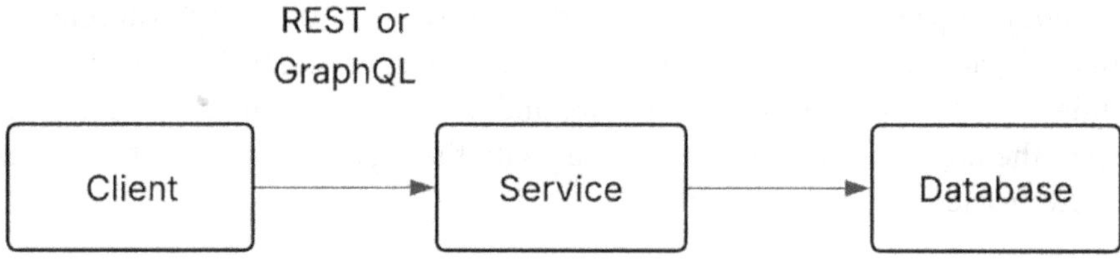

Figure 4.16: CRUD service

Many applications have a strongly biased ratio of reads to writes—there's usually a lot more reading from the database than updating it in a typical app. This means making the reads as fast as possible can yield better performance: reads and writes can now be optimized and scaled separately. CQRS can be used to support this. Other than that, introducing CQRS can help if many writes are competing with each other, or if a track of all the writes needs to be maintained, or if a set of your API users should have read-only access.

Having separate models for reads and writes can allow different teams to work on both sides. The developers working on the read side of things don't need to have a deep understanding of the domain, which is required to perform updates properly. When they make a request, they get a **data transfer object** (**DTO**) from a thin read layer in just one simple call instead of going through the domain model.

If you're not aware of what a DTO is, think of returning item data from the database. If the caller asks for a list of items, you could provide them with an `ItemOverview` object containing just the names and thumbnails of items. On the other hand, if they want items for a specific store, you could also provide a `StoreItem` object containing a name, more pictures, a description, and a price. Both `ItemOverview` and `StoreItem` are DTOs, grabbing data from the same `Item` objects in the database.

The read layer can reside either on top of the data storage used for writes, or it can be a different data storage that gets updated via events, as you can see in the following figure:

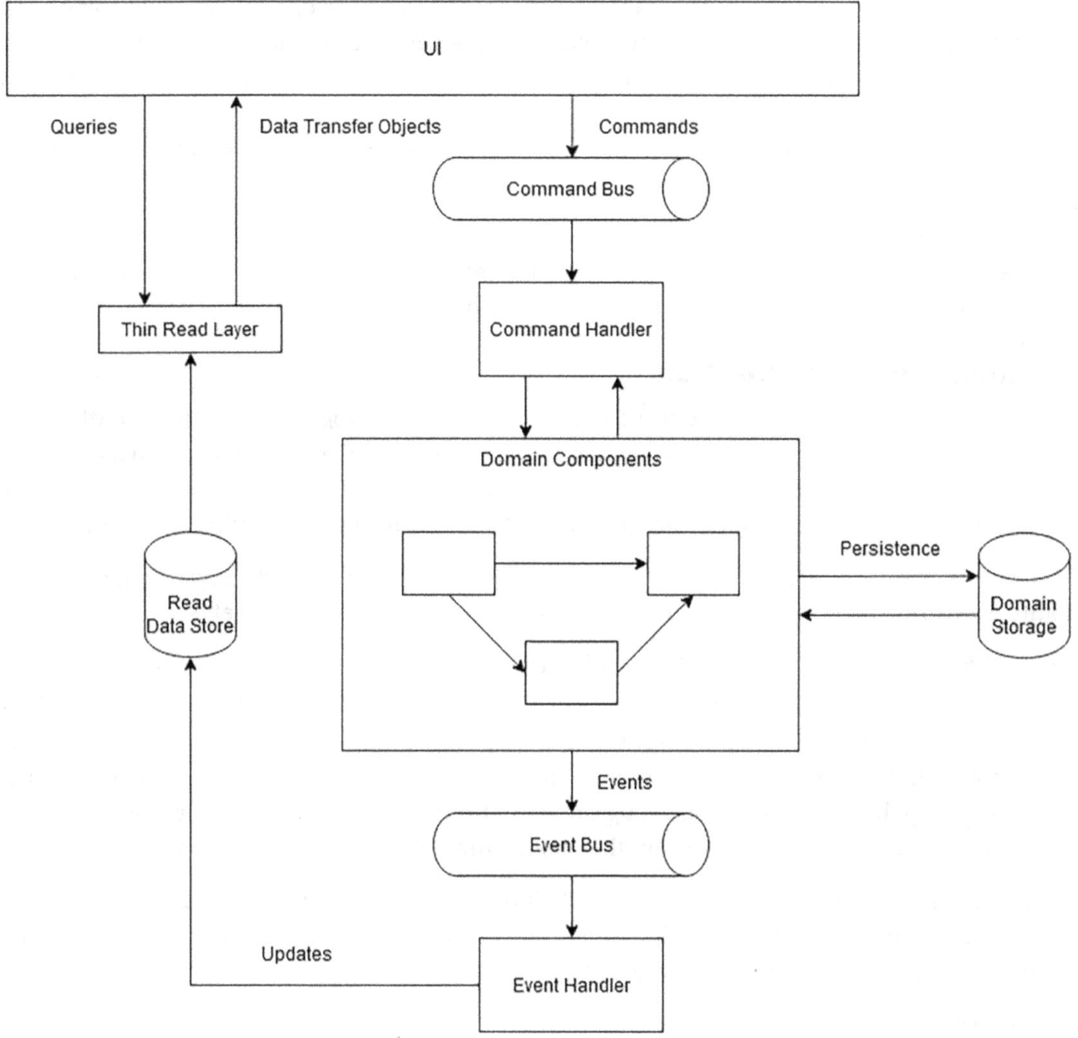

Figure 4.17: CQRS with event sourcing; domain storage on the schema is an event source

Using the approach shown in *Figure 4.17*, you can create as many different commands as you like, each having its own handler. Usually, the commands are asynchronous and don't return any values to the caller. Each handler uses domain objects and persists the changes made. After doing that, events are published, which event handlers can use to update the storage used by read operations. Continuing our last example, item data queries would grab information from a database updated by events such as `ItemAdded` or `ItemPriceChanged`, which could be triggered by commands such as `AddItem` or `ModifyItem`.

Using CQRS allows us to have different data models for read and write operations. For instance, you can create stored procedures and materialized views to speed up reads. Using different types of storage (SQL or NoSQL) for the domain and read stores can also be beneficial because these storage types can be more suitable for either updating or reading data. One efficient way to persist data is to use an Apache Cassandra cluster, while using Elasticsearch is a great way to search through the stored data quickly.

Aside from the preceding pros, CQRS also has its cons. Due to the complexity it introduces, it's usually not a good fit for small or less requiring architectures. It's often useful to apply it only to the parts of your system where it would bring the biggest benefits. You should also notice that updating the read store after the domain store means that now we have eventual consistency instead of strong consistency.

Command query separation

CQRS is based on a simple idea introduced long ago in the Eiffel programming language (the same one that introduced contracts): **command query separation** (CQS). CQS is a principle that devises to separate API calls into, well, commands and queries—just like in CQRS, but regardless of the scale. It plays really well with object-oriented programming and imperative programming in general.

If your function's name starts with `has`, `is`, `can`, or a similar word, it should be just a query and not modify the underlying state or have any side effects. This brings two great benefits:

- **Much easier reasoning about the code**: It's clear that such functions are semantically just *reads*, never *writes*. This can make looking for a change of state much easier when debugging.
- **Fewer heisenbugs**: If you have ever had to debug an error that manifested in a release build but not in the debug one (or the other way around), you have dealt with heisenbugs, which disappear or change behavior when you debug software. It's rarely something pleasurable. Many such errors can be caused by assert calls that modify the state. Following CQS eliminates such bugs.

Similarly to asserts, if you want to have contracts (pre- and post-conditions), it's super important to only use queries in them. Otherwise, disabling some contract checks could also lead to heisenbugs, not to mention how counterintuitive it would be.

Let's now say a few more words about event sourcing.

Event sourcing

As introduced in *Chapter 2, Architectural Styles*, event sourcing means that instead of always storing the whole state of your application, possibly dealing with conflicts during updates, you can just store the changes that happened to your application's state. Using event sourcing can boost your app's performance by eliminating concurrent updates and allowing all interested parties to perform gradual changes to their state. Saving the history of the operations done (for example, market transactions) can allow easier debugging (by replaying them later) and auditing. This also brings more flexibility and extensibility to the table. Some domain models can get much simpler when event sourcing is introduced by reducing their complexity.

One cost of event sourcing is being eventually consistent. Another one is slowing down the startup of your application—unless you make periodic snapshots of the state or can use the read-only store, as in CQRS, discussed in the previous section.

Okay, enough of CQRS and related patterns. Let's now move on to another hot topic when it comes to performance (no pun intended): caching.

Caching patterns

Proper usage of caches can yield better performance, lower latency, reduce the server load (and thus, costs of running in the cloud), and help with scalability concerns (fewer servers required)—what's not to like?

If you're here for tips on CPU caches, you can find them in *Chapter 13, Performance.*

Caching is a big topic, so we'll only cover a few aspects of it here.

Caching works by simply storing the data that is read most often in non-persistent storage with fast access times. There are many different types of caches:

- **Client-side caches**: For storing data specifically for a given customer, often placed on the client's machine or browser.
- **Web server caches**: For speeding up reading from web pages, for instance, through HTTP accelerators such as Varnish, NGINX, or Apache that can cache the web server responses. Many popular sites and web services use NGINX and Varnish together.
- **Database caches**: For improving performance, availability, and scalability through built-in, tunable caching mechanisms.
- **Application caches**: For speeding up your application, which can now read data from a cache instead of reaching out to its database.
- **CDNs can be treated as caches too**: For serving content from a location close to the user for the purpose of reducing latency.

Some types of caches can be replicated or deployed in clusters to provide performance at scale. An alternative can also be to shard them: similarly to how you would shard databases, you can use different instances of your caches for distinct parts of your data.

Let's now go through the different approaches to updating the data in the cache. After all, no one likes to be served stale data.

Updating caches

There are a few strategies for keeping the cached data fresh. Whether it's you who decided how to update cached items or another company, it's worth knowing them. In this section, we'll discuss their pros and cons.

Read-through cache

In this strategy, data is loaded on demand and returned immediately if there's a cache hit. Otherwise, when there's a cache miss, data is fetched from the database before updating the cache and returning data. This cache is for read-heavy workloads, but its downside is some delay in prefetching.

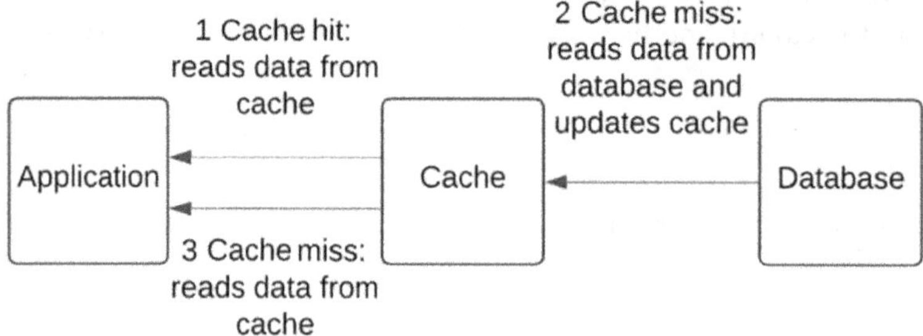

Figure 4.18: Read-through cache

Write-through cache

If you require strong consistency, synchronously updating both the database and the cache is a valid approach for you. This strategy protects you from data loss: if data becomes visible to a user, it means it is already written to the database. A downside of write-through caches is that the latency to perform the update is greater than in the other write strategies.

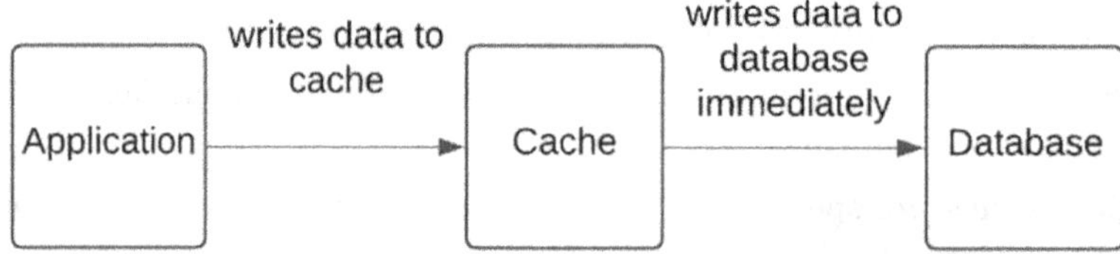

Figure 4.19: Write-through cache

Write-behind cache

Another strategy, also known as **write-back**, is to provide the user with just access to the cache. When the user performs an update, the cache will then queue the incoming update, which will then be asynchronously executed, thus updating the database. The obvious downside here is that if something goes wrong, the data can never be written. It's also not as easy to implement as the other strategies. The upside, however, is low latency and high throughput as seen by the user.

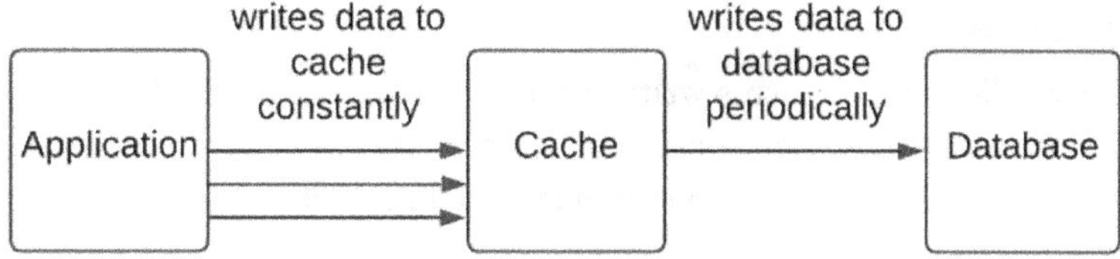

Figure 4.20: Write-behind cache

Cache-aside cache

This strategy, also called **lazy loading**, is about filling the cache on demand. The difference between this strategy and read-through is that the application itself fetches data, updates the cache, and may disable the cache in the case of its failure.

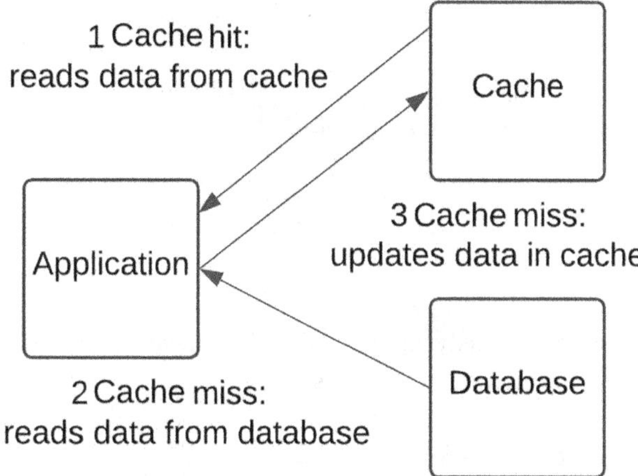

Figure 4.21: Cache-aside cache

This type of caching is often done using Memcached, Valkey, or Redis. It can be really fast and efficient—the cache only contains data that was requested.

However, if data that is not in the cache is often requested, the preceding three calls can increase the latency noticeably. To mitigate this for cache restarts, the cache can be primed (initialized) with selected data from the persistent store.

Write-around cache

In this strategy, the application performs write operations to the database, bypassing the cache, and only subsequent read operations trigger caching. This cache is for write-heavy workloads without polluting the cache, but its downside is the risk of stale data and some delay in prefetching.

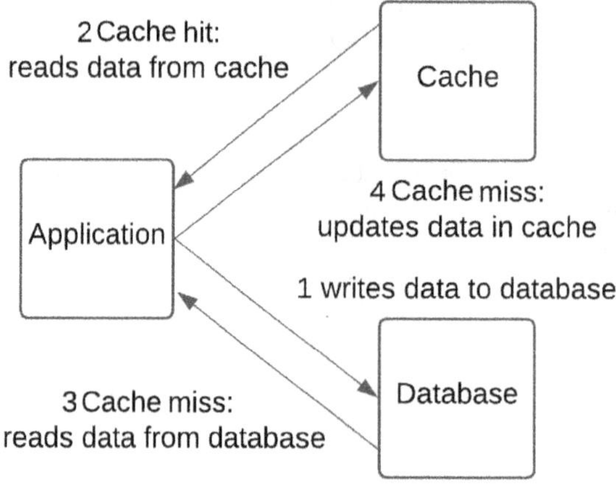

Figure 4.22: Write-around cache

Refresh-ahead cache

The refresh-ahead cache asynchronously and periodically renews the hot data before expiration, but its downside is extra load on the cache and database.

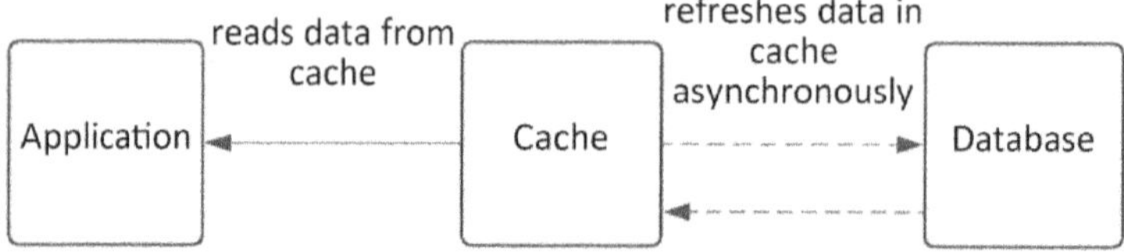

Figure 4.23: Refresh-ahead cache

The items in the cache can become stale, so it's best to set a **time to live** (TTL) for each entry. If the data is to be updated, it can happen in a write-through manner by removing the record from the cache and updating it in the database. Take care when using multi-level caches with just a time-based update policy (for instance, as in DNS caches). This may lead to using stale data for long periods of time, as the cache might not get updated until the TTL expires.

We've discussed the types of caches and strategies to update them, so that's enough about caches for now. Let's move on to a different aspect of providing scalable architectures: designing efficient data storage.

Designing data storage

Let's now discuss the storage for your application. First, let's decide whether you should go with SQL, NoSQL, or something else.

Roughly, a good rule of thumb is to decide on the technology according to the size of your database. For small databases, say, those whose size will never grow into the terabyte area, going with SQL is a valid approach. If you have a very small database or want to create an in-memory cache, you can try SQLite. If you plan to go into single terabytes, again, guaranteeing that the size will never get bigger than that, your best bet would be to go with NoSQL. It's possible in some cases to still stick to SQL databases, but it gets expensive quickly because of the costs of hardware, as you'll need a beast of a server for your master node. Even if it's not an issue, you should measure whether the performance is enough for your needs and be prepared for long maintenance windows. In some cases, it may also suit you to just run a cluster of SQL machines using technologies such as MySQL NDB Cluster or Citus, which is, in essence, a sharded PostgreSQL. However, usually, it's just cheaper and simpler to go with NoSQL in such cases. If the size of your database exceeds 10 TBs or you need to ingest data in real time, consider using a data warehouse instead of NoSQL.

Which NoSQL technology should I use?

The answer to this question depends on several factors. A few are listed here:

- If you want to store time series (save increments at small, regular intervals), then the best option would be to use InfluxDB or VictoriaMetrics.
- If you need something like SQL but could live without joins, or in other words, if you plan to store your data in columns, you can try out Apache Cassandra, ScyllaDB, AWS DynamoDB, or Google's BigTable.
- If that's not the case, then you should think about whether your data is a document without a schema, such as JSON or some kind of application logs. If that's the case, you could go with Elasticsearch, which is great for such flexible data and provides a RESTful API. You could also try out RethinkDB or MongoDB, which store their data in **Binary JSON (BSON)** format and allow MapReduce.

OK, but what if you don't want to store documents? Then you could opt for object storage, especially if your data is large. Usually, going with a cloud provider is OK in this case, which means that using Amazon's S3, MinIO, Google's Cloud Storage, or Microsoft Azure Blob Storage should help your case. If you want to go with something local, you could use OpenStack's Swift or deploy Ceph.

If file storage is also not what you're looking for, then perhaps your case is just about simple key-value data. Using such storage has its benefits as it's fast. This is why many distributed caches are built using it. Notable technologies include Riak, Redis, Valkey, and Memcached (this last one is not suitable for persisting data).

Aside from the previously mentioned options, you could consider using a tree-based database such as BerkeleyDB. Those databases are basically specialized key-value storage with path-like access. If trees are too restrictive for your case, you might be interested in graph-oriented databases such as Neo4j or OrientDB.

After sorting out data storage, another important aspect of building a scalable architecture is planning how to deploy your system in production.

Deploying your system

Even though deploying services sounds easy, there are a lot of things to think about if you take a closer look. This section will describe how to perform efficient deployments, configure your services after installing them, and check that they stay healthy after being deployed, all while minimizing downtime.

The sidecar pattern

Remember Envoy from earlier in this chapter? It's a very useful tool for efficient application development. Instead of embedding infrastructure services such as logging, monitoring, or networking into your application, you can deploy the Envoy proxy along with your app, just like a sidecar would be *deployed* next to a motorbike. Together, they can do much more than the app without the sidekick (another name for this pattern).

Using a sidecar can speed up development, as many of the functionalities it brings would need to be developed independently by each of your microservices. Because it's separate from your application, a sidecar can be developed using any programming language you find best for the job. The sidecar, along with all the functionality it provides, can be maintained by an independent team of developers and updated independently from your main service.

Because sidecars reside right next to the app they enhance, they can use local means of inter-process communication. Usually, it's fast enough and much faster than communicating from another host, but remember that it can cause high system resource consumption.

Even if you deploy a third-party service, deploying your selected sidecar next to it can still provide value: you can monitor the resource usage and the condition of both the host and the service, as well as tracing requests throughout your distributed system. Sometimes it's also possible to reconfigure the service dynamically based on its condition, via editing the config file or a web interface.

In real-world deployments, the sidecar pattern is often paired with other architectural patterns. For example, in Docker and Kubernetes environments, the sidecar pattern is commonly used along with the ambassador and adapter patterns to collect, transmit, and analyze telemetry of containers, and for communication. These patterns are together referred to as a triad. *Figure 4.24* shows how this triad functions.

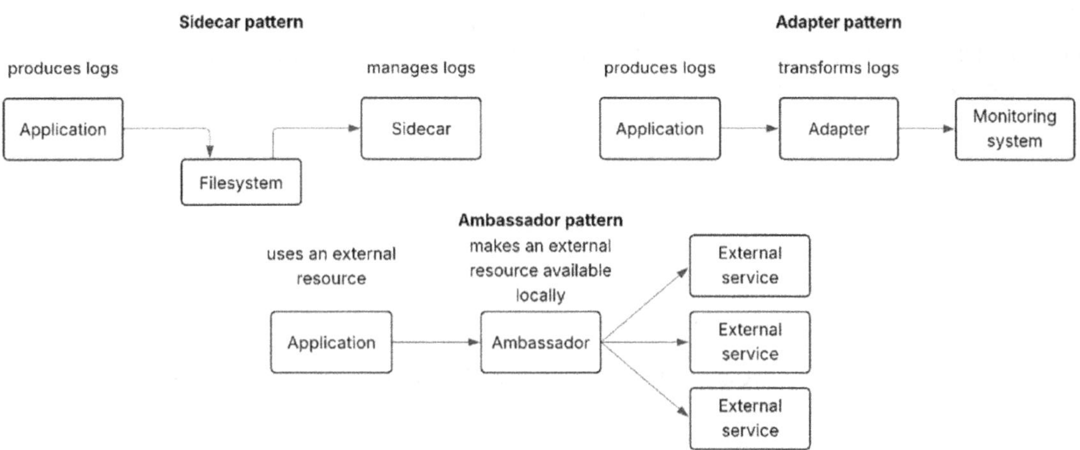

Figure 4.24: Ambassador, adapter, and sidecar patterns

Ambassador is a container functioning as a proxy to other parts of the system, **adapter** is a container transforming the output of the main container, such as logs for a monitoring system, and **sidecar** is an additional container enhancing or extending the functionality of the main container.

Such combined deployment patterns are often essential for building robust, production-ready systems.

Let's now look at a practical implementation of the sidecar pattern using Envoy.

Deploying a service with tracing and a reverse proxy using Envoy

We'll use Envoy as a front proxy for our deployment. In our configuration, Envoy, being a proxy of the front application, will send telemetry to an OpenTelemetry Collector. Start by creating Envoy's configuration file (in our case named `envoy-front_proxy.yaml`) with the address of our proxy:

```
static_resources:
  listeners:
  - address:
      socket_address:
        address: 0.0.0.0
        port_value: 8080
    traffic_direction: INBOUND
```

We've specified that Envoy is going to listen for incoming traffic on port 8080. Later in the configuration, we'll route it to our service. Now, let's specify that we'd like to handle HTTP requests using our set of service instances and adding some tracing capabilities on top. First, let's add an HTTP endpoint:

```
    filter_chains:
      - filters:
          - name: envoy.filters.network.http_connection_manager
            typed_config:
              "@type": type.googleapis.com/envoy.extensions.filters.network.
http_connection_manager.v3.HttpConnectionManager
```

Now, let's specify that requests should have IDs assigned and be traced by the distributed tracing system, OpenTelemetry:

```
              generate_request_id: true
                tracing:
                  provider:
                    name: envoy.tracers.opentelemetry
                    typed_config:
                      "@type": type.googleapis.com/envoy.config.trace.
v3.OpenTelemetryConfig
                      grpc_service:
                        envoy_grpc:
                          cluster_name: opentelemetry_collector
                        timeout: 0.250s
                      service_name: front_proxy
```

We'll create IDs for requests and use the OpenTelemetry tracer. The tracer will report to the OpenTelemetry Collector instance running under the specified address.

We also need to specify that all traffic (see the match section) from all domains shall be routed into our service cluster:

```
              codec_type: auto
              stat_prefix: ingress_http
              route_config:
                name: example_route
                virtual_hosts:
                  - name: front_proxy
                    domains:
                      - "*"
                    routes:
                      - match:
                          prefix: "/"
                        route:
```

```
                cluster: example_service
              decorator:
                operation: example_operation
```

We'll define our `example_service` cluster in a second. Note that each request coming to the cluster will be marked by a predefined operation decorator. We also need to specify what router address to use:

```
          http_filters:
          - name: envoy.filters.http.router
            typed_config:
              @type': type.googleapis.com/envoy.extensions.filters.http.
router.v3.Router
          use_remote_address: true
```

Now we know how to handle and trace the requests, so what's left is to define the clusters we used. Let's start with our service cluster:

```
  clusters:
    - name: example_service
      connect_timeout: 0.250s
      type: strict_dns
      lb_policy: round_robin
      load_assignment:
        cluster_name: example_service
        endpoints:
          - lb_endpoints:
            - endpoint:
                address:
                  socket_address:
                    address: example_service
                    port_value: 5678
    - name: opentelemetry_collector
      type: STRICT_DNS
      lb_policy: ROUND_ROBIN
      typed_extension_protocol_options:
        envoy.extensions.upstreams.http.v3.HttpProtocolOptions:
          "@type": type.googleapis.com/envoy.extensions.upstreams.http.
v3.HttpProtocolOptions
          explicit_http_config:
            http2_protocol_options: {}
      load_assignment:


        cluster_name: opentelemetry_collector
```

```
        endpoints:

          - lb_endpoints:

              - endpoint:

                  address:

                    socket_address:

                      address: opentelemetry
                      port_value: 4317
```

Each cluster can have multiple instances (endpoints) of our service. Here, if we decide to add more endpoints, the incoming requests will be load-balanced using the round-robin strategy.

Let's also add an `admin` interface:

```
admin:
  access_log_path: /tmp/admin_access.log
  address:
    socket_address:
      address: 0.0.0.0
      port_value: 9901
```

Let's now place the config inside a container that will run Envoy using a Dockerfile, which we named `Dockerfile-front_proxy`:

```
FROM envoyproxy/envoy:v1.32-latest
COPY --chmod=644 envoy-front_proxy.yaml /etc/envoy/envoy.yaml
```

Now, let's specify how to run our code in several containers using Docker Compose. Create a Docker Compose (`compose.yaml`) file, starting with the front proxy service definition:

```
services:
  front_proxy:
    build:
      context: .
      dockerfile: Dockerfile-front_proxy
    networks:
      - example_network
    ports:
      - "12345:12345"
      - "
9901:9901"
```

We use our Dockerfile here, a simple network, and we expose two ports from the container on the host: our service and the `admin` interface. Now we add the service our proxy will direct to:

```
  example_service:
    image: hashicorp/http-echo
    networks:
      - example_network
    command: -text "It works!"
```

In our case, the service will just display a predefined string in a simple web server.

Now, we run the OpenTelemetry Collector in another container, exposing its port to the outside world:

```
  opentelemetry-collector:
    image: otel/opentelemetry-collector-contrib

    networks:
      - example_network
    ports:
      - "4317:4317"
      - "4318:4318"
      - "55679:55679"
    volumes:
      - ./collector-config.yaml:/etc/otelcol/config.yaml
```

The last step will be to define our network:

```
networks:
  example_network: {}
```

And we're done. You can now run the service using `docker compose up --build` and point your browser to the endpoints we specified.

Using a sidecar proxy has a benefit: even if your service dies, the sidecar is usually still alive and can respond to external requests while the main service is down. The same applies when your service is redeployed, for example, because of an update. Speaking of which, let's learn how to minimize the related downtime.

Zero-downtime deployments

There are two common ways to minimize the risk of downtime during deployments: blue-green deployments and canary releases. You can use the Envoy sidecar when introducing either of those two.

Blue–green deployment pattern

Blue-green deployments can help you minimize both the downtime and the regression risk (having defects) related to deploying your app. To do so, you'll need two identical production environments, called *blue* and *green*.

While the green one serves the customers, you can perform the update in the blue one. Once the update has been made, the services have been tested, and all looks stable, you can switch the traffic so it now flows to the updated (blue) environment.

If any issues are spotted in the blue environment after the switch, the green one is still there—you can just switch them back. The users probably won't even notice any changes, and because both environments are up and running, no downtime should be visible during the switch.

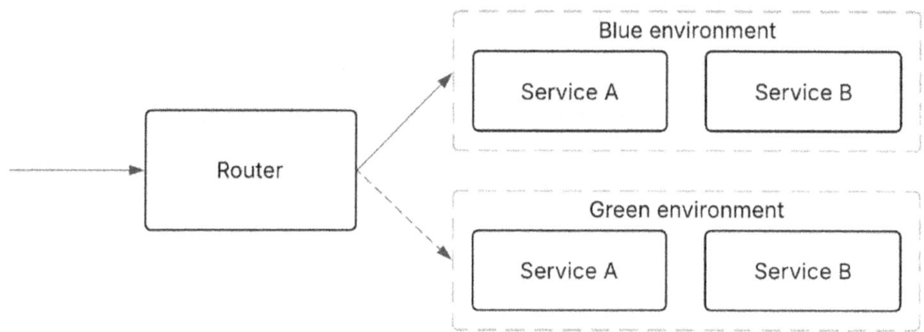

Figure 4.25: Blue-green deployment

Just make sure you won't lose any data during the switch (for example, transactions made in the new environment).

Canary release pattern

The simplest way to not have all your service instances fail after an update is often, well, not updating all of them at once. That's the key idea behind the incremental variant of blue-green deployments, also called a canary release.

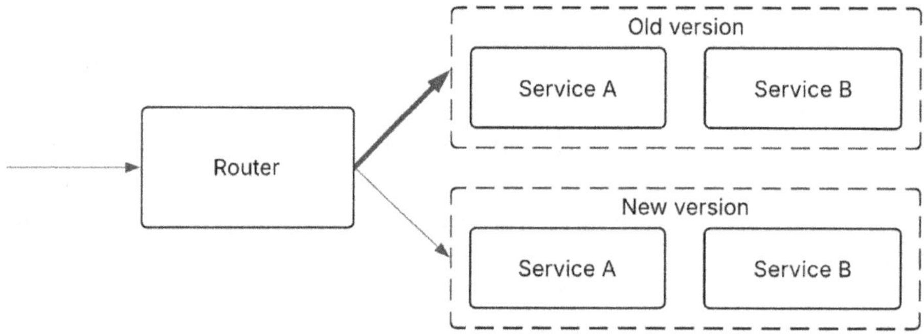

Figure 4.26: Canary release

In Envoy, you could put the following in the `routes` section of your config:

```
- match:
    prefix: "/"
  route:
    weighted_clusters:
```

```
    clusters:
    - name: new_version
      weight: 5
    - name: old_version
      weight: 95
```

You should also remember to define the two clusters from the preceding snippet. Here's the first one, which uses the old version of your service:

```
clusters:
  - name: old_version
    connect_timeout: 0.250s
    type: strict_dns
    lb_policy: round_robin
    load_assignment:
      cluster_name: old_version
      endpoints:
        - lb_endpoints:
            - endpoint:
                address:
                  socket_address:
                    address: old_version
                    port_value: 5678
```

The second cluster will run the new version:

```
  - name: new_version
    connect_timeout: 0.250s
    type: strict_dns
    lb_policy: round_robin
    load_assignment:
      cluster_name: new_version
      endpoints:
        - lb_endpoints:
            - endpoint:
                address:
                  socket_address:
                    address: new_version
                    port_value: 5678
```

When an update gets deployed, the new version of a service will only be seen and used by a small fraction (here, 5%) of your users. If the updated instances remain stable and no checks and verifications fail, you can gradually update more and more hosts in several steps, until all of them are switched to a new version. You can do it either by updating the config files manually or by using the `admin` endpoint. Voila!

Let's now move on to the last deployment pattern that we'll cover here.

External configuration store pattern

If you're deploying a simple application, it can be okay to just deploy its configuration along with it. However, when you want to have a more complex deployment with many application instances, it can quickly become a burden to redeploy a new version of the app just to reconfigure it. At the same time, manual configuration changes are a no-go if you want to treat your services like cattle, not pets. Introducing an external configuration store can be an elegant way to overcome such hurdles.

In essence, your apps can grab their configuration from said store instead of just relying on their local config files. This allows you to provide common settings for multiple instances and tune parameters for some of them, while having an easy and centralized way to monitor all your configs. If you want an arbiter to decide which nodes will be master nodes and which will serve as backup ones, an external configuration store can provide the instances with such information. It's also useful to implement a configuration update procedure so that your instances can be easily reconfigured during operation. You can use ready solutions such as Firebase Remote Config, leverage the Java-based Netflix Archaius, or write a configuration store on your own, leveraging cloud storage and change notifications.

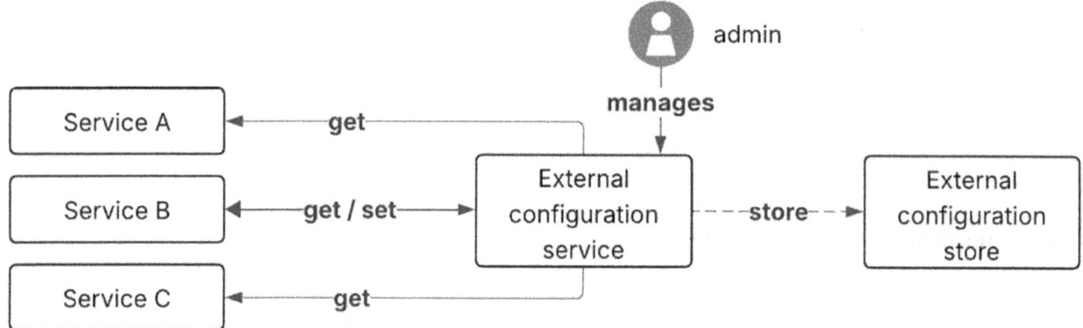

Figure 4.27: External configuration store

Now that we've learned about some useful deployment patterns, let's move to another important topic when it comes to high-level design: APIs.

Managing your APIs

Proper APIs are essential for the success of your development team and product. We can divide this topic into two groups: system-level APIs and component-level APIs. In this section, we'll discuss handling APIs on the first of those levels, while the next chapter will present you with tips on the second.

API management tools

Aside from managing objects, you'll also want to manage your whole API. If you want to introduce policies regarding API usage, control access to said API, gather performance metrics and other analytical data, or just charge your customers based on their use of your interfaces, **API management** (**APIM**) is the solution you're looking for.

Typically, a set of APIM tools consists of these components:

- **An API gateway**: A single entry point for all users of an API. More on this in the next section.
- **Reporting and analytics**: To monitor the performance and latency of your APIs, resources consumed, or data sent. Such tools can be leveraged to detect trends in usage, and know which parts of the API and which components behind them are performance bottlenecks, or what SLAs are reasonable to offer and how to improve them.
- **A portal for developers**: To help them get up to speed with your API quickly, and to subscribe to your APIs at all.
- **A portal for administrators**: To manage policies, users, and package APIs into sellable products.
- **Monetization**: To charge your customers based on how they use your APIs and to aid related business processes.

APIM tools are provided both by cloud providers and independent parties, for example, NGINX's Controller or Tyk.

When designing APIs for a given cloud, get to know the good practices the cloud provider usually documents. For instance, you can find common design patterns for Google Cloud Platform in the *Further reading* section. In their case, lots of the practices revolve around using Protobuf.

Choosing the right way to consume APIs can take you a long way. The simplest way to file requests to your servers is by connecting to the services directly. While easy to set up and okay for small apps, it can lead to performance issues down the road. An API consumer will likely need to call a few different services, leading to high latency. Proper scalability is also impossible to achieve using this approach.

A better approach is to use an API gateway. Such gateways are often an essential part of an APIM solution, but can also be used on their own.

API gateways

An API gateway is an entry point for clients who want to use your API. It can then route the incoming requests to a specific instance or cluster of services. This can simplify your client code, as it no longer needs to know all the backend nodes or how they cooperate with each other. All a client needs to know is the address of an API gateway, as the gateway will handle the rest. Thanks to hiding the backend architecture from the client, it can be easily remodeled without even touching the client's code.

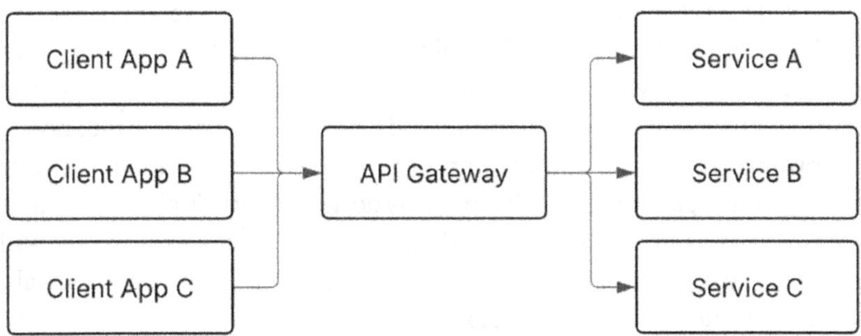

Figure 4.28: An API gateway is an entry point for API calls

The gateway can aggregate multiple parts of your system's API into a single entry point and use **layer-7 routing** based on detailed information such as URLs, HTTP headers, cookies, or message content to direct requests to the appropriate part of the system. This operates at the application layer of the **Open Systems Interconnection** (**OSI**) model, in contrast to **layer-4 routing**, which uses transport-layer details such as protocols and ports, and network-layer information such as IP addresses.

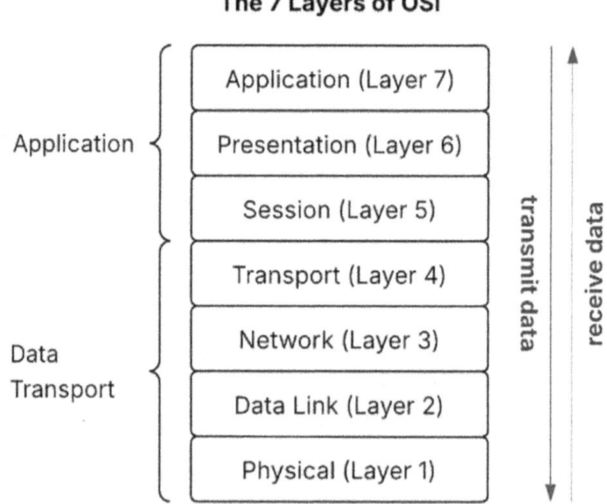

Figure 4.29: The seven layers of the OSI model

As with many patterns described in this chapter, always consider whether it's worth adding more complexity by introducing another pattern to your architecture. Think about how adding it will affect your availability, fault tolerance, and performance if they matter to you. After all, a gateway usually is just a single node, so try not to make it a bottleneck or a single point of failure.

The *backends for frontends* pattern we mentioned in *Chapter 2, Architectural Styles*, can be thought of as a variant of the API gateway pattern. In the *backends for frontends* case, each frontend connects to its own gateway.

Summary

In this chapter, we've learned quite a lot of stuff. You now know when to apply which service model and how to avoid the common pitfalls of designing distributed systems. You've learned about the CAP and PACELC theorems and what practical outcomes they have for distributed architectures. You can now run transactions in such systems successfully, reduce their downtime, prevent issues, and gracefully recover from errors. Dealing with unusually high load is no longer black magic. Integrating parts of your system, even legacy ones, with your newly designed parts is also something you're able to perform. You now also have some tricks up your sleeve to increase the performance and scalability of your system, and design data storage. Deploying and load balancing your system are also demystified, so you can now perform them efficiently. Last but not least, discovering services and designing and managing their APIs are all things that you have now learned to perform. Nice!

In the next chapter, we'll learn how you can use specific C++ features to travel on the road to excellent architecture in a more pleasant and efficient way.

Questions

1. What is event sourcing?
2. What are the common practical consequences of the CAP and PACELC theorems?
3. What can you use Netflix's Chaos Monkey for?
4. Where can caching be applied?
5. How do you prevent your app from going down when a whole data center does?
6. Why use an API gateway?
7. How can Envoy help you achieve various architectural goals?

Further reading

- Microsoft Azure, *Cloud Design Patterns*: `https://docs.microsoft.com/en-us/azure/architecture/patterns/`
- Google API Improvement Proposals, *Design Patterns*: `https://google.aip.dev/general#design-patterns`
- Microsoft, *Microsoft REST API Guidelines*, GitHub: `https://github.com/microsoft/api-guidelines/blob/vNext/Guidelines.md`
- Envoy, *Getting Started*: `https://www.envoyproxy.io/docs/envoy/latest/start/start`
- Jay Runkel, *Active-Active Application Architectures with MongoDB* (Blog), MongoDB: `https://www.mongodb.com/blog/post/active-active-application-architectures-with-mongodb`
- DB-Engines, *DB-Engines Ranking*: `https://db-engines.com/en/ranking`
- Jasper, *How Millisecond Delays May Kill Database Performance* (Blog), Packet-Foo: `https://blog.packet-foo.com/2014/09/how-millisecond-delays-may-kill-database-performance/`
- Istio, *Architecture*: `https://istio.io/latest/docs/ops/deployment/architecture/`

5

Leveraging C++ Language Features

C++, created by Bjarne Stroustrup at AT&T Bell Labs as an extension of the C language, is a high-level, general-purpose, compiled, statically typed programming language supporting procedural, object-oriented, and generic programming.

This language is used in a plethora of cases to build both low- and high-level systems, varying from creating firmware and operating systems, desktop and mobile applications, to server software, frameworks, and services. C++ code runs on all kinds of hardware, is massively deployed on compute clouds, and can even be found in outer space. Such success wouldn't have been possible without the broad set of features this multi-paradigm language has.

In the previous chapter, we introduced architectural patterns that solve high-level system design challenges such as scalability, availability, deployment, and integration in distributed environments. This chapter brings the focus down to the C++ language level, showing how to implement the core components of those systems using modern, safe, and efficient C++ features.

Although C++ allows you to use the well-known object-oriented APIs of the standard libraries that you may be familiar with if you write code in C# or so-called coffee languages (a lighthearted term for Java and its related languages, inspired by Java's coffee cup logo and name) such as Java and Kotlin, it has some other tricks up its sleeves that go beyond object-oriented design. We'll mention a few of them in this chapter.

During this journey, we will demonstrate the best industry practices for ensuring type safety, avoiding memory issues, and creating efficient code. You'll learn about the features and techniques that are available in various standards of C++, ranging from C++98 all the way to C++23. This will include declarative programming, RAII, `constexpr`, `constinit`, `consteval`, monadic interfaces, templates, ranges, and concepts.

In this chapter, we'll cover the following topics:

- Using RAII
- Specifying the interfaces of containers in C++
- Using raw and smart pointers in interfaces
- Specifying preconditions and postconditions
- Employing inline namespaces
- Applying std::optional
- Using monadic interfaces
- Writing declarative code
- Moving computations to compile time
- Leveraging the power of safe types

Without further ado, let's begin this journey.

Technical requirements

You will need the following tools to build the code in this chapter:

- A compiler that supports C++23 (GCC 14+ is recommended)
- CMake 3.28+

The source code for this chapter can be found at `https://github.com/PacktPublishing/Software-Architecture-with-Cpp-2E/tree/main/Chapter05`.

Using RAII

RAII (resource acquisition is initialization) is a crucial idiom popularized by C++ creator Bjarne Stroustrup. It uses stack-based objects, constructors, and destructors to manage all resources, including heap memory, sockets, files, mutexes, disk space, and network connections.

When a class object is declared on the stack, it is initialized by calling its constructor, which captures the resource or throws an exception if an error occurs. When the object goes out of scope, it is popped off the stack, but not before the object's destructor is called to release the captured resource.

This code shows an RAII wrapper class that allocates dynamic memory for an array in its constructor and releases the memory in its destructor:

```
template <typename T>
class Array final {
public:
    explicit Array(std::size_t size) : sz_{size}, data_{new T[size]} {
    std::cout << "Resource acquired\n";
    }

    Array(std::initializer_list<T> list) : Array(list.size()) {
        std::copy(list.begin(), list.end(), data_);
```

```
    }

    ~Array() {
        delete[] data_;
        std::cout << "Resource released\n";
    }

    // Copy constructor and assignment operator are deleted to prevent shallow
copies and multiple deletions of the same dynamic memory.
    // See Chapter 6 for more on copy and move semantics.
    Array(const Array&) = delete;
    Array& operator=(const Array&) = delete;

    T& operator[](std::size_t idx) { return data_[idx]; }
    const T& operator[](std::size_t idx) const { return data_[idx]; }

    [[nodiscard]] std::size_t size() const noexcept { return sz_; }

    std::span<const T> span() { return std::span{data_, sz_}; }

private:
    std::size_t sz_;
    T* data_;
};
```

The copy constructor and copy assignment operator are explicitly deleted in this implementation to prevent shallow copies and potential double deletions of the same dynamic memory. Without these deletions, the compiler would generate implicit versions of these functions. The implicitly provided copy assignment operator could cause the program to crash because it performs a shallow copy of the internal pointers when assigning from a temporary `Array` object. When the temporary object is destroyed, it frees the dynamic memory, leaving the original object with a dangling pointer and leading to a double deletion:

```
Array<int> array{};
array = {1, 2, 3, 4, 5};
Array copy_array{array};
```

Copy and move constructors and assignment operators, including shallow and deep copying, are explained in more detail in the next chapter. Here's a helper function that prints elements of the `Array` class's internal array that cannot be modified because `std::span` is a read-only view of the underlying data:

```
template <typename T> void print_span(std::span<T> s) {
    std::copy(s.begin(), s.end(), std::ostream_iterator<T>(std::cout));
    std::cout << std::endl;
}
```

Now, let's see RAII in action. In the following code, dynamic memory, being a resource, is automatically freed when the arr object leaves the scope of the main() function:

```
Array<char> a{0x74, 0x68, 0x65, 0x20, 0x64, 0x6f, 0x6f, 0x72, 0x20, 0x69, 0x6e,
0x74, 0x6f, 0x20, 0x73, 0x75, 0x6d, 0x6d, 0x65, 0x72};

print_span(a.span());

for (std::size_t i{}; i < a.size(); ++i) {
    a[i] = static_cast<char>(i + 65);
}

print_span(a.span());
```

The code snippet prints messages when the resource is created and destroyed. The for loop replaces characters of the array with uppercase letters:

```
Resource acquired
the door into summer
ABCDEFGHIJKLMNOPQRST
Resource released
```

RAII is a core idiom in C++ that enables deterministic resource management. Unlike garbage-collected languages such as Java, Python, or Go, C++ ensures immediate cleanup via destructors. Languages such as Rust and Ada also adopt similar patterns.

The C++ **Standard Template Library** (**STL**) provides many classes implementing RAII: std::unique_ptr, std::shared_ptr, std::string, std::vector, std::lock_guard, std::unique_lock, and std::shared_lock. The STL is full of thoughtful features that help developers write clean and reusable code. Let's now examine standard containers such as std::array, a fundamental part of the library.

Specifying the interfaces of containers in C++

Implementations of the standard library are great places to search for idiomatic and performant C++ code. For instance, if you want to read some really interesting template code, you should give std::chrono a shot, as it demonstrates some useful techniques and has a fresh approach to this. A link to libstdc++'s implementation can be found in the *Further reading* section.

When it comes to other parts of the library, even a quick peek at its containers shows that even though C++ containers may differ from those in other languages in terms of syntax and implementation, they follow consistent data structures. For example, many C++ standard containers share common type aliases. To show this, let's take a look at a pretty straightforward class from the standard library—std::array—to analyze this pattern:

```
template <class T, size_t N>
struct array {
    // types:
    typedef T& reference;
```

```
    typedef const T& const_reference;
    typedef /*implementation-defined*/ iterator;
    typedef /*implementation-defined*/ const_iterator;
    typedef size_t size_type;
    typedef ptrdiff_t difference_type;
    typedef T value_type;
    typedef T* pointer;
    typedef const T* const_pointer;
    typedef reverse_iterator<iterator> reverse_iterator;
    typedef reverse_iterator<const_iterator> const_reverse_iterator;
```

The first thing you can see when you start reading the class definition is that it creates aliases for some types. This is common across the standard containers, and the names of those aliases are the same in many of them. This happens for a few reasons. One of them is the rule of least surprise—having it this way reduces the time developers spend scratching their heads and trying to understand what you meant and how a specific alias was named. Another reason is that the users of your class and library writers will often depend on such type traits when they're writing their own code. If your container won't provide such aliases, it will make using it with some standard utilities or type traits harder, so the users of your APIs will have to work around this or even use a completely different class.

Having such type aliases can be useful even if you're not using them in your templates. It's not uncommon to rely on those types for function parameters and class member fields, so always remember to provide them if you're writing a class that other people could use. For instance, if you're writing an allocator, many of its consumers will rely on specific type aliases being present.

Let's see what else `std::array` brings us:

```
  // no explicit construct/copy/destroy for aggregate type
```

So, the next interesting thing about `std::array` is that it has no definition of a constructor, including copy/move constructors, assign operators, or destructors. It's simply because having those wouldn't add any value. Often, adding such members when it's not necessary is harmful to performance. If `std::array` were to use a non-default constructor (and `T() {}` is already non-default, as opposed to `T() = default;`), your class would no longer be trivial nor trivially constructible, which would prevent the compiler from applying optimizations to it.

Let's see what other declarations our class has:

```
  constexpr void fill(const T& u);
  constexpr void swap(array<T, N>&) noexcept(is_nothrow_swappable_v<T&>);
```

Now, we can see two member functions, including a member swap. Often, it's profitable to not rely on the default behavior of `std::swap` and to provide our own. For instance, in the case of `std::vector`, the underlying storage is swapped as a whole instead of each element being swapped. When you're writing a member swap function, be sure to also introduce a free function named `swap` so that the custom swap for your type can be detected via **argument-dependent lookup** (**ADL**). It could just call your member's `swap` function.

One more thing regarding the swap function that's worth mentioning is that it's conditionally noexcept. If the stored type can be swapped without throwing exceptions, the array's swap function will be noexcept as well. The non-throwing swap idiom can help you achieve strong exception safety guarantees in copy operations for classes that are storing our type as a member.

As shown in the following code block, now comes a big set of functions that show us another important aspect of many C++ container classes—their iterators:

```
// iterators:
constexpr iterator begin() noexcept;
constexpr const_iterator begin() const noexcept;
constexpr iterator end() noexcept;
constexpr const_iterator end() const noexcept;

constexpr reverse_iterator rbegin() noexcept;
constexpr const_reverse_iterator rbegin() const noexcept;
constexpr reverse_iterator rend() noexcept;
constexpr const_reverse_iterator rend() const noexcept;

constexpr const_iterator cbegin() const noexcept;
constexpr const_iterator cend() const noexcept;
constexpr const_reverse_iterator crbegin() const noexcept;
constexpr const_reverse_iterator crend() const noexcept;
```

Iterators are vital for every container. If you don't provide iterator access for your class, you won't be able to use it in range-based for loops and it won't be compatible with all the useful algorithms from the standard library. This doesn't mean that you need to write your own iterator types—you could just use a simple pointer if your storage is contiguous. Providing const iterators can help you use your class in an immutable manner, and providing reverse iterators can help with enabling more use cases for your container.

Before we move on, let's take a step back and understand what iterators actually are, how they are classified, and how they can be implemented.

Iterators in C++ are classified into six categories that form a hierarchy based on the operations they support. They are usually declared inside the classes they belong to. Starting from the lowest in the hierarchy to the highest, they are as follows:

- The input iterator is a one-way iterator used to access values
- The output iterator is also a one-way iterator, used to assign values
- The forward iterator combines the input and output iterators
- The bidirectional iterator moves forward and backward
- The random-access iterator has all the properties of the bidirectional iterator and random access

- The contiguous iterator is the same as previous one with the addition that logically adjacent elements are also physically adjacent in memory

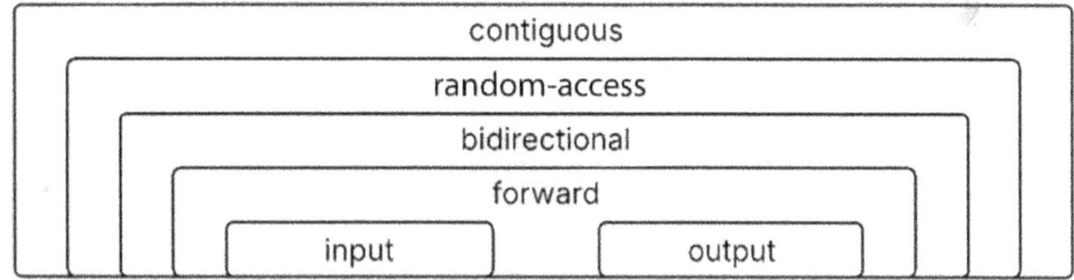

Figure 5.1: Hierarchy of iterators in C++

Traditionally, the iterators are implemented with the help of tagging and common properties: `iterator_category`, `difference_type`, `value_type`, `pointer`, and `reference`. These allow the standard library algorithms to deduce an iterator's capabilities and use it appropriately.

While many standard containers already come with iterators, writing your own is essential when designing a custom container class, such as our RAII-based `Array`. This enables compatibility with range-based loops and STL algorithms. The following example shows how to implement a custom forward iterator for the `Array` class from our earlier example:

```
template<typename T> class Array final {
public:
  ...
    struct Iterator {
        using iterator_category = std::forward_iterator_tag;
        using difference_type = std::ptrdiff_t;
        using value_type = T;
        using pointer = T*;
        using reference = T&;

        Iterator() = default;

        explicit Iterator(pointer ptr) : ptr_{ptr} {}

        reference operator*() const { return *ptr_; }
        pointer operator->() { return ptr_; }

        Iterator& operator++() {
            ++ptr_;
            return *this;
        }
        Iterator operator++(int) {
            Iterator tmp = *this;
            ++(*this);
```

```
            return tmp;
        }
        friend bool operator==(const Iterator& a, const Iterator& b) {
            return a.ptr_ == b.ptr_;
        };
        friend bool operator!=(const Iterator& a, const Iterator& b) {
            return a.ptr_ != b.ptr_;
        };

    private:
        pointer ptr{nullptr};
    };

    [[nodiscard]] Iterator begin() { return Iterator(&data[0]); }
    [[nodiscard]] Iterator end() { return Iterator(&data[sz]); }

    [[nodiscard]] const Iterator begin() const { return Iterator(&data[0]); }`
    [[nodiscard]] const Iterator end() const { return Iterator(&data[sz]); }

private:
  ...
};
```

This implementation equips the `Array` class with a custom forward iterator, allowing it to be used in range-based `for` loops and standard algorithms that expect iterators. It provides both const and non-const versions of `begin()` and `end()`, supporting both mutable and immutable access to elements. The iterator itself supports dereferencing, incrementing, and comparison, thereby meeting the minimal requirements for a forward iterator.

With C++20, concepts provide a cleaner way to express iterator requirements. See the *Further reading* section for a resource that covers iterator concepts. Instead of relying on tags, we can now use `static_assert` to check at compile time whether our `Iterator` type satisfies the `std::forward_iterator` concept, as shown here:

```
template<typename T> class Array final {
public:
  ...
    struct Iterator {
        using difference_type = std::ptrdiff_t;
        using value_type = T;
        using pointer = T*;
        using reference = T&;
  ...
```

```
    static_assert(std::forward_iterator<Iterator>);

private:
  ...
};
```

Here, we have a helper function that uses this iterator to print the elements of the array:

```
template <typename T> void print_array(const Array<T> &arr) {
    for (auto it = arr.begin(); it != arr.end(); ++it) {
        std::cout << *it;
    }
    std::cout << std::endl;
}
```

Here's a `for` loop that transforms all characters in the array to lowercase, demonstrating the use of a range-based `for` loop:

```
for (auto &c : arr) {
    c += 32;
}

print_array(arr);
```

The complete example prints these messages:

```
Resource acquired
the door into summer
ABCDEFGHIJKLMNOPQRST
abcdefghijklmnopqrst
Resource released
```

Let's see what comes next:

```
// capacity:
constexpr size_type size() const noexcept;
constexpr size_type max_size() const noexcept;
constexpr bool empty() const noexcept;

// element access:
constexpr reference operator[](size_type n);
constexpr const_reference operator[](size_type n) const;
constexpr const_reference at(size_type n) const;
constexpr reference at(size_type n);
constexpr reference front();
```

```
constexpr const_reference front() const;
constexpr reference back();
constexpr const_reference back() const;

constexpr T * data() noexcept;
constexpr const T * data() const noexcept;
private:
    // the actual storage, like T elements[N];
};
```

After the iterators, we have a few ways to inspect and modify the container's data. In the case of `Array`, all of them are marked `constexpr`. This means that if we were to write some compile-time code, we could use our `Array` class. We'll look at this in more detail later in this chapter, in the *Moving computations at compile time* section.

Finally, we made it through the whole definition of our `Array`. Its interface doesn't end there, however. Starting with C++17, you can spot lines similar to the following:

```
template<class T, class... U>
    array(T, U...) -> array<T, 1 + sizeof...(U)>;
```

Such statements are called **deduction guides**. They're part of a feature called **class template argument deduction (CTAD)**, which was introduced in C++17. It allows you to omit the template parameters when you're declaring a variable. With `std::array`, now, you can just write the following:

```
auto ints = std::array{1, 2, 3};
```

However, it could be even handier for more complex types, such as maps, as follows:

```
auto legCount = std::unordered_map{ std::pair{"cat", 4}, {"human", 2},
{"mushroom", 1} };
```

There is, however, a catch here: we needed to specify that we're passing the key-value pair when we passed the first argument. Note that we also used a deduction guide for it. Deduction guides give the compiler a hint on how to infer types that are not directly related. With CTAD, you can write such deduction guides yourself.

Since we're on the topic of interfaces, let's point to some other aspects of them.

Using raw and smart pointers in interfaces

The types that you use in your interfaces communicate a lot about how your API is meant to be used. Even if there's documentation, a good API should still be intuitive at a glance. This statement also applies to pointers since the pointer passed to a function determines the use of an interface.

Let's see how different approaches to passing resource parameters to a function—by value, reference, or pointer—can suggest different things to the API consumer.

But before we move on to demonstrating the differences, we need an auxiliary class wrapping the `std::string` type:

```
class Resource final {
    std::string m_s;

public:
    explicit Resource(std::string s) : m_s{std::move(s)} {
        std::cout << "Resource constructor " << m_s << '\n';
    }

    ~Resource() {
        std::cout << "Resource destructor " << m_s << '\n';
    }

    // user-defined conversion function
    explicit operator std::string() const { return m_s; }
};

std::ostream& operator<<(std::ostream& os, const Resource& r) {
    os << static_cast<std::string>(r);
    return os;
}
```

The `Resource` class wraps a string only to print messages when a resource is captured or released, which is useful for tracking resource ownership in smart pointers. Accordingly, the user-defined `std::string()` conversion function returns the wrapped string.

Such conversion functions can be defined for different C++ types instead of implicit type conversion for safer type casting. More on this concept will be covered in *Chapter 12, Security in Code and Deployment*.

Now, consider the following function declarations (the `const` keyword is omitted for brevity):

```
void unique_ptr_val(std::unique_ptr<Resource>);
void unique_ptr_ref(std::unique_ptr<Resource>&);
void unique_ptr_raw(std::unique_ptr<Resource>*);

void shared_ptr_val(std::shared_ptr<Resource>);
void shared_ptr_ref(std::shared_ptr<Resource>&);
void shared_ptr_raw(std::shared_ptr<Resource>*);
```

```
void val(Resource);
void ref(Resource&);
void raw(Resource*);

void weak_ptr_val(std::weak_ptr<Resource>);
void weak_ptr_ref(std::weak_ptr<Resource>&);
void weak_ptr_raw(std::weak_ptr<Resource>*);
```

When should you use which of those functions? When a called function returns a raw pointer to dynamically allocated memory, it is not always clear which code should free the memory: the caller or the callee. This is elegantly resolved by smart pointers that own pointers and automatically free memory when the pointer goes out of scope. The use of smart pointers does not conflict with the use of raw pointers as long as the latter *use* objects rather than *owning* them.

Among smart pointers, `std::unique_ptr` is the default choice. It is moveable, but not copyable, because only one owner can exist at a time. Therefore, this smart pointer has a deleted copy constructor. The ownership of the resource can be moved by applying `std::move`, which triggers the move constructor:

```
void unique_ptr_val(std::unique_ptr<Resource> p) {
    std::cout << "unique_ptr_val: value = " << *p << std::endl;
}

int main() {
    auto p = std::make_unique<Resource>("candy apple");

    // compilation error: deleted copy constructor
    // unique_ptr_val(p);

    // not copyable, but movable
    unique_ptr_val(std::move(p));

    // the resource is moved and destroyed in unique_ptr_val()
    std::cout << "unique_ptr_main: value = "
              << (p != nullptr ? static_cast<std::string>(*p) : "null")
              << std::endl;
}
```

Here's the terminal output:

```
Resource constructor candy apple
unique_ptr_val: value = candy apple
Resource destructor candy apple
unique_ptr_main: value = null
```

We see that a `Resource` object is created and wrapped in a unique smart pointer. Ownership is transferred to the `unique_ptr_val` function, so the original pointer is empty at the end.

Unique pointers are objects like any other, so they can be passed by reference or pointer. However, doing so violates the exclusive ownership principle:

```
void unique_ptr_ref(std::unique_ptr<Resource>& p) {
    std::cout << "unique_ptr_ref: value = " << *p << std::endl;
}

void unique_ptr_raw(std::unique_ptr<Resource>* p) {
    std::cout << "unique_ptr_raw: value = " << **p << std::endl;
}

int main() {
    auto p = std::make_unique<Resource>("jet town");

    // violation: exclusive ownership
    unique_ptr_ref(p);
    unique_ptr_raw(&p);

    // the ownership is not moved
    std::cout << "unique_ptr_main: value = " << *p << std::endl;
}
```

This is the terminal output:

```
Resource constructor jet town
unique_ptr_ref: value = jet town
unique_ptr_raw: value = jet town
unique_ptr_main: value = jet town
Resource destructor jet town
```

This time, the resource ownership is not transferred, so the pointer is not empty.

The ownership can be transferred from a unique pointer to a shared pointer, but not back because the shared resource cannot be exclusively owned, and therefore the unique pointer will be nullified. When `std::shared_ptr` is passed by value, it implies that the callee will be an owner too. Consequently, this invokes atomic increments/decrements of the reference count in the copy constructor and destructor, which incur a performance overhead compared to raw and smart pointers:

```
void shared_ptr_val(std::shared_ptr<Resource> p) {
    std::cout << "shared_ptr_val: value = " << *p << std::endl;
}
```

```
int main() {
    auto up = std::make_unique<Resource>("walkman on");
    std::shared_ptr<Resource> sp = std::move(up);

    // shared ownership
    shared_ptr_val(sp);

    std::cout << "unique_ptr_main: value = "
              << (up != nullptr ? static_cast<std::string>(*up) : "null")
              << std::endl;
    std::cout << "shared_ptr_main: value = " << *sp << std::endl;
}
```

We get this as the terminal output:

```
Resource constructor walkman on
shared_ptr_val: value = walkman on
unique_ptr_main: value = null
shared_ptr_main: value = walkman on
Resource destructor walkman on
```

Shared pointers are also objects like any other, so they can be passed by reference or pointer. This approach does not assume ownership and is used to avoid the overhead of copying, particularly when performance is a concern:

```
void shared_ptr_ref(std::shared_ptr<Resource>& p) {
  std::cout << "shared_ptr_ref: value = " << *p << std::endl;
}

void shared_ptr_raw(std::shared_ptr<Resource>* p) {
  std::cout << "shared_ptr_raw: value = " << **p << std::endl;
}

int main() {
  auto p = std::make_shared<Resource>("playback");

  // no shared ownership
  shared_ptr_ref(p);
  shared_ptr_raw(&p);  // little sense

  std::cout << "shared_ptr_main: value = " << *p << std::endl;
}
```

Here is the terminal output:

```
Resource constructor playback
shared_ptr_ref: value = playback
shared_ptr_raw: value = playback
shared_ptr_main: value = playback
Resource destructor playback
```

Smart pointers are often passed to other functions by constant reference because class type parameters should be passed by reference, preferably by const reference. But if you don't need smart pointers and to pass ownership, use raw pointers as they are faster and make the code more readable. Ideally, if you can avoid dynamic memory allocation, that's even better.

Obviously, raw pointers are acceptable in C++. This could be either a third-party library or performance-critical code. But when you call `get()` on a smart pointer to obtain a raw pointer, there is a risk that the pointers will be deleted, or another smart pointer will acquire the raw pointer, which causes undefined behavior or a dangling pointer because the raw pointer is out of the control of your smart pointer. *Don't allow multiple smart pointers to own the same resource.* Raw pointers should be used in small blocks of code with limited scope, helper functions, and loops:

```
void val(Resource p) {
    std::cout << "val: value = " << p << std::endl;
}

void ref(Resource& p) {
    std::cout << "ref: value = " << p << std::endl;
}

void raw(Resource* p) {
    std::cout << "raw: value = " << *p << std::endl;
}

int main() {
    auto p = std::make_unique<Resource>("tonight");

    // out of control
    val(*p.get());
    ref(*p.get());
    raw(p.get());

    std::cout << "unique_ptr_main: value = "
              << (p != nullptr ? static_cast<std::string>(*p) : "null")
              << std::endl;
}
```

Here is the terminal output that we get:

```
Resource constructor tonight
val: value = tonight
Resource destructor tonight
ref: value = tonight
raw: value = tonight
unique_ptr_main: value = tonight
Resource destructor tonight
```

Weak pointers are rarely used, but they are intended for cases when circular references are required. Sometimes circular references cannot be avoided because shared pointers can reference each other, resulting in mutual failure to free memory. To avoid this, `std::weak_ptr` is used as a weak reference to the strong reference `std::shared_ptr`. By the time a shared pointer is locked, the reference to the shared pointer may have expired, which breaks the circular reference. Locking a shared pointer ensures that the object is still valid before it is accessed:

```
void weak_ptr_val(std::weak_ptr<Resource> wp) {
    if (std::shared_ptr<Resource> sp = wp.lock()) {
        std::cout << "weak_ptr_val: value = " << *sp << std::endl;
    } else {
        std::cout << "weak_ptr_val: expired" << std::endl;
    }
}

void weak_ptr_ref(std::weak_ptr<Resource>& wp) {
    if (std::shared_ptr<Resource> sp = wp.lock()) {
        std::cout << "weak_ptr_ref (shared_ptr): value = " << *sp << std::endl;
    } else {
        std::cout << "weak_ptr_ref: expired" << std::endl;
    }
}

void weak_ptr_raw(std::weak_ptr<Resource>* wp) {
    if (std::shared_ptr<Resource> sp = wp->lock()) {
        std::cout << "weak_ptr_ref (shared_ptr): value = " << *sp << std::endl;
    } else {
        std::cout << "weak_ptr_ref: expired" << std::endl;
    }
}
```

Passing such a weak pointer by value, reference, or constant has no practical difference, since the weak pointer does not affect the reference count of the shared pointer in any way:

```
auto sp = std::make_shared("synth samurai");
std::weak_ptr wp = sp;

weak_ptr_val(wp);
weak_ptr_ref(wp); // little sense
weak_ptr_val(wp); // little sense

std::cout << "shared_ptr_main: value = " << *sp << std::endl;

sp.reset();  // nullified

weak_ptr_val(wp);

std::cout << "shared_ptr_main: value = "
          << (sp != nullptr ? static_cast<std::string>(*sp) : "null")
          << std::endl;
```

The terminal output is as follows:

```
Resource constructor synth samurai
weak_ptr_val: value = synth samurai
weak_ptr_ref (shared_ptr): value = synth samurai
weak_ptr_val: value = synth samurai
shared_ptr_main: value = synth samurai
Resource destructor synth samurai
weak_ptr_val: expired
shared_ptr_main: value = null
```

Now that we've looked at how to use pointers, let's turn to another important aspect of robust code—clearly specifying what functions expect and guarantee.

Specifying preconditions and postconditions

It's not uncommon for a function to have some requirements regarding its parameters. Each requirement should be stated as a precondition or postcondition. If a function guarantees that its parameters or result have some properties—for example, they're non-negative—the function should make that clear as well. Some developers resort to placing comments to inform others about this, but it doesn't really enforce the requirement in any way. Placing `if` statements is better, but it hides the reason for the check. Currently, the C++ standard still doesn't offer a way to deal with this, apart from compile-time assertions—in particular, a `static_assert` declaration or the `assert` macro, which depends on the `NDEBUG` macro to enable or disable compilation of assertions. Contracts are expected to become part of the C++26 standard, though they remain unimplemented at the time of writing. Fortunately, libraries such as Microsoft's **Guideline Support Library** (GSL), recommended in the C++ Core Guidelines, provide their own checks. GSL includes views, ownership pointers, assertions, utilities, and concepts (in particular, smart pointer concepts) to help enforce best practices.

Let's assume that, for whatever reason, we're writing a function that is guaranteed to work with numbers only in a certain range. The function could look like this:

```
int foobar(int n) {
    std::cout << "Expects that n >= 0: " << n << std::endl;
    Expects(n >= 0);

    ++n;

    std::cout << "Ensures that n < 10: " << n << std::endl;
    Ensures(n < 10);

    return n;
}
```

Note that the user doesn't even need access to the implementation to be sure that some checks are in place. The code is also self-documenting as it's clear what the function requires and what the result will be:

```
std::random_device rd;
std::mt19937 gen{rd()};
std::uniform_int_distribution<> dist{-5, 15};

for (int i = 0; i < 5; ++i) {
    std::cout << "Value = " << foobar(dist(gen)) << std::endl;
}
```

This is because the `Expects` and `Ensures` macros act as runtime checks on all release and debug builds and are not optimized away. They check that a condition holds and terminate the program if the condition is not met. These macros enforce the contact that our function offers to its consumers.

Contracts help ensure functions are used correctly. But when working with shared libraries or evolving code over time, it's also important to ensure that different parts of the program can still work together. One way C++ helps with this is through inline namespaces.

Employing inline namespaces

In systems programming, oftentimes, you're not always just writing code against an API; often, you need to care about **application binary interface** (**ABI**) compatibility as well. A famous ABI break happened when GCC released its fifth version, with one of the major changes being the change of the class layout of `std::string`. This meant that libraries working with older GCC versions (or still using the new ABI in newer versions, which is still a thing in recent GCC releases) would not work with code written using a later ABI. In the case of an ABI break, if you receive a linker error, you can consider yourself lucky. In some cases, such as mixing debug code with release code, you'll likely get memory corruption if a class only has members available in one such configuration—for instance, special members being added for better debugging.

Some memory corruptions, which are often hard to debug, can easily be turned into linker errors with the use of C++11's inline namespaces. Consider the following code:

```
#ifdef NDEBUG
inline namespace release {
#else
inline namespace debug {
#endif

struct EasilyDebuggable {
    // ...
#ifndef NDEBUG
    // fields helping with debugging
#endif
};

} // end namespace
```

Because the preceding code uses inline namespaces, the users won't see a difference between the two build types when you're declaring objects of this class: all declarations from an inline namespace are visible in the surrounding scope. The linker, however, will end up with different symbol names, which will cause the linker to fail if it tries to link incompatible libraries, giving us the ABI safety we're looking for and a nice error message mentioning the inline namespace.

For more tips on providing safe and elegant ABIs, please see Arvid Norberg's *The ABI Challenge* talk from *C++Now* 2019, which is linked in the *Further reading* section.

Applying std::optional

Going back from ABIs to APIs, let's mention one more type that we omitted when we were designing great APIs earlier in this book. The hero of this section can save the day when it comes to optional parameters for functions, as it can help your types have components that may or may not hold value, and it can also be used for designing clean interfaces or as a replacement for pointers. This hero is called `std::optional` and was standardized in C++17. If you can't use C++17, you can still find it in Abseil (`absl::optional`) or find a very similar version from Boost (`boost::optional`). A big plus of using those classes is that they express the intent very clearly, which helps with writing clean and self-documenting interfaces. Let's look at some use cases to see it in action.

Optional function parameters

We'll start by passing arguments to functions that can, but may not, hold value. Have you ever stumbled upon a function signature similar to the following?

```
void calculate(int param); // If param equals -1 it means "no value"

void calculate(int param = -1);
```

Sometimes, it's just too easy to pass a `-1` by mistake when you didn't want to if `param` was calculated somewhere else in code—perhaps where it was even a valid value. Modern C++ offers a cleaner and safer way to express optional values:

```
void calculate(std::optional<int> param);
```

This time, it's much clearer what to do if you don't want to pass a value: just pass an empty optional. The intent is clear, and `-1` can still be used as a valid value instead of you having to give it any special meaning in a type-unsafe manner.

That's just one usage of our optional template. Let's see some others.

Optional function return values

Just like with accepting special values to signify the *no value* of a parameter, a function can sometimes return *no value*. Which of the following would you prefer?

```
int try_parse(std::string_view maybe_number);
bool try_parse(std::string_view maybe_number, int &parsed_number);
int *try_parse(std::string_view maybe_number);
std::optional<int> try_parse(std::string_view maybe_number);
```

How can you tell what value the first function will return in case of errors? Or, will it throw an exception instead of returning a magic value? Moving on to the second signature, it looks like `false` will be returned if there is an error, but it's still easy to just forget to check it and read `parsed_number` directly, potentially causing trouble. In the third case, while it's relatively safe to assume `nullptr` will be returned in case of errors and an integer in case of success, it's now unclear whether the returned `int` should be freed.

With the last signature, it's clear by just looking at it that an empty value will be returned in case of errors and that there's nothing else that needs to be done. It's simple, understandable, and elegant.

For comparison, the other candidates that can be used to return an optional value are `std::pair`, `std::tuple`, `std::variant`, and `std::any`. When you need some dummy value instead of a result in case of an error return, `std::pair` and `std::tuple` are common, but not as elegant. The `std::variant` class template can be a better alternative. It represents a type-safe union and holds one value of a predefined set of types or a placeholder such as `std::monostate`. If you know the types, `std::any` is probably not the proper tool. But this type contains a value of any type or nothing, and objects within `std::any` are stored without dynamic memory allocation depending on the implementation.

Here are function signatures showing how these types might be used:

```
std::pair<bool, int> try_parse(std::string_view maybe_number);
std::tuple<bool, int, std::string> try_parse(std::string_view maybe_number);
std::variant<int, parse_error> try_parse(std::string_view maybe_number);
std::any try_parse(std::string_view maybe_number);
```

A good choice is C++23's `std::expected`, which represents either of two values: expected or unexpected. The `std::expected` class template is like `std::variant` but more ergonomic in handling the expected type:

```
enum class parse_error
{
    empty,
    invalid_input,
    out_of_range
};
std::expected<int, parse_error> try_parse(std::string_view maybe_number);
```

You can use `std::unique_ptr` to represent an optional value with `nullptr` denoting absence, but memory allocation incurs a runtime cost and can fail:

```
bool try_parse(std::string_view maybe_number, std::unique_ptr<int> &parsed_
number);
std::unique_ptr<int> try_parse(std::string_view maybe_number);
```

Optional return values can also be used to just mark a *no value* being returned, not necessarily that an error has occurred. Having said that, let's move on to our last use case for optionals.

Optional class members

Achieving coherence in a class state is not always an easy task. For instance, sometimes, you want to have a member or two that can simply not be set. Instead of creating another class for such a case (which increases code complexity) or reserving a special value (which is easy to pass unnoticed), you can use an optional class member. Consider the following type:

```
struct UserProfile {
    std::string nickname;
    std::optional <std::string> full_name;
    std::optional <std::string> address;
    std::optional <PhoneNumber> phone;
};
```

Here, we can see which fields are necessary and which ones don't need to be filled. The same data could be stored using empty strings, but this wouldn't be clearly visible just from the struct's definition. Another alternative would be to use `std::unique_ptr`, but then we would lose data locality, which is often essential for performance. For such cases, `std::optional` can be of great value. It should definitely be a part of your toolbox when you want to design clean, high-quality, and intuitive APIs.

There's one more thing you can do to improve them further that will also help you write less buggy code by default. We will discuss this in the next section.

Using monadic interfaces

Monadic interfaces are based on functional programming principles. Functional programming is a paradigm that solves problems by decomposing them into functions. It is a declarative programming paradigm based on key concepts such as recursion, the immutability of variables, pure functions (which produce the same output with the same input without side effects), higher-order functions (which accept or return functions), and first-class functions (functions that are treated like any other variable). As a result of this approach, functional programs are easy to read, debug, and parallelize. However, recursive functions can be costly due to higher memory usage.

Monads are a subtype of functors used in functional programming languages to specify an imperative sequence of operations on values. They are a simple and powerful compositional design pattern to manage a core challenge in functional programming—handling side effects, where a function not only produces the same output with the same input but also does something else. Examples of side effects include displaying something on the screen, writing something to a file, or changing something inside some other variable in the program. The principle behind monads is to encapsulate computations that contain side effects while preserving the purity of the language.

Since monads have mathematical roots, it can be useful to understand the laws that apply to them. We briefly cover the mathematical background here for those interested, but it's not essential to grasp these details to use monads effectively in practice.

The concept of a monad belongs to a mathematical theory named **category theory**, which might make it seem complicated and abstract, but this pattern is very convenient and universal.

While this book is not about functional programming languages, we briefly refer to concepts common in functional programming languages such as Haskell because they provide a concise and canonical way to express the monadic pattern:

```
-- m is a variable and `m a` is a monad of some polymorphic type
data m a = ...
-- (aka unit) a function to wrap a value into a monad
return :: a -> m a
-- a function for combining monadic calculations
bind :: m a -> (a -> m b) -> m b
```

Monads follow three laws, which state that `return` acts as a neutral element for `bind` and `bind` is an associative operation:

- Left identity: `return a >>= h = h a`
- Right identity: `m >>= return = m`
- Associativity: `(m >>= g) >>= h = m >>= (\x -> g x >>= h)`

In mathematics, function calls are written as `h(g(f(x)))`, which is not always convenient. Therefore, in programming, it is often better to apply method chaining for calling methods one by one as `x.f().g().h()`. This improves code readability and allows you to skip optional steps. Monads can use both approaches, but monadic operations in `std::optional` and `std::expected` classes are based on method chaining in C++23.

The following two code snippets demonstrate the difference in use of `std::optional` and `std::expected`. The first two snippets do not perform any monadic operations; they merely define and use `std::optional` or `std::expected` without chaining transformations using monadic methods.

The following function demonstrates how `std::optional` is used to return a value or nothing. This function indicates success or failure without explaining the cause to its caller:

```
std::optional<int> parse_int(const std::string& s) {
    try {
        std::println("Parsing {} to integer", s);
        return std::stoi(s);
    } catch (const std::invalid_argument& ex) {
        std::println(std::cerr, "std::invalid_argument::what(): {}",
ex.what());
        return std::nullopt;
    } catch (const std::out_of_range& ex) {
        std::println(std::cerr, "std::out_of_range::what(): {}", ex.what());
        return std::nullopt;
    }
}
```

The next function also does string-to-number conversion, but optionally can return a value or detailed error in the same object. This feature is used to distinguish expected and unexpected values because `std::expected` is intended for error handling. Moreover, this class provides performance benefits due to the lack of need for stack unwinding, unlike exceptions:

```
std::expected<int, std::string> parse_int(const std::string& s) {
    try {
        std::println("Parsing {} to integer", s);
        return std::stoi(s);
    } catch (const std::invalid_argument& ex) {
        std::println(std::cerr, "std::invalid_argument::what(): {}",
ex.what());
        return std::unexpected{"invalid argument"};
    } catch (const std::out_of_range& ex) {
        std::println(std::cerr, "std::out_of_range::what(): {}", ex.what());
        return std::unexpected{"out of range"};
    }
}
```

C++23 extended the functionality of the `std::optional` class by adding monadic operations to apply functional programming patterns:

```
std::string s;
std::getline(std::cin, s);
auto input = std::make_optional(s);

auto res =
    input.and_then(parse_int)
         .transform([](int n) {
             std::println("Squaring {}", n);
             return n * n;
         })
         .transform([](int n) {
             std::println("Converting {} to a string", n);
             return std::to_string(n);
         })
         .or_else([]() {
             std::println(std::cerr, "Handled error");
             return std::optional<std::string>{"*missing*"};
         });

if (res.has_value()) {
    std::println("Square number: {}", *res);
} else {
    std::println(std::cerr, "no value");
}
```

With the new functions, there is no need to check for `std::optional` being empty to perform transformations on the data. The `and_then` operation chains functions that produce an `std::optional` object.

The `transform` operation is similar to `and_then`, but it calls the provided function operating on a plain value, not `std::optional`.

The `or_else` operation is a fallback applied if `std::optional` is empty.

The following example demonstrates the use of monadic operations introduced in C++23 with `std::expected`:

```
std::string s;
std::getline(std::cin, s);
auto input = std::expected<std::string, std::string>(s);

auto res =
    input.and_then(parse_int)
```

```
        .transform([](int n) {
            std::println("Squaring {}", n);
            return n * n;
        })
        .transform([](int n) {
            std::println("Converting {} to a string", n);
            return std::to_string(n);
        })
        .transform_error([](const std::string &error) -> std::string {
            return "Error encountered: " + error;
        })
        .or_else([](const std::string &error) {
            std::println(std::cerr, "Handled Error ({})", error);
            return std::expected<std::string, std::string>(
                std::unexpected(error));
        });

if (res.has_value()) {
    std::println("Square number: {}", *res);
} else {
    std::println(std::cerr, "{}", res.error());
}
```

The and_then operation chains functions that produce an `std::expected` object.

The `transform` operation is similar to and_then, but it calls the provided function operating on a plain value, not `std::expected` if the `std::expected` object holds a value. The `transform_error` operation is similar to `transform` and the `or_else` operation is a fallback applied if the `std::expected` object holds an error.

Thus, `std::expected` allows you to act upon detailed error information, giving more control over the execution than `std::optional`.

In essence, `std::expected` returns a value or an error reason, effectively combining exceptions in C++ and error codes in C, but `std::optional` just tells you whether a value exists or not without saying why it might be missing.

We discussed how monads relate to functional programming—a subset of declarative programming that emphasizes *what* to do rather than *how* to do it. This mindset is increasingly relevant in modern C++ programming. Let's explore what declarative programming looks like in practice.

Writing declarative code

Are you familiar with imperative versus declarative coding styles? The former is when your code tells the machine *how* to achieve what you want step by step. The latter is when you tell the machine just *what* you want to achieve. Certain programming languages favor one over the other. For instance, C and Pascal are imperative, while SQL, HTML, and CSS are declarative, just like many functional languages. Some languages allow you to mix the styles—think of LINQ in C#.

C++ is a multi-paradigm programming language supporting procedural, object-oriented, and functional programming. Is there one you should prefer? It turns out that when you're writing declarative code, usually a higher level of abstraction is kept, which leads to fewer bugs and easier-to-spot errors. So, how can we write C++ declaratively? There are two main tactics to apply.

The first one is to write functional-style C++, which is where you prefer a pure functional style (no side effects of functions) if possible. Instead of writing manually, you should try the STL algorithm library.

Consider the following code. This function searches for two adjacent elements whose distance is greater than 5 and returns the index of the first element in such a pair, if one is found:

```
std::optional<std::size_t> imperative_adjacent_distance() {
  constexpr auto temperatures = std::array{-3.0, 2.0, 0.0, 8.0, -10.0, -7.0};
  constexpr std::size_t size = temperatures.size();
  for (std::size_t i = 0; i < size - 1; ++i) {
    if (std::abs(temperatures[i] - temperatures[i + 1]) > 5) {
      return i;
    }
  }
  return std::nullopt;
}
```

Now, compare the preceding code with the following snippet, which does the same:

```
std::optional<std::size_t> declarative_adjacent_distance() {
    constexpr auto temperatures = std::array{-3.0, 2.0, 0.0, 8.0, -10.0, -7.0};
    const auto it = std::ranges::adjacent_find(
        temperatures, [](double first, double second) {
            return std::abs(first - second) > 5;
        });

    if (it != std::end(temperatures)) {
        return std::distance(std::begin(temperatures), it);
    }
    return std::nullopt;
}
```

Which one of those would you rather read? Which one is easier to understand? Even if you're not that familiar with C++ algorithms now, after encountering them a few times, the second version just feels simpler, safer, and cleaner than hand-crafted loops. That's because it often is, but depending on your program, the first approach may be suitable too.

The second tactic for writing declarative code in C++ is already somewhat present in the previous snippet. You should prefer using declarative APIs, such as the one from the ranges library. Although no range views were used in our snippet, they can make a lot of difference. Consider the following snippet:

```
using namespace std::ranges;
auto is_even = [](auto x) { return x % 2 == 0; };
auto to_string = [](auto x) { return std::to_string(x); }
auto my_range = views::iota(1)
              | views::filter(is_even)
              | views::take(2)
              | views::reverse
              | views::transform(to_string);
std::cout << std::accumulate(begin(my_range), end(my_range), ""s) << '\n';
```

This is a great example of declarative coding: you just specify what should happen, not how. The preceding code takes the first two even numbers, reverses their order, transforms them into strings, and then prints the result: 42—the famous answer to life, the universe, and everything. All of this is done in an intuitive and easily modifiable way.

Enough with the toy examples, though. Let's move on to an example that better mirrors real-world scenarios.

Showcasing a featured items gallery

Remember our trade fair application from *Chapter 3, Functional and Nonfunctional Requirements*? Let's write a component that will select and display a few featured items from the stores that a customer saved as their favorites. This can be pretty handy when we're writing a mobile app, for example.

Let's start with a mostly C++17 implementation, which we'll update to C++20 throughout this chapter. This will include adding support for ranges.

First, let's start with some code for obtaining information about the current user:

```
int get_current_customer_id() {
    return 42;
}
```

Now, let's add the store owners:

```
struct Merchant {
    int id{};
};
```

The stores also need to have items in them:

```
struct Item {
    std::string name;
    std::optional<std::string> photo_url;
    std::string description;
    std::optional<float> price;
    std::chrono::time_point<std::chrono::system_clock> date_added{};
    bool featured{};
};
```

Some items may not have photos or prices (in cases such as promotional giveaways or gifts), which is why we used `std::optional` for those fields.

We also need to handle the `date_added` field and display its content in a human-readable format, which requires converting it to a string. However, doing this across compilers would involve some considerations. The date-to-string conversion in pre-C++20 looks like this:

```
auto date_added = system_clock::to_time_t(item->date_added);
std::put_time(std::localtime(&date_added), "%c %Z");
```

But the **Microsoft Visual C++ (MSVC)** compiler deprecates the `localtime` function as an unsafe function, issuing a warning or refusing to compile the code if warnings are treated as errors. Alternative functions, `localtime_r` and `localtime_s`, help resolve this issue, but not all C++ compilers support these functions. As an option, the `_CRT_SECURE_NO_DEPRECATE` preprocessor directive can suppress that warning, but C++20 has a better solution—the `<format>` library, offering the universal `std::format` function.

Next, let's add some code that describes our items using the `<format>` library:

```
std::ostream &operator<<(std::ostream &os, const Item &item) {
    auto stringify_optional = []<typename T>(const T &optional) {
        using optional_value_type = typename std::remove_cvref_t<T>::value_
type;
        if constexpr (std::is_same_v<optional_value_type, std::string>) {
            return optional ? *optional : "missing";
        } else {
            return optional ? std::to_string(*optional) : "missing";
        }
    };

    auto time_added = std::chrono::system_clock::to_time_t(item.date_added);

    os << "name: " << item.name
       << ", photo_url: " << stringify_optional(item.photo_url)
       << ", description: " << item.description
```

```
        << ", price: " << stringify_optional(item.price)
        << ", date_added: " << std::format("{:%c %Z}", item.date_added)
        << ", featured: " << item.featured;
    return os;
}
```

First, we created a helper lambda for converting our optionals into strings. Since we only want to use this logic in our << operator, we defined it inside it. Note how we used C++14's generic lambdas (the `typename` keyword alternative to the `auto` parameter), along with C++17's `constexpr` and the `is_same_v` type trait, so that we have a different implementation when we're dealing with an optional `<string>` versus other cases. Achieving the same pre-C++17 would have required writing templates with overloads, resulting in more complicated code.

Now let's define item categories using modern C++:

```
enum class Category {
    Food,
    Antiques,
    Books,
    Music,
    Photography,
    Handicraft,
    Artist,
};
```

Finally, we can define the store itself:

```
struct Store {
    gsl::not_null<const Merchant *> owner;
    std::vector<Item> items;
    std::vector<Category> categories;
};
```

What's worth noting here is the use of the `gsl::not_null` template from the GSL, which signals that the owner will always be set. Why not use just a plain old reference? That's because we may want our store to be movable and copyable. Using a reference would hinder that. The alternative is `std::reference_wrapper<T>`, which does not rely on runtime null checks but supports copy and move semantics.

Now that we have those building blocks, let's define how to retrieve a customer's favorite stores. For simplicity, let's assume we're dealing with hardcoded stores and merchants instead of integrating with external data stores.

First, let's define a type alias for the stores and begin our function definition:

```
using Stores = std::vector<gsl::not_null<const Store *>>;
Stores get_favorite_stores_for(int customer_id) {
```

Next, let's hardcode some merchants, as follows:

```
static const auto merchants = std::vector<Merchant>{{17}, {29}};
```

Now, let's add a store with some items, as shown here:

```
static const auto stores = std::vector<Store>{
    {
        .owner = &merchants[0],
        .items = {
            {
                .name = "Honey",
                .photo_url = {},
                .description = "Straight outta Compton's apiary",
                .price = 9.99f,
                .date_added = system_clock::now(),
                .featured = false
            },
            {
                .name = "Oscypek",
                .photo_url = {},
                .description = "Tasty smoked cheese from the Tatra mountains",
                .price = 1.23f,
                .date_added = system_clock::now() - 1h,
                .featured = true
            }
        },
        .categories = {Category::Food}
    }
    // more stores can be found in the complete code on GitHub
};
```

Once we've defined our stores, we can write the last part of our function, which will do the actual lookup:

```
static auto favorite_stores_by_customer =
    std::unordered_map<int, Stores>{{42, {&stores[0], &stores[1]}}
    };
return favorite_stores_by_customer[customer_id];
```

Here, we introduced our first C++20 feature in this function. You might not be familiar with the `.field = value;` syntax unless you've coded in C99 or newer. Starting from C++20, you can use this notation (officially called designated initializers) to initialize aggregate types. It's more constrained than in C99 because the order is important, although it has some other minor differences. Without those designated initializers, it can be hard to understand which value initializes which field. With them, the code is more verbose but easier to comprehend, even for people unfamiliar with programming.

Now that we have our stores, let's write some code to obtain the featured items for those stores:

```
using Items = std::vector<gsl::not_null<const Item *>>;

Items get_featured_items_for_store(const Store &store) {
    auto featured = Items{};

    for (const auto &items = store.items; const auto &item : items) {
        if (item.featured) {
            featured.emplace_back(&item);
        }
    }
    return featured;
}
```

The preceding code was for obtaining items from one store. Let's also write a function that will obtain items from all the given stores:

```
Items get_all_featured_items(const Stores &stores) {
    auto all_featured = Items{};
    for (const auto &store : stores) {
        const auto featured_in_store = get_featured_items_for_store(*store);
        all_featured.reserve(all_featured.size() + featured_in_store.size());
        std::copy(std::begin(featured_in_store), std::end(featured_in_store),
std::back_inserter(all_featured));
    }
    return all_featured;
}
```

The preceding code uses `std::copy` to insert elements into a vector, with memory preallocated by the reserve call.

Now that we have a way to obtain interesting items, let's sort them by "freshness" so that the most recently added ones will appear first:

```
void order_items_by_date_added(Items &items) {
    // left and right are gsl::not_null<const Item *>
    auto date_comparator = [](const auto &left, const auto &right) {
        return left->date_added > right->date_added;
    };
    std::sort(std::begin(items), std::end(items), date_comparator);
}
```

As you can see, we used std::sort with a custom comparator. If you like, you could also force the same type for both left and right. To do so in a generic manner, let's use another C++20 feature: template lambdas. Let's apply them to the preceding code:

```
void order_items_by_date_added(Items &items) {
    auto date_comparator = []<typename T>(const T &left, const T &right) {
        return left->date_added > right->date_added;
    };
    std::sort(std::begin(items), std::end(items), date_comparator);
}
```

The T type for the lambda will be deduced just like it would for any other template.

The last two parts that are missing are the actual rendering code and the main function to glue it all together. In our example case, rendering will be as simple as printing to ostream:

```
void render_item_gallery(const Items &items) {
    std::copy(
        std::begin(items), std::end(items),
        std::ostream_iterator<gsl::not_null<const Item *>>(std::cout, "\n"));
}
```

In our case, we just copy each element to the standard output and insert a newline between the elements. Using copy and ostream_iterator allows you to handle the element's separators for yourself. This can be handy in some cases; for instance, if you don't want a comma (or a newline, in our case) after the last element.

Finally, our main function will look like this:

```
int main() {
    const auto fav_stores = get_favorite_stores_for(get_current_customer_id());
    auto selected_items = get_all_featured_items(fav_stores);
    order_items_by_date_added(selected_items);
    render_item_gallery(selected_items);
}
```

Voila! Feel free to run the code to see how it prints our featured items:

```
name: Handmade painted ceramic bowls, photo_url: http://example.com/beautiful_
bowl.png, description: Hand-crafted and hand-decorated bowls made of fired
clay, price: missing, date_added: Sun Dec  3 12:54:38 2024 CET, featured: 1
name: Oscypek, photo_url: missing, description: Tasty smoked cheese from the
Tatra mountains, price: 1.230000, date_added: Sun Dec  3 12:06:38 2024 CET,
featured: 1
```

Now that we're done with our base implementation, let's see how we can improve it by using some new language features from C++20.

Applying standard ranges

Our first addition will be the ranges library. As you may recall, it can help us achieve elegant, simple, and declarative code. For brevity, first, we will pull in the `ranges` namespace:

```
#include <ranges>

using namespace std::ranges;
```

We'll leave the code-defining merchants, items, and stores as is. Let's start our modifications by using the `get_featured_items_for_store` function:

```
Items get_featured_items_for_store(const Store &store) {
    auto items = store.items
                 | views::filter(&Item::featured)
                 | views::transform([](const auto &item) {
                     return gsl::not_null<const Item *>(&item);
                 });
    return {std::begin(items), std::end(items)};
}
```

As you can see, making a range out of a container is straightforward: just pass it to a pipe operator. Instead of our hand-crafted loop to filter featured elements, we now use the `views::filter` expression, passing it a member pointer as the predicate. Due to the magic of `std::invoke` under the hood, this will correctly filter out all items that have our Boolean data member set to `false`.

Next, we converted each item into a `gsl::not_null` pointer so that we can avoid unnecessary item copies. Finally, we return a vector of such pointers, the same as in our base code.

Now, let's see how we can use the preceding function to obtain all the featured items from all our stores:

```
Items get_all_featured_items(const Stores &stores) {
    auto all_featured = stores
                        | views::transform([](auto elem) {
                            return get_featured_items_for_store(*elem);
                        });

    Items ret{};
    for_each(all_featured, [&](const Items &elem) {
        ret.reserve(ret.size() + elem.size());
        std::copy(std::begin(elem), std::end(elem),  std::back_inserter(ret));
    });
    return ret;
}
```

Here, we created a range from all the stores and transformed them using the function we created in the previous step. Because we needed to dereference each element first, we used a helper lambda. Views are lazily evaluated, so each transform will be done only when it is about to be consumed. This can sometimes save you lots of time and computations: assuming you would only want the first N items, you can skip the unnecessary calls to `get_featured_items_for_store`.

Once we have our lazy view, similar to our base implementation, we can reserve space in the vector and copy items there from each nested vector in the `all_featured` view. Range algorithms are more concise to use if you take the whole container. Look how `std::ranges::copy` doesn't require us to write `std::begin(elem)` and `std::end(elem)`.

Now that we have our items, let's simplify our sorting code by using ranges to process them:

```
void order_items_by_date_added(Items &items) {
    sort(items, greater{}, &Item::date_added);
}
```

Again, you can see how ranges can help you write more concise code. The preceding copy operation and the `sort` here are both range *algorithms*. As opposed to *views*, they are eager and allow you to use projections. In our case, we passed another member of our `Item` class so that it can be used for comparison when sorting. Effectively, each item will be projected as just its `date_added` value, which will then be compared using `greater{}`.

But wait—our items are actually `gsl::not_null` pointers to `Item`. How does this work? It turns out that our projection will dereference the `gsl::not_null` pointer first because of the cleverness of `std::invoke`. Neat!

The last change that we can make is in our "rendering" code:

```
void render_item_gallery(const Items &items) {
    copy(items, std::ostream_iterator<gsl::not_null<const Item *>>(std::cout,
"\n"));
}
```

Here, ranges just help us remove some boilerplate code.

When you run our updated version of the code, you should get the same output as in the base case.

You already know that using lazy evaluation in `std::ranges::views` can help with performance by eliminating unnecessary compute. It turns out we can also use ranges to reduce the memory overhead in our example. Let's revisit our code for obtaining featured items from a store. It can be shortened down to the following:

```
auto get_featured_items_for_store(const Store &store) {
    return store.items | views::filter(&Item::featured) | views::transform(
            [](const auto &item) { return gsl::not_null(&item); });
}
```

Note that our function no longer returns items; instead, it relies on C++14's auto return type deduction. In our case, instead of returning a vector, our code will return a lazy view.

Let's learn how to consume this for all stores:

```
Items get_all_featured_items(const Stores &stores) {
    auto all_featured = stores | views::transform([](auto elem) {
                            return get_featured_items_for_store(*elem);
                        }) |
                        views::join;
    auto as_items = Items{};
    as_items.reserve(distance(all_featured));
    copy(all_featured, std::back_inserter(as_items));
    return as_items;
}
```

Now, because our preceding function returns a view instead of the vector, we end up with a view of views after calling `transform`. This means we can use yet another standard view called join to join our nested views into just one that's unified.

Next, we use `std::ranges::distance` to preallocate space in our destination vector, after which we make our copy. Some ranges are sized, in which case you could call `std::ranges::size` instead. The resulting code has just one call to `reserve`, which should give us a nice performance boost.

This concludes introducing ranges to our code. Since we ended this section on a performance-related note, let's talk about one more topic that's important for this aspect of C++ programming.

Moving computations to compile time

Starting with the advent of modern C++ in the early 2000s, C++ programming became more about computing things during compilation instead of deferring them to runtime. It's much cheaper to detect errors during compilation than to debug them afterward. Similarly, it's much faster to have the result ready before the program is started instead of calculating it later.

At first, there was template metaprogramming, but with C++11 onward, each new standard brought additional features for compile-time compute: be it type traits, constructs such as `std::enable_if` or `std::void_t`, or C++20's `constinit` and `consteval` for computing stuff only at compile time.

The `constinit` keyword enforces constant initialization and guarantees that a static or thread-local variable is initialized before any dynamic initialization happens, thus preventing the static initialization order fiasco, even though the variables themselves may not be `const`. On the other hand, the `consteval` keyword enforces constant evaluation and marks *immediate functions* that must be evaluated at compile time, and any call to such a function results in a compile-time constant expression.

One feature that has improved over the years is the `constexpr` keyword and its related code. C++20 really improved and extended `constexpr`. By C++20, you could not only write regular, simple `constexpr` functions thanks to the previous standards (quite an improvement from C++11's single-expression ones) but you could also use dynamic allocations and exceptions inside them, not to mention `std::vector` and `std::string`!

C++23 expands the scope of this keyword: even virtual functions can now be `constexpr`. Overload resolution happens as usual, but if a given one is `constexpr`, it can get called at compile time. The `constexpr` keyword, intended for program optimizations, declares that functions and variables can be evaluated at compile time, but a compiler ultimately decides whether to compute at compile time or runtime.

Yet another improvement was made to standard algorithms. Their non-parallel versions are all ready for you to use in your compile-time code. Consider the following example, which can be used to check whether a given merchant is present in a container:

```
#include <algorithm>
#include <array>

struct Merchant { int id; };

bool has_merchant(const Merchant &selected) {
    auto merchants = std::array{Merchant{1}, Merchant{2}, Merchant{3},
Merchant{4}, Merchant{5}};
    return std::ranges::binary_search(merchants, selected, [](auto a, auto b) {
return a.id < b.id; });
}
```

As you can see, we're doing a binary search for an array of merchants, sorted by their IDs.

To gain insight into the code and its performance, we recommend that you take a quick look at the assembly that this code generates. Along with the advent of compile-time computations and chasing performance, one of the invaluable tools that emerged is `https://godbolt.org`. It can be used to quickly play with code to see how different architectures, compilers, flags, library versions, and implementations influence the generated assembly.

We tested the preceding code using the GCC trunk with `-O3` and `--std=c++2a`. In our case, we checked the generated assembly with the following code:

```
int main() { return has_merchant({4}); }
```

You can see a few dozen assembly lines using the following link: `https://godbolt.org/z/PYMTYx`.

But wait—you could say that there's a function call in the assembly, so maybe we could inline it so it can be optimized better? That would be a valid point. Often, this helps a lot, although now, we just get the assembly inlined (see: `https://godbolt.org/z/hPadxd`).

So, now, try changing the signature to the following:

```
constexpr bool has_merchant(const Merchant &selected)
```

The `constexpr` functions are implicitly inline, so we removed the `inline` keyword. If we examine the assembly, we will see that some magic happened: the search was optimized away at compile time! As you can see at `https://godbolt.org/z/v3hj3E`, all the assembly that was left was as follows:

```
main:
        mov     eax, 1
        ret
```

The compiler optimized our code so that the only thing left is our pre-computed result being returned. That's pretty impressive, isn't it?

Helping the compiler help you by using const

Compilers can optimize your code pretty well, even if you don't give them `inline` or `constexpr` keywords, as in the preceding example. One thing that helps them achieve performance for you is marking variables and functions as `const`. Perhaps even more importantly, it also helps you avoid making mistakes in your code. Many languages have immutable variables by default, which can lead to fewer bugs, code that's easier to reason about, and often faster multi-threaded performance.

Even though C++ has mutable variables by default and you need to explicitly type `const`, we encourage you to do so. It can really help you stop making tricky typos related to modifying a variable that you shouldn't.

Using `const` (or `constexpr`) code is part of a bigger philosophy called type safety. Let's say a few words about it.

Leveraging the power of safe types

C++ relies heavily on mechanisms that help you write type-safe code. Language constructs such as explicit constructors and conversion operators have been baked into the language for a long time. More and more safe types are being introduced to the standard library. There's `optional` to help you avoid referencing empty values, `string_view` to help you avoid going out of a range, and `any` as a safe wrapper for any type, just to name a few. Moreover, with its zero-cost abstractions, it's recommended that you create your own types that are useful and hard or impossible to misuse.

Often, using C-style constructs can lead to type-unsafe code. One example would be C-style casts. They can resolve to `const_cast, static_cast`, `reinterpret_cast`, or a combination of one of these with `const_cast`. Accidentally writing to a `const` object that was `const_cast` is undefined behavior. So is reading memory returned from a `reinterpret_cast<T>`, if T was not the original type of the object (C++20's `std::bit_cast` can help here). Both of those cases are much more easily avoided if C++ casts are used.

C was perhaps too permissive when it came to types. Fortunately, C++ introduces many type-safe alternatives to problematic C constructs. There are streams and `std::format` instead of `printf` et al., and there's `std::copy` and other similar algorithms instead of the unsafe `memcpy`. Finally, there are templates instead of functions taking a void * (and paying a price in terms of performance). With C++, templates get even more type safety through a feature called concepts. Let's see how we can improve our code by using them.

Constraining template parameters

The first way concepts can improve your code is by making it more generic. Do you remember the cases where you needed to change the container type in one place, which caused a cascade of changes in other places too? If you weren't changing the container to one with totally different semantics and that you had to use in a different way, that means your code may not have been generic enough.

On the other hand, have you ever written a template or sprinkled `auto` over your code and later wondered if your code would break if someone changed the underlying type?

Concepts are all about putting the right level of constraints on the types you're operating on. They constrain what types your template can match and are checked at compile time. For instance, let's say you write the following:

```
template<typename T>
void foo(T& t) {...}
```

Now, you can write the following instead:

```
void foo(std::swappable auto& t) {...}
```

Here, `foo()` must be passed a type that supports `std::swap` to work.

Do you recall some templates that matched just too many types? Before concepts, developers relied on techniques such as tag dispatch (tagging iterators), `if constexpr` (since C++17), or **substitution failure is not an error** (**SFINAE**)-based type traits (for example, `std::enable_if` and `std::void_`) to enforce constraints. Tag dispatch selects overloads based on type tags describing an argument's capabilities; `if constexpr` enables compile-time branching inside templates based on type properties; and SFINAE relies on the rule that when a template substitution is invalid, it is silently removed from the overload set instead of causing a compilation error.

However, the use of type traits and similar techniques is a bit cumbersome and can slow down your compilation times. Concepts (since C++20) are usually preferred over these methods because they are more concise and expressive.

There are a few dozen standard concepts in C++20. Most of them live in the `<concepts>` header and can be divided into four categories:

- Core language concepts, such as `derived_from`, `integral`, `swappable`, and `move_constructible`
- Comparison concepts, such as `boolean-testable`, `equality_comparable_with`, and `totally_ordered`
- Object concepts, such as `movable`, `copyable`, `semiregular`, and `regular`
- Callable concepts, such as `invokable`, `predicate`, and `strict_weak_order`

Additional ones are defined in the `<iterator>` header. These can be divided into the following categories:

- Indirect callable concepts, such as `indirect_binary_predicate` and `indirectly_unary_invocable`

- Common algorithm requirements, such as `indirectly_swappable`, `permutable`, `mergeable`, and `sortable`

Finally, a dozen can be found in the `<ranges>` header. Examples include `range` (duh), `contiguous_range`, and `view`.

If that's not enough for your needs, you can declare your own concepts similarly to how the standard defines the ones we just covered. For instance, the `movable` concept, used to specify whether an object can be moved and swapped, is implemented like so:

```
template <class T>
concept movable = std::is_object_v<T> && std::move_constructible<T> &&
std::assignable_from<T&, T> && std::swappable<T>;
```

Furthermore, if you look at `std::swappable`, you'll see the following:

```
template<class T>
concept swappable = requires(T& a, T& b) { ranges::swap(a, b); };
```

This means a type, `T`, will be `swappable` if `ranges::swap(a, b)` compiles for two references of this type.

When defining your own concepts, be sure that you cover the semantic requirements for them. Specifying and using a concept when defining an interface is a promise that's made to the consumers of that interface.

Often, you can go with the so-called shorthand notation in declarations for brevity:

```
void sink(std::movable auto& resource);
```

For readability and type safety, it's recommended that you use `auto` together with a concept to constrain the type and let your readers know the kind of object they're dealing with. Code written in this manner will retain the perks of auto-like genericity. You can use this in both regular functions and lambdas.

A great bonus of using concepts is shorter error messages. It's not uncommon to cut dozens and dozens of lines about one compilation error down to just a few lines. Yet another bonus is that you can overload on concepts.

Now, let's go back to our trade fair example. This time, we'll add some concepts to see how they can improve our implementation.

First, let's make `get_all_featured_items` return just a range of items. We can do so by adding the concept to the return type, like so:

```
range auto get_all_featured_items(const Stores &stores);
```

So far, so good. Now, let's add yet another requirement to this type that will be enforced when we call `order_items_by_date_added`: our range must be sortable. The `std::sortable` concept has already been defined for a range iterator, but for our convenience, let's define a new concept called `sortable_range`:

```
template <typename Range, typename Comp, typename Proj>
concept sortable_range =
    random_access_range<Range> && std::sortable<iterator_t<Range>, Comp, Proj>;
```

Like its standard library counterpart, we can accept a comparator and a projection (which we introduced with ranges). Our concept is satisfied by (will be matched by) types that satisfy the `random_access_range` concept, as well as having an iterator that satisfies the aforementioned sortable concept. It's as simple as that.

When defining concepts, you can also use the `requires` clause to specify additional constraints. For instance, if you want our range to store elements with a `date_added` member only, you could write the following:

```
template <typename Range, typename Comp>
concept sortable_indirectly_dated_range =
    random_access_range<Range> && std::sortable<iterator_t<Range>, Comp> &&
requires(range_value_t<Range> v) { { v->date_added }; };
```

However, in our case, we don't need to constrain the type that much, as you should leave some flexibility when you're using concepts and define them so that it will make sense to reuse them.

What's important here is that you can use the `requires` clause to specify what code should be valid to call on your type when it meets the requirements for a concept. If you want, you can specify constraints on the type that's returned by each subexpression; for instance, to define something incrementable, you could use the following:

```
requires(I i) {
    { i++ } -> std::same_as<I>;
}
```

Now that we have our concept, let's redefine the `order_items_by_date_added` function:

```
void order_items_by_date_added(
    sortable_range<greater, decltype(&Item::date_added)> auto &items) {
    sort(items, greater{}, &Item::date_added);
}
```

Now, our compiler will check whether any range we pass to it is a sortable one and contains a `date_added` member that can be sorted using `std::ranges::greater{}`.

If we were to use the more constrained concept here, the function would look like this:

```
void order_items_by_date_added(
    sortable_indirectly_dated_range<greater> auto &items) {
```

```
    sort(items, greater{}, &Item::date_added);
}
```

Finally, let's redo our rendering function:

```
template <input_range Container>
requires std::is_same_v<typename Container::value_type, gsl::not_null<const
Item *>>
void render_item_gallery(const Container &items) {
    copy(items, std::ostream_iterator<typename Container::value_
type>(std::cout, "\n"));
}
```

Here, you can see that a concept name can be used instead of the `typename` keyword in a template declaration. One line below this, you can see that the `requires` keyword can also be used to further constrain the appropriate types based on their traits. This can be handy if you don't want to specify a new concept.

C++20 also has `requires` clauses and `requires` expressions, which are like `noexcept` clauses and `noexcept` expressions in C++11. A `requires` expression is a compile-time expression of type `bool`, primarily used to create concepts. However, it can be applied to check whether template parameters have the required interfaces. The `requires` clause constrains a template argument or function declaration to determine whether it is applicable in a particular scope. The following code uses both `requires` clauses and `requires` expressions:

```
template<typename T>
requires requires (T a, T b) { a + b; }
auto sum(T a, T b) { return a + b; }
```

Here, we nested a `requires` expression within a `requires` clause, which is completely grammatically correct but can be perceived as bad style. In some cases, it is better to define the concepts explicitly because they are created to make template metaprogramming simpler and more readable:

```
template<typename T>
concept is_digit = requires (T a, T b) { a + b; a - b ; };
template<typename T>
requires is_digit<T>
auto sum(T a, T b) { return a + b; }
```

That's it for concepts. Let's summarize what we've learned.

Summary

In this chapter, we learned about many C++ features and their impact on writing concise, expressive, and performant C++ code. We learned about providing proper C++ component interfaces. You're now able to apply principles such as RAII to write elegant code that's free from resource leaks. You also know how to use types such as `std::optional` to express your intent better in your interfaces.

Next, we explored monadic interfaces and demonstrated how to use features such as generic and template lambdas, as well as `if constexpr`, to write less code that will work with many types. You're now also able to define objects in a clear manner using designated initializers.

Afterward, you learned how to write simple code in a declarative style using standard ranges, how to write code that can be executed at both compile time and runtime using `constexpr`, and how to write more constrained templated code using concepts.

In the next chapter, we'll discuss how to design C++ code so that we can build upon the available idioms and patterns.

Questions

1. How can you ensure that each file of your code that's open will be closed when no longer in use?
2. When should you use raw pointers (not encapsulated in smart pointers) in C++ code?
3. What is a deduction guide?
4. When should you use `std::optional` and `gsl::not_null`?
5. When should you use `std::optional` and `std::expected`?
6. When should you use `const`, `constexpr`, `consteval`, and `constinit`?
7. How are range algorithms different than views?
8. How can you constrain your type by doing more than just specifying the concept's name when you're defining a function?

Further reading

- Arvid Norberg, *The ABI Challenge* (YouTube Video), C++Now 2019: https://www.youtube.com/watch?v=ncyQAjTyPwU
- ISO C++, *C++ Core Guidelines: T.10 Specify Concepts for All Template Arguments,* GitHub: https://isocpp.github.io/CppCoreGuidelines/CppCoreGuidelines#t10-specify-concepts-for-all-template-arguments
- ISO C++, *C++ Core Guidelines: Guidelines Support Library (GSL)*, GitHub: https://isocpp.github.io/CppCoreGuidelines/CppCoreGuidelines#gsl-guidelines-support-library
- GCC, *libstdc++: Implementation of* std::chrono, GitHub: https://github.com/gcc-mirror/gcc/blob/trunk/libstdc%2B%2B-v3/include/std/chrono
- C++ Reference, *Standard Format Specification (Since C++20)*: https://en.cppreference.com/w/cpp/utility/format/spec
- C++ Reference, std::formatter<std::chrono::duration>: https://en.cppreference.com/w/cpp/chrono/duration/formatter
- C++ Reference, *Iterator Tags*: https://en.cppreference.com/w/cpp/iterator/iterator_tags.html
- C++ Reference, *Iterator Library*: https://en.cppreference.com/w/cpp/iterator.html
- C++ Reference, *Contract Assertions (Since C++26)*: https://en.cppreference.com/w/cpp/language/contracts.html

6

Design Patterns and C++ Idioms

In the previous chapter, we saw how to implement the core components of a system using modern, safe, and efficient C++ features. This chapter builds on that by introducing idioms and design patterns that make those components more maintainable, reusable, and extensible.

It's important to note that C++ is not just an object-oriented language, and it doesn't just offer dynamic polymorphism, so design in C++ is not just about the Gang of Four design patterns. In this chapter, you will learn about the commonly used C++ idioms and design patterns and where to use them.

The following topics will be covered in this chapter:

- Writing idiomatic C++
- Applying the curiously recurring template pattern
- Implementing `deducing this`
- Creating objects
- Tracking state and visiting objects in C++
- Dealing with memory efficiently

That's quite a list! Let's not waste time and jump right in.

Technical requirements

The code from this chapter requires the following tools to build and run it:

- A compiler supporting C++23
- CMake 3.28+

The source code snippets from the chapter can be found at `https://github.com/PacktPublishing/Software-Architecture-with-Cpp-2E/tree/main/Chapter06`.

Writing idiomatic C++

If you're familiar with object-oriented programming languages, you must have heard of the Gang of Four design patterns that are often implementations of the **General Responsibility Assignment Software Patterns** (GRASP) design principles. While they can be implemented in C++ (and often are), this multi-paradigm language often takes a different approach to achieve the same goals.

For example, if you want to beat the performance of managed programming languages such as Go, C#, or Java, sometimes paying the cost of virtual dispatch is too much. In many cases, you'll know upfront what types you'll deal with. If that happens, you can often write more performant code using the tools available both in the language and in the standard library. Out of many, there's a group that we will start this chapter with—the language idioms. Let's start our journey by looking at a few of them.

By definition, an idiom is a construct that recurs in a given language, an expression that's specific to the language. "Native speakers" of C++ should know its idioms by intuition. We already mentioned smart pointers in the previous chapter, which are one of the most common ones.

Automating scope exit actions using RAII guards

One of the most powerful expressions in C++ is the brace closing a scope. This is the place where destructors get called and the RAII magic happens. To harness this construct, you don't need to use smart pointers. All you need is an RAII guard—an object that, when constructed, will remember what it needs to do when destroyed. This way, regardless of whether the scope exits normally or by an exception, the work will happen automatically.

The best part—you don't even need to write an RAII guard from scratch. Well-tested implementation already exists in various libraries. If you're using GSL, which we mentioned in the previous chapter, you can use `gsl::finally()` to execute a final action before leaving the scope. Consider the following example:

```
using namespace std::chrono;

void self_measuring_function() {
    auto timestamp_begin = high_resolution_clock::now();

    auto cleanup = gsl::finally([timestamp_begin] {
        auto timestamp_end = high_resolution_clock::now();
        std::cout << "Execution took: " << duration_
cast<microseconds>(timestamp_end - timestamp_begin).count() << " us";
  });
    // simulate some operations that might
    // throw std::runtime_error{"Unexpected fault"};
}
```

Here, we take a timestamp at the start of the function and another one at the end. Try running this example and see how uncommenting the `throw` statement affects the execution. In both cases, our RAII guard will properly print the execution time (assuming the exception is caught somewhere).

Let's now discuss a few more popular C++ idioms.

Managing copyability and movability

When designing a new type in C++, deciding how to manage copying and moving is essential. Even more important is implementing those semantics for a class correctly.

By default, C++ provides a copy constructor and copy assignment operator that perform memberwise copies. In such a copy, an object is copied as is, with all its data elements, including pointers. If the class manages dynamic memory, this results in a shallow copy. In that case, both objects end up referring to the same dynamic memory addresses. This causes runtime errors when objects are destroyed, as both objects attempt to release the same dynamic memory. The resolution is to define custom copy constructors and assignment operators to perform deep copying. A deep copy duplicates the object and all its recursively copied data members. Thus, the deep copy does not refer to the same addresses of dynamic memory as the original object.

Move semantics, on the other hand, enable transferring ownership of resources from one object to another instead of copying it, which is generally less expensive than performing a copy operation. The copy functions take a `const` l-value reference as a parameter, while the move functions take a non-`const` r-value reference as a parameter. In some cases, copy and move constructors and assignment operators are optionally deleted so that they are never performed.

Let's discuss those decisions now.

Implementing non-copyable types

There are cases when you don't want your class to be copied. One common scenario is classes that are very expensive to copy. In the STL, such classes include `std::unique_ptr`, which is not copyable but movable, transferring resource ownership. Another example is `std::mutex`, which is conceptually neither copyable nor movable because the behavior of a program would be undefined if a mutex were destroyed while still being owned by some thread.

Another scenario involves classes subject to error due to object slicing, which occurs when an object of a subclass type is copied to an object of a superclass type.

Here's one way you can make a class non-copyable by deleting its copy operations:

```
struct NonCopyable {
    NonCopyable() = default;
    NonCopyable(const NonCopyable&) = delete;
    NonCopyable& operator=(const NonCopyable&) = delete;

    // NOTE: also non-movable
    // without defined move constructor and assignment operator
    // NonCopyable(NonCopyable &&) = default;
    // NonCopyable &operator=(NonCopyable &&) = default;
};

class MyType : NonCopyable {};
```

Note, however, that such a class is also not movable, although it's easy not to notice it when reading the class definition. A better approach would be to just explicitly declare the move constructor and move assignment operator as deleted.

Prior to C++11, a common way to prevent such objects from copying was by restricting copy semantics by declaring but not defining copy operations as private:

```
struct NonCopyable {
    NonCopyable() {}

private:
    NonCopyable(const NonCopyable &);
    NonCopyable &operator=(const NonCopyable &);
};
```

As a rule of thumb, when declaring such special member functions, always declare all of them. This means that from C++11 onward, the preferred way is to write the following:

```
struct MyTypeV2 {
    MyTypeV2() = default;
    MyTypeV2(const MyTypeV2 &) = delete;
    MyTypeV2 & operator=(const MyTypeV2 &) = delete;
    MyTypeV2(MyTypeV2 &&) = delete;
    MyTypeV2 & operator=(MyTypeV2 &&) = delete;
    virtual ~MyTypeV2() = default;
};
```

This time, the members were defined directly in the target type without the inherited helper `NonCopyable` type.

Adhering to the rules of three and five

There's one more thing to mention when discussing special member functions: if you don't delete them and are providing your own implementations, most probably you need to define all of them, including the destructor, too. This was called the rule of three in C++98—due to the need to define three functions: the copy constructor, the copy assignment operator, and the destructor. After C++11 introduced move operations, it is now replaced by the rule of five, which adds the move constructor and the move assignment operator. Applying these rules can help you avoid resource management issues.

Adhering to the rule of zero

If, on the other hand, you're good to go with just the default implementations of all special member functions, then just don't declare them at all. This is a clear sign that you want the default behavior. It's also the least confusing. Consider the following type:

```
class PotentiallyMisleading final {
public:
    PotentiallyMisleading() = default;
    PotentiallyMisleading(const PotentiallyMisleading &) = default;
    PotentiallyMisleading &operator=(const PotentiallyMisleading &) = default;
    PotentiallyMisleading(PotentiallyMisleading &&) = default;
    PotentiallyMisleading &operator=(PotentiallyMisleading &&) = default;
    ~PotentiallyMisleading() = default;

private:
    std::unique_ptr<int> value;
};
```

Even though we defaulted all the members, the class is still non-copyable. That's because it has a `unique_ptr` member that is non-copyable itself. Fortunately, C++ compilers can warn you about this, but compiler warnings depend on compiler settings and enabled warning flags. A better approach would be to apply the rule of zero and instead write the following:

```
class RuleOfZero final {
    // would be implicitly non-movable
    // ~RuleOfZero() = default;

    std::unique_ptr<int> value;
};
```

Now we have less boilerplate code, and by looking at the members, it's easier to notice that it does not support copying.

There's one more important idiom to know about when it comes to copying that you'll get to know in a minute. Before that happens, we shall touch on yet another idiom, which can (and should) be used to implement the former.

Using hidden friends

In essence, hidden friends are non-member functions defined in the body of the type that declares them as a friend. This makes such functions impossible to call in ways other than by using **argument-dependent lookup (ADL)**, effectively making them hidden. (ADL, also known as **Koenig lookup**, is the set of rules for looking up unqualified function names in function-call expressions.)

By reducing the number of overloads a compiler considers, hidden friends speed up compilation. A bonus of this is that they provide shorter error messages than their alternatives. Another interesting property is that they cannot be called if an implicit conversion should happen first. This can help you avoid such accidental conversions.

Although friends in C++ are generally not recommended, things look different for hidden friends. If the advantages from the previous paragraph don't convince you, you should also know that they should be the preferred way of implementing customization points, as properly implemented hidden friends enhance encapsulation.

Now, you're probably wondering what those customization points are. Briefly speaking, they are callables used by the library code that the user can specialize in for their types. The standard library reserves quite a lot of names for those, such as `begin`, `end`, and their reverse and `const` variations, `swap`, `(s)size`, `(c)data`, and many operators, among others. If you decide to provide your own implementation for any of those customization points, it had better behave as the standard library expects.

Okay, enough theory for now. Let's see how to provide a customization point specialization using a hidden friend in practice. For example, let's create an oversimplified class to manage arrays of types:

```
template <typename T> class Array final {
public:
    Array(T *array, std::size_t size) : array_{array}, size_{size} {}

    ~Array() { delete[] array_; }

    T &operator[](std::size_t index) { return array_[index]; }
    [[nodiscard]] std::size_t size() const noexcept { return size_; }

    friend void swap(Array &left, Array &right) noexcept {
        using std::swap;
        swap(left.array_, right.array_);
        swap(left.size_, right.size_);
    }

private:
    T *array_;
    std::size_t size_;
};
```

As you can see, we defined a destructor, which means we should provide other special member functions too. We implement them in the next section, using our hidden friend `swap`. Note that despite being declared in the body of our `Array` class, this `swap` function is still a non-member function. It accepts two `Array` instances and doesn't have access to `this` (a pointer to the current instance of a class).

The line `using std::swap;` makes the compiler first look for `swap` functions in the namespaces of the swapped members. If not found, it will fall back to `std::swap`. This is called the **two-step ADL and fallback idiom**, or **two-step** for short, because we first make `std::swap` visible, and then call `swap`.

The `noexcept` keyword tells the compiler that our `swap` function does not throw, which allows it to generate faster code in certain situations. Aside from `swap`, always mark your default and move constructors with this keyword too for the same reason. The primary benefit of `noexcept` on `swap`, move constructors, and assignment operators is enabling optimizations in the standard library containers. For instance, `std::vector` can move elements during reallocation if move operations are `noexcept`; otherwise, it might copy.

Note that the `Array` class owns a raw pointer and always deletes it in the destructor. That means the pointer you pass in must come from `new[]`. If you pass the address of a stack array or memory not allocated with `new[]`, the program will hit undefined behavior. The raw pointers here are intentional to demonstrate hidden-friend usage. In real-world code, you'd typically wrap it in a smart pointer (`std::unique_ptr<Array>`) or use an STL container.

As discussed in the previous chapter, raw pointers are low-level building blocks, while smart pointers provide safer and clearer memory management.

As mentioned, our `Array` class is intentionally low-level. It wraps a raw pointer much like an STL container would. Thus, its instances should be placed on the stack or wrapped in smart pointers to manage memory automatically and safely to avoid memory leaks. Its constructor has no memory leaks because the objects are not partially constructed and the destructor is never called on not constructed objects.

However, because this class owns a raw pointer, the compiler-generated copy operations would result in shallow copies and double deletions. We will fix this by defining safe copy and move operations using the **copy-and-swap idiom**.

Providing exception safety using the copy-and-swap idiom

As we mentioned in the previous section, because our `Array` class defines a destructor, according to the rule of five, it should also define other special member functions. In this section, you'll learn about an idiom that lets us do this without boilerplate, while also adding strong exception safety as a bonus.

If you're not familiar with the exception safety levels, here's a quick recap of the levels your functions and types can offer:

- **No guarantee**: This is the most basic level. No guarantees are made about the state of your object after an exception is thrown while it's being used.
- **Basic exception safety**: Side effects are possible, but your object won't leak any resources, will be in a valid state, and will contain valid data (not necessarily the same as before the operation). Your types should always offer at least this level.
- **Strong exception safety**: No side effects will happen. The object's state will be the same as before the operation.
- **No-throw guarantee**: Operations will always succeed. If an exception is thrown during the operation, it will be caught and handled internally, so the operation does not throw exceptions outside. Such operations can be marked as `noexcept`.

So, how can we achieve these goals: write boilerplate-free special members while also providing strong exception safety? It's pretty easy, actually. As we have our `swap` function, let's use it to implement the assignment operators:

```
Array &operator=(Array other) noexcept {
    swap(*this, other);
    return *this;
}
```

In our case, a single operator suffices for both the copy and move assignments. Nonetheless, implementing a separate move operator can still be valuable for expensive-to-copy types, as it offers performance benefits by avoiding the creation/destruction of the temporary objects.

Note that C++ typically supports copy constructor syntax that accepts an object passed by `const` reference, which prevents modification operations, but this option does not provide exception-safety.

In our case, we take the parameter by value, which means a copy or move occurs when the argument is passed. This copy acts as temporary, protecting the original object from modification. Then, all we need to do is swap the members with this temporary copy. Thus, the temporary object is destroyed automatically, and this approach does not require allocating memory in the constructor. We have not only achieved strong exception safety but were also able not to throw from the assignment operator's body. However, an exception can still be thrown right before the function gets called, when the copy is created. In the case of the move assignment, no copy is made because the parameter is initialized by moving the argument into the function.

Now, let's define the copy constructor:

```
Array(const Array &other) : array_{new T[other.size_]}, size_{other.size_}
{
    std::copy_n(other.array_, size_, array_);
}
```

This constructor can throw an exception depending on `T` and because it allocates memory, but an instance of this class is not partially constructed since the pointer field is single. Thus, memory does not leak here if the allocation itself throws, because the constructor body is never entered and the destructor is not called. For trivial types such as `int`, the risk of memory leaks or exceptions isn't an issue, but for general types, this implementation is not exception-safe.

Now, let's define the move constructor too:

```
Array(Array &&other) noexcept
    : array_{std::exchange(other.array_, nullptr)}, size_{std::exchange(other.
size_, 0)} {}
```

Here, we use `std::exchange` so that our members get initialized and members of `other` get cleaned up, all within the initialization list. The constructor is declared `noexcept` for performance reasons. For instance, `std::vector` can move its elements when it grows only if they're `noexcept` move-constructible, and copies otherwise.

That's it. We've created the `Array` class, providing strong exception safety with little effort and no code duplication.

Writing niebloids

This C++ idiom can be spotted in a few places in the standard library. Niebloids, named after Eric Niebler, are a type of function object, also known as a functor, that the standard uses for customization points from C++17 onward. With the introduction of standard ranges described in *Chapter 5, Leveraging C++ Language Features*, their popularity started to grow, but they were first proposed by Niebler back in 2014. *Their purpose is to disable ADL where it's not wanted, so overloads from other namespaces are not considered by the compiler since non-function symbols inhibit ADL.* Remember the two-step idiom from the previous sections? Because it's inconvenient and easy to forget, the notion of *customization point objects* was introduced. In essence, these are function objects performing the *two-step* for you.

If your libraries should provide customization points, it's probably a good idea to implement them using niebloids. All the customization points in the standard library introduced in C++17 and later are implemented this way for a reason. Even if you just need to create a function object, still consider using niebloids. They offer all the good parts of ADL while reducing the drawbacks. They allow specialization, and together with concepts, they give you a way to customize the overload set of your callables. They also allow better customization of algorithms, all at the slight cost of writing a bit more verbose code than usual.

In this section, we'll create a simple range algorithm that we'll implement as a niebloid. Let's call our niebloid `contains_fn`, as it simply returns a boolean value denoting whether a given element is found in the range or not. First, let's create the function object itself, starting with the declaration of its iterator-based call operator:

```
namespace detail {
struct contains_fn final {
    template <std::input_iterator It, std::sentinel_for<It> Sent, typename T,
typename Proj = std::identity>
    requires std::indirect_binary_predicate<std::ranges::equal_to,
std::projected<It, Proj>, const T *>
    constexpr bool operator()(It first, Sent last, const T &value, Proj
projection = {}) const {
```

It looks verbose, but all this code has a purpose. We make our struct `final` to aid the compiler in generating more efficient code. If you look at the template parameters, you'll see an iterator and a sentinel—the basic building blocks of each standard range. The sentinel is often an iterator, but it can be any semiregular type that can be compared with the iterator (a semiregular type is copyable and default-initializable). Next, `T` is the type of element to search for, while `Proj` denotes a projection—an operation to apply to each range element before comparison (the default of `std::identity` simply passes its input as output).

After the template parameters, there come the requirements for them; the operator requires that we can compare the projected value and the searched-for value for equality. After those constraints, we simply specify the function parameters.

Let's now see how it's implemented:

```
while (first != last && std::invoke(projection, *first) != value) {
    ++first;
}
return first != last;  }
```

Here, we simply iterate over the elements, invoking the projection on each element and comparing it with the searched-for value. We return `true` if found and `false` otherwise (when `first == last`).

The preceding function would work even if we didn't use standard ranges, but we also need an overload that accepts a range directly. The declaration of the overload can be as follows:

```
template <std::ranges::input_range Range, typename T, typename Proj =
std::identity>
requires std::indirect_binary_predicate<std::ranges::equal_to,
std::projected<std::ranges::iterator_t<Range>, Proj>, const T *>
constexpr bool operator()(Range &&range, const T &value, Proj projection = {})
const {
```

This time, we take a type satisfying the `input_range` concept, the element value, and the type of projection as template parameters. We require that the range's iterator after calling the projection can be compared for equality with objects of type `T`, similar to before. Finally, we use the range, the value, and the projection as our overload's parameters.

The body of this operator will be pretty straightforward, too:

```
    return (*this)(std::ranges::begin(range), std::ranges::end(range), value,
std::move(projection));
    }
};
}  // namespace detail
```

We simply call the previous overload using an iterator and sentinel from the given range, while passing the value and our projection unchanged. Now, for the last part, we need to provide a `contains` niebloid instead of just the `contains_fn` callable:

```
inline constexpr detail::contains_fn contains{};
```

By declaring an inline variable named `contains` of type `contains_fn`, we allow anyone to call our niebloid using the variable name. Now, let's call it ourselves to see whether it works:

```
int main() {
    auto ints = std::ranges::views::iota(0) | std::ranges::views::take(5);

    return contains(ints, 42);
}
```

And that's it. Our ADL-inhibiting functor works as intended.

If you think all of this is a tad too verbose, then you might be interested in `tag_invoke`, which might become part of the standard at some point in the future. Refer to the *Further reading* section for a paper on this topic and a YouTube video that explains ADL, niebloids, hidden friends, and `tag_invoke` nicely.

Let's now move on to yet another useful C++ idiom.

Using the policy-based design idiom

Policy-based design was first introduced by Andrei Alexandrescu in his excellent *Modern C++ Design* book. Although published in 2001, many ideas shown in it are still used today. The **policy idiom** is basically a compile-time equivalent of the Gang of Four's Strategy pattern. If you need to write a class with customizable behavior, you can make it a template with the appropriate policies as template parameters. A real-world example of this could be standard allocators, passed as a policy to many C++ containers as the last template parameter.

Let's return to our `Array` class and add a policy for debug printing:

```
template <typename T, typename DebugPrintingPolicy = NullPrintingPolicy>
class Array {
```

As you can see, we can use a default policy (`NullPrintingPolicy`) that won't print anything. `NullPrintingPolicy` can be implemented as follows:

```
struct NullPrintingPolicy {
    template <typename... Args> void operator()(Args...) {}
};
```

As you can see, regardless of the arguments given, it won't do anything. The compiler will completely optimize it out, so no overhead will be paid when the debug printing feature is not used.

If we want our class to print texts, we can use a different policy:

```
struct CoutPrintingPolicy {
    void operator()(std::string_view text) { std::cout << text << std::endl; }
};
```

This time, we'll simply print the text passed to the policy to `cout`. We also need to modify our class to actually use our policy:

```
    Array(T *array, int size) : array_{array}, size_{size} {
        DebugPrintingPolicy{}("constructor");
    }

    Array(const Array &other) : array_{new T[other.size_]}, size_{other.size_}
{
```

```
        DebugPrintingPolicy{}("copy constructor");
        std::copy_n(other.array_, size_, array_);
    }

    // ... other members ...
```

We simply call the policy's `operator()`, passing the text to be printed. Since our policies are stateless, we can instantiate them each time we need to use them without extra cost. An alternative could also be to just call a static function from the policy.

Now, all we need to do is to instantiate our `Array` class with the desired policy and use it:

```
Array<T, CoutPrintingPolicy>(new T[size], size);
```

One drawback of using compile-time policies is that the template instantiations using different policies are of different types. This means more work is required to, for instance, assign from a regular `Array` class to one with `CoutPrintingPolicy`. To do so, you would need to implement assignment operators as template functions with the policy as the template parameter.

Sometimes, an alternative to policy-based design is to use traits. Policies define custom behavior for generic functions and types, while traits provide additional properties of a template parameter. As an example, take `std::iterator_traits`, which can be used to use various information about iterators when writing algorithms that use them. An example could be `std::iterator_traits<T>::value_type`, which can work for both custom iterators defining a `value_type` member, and simple ones such as pointers (in which case, `value_type` would refer to the pointed-to type).

Enough about policy-based design. Next on our list is a powerful idiom that can be applied in multiple scenarios.

Applying the curiously recurring template pattern

Despite having *pattern* in its name, the **Curiously Recurring Template Pattern** (**CRTP**) is an idiom in C++. It can be used to implement other idioms and design patterns, and to apply static polymorphism, to name a couple of things. Let's start with this last one, as we'll cover the others later on.

Knowing when to use dynamic versus static polymorphism

When mentioning polymorphism, many programmers will think of dynamic polymorphism (runtime polymorphism), where the information needed to perform a function call is gathered at runtime. In contrast to this, static polymorphism is about determining the calls at compile time. An advantage of the former is that you can modify the list of types at runtime, allowing you to extend your class hierarchies through plugins and libraries. The big advantage of the latter is that it can get better performance if you know the types upfront. Sure, in the first case, you can sometimes expect your compiler to devirtualize your calls, but you cannot always count on it doing so. However, in the second case, you can get longer compilation times.

Looks like you cannot win in all cases. Still, choosing the right type of polymorphism for your types can go a long way. If performance is at stake, we strongly suggest you consider static polymorphism. CRTP is an idiom that can be used to apply it. If you're writing performance-oriented code (and you probably are if you chose C++), you should know that using dynamic polymorphism can be a bad idea in terms of performance, especially on the hot path, because dynamic method dispatch has a performance overhead compared to static method calls when a program decides at runtime which method to call. To give you a concrete sense of the difference, consider the benchmark reported by Eli Bendersky in his detailed article on the cost of dynamic virtual calls versus static CRTP dispatch in C++. The link is provided in the *Further reading* section.

Many design patterns can be implemented in one way or another. As the cost of dynamic polymorphism is not always worth it, the Gang of Four design patterns are often not the best solution in C++. If your type hierarchy should be extended at runtime, or compile times are a much bigger issue than performance for you (and you don't plan on using modules any time soon), then the classical implementations of the Gang of Four patterns may be a good fit. Otherwise, you can try to implement them using static polymorphism or by applying simpler C++-focused solutions, some of which we describe in this chapter. It's all about choosing the best tool for the job.

Implementing static polymorphism

Let's now implement our statically polymorphic class hierarchy. We'll need a base template class:

```
template <typename ConcreteItem> class GlamorousItem {
public:
    void appear_in_full_glory() {
        static_cast<ConcreteItem *>(this)->appear_in_full_glory();
    }
};
```

The template parameter for the base class is the derived class itself. This may seem odd at first, but it allows us to apply static type casting at compile time using `static_cast` to convert `this` to the correct derived type. In our interface function, called `appear_in_full_glory`, we then call the implementation of this function in a derived class. Derived classes could be implemented like so:

```
class PinkHeels : public GlamorousItem<PinkHeels> {
public:
    void appear_in_full_glory() {
        std::cout << "Pink high heels suddenly appeared in all their beauty\n";
    }
};

class GoldenWatch : public GlamorousItem<GoldenWatch> {
public:
    void appear_in_full_glory() {
        std::cout << "Everyone wanted to watch this watch\n";
    }
};
```

Each of these classes derives from our `GlamorousItem` base class using itself as the template argument. Each also implements the required function.

Note that, as opposed to dynamic polymorphism, the base class in CRTP is a template, so you'll get a different base type for each of your derived classes. This means you can't easily create a container of your `GlamorousItem` base class. What you can do, however, is several things:

- Store objects in a tuple.
- Create a `std::variant` of your derived classes.
- Add one common class to wrap all instantiations of the base. You can use a variant for this one as well.

In the first case, we could use the class as follows. First, create the tuple of instances of `base`:

```
template <typename... Args>
using PreciousItems = std::tuple<GlamorousItem<Args>...>;

auto glamorous_items = PreciousItems<PinkHeels, GoldenWatch>{};
```

Our type-aliased tuple will be able to store any glamorous items. Now, all we need to do is call the `appear_in_full_glory()` function:

```
std::apply(
    []<typename... T>(GlamorousItem<T>&... items) {
        (items.appear_in_full_glory(), ...);
    },
    glamorous_items);
```

Because we're trying to iterate a tuple, the easiest way to do so is to call `std::apply`, which invokes the given callable on all the elements of the given tuple. In our case, the callable is a lambda that accepts only the `GlamorousItem` base class. We use fold expressions, introduced in C++17, to ensure our function will be called for all elements.

If we were to use a variant instead of a tuple, we'd need to use `std::visit`, like so:

```
using GlamorousVariant = std::variant<PinkHeels, GoldenWatch>;
auto glamorous_items = std::array{GlamorousVariant{PinkHeels{}},
GlamorousVariant{GoldenWatch{}}};

    for (auto& elem : glamorous_items) {
        std::visit([]<typename T>(GlamorousItem<T> item){ item.appear_in_full_
glory();
    }, elem);
}
```

The `std::visit` function basically takes the variant and calls the passed lambda on the object stored in it. Here, we create an array of our glamorous variants, so we can just iterate over it like any other container, visiting each variant with the appropriate lambda.

If you find it's not intuitive to write from the interface user's perspective, consider this next approach, which wraps the variant into yet another class, in our case called `CommonGlamorousItem`:

```
class CommonGlamorousItem {
public:
    template <typename T> requires std::is_base_of_v<GlamorousItem<T>, T>
    explicit CommonGlamorousItem(T &&item)
        : item_{std::forward<T>(item)} {}
private:
    GlamorousVariant item_;
};
```

To construct our wrapper, we use a forwarding constructor (`templated T&&` being its parameter). We then forward instead of moving to create the `item_` wrapped variant, as this way we only move r-value inputs. We also constrain the template parameters, so on one hand, we only wrap the `GlamorousItem` base class, and on the other, our template is not used as a move or copy constructor.

We also need to wrap our member function:

```
void appear_in_full_glory() {
    std::visit(
        []<typename T>(GlamorousItem<T> item) {
            item.appear_in_full_glory(); },
        item_);
}
```

This time, the `std::visit` call is an implementation detail. The user can use this wrapper class in the following way:

```
auto glamorous_items = std::array{CommonGlamorousItem{PinkHeels{}},
CommonGlamorousItem{GoldenWatch{}}};

    for (auto& elem : glamorous_items) {
        elem.appear_in_full_glory();
    }
```

This approach lets the user of the class write easy-to-understand code, but still keep the performance of static polymorphism.

To offer a similar user experience, albeit with worse performance due to dynamic polymorphism and hidden type information used by a C++ compiler to optimize generated code, you can also use a technique called type erasure, which we'll discuss next.

Interlude: using type erasure

Although type erasure isn't related to CRTP, it fits in nicely with our current example, which is why we're showing it here.

The **type erasure idiom** is about hiding the concrete type under a polymorphic interface. A great example of this approach can be found in Sean Parent's talk *Inheritance Is The Base Class of Evil* from the GoingNative 2013 conference. We highly recommend you watch it in your spare time; you can find a link to it in the *Further reading* section. In the standard library, you can find it in `std::function`, the deleter in `std::shared_ptr`, or `std::any`, among others.

However, the convenience of use and flexibility comes at a price—this idiom needs to use pointers and virtual dispatch, which makes the mentioned utilities from the standard library bad to use in performance-oriented use cases. Beware.

To introduce type erasure to our example, we no longer need CRTP. This time, our `GlamorousItem` class will wrap dynamically polymorphic objects in a smart pointer:

```
class GlamorousItem {
public:
    template <class T>
    explicit GlamorousItem(T &&t)
        : item_{std::make_unique<TypeErasedItem<T>>(std::forward<T>(t))} {}

    void appear_in_full_glory() {
        item_->appear_in_full_glory_impl();
    }

private:
    std::unique_ptr<TypeErasedItemBase> item_;
};
```

This time, we store a pointer to base (`TypeErasedItemBase`), which will point to derived wrappers for our items (`TypeErasedItem<T>s`). The base class can be defined as follows:

```
struct TypeErasedItemBase {
    virtual ~TypeErasedItemBase() = default;
    virtual void appear_in_full_glory_impl() = 0;
};
```

Each derived wrapper needs to implement this interface, too:

```
template <class T> class TypeErasedItem final : public TypeErasedItemBase {
    public:
        explicit TypeErasedItem(T &&t) : t_{std::forward<T>(t)} {}
        void appear_in_full_glory_impl() override { t_.appear_in_full_glory();
    }
```

```
private:
    T t_;
};
```

The base class's interface is implemented by calling the function from the wrapped object. Note that the idiom is called *type erasure* because the `GlamorousItem` class doesn't know what `T` it is actually wrapping. The `information` type gets erased when the item gets constructed, but it all works because `T` implements the required methods.

The concrete items can be implemented in a simpler manner, as shown next:

```
class PinkHeels {
public:
    void appear_in_full_glory() {
        std::cout << "Pink high heels suddenly appeared in all their beauty\n";
    }
};

class GoldenWatch {
public:
    void appear_in_full_glory() {
        std::cout << "Everyone wanted to watch this watch\n";
    }
};
```

This time, they don't need to inherit from any base. All we need is duck typing—if it quacks like a duck, it's probably a duck. And if it can appear in full glory, it's probably glamorous.

Our type-erased API can be used as follows:

```
auto glamorous_items = std::array{GlamorousItem{PinkHeels{}},
GlamorousItem{GoldenWatch{}}};

    for (auto &item : glamorous_items) {
        item.appear_in_full_glory();
    }
```

We just create an array of our wrappers and iterate over it, all using simple, value-based semantics. We find it the most pleasant to use, as the polymorphism is hidden from the caller as an implementation detail.

However, a drawback of this approach is, as we mentioned before, performance. Type erasure comes at a price, so it should be used sparingly and definitely not in the hot path. In general, you need to test performance on a case-by-case basis, where you use type erasure.

For comparison, we will apply `deducing this`, a C++23 feature, to examples from the CRTP topic so you can compare changes side by side.

Implementing deducing this

C++23 introduced an explicit object parameter, also known as `deducing this`. The parameter does not change type deduction, but allows you to declare the implicit `this` parameter explicitly. This opens up new horizons for us, such as code deduplication, recursive lambdas, and CRTP replacement.

Combined with type deduction, the explicit object parameter allows us to define one generic method instead of four declared with `cv`- or `ref`-qualifiers (&, `const&`, &&, `const&&`), which reduces boilerplate code.

However, functions declared with the explicit object parameter cannot be declared as static or virtual, nor can they have `cv`- or `ref`-qualifiers. Inheritance is supported as the explicit objects deduce the types of derived objects. Moreover, the only way to interact with a class object inside such functions is through the explicit object parameter, because the function behaves like a static member function, so `this`, a pointer to the current instance of a class, is not available.

To illustrate the power of `deducing this`, let's refactor the `GlamorousItem` example from the previous section.

Let's start with refactoring the base class. Both of the implementations that follow can be used interchangeably.

Here's the first one:

```
class GlamorousItem {
public:
    void appear_in_full_glory(this auto&& self) { self.appear_in_full_glory_
impl();
    }
};
```

Here, the type of `self` is deduced automatically using `auto`.

Alternatively, you can explicitly declare the type as a template parameter:

```
class GlamorousItem {
public:
    template <typename Self>
    void appear_in_full_glory(this Self&& self) {
        self.appear_in_full_glory_impl();
    }
};
```

In this case, the template parameter is not necessarily required.

Derived classes could be implemented like so:

```
class PinkHeels : public GlamorousItem {
public:
    void appear_in_full_glory_impl() {
        std::cout << "Pink high heels suddenly appeared in all their beauty\n";
    }
};

class GoldenWatch : public GlamorousItem {
public:
    void appear_in_full_glory_impl() {
        std::cout << "Everyone wanted to watch this watch\n";
    }
};
```

Note that you still can't create a container of your `GlamorousItem` base class directly. Instead, you can use a few alternatives.

You can use a tuple constrained by concepts:

```
/*template <typename... Args> requires(std::derived_from<Args, GlamorousItem>
&& ...)*/

template <std::derived_from<GlamorousItem>... Args>
using PreciousItems = std::tuple<Args...>;

int main() {
    auto glamorous_items = PreciousItems<PinkHeels, GoldenWatch>{};
    std::apply([]<std::derived_from<GlamorousItem>... T>(T&... items) { (items.
appear_in_full_glory(), ...);
    },
    glamorous_items);
}
```

You can create a `std::variant` class template of your derived classes:

```
using GlamorousVariant = std::variant<PinkHeels, GoldenWatch>;

int main() {
    auto glamorous_items = std::array{GlamorousVariant{PinkHeels{}},
GlamorousVariant{GoldenWatch{}}
    };
    for (auto& elem : glamorous_items) {
        std::visit([]<std::derived_from<GlamorousItem> T>(T& item) { item.
```

```
appear_in_full_glory();
            },
            elem);
    }
}
```

You can add one common class to wrap all instantiations of the base class:

```
class CommonGlamorousItem {
public:
    template <typename T>
        requires std::is_base_of_v<GlamorousItem, T>
    explicit CommonGlamorousItem(T&& item) : item_{std::forward<T>(item)} {}

    void appear_in_full_glory() {
        std::visit([]<typename T>(T& item) { item.appear_in_full_glory(); },
item_);
    }

private:
    GlamorousVariant item_;
};

int main() {
    auto glamorous_items = std::array{CommonGlamorousItem{PinkHeels{}},
CommonGlamorousItem{GoldenWatch{}}};

    for (auto& elem : glamorous_items) {
        elem.appear_in_full_glory();
    }
}
```

Finally, the RAII-style `Array` class from the previous chapter can be simplified by applying `deducing this`, since this feature deduplicates overloads of the subscript operator into a single function:

```
// Use an explicit object parameter (self) and auto&&
// to differentiate const vs non-const
auto &&operator[](this auto &&self, std::size_t idx) {
    return self.data_[idx];
}
```

With the `deducing this` feature in place, let's turn to another important aspect—object creation.

Creating objects

In this section, we'll discuss common solutions to problems related to object creation. However, we'll take a slightly different approach from the Gang of Four patterns when describing their solutions. They proposed complex, dynamically polymorphic class hierarchies as proper implementations of their patterns. In the C++ world, many patterns can be applied to real-world problems without introducing as many classes and the overhead of dynamic dispatch. That's why, in our case, the implementations will be different and in many cases simpler or more performant (although more specialized and less "generic" in the Gang of Four sense). Let's dive right in.

Using factories

The first type of creational patterns we'll discuss here is factories. They're useful when the object construction can be done in a single step, but when the constructor just isn't good enough on its own. There are three types of factories: factory methods, factory functions, and factory classes. Let's introduce them one by one.

Using factory methods

Factory methods, also called the **named constructor idiom**, are basically member functions that call a private constructor for you. When do we use them? Here are a few scenarios:

- **When there are many different ways to construct an object, which would make errors likely:** For example, imagine constructing a class for storing different color channels for a given pixel; each channel is represented by a one-byte value. Using just a constructor would make it too easy to pass the wrong order of channels or values meant for a different color palette entirely. Also, switching the pixel's internal representation of colors would get tricky pretty fast. You could argue that we should have different types representing colors in those different formats, but often, using a factory method is a valid approach as well.
- **When you want to force the object to be created on the heap or in another specific memory area:** If your object takes up loads of space on the stack and you're afraid you'll run out of stack memory, using a factory method is a solution. The same goes if you require all instances to be created in some area of memory on a device, for instance.
- **When constructing your object can fail, but you cannot throw exceptions:** You should use exceptions instead of other methods of error handling. When used properly, they can yield cleaner and better-performing code. However, some projects or environments require that exceptions are disabled. In such cases, using a factory method will allow you to report errors happening during construction.

Factory methods help manage errors that occur during object construction by providing controlled creation mechanisms. Similarly, it's important to handle errors safely during object destruction, because exceptions escaping destructors can cause program termination. Although throwing exceptions is preferred for managing errors during construction, the exact opposite applies to destructors: don't let exceptions escape the destructors. C++ defines a harsh rule, which says that an uncaught exception thrown from a destructor during stack unwinding caused by handling another exception terminates the program. In more detail, the **runtime library** (**RTL**) looks for a handler whose type matches the type of thrown object upward in the call stack.

Then, the RTL destroys all local objects in the stack frames up to the exception handler before executing the handler that exists. But if a destructor also throws an exception and that exception is not caught in the destructor, then the program terminates by calling `std::terminate`. Deallocation functions without the `noexcept` specifier are treated as if declared with `noexcept(true)` **implicitly**. Declaring destructors as throwing exceptions with `noexcept(false)` is rare and potentially dangerous due to unexpected behavior.

A factory method for the first case we described could look as follows:

```
class Pixel final {
public:
    static Pixel fromRgba(std::byte r, std::byte b, std::byte g, std::byte a) {
      return Pixel{r, g, b, a};
    }
    static Pixel fromBgra(std::byte b, std::byte g, std::byte r, std::byte a) {
        return Pixel{r, g, b, a};
    }

    // other members

private:
    Pixel(std::byte r, std::byte g, std::byte b, std::byte a)
        : r_(r), g_(g), b_(b), a_(a) {}
    std::byte r_, g_, b_, a_;
}
```

The `Pixel` class here defines two factory methods (actually, the C++ standard doesn't recognize the term *method*, calling them *member functions* instead): `fromRgba` and `fromBgra`. Now it's harder to make a mistake and initialize the channels in the wrong order.

Note that the constructor of `Pixel` is private, and having a private constructor effectively inhibits any class from inheriting from your type, as without access to its constructor, no instances can be created. If that's your goal, however, you should prefer to just mark your class as `final`.

Using factory functions

As opposed to using factory member functions, we can also implement them using non-member ones. This way, we can provide better encapsulation, as described by Scott Meyers in his article linked in the *Further reading* section.

In the case of `Pixel`, we could also create a free function to fabricate its instances. This way, our type could have simpler code:

```
struct Pixel {
    std::byte r, g, b, a;
};

Pixel makePixelFromRgba(std::byte r, std::byte b, std::byte g, std::byte a) {
    return Pixel{r, g, b, a};
}

Pixel makePixelFromBgra(std::byte b, std::byte g, std::byte r, std::byte a) {
    return Pixel{r, g, b, a};
}
```

Using this approach makes our design conform to the open-closed principle described in *Chapter 1, Importance of Software Architecture and Principles of Great Design*. It's easy to add more factory functions for other color palettes without the need to modify the `Pixel` struct itself.

This implementation of `Pixel` allows the user to initialize it manually instead of using one of our provided functions. If we want, we can inhibit this behavior by changing the class declaration. Here's how it could look after the fix:

```
struct Pixel {
    std::byte r, g, b, a;

private:
    Pixel(std::byte r, std::byte g, std::byte b, std::byte a)
        : r(r), g(g), b(b), a(a) {}
    friend Pixel makePixelFromRgba(std::byte r, std::byte g, std::byte b,
std::byte a);
    friend Pixel makePixelFromBgra(std::byte b, std::byte g, std::byte r,
std::byte a);
};
```

This time, our factory functions are friends of our class. However, the type is no longer an aggregate, so we can no longer use aggregate initialization (`Pixel{}`), including designated initializers. Also, we gave up on the open-closed principle. The two approaches offer different trade-offs, so choose wisely.

Choosing the return type of a factory

Yet another thing you should choose when implementing an object factory is the actual type it should return. Let's discuss the various approaches.

In the case of `Pixel`, which is a value type and not a polymorphic one, the simplest approach works the best—we simply return by value. If you produce a polymorphic type, return it by a smart pointer (*never* use a naked pointer for this, as this will yield memory leaks at some point) unless you are following framework-specific memory ownership rules (e.g., Qt, Unreal Engine). If the caller should own the created object, usually returning it in `unique_ptr` to the base class is the best approach. In the not-so-common cases where your factory and the caller must both own the object, use `shared_ptr` or another reference-counted alternative. Sometimes it's enough that the factory keeps track of the object but doesn't store it. In such cases, store `weak_ptr` inside the factory and lock `shared_ptr` outside.

Some C++ programmers would argue that you should return specific types using an out parameter, but that's not the best approach in most cases. In the case of performance, returning by value is usually the best choice, as compilers will not make extra copies of your object. If the issue is with the type being non-copyable, from C++17 onward, the standard specifies where copy elision is mandatory, so returning such types by value is usually not an issue. If your function returns multiple objects, use a pair, tuple, struct, or container.

If something goes wrong during construction, you have several choices:

- Return `std::optional` of your type if there's no need to provide error messages to the caller
- Throw an exception if errors during construction are rare and should be propagated
- Return `std::expected` (since C++23) or `absl::StatusOr` of your type if errors during construction are common (see Abseil's documentation for this template in the *Further reading* section)

Now that you know what to return, let's discuss our last type of factory.

Using factory classes

Factory classes are types that can fabricate objects for us. They can help decouple polymorphic object types from their callers. They can allow using object pools (in which reusable objects are kept so that you don't need to constantly allocate and free them) or other allocation schemes. Those are just a few examples of how they can be useful. Let's take a closer look at yet another one. Imagine you need to create different polymorphic types based on input parameters. In some cases, a polymorphic factory function such as the one shown next is not enough:

```
std::unique_ptr<IDocument> open(const std::string &path) {
    const auto extension = std::filesystem::path(path).extension();
    if (extension == ".pdf") return std::make_unique<PdfDocument>(path);
    if (extension == ".html") return std::make_unique<HtmlDocument>(path);

    return nullptr;
}
```

What if we wanted to open other kinds of documents as well, such as OpenDocument text files? It may be ironic to discover that the preceding open factory is not open for extension. It might not be a big issue if we own the code base, but if the consumers of our library need to register their own types, this can be an issue. To solve it, let's use a factory class that will allow registering functions to open different kinds of documents, as shown next:

```
class DocumentOpener final {
public:
    using DocumentType = std::unique_ptr<IDocument>;
    using ConcreteOpener = DocumentType (*)(const std::string&);
    // using ConcreteOpener = std::function<DocumentType(const std::string&)>;

private:
    std::unordered_map<std::string, ConcreteOpener> openerByExtension;
};
```

The class doesn't do much yet, but it has a map from extensions to functions that should be called to open files of given types. Now we'll add two public member functions. The first one will register new file types:

```
    void register_plugin(const std::string &extension, const ConcreteOpener
&opener) {
        openerByExtension.emplace(extension, opener);
    }
```

Now we have a way of filling the map. The second new public function will open the documents using an appropriate opener:

```
    DocumentType open(const std::string &path) {
        if (const auto p = std::filesystem::path(path); p.has_extension()) {
            return openerByExtension.at(p.extension().string())(path);
        }
        throw std::invalid_argument{"Trying to open a file with no extension"};
    }
```

Basically, we extract the extension from the file path, throw an exception if it's empty, and if not, we look for an opener in our map. If found, we use it to open the given file, and if not, the map will throw another exception for us.

Now we can instantiate our factory and register custom file types such as the OpenDocument text format:

```
auto document_opener = DocumentOpener{};

document_opener.register_plugin(
    ".odt", [](const auto &path) -> DocumentOpener::DocumentType {
```

```
        return std::make_unique<OdtDocument>(path);
    });
```

Notice that we're registering a lambda because it can be converted to our `ConcreteOpener` type, which is a function pointer. However, if our lambda had state, this wouldn't be the case. In such cases, we need a wrapper that can hold state. One such thing could be `std::function`, but the drawback of this would be the need to pay the cost of type erasure each time we would want to run the function. In the case of opening files, that's probably okay. If you need better performance, however, consider using a type such as `std::function_ref` (expected to be introduced in C++26 and supported by the major compilers in the future).

Okay, now that we have our opener registered in the factory, let's use it to open a file and extract some text out of it:

```
auto document = document_opener.open("file.odt");
std::cout << document->extract_text().front();
```

And that's all! If you want to provide the consumers of your library with a way to register their own types, they must have access to your map at runtime. You can either provide them with an API to reach it or make the factory static and allow them to register from anywhere in the code.

That does it for factories and building objects in a single step. Let's discuss another popular pattern to be used if factories aren't a good fit.

Using builders

Builders are similar to factories, a creational pattern coming from the Gang of Four. Unlike factories, they can help you build more complex objects: those that cannot be built in a single step, such as types assembled from many separate parts. They also provide you with a way to customize the construction of objects. In our case, we'll skip designing complex hierarchies of builders. Instead, we'll show how a builder can help. We'll leave implementing hierarchies to you, as an exercise.

Builders are needed when an object cannot be produced in a single step. Even when single-step creation is possible, having a fluent interface can just make builders pleasant to use. Let's demonstrate creating fluent builder hierarchies using CRTP.

In our case, we'll create a CRTP, `GenericItemBuilder`, which we'll use as our base builder, and `FetchingItemBuilder`, which will be a more specialized one that can fetch data using a remote address if that's a supported feature. Such specializations can even live in different libraries, for instance, consuming different APIs that may or may not be available at build time.

For demo purposes, we'll build instances of our `Item` struct from *Chapter 5, Leveraging C++ Language Features*:

```
struct Item {
    std::string name;
    std::optional<std::string> photo_url;
    std::string description;
```

```
    std::optional<float> price;
    time_point<system_clock> date_added{};
    bool featured{};
};
```

If you want, you can enforce that `Item` instances are built using a builder by making the default constructor private and making the builders friends:

```
template <typename ConcreteBuilder> friend class GenericItemBuilder;
```

Our builder's implementation can be started as follows:

```
template <typename ConcreteBuilder> class GenericItemBuilder {
public:
    explicit GenericItemBuilder(std::string name)
        : item_{.name = std::move(name)} {}
protected:
    Item item_;
```

Although it's generally not recommended to create protected members, we want our descendant builders to be able to reach our item. An alternative would be to use just the public methods of our base builder in derived ones.

We take the item's name as a parameter in the builder's constructor, as it's a single input coming from the user that needs to be set when we create our item. This way, we make sure that it will be set. An alternative would be to check whether it's okay at the final stage of building, when the object is being released to the user. In our case, the build step can be implemented as follows:

```
Item build() && {
    item_.date_added = system_clock::now();
    return std::move(item_);
}
```

We enforce that the builder is "consumed" when this method is called; it must be an r-value. This means we can either use the builder in one line or move it to the last step to mark the end of its work. We then set the creation time for our item and move it outside of the builder.

Our builder's API could offer functions such as the following:

```
ConcreteBuilder &&with_description(std::string description) {
    item_.description = std::move(description);
    return static_cast<ConcreteBuilder &&>(*this);
}

ConcreteBuilder &&marked_as_featured() {
    item_.featured = true;
    return static_cast<ConcreteBuilder &&>(*this);
}
```

Each of them returns the concrete (derived) builder object as an r-value reference. Perhaps counter-intuitively, this time, such a return type should be preferred to returning by value. This is to avoid unnecessary copies of `item_` when building. On the other hand, returning by an l-value reference could lead to dangling references and would make calling `build()` harder because the returned l-value reference wouldn't match the expected r-value one.

The final builder type could look as follows:

```
class ItemBuilder final : public GenericItemBuilder<ItemBuilder> {
    using GenericItemBuilder<ItemBuilder>::GenericItemBuilder;
};
```

It's just a class that reuses the constructors from our generic builder. It can be used as follows:

```
auto directly_loaded_item = ItemBuilder{"Pot"}.with_description("A decent
one").with_price(100).build();
```

As you can see, the final interface can be called using function chaining, and the method names make the whole invocation fluent to read, hence the name *fluent interfaces*.

What if we were to not load each item directly, but rather use a more specialized builder that could load parts of the data from a remote endpoint? We could define it as follows:

```
class FetchingItemBuilder final
    : public GenericItemBuilder<FetchingItemBuilder> {
public:
    explicit FetchingItemBuilder(std::string name)
        : GenericItemBuilder(std::move(name)) {}

    FetchingItemBuilder&& using_data_from(std::string_view url) && {
        item_ = fetch_item(url);
        return std::move(*this);
    }
};
```

We also use CRTP to inherit from our generic builder and ensure that a name is provided. This time, however, we extend the base builder with our own function to fetch the contents and put them in the item we're building. Thanks to CRTP, when we call a function from our base builder, we'll get the derived one returned, which makes the interface much easier to use. It can be called in the following manner:

```
auto fetched_item = FetchingItemBuilder{"Linen blouse"}.using_data_
from("https://example.com/items/linen_blouse").marked_as_featured().build();
```

All nice and dandy!

Builders can also come in handy if you need to always create immutable objects. As the builder has access to private members of the class, it can modify them, even if the class doesn't provide any setters for them.

Another advantage of builders is that they compensate for the lack of named parameters in C++. Since C++ only supports positional parameters, builders can be used to construct proxy objects to pass function parameters, a technique called **named parameter idiom**. You may use designated initializers for the same purpose to name parameters.

These are, of course, not the only cases when you can benefit from using builders. They are flexible patterns that prove useful in a variety of scenarios.

A case where you would need to use a builder is when creating a composite. A composite is a design pattern in which a group of objects is treated as one, all sharing the same interface (or the same base type). An example would be a graph, which you could compose out of subgraphs, or a document, which could nest other documents. When you call `print()` on such an object, all its sub-objects will get their `print()` functions called in order to print the whole composite. The builder pattern can be useful for creating each sub-object and composing them all together.

Using prototypes

Prototype is yet another pattern that can be used for object construction. If your type is very costly to create anew, or you just want to have a base object to build upon, you might want to use this pattern. It boils down to providing a way to clone your object, which you could later either use on its own or modify so it becomes what it should be. In the case of a polymorphic hierarchy, just add `clone()` like so:

```
class Map {
public:
    virtual std::unique_ptr<Map> clone() const;
    // ... other members ...
};

class MapWithPointsOfInterests {
public:
    std::unique_ptr<Map> clone() override const;
    // ... other members ...
private:
    std::vector<PointOfInterest> pois_;
};
```

Our `MapWithPointsOfInterests` object could clone the points too, so we don't need to re-add each of them manually. This way, we can have some default provided to the end user when they create their own map. Note also that in some cases, instead of using a prototype, a simple copy constructor would suffice.

We have now covered object creation. We touched on variants along the way, so why not revisit them (pun intended) to see how else they can help us?

Tracking state and visiting objects in C++

State is a design pattern meant to help change the behavior of an object when its internal state changes. The behavior for different states should be independent of each other so that adding new states doesn't affect the current ones. The simple approach of implementing all the behavior in the stateful object doesn't scale and is not open for extension. Using the state pattern, new behavior can be added by introducing new state classes and defining the transitions between them.

In this section, we'll show a way to implement states and a state machine leveraging `std::variant` and statically polymorphic double dispatch. In other words, we'll build a finite state machine by joining the state and visitor patterns in a C++ way.

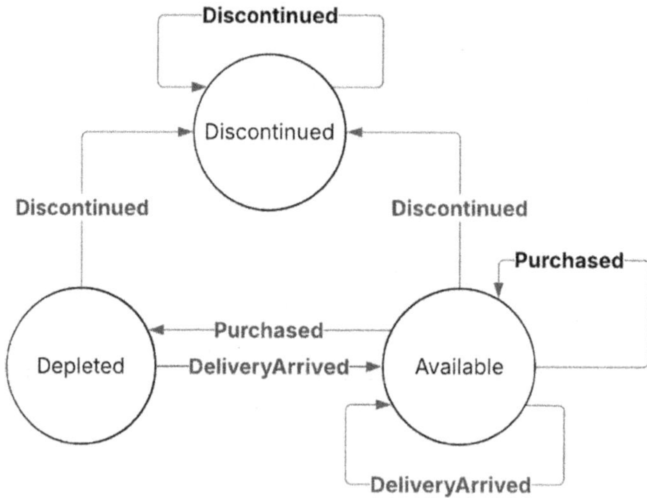

Figure 6.1: State machine for store items

First, let's define our states. In our example, let's model the states of a product in a store. They can be as follows:

```
namespace state {

struct Depleted {};

struct Available {
    int count;
};

struct Discontinued {};
} // namespace state
```

Our states can have properties of their own, such as the count of items left. Also, as opposed to dynamically polymorphic ones, they don't need to inherit from a common base. Instead, they are all stored in one variant, as shown next:

```
using State = std::variant<state::Depleted, state::Available,
state::Discontinued>;
```

Aside from states, we also need events for state transitions. Check the following code:

```
namespace event {

struct DeliveryArrived {
    int count;
};

struct Purchased {
    int count;
};

struct Discontinued {};

} // namespace event
```

As you can see, our events can also have properties and don't inherit from a common base. Now, we need to implement the transitions between the states. This can be done as follows:

```
State on_event(state::Available available, event::DeliveryArrived delivered) {
    available.count += delivered.count;
    return available;
}

State on_event(state::Available available, event::Purchased purchased) {
    available.count -= purchased.count;
    if (available.count > 0)
        return available;
    return state::Depleted{};
}
```

If a purchase is made, the state can change (`Depleted`), but it can also stay the same (`Available`). We can also use templates to handle multiple states transitioning to the same next state:

```
template <typename S> State on_event(S, event::Discontinued) {
    return state::Discontinued{};
}
```

If an item gets discontinued, it doesn't matter what state it was in because this state is terminal.

Okay, let's now implement the last supported transition:

```
State on_event(state::Depleted depleted, event::DeliveryArrived delivered) {
    return state::Available{delivered.count};
}
```

The next piece of the puzzle we need is a way to define multiple call operators in one object generically so that the best-matching overload can be called. We'll use it later to call the transitions we just defined. Our helper implementing the overload pattern based on `std::variant` can look as follows in C++17:

```
template<class... Ts>
struct overload : Ts... {
    using Ts::operator()...;
};
template<class... Ts>
overload(Ts...) -> overload<Ts...>;
```

We create an `overload` struct that will provide all the call operators passed to it during construction, using variable templates, a fold expression, and a class template argument deduction guide.

The implementation in C++20 is shorter due to extensions to **class template argument deduction (CTAD)** for aggregates and does not need a custom deduction guide:

```
template <class... Ts>
struct overload : Ts... {
    using Ts::operator()...;
};
```

In C++23, the implementation is even safer because it catches unimplemented overloads at compile time. This feature is mentioned here for your information, but we do not need it for our state machine. For a more in-depth explanation of this, along with alternative ways of implementing visitations, refer to Bartłomiej Filipek's and Andreas Fertig's blog posts in the *Further reading* section:

```
template <class... Ts>
struct overload : Ts... {
    using Ts::operator()...;

    consteval void operator()(auto) const {
        static_assert(false, "Unsupported type");
    }
};
```

We can now start implementing the state machine itself:

```
class ItemStateMachine {
```

```
public:
    template <typename Event> void process_event(Event &&event) {
        state_ = std::visit(overload{[&](const auto &state) requires std::is_
same_v<decltype(on_event(state, std::forward<Event>(event))), State>{
            return on_event(state, std::forward<Event>(event));
        },
        [](const auto &unsupported_state) -> State {
            throw std::logic_error{"Unsupported state transition"};
        }
    },
    state_);
}

private:
    State state_;
};
```

Our `process_event` function will accept any of our defined events. It will call an appropriate `on_event` function using the current state and the passed event and switch to the new state. If an `on_event` overload is found for the given state and event, the first lambda will get called. Otherwise, the constraint won't be satisfied, and the second, more generic overload will get called. This means if there's an unsupported state transition, we'll just throw an exception.

Now, let's provide a way to report the current state:

```
std::string report_current_state() {
    return std::visit(overload{[](const state::Available &state) -> std::string
{
        return std::to_string(state.count) +" items available";
        },
        [](const state::Depleted) -> std::string {
            return "Item is temporarily out of stock";
        },
        [](const state::Discontinued) -> std::string {
            return "Item has been discontinued";
        }
    },
    state_);
}
```

Here, we use our overload to pass three lambdas, each returning a report string generated by visiting our state object.

We can now call our solution:

```
auto fsm = ItemStateMachine{};
std::cout << fsm.report_current_state() << '\n';
fsm.process_event(event::DeliveryArrived{3});
std::cout << fsm.report_current_state() << '\n';
fsm.process_event(event::Purchased{2});
std::cout << fsm.report_current_state() << '\n';
fsm.process_event(event::DeliveryArrived{2});
std::cout << fsm.report_current_state() << '\n';
fsm.process_event(event::Purchased{3});
std::cout << fsm.report_current_state() << '\n';
fsm.process_event(event::Discontinued{});
std::cout << fsm.report_current_state() << '\n';
// fsm.process_event(event::DeliveryArrived{1});
```

Upon running, this will yield the following output:

```
Item is temporarily out of stock
3 items available
1 items available
3 items available
Item is temporarily out of stock
Item has been discontinued
```

That is, unless you uncomment the last line with the unsupported transition, in which case an exception will be thrown at the end.

Our solution is much more performant than dynamic polymorphism-based implementations, which suffer from indirection through virtual function tables (vtables) when calling methods. However, it only supports states and events known at compile time. For more information on states, variants, and the various ways to implement visitation, see Mateusz Pusz's talk from CppCon 2018, also listed in the *Further reading* section.

Before we close this chapter, one last thing we'd like for you to learn about is handling memory. Let's begin our last section.

Dealing with memory efficiently

Even if you don't have very limited memory, it's a good idea to look at how you use it. Usually, memory throughput is the performance bottleneck of modern-day systems, so it's always important to make good use of it. Performing too many dynamic allocations can slow down your program and lead to memory fragmentation. Let's learn a few ways to mitigate those issues.

Reducing dynamic allocations using SSO/SBO/SOO

Dynamic allocations can sometimes cause you more trouble than just throwing exceptions when you construct objects despite not having enough memory. They often cost you CPU cycles and can cause memory fragmentation. Fortunately, there is a way to protect against it. If you've ever used `std::string` (post GCC 5.0), you most probably used an optimization called **small string optimization (SSO)** or **small buffer optimization (SBO)**. This is one example of a more general optimization named **small object optimization (SOO)**, which can be spotted in types such as Abseil's `InlinedVector`.

The main idea is pretty straightforward: if the dynamically allocated object is small enough, it should be stored inside the class that owns it instead of being dynamically allocated to avoid additional dynamic memory allocations. In the case of `std::string`, usually, there's a capacity, length, and the actual string to store. If the string is short enough (in GCC's case, on 64-bit platforms, it's 15 bytes), it will be stored in some of those members.

Storing objects in place instead of allocating them somewhere else and storing just the pointer has one more benefit: less pointer chasing. Each time you need to access data stored behind a pointer, you increase the pressure on the CPU caches and risk needing to fetch data from the main memory. If this is a common pattern, it can influence the overall performance of your app, especially if the pointed-to addresses aren't guessed by the CPU's prefetcher. Using techniques such as SSO, SBO, and SOO is invaluable in reducing those issues.

This example implements the technique, including the implementation of copy and move constructors and assignment operators.

First, the class is defined with dual storage—a fixed-size inline buffer for short strings and a heap-allocated buffer for longer ones:

```
class String final {
    static const std::size_t BUF_SIZE = 15;

    union {
        char buffer[BUF_SIZE + 1];
        char* data;
    };
    std::size_t size{};
```

Here, the class uses a union to hold either the inline buffer or a pointer to heap memory. Both members occupy the same memory location, which allows the class to switch between inline and dynamic storage depending on the string length.

Next, we define a helper function to determine which field of the union to use: the built-in fixed-length array, `buffer`, or the pointer to dynamic memory, `data`:

```
[[nodiscard]] bool is_small_string() const noexcept { return size <= BUF_SIZE;
}
public:
```

In the next code snippet, the constructor fixes the string's storage mode at initialization, so its memory location or length does not change later:

```
explicit String(const char *s) {
    size = strlen(s);
    data = !is_small_string() ? new char[size] : buffer;
    memcpy(data, s, size + 1);
};

~String() {
    if (!is_small_string()) {
        delete[] data;
    }
}
```

The copy and move constructors call their corresponding assignment operators recursively, which simplifies the implementation and avoids code duplication:

```
String(const String& other) {*this = other;}
    String &operator=(const String &other) {
        if (this != &other) {
            if (!is_small_string()) {
                delete[] data;
        }

       size = other.size;
       if (!is_small_string()) {
           data = new char[size];
           memcpy(data, other.data, size + 1);
        } else {
            memcpy(buffer, other.buffer, size + 1);
        }
    }
    return *this;
};

String(String &&other) noexcept { *this = std::move(other); }
```

```
String &operator=(String &&other) noexcept {
    if (this != &other) {
        size = other.size;
        if (!is_small_string()) {
            data = other.data;
        } else {
            memcpy(buffer, other.buffer, size + 1);
        }

        other.size = 0;
        other.data = nullptr;
        }
    return *this;
}
```

This implementation follows the common pattern of SSO/SBO described in Raymond Chen's blog and similar discussions. While this simplified version illustrates the idea clearly, real-world implementations also add refinements such as better exception safety (using copy-and-swap).

Then, one array subscript operator is used to get and set values:

```
char &operator[](std::size_t idx) {
    return !is_small_string() ? data[idx] : buffer[idx];
}
```

This `const` function copies the return value because `char` is a primitive type. In general, such a member function returns a `const&` reference:

```
char operator[](std::size_t idx) const {
    return !is_small_string() ? data[idx] : buffer[idx];
}

[[nodiscard]] std::size_t length() const noexcept { return size; }
```

Here, the `friend` function is justified because it simplifies the implementation and encapsulates the internal details of the class:

```
    friend std::ostream &operator<<(std::ostream &os, const String &s) {os <<
(!s.is_small_string() ? s.data : s.buffer);
    return os;
    }
};
```

Before SSO became the norm, some `std::string` implementations used a different strategy.

Saving memory by herding COWs

Older `std::string` implementations used a different optimization called **copy-on-write** (COW). In this implementation, multiple instances created with the same underlying character array shared the same memory address for the array. When the string was written to, the underlying storage was copied—hence the name.

However, retaining pointers and references to internal string data is still unsafe because the internal data may be reallocated when the string is modified. This optimization was dropped in C++11 due to dangling pointers and references in some cases.

In our example, the string `s` and its copy share the same underlying data, but the call to `operator[]` triggers memory reallocation. Therefore, `p` becomes a dangling pointer when the copy goes out of scope:

```
std::string s("sample");
const char* p = s.data();
{
    std::string copy = s;
```

```
    std::cout << s[0] << std::endl; // COW triggers memory reallocation
  }
  std::cout << *p << '\n';  // p is dangling
```

This technique helped save memory and keep the caches hot and often offered solid performance on a single thread. Beware of using it in multi-threaded contexts, though. The need for using locks can be a real performance killer. As with any performance-related topic, it's best to just measure whether, in your case, it's the best tool for the job.

Let's now discuss a feature of C++17 that can help you achieve good performance with dynamic allocations.

Leveraging polymorphic allocators

The feature we're talking about is polymorphic allocators. To be specific, `std::pmr::polymorphic_allocator` and the polymorphic `std::pmr::memory_resource` class that the allocator uses to allocate memory.

In essence, these allocators allow you to easily chain memory resources to make the best use of your memory. Chains can be as simple as one resource that reserves a big chunk and distributes it, falling back to another that simply calls `new` and `delete` if it depletes memory. They can also be much more complex: you can build a long chain of memory resources that handle pools of different sizes, offer thread-safety only when needed, bypass the heap and go for the system's memory directly, return the last freed chunk of memory to provide cache hotness, and do other fancy stuff. Not all these capabilities are offered by the **Polymorphic Memory Resource** (**PMR**) library, but thanks to their design, it's easy to extend them.

Let's first tackle the topic of memory arenas.

Using memory arenas

A memory arena, also called a region, zone, area, or memory context, is just a large chunk of memory that exists for a limited time. You can use it to allocate smaller objects that you use for the lifetime of the arena. Objects in the arena can be either deallocated as usual or erased all at once in a process called *winking out*. We'll describe it later on.

Arenas have several great advantages over the usual allocations and deallocations—they increase performance because they limit the memory allocations that need to grab upstream resources. Region-based memory management also reduces the fragmentation of memory, because any fragmentation that happens will happen inside the arena. Once an arena's memory is released, the fragmentation is no more either. A great idea is to create separate arenas per thread. If only a single thread uses an arena, it doesn't need to use any locking or other thread-safety mechanisms, reducing thread contention and giving you a nice boost in performance.

To effectively use memory arenas, you need a way to construct objects directly inside a pre-allocated block of memory. This is where placement new comes into the picture. Placement new is a C++ feature that allows you to explicitly construct objects at specific memory addresses without performing additional allocations.

Historically, C++ has provided placement new and delete operators to construct and destruct objects at specific addresses, including memory-mapped hardware regions. Bjarne Stroustrup described placement syntax in his book *The Design and Evolution of C++* in 1994. Placement syntax is useful to control where objects are placed in memory for implementing custom memory management, object pools, placement in shared memory, constructing objects in pre-allocated buffers, preventing exceptions, and performance optimizations in embedded systems or real-time applications.

C++ also provides the `std::nothrow` constant from `<new>`, which returns `nullptr` instead of throwing a `std::bad_alloc` exception. Moreover, standard containers such as `std::vector` use placement new to construct elements in pre-allocated buffers.

Here is a simple example using placement syntax that just capitalizes three letters in the buffer. It demonstrates the fundamental idea behind placement new: constructing objects directly at specific memory locations:

```
char buffer[] = "into the eagle's nest";

const auto p1 = new (buffer) cha('I');
const auto p2 = new (buffer + 9) char('E');
const auto p3 = new (buffer + 17) char('N');
```

Avoid this syntax as much as possible unless you really need it and know what you are doing because this syntax causes errors that are hard to work with both at compile time and runtime.

Before we go further, let's create the simple `Point` structure, which will be used in the following examples:

```
struct Point {
    double x, y;

    constexpr bool operator==(const Point &) const noexcept = default;
};
```

C++20 introduced `std::construct_at` and `std::ranges::construct_at` functions as safer alternatives to create an object initialized with given arguments at a given address. Note the latter one is invisible to ADL. These functions may be used in the evaluation of constant expressions evaluated at compile time. There are several approaches to apply them:

```
constexpr auto N = 51.528100;
constexpr auto E = 45.977859;

alignas(Point) unsigned char buf[sizeof(Point)];
Point *ptr = std::construct_at(reinterpret_cast<Point *>(buf), N, E);
const bool res{*ptr == Point{N, E}};
std::destroy_at(ptr);
```

Since `reinterpret_cast` is not a constant expression, a safer alternative for trivially copyable objects is `std::bit_cast`, which can be evaluated at compile time. (Trivially copyable means that an object can be copied using primitive memory operations such as `memcpy` or `memmove`.)

Regardless of whether you use `reinterpret_cast` or `bit_cast`, you must still explicitly destroy the object when done. The `std::destroy_at` function template handles this:

```
alignas(Point) unsigned char buf[sizeof(Point)];
auto p = std::bit_cast<Point>(buf);
std::destroy_at(&p);

Point *ptr = std::construct_at(std::addressof(p), N, E);
const bool res{*ptr == Point{N, E}};
std::destroy_at(ptr);
```

Now that we've seen the library-based approach with `construct_at` and `bit_cast`, let's return to the placement new syntax itself and look at how it can be extended through operator overloading.

Placement syntax allows overloading the operator new and operator delete functions to support custom allocators and arenas. The `void* operator new (size_t, void* buffer)` and `void operator delete(void*, void*)` functions are in the `<new>` header and cannot be redefined, but you can add class-specific overloads that take additional arguments:

```
struct Point final {
    double x, y;

    Point(double x, double y) : x(x), y(y) {
        std::cout << "Point(" << x << ',' << y << ')' << std::endl;
        // throw std::runtime_error("Point(): std::runtime_error");
    }
    Point() : Point(0, 0) { std::cout << "Point(0, 0)" << std::endl; }

    ~Point() { std::cout << "~Point()" << std::endl; }
};

void *operator new(std::size_t size, std::byte *buffer) {
    std::cout << "operator new " << size << " bytes" << std::endl;
    return ::operator new(size, static_cast<void *>(buffer));
}

void operator delete(void *ptr, std::byte *buffer) {
    std::cout << "operator delete at " << ptr << std::endl;
    ::operator delete(ptr, static_cast<void *>(buffer));
}
```

Placement syntax has its own peculiarities, and when using custom placement new/delete, a few rules are worth remembering: You need to call the destructors explicitly, but not the delete operator; you can omit the destructors if the objects are entirely in the buffer and do not manage other resources. Also, the placement delete operator is only called to prevent a memory leak if a constructor throws an exception while constructing an object with placement new:

```
try {
    std::array<std::byte, 1024> buffer;
    auto *p1 = new (buffer.data()) Point{48.290178, 37.171792};
    p1->x = 52.194845;
    p1->y = 20.924213;
const auto *p2 = new (&buffer[sizeof(Point)]) Point{53.946519, 27.688998};

    std::cout << "p1.x=" << p1->x << " p1.y=" << p1->y << std::endl;
    std::cout << "p2.x=" << p2->x << " p2.y=" << p2->y << std::endl;

    p1->~Point();
    p2->~Point();
} catch (const std::exception &ex) {
    std::cout << ex.what() << '\n';
}
```

The preceding examples illustrate why placement new is important—it enables creating objects directly within existing storage. It would be impossible to create objects within existing storage without features such as placement new or `std::construct_at`. These give you fine-grained, low-level control over object construction in existing memory. C++17 added a higher-level abstraction for managing memory more flexibly—the PMR library, found primarily in the `<memory_resource>` header and `std::pmr` namespace.

For example, if your program is single-threaded, a low-cost solution to increase its performance could be as follows:

```
auto single_threaded_pool = std::pmr::unsynchronized_pool_resource();
std::pmr::set_default_resource(&single_threaded_pool);
```

The default resource, if you don't set any explicitly, will be `new_delete_resource`, which calls `new` and `delete` each time—just like regular `std::allocator` does—with all the thread-safety it provides (and costs).

If you use the preceding code snippet, all the allocations done using `pmr` allocators will be done with no locks. You still need to use the `pmr` types, though. To do so with standard containers, for instance, you need to simply pass `std::pmr::polymorphic_allocator<T>` as the allocator template parameter. Many standard containers have `pmr`-enabled type aliases. The two variables created next are of the same type, and both will use the default memory resource:

```
auto ints = std::vector<int, std::pmr::polymorphic_
allocator<int>>(std::pmr::get_default_resource());
auto also_ints = std::pmr::vector<int>{};
```

The first one gets the resource passed explicitly, though. Let's now go through the resources available in `pmr`.

Using the monotonic memory resource

The first one we'll discuss is `std::pmr::monotonic_buffer_resource`. It's a resource that only allocates memory and doesn't do anything on deallocation. It will only deallocate memory when the resource is destroyed, or on an explicit call to `release()`. This, connected with no thread safety, makes this type extremely performant. If your application occasionally needs to perform a task that does lots of allocations on a given thread, then releases all the objects used at once afterward, using monotonic resources will yield great gains. It's also a great base building block for chains of resources.

Using pool resources

A common combo of two resources is to use a pool resource on top of a monotonic buffer resource. The standard pool resources create pools of different-sized chunks. There are two types in `std::pmr`, `unsynchronized_pool_resource` for use when only one thread allocates and deallocates from it, and `synchronized_pool_resource` for multi-threaded use. Both should provide you with much better performance compared to the global allocator, especially when using the monotonic buffer as their upstream resource. If you're wondering how to chain them, here's how:

```
auto buffer = std::array<std::byte, 1 * 1024 * 1024>{};
auto monotonic_resource = std::pmr::monotonic_buffer_resource{buffer.data(),
buffer.size()};
auto pool_options = std::pmr::pool_options{.max_blocks_per_chunk = 0,.largest_
required_pool_block = 512};
auto arena =std::pmr::unsynchronized_pool_resource{pool_options, &monotonic_
resource};
```

We create a 1 MB buffer for the arena to reuse. We pass it to a monotonic resource, which is then passed to an unsynchronized pool resource, creating a simple yet efficient chain of allocators that won't call `new` until all the initial buffer is used up.

You can pass a `std::pmr::pool_options` object to both the pool types to limit the max count of blocks of a given size (`max_blocks_per_chunk`) or the size of the largest block (`largest_required_pool_block`). Passing `0` causes the implementation's default to be used. In the case of GCC's library, the actual blocks per chunk differ depending on the block size. If the max size is exceeded, the pool resource will allocate directly from its upstream resource. It also goes to the upstream resource if the initial memory was depleted. In this case, it allocates geometrically growing chunks of memory.

Writing your own memory resource

If the standard memory resources don't suit all your needs, you can always create a custom one quite simply. For instance, a good optimization that not all standard library implementations offer is to keep track of the last chunks of a given size that were released and return them on the next allocations of given sizes. This `Most Recently Used` cache can help you increase the hotness of data caches, which should help your app's performance. You can think of it as a set of last-in, first-out queues for chunks.

Sometimes you might also want to debug allocations and deallocations. The following snippet shows a simple resource that can help you with this task:

```
class verbose_resource : public std::pmr::memory_resource {
    std::pmr::memory_resource *upstream_resource_;
public:
    explicit verbose_resource(std::pmr::memory_resource *upstream_resource)
        : upstream_resource_(upstream_resource) {}
```

The `verbose resource` class inherits from the polymorphic base resource. It also accepts an upstream resource, which it will use for actual allocations. It has to implement three private functions—one for allocating, one for deallocating, and one for comparing instances of the resource itself. Here's the first one:

```
private:
    void *do_allocate(size_t bytes, size_t alignment) override {
        std::cout << "Allocating " << bytes << " bytes\n";
        return upstream_resource_->allocate(bytes, alignment);
    }
```

All it does is print the allocation size on the standard output and then use the upstream resource to allocate memory. The next one will be similar:

```
void do_deallocate(void *p, size_t bytes, size_t alignment) override {
    std::cout << "Deallocating " << bytes << " bytes\n";
    upstream_resource_->deallocate(p, bytes, alignment);
}
```

We log how much memory we deallocate and use the upstream to perform the task. The last required function is stated next:

```
[[nodiscard]] bool
do_is_equal(const memory_resource &other) const noexcept override {
    return this == &other;
}
```

We simply compare the addresses of the instances to know whether they're equal. The `[[nodiscard]]` attribute helps us be sure that the caller actually consumes the returned value, which can help us avoid accidental misuse of our function.

That's it. For a powerful feature such as the pmr allocators, the API isn't that complex now, is it?

Aside from tracking allocations, we can also use pmr to guard us against allocating when we shouldn't.

Ensuring there are no unexpected allocations

The special `std::pmr::null_memory_resource()` call will throw an exception when anyone tries to allocate memory using it. You can safeguard from performing any allocations using pmr by setting it as the default resource, as shown next:

```
std::pmr::set_default_resource(null_memory_resource());
```

You can also use it to limit allocation from the upstream when it shouldn't happen. Check the following code:

```
auto buffer = std::array<std::byte, 640 * 1024>{}; // 640K ought to be enough
for anybody
auto resource = std::pmr::monotonic_buffer_resource{
    buffer.data(), buffer.size(), std::pmr::null_memory_resource()};
```

If anybody tries to allocate more than the buffer size we set, `std::bad_alloc` will be thrown.

Let's move on to our last item in this chapter.

Winking out memory

Sometimes, not having to deallocate the memory, as the monotonic buffer resource does, is still not enough for performance. A special technique called **winking out** can help here. Winking out objects means that they're not only not deallocated one by one, but their destructors aren't called either. All the objects simply evaporate at once, and the used arena memory is reclaimed, saving time that would normally be spent calling destructors for each object and their members (and their members...) in the arena. Therefore, no side effects are allowed in destructors when using the technique! Objects in the arena should not acquire resources outside the arena because those resources are not released when destructors are skipped.

This is an advanced topic. Be careful when using this technique and only use it if the possible gain is worth it.

This technique can save your precious CPU cycles, but it's not always possible to use it. Avoid winking out memory if your objects handle resources other than memory. Otherwise, you will get resource leaks. The same goes if you depend on any side effects the destructors of your objects would have.

Let's now see winking out in action:

```
auto verbose = verbose_resource(std::pmr::get_default_resource());
auto monotonic = std::pmr::monotonic_buffer_resource(&verbose);
std::pmr::set_default_resource(&monotonic);
```

```
auto alloc = std::pmr::polymorphic_allocator{};
auto *vector = alloc.new_object<std::pmr::vector<std::pmr::string>>();
vector->push_back("first one");
vector->emplace_back("long second one that must allocate");
```

Here, we created a polymorphic allocator manually that'll use our default resource—a monotonic one that logs each time it reaches upstream. To create objects, we use a C++20 addition to `pmr`, the `new_object` function. We create a vector of strings. We can pass the first one using `push_back`, because it's small enough to fit into the small-string buffer we have, thanks to SSO. The second string would need to allocate a string using the default resource and only then pass it to our vector if we used `push_back`. Emplacing it causes the string to be constructed inside the vector's functions (not before the call), so it will use the vector's allocator. Finally, we don't call the destructors of allocated objects anywhere and just deallocate everything at once when we exit the scope. This should give us hard-to-beat performance.

Let's look at one more example. This `Test` class prints messages for demonstration purposes when an object is created and destroyed:

```
struct Test final {
    std::string name;

    explicit Test(std::string n) : name(std::move(n)) {
        std::cout << "Constructed: " << name << '\n';
    }

    ~Test() {
        std::cout << "Destructed: " << name << '\n';
    }
};
```

This snippet creates a PMR arena and places objects in the arena by using placement syntax:

```
std::cout << "Creating arena and constructing objects manually...\n";

std::byte buffer[1024];
std::pmr::monotonic_buffer_resource arena{buffer, sizeof(buffer)};

void* mem1 = arena.allocate(sizeof(Test), alignof(Test));
new (mem1) Test("Alpha");

void* mem2 = arena.allocate(sizeof(Test), alignof(Test));
new (mem2) Test("Beta");
```

```
std::cout << "Constructed 2 objects. Exiting scope...\n";

// No destructors are called!
```

The allocated memory is deallocated when the PMR allocator goes out of scope. The example prints the "Constructed" messages, but no "Destructed" messages, because the destructor is not called at all. The objects are *winked out*:

```
Creating arena and constructing objects manually...
Constructed: Alpha
Constructed: Beta
Constructed 2 objects. Exiting scope...
```

That was the last item on our list for this chapter. Let's summarize what we've learned.

Summary

In this chapter, we went through various idioms and patterns used in the C++ world. You should now be able to write fluent, idiomatic C++. We've demystified how to perform automatic cleanup and write safer types that properly move, copy, and swap. You learned how to use ADL to improve both compilation performance and the design of customization points. We discussed how to choose between static and dynamic polymorphism. We also learned how to introduce policies to your types and when to use type erasure and the explicit object parameter, a C++23 feature known as `deducing this`.

What's more, we discussed how to create objects using factories and fluent builders. We also explored region-based memory management with arenas. Also, writing state machines with tools such as `std::variant` should no longer be a mystery to you.

We did all that while also touching on extra topics down the road. Phew! The next stop on our journey will be building your software and packaging it.

Questions

1. What are the rules of three, five, and zero?
2. When do we use niebloids versus hidden friends?
3. How can array interfaces be improved to be more production-ready?
4. What are fold expressions?
5. When shouldn't you use static polymorphism?
6. What facilities does C++ have for placing objects in a pre-allocated buffer? What are the reasons for this?
7. How can we save on one more allocation in the winking out example?

Further reading

- Lewis Baker, Eric Niebler, and Kirk Shoop, *tag_invoke: A General Pattern for Supporting Customisable Functions* (ISO C++ proposal P1895): `https://www.open-std.org/jtc1/sc22/wg21/docs/papers/2019/p1895r0.pdf`

- Gašper Ažman, *tag_invoke :: niebloids Evolved* (Conference talk), Core C++ Meetup: `https://www.youtube.com/watch?v=oQ26YL0J6DU`
- Sean Parent, *Inheritance Is The Base Class of Evil* (Conference talk), GoingNative 2013: `https://learn.microsoft.com/en-us/shows/goingnative-2013/inheritance-base-class-of-evil`
- Scott Meyers, *How Non-Member Functions Improve Encapsulation*: `https://www.aristeia.com/Papers/CUJ_Feb_2000.pdf`
- Abseil, *Returning a Status or a Value, Status User Guide*: `https://abseil.io/docs/cpp/guides/status#returning-a-status-or-a-value`
- Bartłomiej Filipek, *How To Use std::visit with Multiple Variants and Parameters* (Blog), C++ Stories: `https://www.bfilipek.com/2018/09/visit-variants.html`
- Andreas Fertig, *Visiting a std::variant Safely* (Blog), Andreas Fertig's Blog: `https://andreasfertig.com/blog/2023/07/visiting-a-stdvariant-safely/`
- Mateusz Pusz, *Effective Replacement of Dynamic Polymorphism with std::variant* (Conference talk), CppCon 2018: `https://www.youtube.com/watch?v=gKbORJtnVu8`
- C++ Reference, *Constrained Algorithms (Since C++20)* (niebloids): `https://en.cppreference.com/w/cpp/algorithm/ranges`
- C++ Reference, *C++ Named Requirements: Allocator*: `https://en.cppreference.com/w/cpp/named_req/Allocator`
- C++ Reference, *Explicit Object Member Functions* (deducing this): `https://en.cppreference.com/w/cpp/language/member_functions#Explicit_object_member_functions`
- ISO C++, *What is "Placement New" and Why Would I Use It?*: `https://isocpp.org/wiki/faq/dtors#placement-new`
- ISO C++, *Is There a Placement Delete?*: `https://isocpp.org/wiki/faq/dtors#placement-delete`
- Eli Bendersky, *The Cost of Dynamic (Virtual Calls) vs. Static (CRTP) Dispatch in C++*, Eli Bendersky's Website: `https://eli.thegreenplace.net/2013/12/05/the-cost-of-dynamic-virtual-calls-vs-static-crtp-dispatch-in-c`
- Raymond Chen, *Inside STL: The String*, Microsoft: `https://devblogs.microsoft.com/oldnewthing/20230803-00/?p=108532`

7

Building and Packaging

Now that we've explored how to design robust systems and their components using modern C++ and established patterns, this chapter focuses on how to build and package those systems for production.

This chapter will explain all the elements that make up the build process. From compiler flags to automation scripts and beyond, we will guide you to the point where each possible module, service, and artifact is versioned and prepared for deployment. We will mainly focus on CMake.

You will learn how to create build systems based on Modern CMake, use external code in CMake, build reusable components, and create DEB, RPM, and AppImage packages using CPack.

In this chapter, you'll learn about the following:

- Getting the most out of compilers
- Abstracting the build process
- Using external modules
- Reusing quality code

After reading this chapter, you'll know how to write state-of-the-art code for building and packaging your project.

Technical requirements

To replicate the examples from this chapter, you should install a recent version of **GCC** and **Clang**, CMake 3.28 or higher, Conan, and Ninja.

The source code snippets from the chapter can be found at `https://github.com/PacktPublishing/Software-Architecture-with-Cpp-2E/tree/main/Chapter07`.

Getting the most out of compilers

Compilers are one of the most important tools in every programmer's workshop. That's why getting to know them well can help you out in many different ways, on countless occasions. In this section, we'll describe a few tips to use them effectively.

This will only touch the tip of the iceberg, as whole books can be written about these tools and their vast variety of available flags, optimizations, functionalities, and other specifics. GCC even has a wiki page with a list of books about compilers! You can find it in the *Further reading* section at the end of this chapter.

In the following sections, we'll explore several practical ways to get more out of your compiler and your build process. We'll start by looking at how using multiple compilers can improve portability, catch more issues, and help optimize performance. Then, we'll discuss strategies for reducing build times. Next, we'll cover how to find potential code issues early by enabling the right warnings and using diagnostic options effectively. Finally, we'll examine compiler-centric tools that can automate formatting, perform static analysis, and help you detect subtle bugs before they reach production.

Using multiple compilers

One of the things you should consider in your build process is using multiple compilers instead of just one, the reason being the several benefits that come with it. For instance, they can detect different issues with your code. As an example, **Microsoft Visual** C++ (**MSVC**) has signedness checks enabled by default. Moreover, using several compilers can help with potential portability issues you may encounter in the future, especially when a decision is made to also compile your code on a different **operating system** (**OS**), such as moving from Linux to Windows or the other way. To go to such efforts at no cost, you should strive to write portable, ISO C++-compliant code.

Each compiler has its benefits with respect to conformation with standards. For example, **Clang** strives for compliance with the C++ standards more than GCC. If you're using **MSVC**, try adding the `/permissive-` option (available since Visual Studio 2017 version 15.5; enabled by default for projects created using version 15.5+) to ensure standard compliance. When using **GCC**, try not to use the GNU variants when choosing the C++ standard for your code; instead, prefer, for example, `-std=c++17` over `-std=gnu++17`, to avoid GNU-specific extensions and ensure your code remains fully portable.

If performance is your goal, being able to build your software with a wide range of compilers will also allow you to pick the one that will offer the fastest binaries for your specific use cases.

Regardless of which compiler you choose for your release builds, consider using Clang for development. It runs on macOS, Linux, and Windows, supports the same set of flags as GCC, and aims to provide the fastest build times and concise compilation errors.

Using multiple compilers also facilitates a valuable strategy called cross-compilation, which means creating executables for a platform other than the one on which the compilation occurs. It helps catch implicit type errors, since the same library, depending on the OS, can use different data types. For instance, the C++ REST SDK defines the `utility::string_t` type, which resolves to two incompatible string types depending on the OS: as `std::wstring` using UTF-16 on Windows and as `std::string` using UTF-8 on **Portable Operating System Interface** (**POSIX**) platforms—in particular, Linux, macOS, Solaris, FreeBSD, Android, and iOS. The statement "it works on my machine" is not an argument. This discrepancy often stems from differences in environments.

To take advantage of multi-compiler builds and cross-compilation, you'll need a flexible build system. This is where CMake comes in, being a software development tool for building, testing, packaging, and distributing cross-platform software via compiler-independent instructions. If you're using CMake, you have two common ways to add another compiler. One is to pass the appropriate compilers when invoking CMake, like so:

```
cmake -S . -B ./build -DCMAKE_BUILD_TYPE=Release -DCMAKE_C_COMPILER=/usr/bin/
gcc -DCMAKE_CXX_COMPILER=/usr/bin/g++
```

It's also possible to just set CC and CXX before invoking CMake, but those variables are not honored by all build generators (for example, Visual Studio on Windows) and must be set before running CMake in a new build directory:

```
export CC=/usr/bin/clang
export CXX=/usr/bin/clang++
cmake -S . -B ./build -DCMAKE_BUILD_TYPE=Release
```

Another approach is to use toolchain files. It's probably overkill if you just need to use a different compiler, but it's the go-to solution when you want to cross-compile. To use a toolchain file, you should pass it as a CMake argument: `-DCMAKE_TOOLCHAIN_FILE=toolchain.cmake`.

The toolchain file describes the target platform and therefore contains mandatory and optional settings such as `CMAKE_SYSTEM_NAME`, `CMAKE_SYSTEM_VERSION`, `CMAKE_SYSTEM_PROCESSOR`, `CMAKE_C_COMPILER`, and `CMAKE_CXX_COMPILER`. Here's an example:

```
SET(CMAKE_SYSTEM_NAME Linux)
SET(CMAKE_SYSTEM_PROCESSOR x86_64)
SET(CMAKE_CROSSCOMPILING FALSE
SET(CMAKE_C_COMPILER gcc
SET(CMAKE_CXX_COMPILER g++)

if(CMAKE_BUILD_TYPE MATCHES "Debug")
  ADD_DEFINITIONS(-rdynamic)
endif()
```

Now that we've explored how using multiple compilers can improve portability and performance, let's turn to another equally important aspect of working with compilers—reducing build times.

Reducing build times

Every year, programmers spend countless hours waiting for their builds to complete. Reducing build times is an easy way to improve the productivity of whole teams, so let's discuss a few compiler- and toolchain-related approaches to doing it.

Using a fast compiler

One of the simplest ways to have faster builds is sometimes to upgrade your compiler. For instance, Clang 7.0.0 introduced **precompiled header (PCH)** files, which can significantly reduce build times as they work by compiling commonly used headers once and reusing them, instead of compiling them repeatedly for every source file. Since Clang 9, the `-ftime-trace` option has been added, which can provide you with information on the compilation times of all the files it processes; other compilers offer similar capabilities, too: check out GCC's `-ftime-report` or MSVC's `/Bt` and `/d2cgsummary`. These tools reveal where compilation time is spent and, therefore, can help you identify which compiler and configuration work best for your workflow. Sometimes, you can get faster compiles by switching the compiler, which is especially useful on your development machine, but the impact varies by project and environment.

Once you have a fast compiler, let's take a look at what it needs to compile.

Rethinking templates

Different parts of the compilation process take different amounts of time to complete. This is especially important for compile-time constructs and templates. For instance, the `qsort` function from C is compiled faster than `std::sort` from C++ because the C++ function is a template, and almost every use of `std::sort` creates a different instance of this template when parsed in a translation unit.

One of Odin Holmes' interns, Chiel Douwes, created the so-called **Rule of Chiel**, based on benchmarking the compile-time costs of various template operations. This rule describes which C++ constructs are the most difficult ones for the compiler. So, avoid these constructs whenever possible to reduce compilation times. This, and other type-based template metaprogramming tricks, can be seen in the *Type Based Template Metaprogramming is Not Dead* lecture by Odin Holmes, which has performance charts. In C++20, it is also tempting to start using concepts and `requires`-clauses instead of SFINAE.

According to the rule, operations can be ranked from fastest to slowest in terms of compile-time cost, as follows:

- Looking up a memoized type (by retrieving it from cache instead of performing repeated computations)
- Adding a parameter to an alias call
- Adding a parameter to a type
- Calling an alias
- Instantiating a type
- Instantiating a function template
- **Substitution failure is not an error** (SFINAE)

To demonstrate this rule, consider the following code, in which the compiler only needs to look up a memoized type via an alias (the fastest operation on the list):

```
template<bool>
struct conditional {
  template<typename T, typename F>
```

```
    using type = F;
};

template<>
struct conditional<true> {
    template<typename T, typename F>
    using type = T;
};

template<bool B, typename T, typename F>
using conditional_t = conditional<B>::template type<T, F>;
```

It defines a `conditional` template alias, which stores a type that resolves as `T` if condition `B` is true, and to `F` otherwise.

The traditional way to write such a utility would be as follows:

```
template<bool B, class T, class F>
struct conditional {
    using type = T;
};

template<class T, class F>
struct conditional<false, T, F> {
    using type = F;
};

template<bool B, class T, class F>
using conditional_t = conditional<B,T,F>::type;
```

However, this second way is slower to compile than the first because it relies on creating template instances instead of type aliases, which requires the compiler to generate new specializations rather than reuse existing types.

Let's now take a look at what tools and their features you can use to keep compile times low.

Leveraging tools

A common technique that can make your builds faster is to use a **single compilation unit build**, or a **unity build**. It won't speed up every project, but it may be worth a shot if there's plenty of code in your header files. Unity builds work by just including all your `.cpp` files in one translation unit.

But the fusion of header and source files in this way eliminates the separation of interface and implementation, and not all valid C++ code continues to compile due to clashes of defined symbols and leaked preprocessor identifiers. Moreover, compilation of a translation unit might require a lot of memory depending on the number of included files.

The `static` keyword also has no meaning since all C++ files are included in one translation unit. In a unity build, everything is compiled every time at once and not parallelized. Therefore, the order of inclusion and composition of unity builds matter.

Another similar idea is to use PCHs. CMake 3.16 added native support for both unity builds and PCHs. You can enable unity builds either for one target, `set_target_properties(<target> PROPERTIES UNITY_BUILD ON)`, or globally by setting `CMAKE_UNITY_BUILD` to `true`. For PCHs, you might want to take a look at CMake 3.16's `target_precompile_headers`. In this case, when building the target, a header file including all the necessary headers is created first, which is used to generate the precompiled header file artifact, to speed up subsequent compilations.

If you feel like you are including too much in your C++ files, consider using a tool named **include-what-you-use** to tidy them up. Preferring forward-declaring types and functions to including header files can also go a long way in reducing the compilation times.

C++20 offered C++ modules as a modern alternative to PCHs. Modules are self-contained, reusable units of code replacing source file inclusion with a structured binary interface. Only exported names are visible outside these modules, not macros, preprocessor directives, or internal declarations, which often significantly reduces compilation times. According to Alibaba, the use of C++ modules over traditional header files reduced the compilation time of their Alibaba Hologres project, a unified real-time data warehousing service, by 42% (`https://www.alibabacloud.com/blog/601974`). C++ modules are described in *Chapter 9, The Future of C++ Code Reuse: Using Modules*.

If your project takes forever to link, there are some ways to deal with this as well. Using a different linker, such as LLVM's LLD or GNU's Gold, can help a lot, especially since they allow multi-threaded linking. If you can't afford to use a different linker, you can always experiment with flags such as `-fvisibility-hidden` or `-fvisibility-inlines-hidden` and mark only the functions you want to have visible in your shared library with an appropriate annotation in the source code. This way, the linker will have less work to perform. If you're using link-time optimization, try to only do that for the builds that are performance-critical: those that you plan to profile and those meant for production. Otherwise, you'll probably just waste your developers' time.

If you're using CMake and aren't tied to a specific generator, you can replace the default Make generator with a faster one. **Ninja** is a great one to start with, as it was created specifically to reduce build times. To use it, just pass `-G Ninja` when invoking CMake.

There are still two more great tools that will surely give you a boost. One of them is **Ccache**. It's a tool that runs its cache of C and C++ compilation outputs. If you're trying to build the same thing twice, it will get the results from the cache instead of running the compilation. It keeps the statistics, such as cache hits and misses, can remember the warnings that it should emit when compiling a specific file, and has many configuration options that you can store in the `~/.ccache/ccache.conf` file. To obtain its statistics, just run `ccache --show-stats`.

The second tool is **IceCC** (or **Icecream**). It's a fork of distcc, essentially a tool to distribute your builds across hosts. With IceCC, it's easier to use a custom toolchain. It runs the `iceccd` daemon on each host and an `icecc-scheduler` service that manages the whole cluster. The scheduler, unlike in distcc, makes sure to only use the idle cycles on each machine, so you won't end up overloading other people's workstations.

To use both IceCC and Ccache for your CMake builds, just add the following to your CMake invocation:

```
-DCMAKE_C_COMPILER_LAUNCHER="ccache;icecc"
-DCMAKE_CXX_COMPILER_LAUNCHER="ccache;icecc"
```

If you're compiling on Windows, instead of the last two tools, you could use clcache and Incredibuild or look for other alternatives such as sccache, homcc, or FASTBuild.

Now that you know how to build fast, let's move on to another important topic.

Finding potential code issues

Even the quickest builds aren't worth much if your code has bugs. There are dozens of compiler flags to warn you of potential issues in your code. This section will try to answer which ones you should consider enabling.

First, let's start with a slightly different matter: how not to get warned about issues with code from other libraries. Getting warned about issues that you can't really fix isn't useful. Fortunately, there are compiler switches to disable such warnings. In GCC, for instance, you have two types of `include` files: regular (passed using `-I`) and system ones (passed using `-isystem`). If you specify a directory using the latter, you won't get warnings from the headers it contains. MSVC has `-isystem`: `/external:I` to offer the same functionality. Additionally, it has other flags to handle external includes, such as `/external:anglebrackets`, which tells the compiler to treat all files included using angle brackets as external ones, thus disabling warnings for them. You can specify a warning level for external files. You can also keep warnings coming from template instantiations caused by your code using `/external:templates-`. If you're looking for a portable way to mark `include` paths as system/external ones, and you're using CMake, you can add the `SYSTEM` keyword to a `target_include_directories` directive.

Speaking of portability, if you want to be conformant to a C++ standard (and you should), consider adding `-pedantic` to your compile options for GCC or Clang, or the `/permissive-` option for MSVC. This way, you'll get informed about every non-standard extension that you might be using. If you're using CMake, add the following line for each of your targets: `set_target_properties(<target> PROPERTIES CXX_EXTENSIONS OFF)`, to disable compiler-specific extensions. The most convenient option is to set the global behavior with `set(CMAKE_CXX_EXTENSIONS OFF)`. However, this may not be feasible if your `CMakeLists.txt` is included from some higher-level project. The other usually set options are `CMAKE_CXX_STANDARD` and `CMAKE_CXX_STANDARD_REQUIRED`.

If you're using MSVC, strive to compile your code with `/W4/WX`, since it enables most of the important warnings. For GCC and Clang, try to use `-Wall -Wextra -Wpedantic -Werror`. The first one, despite its name, enables only some common warnings. The second, however, adds another bunch of warnings. The third one is based on the tips from a great book by Scott Meyers, titled *Effective C++* (it's a set of good warnings, but check that it's not too noisy for your needs). The last two are about type conversions and signedness conversions. All those flags together create a sane safety net, but you can, of course, look for more flags to enable. Clang has a `-Weverything` flag. Try to periodically run a build with it to discover new, potential warnings that could be worth enabling in your code base. You might be surprised at how many messages you get with this flag, although enabling some of the warning flags might not be worth the hassle. An MSVC alternative is named `/Wall`. Take a look at the following tables to see some other interesting options that are not enabled by the preceding ones:

Flag	**Meaning**
`-Wduplicated-cond`	Warn when the same condition is used in `if` and `else-if` blocks.
`-Wduplicated-branches`	Warn if both branches contain the same source code.
`-Wlogical-op`	Warn when operands in logical operations are the same and when a bitwise operator should be used instead.
`-Wnon-virtual-dtor`	Warn when a class has virtual functions but not a virtual destructor.
`-Wnull-dereference`	Warn about null dereferences. This check may be inactive in unoptimized builds.
`-Wuseless-cast`	Warn when casting to the same type.
`-Wshadow`	A whole family of warnings about declarations that shadow other, previous declarations.

Table 5.1: Additional GCC/Clang warning flags

Flag	**Meaning**
`/w44640`	Warn on non-thread-safe static member initialization.

Table 5.2: Additional MSVC warning flags

One last thing worth mentioning is this: whether to use `-Werror` (or `/WX` on MSVC) or not. This really depends on your personal preferences, as issuing errors instead of warnings has its pros and cons. On the plus side, you won't let any of your enabled warnings slip by. Your CI build will fail, and your code won't compile. When running multi-threaded builds, you won't lose any warnings in the quickly passing compilation messages.

However, there are certain downsides too. You won't be able to upgrade your compiler if it enables any new warnings or just detects more issues. The same goes for dependencies, which can deprecate some functions they provide. You won't be able to deprecate anything in your code if it's used by other parts of your project.

Fortunately, you can always use a mixed solution: strive to compile with `-Werror`, but unset this option (for example, by removing it from your compiler flags) when you need to do the things it inhibits. This requires discipline, as if any new warnings are to slip in, you may have a hard time eliminating them.

The next section covers the powerful ecosystem of compiler-centric tools.

Using compiler-centric tools

Nowadays, compilers allow you to do much more with them than a few years back. This is owing to the introduction of LLVM and Clang. By providing APIs and a modular architecture allowing easy reuse, LLVM and Clang have enabled tools such as sanitizers, automatic refactoring utilities, and code completion engines to flourish. You should consider taking advantage of what this compiler infrastructure offers you.

Use `clang-format`, a tool to format C/C++ code, to ensure all the code in your code base conforms to a given coding style, resulting in a consistent and readable code base. Consider adding pre-commit hooks using the `pre-commit` tool to reformat new code before it is committed. You can also add Python and CMake formatters to the mix. Statically analyze source code using Clang diagnostics, Clang static analyzer and `clang-tidy`—a linter tool for diagnosing and fixing typical programming errors such as style violations, interface misuse, and errors deduced via static analysis. There's a ton of different checks this tool can perform for you, so be sure to customize the list and options to your specific needs. You can also run nightly or weekly tests of your software with sanitizers enabled. This way, you can detect threading issues, undefined behavior, memory access, management issues, and more. Running tests using debug builds can also be of value if your release builds have assertions disabled.

If you think that more could be done, you can consider writing your own code refactorizations using Clang's infrastructure. There's already a `clang-rename` tool if you want to see how to create an LLVM-based tool of your own. Additional checks and fixes for clang-tidy are also not that hard to create, and they can save you hours of manual labor.

Beyond Clang-based tools, there are many other tools you can integrate into your building process. The alternatives to Clang tools are static analyzers such as cppheck, PVS-Studio, Coverity Scan, and OCLint; dynamic analyzers such as Valgrind, CHAP, and Google sanitizers; and linters such as cpplint and SonarLint.

Since the build system is at the heart of managing such integrations, let's now turn to that topic.

Abstracting the build process

In modern C++ development, you rarely interact directly with low-level build tools, as maintaining separate build scripts for each environment is time-consuming and error-prone. Therefore, you work through an abstraction layer that hides platform-specific details and lets you describe what to build rather than how to build it.

In this section, we'll discuss CMake, the de facto standard for this role. It is a build system generator used for C++ projects worldwide. What does it mean that CMake is a build system generator and not a build system per se? Simply that CMake can be used to generate various types of build systems. You can use it to generate build files for a wide range of environments, including Visual Studio projects, Makefile projects, Ninja-based ones, Sublime, Eclipse, and Xcode.

CMake also comes with a set of other tools, such as CTest for executing tests, CDash for aggregating, analyzing, and displaying the test results, and CPack for packaging and creating setup programs. CMake itself allows exporting and installing targets too.

Many popular IDEs, such as CLion, C++ Builder, Qt Creator, KDevelop, Visual Studio, and VSCode (via a plugin), support CMake. Competing build system generators and meta-build tools include Ninja, Meson, and Bazel, as well as Xmake, Pixi, Mamba, Premake, SCons, and BitBake.

Getting started with CMake

CMake's generators can be either single-configuration, such as Make or NMAKE, or multi-configuration, such as Visual Studio or Ninja Multi-Config. For single-configuration ones, you should pass the `CMAKE_BUILD_TYPE` flag when running the generation for the first time in a folder. For instance, to configure a debug build, you could run the following:

```
cmake <project_directory> -DCMAKE_BUILD_TYPE=Debug
```

CMake will then produce a configuration log to record certain events that occurred during the configuration step. Other predefined configurations are `Release`, `RelWithDebInfo` (release with debug symbols), and `MinSizeRel` (release optimized for minimum binary size). To keep your source directories clean, always create a separate build folder and run CMake generation from there.

Although it's possible to add your own build type, you should really strive not to do so, as this complicates usage of some IDEs and doesn't scale well. A much better option is to use, well, `option`.

CMake files can be written in two styles: an obsolete one, based on variables, and a target-based Modern CMake style. We'll focus just on the latter here. Try to avoid setting things through global variables, as this causes issues when you want to reuse your targets.

Starting with CMake 3.27, you can debug CMake scripts by using debuggers such as GDB, LLDB, and Visual Studio Debugger, and IDEs such as CLion, Qt Creator, Visual Studio, and VS Code supporting the **Debug Adapter Protocol** (**DAP**), which makes the development simpler. Previously, CMake scripts were debugged only by outputting execution information.

Creating CMake projects

Each CMake project should have the following lines in its top-level `CMakeLists.txt` file:

```
cmake_minimum_required(VERSION 3.28...3.31)

project(
  Customer
  VERSION 0.0.1
  LANGUAGES CXX)
```

Setting a minimum and a maximum supported version is important as it influences how CMake will behave by setting policies, but usually a minimum version is enough. You can also set them manually if needed by using the `cmake_policy()` command.

The definition of our project specifies its name, version (which will be used to populate a few variables), and the programming languages that CMake will use to build the project (which populates many more variables and finds the required tools).

A typical C++ project has the following directories:

```
cmake: For CMake scripts
include: For public headers, usually with a subfolder named after the project
src: For source files and private headers
test: For tests
```

Some projects add directories for third-party libraries via Git submodules or by simply copying, but this approach can complicate maintenance and updates. Thus, it is recommended to link external libraries to projects by means of package managers.

You can use the CMake directory to store your custom CMake modules. To have easy access to scripts from this directory, you can add it to CMake's `include()` search path, like so:

```
list(APPEND CMAKE_MODULE_PATH "${CMAKE_CURRENT_LIST_DIR}/cmake")
```

When including CMake modules, you can omit the `.cmake` suffix. This means `include(CommonCompileFlags.cmake)` is equal to just `include(CommonCompileFlags)`.

Navigating through the directories in CMake has a common pitfall: not everyone is aware of the subtle differences between its built-in directory variables. The next section explains these variables and how to distinguish between them.

Distinguishing between CMake directory variables

Try to distinguish between the following built-in variables when writing CMake scripts:

```
PROJECT_SOURCE_DIR: The directory where the project command was last called
from a CMake script.
PROJECT_BINARY_DIR: Like the preceding one, but for the build directory tree.
```

```
CMAKE_SOURCE_DIR: Top-level source directory (this may be in another project
that just adds ours as a dependency/subdirectory).
CMAKE_BINARY_DIR: Like CMAKE_SOURCE_DIR, but for the build directory tree.
CMAKE_CURRENT_SOURCE_DIR: The source directory corresponding to the currently
processed CMakeLists.txt file.
CMAKE_CURRENT_BINARY_DIR: The binary (build) directory matching CMAKE_CURRENT_
SOURCE_DIR.
CMAKE_CURRENT_LIST_DIR: The directory of CMAKE_CURRENT_LIST_FILE. It can be
different from the current source directory if the current CMake script was
included from another one (common for CMake modules that are included).
```

Having cleared that up, let's now start navigating through those directories.

In your top-level `CMakeLists.txt` file, you will probably want to call `add_subdirectory(src)` so that CMake will process that directory.

After learning how CMake organizes and references its various directories, the next step is to put that knowledge to use by defining actual build outputs.

Specifying CMake targets

In the `src` directory, you should have another `CMakeLists.txt` file, this time probably defining a target or two. Let's add an executable for a customer microservice for the trade fair system we mentioned earlier in the book:

```
add_executable(customer main.cpp)
```

Source files can be specified as in the preceding code line or added later using `target_sources`.

A common CMake antipattern is the use of globs to specify source files. A big drawback of using them is that CMake will not know whether a file was added until it reruns generation. A common consequence of that is that if you pull changes from a repository and simply build, you can miss compiling and running new unit tests or other code. Even if you used globs with `CONFIGURE_DEPENDS`, the build time will get longer because globs must be checked as part of each build when the build system traverses the dependency graph. Besides, the flag may not work reliably with all generators. Even the CMake authors discourage using it in favor of just explicitly stating the source files.

Okay, so we defined our sources. Now, we specify that our target requires C++17 support from the compiler:

```
target_compile_features(customer PRIVATE cxx_std_17)
```

The `PRIVATE` keyword specifies that this is an internal requirement, that is, it is just visible to this specific target and not to any targets that will depend on it. In any case, mixing C++ language dialects across targets is impossible. If you were writing a header-only library that provided a user with a C++ API, you could use the `INTERFACE` keyword. To specify both the interface and internal requirements, you could use the `PUBLIC` keyword. When the consumer links to our target, CMake will then automatically require C++17 support for it as well. If you were writing a target that is not built (that is, a header-only library or an imported target), using the `INTERFACE` keyword is usually enough.

You should also note that specifying that our target wants to use C++17 features doesn't enforce the C++ standard or disallow compiler extensions for our target. To do so, you should instead call the following:

```
set_target_properties(customer PROPERTIES
  CXX_STANDARD 17
  CXX_STANDARD_REQUIRED YES
  CXX_EXTENSIONS NO)
```

If you want to have a set of compiler flags to pass to each target, you can store them in a variable and call the following if you want to create a target that has those flags set as `INTERFACE`, doesn't have any source, and uses this target in `target_link_libraries`:

```
target_compile_options(customer PRIVATE ${BASE_COMPILE_FLAGS})
```

The command automatically propagates include directories, options, macros, and other properties, aside from just adding a linker flag. Speaking of linking, let's create a library that we shall link with:

```
add_library(libcustomer responder.cpp controller.cpp)
add_library(tradefair::libcustomer ALIAS libcustomer)
set_target_properties(libcustomer PROPERTIES OUTPUT_NAME customer)
# ...
target_link_libraries(customer PRIVATE libcustomer)
```

The `add_library` command can be used to create static, shared, object, and interface (think header-only) libraries, as well as defining any imported libraries.

The `ALIAS` version of it creates a namespaced target, which helps debug many CMake issues and is a recommended Modern CMake practice.

Because we gave our target a `lib` prefix already, we set the output name to have `libcustomer.a` instead of `liblibcustomer.a`.

Finally, we link our executable with the added library. Try to always specify the `PUBLIC`, `PRIVATE`, or `INTERFACE` keyword for the `target_link_libraries` command, as this is crucial for CMake to effectively manage the transitivity of the target dependencies.

With our targets defined, the next step is deciding where CMake should place the build outputs.

Specifying the output directories

Once you build your code using commands such as `cmake --build .`, you might want to know where to find the build artifacts. By default, CMake will create them in a directory matching the source directory they were defined in. For instance, if you have a `src/CMakeLists.txt` file with an `add_executable` directive, then the binary will land in your build directory's `src` subdirectory by default. We can override this using code such as the following:

```
set(CMAKE_RUNTIME_OUTPUT_DIRECTORY ${PROJECT_BINARY_DIR}/bin)
set(CMAKE_ARCHIVE_OUTPUT_DIRECTORY ${PROJECT_BINARY_DIR}/lib)
set(CMAKE_LIBRARY_OUTPUT_DIRECTORY ${PROJECT_BINARY_DIR}/lib)
```

This way, the binaries and **dynamic link library** (DLL) files will land in the `bin` subdirectory of your project's build directory, while static and shared Linux libraries will be placed in the `lib` subdirectory.

With the basics in place, we can take advantage of one of CMake's most powerful features—generator expressions.

Using generator expressions

Setting compile flags in a way to support both single- and multi-configuration generators can be tricky, as CMake executes `if` statements and many other constructs at configure time, not at build/install time.

This means that the following is a CMake antipattern:

```
if(CMAKE_BUILD_TYPE STREQUAL Release)
  target_compile_definitions(libcustomer PRIVATE RUN_FAST)
endif()
```

Instead, generator expressions are the proper way to achieve the same goal, as they're processed at a later time. Let's see an example of their use in practice. Assuming you want to add a preprocessor definition just for your `Release` configuration, you could write the following:

```
target_compile_definitions(libcustomer PRIVATE "$<$<CONFIG:Release>:RUN_FAST>")
```

This will resolve to `RUN_FAST` only when building that one selected configuration. For others, it will resolve to an empty value. It works for both single- and multi-configuration generators. That's not the only use case for generator expressions, though.

Some aspects of our targets may vary when used by our project during builds and by other projects when the target is installed. A good example is **include directories**. A common way to deal with this in CMake is as follows:

```
target_include_directories(libcustomer PUBLIC $<INSTALL_INTERFACE:include>
                                              $<BUILD_INTERFACE:${PROJECT_SOURCE_DIR}/include>)
```

In this case, we have two generator expressions. The first one tells us that, when installed, the include files can be found in the `include` directory, relative to the install prefix (the root of the installation). If we're not installing, this expression will become an empty one. This is why we have another expression for building. This one will resolve as the `include` subdirectory of the directory where the last used `project()` was found.

Don't use `target_include_directories` with a path outside of your module. If you do, you're *stealing* someone's headers. This is a CMake antipattern. Instead, explicitly declare a library/target dependency.

CMake defines many generator expressions that you can use to query the compiler and platform, as well as the targets (such as full name, the list of object files, any property values, and so on). Aside from these, there are expressions that run Boolean operations, conditional statements, string comparisons, and more.

Now, for a more complex example, assuming you'd like to have a set of compile flags that you use across your targets and that depend on the compiler used, you could define it as follows:

```
list(
  APPEND
  BASE_COMPILE_FLAGS
  "$<$<OR:$<CXX_COMPILER_ID:Clang>,$<CXX_COMPILER_ID:AppleClang>,$<CXX_
COMPILER_ID:GNU>>:-Wall;-Wextra;-pedantic;-Werror>"
  "$<$<CXX_COMPILER_ID:MSVC>:/W4;/WX>")
```

This will append one set of flags if the compiler is Clang or AppleClang, or GCC and another one if MSVC is being used instead. Note that we separate the flags with a semicolon because that's how CMake separates elements in a list.

Let's now see how we could add external code to our projects.

Using external modules

There are several ways for you to fetch the external projects you depend on. For instance, you could add them as a Conan dependency, use CMake's `find_package` to look for a version provided by the OS or installed in another way, or fetch and compile the dependency yourself. The Conan package manager is described in the next chapter.

The key message of this section is: if you can, you should use a package manager. This way, you'll end up using one version of the dependency that matches your project's and its dependencies' requirements. Other well-known C++ package managers are vcpkg, Hunter, CPM, xrepo, Spack, and lesser-known ones are Buckaroo, Biicode, CGet, Teaport, and C++ Archive Network.

If you're aiming to support multiple platforms, or even multiple versions of the same distribution, using a package manager such as Conan or compiling everything yourself is the way to go. This way, you'll use the same dependency version regardless of the OS you compile on.

Fetching dependencies

One of the possible ways to prepare your dependencies from the source is to use CMake's built-in `FetchContent` module. It will download your dependencies and then build them for you as a regular target.

The feature arrived in CMake 3.11. It's a replacement for the `ExternalProject` module, which had many flaws. One of them was that it cloned the external repository during build time, so CMake couldn't reason about the targets that the external project defined, or their dependencies. This made many projects resort to manually defining the `include` directories and library paths of such external targets and ignoring their required interface compilation flags and dependencies completely. Ouch. `FetchContent` doesn't have such issues, so it's recommended you use it instead.

Before we show how to use it, you must know that both `FetchContent` and `ExternalProject` (as well as using Git submodules and similar methods) have one important flaw. If you have many dependencies using the same third-party library, you might end up with multiple versions of the same project, such as a few versions of Boost. Using package managers such as Conan can help you avoid such issues.

For the sake of an example, let's demonstrate how to integrate **GTest** into your project using the aforementioned `FetchContent` feature. First, create a `FetchGTest.cmake` file and put it in the `cmake` directory in our source tree. Our `FetchGTest` script will be defined as follows:

```
include(FetchContent)

FetchContent_Declare(
  googletest
  GIT_REPOSITORY https://github.com/google/googletest.git
  GIT_TAG v1.15.2
  EXCLUDE_FROM_ALL)

# For Windows: Prevent overriding the parent project's compiler/linker settings
set(gtest_force_shared_crt
    ON
    CACHE BOOL "" FORCE)
FetchContent_MakeAvailable(googletest)
message(STATUS "GTest binaries are present at ${googletest_BINARY_DIR}")
```

First, we include the built-in `FetchContent` module. Once the module is loaded, we declare the dependency using `FetchContent_Declare`. Then, we name our dependency and specify the repository that CMake will clone, along with the revision that it will check out. The `EXCLUDE_FROM_ALL` option will tell CMake not to build targets that are not needed by other targets when we run a command such as `make all`.

Now, we can make our external library available to the project if that wasn't done already. After successfully processing the library, our script will print a message denoting the directory in which GTests libraries will land after being built.

That chain of commands can be replaced with `CPM.cmake`, a configurable CMake script that wraps the `FetchContent` module to add dependency management capabilities to CMake: version checking, dependency caching, package lock files. You need to add `CPM.cmake` to your project to use this package manager. The link to detailed instructions is in the *Further reading* section. This script does what the preceding script does, additionally calling the `find_package()` command:

```
include(CPM)

CPMAddPackage(
```

```
  NAME googletest
  GITHUB_REPOSITORY google/googletest
  GIT_TAG v1.17.0
  VERSION 1.17.0
  EXCLUDE_FROM_ALL
  OPTIONS "BUILD_GMOCK OFF" "INSTALL_GTEST OFF" "gtest_force_shared_crt")
```

CMake 3.24 introduced dependency providers, which take integration a step further. A dependency provider controls how dependencies are provided to the project. This method connects third-party package managers to provide their libraries, include directories, and other details directly to CMake. An example of such a provider is the CMake-Conan dependency provider, a wrapper for Conan C and C++ package manager. IDEs such as CLion, Qt Creator, Visual Studio, and Visual Studio Code allow us to configure CMake in this way. You can pass the path to this provider as a CMake argument: `-DCMAKE_PROJECT_TOP_LEVEL_INCLUDES=conan_provider.cmake`. If your project depends on Conan, this provider completely takes care of downloading and installing project dependencies with the Conan package manager:

```
cmake -S . -B build -DCMAKE_PROJECT_TOP_LEVEL_INCLUDES=[path-to-cmake-conan]/
conan_provider.cmake -DCMAKE_BUILD_TYPE=Release
cmake --build build
```

If you're not fond of building your dependencies together with your project, perhaps the next way of integrating your dependencies will be more suitable for you.

Using find scripts

Assuming your dependency is available somewhere on your host, you can just call `find_package` to try to search for it. If your dependency provides a config or targets files (more on those later), then just writing this one simple command is all you need. That is, of course, assuming that the dependencies are already available on your machine. If not, it's your responsibility to install them before running CMake for your project.

To create the preceding files, your dependency would need to use CMake, which is not always the case. How could you deal with those libraries that don't use CMake? If the library is popular, chances are someone has already created a find script for you to use. The Boost libraries in versions older than 1.70 were a common example of this approach. CMake comes with a `FindBoost` module that you can execute by just running `find_package(Boost)`.

To find Boost using the preceding module, you would first need to install it on your system. After that, in your CMake lists, you should set any options that you find reasonable. For instance, to use dynamic and multi-threaded Boost libraries, not linked statically to the C++ runtime, specify the following:

```
set(Boost_USE_STATIC_LIBS OFF)
set(Boost_USE_MULTITHREADED ON)
set(Boost_USE_STATIC_RUNTIME OFF)
```

Then, you need to search for the library, as shown next:

```
find_package(Boost 1.69 EXACT REQUIRED COMPONENTS Beast)
```

Here, we specified that we want to just use Beast, a great networking library that comes as part of Boost. Once found, you could link it to your target as follows:

```
target_link_libraries(MyTarget PUBLIC Boost::Beast)
```

Now that you know how to properly use a find script, let's learn how to write one on your own.

Writing find scripts

If your dependency is neither providing config and target files nor has anyone written a find module for it, you can always write such a module yourself.

This is not something you'll do very often, so we'll try to just skim the topic. For an in-depth description, you should also read the guidelines in the official CMake documentation (linked in the *Further reading* section) or just look at a few find modules installed with CMake (usually in a directory such as `/usr/share/cmake-3.17/Modules` on Unix systems). For simplicity, we assume there's just one configuration of your dependency that you'd like to find, but it's possible to find `Release` and `Debug` binaries separately. This will result in different targets with different associated variables being set.

The script name determines the argument you'll pass to `find_package`; for example, if you wish to end up with `find_package(Foo)`, then your script should be named as follows:

```
FindFoo.cmake
```

`find_package()` has several search modes:

- MODULE looks for `Find<PackageName>.cmake`
- CONFIG looks for one of these: `<lowercasePackageName>-config.cmake`, `<PackageName>Config.cmake`, `<lowercasePackageName>-config-version.cmake`, or `<PackageName>ConfigVersion.cmake`
- Also, a call to `find_package()` can be redirected internally to a package provided by the `FetchContent` module

A good practice is to start your script with a `reStructuredText` section describing what your script will do, which variables it will set, and so on. An example of such a description could be as follows:

```
#.rst:
# FindMyDep
# ----------
#
# Find my favorite external dependency (MyDep).
#
# Imported targets
# ^^^^^^^^^^^^^^^^
```

```
#
# This module defines the following :prop_tgt:`IMPORTED` target:
#
# ``MyDep::MyDep``
#   The MyDep library, if found.
#
```

Usually, you'll also want to describe the variables your script will set:

```
# Result variables
# ^^^^^^^^^^^^^^^^
#
# This module will set the following variables in your project:
#
# ``MyDep_FOUND``
#   whether MyDep was found or not
# ``MyDep_VERSION_STRING``
#   the found version of MyDep
```

If `MyDep` has any dependencies itself, now is the time to find them:

```
find_package(Boost REQUIRED)
```

Now we can start our search for the library. A common way to do so is to use `pkg-config`:

```
find_package(PkgConfig)
pkg_check_modules(PC_MyDep QUIET MyDep)
```

If `pkg-config` has information on our dependency, it will set some variables we can use to find it.

A good idea might be to have a variable that the user of our script can set to point us to the location of the library. As per CMake conventions, it should be named `MyDep_ROOT_DIR`. To provide CMake with this variable, the user can either invoke CMake with `-DMyDep_ROOT_DIR=some/path`, modify the variable in `CMakeCache.txt` in their build directory, or use the `ccmake` (TUI) or `cmake-gui` programs.

Now, we can search for the headers and libraries of our dependency using the aforementioned paths:

```
find_path(
  MyDep_INCLUDE_DIR
  NAMES MyDep.h
  PATHS "${MyDep_ROOT_DIR}/include" "${PC_MyDep_INCLUDE_DIRS}"
  PATH_SUFFIXES MyDep)

find_library(
  MyDep_LIBRARY
  NAMES mydep
  PATHS "${MyDep_ROOT_DIR}/lib" "${PC_MyDep_LIBRARY_DIRS}"
```

Then, we also need to set the found version, as we promised in the header of our script. To use the one found from `pkg-config`, we could write the following:

```
set(MyDep_VERSION ${PC_MyDep_VERSION})
```

Alternatively, we can just manually extract the version from the contents of the header file, from components of the library path, or using any other means. Once this is done, let's leverage CMake's built-in scripts to decide whether the library was successfully found while handling all the possible parameters to the `find_package` invocation:

```
include(FindPackageHandleStandardArgs)

find_package_handle_standard_args(
  MyDep
  FOUND_VAR MyDep_FOUND
  REQUIRED_VARS MyDep_LIBRARY MyDep_INCLUDE_DIR
  VERSION_VAR MyDep_VERSION)
```

As we decided to provide a target and not just a bunch of variables, now it's time to define that target:

```
if(MyDep_FOUND AND NOT TARGET MyDep::MyDep)
  add_library(MyDep::MyDep UNKNOWN IMPORTED)
  set_target_properties(
    MyDep::MyDep
    PROPERTIES IMPORTED_LOCATION "${MyDep_LIBRARY}"
               INTERFACE_COMPILE_OPTIONS "${PC_MyDep_CFLAGS_OTHER}"
               INTERFACE_INCLUDE_DIRECTORIES "${MyDep_INCLUDE_DIR}")
endif()
```

Finally, let's hide our internally used variables for users who don't want to deal with them:

```
mark_as_advanced(MyDep_INCLUDE_DIR MyDep_LIBRARY)
```

Now, we have a complete find module that we can use in the following way:

```
find_package(MyDep REQUIRED)
target_link_libraries(MyTarget PRIVATE MyDep::MyDep)
```

This is how you can write the find module yourself.

Don't write `Find\*.cmake` modules for your own packages. Those are meant for packages that don't support CMake. Instead, write a `Config\*.cmake` module (as described later in this chapter).

Once our dependencies are set up, we can focus on testing our code.

Adding tests

CMake has its own test driver program named `CTest`. It's easy to add new test suites to it from your `CMakeLists` either on your own or using the many integrations provided by testing frameworks. We'll discuss testing in depth in *Chapter 10, Writing Testable Code,* but let's first show how to quickly and cleanly add unit tests based on the GoogleTest, or GTest, testing framework.

Usually, to define your tests in CMake, you'll want to write the following:

```
if(CMAKE_PROJECT_NAME STREQUAL PROJECT_NAME)
  include(CTest)
  if(BUILD_TESTING)
    add_subdirectory(test)
  endif()
endif()
```

The preceding snippet will first check whether the current project is the main project that's being built or not. Usually, you just want to run tests for your project and omit even building the tests for any third-party components you use. This is why the project name is checked. Since version 3.21, CMake provides the `PROJECT_IS_TOP_LEVEL` variable for this purpose, which simplifies the check:

```
if(PROJECT_IS_TOP_LEVEL)
  include(CTest)
  if(BUILD_TESTING)
    add_subdirectory(test)
  endif()
endif()
```

If we are to run our tests, we include the `CTest` module. This loads the whole testing infrastructure CTest offers, defines its additional targets, and calls a CMake function called `enable_testing`, which will, among other things, enable the `BUILD_TESTING` flag. This flag is cached, so you can disable all testing when building your project by simply passing a `-DBUILD_TESTING=OFF` argument to CMake when generating the build system.

All such cached variables are stored in a text file named `CMakeCache.txt` in your build directory. Feel free to modify the variables there to change what CMake does; it won't overwrite the settings there until you remove the file. You can do so using `ccmake`, `cmake-gui`, or manually.

If `BUILD_TESTING` is true, we simply process the `CMakeLists.txt` file in our test directory. It could look like so:

```
include(FetchGTest)
include(GoogleTest)

add_subdirectory(customer)
```

The first `include` calls the script for providing us with GTest that we described previously. After fetching GTest, our current `CMakeLists.txt` loads helper functions defined in the GoogleTest CMake module by invoking `include(GoogleTest)`. This enables us to integrate our tests into `CTest` more easily. Finally, we call `add_subdirectory(customer)` to tell CMake to dive into a directory that contains some tests.

The `test/customer/CMakeLists.txt` file will simply add an executable with tests that is compiled with our predefined set of flags and links to the tested module and GTest. Then, we call the CTest helper function that discovers the defined tests. All of this is just four lines of CMake code:

```
add_executable(unittests unit.cpp)
target_compile_options(unittests PRIVATE ${BASE_COMPILE_FLAGS})
target_link_libraries(unittests PRIVATE tradefair::libcustomer gtest_main)
gtest_discover_tests(unittests)
```

Voilà! `gtest_discover_tests()`, introduced in CMake 3.10, dynamically discovers tests. Alternatively, you can use `gtest_add_tests()` or `enable_testing()` with `add_test()` commands:

```
enable_testing()
add_test(NAME unittests COMMAND $<TARGET_FILE:unittests>)
```

You can now build and execute your tests by simply going to the `build` directory and calling the following:

```
cmake --build . --target unittests
ctest # or cmake --build . --target test
```

You can pass a `-j` flag for `CTest` to parallelize the test execution. It works just like with Make or Ninja invocations.

If you want to have a shorter command for building, just run your build system, that is, by invoking `make`.

In scripts, it's usually better to use the longer form of the command; this will make your scripts easier to comprehend and maintain.

Run the `cmake --build . --target help` command to get a *textual* list of targets.

In addition, CMake generates Graphviz target dependency graphs for C, C++, and Fortran, showing the dependencies between the targets in a project *visually* (see *Figure 7.1*):

```
cmake --graphviz=project.dot .. # point to a source directory
dot -T svg project.dot -o project.svg # or dotty project.dot
```

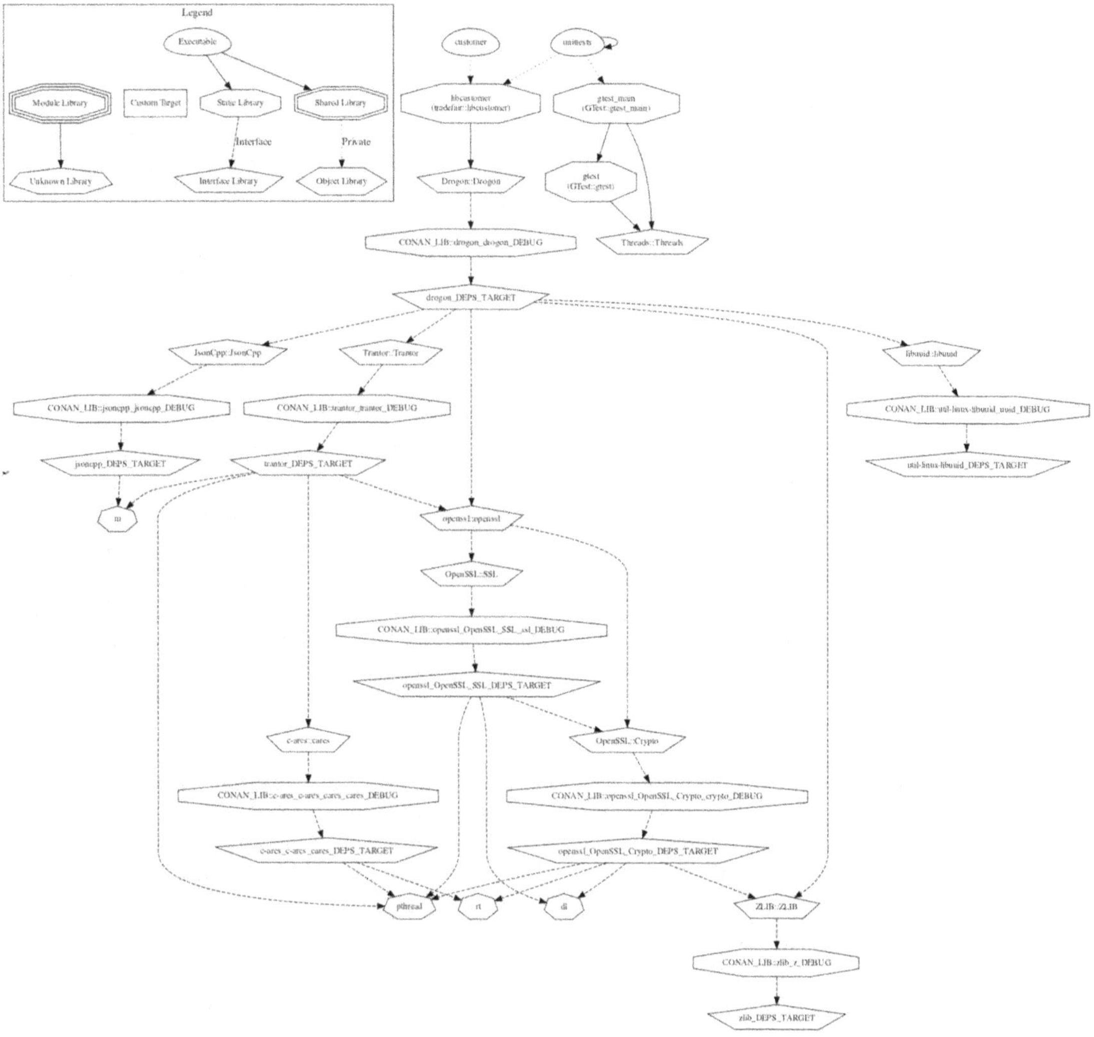

Figure 7.1: Visualizing module dependencies with CMake and Graphviz

Quick tip: Need to see a high-resolution version of this image? Open this book in the next-gen Packt Reader or view it in the PDF/ePub copy.

The next-gen Packt Reader and a **free PDF/ePub copy** of this book are included with your purchase. Scan the QR code OR visit `https://packtpub.com/unlock`, then use the search bar to find this book by name. Double-check the edition shown to make sure you get the right one.

Once your tests have passed, we can think about sharing them with a wider audience.

Reusing quality code

CMake has built-in utilities that can go a long way when it comes to distributing the results of your builds. This section will describe installing and exporting utilities, explain the differences between them, and show how to package your code using CPack.

Installing and exporting are not that important for microservices per se, but very useful if you're delivering libraries for others to reuse.

Installing

If you have written or used Makefiles, you've most probably invoked `make install` at one point and seen how the deliverables of a project were installed either in the OS directories or in another directory of your choosing. If you're using `make` with CMake, using the steps from this section will allow you to install the deliverables in the same way. If not, you'll still be able to call the install target, of course. Aside from that, in both cases, you will then have an easy way to leverage CPack for creating packages based on your installation commands.

If you're on Linux, it's probably a good idea to preset some installation directories based on the conventions of the OS by calling the following:

```
include(GNUInstallDirs) # set CMAKE_INSTALL_PREFIX to change the destination
```

This will make the installer use a directory structure made of `bin`, `lib`, and similar other directories. Such directories can also be set manually using a few CMake variables.

Creating an install target consists of a few more steps. First, define the targets we want to install, which in our case will be the following:

```
install(
  TARGETS libcustomer customer
  EXPORT CustomerTargets
  LIBRARY DESTINATION ${CMAKE_INSTALL_LIBDIR}
  ARCHIVE DESTINATION ${CMAKE_INSTALL_LIBDIR}
  RUNTIME DESTINATION ${CMAKE_INSTALL_BINDIR})
```

This tells CMake to expose our library and executable defined earlier in this chapter as `CustomerTargets`, using the directories we set earlier.

If you plan to install different configurations of your library in different folders, you could use a few invocations of the preceding command, like so:

```
install(
  TARGETS libcustomer customer
  CONFIGURATIONS Debug
  # destinations for other components go here...
```

```
    RUNTIME DESTINATION Debug/bin)
install(
    TARGETS libcustomer customer
    CONFIGURATIONS Release
    # destinations for other components go here...
    RUNTIME DESTINATION Release/bin)
```

You will notice that we specify the directories for executables and libraries, but not for include files. We need to provide them in another command, like so:

```
install(
    DIRECTORY ${PROJECT_SOURCE_DIR}/include/ # the last slash is important here
    DESTINATION include)
```

This means that the top-level `include` directory's contents will be installed in the `include` directory under the installation root. The slash after the first path fixes some path issues, so take note to use it.

So, we have our set of targets; now we need to generate a file that another CMake project could read to understand our targets. This can be done in the following way:

```
install(
    EXPORT CustomerTargets
    FILE CustomerTargets.cmake
    NAMESPACE tradefair::
    DESTINATION ${CMAKE_INSTALL_LIBDIR}/cmake/Customer)
```

This command takes our target set and creates a `CustomerTargets.cmake` file that will contain all the info about our targets and their requirements. Each of our targets will get prefixed with a namespace; for example, `customer` will become `tradefair::customer`. The generated file will get installed in a subdirectory of the library folder in our installation tree.

To allow dependant projects to find our targets using CMake's `find_package` command, we need to provide a `CustomerConfig.cmake` file. If your target doesn't have any dependencies, you can just export the preceding targets directly to that file instead of the `targets` file. Otherwise, you should write your own config file that will include the preceding `targets` file.

In our case, we want to reuse some CMake variables, so we need to create a template and use the `configure_file` command to fill it in:

```
configure_file(${PROJECT_SOURCE_DIR}/cmake/CustomerConfig.cmake.in
               CustomerConfig.cmake @ONLY)
```

Our `CustomerConfig.cmake.in` file will begin by dealing with our dependencies:

```
include(CMakeFindDependencyMacro)
find_dependency(drogon 1.9.10)
```

The `find_dependency` macro is a wrapper for `find_package` that is meant to be used in config files. Although we relied on the Conan package manager to provide us with the Drogon Framework 1.9.10 during development, as defined in `conanfile.txt`, here we need to specify the dependency once more. This package manager is described in the next chapter and mentioned here because it is important that the versions of Drogon match. Our package can be used on another machine, so we require that our dependency be installed there too. If you want to use Conan on the target machine, you can install the Drogon framework as follows:

```
conan install drogon/1.9.10
```

After dealing with the dependencies, our config file template will include the `targets` file that we created earlier:

```
if(NOT TARGET tradefair::@PROJECT_NAME@)
  include("${CMAKE_CURRENT_LIST_DIR}/@PROJECT_NAME@Targets.cmake")
endif()
```

When `configure_file` executes, it will replace all those `@VARIABLES@` with the contents of their matching `${VARIABLES}` defined in our project. This way, based on our `CustomerConfig.cmake.in` file template, CMake will create a `CustomerConfig.cmake` file.

When finding a dependency using `find_package`, you'll often want to specify a version of the package to find. To support that in our package, we must create a `CustomerConfigVersion.cmake` file. CMake offers us a helper function that will create this file for us. Let's use it as follows:

```
include(CMakePackageConfigHelpers)
write_basic_package_version_file(CustomerConfigVersion.cmake
                                 VERSION ${PACKAGE_VERSION}
                                 COMPATIBILITY AnyNewerVersion)
```

The `PACKAGE_VERSION` variable will get populated according to the `VERSION` argument we passed when calling `project` at the top of our top-level `CMakeLists.txt` file.

`AnyNewerVersion COMPATIBILITY` means our package will be accepted by any package search if it is newer or the same as the requested version. Other compatibility modes are `SameMajorVersion`, `SameMinorVersion`, and `ExactVersion`. Semantic versioning uses four numbers: major for incompatible API changes, minor for backward compatible changes, patch for backward compatible bug fixes, and the build number. These compatibility modes are taken into account by the `find_package()` command when working with version ranges, and they determine which CMake package will be selected.

Once we have created our config and config version files, let's tell CMake that they should be installed along with the binaries and our target file:

```
install(FILES ${CMAKE_CURRENT_BINARY_DIR}/CustomerConfig.cmake
              ${CMAKE_CURRENT_BINARY_DIR}/CustomerConfigVersion.cmake
        DESTINATION ${CMAKE_INSTALL_LIBDIR}/cmake/Customer)
```

One last thing we should install is the license for our project. We'll leverage CMake's command for installing files to put them in our documentation directory:

```
install(FILES ${PROJECT_SOURCE_DIR}/LICENSE
        DESTINATION ${CMAKE_INSTALL_DOCDIR})
```

That's all you need to know to successfully create an install target in the root of your OS. You may ask how to install the package in another directory, such as just for the current user. To do so, you would need to set the `CMAKE_INSTALL_PREFIX` variable, for example, when generating the build system.

Note that if we don't install into the root of our Unix tree, we'll have to provide the dependent project with a path to the installation directory, such as by setting `CMAKE_PREFIX_PATH`.

Let's now look at yet another way you could reuse what you just built.

Exporting

Exporting is a technique to add information about a package that you built locally to CMake's package registry. This is useful when you want your targets to be visible right from their build directories, even without installation. A common use for exporting is when you have several projects checked out on your development machine and you build them locally.

It's quite easy to add support for this mechanism from your `CMakeLists.txt` files. In our case, it can be done in this way:

```
export(
  TARGETS libcustomer customer
  NAMESPACE tradefair::
  FILE CustomerTargets.cmake)

set(CMAKE_EXPORT_PACKAGE_REGISTRY ON)
export(PACKAGE tradefair)
```

This way, CMake will create a targets file similar to the one from the *Installing* section, defining our library and executable targets in the namespace we provided. From CMake 3.15, the package registry is disabled by default, so we need to enable it by setting the appropriate preceding variable. Then, we can put the information about our targets right into the registry by exporting our package.

Note that we now have a `targets` file without a matching config file. This means that if our targets depend on any external libraries, they must be found before our package is found. In our case, the calls must be ordered in the following way:

```
find_package(drogon 1.9.10)
find_package(tradefair)
```

First, we find the Drogon framework, and only afterward do we look for our package that depends on it. That's all you need to know to start exporting your targets. Much easier than installing them, isn't it?

Let's now move on to a third way of exposing your targets to the external world.

Using CPack

In this section, we'll describe how to use CPack, the packaging tool that comes with CMake.

CPack allows you to easily create packages in various formats, ranging from ZIP and TGZ archives through to DEB and RPM packages, and even installation wizards such as NSIS or a few macOS-specific ones. Once you have your installation logic in place, it's not hard to integrate the tool. Let's show how to use CPack to package our project.

First, we need to specify variables that CPack will use when creating the packages:

```
set(CPACK_PACKAGE_VENDOR "Authors")
set(CPACK_PACKAGE_CONTACT "author@example.com")
set(CPACK_PACKAGE_DESCRIPTION_SUMMARY
    "Library and app for the Customer microservice")
set(CPACK_PACKAGE_DIRECTORY packages)
```

We need to give some information manually, but some variables can be filled based on our project version, specified when we defined our project. There are many more CPack variables, and you can read about all of them at the CPack link in the *Further reading* section at the end of the chapter. Some of them are common for all package generators, while some are specific to a few of them. For instance, if you plan to use the installers, you could set the following two:

```
set(CPACK_RESOURCE_FILE_LICENSE "${PROJECT_SOURCE_DIR}/LICENSE")
set(CPACK_RESOURCE_FILE_README "${PROJECT_SOURCE_DIR}/README.md")
```

Once you've set all the interesting variables, it's time to choose the generators for CPack to use. Let's start with putting some basic ones in `CPACK_GENERATOR`, which is a variable CPack relies on to execute chosen CPack generators:

```
list(APPEND CPACK_GENERATOR TGZ ZIP)
```

This will cause CPack to generate those TGZ and ZIP archives based on the installation steps we defined earlier in the chapter.

You can select different package generators based on many things—for example, the tools available on the machine you're running on. An example would be to create Windows installers when building on Windows and a DEB or RPM package if building on Linux with the appropriate tools installed. For instance, if you're running Linux, you could check whether `dpkg` is installed and, if so, create DEB packages:

```
if(LINUX)
  find_program(DPKG_PROGRAM dpkg)
  if(DPKG_PROGRAM)
    list(APPEND CPACK_GENERATOR DEB)
    set(CPACK_DEBIAN_PACKAGE_DEPENDS
        "${CPACK_DEBIAN_PACKAGE_DEPENDS} libdrogon1t64 (>= 1.8.7)"))
    set(CPACK_DEBIAN_PACKAGE_SHLIBDEPS ON)
```

```
  else()
    message(STATUS "dpkg not found - won't be able to create DEB
packages")
  endif()
endif()
```

We used the `CPACK_DEBIAN_PACKAGE_DEPENDS` variable to make the DEB package require the Drogon framework to be installed first.

For RPM packages, you could manually check for `rpmbuild`:

```
  find_program(RPMBUILD_PROGRAM rpmbuild)
    if(RPMBUILD_PROGRAM)
      list(APPEND CPACK_GENERATOR RPM)
      # The package does not exist for RPM-based Linux distributions, but #the
principle is the same
      # set(CPACK_RPM_PACKAGE_REQUIRES "${CPACK_RPM_PACKAGE_REQUIRES}")
    else()
      message(STATUS "rpmbuild not found - won't be able to create RPM
packages")
    endif()
  endif()
```

Nifty, right?

These generators offer a plethora of other useful variables, so feel free to look at CMake's documentation if you need anything more than those basic needs described here.

One last thing when it comes to variables—you can also use them to avoid accidentally packaging undesired files. This can be done by using the following:

```
set(CPACK_SOURCE_IGNORE_FILES /.git /dist /.*build.* /\\\\.DS_Store)
```

Once we have all that in place, we can include CPack itself from our CMake lists:

```
include(CPack)
```

Remember to always do this as the last step, as CMake won't propagate any variables you used later to CPack.

To run it, directly invoke either just `cpack` or the longer form, which will also check whether anything needs rebuilding first: `cmake --build . --target package`. You can easily override the generators if you just need to rebuild one type of package using the `-G` flag—for example, `-G DEB` to build just the DEB package, `-G WIX -C Release` to pack a release MSI executable, or `-G DragNDrop` to obtain a DMG installer.

Let's now discuss a more barbaric way of building packages. Some disadvantages of formats such as RPM and DEB are dependencies on other packages, which makes it difficult to install a package on another Linux distro or even a version of the same distro. There is even a term to describe this situation: dependency hell, like the DLL hell of Windows. Package formats such as Snap, Flatpak, and AppImage are intended to resolve this issue and make software distribution easier on Linux. All these formats bundle an application with its dependencies into a single package dependent on its runtime environment.

AppImage packages are regular executable files. `linuxdeploy` is a tool for assembling portable software in this format, which is not as popular as Snap or Flatpak. But AppImages does not require preparing a specific development environment, and that's the reason why we chose it to demonstrate custom packaging with the CPack External generator:

```
# linuxdeploy detects an executable file in this directory set(CPACK_PACKAGING_
INSTALL_PREFIX "/usr")
find_program(LINUXDEPLOY_PROGRAM NAMES linuxdeploy linuxdeploy-x86_64.AppImage
                                       linuxdeploy-aarch64.AppImage)
if(LINUXDEPLOY_PROGRAM)
  list(APPEND CPACK_GENERATOR External)
  configure_file(../../cmake/CPackExternal.cmake.in
                 "${CMAKE_BINARY_DIR}/CPackExternal.cmake" COPYONLY)
  set(CPACK_EXTERNAL_PACKAGE_SCRIPT
      "${CMAKE_BINARY_DIR}/CPackExternal.cmake")
  set(CPACK_EXTERNAL_ENABLE_STAGING YES)
  configure_file(../../resources/customer.desktop
                 "${CMAKE_BINARY_DIR}/customer.desktop" COPYONLY)
  configure_file(../../resources/customer.svg
                 "${CMAKE_BINARY_DIR}/customer.svg" COPYONLY)
else()
  message(STATUS"linuxdeploy not found - won't be able to create AppImage
executables")
endif()
```

The `customer.desktop` file is a desktop entry file. AppImage requires such files as entry points to run executables. The `configure_file()` command can replace variable references in text with their values:

```
[Desktop Entry]
Type=Application
Name=customer
Exec=customer
Icon=customer
Categories=Network
```

The CPACK_EXTERNAL_PACKAGE_SCRIPT variable points to a static or dynamically created CMake script. Regardless of how it is created, this script is isolated from the main project because CPack injects a limited set of variables into its environment. Therefore, the find_program() command is executed twice—once in the main project and once in the CPackExternal.cmake script.

This solution uses the fact that the CMAKE_CURRENT_LIST_DIR variable points to the CMAKE_BINARY_DIR directory, where the build resources are located. This works because, in our example, the CPackExternal.cmake script is copied to this directory:

```
find_program(LINUXDEPLOY_PROGRAM
NAMES linuxdeploy linuxdeploy x86_64.AppImage linuxdeploy-aarch64.AppImage
)
if(LINUXDEPLOY_PROGRAM)
    execute_process(
        COMMAND
         ${CMAKE_COMMAND} -E env
         LDAI_OUTPUT=${CPACK_PACKAGE_FILE_NAME}.appimage
         LINUXDEPLOY_OUTPUT_VERSION=$<IF:$<BOOL:${CPACK_PACKAGE_VERSION}>,
                ${CPACK_PACKAGE_VERSION},0.0.1>
                ${LINUXDEPLOY_PROGRAM}
                --output=appimage
                --appdir=${CPACK_TEMPORARY_DIRECTORY}
                --desktop-file=${CMAKE_CURRENT_LIST_DIR}/customer.desktop
                --icon-file=${CMAKE_CURRENT_LIST_DIR}/customer.svg
                --verbosity=2
        WORKING_DIRECTORY ${CPACK_PACKAGE_DIRECTORY}
    )
endif()
```

The configure_file() command has two ways to replace CMake variables in a text with actual values: ${VAR} and @VAR@, or @ONLY with @VAR@. In our case, the CPackExternal.cmake script is copied without any replacement. This script is rewritten when the CMake project is reconfigured and the linuxdeploy tool is found.

The customer.desktop entry file and customer.svg image can be copied to the /usr/share/applications/ and /usr/share/icons/hicolor/scalable/apps/ directories inside the AppImage package without passing them as -desktop-file and -icon-file options, because linuxdeploy can detect these files automatically. However, this approach is not used in our example.

A distributed AppImage package can be signed, and the signature validated, but this feature depends on OpenPGP encryption and signing tools. Please refer to Applmage, gpg, or gpg2 documentation for additional information.

Further, AppImage files can be mounted to observe or extract their content. Just add the `--appimage-mount` option when you run an AppImage executable file. This is a convenient format for distributing your programs that has its advantages and disadvantages.

Summary

In this chapter, you've learned a lot about building and packaging your code. You're now able to write faster-building template code, know how to choose the tools to compile your code faster, and know how to find potential code issues and use compiler-centric tools.

Aside from that, you can now define your build targets and test suites using Modern CMake, manage external dependencies using find modules and `FetchContent`, create packages and installers in various formats, and last but not least, use package managers to install your dependencies.

In the next chapter, we will look at package management, including project dependencies and building executables with Conan and Conan packages.

Questions

1. What's the difference between installing and exporting your targets in CMake?
2. How do you make your template code compile faster?
3. How can we ensure we force a specific C++ standard in CMake?
4. How would you build documentation in CMake and ship it along with your DEB and RPM packages?

Further reading

- GCC Wiki, *List of Compiler Books*: `https://gcc.gnu.org/wiki/ListOfCompilerBooks`
- C++ Reference, *C++ Compiler Support*: `https://en.cppreference.com/w/cpp/compiler_support`
- Odin Holmes, *Type Based Template Metaprogramming Is Not Dead* (Presentation), C++Now 2017: `https://youtu.be/EtU4RDCCsiU` `https://github.com/boostcon/cppnow_presentations_2017/blob/master/05-17-2017_wednesday/type_based_template_metaprogramming_is_not_dead__odin_holmes__cppnow_05-17-2017.pdf`
- Henry Schreiner, *An Introduction to Modern CMake*: `https://cliutils.gitlab.io/modern-cmake`
- *CPM.cmake*, GitHub: `https://github.com/cpm-cmake/CPM.cmake/`
- CMake, *A Sample Find Module* (Documentation on creating find scripts): `https://cmake.org/cmake/help/latest/manual/cmake-developer.7.html#a-sample-find-module`
- CMake, *CPack*: `https://cmake.org/cmake/help/latest/module/CPack.html`
- Rafał Świdziński, *Modern CMake for C++: Effortlessly Build Cutting-Edge C++ Code and Deliver High-Quality Solutions*, Second Edition, Packt Publishing: `https://www.packtpub.com/en-us/product/modern-cmake-for-c-9781805123361`

- Tom Hulton-Harrop, *Minimal CMake: Learn the Best Bits of CMake to Create and Share Your Own Libraries and Applications*, Packt Publishing: `https://www.packtpub.com/en-us/product/minimal-cmake-9781835080658`
- Dominik Berner and Mustafa Kemal Gilor, *CMake Best Practices: Upgrade Your C++ Builds with CMake for Maximum Efficiency and Scalability*, Second Edition, Packt Publishing: `https://www.packtpub.com/en-us/product/cmake-best-practices-9781835880654`
- Conan.io, *cmake-conan*, GitHub: `https://github.com/conan-io/cmake-conan`
- *Drogon Framework* (Documentation), GitHub: `https://drogonframework.github.io/drogon-docs/#/`
- Canonical Snapcraft, *About Snaps*: https://snapcraft.io/about
- Flatpak Documentation, *Terminology*: `https://docs.flatpak.org/en/latest/introduction.html#terminology`
- AppImage, *Packaging Native Binaries*: `https://docs.appimage.org/packaging-guide/from-source/native-binaries.html`
- *linuxdeploy*, GitHub: `https://github.com/linuxdeploy/linuxdeploy`
- Freedesktop.org, *Icon Theme Specification*: `https://specifications.freedesktop.org/icon-theme-spec/latest/`
- AppImage, *Signing AppImages*: `https://docs.appimage.org/packaging-guide/optional/signatures.html`
- Arch Linux Wiki, *GnuPG*: `https://wiki.archlinux.org/title/GnuPG`
- Alibaba Cloud, *42% Boost in Compilation Efficiency! A Practical Analysis of C++ Modules* (Blog): `https://www.alibabacloud.com/blog/42%25-boost-in-compilation-efficiency-a-practical-analysis-of-c%2B%2B-modules_601974`

8

Package Management

In the previous chapter, we briefly touched on package managers, noting that they can simplify dependency management and ensure consistency across environments. In this chapter, we will explore them in more detail, with a focus on Conan, a package manager dedicated to C and C++. Conan is feature-rich, integrates smoothly with CMake, and supports multiple platforms and compilers, making it worthy of detailed consideration.

The application of package management is a widely adopted practice because the compilation and installation of programs from source code on a target system may quickly lead to version conflicts or even the inability to update the system without breaking the applications. Packages help resolve these issues as they bundle source code, binaries, scripts, settings, and documentation, along with versioning requirements.

Package managers make life easier, especially compared to installing project dependencies manually. However, while CMake scripts have been backward compatible for many years, this is not the case with the Conan package manager. Conan versions 1 and 2 are not backward compatible, and there's a risk that this situation may repeat itself in the future. So, when choosing this package manager, you should be aware that migration from version to version requires some effort.

In this chapter, you'll learn about the following topics:

- Introduction to package management
- Using the Conan package manager
- Packaging using Conan

After reading this chapter, you'll also know how to install project dependencies, build artifacts with Conan, create Conan packages, and share them.

Technical requirements

You will need the following tools to build the code in this chapter: GCC14+ or Clang19+, CMake 3.28 or higher, and Conan.

The source code snippets from the chapter can be found at `https://github.com/PacktPublishing/Software-Architecture-with-Cpp-2E/tree/main/Chapter08`.

For instructions on setting up the Conan package manager, you should refer to this link: `https://github.com/PacktPublishing/Software-Architecture-with-Cpp-2E/tree/main/devenv_readme`.

Conan itself provides platform-specific installers here: `https://conan.io/downloads`.

Introduction to package management

Package management is the process of systematically installing, updating, configuring, and removing software packages. Package managers automate these tasks, ensuring that the required versions of packages are installed and their dependencies are resolved reliably.

Package management enhances code reuse and collaboration by facilitating the sharing and integration of libraries, tools, and frameworks across projects. It also simplifies project maintenance, saves cost and time, provides effortless environment setup, and ensures consistency across environments. Moreover, package managers must ensure that software comes from trusted sources and has not been tampered with. To achieve this, cryptographic signatures of packages are verified to confirm the packages' integrity. Additionally, it is recommended to update packages regularly to mitigate discovered vulnerabilities.

There are two common ways to classify packages and package managers. At the package level, we have ordinary packages and development packages. The former contains the files required for running software, while the latter also includes headers, libraries, and other files needed for building, testing, and publishing software. Thus, one could say that the distinction is not very significant. It mainly exists to hide internal details from end users, but they cannot be removed entirely because operating systems and software ecosystems are complex.

Different operating systems handle this distinction in different ways. Many Linux distributions come with separate development packages for building software from source and integrating this software with the distributions. On macOS, Homebrew (a popular package manager for macOS) does not differentiate these types of packages, as both are included by default. Windows installers, in contrast, usually do not have development packages, since applications are distributed primarily for end users rather than developers.

At the package-manager level, we distinguish between system-level and application-level package managers. System-level package managers (such as RPM, **Debian Package (dpkg)**, pacman, WinGet, and Homebrew) are used to install and manage software, libraries, and tools within an operating system. Application-level package managers (such as `pip` for Python, `npm` for the JavaScript runtime Node.js, NuGet for .NET, Cargo in Rust, and Alire in Ada) intend to manage dependencies and libraries at the project level. Conan fulfills this role for C and C++, serving as an application-level package manager dedicated to these languages.

In the next section, we will learn how to work with Conan effectively.

Using the Conan package manager

Conan is an open source, decentralized package manager for C and C++ that stores source code and precompiled binaries. Decentralization means that clients can fetch packages from as well upload packages to different servers. In contrast, a centralized system relies on a central repository where all packages are stored.

This package manager supports multiple platforms (Linux, FreeBSD, macOS, Solaris, Windows, Android, iOS, STM32, and ESP32) and compilers (GCC, Clang, and MSVC Compiler). The official documentation declares that Conan can be integrated with multiple build systems (CMake, Bazel, Meson, and Premake) and IDEs (CLion, Visual Studio, Android Studio, Xcode, and Qt Creator).

Any **integrated development environment** (**IDE**) can be integrated with Conan if the IDE supports customized CMake parameters. It is feasible as CMake 3.24 introduced dependency providers, which expand the scope of package managers. All you need is to configure the variable as follows:

```
CMAKE_PROJECT_TOP_LEVEL_INCLUDES=[path-to-cmake-conan]/conan_provider.cmake
```

This dependency provider will fetch and install Conan packages automatically.

Once integrated into the workflow, Conan relies on repositories for package distribution. Conan fetches packages from existing repositories. Once built, Conan packages can also be uploaded to either public or private Conan repositories. There are two options if you need to deploy your own repository: `conan_server` (for basic use) and JFrog Artifactory server (for enterprise workflows). Uploading binaries and sharing them is useful because it speeds up development since no one else, including you, needs to spend time compiling those binaries again.

Preparing Conan profiles

If this is the first time you're running Conan, it will create a default profile based on your environment. You might want to modify some of its settings either by creating a new profile or by updating the default one. Assuming we're using Linux and want to compile everything using GCC 14, we could run the following to create a Conan profile and adjust auto-detected values:

```
conan profile detect --name hosacpp
conan profile detect --name ./hosacpp
conan profile detect --name ../hosacpp
```

The profiles can be located in different folders, as absolute paths, relative paths, or within the `[CONAN_HOME]/profiles` directory. By default, `CONAN_HOME` points to the `<username>/.conan2` directory, and profile settings are written to the `<username>/.conan2/profiles/hosacpp` file. A sample configuration might look like this (note that `libstdc++` is an old ABI and `libstdc++11` is new):

```
[settings]
arch=x86_64
build_type=Release
compiler=gcc
```

```
compiler.cppstd=gnu23
compiler.cstd=gnu17
compiler.libcxx=libstdc++11
compiler.version=14
os=Linux
```

Conan profiles are Jinja2 templates, which are structured files containing tag blocks, variables, and instructions to generate settings dynamically. Jinja2 is a template engine written in Python, which allows Conan profiles to use variables and, if needed, import Python modules or include other files.

For example, consider a Conan profile named `Linux-x86_64-gcc-14`. Instead of writing its settings manually, we can define a template like this:

```
{% set os, arch, compiler, compiler_version = profile_name.split('-') %}
[settings]
os={{ os }}
arch={{ arch }}
compiler={{ compiler }}
compiler.version={{ compiler_version }}
```

The `conan profile show --profile Linux-x86_64-gcc-14` command generates these Conan profiles using the Jinja2 template:

```
Host profile:
[settings]
arch=x86_64
compiler=gcc
compiler.version=14
os=Linux

Build profile:
[settings]
arch=x86_64
build_type=Release
compiler=gcc
compiler.cppstd=gnu17
compiler.libcxx=libstdc++11
compiler.version=14
os=Linux
```

The preceding outcome shows that Conan has two profile models intended to cross-compile applications: `build`, where the binaries are built, and `host`, where the built binaries run.

If dependencies come from other repositories than the default ones, they are added using the `conan remote add <repo> <repo_url>` command.

Now that we've set Conan up, let's see how to define our dependencies using Conan and integrate them into our CMake scripts.

Specifying Conan dependencies

Our project relies on the Drogon web framework and GoogleTest, a testing and mocking framework. To tell this to Conan, we need to create either a `conanfile.txt` recipe file or a `conanfile.py` recipe script, but not both in the same directory, as this leads to ambiguity of which one to apply because they are mutually exclusive.

Here's an example of `conanfile.txt`:

```
[requires]
drogon/1.9.10

[test_requires]
gtest/1.16.0

[generators]
CMakeDeps
```

You can specify as many dependencies as you want here. Each can have a fixed version, a version range, or a specific recipe revision.

The `[generators]` section is where you specify what build systems you want to use. For CMake projects, you should use `CMakeDeps`. You can also generate lots of others, including ones for generating compiler arguments, CMake toolchain files, virtual environments, and many more.

In our case, we also disable Boost and database **object-relational mapping** (**ORM**), which are not used:

```
[options]
drogon/*:with_boost=False
drogon/*:with_orm=False
```

As seen in the preceding code, you can easily configure variables and dependencies for your package by adding an `[options]` section.

The `conanfile.txt` file is a simplified version of the more flexible `conanfile.py` script. While the former is suitable for basic dependency management and consumption, the latter is aimed at creating packages and expressing conditional requirements. The `conanfile.py` approach is flexible because Conan packages can be customized for different conditions: operating system, compilers and their versions, package versions, optional dependencies, and so on. This flexibility is often used to maintain backward compatibility of Conan packages.

Here's an example of `conanfile.py`. Each Conan recipe has logical blocks. This block defines metadata, default configuration, settings, and the other attributes of a package:

```
from conan import ConanFile
from conan.tools.build import can_run
from conan.tools.cmake import cmake_layout, CMake, CMakeDeps, CMakeToolchain

class CustomerConan(ConanFile):
    name = "customer"
    version = "0.0.1"
    license = "MIT"
    author = "Authors"
    homepage = "https://example.com"
    url = "https://github.com/PacktPublishing/Software-Architecture-with-Cpp-2E"
    description = "Library and app for the Customer microservice"
    topics = ("Customer", "tradefair")
    settings = "os", "compiler", "build_type", "arch"
    default_options = {"drogon/*:with_boost": "False", "drogon/*:with_orm": "False"}

    # export sources to generate the package
    exports_sources = "CMakeLists.txt", "LICENSE", "README.md", "cmake/*", "include/*", "src/*", "test/*"
```

In the preceding code, the attributes are obvious, except `topics` and `exports_sources`. The `topics` attribute is used to group related packages together and serves as a search filter. The `exports_sources` attribute (or function) is intended to copy files from the user folder to the Conan cache folders when running the `conan export` and `conan create` commands. In our example, the `default_options` attribute disables dependencies of the Drogon framework: the Boost library and ORM support used to map database tables and classes.

This block defines the requirements of the package:

```
    def requirements(self):
        # specifies the dependencies
        self.requires("drogon/1.9.10")

    def build_requirements(self):
        # specifies the test dependencies and build tools
        self.test_requires("gtest/1.15.0")
```

This block defines the project layout and prepares the build:

```
    def layout(self):
        # defines the project layout
        cmake_layout(self)

    def generate(self):
        # prepares the build
        deps = CMakeDeps(self)
        deps.generate()
        tc = CMakeToolchain(self)
        tc.generate()
```

This block handles building, installing, and testing the package:

```
    def build(self):
        # invokes the build system
        cmake = CMake(self)
        cmake.configure()
        cmake.build()
        if can_run(self):
            # runs tests particularly CTest
            cmake.test()

    def package(self):
        # copies files from the build to package folder
        cmake = CMake(self)
        cmake.install()
```

The last block defines how the package is consumed by others:

```
    def package_info(self):
        # provides information to consumers of this package
        self.cpp_info.libs = ["customer"] # the lib to link
```

Once we have `conanfile.py` in place, let's tell Conan to install the dependencies so Conan can use them in our project.

Installing Conan dependencies

To use our Conan packages in CMake code, we must first install them. In Conan, this means downloading the source code and building the packages or downloading prebuilt binaries. Moreover, Conan creates configuration files that we'll use in CMake to find packages provided by Conan.

To make Conan handle this for us, we should create the Conan profile and simply run the following (hosacpp is a Conan profile presented earlier in the chapter):

```
conan install . --build=missing -s build_type=Release -pr:a=hosacpp
```

By default, Conan wants to download all the dependencies as prebuilt binaries. If the server doesn't have them prebuilt, Conan will build them instead of bailing out as we passed the `--build=missing` flag. We tell it to grab the release versions built using the same compiler and environment as we have in our profile. You can install packages for more than one build type by simply invoking another command with `build_type` set to other CMake build types. This can help you quickly switch between them if needed. If you want to use the default profile (the one Conan can detect for you automatically), just don't pass the `-pr` flag.

If the CMake generator was not specified in `conanfile.txt`, we could append it to the preceding command. For instance, to use the `CMakeDeps` generator, we should append `--generator=CMakeDeps` to the preceding command.

Using Conan targets from CMake

Once Conan finishes downloading, building, and configuring our dependencies, we need to tell CMake to use them.

If you're using Conan with the `CMakeDeps` generator, be sure to specify a `CMAKE_BUILD_TYPE` value. Without this, CMake will be unable to use the packages configured by Conan. Here's an example invocation of our CMake project (run from the same directory you ran Conan):

```
cmake -S path/to/source/directory/containing/CMakeLists.txt
      -B path/to/build/directory/containing/Conan/dependencies
      -DCMAKE_BUILD_TYPE=Release
```

This way, we would build our project in release mode. The `CMAKE_BUILD_TYPE` value must match one of the types we installed using Conan.

To find our dependencies, we can just use CMake's `find_package()`:

```
list(APPEND CMAKE_PREFIX_PATH "${CMAKE_BINARY_DIR}")
find_package(Drogon REQUIRED)
```

First, we add the root build directory to the path CMake will try to find package files in. Then, we find the package files generated by Conan.

To pass Conan-defined targets as our targets' dependencies, it's best to use the namespaced target name:

```
target_link_libraries(libcustomer PUBLIC Drogon::Drogon)
```

This way, we'll get an error during CMake's configuration when the package is not found. Without the alias, we'd get an error when trying to link.

Now that we have compiled and linked our targets just the way we wanted, it's time to test, package, and publish our Conan package.

Packaging using Conan

The core packaging step in Conan involves the creation of a package. However, in practice, this step is usually preceded by testing and followed by publishing. In this section, we cover the complete workflow: testing, creating, and publishing a Conan package.

Packages should be validated before their publication, as malfunctioning packages can break development. Conan supports this validation process through a test package, which is used only during testing. Thus, the process of creating a Conan package involves two scripts, one of which is published, and the other that is not published but needed only for testing the package.

Testing our Conan package

Once Conan builds a package, it should test whether the package was properly built and can be correctly linked and reused by consumers in their own projects. In order to do so, let's start by creating a `test_package` subdirectory. It will include a `conanfile.py` script, but this time, a shorter one. It should start as follows:

```
import os
from conan import ConanFile
from conan.tools.build import can_run
from conan.tools.cmake import CMake, cmake_layout

class CustomerTestConan(ConanFile):
    settings = "os", "compiler", "build_type", "arch"
    generators = "CMakeDeps", "CMakeToolchain"
```

Nothing too fancy here. Now, we should provide the logic to build the test package:

```
    def layout(self):
        cmake_layout(self)

    def build(self):
        cmake = CMake(self)
        cmake.configure()
        cmake.build()
```

Then comes the heart of our package testing logic, which is the `test` method in `test_package/conanfile.py`:

```
    def test(self):
        if can_run(self):
            cmd = os.path.join(self.cpp.build.bindir, "example")
            self.run(cmd, env="conanrun")
```

We want to run it if we're building for our native architecture. Otherwise, we would most probably be unable to run the compiled executable.

Let's now define our `CMakeLists.txt` file:

```
cmake_minimum_required(VERSION 3.12)
project(PackageTest CXX)

list(APPEND CMAKE_PREFIX_PATH "${CMAKE_BINARY_DIR}")

find_package(customer CONFIG REQUIRED)

add_executable(example example.cpp)
target_link_libraries(example customer::customer)

# CTest tests can be added here
```

Simple as that. We link to all the Conan libraries provided (in our case, just our `customer` library).

Finally, let's write our `example.cpp` file with just enough logic to check whether the package was successfully created:

```
#include <customer/responder.h>
int main() { responder{}.prepare_response("Conan"); }
```

This test is automatically invoked at the end of commands such as `conan create` and `conan export-pkg` to verify that the package is created correctly. But the `customer` library can be tested explicitly by running `conan test test_package customer/0.0.1`.

Now, let's dive into creating and publishing Conan packages.

Creating and publishing our Conan package

In Conan, packages are first created in the local cache, where build systems can find them. For exporting files from the package folder to those Conan folders, you should declare the interchangeable `exports_sources` attribute or the `export_sources` method, but not both simultaneously, before executing the `conan create` and `conan export` commands, which create the package and export the recipe, respectively.

Once the attribute or method is defined, you can create the package by running one command:

```
conan create . --build=missing -pr:a=hosacpp
```

This command performs all recipe stages in the Conan cache folders rather than in the current project folder, except for running package tests in the `test_package` directory, which are run from the project folder to validate the built package.

Creating Conan packages without specifying exports_sources/export_sources is possible too. In this case, you need to install dependencies, then build and export the package by running several commands. This scenario is also used when developing Conan packages:

```
conan install . --build=missing -pr:a=hosacpp
conan build . -pr:a=hosacpp
conan export-pkg . -pr:a=hosacpp
```

Once a package is created and stored in the Conan local cache, the package can be uploaded to a Conan repository to be reused in other projects or on different machines. Conan packages are signed, and the signatures are validated, but this feature is currently under development.

Let's assume that a Conan server was deployed and the local repository (conan-local) was created on the server. To upload your package to this server, you need to add this remote repository to your local Conan configuration and log in with your credentials. In our case, the local server has the address localhost:8081. By default, the credentials are admin:password:

```
conan remote add hinrg-tapps  http://localhost:8081/artifactory/api/conan/
conan-local
conan remote login hinrg-tapps admin -p password
```

Then, upload the built customer package to the added remote repository and search for this package:

```
conan upload customer -r=hinrg-tapps
conan search "customer" -r=hinrg-tapps
```

You can deploy the JFrog Artifactory **Community Edition** (CE) server for C and C++ on Linux, macOS, and Windows for hosting, managing, and distributing binaries and artifacts, or choose the commercial product. If everything is correctly configured and the uploaded package is found on the server, then you will see the output of the last command, like this:

```
Connecting to remote 'hinrg-tapps' with user 'admin'
Found 1 pkg/version recipes matching customer in hinrg-tapps
hinrg-tapps
  customer
    customer/0.0.1
```

This output confirms that the package was uploaded and is now available in the remote repository.

You can also verify the uploaded package via the JFrog Artifactory web interface, as shown in *Figure 8.1*:

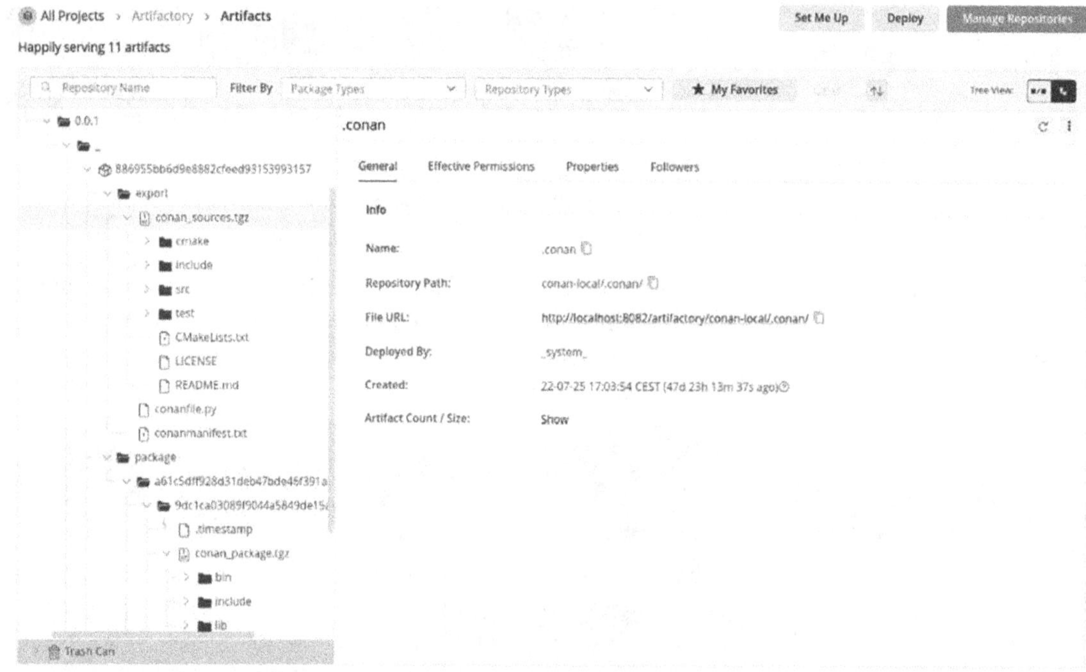

Figure 8.1: An overview of JFrog Artifactory CE for C/C++

Quick tip: Need to see a high-resolution version of this image? Open this book in the next-gen Packt Reader or view it in the PDF/ePub copy.

The next-gen Packt Reader and a **free PDF/ePub copy** of this book are included with your purchase. Scan the QR code OR visit `https://packtpub.com/unlock`, then use the search bar to find this book by name. Double-check the edition shown to make sure you get the right one.

Conan also supports creating new recipes from either predefined or user-defined templates, managing shared configurations, and computing dependency graphs. The fact that there are such package managers as vcpkg (Microsoft), xrepo, and Conan (JFrog) for C and C++ is impressive, but their usage comes with trade-offs.

While it's obvious that having tested and compatible versions of libraries is necessary, updates and bug fixes, including critical bugs and even vulnerabilities, often take a long time due to the centralization of repositories: it may take days, weeks, or even months.

Also, Conan provides a limited set of supported versions. As a result, you may need your own Conan repository for your projects.

Another trade-off is the learning curve, since using a package manager introduces additional tooling that you need to learn.

Summary

In this chapter, you learned the essentials of working with Conan packages. You're now able to consume existing Conan packages, create, test, and share your own packages, install dependencies of the projects with Conan, use Conan targets from CMake scripts, and create your own artifacts.

In the next chapter, you will be introduced to C++ modules—a modern approach to code reuse—and learn how they are used. Moreover, you will build on the skills developed in this chapter by learning how to integrate them with CMake and Conan.

Questions

1. How do you use multiple compilers with Conan?
2. What would you do if you'd like to compile your Conan dependencies with the pre-C++11 GCC ABI?
3. What is the purpose of using `conanfile.txt` and `conanfile.py`?
4. Which approach is used in Conan to test packages?
5. Why is the `exports_sources` attribute or `export_sources` method declared in `conanfile.py`?

Further reading

- Conan Center, *Conan Recipes*, JFrog: `https://conan.io/center/recipes`
- Conan Documentation, *Local Package Development Flow* (tutorial), JFrog: `https://docs.conan.io/2/tutorial/developing_packages/local_package_development_flow.html`
- Conan Documentation, *Testing Conan Packages* (Tutorial), JFrog: `https://docs.conan.io/2/tutorial/creating_packages/test_conan_packages.html`
- Conan Extensions, *Migration Commands*, Conan, GitHub: `https://github.com/conan-io/conan-extensions/tree/main/extensions/commands/migrate`
- JFrog, *Conan Package Manager* (JFrog Integrations): `https://jfrog.com/integrations/conan-package-manager/`
- JFrog, *JFrog & Conan* (JFrog Integrations): `https://jfrog.com/integrations/conan-xray/`
- JFrog, *JFrog Artifactory Open Source for Artifact Life-Cycle Management* (JFrog Community): `https://jfrog.com/community/download-artifactory-oss/`
- JFrog, *Downloads* (JFrog Community): `https://jfrog.com/community/open-source/`

9

The Future of C++ Code Reuse: Using Modules

Modularity is a fundamental aspect of all successful large programs.

– Bjarne Stroustrup, The C++ Programming Language, Special Edition, 1998

C++ programmers have been facing the shortcomings of the preprocessor-based approach of including header files through the `#include` system. These include weak encapsulation, heavy macro usage, and slow compilation. C++ modules change the way code is organized and compiled, which helps resolve these issues. They replace textual inclusion with a structured binary interface, which improves code isolation and compilation speed and provides clearly defined interfaces.

However, it is difficult to predict when the C++ community will replace header files in favor of modules, as maintaining backward compatibility with older projects continues to slow down the transition. Therefore, the approach where C++ libraries provide both headers and module interfaces may become a de facto standard for projects that have not migrated to using C++ modules completely and for backward compatibility.

The concept of modularity is not new and is based on principles of separation of concerns and information hiding. According to the principle of separation of concerns, a program should be divided into modules, where each module performs only one, clearly defined task. As per the principle of information hiding, the internal structure of a module should be hidden from the outside world, and interaction with it should only be available through a clearly defined interface. As long as the interface remains the same, the program remains protected from unintentional changes; moreover, its further development is simplified, since the internal implementation of the module does not affect other parts of the program.

> *The single most important factor that distinguishes a well-designed module from a poorly designed one is the degree to which the module hides its internal data and other implementation details.*
>
> *– Joshua Bloch, Effective Java, 2001*

Thus, we can say that modular programming is based on the divide and conquer paradigm, which simplifies software design, code reuse, and replaceability, enables parallel development by separate teams and better scalability of projects, reduces the likelihood of errors, and improves testability.

The concept of modularity was pioneered by Canadian programmer David Parnas in his seminal 1972 paper *On the Criteria to Be Used in Decomposing Systems into Modules*. He proposed that to create a module, a minimal set of knowledge about the content of others is sufficient. He also said that *"the sequence of instructions necessary to call a given routine and the routine itself are part of the same module."*

At that time, a module was understood as any procedure or function written according to certain rules. However, syntactical constructs such as procedures and functions available in programming languages in the 1970s could not provide reliable information hiding due to global variables, which caused hidden dependencies and side effects.

The first specialized syntactical construct of a module was proposed by Niklaus Wirth in 1975 and included in his new language Modula. Following this, Modula-2 was introduced in the late 1970s, heavily influenced by the MESA language that he saw during his 1976 sabbatical at Xerox PARC, and also built upon the foundation of his earlier Pascal language. The research center was the birthplace of many foundations of modern computing: **windows, icons, menus, and pointing device** (**WIMP**), the **graphical user interface** (**GUI**), the **model–view–controller** (**MVC**) pattern, Ethernet networking, the computer mouse, the laser printer, the bit-mapped display, the **what you see is what you get** (**WYSIWYG**) paradigm, and the Xerox Alto (the first personal computer).

The module structure includes an interface that defines public declarations visible and accessible to other modules, while the implementation contains private code and data accessible only within the module itself.

Nowadays, most modern programming languages support modular programming, including languages such as C++, C#, Ada, Erlang, Haskell, Go, Java, JavaScript, Perl, Python, Ruby, and Zig.

Modular programming is possible even without explicitly assigning names to modules, since the principle of modularity is based on dividing the program into logically independent parts (units or modules).

In C++, modularity additionally improves using namespaces to organize code more efficiently and prevent naming conflicts that may arise, especially if your code base includes multiple libraries, by grouping the identifiers (the names of types, functions, variables, and so on) under a single namespace and providing a scope to them inside it.

Of course, modular architecture is a term used not only in software development. Examples of modular systems include modular buildings, solar panels, modularized wind turbines, consumer electronics such as modular PCs and smartphones, and modular car platforms in transportation.

Traditionally, modularity in C++ is achieved by dividing code into separate units (modules) by using header files (`.h`) and source code files (`.cpp`). Since C++20, the built-in module system can also be used for this purpose, which improves dependency management and reduces compilation times.

In this chapter, we'll cover the following topics:

- Introduction to C++ modules
- Consuming modules
- Creating your own modules
- Migrating existing code bases to modules
- Using modules with CMake
- Using modules with Conan

Technical requirements

You will need the following tools to build the code in this chapter:

- **A compiler that supports C++23:** GCC 15, Clang 20, and MSVC 19.50 (VS 2026) are recommended. The examples are also compatible with earlier versions of C++ compilers (GCC 14, Clang 19, and MSVC 19.44), but not all of them, especially experimental features.
- CMake 4.0+.
- Ninja (a build system).

The source code for this chapter can be found at `https://github.com/PacktPublishing/Software-Architecture-with-Cpp-2E/tree/main/Chapter09`.

Introduction to C++ modules

C++ has used header file inclusion since its introduction in 1985. Originally, C++ was called *C with classes*, but the name was soon changed to C++ because the increment operator in C symbolizes adding new features to the language. Header files are inherent for the C language since its development in the early 1970s, when programmers began using them to organize and reuse code. They allow declarations of functions, classes, structures, macros, and variables to be included in the source file; this makes the code modular, maintainable, and reusable by separating the interface and implementation.

However, this classic textual inclusion has its flaws, as listed here:

Due to the need to process large volumes of text, compilation is slow. Even a simple *Hello World* is around half a million lines of code after the C++ preprocessor includes header files in the source file before the compilation. This approach can also lead to **one-definition rule** (**ODR**) violations, conflicts from macros, and naming conflicts.

ODR is a fundamental principle of the C++ language and requires that any entity, such as a variable, function, class type, enumeration type, concept (since C++20), or template, has exactly one definition throughout the entire program, although it may have multiple declarations in different files. An ODR violation, if not detected during compilation and linking the program, leads to undefined behavior. The ODR rule might be violated if an entity defined in a header file is included in multiple source files rather than being defined in a source file—for instance, if a function or class is differently included in different translation units depending on the macros. Name conflicts in C++ are usually resolved using namespaces and the scope resolution operator.

The order of your `#include` directives matters, but it shouldn't. The order of inclusion can matter due to macro definitions, header guards, and conditional compilation. Google C++ Style Guide recommends including C++ headers in the following order to ensure headers are self-contained and to catch hidden dependencies: headers related to a C++ source file, C system headers, C++ standard library headers, third-party library headers, and project headers.

It's hard to encapsulate stuff that just needs to be in header files. Even if you put such code in a detailed namespace, someone will use it, as Hyrum's law, or the Law of Implicit Interfaces, states. Over time, users will depend on all observable behaviors of an API, not only those specified in its contract. This law highlights the challenges of maintaining backward compatibility and managing expectations as systems grow and evolve. The gist of the law is that as an API attracts more and more users, people begin to rely on behavior that the developers didn't intend or document. Eventually, even small, undocumented features or edge cases become features that users depend on, making it difficult to make changes or improvements to the API without breaking someone's interests. When users rely on undocumented features of a system, the smooth development of that system becomes much more difficult. C++20 modules are a way of defining a public API. Hence, they mitigate the problem by replacing textual inclusion with a structured binary interface and allowing developers to explicitly hide implementation details, but they don't eliminate Hyrum's Law.

> *With a sufficient number of users of an API, it does not matter what you promise in the contract: all observable behaviors of your system will be depended on by somebody.*
>
> *– Hyrum Wright, Hyrum's Law, hyrumslaw.com, 2012*

The following diagram shows the process of building an executable file. The first stage is to include header files in a source file with the preprocessor. After this, the preprocessed source file is compiled into an object file. Many such object files can be created. The linker combines them and external libraries into an executable file.

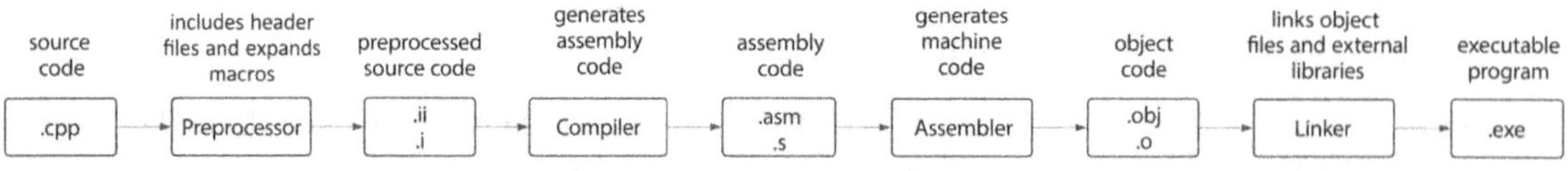

Figure 9.1: The C++ build process

Fortunately, this is when modules enter the game. They solve some of the aforementioned flaws, speeding up build times and offering better C++ scalability when it comes to building, because they are a replacement for the preprocessor and C/C++ `#include` directives, which replace the directive line with the content of the specified file. They also improve encapsulation by explicitly controlling the visibility of symbols and make large projects easier to manage.

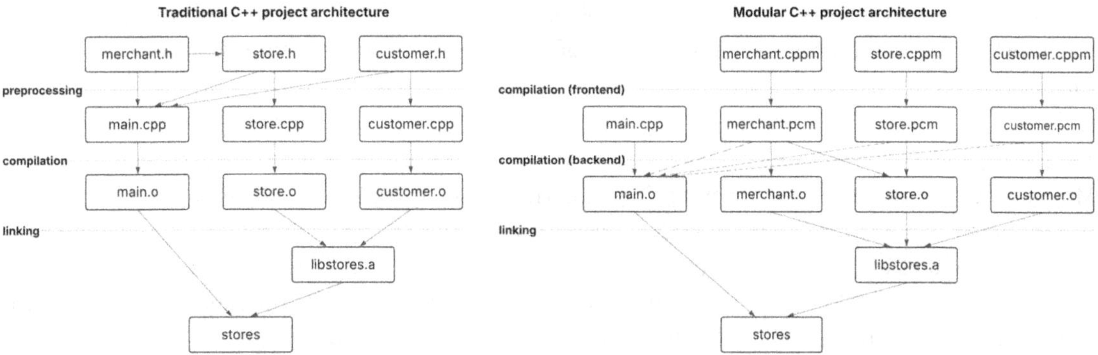

Figure 9.2: Traditional and modular C++ project architectures (using Clang)

Modules are selective with what to make public because everything is private by default. With modules, you only export what you want to export, which results in good encapsulation natively. This also applies to third-party libraries, as modules help resolve name collisions and ODR violations by exporting only the necessary library entities and hiding the module implementations from their importers.

The C++ standard does not require that names of module units match module names because C++ organizes modules into logical units. These consist of public module interface units and private module implementation units. Because these module units are compiled as logical entities, C++ modules avoid text inclusion by parsing code only once per build, unlike header files.

Having a specific order of dependency inclusion is no longer an issue either, because the modules can be imported in any order, but the modules are compiled in the dependency order. Thus, they do not support circular dependencies, which is not a standard in C++. Their compilation would be impossible because dependency modules are compiled before others.

Now let's see how modules are used in practice. Working with modules involves either consuming modules that others provide or creating your own.

Consuming modules

Each module, after compilation, is compiled not only into the object file but also into a module interface file.

An object file is an intermediate, machine-readable file generated by the compiler that contains machine code and metadata such as a symbol table, which the linker needs to combine the object file with other object files and libraries into a final executable.

Functionally, a modular interface file is similar to the header file, but it significantly speeds up compilation and reduces build times by pre-compiling and reusing module interface files. The interface file is binary and exports only public entities such as types, functions, templates, and variables. So, the compiler quickly scans this pre-parsed file instead of re-parsing the source code and its dependencies repeatedly.

This approach separates concerns because the object file contains the compiled implementation, while the interface file contains the declarations and definitions needed by other source files to import (use) the module, as follows:

```
import module;
```

Modules most commonly have the extension `.cppm` in the Clang and GCC toolchains, adding the suffix `m` (to denote module) to the traditional C++ file extension `.cpp`. In the MSVC toolchain, the extension for C++20 modules is `.ixx`, which stands for *interface*. There is no standard naming convention. Clang's convention is that importable module unit files should have the extension `.cppm` (or `.ccm`, `.cxxm`, `.c++m`), and module implementation unit files should have the extension `.cpp` (or `.cc`, `.cxx`, `.c++`). The extensions `.mxx` and `.mpp` are used quite rarely.

Creating your own modules

In addition to the basic `export` and `import` keywords, C++20 adds concepts such as **module unit**, **module partition**, **module linkage**, and **header unit**.

Module units have two types: module interface units and module implementation units. A named module consists of one or more module units that share the same module name.

A module interface unit exports a module name or module partition name using the `export` keyword in its declaration, while a module implementation unit does not export anything, but only implements the things exported by the module. Besides, a primary module interface unit exports the module name, and the named module can have only one such unit. A complete module can be defined in a single source file.

A module interface unit in C++ can have several sections called fragments.

An optional global module fragment starts with the `module` keyword and ends with the `export module` keyword. This fragment is intended for any preprocessor directives, including `#include` and macro definitions that must be processed before the module itself is defined. This is necessary for modules interacting with code depending on the preprocessor, but macros defined here do not affect header files included in the module after this fragment. Therefore, non-module units are considered part of the global module, which is anonymous, has no interface, and contains regular non-module code.

An optional private module fragment begins with the `module :private` declaration. It entirely hides the implementation details of the module from its importers. This option is often used to implement a primary interface module as a complete module in a single file.

The global fragment precedes the module purview, where functions, types, templates, and so on are exported from the module. The module purview can be considered the entire scope of the module unit, extending from the module declaration to the end of the translation unit.

C++ module partitions divide large modules into smaller, more manageable internal parts, simplifying development and helping manage complexity. They are accessible only within the named module itself. Hence, translation units outside the named modules cannot import their module partitions directly.

Another method offered by C++20 for combating code complexity is submodules. Unlike module partitions, submodules create a hierarchy of independent modules that can be imported separately or together. For example, a huge math module can be broken down into `math.algebra`, `math.calculus`, `math.geometry`, `math.trigonometry`, and so on.

Therefore, module decomposition (breaking down large modules into smaller modules) is achieved using both partitions and submodules.

Header units are designed to effectively replace traditional header files. Unlike the text inclusion approach, they are compiled into binary format. This speeds up compilation, helps avoid re-inclusion, and provides stronger encapsulation. Header units are not affected by macro definitions outside of the header unit itself. They are a smooth way to transition from header files to named modules in cases where you rely on macros defined in header files, since C++ named modules do not export macros. They are imported just like modules:

```
// before
#include <iostream>
// after
import <iostream>;
```

For a long time, C++ had two primary types of linkage: internal and external. An entity with internal linkage is only visible to the linker within a single translation unit (a source file and its included headers), while an entity with external linkage is visible across all translation units in a program. C++20 introduced module linkage, a new type of linkage where entities are visible across all translation units that belong to the same named module.

Having two exported entities with the same name and signature in two different modules when imported into the global namespace leads to an **ill-formed no diagnostic required** (**IFNDR**) situation, which is almost identical to an ODR violation. This occurs because, unlike some other languages, C++ does not implicitly create a namespace when importing a C++ module. Therefore, export declarations, which include variables, classes, structs, functions, namespaces, template functions/classes, and concepts, must be made at the namespace level. It is recommended to introduce namespaces with the same names as modules.

Without further ado, let's return to our trade fair example and show how to use modules in practice. First, let's create our first module for the customer code, starting with the following directive:

```
module;
```

This statement starts a global module fragment, which is a good place to put includes and other content that won't be exported.

Next, we specify the name of the module:

```
export module customer;
```

This will be the name we'll use to import the module later. It must come before the exported contents.

Now, let's specify what our module will export, prefixing the definitions with the `export` keyword. Optionally, the export declarations and definitions can be separated, including namespaces. It is useful for better readability or to move implementations either into module implementation units or private module fragments to split the interfaces and implementations:

```
export namespace trade_fair {
using CustomerId = int;

CustomerId get_current_customer_id() { return 42; }
}
```

Quick tip: Enhance your coding experience with the **AI Code Explainer** and **Quick Copy** features. Open this book in the next-gen Packt Reader. Click the **Copy** button

(1) to quickly copy code into your coding environment, or click the **Explain** button

(2) to get the AI assistant to explain a block of code to you.

```
function calculate(a, b) {
  return {sum: a + b};
};
```

Copy (1) Explain (2)

The next-gen Packt Reader is included for free with the purchase of this book. Scan the QR code OR go to `https://packtpub.com/unlock`, then use the search bar to find this book by name. Double-check the edition shown to make sure you get the right one.

And done! Our first module is ready to be used.

Let's create another one for the merchant:

```
module;

export module merchant;
```

```
export namespace trade_fair {
struct Merchant {
  int id;
};
}
```

Like our first module, here, we specified the name and the type to be exported (as opposed to a type alias and a function for the first one). You can export other definitions, such as templates, too. It gets tricky with macros, though, as you need to import `<header_file>` for them to be visible.

By the way, a good advantage of modules is that they don't allow macros to propagate to imported modules. This means that when you write code such as the following, the module won't have `MY_MACRO` defined:

```
#define MY_MACRO
import my_module;
```

It helps to have determinism in modules as it protects you from breaking code in other modules.

Now, let's define the third and fourth modules for our stores and items in the stores. We won't discuss exporting other functions, enums, and other types, as they won't differ from the previous two modules. What's interesting is how the module file starts. First, let's include what we need for the stores in a global module fragment intended for C++ header files:

```
module;

#include <vector>
```

Now, let's see what happens next:

```
export module store;

export import merchant;
```

Our `store` module imports the `merchant` module we defined previously and then re-exports it as part of the store's interface. This can be handy if a module is a facade for other ones. This technique is also applied to module partition interface units to reexport their exported entities from module interface units. For example, the `store:item` partition exports the `Item` structure and an overload of the `operator<<` function that targets this structure:

```
export module store:item;

export namespace trade_fair {
struct Item {
  ...
};
```

```
std::ostream &operator<<(std::ostream &os, const Item &item) {
  ...
}
}
```

Then, these entities from the partition are re-exported in the primary module interface unit of the store module, as follows:

```
export module store;

export import :item;
```

In C++20, standard library headers are not modules, but C++23 introduces standard named modules, `std` and `std.compat`, but their availability depends on compiler support and may remain experimental:

```
export module store:item;

import std;

using namespace std::chrono;

export namespace trade_fair {
struct Item {
  ...
};

...
}
```

This version does not need to include the global module fragment because the named modules `std` and `std.compat` export declarations from the `std` namespace of the C++ standard library. At the time of writing the book, this was an experimental feature.

As stated earlier in this chapter, migration to C++ modules is proceeding with some difficulty, and they will not be widely adopted for some time. Moreover, such things do not happen overnight, and since these modules are backward compatible, they are used in existing C++ code as hybrid solutions. This is what we will do in the next topic, showing how such a migration can occur.

Migrating existing code bases to modules

Ideally, the best option is to start a new project using C++ modules, but this is not always possible, especially with existing code bases. Therefore, many C++ libraries provide both C++ header files and module interface units, so as not to break compatibility. This approach ensures gradual migration by using the C++ module interface unit to include C++ headers and re-export their entities.

The following code from customer.h shows how this approach works in practice. These header and source files are quite traditional for C++ programs:

```
namespace trade_fair {
using CustomerId = int;

CustomerId get_current_customer_id();
}
```

The following code from customer.cpp defines the function declared in customer.h:

```
trade_fair::CustomerId trade_fair::get_current_customer_id() { return 42; }
```

customer.cppm re-exports the declarations from the customer header file. The export block is applied to group many declarations:

```
module;

#include "stores/customer.h"
export module customer;

// re-export
export {
  using trade_fair::CustomerId;
  using trade_fair::get_current_customer_id;
}
```

So, main.cpp can either include the header file or import the module. The latter is preferable, but the program may use C++ standards earlier than C++20:

```
...
// #include "stores/customer.h"
import customer;
```

In our implementation, the module interface unit and the header file are interchangeable. The conditional compilation approach is often used in C++ libraries to support clients using different C++ standards. Similarly, there are two versions: one with support for C++ modules for those who use them, and a more traditional version based on header files.

Using modules with CMake

This CMake code supports both approaches: header files and module interfaces. As described previously, this is a hybrid solution, and here is an example of how to build such a program:

```
add_library(libstores)
add_library(stores::libstores ALIAS libstores)
set_target_properties(libstores PROPERTIES OUTPUT_NAME stores)
target_compile_options(libstores PUBLIC ${BASE_COMPILE_FLAGS})
```

This configuration links both module units and the source file with its header file to the `libstores` library. Accordingly, in a fully modular implementation, neither this source file nor its header file is needed:

```
target_sources(
  libstores
  PRIVATE src/stores/customer.cpp
  PUBLIC FILE_SET
         CXX_MODULES
         BASE_DIRS
         src/stores
         FILES
         src/lib/customer.cppm
         src/lib/merchant.cppm
         src/lib/store.cppm
         src/lib/store_item.cppm)

target_sources(libstores PUBLIC FILE_SET HEADERS BASE_DIRS include FILES
                                 include/stores/customer.h)

add_executable(stores src/main.cpp)
target_link_libraries(stores PRIVATE libstores) target_compile_options(stores
PRIVATE ${BASE_COMPILE_FLAGS})
...
```

The code is practically no different from the code described in *Chapter 7, Building and Packaging*, except for the keywords associated with the modules, such as `CXX_MODULES`, and the `target_sources` command, which adds sources to the target.

Once your targets are configured, the next step is to install and export both the header files and module interface units so that consumers can reuse them:

```
...
install(
 TARGETS libstores stores
 EXPORT StoresTargets
 FILE_SET HEADERS
 DESTINATION ${CMAKE_INSTALL_INCLUDEDIR}
 FILE_SET CXX_MODULES
 DESTINATION ${CMAKE_INSTALL_LIBDIR}
 LIBRARY DESTINATION ${CMAKE_INSTALL_LIBDIR}
 ARCHIVE DESTINATION ${CMAKE_INSTALL_LIBDIR}
 RUNTIME DESTINATION ${CMAKE_INSTALL_BINDIR})
```

```
install(
 EXPORT StoresTargets
 FILE StoresTargets.cmake
 NAMESPACE stores::
 DESTINATION ${CMAKE_INSTALL_LIBDIR}/cmake/Stores)
```

Unlike header files, there is no default destination for `CXX_MODULES`. Many projects treat module interface units as header-like files and install them under `${CMAKE_INSTALL_INCLUDEDIR}` or in a dedicated modules directory. Other projects install them under `${CMAKE_INSTALL_LIBDIR}`, as shown in the example.

Because the examples in this book use the Conan package manager and there's a chapter dedicated to that package manager, the following topic describes how to publish a Conan package for a project that uses C++ modules, and what issues existed in this regard at the time of writing.

Using modules with Conan

Conan has no native module awareness, and, therefore, building and integration of C++ modules is handled by the build system—typically, CMake. CMake supports C++ modules since version 3.28 and experimentally imports the `std` module since version 3.29. At the time of writing, there is no official approach to distributing C++ modules with CMake. So, we use a workaround to achieve this. The other build systems—in particular, Xmake, Build2, Meson, and MSVC Build Tools—also support C++ modules to varying degrees.

Creating and testing Conan packages is described in *Chapter 8*, *Package Management*. Our Conan script follows almost the same approach, except for a few key differences—this example does not require external libraries, and only Ninja and Visual Studio generators support scanning sources required for C++ modules to find their dependencies:

```
class StoresConan(ConanFile):
    name = "stores"
    ...
    def generate(self):
        deps = CMakeDeps(self)
        deps.generate()
        tc = CMakeToolchain(self, generator="Ninja")
        tc.generate()
    ...
    def package_info(self):
        self.cpp_info.libs = ["stores"]
};
```

This configuration works with GCC, Clang, and MSVC compilers. For verifying that the published Conan package behaves correctly, we use a test package similar to the one described in the previous chapter:

```
class StoresTestConan(ConanFile):
    ...
    def generate(self):
        deps = CMakeDeps(self)
        deps.generate()
        tc = CMakeToolchain(self, generator="Ninja")
        tc.generate()
    ...
    def test(self):
        if can_run(self):
            cmd = os.path.join(self.build_folder, "example")
            self.run(cmd, env="conanrun")
    ...
```

Here is the workaround for linking C++ modules from an external library, since the `find_package()` command does not provide any module metadata. This solution is unlikely to be a convenient and long-term strategy, which limits the widespread use of C++ modules:

```
find_package(stores CONFIG REQUIRED)

string(TOUPPER "${CMAKE_BUILD_TYPE}" config_suffix)
set(stores_lib_base_dir ${stores_LIB_DIRS_${config_suffix}})
set(stores_lib_files "${stores_lib_base_dir}/customer.cppm" "${stores_lib_base_
dir}/merchant.cppm" "${stores_lib_base_dir}/store.cppm" "${stores_lib_base_
dir}/store_item.cppm")

add_library(stores_lib)
target_sources(
  stores_lib PUBLIC FILE_SET CXX_MODULES BASE_DIRS ${stores_lib_base_dir} FILES
                  ${stores_lib_files})
target_compile_features(stores_lib PUBLIC cxx_std_20)
target_link_libraries(stores_lib PUBLIC stores::stores)

add_executable(example example.cpp)
target_compile_features(example PUBLIC cxx_std_20)
target_link_libraries(example stores_lib)
```

This CMake code uses a path to the `stores` library from the `stores_LIB_DIRS_<CONFIG>` CMake variable, defines the new `stores_lib` library, adds module interface units, and links the `stores` library to the newly defined library. Then, the combined library is linked to the executable.

This workaround is applied because compiler-generated module interfaces, informally called **binary module interfaces** (**BMIs**), are implementation-specific and, therefore, may be incompatible across different compiler versions, and, moreover, they are incompatible between different C++ compilers. Thus, distributing BMIs is a poor approach, unlike the case with C++ object files, which are standardized.

For dependency scanning, module interface units must be visible to the build system so that it can generate compatible BMIs during compilation. C++ compilers use mappings between C++ modules and their usages in source code. So, module mappers match imported modules to their declarations and definitions, handle dependencies between modules efficiently, and allow modules to be used as a faster and more robust alternative to header files, making it possible to effectively exploit this feature of the C++ language.

Each C++ compiler has its own implementation strategy for handling modules. For example, in addition to BMIs, GCC uses temporary binary **compiled module interface** (**CMI**) files when compiling named module interfaces, module partitions, or header units; these files are then read when the module is imported. For the same purpose, MSVC produces module **interface** (**IFC**) files and Clang **precompiled module** (**PCM**) files with prebuilt module information. These files speed up the compilation process because the compilers do not need to re-process each source code module when building. Toolchains such as Clang, MSVC, and GCC continue to evolve support for C++ modules, but as of 2025, full interoperability is still a work in progress.

This concludes the modules and the major C++ features that we planned for this chapter.

Summary

In this chapter, we explored how C++20 modules address limitations faced with traditional header files. We discussed how to consume and create C++ modules. We also looked at practical strategies for migrating existing code bases, where header files and modules coexist to maintain backward compatibility. We then demonstrated how to build and distribute modules using CMake and Conan, including workarounds for current limitations such as the lack of native module metadata in `find_package()`. Overall, we saw how C++ modules can fit into modern C++ workflows.

In the next chapter, we'll discuss how to write testable code, which includes important aspects such as the hierarchy of different types of testing in the testing pyramid, since choosing the right strategy affects both the time spent on testing and especially its cost, as well as the time spent on finding the causes of errors in projects. It also introduces the features of different testing frameworks and explains the benefits of test doubles.

Questions

1. What flaws do header files have, and how do modules resolve them?
2. What approaches to code organization do modules support?
3. How is `import X` different than `import <X>`?

Further reading

- Are We Modules Yet? *Are We Modules Yet?* (Homepage): `https://arewemodulesyet.org/`
- CMake, *cmake-cxxmodules(7)*: `https://cmake.org/cmake/help/latest/manual/cmake-cxxmodules.7.html`
- CMake, *CMake Experimental Features Guide*, GitHub: `https://github.com/Kitware/CMake/blob/master/Help/dev/experimental.rst`
- Princeton University, *A Brief History of Modularity in Programming*: `https://www.cs.princeton.edu/courses/archive/spr16/cos217/lectures/09_ModularityHistory.pdf`
- LLVM, *Clang: Transitioning to Modules*: `https://clang.llvm.org/docs/StandardCPlusPlusModules.html#transitioning-to-modules`
- LLVM, *Clang: Modules*: `https://clang.llvm.org/docs/Modules.html`
- GCC, *C++ Modules*: `https://gcc.gnu.org/onlinedocs/gcc/C_002b_002b-Modules.html`
- Microsoft, *Header Units/Modules*: `https://learn.microsoft.com/en-us/cpp/build/reference/compiler-options-listed-by-category?view=msvc-170#header-unitsmodules`
- Microsoft, *SDK for the IFC Specification*, GitHub: `https://github.com/microsoft/ifc`
- Phil Nash, *C++20 Modules: The Packaging and Binary Redistribution Story*, GitHub: `https://github.com/philsquared/cpponsea2024-slides/blob/main/Presentations/Cpp_Modules_the_packaging_story.pdf`
- Alibaba Cloud Community, *42% Boost in Compilation Efficiency! A Practical Analysis of C++ Modules*: `https://www.alibabacloud.com/blog/42%25-boost-in-compilation-efficiency-a-practical-analysis-of-c%2B%2B-modules_601974`
- CppCat, *C++ Modules in Embedded Systems: A Comprehensive Guide*: `https://cppcat.com/c-modules-in-embedded-systems/`

Part 3

Architectural Quality Attributes

This part focuses more on high-level concepts that together make a software project a success. Where possible, we will also show tooling that helps in maintaining the high quality we want to achieve.

This part contains the following chapters:

- *Chapter 10, Writing Testable Code*
- *Chapter 11, Continuous Integration and Continuous Deployment*
- *Chapter 12, Security in Code and Deployment*
- *Chapter 13, Performance*

10

Writing Testable Code

The ability to test code is the most important quality of any software product. Without proper testing, it is prohibitively expensive to refactor the code or to improve any other part of it, such as its security, scalability, or performance. In this chapter, we'll learn how to design and manage automated tests and how to correctly use fakes and mocks when it is necessary to do so.

The following topics will be covered in this chapter:

- Why do you test code?
- Runtime testing frameworks
- Compile-time testing techniques
- Understanding test doubles
- Test-driven class design
- Automating application tests for **continuous integration/continuous deployment** (CI/CD)
- Automating infrastructure validation for CI/CD

Technical requirements

The sample code for this chapter can be found at `https://github.com/PacktPublishing/Software-Architecture-with-Cpp-2E/tree/main/Chapter10`.

The software that we will be using in this chapter's examples is as follows:

- CMake 3.28+
- GCC 14+ or Clang 19+
- Conan 2+
- GoogleTest 1.15+
- Catch2 3.7+
- Doctest 2.4+
- [Boost].UT 2.1+
- CppUTest 4.0+
- Drogon 1.9+

Why do you test code?

Software engineering and software architecture are complex disciplines, and the natural way to deal with uncertainties is to insure yourself against potential risks. We do it all the time with life insurance, health insurance, and car insurance. Yet when it comes to software development, we tend to forget about all the safety precautions and just hope for an optimistic outcome.

Knowing that things not only may but *will* go wrong, it is unbelievable that the topic of testing software is still a controversial one. Whether it's from having a lack of skill or from a lack of budget, there are still projects that lack even some of the most basic tests. And when the client decides to change the requirements, a simple correction may result in endless reworks and firefights.

The time that's saved from not implementing proper testing is lost when the first rework happens. If you think this rework will not happen very soon, you are most probably mistaken. In the agile environment we live in nowadays, rework is a part of our daily life. Our evolving knowledge about the world and our customers' changes leads to changes in requirements, which in turn call for changes to our code.

Therefore, testing's main purpose is to protect your precious time later in the project. Sure, it's an investment early on when you must implement various tests instead of focusing solely on the features, but it's an investment you won't regret. Like an insurance policy, testing takes a little from your budget when things are going according to plan, but when things go wrong, you'll get a generous payout.

The Great IT Outage of 2024, caused by a faulty update to CrowdStrike's security software, illustrates this. A logical error in a 40 KB file led to a global IT outage, shutting down millions of computers around the world. This example is evidence that an error can go unnoticed even after thorough testing. Of course, this is not the only such failure in history. A single overlooked detail can break a huge system, and that's why rigorous testing is so important.

The testing pyramid

There are different types of automated testing you may encounter when designing or implementing a software system, each serving a slightly different purpose. A useful way to think about them is through the testing pyramid, with low-level tests forming the base and high-level ones occupying the top.

One common hierarchy, from bottom to top, is as follows:

- **Unit testing**: Code
- **Integration testing**: Design
- **System testing**: Requirements
- **Acceptance testing (end-to-end testing)**: Client needs

This distinction is not absolute, and you may often see other categorizations, such as the following:

- Unit testing
- Service testing
- UI testing (end-to-end testing)

In both categorizations, unit testing, also known as component testing or module testing, lies at the base. Service testing combines integration testing and system testing. Integration testing includes component integration testing and consumer-driven contract testing. (In fact, component integration testing is often confused with component testing.) UI testing corresponds to acceptance testing.

The following diagram shows the testing pyramid, which illustrates how automated tests should ideally be distributed across layers:

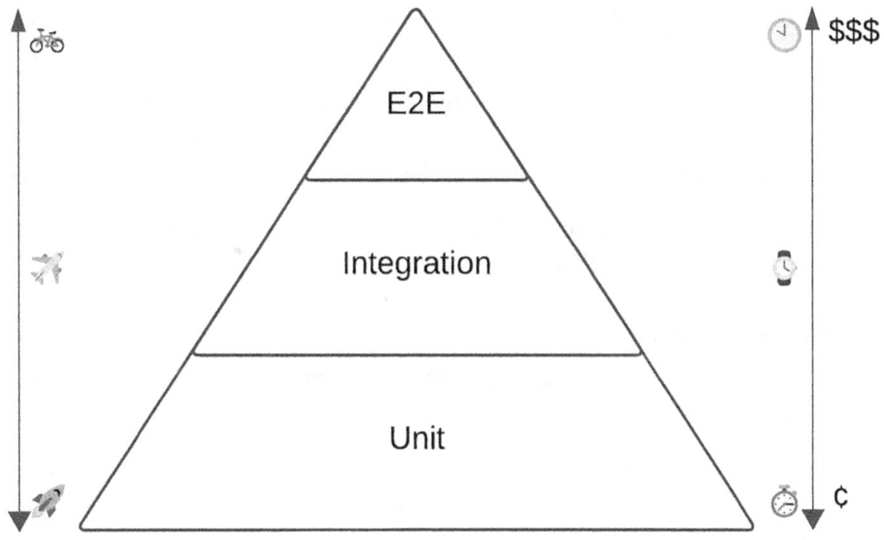

Figure 10.1: Testing pyramid

It's worth noting that unit tests are not only the cheapest to build, but that they also execute pretty quickly and can often run in parallel. This means they make for a great CI gating mechanism. Not only that, but they also often provide quick feedback about the health of your system. Higher-level tests are not only harder to write properly, but they may also be less robust. This can lead to flickering test results, with one in every few test runs failing. They are also more prone to flakiness—tests that pass or fail unpredictably regardless of whether the code or test environment changes or not. If the failure in the higher-level test is not correlated with any failure at the unit test level, chances are that the problem may be with the test itself and not in the system under test.

Flaky tests should not be the norm, as such tests corrode trust in test suites and create uncertainty, reduce development velocity and affect team morale, waste time and resources, and hide the real issues. To identify flaky tests, repeat failed tests in sequential and parallel runs in different environments, compare the environments, and analyze the results. Moreover, to prevent such tests, check external dependencies, stabilize, replicate and clean test environments, isolate tests, eliminate the randomness, simplify the test logic, check the sufficiency of test assertions, address concurrency issues, adjust the timings and waits, and continuously monitor tests.

We don't want to say that the higher-level tests are entirely useless and that you should only focus on writing unit tests. That's not the case. The pyramid has its shape because there should be a solid base covered by unit tests. On that base, however, you should also have all the higher-level tests in an appropriate proportion, which means that the number of underlying ones must be much greater than the above ones to form the shape of the metaphoric test automation pyramid. After all, it is not very hard to imagine a system where all the unit tests are passing, but the system itself doesn't provide any value to the customer. An extreme example would be a perfectly working backend without any user interface (be it graphical or in the form of an API) present. Sure, it passes all the unit tests, but that's no excuse!

As you may imagine, the opposite of the testing pyramid is known as an ice cream cone, and it is an antipattern. Violating the testing pyramid often leads to fragile code and hard-to-trace bugs. This makes debugging much more expensive and doesn't introduce savings in test development either.

What we've covered are so-called **functional tests**. Their aim is to check whether the system under test fulfills the functional requirements.

Non-functional testing

There are other types of requirements besides functional ones that we may want to control. Some of them are as follows:

- **Performance**: Your application may behave according to requirements in terms of functionality, but still be unusable for end users due to weak performance. We will focus more on improving performance in *Chapter 13, Performance*.
- **Endurance**: Even if your system can be really performant, it doesn't mean it can survive a continuously high workload. And when it does, can it survive some of the malfunctions of the components? When we embrace the idea that every piece of software is vulnerable and may break at any given moment, we start designing systems that can be failure-resistant. This forms the foundation of fault-tolerant design, as well as of chaos engineering, where failures are intentionally introduced in systems in controlled ways to expose their weaknesses.
- **Security**: Nowadays, there should be no need to repeat that security is crucial. But since it still isn't treated with all the seriousness the matter requires, we will bore you with saying this yet again. Every system that is connected to the network can—and most probably will—be broken. Performing security tests early on during development gives the same benefits as other kinds of tests: you can catch problems before they are too expensive to fix.
- **Availability**: Whereas poor performance may discourage your end users from using your product, poor availability may prevent them from even accessing said product. While availability problems may arise due to performance overload, there are also other causes of lost availability.
- **Integrity**: Your customers' data should not only be safe from outside attackers, but it should also be safe from any alterations or losses due to software malfunction. Protection against bit rot, snapshotting, and backups are ways to prevent integrity loss. By comparing the current version with previously recorded snapshots, you can identify whether the difference resulted only from the action that was taken or whether it was caused by errors.

- **Usability**: Even a product that ticks all of the previous boxes may still be unsatisfactory for the users if it has a clunky interface and unintuitive interaction. Usability tests are mostly performed manually. It's important to perform a usability assessment each time the UI or the workflow of the system changes.

Regression testing

Regression tests are usually end-to-end tests that should prevent you from making the same mistake twice. However, they are not limited to this level and can exist at any level of the testing pyramid. When you (or your QA team or customers) discover a bug in a production system, it is not sufficient to apply a hotfix and forget all about it. A regression test should be added to ensure that the issue never reappears.

Broadly, regression testing is a collective name for various types of software testing to confirm that the new functionality does not affect the old one and detect errors in already tested source code. A well-written regression test should prevent the same error from ever entering the production system again. In fact, good regression tests can even prevent the entire *class* of errors from entering production. After all, once you know what you did wrong, you can imagine other ways to mess things up. Another thing you can do is perform root cause analysis.

The **regression test selection** (**RTS**) strategy speeds up regression testing by identifying and running only the tests that are likely to be affected by recent code changes, thereby reducing the cost of regression testing.

Root cause analysis

Root cause analysis is a process that helps you uncover what the original source of the problem was, not only its manifestation. The most common way to perform root cause analysis is to use the method of the *5 Whys*, which was made famous by the Toyota company. This method consists of peeling off all the superficial layers of the problem's manifestation to uncover the root cause hidden underneath. You do this by asking *why* at each layer until you find the root cause you are looking for.

Let's look at an example of this method in action.

The problem in this example is that we didn't get payments for some of the transactions.

Why? The system didn't send the appropriate emails to the customers.

Why? The email sending system doesn't support special characters in customers' names.

Why? The email sending system wasn't tested properly.

Why? There was no time for proper testing due to the need to develop new features.

Why? Our time estimates for the features were incorrect.

In this example, the problem with time estimates may be the root cause of the bug that was found in the production system, but it may as well be another layer to peel. The framework gives you a heuristic that should work most of the time, but if you don't feel entirely sure that what you got is what you are looking for, you can keep on peeling additional layers until you find what caused all the trouble.

Given that many bugs result from the exact same and often repeatable root causes, finding the root cause is extremely beneficial because you can protect yourself from making the same mistake in the future *on several different levels*. This approach aligns with the principle of **defense in depth** applied to software testing and problem-solving. This principle assumes multiple, complementary safeguards in case any security control fails or is vulnerable.

The groundwork for further improvement

Having your code tested protects you from making accidental errors. But it also opens up different possibilities. When your code is covered by test cases, you don't have to fear refactoring. Refactoring is the process of transforming code that works into code that is functionally similar, except it has better internal organization. You may be wondering why you need to change the code's organization. There are several reasons for this.

First of all, your code may no longer be readable, which means every modification takes too much time. Second, fixing a bug will make some other features behave incorrectly as the code gathers too many workarounds and special cases over time. Both of those reasons can be summed up as productivity improvements. They will make maintenance cheaper in the long run.

Apart from productivity, you may also want to improve performance. This can mean either runtime performance (how the application behaves in production) or compile-time performance (which is basically another form of productivity improvement).

You can refactor for runtime performance by replacing the current suboptimal algorithms with more efficient ones or by changing the data structures that are used in the module you are refactoring. Refactoring for compile-time performance usually consists of moving parts of code to different compilation units, reorganizing headers, or reducing dependencies.

No matter what your end goal is, refactoring is generally a risky business. You take something that mostly works correctly and can end up with either a better version or a worse one. How would you know which case is yours? Here, testing comes to the rescue.

If the current feature set is thoroughly covered and you want to fix the recently uncovered bug, all you need to do is add another test case that will fail at that time. If your entire test suite starts passing again, it means your refactoring efforts were successful. The worst-case scenario is that you must abort the refactoring process if you cannot satisfy all the test cases within a specified timeframe.

You would undertake a similar procedure if you wanted to improve performance, but instead of unit tests (or end-to-end tests), you would focus on performance testing.

With the recent rise of automated tools that aid in refactoring, such as ReSharper C++ (`https://www.jetbrains.com/resharper-cpp/features/`) and code maintenance, you can even go as far as outsourcing a part of coding solely to the external software services. Services such as Mend Renovate (`https://www.mend.io/renovate/`) and Snyk (`https://snyk.io/`) support C++ dependencies. Having solid test coverage will let you use them without the fear of breaking your application during dependency updates.

Since keeping your dependencies up to date in terms of security vulnerabilities is something you should always consider, such services can reduce the burden significantly. Therefore, testing not only protects you from making mistakes, but it also reduces the effort necessary to introduce new features. It can also help you improve your code base and keep it stable and secure!

It's easy to assume that we're testing enough, but in reality, we may miss out on some critical tests. This unpredictability is part of the development process. Fortunately, coverage tools help remediate this situation by measuring the quantity and quality of your testing.

You can measure code coverage of C++ applications and tests with tools such as Squish Coco, BullseyeCoverage, RKTracer, Parasoft C/C++test, Testwell CTC++, VectorCast, Codecov, and CANTATA. For instance, the C++ IDE CLion relies on open source coverage tools (`llvm-cov` and `gcov`) that require special compiler flags:

- GCC:

  `-fprofile-arcs -ftest-coverage` or `-coverage`

- Clang:

  `-fprofile-instr-generate -fcoverage-mapping`

  `-ftest-coverage` or `-coverage` for the gcov-style coverage

Now that we understand the need for testing, we want to start writing our own tests. It is possible to write tests without any external dependencies, but that would shift the focus toward managing test results and reporting. Since we'd like to focus just on the testing logic, we will select a testing framework/technique to handle the tedious job for us. In the next two sections, we will introduce some of the most popular testing frameworks/techniques.

Runtime testing frameworks

As for the frameworks, the current de facto standard is **GoogleTest** (**GTest**). Together with its companion **Google Mock** (**gMock**), it forms a small suite of tools that allows you to follow the best practices of testing in C++.

Other popular alternatives to the GTest/gMock duo are Catch2, Boost.Test, Doctest, CppUTest, and [Boost].UT. All these frameworks support the modern C++ standards—in particular, C++14, C++17, C++20, and C++23.

To compare these testing frameworks, we will use the same code base that we want to test. Using it as a basis, we will then implement tests in each of the frameworks. There is no universal recipe, as the framework choice depends on your projects and needs.

Some testing frameworks, such as DrogonTest and Qt Test, are provided with libraries, which may be suitable in cases where you need to test systems based on these libraries and using their specific features.

GTest example

GTest is an xUnit test framework that offers comprehensive support for modern C++ testing requirements. xUnit is a family of unit testing frameworks having a common architecture based on test cases, test suites, test fixtures, test runners, and assertions.

GTest supports features such as the following:

- **Test discovery**, so that tests are discovered automatically without manual registration
- **Value- and type-parameterized tests**, to let the same test run with multiple values or types
- **Floating-point comparison**, to allow for small rounding differences when comparing numbers
- **Event listeners**, to plug in custom actions or reports while tests run
- **Mocking and dependency injection (via gMock)**, to replace real components with fakes so you can test in isolation
- **Fixtures**, to share common setup or cleanup code across a group of related tests
- **Logging with additional information**, to capture extra details about what happened during a test
- **Sanitizer integration**, to work with tools that catch memory and threading errors while tests run
- **XML and JSON reports**, to output test results in standard formats for CI/CD systems
- **Private code testing**, to test private class members by making test classes friends

The framework also has a rich set of assertions—checks inside a test that verify whether conditions hold true. These include user-defined assertions and built-in trace support to help in debugging. Moreover, there are various options for running the tests: they can be configured to run selectively, repeatedly, in randomized order, or in distributed setups.

GTest isolates tests, but resources can be shared between tests in the same test suite.

Here is an example test for our `customer` library:

```
#include <gtest/gtest.h>

#include "customer/responder.h"

TEST(basic_responses, given_name_when_prepare_responses_then_greets_friendly) {
  const auto name = "Leo";
  const auto [status, value] = responder{}.prepare_response(name);
  ASSERT_EQ(status, drogon::k200OK);
  ASSERT_EQ(value, "Hello, Leo!");
}
```

In this test, most of the tasks that are commonly done during testing have been abstracted. We're mostly focused on providing the action we want to test (`prepare_response`) and the desired behavior (both `ASSERT_EQ` lines).

Catch2 example

The main advantage of Catch2 is simplicity and natural syntax. This framework supports test fixtures, assertions, data generators (built-in utilities to feed values or ranges of values into a test case), floating-point matchers, logging, event listeners, and reporters (components that format and output test results), including JUnit format (a Java reporting standard) and Hamcrest-style matchers (an expressive matching style implemented in a number of languages).

Catch2 also has some basic support for **behavior-driven development** (BDD)-style testing, where test cases are written in natural language. It also supports micro-benchmarking features.

Here is an example test for our `customer` library:

```
#include <catch2/catch_all.hpp>

#include "customer/responder.h"

TEST_CASE("Basic responses",
          "Given Name When Prepare Responses Then Greets Friendly") {
  const auto name = "Mikey";
  const auto [status, value] = responder{}.prepare_response(name);
  REQUIRE(status == drogon::k200OK);
  REQUIRE(value == "Hello, Mikey!");
}

int main(const int argc, char* argv[]) {
  return Catch::Session().run(argc, argv);
}
```

It looks pretty similar to the previous one. Some keywords differ (`TEST` and `TEST_CASE`), and there's a slightly different way to check the results (`REQUIRE(a == b)` instead of `ASSERT_EQ(a,b)`). Both are pretty compact and readable anyway.

CppUTest example

CppUTest is a C/C++ based xUnit test framework designed for embedded programming. This framework supports fixtures, assertions, and mocking. Moreover, it has plugins such as memory leak detection, along with built-in features such as a pointer restore mechanism (resetting pointers to avoid side effects across tests) and IEEE754 floating-point exception handling (a technical standard for floating-point arithmetic).

CppUTest provides integration code to link and run GTest tests under the CppUTest runner and also supports using gMock in the same project. But CppUTest and GTest are two competing C++ unit testing frameworks. While GTest is widely adopted because of its rich set of features, CppUTest focuses on simplicity and embedded systems.

Here is an example test for our customer library:

```
#include "customer/responder.h"

#include <CppUTest/CommandLineTestRunner.h>
#include <CppUTest/TestHarness.h>

TEST_GROUP(basic_responses){};

TEST(basic_responses, given_name_when_prepare_responses_then_greets_friendly) {
  const auto name = "Raph";
  const auto [status, value] = responder{}.prepare_response(name);
  CHECK_EQUAL(status, drogon::k200OK);
  CHECK(value == "Hello, Raph!");
}

int main(const int ac, char **av) {
  return CommandLineTestRunner::RunAllTests(ac, av);
}
```

Compared to GTest and Catch2, CppUTest uses a different syntax (`TEST_GROUP/TEST`) and simpler assertions (`CHECK` and `CHECK_EQUAL`), and it requires an explicit `main()` function to run tests.

Doctest example

Doctest is a single-header testing framework that's very light, unintrusive, portable, and thread-safe. This framework supports assertions, logging, event listeners, reporters, crash handling, parameterized tests, floating-point comparison, stringification of user types (lets you print custom types in assertion messages), test discovery, extensions, and BDD-style tests.

Here is an example test for our customer library:

```
#include <tuple>

#include "customer/responder.h"

#define DOCTEST_CONFIG_IMPLEMENT_WITH_MAIN
#include <doctest/doctest.h>

TEST_CASE("Basic responses") {
  auto name = "Donnie";
  drogon::HttpStatusCode status;
  Json::Value value;
  std::tie(status, value) = responder{}.prepare_response(name);
```

```
  REQUIRE(status == drogon::k200OK);
  REQUIRE(value == "Hello, Donnie!");
}
```

Once again, it's quite clean and easy to understand. The main selling point of Doctest is that it's the fastest both at compile-time and at runtime compared to the other similarly featured alternatives.

Boost.Test example

Boost.Test is a customizable and configurable framework that supports self-registering, parameterized and dataset tests, assertions, and detailed reporting, including XML and JUnit, but its large and complex API can be challenging. Its fixtures can be consumed by a test case, a test suite, or globally.

Here is an example test for our `customer` library:

```
#define BOOST_TEST_MODULE basic_responses
#include <boost/test/included/unit_test.hpp>

#include "customer/responder.h"

BOOST_AUTO_TEST_CASE(given_name_when_prepare_responses_then_greets_friendly) {
  const auto name = "Bulk Bogan";
  const auto [status, value] = responder{}.prepare_response(name);
  BOOST_CHECK_EQUAL(status, drogon::k200OK);
  BOOST_CHECK_EQUAL(value, "Hello, Bulk Bogan!");
}
```

This example looks clean as well, but Boost.Test is more heavyweight than the other frameworks. Although it is flexible and rich in features, it calls for a steeper learning curve.

DrogonTest example

DrogonTest is a minimal testing framework inspired by both GTest and Catch2 and built into the Drogon framework. This framework has a variety of assertions and native asynchronous testing support.

Here is an example for our `customer` library:

```
#define DROGON_TEST_MAIN
#include <drogon/drogon_test.h>

#include "customer/responder.h"

DROGON_TEST(given_name_when_prepare_responses_then_greets_friendly) {
  const auto name = "Zero Cool";
  const auto [status, value] = responder{}.prepare_response(name);
  CHECK(status == drogon::k200OK);
```

```
  CHECK(value == "Hello, Zero Cool!");
}

int main(const int argc, char** argv) { return drogon::test::run(argc, argv); }
```

This example is straightforward. The framework is a convenient choice for projects built with Drogon, especially when testing asynchronous code.

[Boost].UT example

[Boost].UT or µ(micro) is a single header/module framework that's macro-free and supports parameterized tests, assertions, matchers, runners, reporters, and logging. Tests can be written using BDD methodology (including Gherkin specification and Spec notation).

The framework utilizes C++20 features to implement these features:

- Avoiding unique types for lambda expressions, which speeds up compilation by 5x since no new type is introduced for each lambda
- Type-name erasure, allowing type/function memoization (storing results of expensive computations), which also speeds up compilation
- Assertions combined with the C++20 `source_location` class, which represents specific information about source code such as filenames, line numbers, and function names, useful for logging, testing, or debugging purposes, instead of predefined macros such as `__FILE__` (the current source file), `__FUNCTION__` (the enclosing function), and `__LINE__` (a line number in the current source file)
- Specifying configuration options with designated initializers for writing more concise code
- Constant matchers accepting non-type template parameters
- Parameterized tests supporting template parameter lists for generic lambdas
- C++20 concepts defining constraints of templates and C++20 modules

Here is an example test for our `customer` library:

```
#define BOOST_UT_DISABLE_MODULE
#include <boost/ut.hpp>
// import boost.ut;

#include "customer/responder.h"
namespace ut = boost::ut;

ut::suite<"responder tests"> _ = [] {
  using namespace boost::ut;
  "basic_responses"_test = [] {
    const auto name = "Kelvin Torbo";
    const auto [status, value] = responder{}.prepare_response(name);
    should("given_name_when_prepare_responses_then_greets_friendly") =
```

```
    [status, value] {
      expect(status == drogon::k200OK);
      expect(value == "Hello, Kelvin Torbo!");
    };
  };
};

int main() {}
```

This example highlights [Boost].UT's modern, macro-free style, where tests are defined with BDD-style `should` blocks.

While the preceding frameworks help with testing runtime execution, C++ also allows compile-time testing, which we cover next.

Compile-time testing techniques

Template metaprogramming allows us to write C++ code that is executed during compile-time as opposed to the usual runtime execution. The `constexpr` keyword, which was added in C++11, allows us to make more extensive use of compile-time logic, and the `consteval` keyword from C++20 aims to give us greater control over the way the code is evaluated during compilation.

One of the problems with compile-time programming is that there is no easy way to test it. While unit testing frameworks for execution time code are abundant (as we just saw), there are not that many resources regarding compile-time programming. Part of this may stem from the fact that compile-time programming is still considered complicated and only aimed at experts.

However, just because something isn't easy doesn't mean it is impossible. Just like execution time tests rely on assertions being checked during runtime, you can check your compile-time code for correct behavior using `static_assert`, which was introduced alongside `consteval` in C++20.

The following is a simple example of using `static_assert`:

```
#include <cstdint>
#include <string_view>

consteval uint64_t  generate_lucky_number(std::string_view name) {
  uint64_t number = 1;
  for (const auto letter : name) {
    number = number * 7 + static_cast<uint64_t>(letter);
  }
  return number;
}

static_assert(generate_lucky_number("Paul and Jessica") == 491752089676924,
              "Generate the lucky number for Paul and Jessica");
```

Here, the second argument to `static_assert` provides a custom message. If the check fails, the compiler will stop the build and report an error such as the following:

```
error: static assertion failed: Generate the lucky number for Paul and Jessica.
```

Since the results of these function calls are computed during compile time, we can effectively use the compiler as our testing framework. The limitation, however, is that compile-time failures stop compilation immediately, and unlike runtime frameworks, there is no aggregation of multiple test results.

While compile-time testing could be helpful, most real-world applications still rely heavily on runtime interactions. These interactions bring their own challenges when it comes to testing. That's where techniques such as using test doubles come into play.

Understanding test doubles

As long as you are testing functions that do not interact too much with the outside world, things are pretty easy. The problems start when the units you are testing interface with third-party components such as databases, HTTP connections, and specific files.

On the one hand, you want to see how your code behaves due to various circumstances. On the other hand, you don't want to wait for the database to boot, and you definitely don't want to have several databases containing different versions of data so that you can check all the necessary conditions.

How can we deal with such cases? The idea is not to execute the actual code that triggers all those side effects, but instead to use test doubles. Test doubles are constructions in code that mimic the actual API, except they don't perform the actions of the mimicked functions or objects.

The most common test doubles are mocks, spies, dummies, fakes, and stubs. Many people tend to mistake one for the other as they are similar, though not the same.

Different test doubles

Mocks are test doubles that verify interactions. They are pre-programmed with expectations about which calls should be made, and the test fails if those expectations are not met.

Spies record information about how they were called (for example, arguments or number of calls), so that tests can verify interactions after execution.

Dummies are placeholder objects that are never actually used. They satisfy parameter requirements in constructors, functions, or methods without affecting the test logic.

Stubs return predefined values but do not contain logic. For example, a `StubRandom.randomInteger()` method might always return the same value (for example, `3`), but it may be a sufficient stub implementation when we are testing the type of the returned value or the fact that it does return a value at all. The exact value may not be that important. Besides, random values, such as timestamps, can cause tests to fail if they are not predictable.

Finally, fakes are lightweight objects that have a working implementation and behave mostly like the actual implementation. The main difference is that fakes may take various shortcuts, such as avoiding calling the production database or filesystem, which makes them unsuitable for production.

Fakes can also be used, to a limited extent, outside of testing. For example, in-memory processing data without resorting to database access can also be great for prototyping or when you're hitting performance bottlenecks. But their use in these scenarios has nothing to do with test doubles.

When implementing the **command query separation** (CQS) design pattern, you will usually want to double queries with stubs (since they return values) and commands with mocks (since they represent actions that need to be verified).

Writing test doubles

To write test doubles, we typically use an external library, just as we do with unit tests. Some of the most popular solutions are as follows:

- **Google Mock** (also known as **gMock**) is now a part of the GoogleTest library.
- **Trompeloeil** focuses on C++14, integrates well with many testing libraries, such as Catch2, Doctest, and GTest.
- **CppUMock**, a part of CppUTest, integrates with GTest and gMock.
- **FakeIt** is a single header framework written in C++11 and easily integrated with GTest, MS Test, and Boost.Test. FakeIt's syntax closely resembles gMock; that's why we have not presented a separate example. If you are already familiar with gMock, picking up FakeIt will require only a little effort.

The code in the following sections will show you how to use gMock, Trompeloeil, and CppUMock. To keep things consistent, we will continue using the example we utilized earlier in this chapter.

gMock example

Since gMock is part of GTest, we will present them together.

In the example, we'll use mocks for the merchant and responder to check interactions, and a fake review store that keeps data in memory. This way, we can test the logic without real external systems.

This helper test class provides and stores posted customer reviews of merchants:

```
#pragma once
#include <optional>
#include <unordered_map>
#include "merchants/reviews.h"

class fake_customer_review_store : public i_customer_review_store {
public:
  explicit fake_customer_review_store(review::customer_id_t customer_id)
      : customer_id_(customer_id) {}

  std::optional<review> get_review_for_merchant(
```

```
      review::merchant_id_t merchant_id) final {
    if (auto it = reviews_.find(merchant_id); it != std::end(reviews_)) {
      return it->second;
    }
    return {};
  }

  void post_review(review r) final {
    if (r.customer != customer_id_) {
      throw std::invalid_argument{
          "Trying to post a review under a different customer ID"};
    }
    reviews_[r.merchant] = std::move(r);
  }

private:
  review::customer_id_t customer_id_;
  std::unordered_map<review::merchant_id_t, review> reviews_;
};
```

Mock classes are defined as normal classes, with macros to generate mocked methods and specify their behavior. In our case, the `MOCK_METHOD` macro generates the mocked methods inside the `merchant` class, and the `ON_CALL` macro defines their default actions:

```
#include <gmock/gmock.h>
#include <merchants/visited_merchant_history.h>
#include "fake_customer_review_store.h"
#include "merchants/reviews.h"

namespace {

class mock_visited_merchant : public i_visited_merchant {
public:
  explicit mock_visited_merchant(fake_customer_review_store &store,
                                 merchant_id_t id)
      : review_store_{store},
        review_{store.get_review_for_merchant(id).value()} {
    ON_CALL(*this, post_rating).WillByDefault([this](stars s) {
      review_.rating = s;
      review_store_.post_review(review_);
    });
    ON_CALL(*this, get_rating).WillByDefault([this] { return review_.rating;
```

```
});
  }

  MOCK_METHOD(stars, get_rating, (), (override));
  MOCK_METHOD(void, post_rating, (stars s), (override));

private:
  fake_customer_review_store &review_store_;
  review review_;
};

} // namespace
```

GTest fixtures support the `SetUp()` and `TearDown()` methods to initialize and clean up test data. The following fixture class, `history_with_one_rated_merchant`, contains a fake review store and a mocked merchant for the tests:

```
class history_with_one_rated_merchant : public ::testing::Test {
public:
  static constexpr std::size_t CUSTOMER_ID = 7777;
  static constexpr std::size_t MERCHANT_ID = 1234;
  static constexpr const char *REVIEW_TEXT = "Blue Manic Monday";
  static constexpr stars RATING = stars{5.f};

protected:
  void SetUp() final {
    fake_review_store_.post_review(
        {CUSTOMER_ID, MERCHANT_ID, REVIEW_TEXT, RATING});

    // nice mock will not warn on "uninteresting" call to get_rating
    auto mocked_merchant =
        std::make_unique<::testing::NiceMock<mock_visited_merchant>>(
            fake_review_store_, MERCHANT_ID);

    merchant_index_ = history_.add(std::move(mocked_merchant));
  }

  fake_customer_review_store fake_review_store_{CUSTOMER_ID};
  history_of_visited_merchants history_{};
  std::size_t merchant_index_{};
};
```

The `TEST_F` macro creates an instance of the test fixture and provides access to objects and subroutines in the instance. The `EXPECT_CALL` macro sets expectations, which means that either the expected methods are called a certain number of times, including zero, or the test fails. Notice that the `post_rating` method is mocked:

```
TEST_F(history_with_one_rated_merchant,
       when_user_changes_rating_then_the_review_is_updated_in_store) {
  const auto &mocked_merchant = dynamic_cast<const mock_visited_merchant &>(
      history_.get_merchant(merchant_index_));
  EXPECT_CALL(mocked_merchant, post_rating);
  constexpr auto new_rating = stars{4};
  static_assert(RATING != new_rating);
  history_.rate(merchant_index_, stars{new_rating});
}

TEST_F(history_with_one_rated_merchant,
       when_user_selects_same_rating_then_the_review_is_not_updated_in_store) {
  const auto &mocked_merchant = dynamic_cast<const mock_visited_merchant
&>(history_.get_merchant(merchant_index_));
  EXPECT_CALL(mocked_merchant, post_rating).Times(0);
  history_.rate(merchant_index_, stars{RATING});
}
```

Here is another example test for our `customer` library. This example is like the previous one, but it defines a custom matcher, `contains_value`, with the `MATCHER_P` macro and does not rely on fixtures:

```
#include <gmock/gmock.h>
#include "customer/responder.h"
using namespace ::testing;
namespace {

class responder_mock {
public:
  MOCK_METHOD(
      (std::pair<drogon::HttpStatusCode, Json::Value>),  // note the
parentheses
      prepare_response, (const std::string &name), ());
  MOCK_METHOD(void, respond,
              (drogon::HttpStatusCode status, const Json::Value &response,
               std::function<void(const drogon::HttpResponsePtr &)>
               &&callback),
               ());
};
```

```
MATCHER_P(contains_value, value, "") { return arg == value; }

} // namespace
```

The first expectation returns a test response when the prepare_response method is called. The second one verifies that a value passed to the respond method matches the expected value:

```
TEST(basic_responses,
     given_name_when_handle_get_then_response_is_prepared_and_sent) {
  drogon::HttpRequestPtr request = drogon::HttpRequest::newHttpRequest();
  request->setMethod(drogon::HttpMethod::Get);
  request->setPath("/customer");
  request->setParameter("name", "Rotoro");
  auto responder = StrictMock<responder_mock>{};
  const auto response = Json::Value("Bizarre Club");

  EXPECT_CALL(responder, prepare_response("Rotoro"))
  WillOnce(Return(std::pair{drogon::k200OK, response}));
  EXPECT_CALL(responder, respond(drogon::k200OK, contains_value(response), _));
  handle_get(request, responder, [](const drogon::HttpResponsePtr &) {});
}
```

GTest is the most popular C++ testing framework at the time of writing this book. Its integration with gMock means that gMock is already available for you in your project. This combination is intuitive to use and fully featured, so there's no reason to look for alternatives if you're already invested in GTest.

Trompeloeil example

To contrast this example with the previous one, this time, we are using Trompeloeil for test doubles and Catch2 as a testing framework:

```
#include <merchants/visited_merchant_history.h>

#include <catch2/catch_all.hpp>
#include <catch2/trompeloeil.hpp>
#include <memory>

#include "fake_customer_review_store.h"
#include "merchants/reviews.h"

using trompeloeil::_;
```

The `MAKE_MOCKn` macro creates mock implementations of the member functions:

```
class mock_visited_merchant final : public i_visited_merchant {
public:
  MAKE_MOCK0(get_rating, stars(), override);
  MAKE_MOCK1(post_rating, void(stars s), override);
};
```

This test uses BDD-style syntax with the `GIVEN`, `WHEN`, and `THEN` macros in Gherkin style. In this example, test fixtures are not needed because the test data is in the scope of the macros:

```
SCENARIO("merchant history keeps store up to date", "[mobile app]") {
  GIVEN("a history with one rated merchant") {
    static constexpr std::size_t CUSTOMER_ID = 7777;
    static constexpr std::size_t MERCHANT_ID = 1234;
    static constexpr const char *REVIEW_TEXT = "I'm like TT, just like TT";
    static constexpr stars RATING = stars{5.f};

    auto fake_review_store_ = fake_customer_review_store{CUSTOMER_ID};
    fake_review_store_.post_review(
        {CUSTOMER_ID, MERCHANT_ID, REVIEW_TEXT, RATING});

    auto history_ = history_of_visited_merchants{};
    const auto merchant_index_ =
        history_.add(std::make_unique<mock_visited_merchant>());

    auto &mocked_merchant = const_cast<mock_visited_merchant &>(
        dynamic_cast<const mock_visited_merchant &>(
            history_.get_merchant(merchant_index_)));

    auto review_ = review{CUSTOMER_ID, MERCHANT_ID, REVIEW_TEXT, RATING};
```

The `ALLOW_CALL`, `LR_SIDE_EFFECT`, `LR_RETURN`, `REQUIRE_CALL`, and `FORBID_CALL` macros set expectations. For calls that match these expectations, the first `ALLOW_CALL` macro causes side effects (updating the review and posting it), and the second specifies what `get_rating()` should return:

```
    ALLOW_CALL(mocked_merchant, post_rating(_))
        .LR_SIDE_EFFECT(review_.rating = _1;
                        fake_review_store_.post_review(review_););
    ALLOW_CALL(mocked_merchant, get_rating()).LR_RETURN(review_.rating);

    WHEN("a user changes rating") {
      constexpr auto new_rating = stars{4};
      static_assert(RATING != new_rating);
```

```
      THEN("the review is updated in store") {
        REQUIRE_CALL(mocked_merchant, post_rating(_));
        history_.rate(merchant_index_, stars{new_rating});
      }
    }

    WHEN("a user selects same rating") {
      THEN("the review is not updated in store") {
        FORBID_CALL(mocked_merchant, post_rating(_));
        history_.rate(merchant_index_, stars{RATING});
      }
    }
  }
}
```

One of the great features of Catch2 is that it makes it easy to write BDD-style tests, such as the one shown here. If you prefer this style, then Catch2 with Trompeloeil would be a good choice, as they integrate very well.

CppUMock example

CppUTest supports mocks and their scopes with CppUMock, which mocks functions, class methods, and values, sets expectations, verifies parameters, and returns values, including objects of different types.

This example uses only a few features of this framework:

```
#include "fake_customer_review_store.h"
#include "merchants/reviews.h"
#include "merchants/visited_merchant_history.h"

#include <CppUTest/CommandLineTestRunner.h>
#include <CppUTest/TestHarness.h>
#include <CppUTestExt/MockSupport.h>

namespace {
class mock_visited_merchant final : public i_visited_merchant {
public:
  explicit mock_visited_merchant(fake_customer_review_store &store,
                                 const merchant_id_t id)
      : review_store_{store},
        review_{store.get_review_for_merchant(id).value()} {}

  stars get_rating() override { return review_.rating; }
```

Here, `MockSupport` registers that the test double's `post_rating()` method was called on this particular instance, via the `mock().actualCall(__func__).onObject(this)` call:

```
  void post_rating(const stars s) override {
    mock().actualCall(__func__).onObject(this);
    review_.rating = s;
    review_store_.post_review(review_);
  }

private:
  fake_customer_review_store &review_store_;
  review review_;
};
} // namespace
```

Every test group in CppUTest can have setup and teardown methods to initialize and clean up test data. In the teardown method, `MockSupport` verifies that expectations were met and then clears the `mock` state:

```
TEST_GROUP(history_with_one_rated_merchant) {
  static constexpr std::size_t CUSTOMER_ID = 7777;
  static constexpr std::size_t MERCHANT_ID = 1234;
  static constexpr const char *REVIEW_TEXT =
      "It's not 'Door to Heaven' it is...";
  static constexpr stars RATING = stars{5.f};

  TEST_SETUP() {
    fake_review_store_.post_review(
        {CUSTOMER_ID, MERCHANT_ID, REVIEW_TEXT, RATING});

    merchant_index_ = history_.add(std::make_unique<mock_visited_merchant>(
        fake_review_store_, MERCHANT_ID));
  }

  TEST_TEARDOWN() {
    mock().checkExpectations();
    mock().clear();
  }

  fake_customer_review_store fake_review_store_{CUSTOMER_ID};
  history_of_visited_merchants history_{};
  std::size_t merchant_index_{};
};
```

Here, MockSupport sets the expectation that the post_rating() member function of mocked_merchant is called exactly once; otherwise, the test fails:

```
TEST(history_with_one_rated_merchant,
      when_user_changes_rating_then_the_review_is_updated_in_store) {
  const auto &mocked_merchant = history_.get_merchant(merchant_index_);
  mock()
      .expectOneCall("post_rating")
      .onObject(const_cast<i_visited_merchant *>(&mocked_merchant));

  constexpr auto new_rating = stars{4};
  static_assert(RATING != new_rating);
  history_.rate(merchant_index_, stars{new_rating});
}
```

Here, MockSupport sets the expectation that the post_rating() member function of mocked_merchant is never called; otherwise, the test fails:

```
TEST(history_with_one_rated_merchant,
      when_user_selects_same_rating_then_the_review_is_not_updated_in_store) {
  const auto &mocked_merchant = history_.get_merchant(merchant_index_);
  mock()
      .expectNCalls(0, "post_rating")
      .onObject(const_cast<i_visited_merchant *>(&mocked_merchant));

  history_.rate(merchant_index_, stars{RATING});
}
```

Finally, the test runner executes all tests:

```
int main(const int ac, char **av) { return RUN_ALL_TESTS(ac, av); }
```

CppUTest's main strength lies in its simplicity and suitability for embedded systems. With CppUMock, you can set clear expectations and verify interactions in a lightweight way. However, compared to larger frameworks such as GTest, its mocking capabilities are limited, so it may not be the best choice for complex projects outside embedded contexts.

Using test doubles makes testing convenient, but they won't help if your classes are difficult to test in the first place. This is why test-driven design is the way to go.

Test-driven class design

It's not enough to distinguish between different types of tests and learn a particular testing framework (or several). When you start testing your actual code, you will soon notice that not all classes can be tested easily. Sometimes, you may feel the need to access private attributes or methods. Resist this urge if you want to maintain the principles of good architecture! Instead, consider either testing the business requirements that are available through the type's public API or refactoring the type so that there's another unit of code you can test.

When tests and class design clash

The problem you may be facing is not that the testing frameworks are inadequate. Usually, what you encounter are inappropriately designed classes. Even though your classes may behave correctly and may look correct unless they allow for testing, they are not designed correctly.

The good news is that testing reveals flaws in class design. It means that you can repair the problem before it's inconvenient to do so. The class design will probably haunt you later on when you start building a class hierarchy based on it. Fixing the design during test implementation will simply reduce the possible technological debt.

The boring refrain: write your tests first

This has been said many times, yet many people tend to "forget" this rule. When you write your tests, the first thing you must do is reduce the risk of creating classes that are hard to test. You start with API usage and need to bend the implementation to best serve the API. This way, you usually end up with APIs that are both more pleasant to use and easier to test. When you're implementing **test-driven development** (TDD) or writing tests before code, you'll also end up implementing dependency injection, which means your classes can be more loosely coupled.

Doing this the other way around (writing your classes first and only then adding unit tests to them) may result in code that is easier to write but harder to test. And when testing gets harder, you may feel the temptation to skip it.

To make testing effective across the entire development life cycle, not just during implementation, you also need to automate those tests.

Defensive programming

Unlike its name may suggest, defensive programming is not a security feature. Its name comes from defending your classes and functions from being used contrary to their original intention. It's not directly related to testing, but it's a great design pattern to use since it improves your code's quality, making your project future-proof.

Defensive programming starts with static typing. For example, if you create a function that handles a custom-defined type as a parameter, you must make sure nobody will call it with an accidental value. A user will have to consciously check what the function expects and prepare the input accordingly.

In C++, we can also leverage type-safety features when we're writing template code. When we're creating a container for our customers' reviews, we could accept a list of any type and copy from it. To get nicer errors and well-crafted checks, we could write the following:

```
class CustomerReviewStore : public i_customer_review_store {
 public:
  CustomerReviewStore() = default;
  explicit CustomerReviewStore(const std::ranges::range auto
                                  &initial_reviews) {
   static_assert(is_range_of_reviews_v<decltype(initial_reviews)>,
                 "Must pass in a collection of reviews");
   std::ranges::copy(begin(initial_reviews), end(initial_reviews),
                     begin(reviews_));
  }
 // ...
 private:
  std::vector<review> reviews_;
};
```

The `explicit` keyword protects us from unwanted implicit casts. By specifying that our input parameter satisfies the `range` concept, we ensure that we're only going to compile with a valid container. Thanks to using concepts, we can get clearer error messages from our defense against invalid use. Using `static_assert` in our code is also a great defensive measure, as it allows us to provide a meaningful error message if needed. Our `is_range_of_reviews` check could be implemented as follows:

```
template <typename T>
constexpr bool is_range_of_reviews_v =
    std::is_same_v<std::ranges::range_value_t<T>, review>;
```

This way, we ensure that the range we got really contains reviews of the type we desire.

Static typing will not prevent invalid runtime values from being passed to the function. That's why the next form of defensive programming is checking preconditions. This way, your code will fail as soon as the first sign of a problem arises, which is always better than returning an invalid value that propagates to other parts of the system. Until we have contracts in C++, we can use the GSL library we mentioned in earlier chapters to check the pre- and post-conditions of our code:

```
void post_review(review review) final {
  Expects(review.merchant);
  Expects(review.customer);
  Ensures(!reviews_.empty());

  reviews_.push_back(std::move(review));
}
```

Here, by using the `Expects` macro, we're checking that our incoming review has the IDs of the merchant and reviewer set. Aside from the cases where it doesn't, we are also defending ourselves against cases where adding a review to our storage failed when we use the `Ensures` post-condition macro.

When it comes to runtime checks, one of the first things that comes to mind is checking whether one or more attributes are not a `nullptr` type. The best way to guard yourself against this problem is to distinguish nullable resources (those that can take `nullptr` as a value) from non-nullable ones. There's a great tool you can use for this, which is available in the standard library from C++17: `std::optional`. If you can, use it in all the APIs that you design.

In the next section, we'll look at how automated testing fits into CI/CD workflows.

Automating application tests for CI/CD

In the next chapter, we will focus on CI/CD. For a CI/CD pipeline to work properly, you need to have a set of tests that catch the bugs before they enter production. It is up to you and your team to make sure all the business requirements are properly expressed as tests.

Tests are useful on several levels. With BDD, which we mentioned in the previous section, business requirements form a basis for automated tests. But the system you are building doesn't consist solely of business requirements. You want to make sure all the third-party integrations are working as expected. You want to make sure all your subcomponents (such as microservices) can interface with each other. Finally, you want to make sure that the functions and classes you are building are free of any bugs you could have imagined.

Each test that you can automate is a candidate for a CI/CD pipeline. Each of them also has its place somewhere in this pipeline. For example, end-to-end tests make the most sense after the deployment as acceptance tests. On the other hand, unit tests make the most sense when they're executed directly after compilation. After all, our aim is to break the circuit as soon as we find any possible divergence from the specification.

You don't have to run all the tests that you have automated each time you run a CI/CD pipeline. It's better if the runtime of each pipeline is relatively short. Ideally, it should finish within a couple of minutes of the commit. How can we make sure everything is properly tested, then, if we want to keep the runtime minimal?

One answer is to prepare different suites of tests for different purposes. For example, you can have minimal tests for commits to a feature branch. With many commits coming to feature branches every day, this means they will only be tested briefly, and the answer will be available fast. Merging feature branches to the shared development branch then requires a slightly larger set of test cases. This way, we make sure we haven't broken anything that other team members will be using. Finally, a more extensive set of cases will be run for merges to production branches. After all, we want the production branches to be tested thoroughly, even if the testing takes quite a long time.

Another answer is to use the trimmed-down set of test cases for CI/CD purposes and have an additional continuous testing process. This process runs regularly and performs in-depth checks on the current state of a particular environment. The tests can go as far as security tests and performance tests, and may thus assess the eligibility of the environment to be promoted.

Promotion occurs when we select an environment and acknowledge that this environment has all the qualities to become a more mature environment (for example, from the development environment to the next staging environment, or from staging to production). If this promotion happens automatically, it is also a good practice to provide automatic rollback in case the subtle differences (such as in terms of domain name or traffic) make the freshly promoted environment no longer pass the tests.

This also presents another important practice: to always run tests on the production environment. Such tests have to be the least intrusive, of course, but they should tell you that your system is performing correctly at any given time.

Automating infrastructure validation for CI/CD

If you want to incorporate the concepts of configuration management, **infrastructure as code** (IaC), or immutable deployments into the software architecture of your application, you should also consider validating the infrastructure setup itself. This means checking that servers, containers, and environments are in the expected state before application tests run. There are several tools you can use to do this, including Serverspec, Testinfra, Goss, and Terratest, which are among some of the more popular ones.

These tools slightly differ in scope, as stated here:

- **Serverspec** and **Testinfra** focus more on testing the actual state of the servers that are configured via configuration management tools, such as SaltStack (or simply Salt), Ansible, Puppet, CFEngine, and Chef. They're written in Ruby and Python, respectively, and they plug into the testing engines of their respective languages. This means RSpec for Serverspec and pytest for Testinfra.
- **Goss** is a bit different both in terms of scope and form. Besides testing the servers, you can also use Goss to test the containers you use in your project with the `dgoss` wrapper. As for its form, it doesn't use the imperative code you would see in Serverspec or Testinfra. Rather, similar to Ansible or Salt, it uses a YAML file to describe the desired state we want to check for. If you're already using a declarative approach to configuration management (such as the aforementioned Ansible or Salt), Goss may be more intuitive and thus a much better fit for testing.
- Finally, **Terratest** is a tool that allows you to test the output of IaC tools such as Packer and Terraform (hence the name). Just like Serverspec and Testinfra use testing engines of their respective languages to write tests for servers, Terratest leverages Go's testing package to write the appropriate test cases.

Tools such as Serverspec, Testinfra, and Goss are included here because they show how infrastructure validation usually works. They are commonly used in CI/CD pipelines alongside C++ projects, even though they are not written in C++. Terratest, on the other hand, is focused on testing IaC tools such as Terraform and Packer. Since that scope goes beyond what's usually needed in C++ workflows, we mention it here for completeness but do not provide code examples.

Let's see how we can use Serverspec, Testinfra, and Goss to validate that the deployment went according to plan (at least from the infrastructure's point of view).

Testing with Serverspec

The following is an example of a test for Serverspec that checks the availability of Git in a specific version and the Let's Encrypt configuration file:

```
# We want to have git 1:2.1.4 installed if we're running Debian
describe package('git'), :if => os[:family] == 'debian' do
  it { should be_installed.with_version('1:2.1.4') }
end
# We want the file /etc/letsencrypt/config/example.com.conf to:
describe file('/etc/letsencrypt/config/example.com.conf') do
  it { should be_file } # be a regular file
  it { should be_owned_by 'letsencrypt' } # owned by the letsencrypt user
  it { should be_mode 600 } # access mode 0600
  it { should contain('example.com') } # contain the text example.com
                                       # in the content
end
```

The Ruby DSL syntax should be readable even by those who do not use Ruby daily. However, you may need to get used to writing the code.

Testing with Testinfra

Here's how the same checks are implemented using Testinfra:

```
# We want Git installed on our host
def test_git_is_installed(host):
    git = host.package("git")
    # we test if the package is installed
    assert git.is_installed
    # and if it matches version 1:2.1.4 (using Debian versioning)
    assert git.version.startswith("1:2.1.4")
# We want the file /etc/letsencrypt/config/example.com.conf to:
def test_letsencrypt_file(host):
    le = host.file("/etc/letsencrypt/config/example.com.conf")
    assert le.user == "letsencrypt" # be owned by the letsencrypt user
    assert le.mode == 0o600 # access mode 0600
    assert le.contains("example.com") # contain the text example.com in the
contents
```

Testinfra uses plain Python syntax. It should be readable, but just like Serverspec, you may need some training to confidently write tests in it.

Testing with Goss

The following is an example of a YAML file for Goss that implements the same checks:

```
# We want Git installed on our host
package:
  git:
    installed: true # we test if the package is installed
  versions:
  - 1:2.1.4 # and if it matches version 1:2.1.4 (using Debian versioning)
file:
  # We want the file /etc/letsencrypt/config/example.com.conf to:
  /etc/letsencrypt/config/example.com.conf:
    exists: true
  filetype: file # be a regular file
  owner: letsencrypt # be owned by the letsencrypt user
  mode: "0600" # access mode 0600
  contains:
  - "example.com" # contain the text example.com in the contents
```

YAML's syntax will probably require the least preparation, both to read and write it. However, if your project already uses Ruby or Python, you may want to stick to Serverspec or Testinfra when it comes to writing more complicated tests.

Summary

This chapter focused on both the architectural and technical aspects of testing different parts of the software. We looked at the testing pyramid to understand how different kinds of tests contribute to the overall health and stability of a software project. Since testing can be both functional and non-functional, we saw some examples of both types.

One of the most important things to remember from this chapter is that tests are not the end stage. We want to have them not because they bring immediate value, but because we can use them to check for known regressions when refactoring, or when we're changing the behavior of existing parts of the system. Tests can also prove useful when we want to perform root cause analysis, as they can quickly verify different hypotheses.

Having established the theoretical requirements, we showed examples of the different testing frameworks and libraries we can use to write test doubles. Even though writing tests first and their implementation later requires some practice, it has an important benefit. This benefit is a better class design.

Finally, to highlight that modern architecture is something more than just software code, we also looked at a few tools for testing infrastructure and deployment.

Testing is crucial for automation pipelines that run checks consistently and enforce quality at every step. In the next chapter, we will see how CI and CD bring better service quality and robustness to the applications you design and architect.

Questions

1. What is the base layer of the testing pyramid?
2. What kinds of non-functional tests are there?
3. What is the name of the famous method for root cause analysis?
4. Is it possible to test the compile-time code in C++?
5. What should you use when you're writing unit tests for code with external dependencies?
6. What is the role of unit tests in CI/CD?
7. What are some tools that allow you to test infrastructure code?
8. Is it a good idea to access the class's private attributes and methods in a unit test?

Further reading

- Marius Bancila, *Modern C++ Programming Cookbook: Master Modern C++ with Comprehensive Solutions for C++23 and All Previous Standards*, Third Edition, Packt Publishing: `https://www.packtpub.com/en-us/product/modern-c-programming-cookbook-9781835080542`
- Martin Fowler, *Mocks Aren't Stubs*: `https://martinfowler.com/articles/mocksArentStubs.html`
- Martin Fowler, *Test Pyramid*: `https://martinfowler.com/bliki/TestPyramid.html`
- LLVM Project, *Clang: Source-Based Code Coverage*: `https://clang.llvm.org/docs/SourceBasedCodeCoverage.html`
- GNU Project, *gcov—A Test Coverage Program*: `https://gcc.gnu.org/onlinedocs/gcc/Gcov.html`
- SmartBear, *How to Avoid 7 Common Software-Testing Problems*: `https://smartbear.com/resources/ebooks/how-to-avoid-7-common-software-testing-problems/`
- Pact, *Should you use Pact? Convince me*: `https://docs.pact.io/faq/convinceme`
- Pact, *README* (Pact C++ implementation guide): `https://docs.pact.io/implementation_guides/cpp`

11

Continuous Integration and Continuous Deployment

In *Chapter 7, Building and Packaging*, we learned about different build systems and different packaging systems that our application can use. These form the foundation of automated pipelines. In this chapter, we build on that knowledge by introducing **continuous integration** (CI) and **continuous deployment** (CD)—practices that improve service quality and the robustness of the application we are developing. While CI/CD is often associated with DevOps workflows, it's equally relevant for C++ architects and developers who need to ensure that systems can evolve safely and be released predictably.

CI and CD rely on good test coverage. A CI pipeline uses mostly unit tests and integration tests, whereas CD depends more on smoke tests (a minimal set of tests passing, which shows that the product is ready for further testing to save time and resources by identifying critical errors at an early stage) and end-to-end tests, to ensure the application behaves correctly. You have already gained insights about the different aspects of testing in the previous chapter. With this knowledge, you are ready to build a CI/CD pipeline.

In this chapter, we'll cover the following topics:

- Understanding and implementing CI
- Exploring gating mechanisms
- Reviewing code changes
- Exploring test-driven automation
- Managing deployment as code
- Building deployment code
- Understanding and implementing CD
- Using immutable infrastructure

Along the way, you'll gain hands-on experience with GitLab and GitHub CI/CD pipelines, which are fundamental building blocks of CI/CD, as well as supporting tools such as Ansible, Packer, and Terraform, giving you a practical foundation for designing robust CI/CD workflows.

Technical requirements

The sample code of this chapter can be found at `https://github.com/PacktPublishing/Software-Architecture-with-Cpp-2E/tree/main/Chapter11`.

To understand the concepts explained in this chapter, you'll require the following installations:

- A free GitLab account
- A free GitHub account
- Ansible version 11.1+
- Terraform version 1.11+
- Packer version 1.12+

Understanding and implementing CI

CI is the process of shortening integration cycles by merging changes in code frequently. While in traditional software, many different features are developed separately and only integrated prior to release, in projects developed with CI, integration can occur several times a day.

Usually, each change a developer makes is tested and integrated at the same time into the central repository. Since testing occurs each time a change occurs, the feedback loop is much quicker as issues are identified and resolved quickly, often while the change is still fresh in the developer's mind. Thus, in contrast to the traditional approach of testing just prior to release, CI saves a lot of work and improves the quality of software.

In this section, we'll explore the philosophy that led to CI and the benefits CI brings to a workflow. Finally, we'll go into implementation and build a CI pipeline using GitLab.

Release early, release often

Have you ever heard the saying *"release early, release often"*? This is a software development philosophy that emphasizes the importance of short release cycles. Short release cycles, in turn, provide a much shorter feedback loop between planning, development, and validation. When something breaks, it should break as early as possible so that the costs of fixing the problem are relatively small.

This philosophy was popularized by Eric S. Raymond (also known as ESR) in his 1997 essay entitled *The Cathedral and the Bazaar*. There's also a book with the same title that contains this and other essays by the author. Considering ESR's activity within open source movements, the *release early, release often* mantra became synonymous with how open source projects operated.

Some years later, the same principle moved beyond just open source projects. With the rising interest in Agile methodologies, such as Scrum, the mantra became synonymous with development sprints that end with a product increment. This increment is, of course, a software release, but usually, there are many other releases that happen during the sprint.

So, how can you achieve such short release cycles? One answer is to rely on automation as much as possible. Ideally, every commit to the code repository should end as a release. Whether this release ends up facing the customers is another matter. What's important is that every code change can result in a usable product.

Of course, building and releasing every single commit to the public would be a tedious job for any developer. Even when everything is scripted, this can add unnecessary overhead to the usual chores. This is why you would want to set up a CI system to automate the releases for you and your development team.

Merits of CI

CI is the concept of integrating the work of several developers into a shared repository, at least daily. As already discussed, sometimes it can mean several times a day. Every commit that enters the repository is integrated and validated separately. The build system checks whether the code can be built without errors. The packaging system may create a package that is ready to be saved as an artifact or even deployed later on when CD is used. Finally, the automated tests check that no known regression occurred in relation to the change. Let's now see its merits in detail:

- CI allows for the rapid solving of problems. If one of the developers forgot a semicolon at the end of the line, the compiler on the CI system will catch that error right away before this incorrect code reaches other developers, thereby impeding their work. Of course, developers should always build the changes and test them before committing the code, but minor typos can go unnoticed on the developer's machine and enter the shared repository anyway.
- CI prevents the common "works on my machine" excuse. If a developer forgets to commit a necessary file, the CI system will fail to build the changes, yet again preventing them from spreading further and causing mischief to the whole team. The special configuration of one developer's environment also stops being an issue. If a change builds on two machines, the developer's computer and the CI system, we are safe to assume that it should build on other machines as well.

Implementing the pipeline with GitLab

Throughout this chapter, we will use popular open source tools to build a full CI/CD pipeline that incorporates gating mechanisms, automated deployment, and infrastructure automation concepts.

The first such tool is GitLab. You may have heard about it as a Git-based hosting solution, but in reality, it's much more than that. GitLab comes in several distributions:

- An open source solution that you can host on your own premises
- Self-hosted paid versions that offer additional features over the open source community edition
- And finally, a **Software as a Service** (**SaaS**) managed offering hosted under `https://gitlab.com`

For the purposes of this book, each of the distributions has all the necessary features. We will, therefore, focus on the SaaS version, as this requires the least amount of preparation.

Although `https://gitlab.com` is mainly targeted at open source projects, you can also create private projects and repositories if you don't feel like sharing your work with the entire world. This allows us to create a new private project in GitLab and populate it with the code we have already demonstrated in *Chapter 7, Building and Packaging*.

While a lot of modern CI/CD tools could work instead of GitLab CI/CD, such as GitHub Actions, Travis CI, CircleCI, Jenkins, Jenkins X, and Tekton, we've chosen GitLab as it can be used both in SaaS form and on-premises, so it should accommodate a lot of different use cases.

We will now use our previous build system to create a simple CI pipeline in GitLab. These pipelines are described in the YAML file as a series of steps and metadata. An example pipeline that builds all the required dependencies and the sample project from *Chapter 7, Building and Packaging*, would look like this:

```
# The pipeline name is interpolated
workflow:
  name: 'Pipeline for branch: $CI_COMMIT_BRANCH'

# The Docker executor runs jobs on this Docker image
default:
  image: ubuntu:25.04

variables:
  PIP_CACHE_DIR: "$CI_PROJECT_DIR/.cache/pip"
  CONAN_HOME: "$CI_PROJECT_DIR/.conan2"

# For caching the Conan home folder, pip's wheel cache and CMake build
directory
cache:
  key: build-cache
  paths:
    - .cache/pip
    - .conan2
    - build

stages:
  - build

# This script is executed before each job
before_script:
  - apt update && DEBIAN_FRONTEND=noninteractive apt install -y cmake ninja-
build rpm file

# Configure Conan and build the project
build:
  stage: build
  script:
    - DEBIAN_FRONTEND=noninteractive apt install -y build-essential git
python3-venv python3-pip
```

```
    - python3 -m venv venv && source ./venv/bin/activate
    - pip install conan
    - conan profile detect -f
    - mkdir -p build && cd build
    - conan install ../Chapter10/customer --build=missing -s build_type=Release
-s compiler=gcc -s compiler.cppstd=gnu20 -of .
    - cmake -GNinja -DBUILD_TESTING=ON -DCMAKE_BUILD_TYPE=Release ../Chapter10/
customer
    - cmake --build .
```

In the preceding `default: image` setting, we use a non-LTS base here to ensure compatibility with GCC 14 and Clang 20 without complicating the pipeline. In production, prefer an LTS image or a custom LTS image preloaded with the required toolchains.

Conan is a Python application, so the pipeline caches Python packages from the `.cache/pip` directory. The contents of the cached directories are restored before and saved after each job in the pipeline and between pipeline runs, which reduces execution time. That `cache.key` value can be computed or static.

Saving the preceding file as `.gitlab-ci.yml` in the root directory of your Git repository will automatically enable CI in GitLab and run the pipeline with each subsequent commit.

With this baseline pipeline in place, the next step is to make the configuration more maintainable. In GitLab CI, `before_script` and `after_script` commands aren't the only ways to avoid repeating code across jobs. You can optimize repeated YAML sections with the `extends` keyword, `!reference` tags, or YAML-specific features such as anchors (&), aliases (*), and map merging (<<).

For example, commands from the global `default` section in our example can be moved to the `build` job to be executed only before this job. That's possible because `before_script` and `after_script` keywords can also be defined at the job level. The following snippet demonstrates this approach using `<<: *job_before_script`:

```
.job_before_script: &job_before_script
  before_script:
    - apt update && DEBIAN_FRONTEND=noninteractive apt install -y cmake ninja-
build rpm file

build:
  stage: build
  <<: *job_before_script
  script:
      # contains the same commands as in the previous example
    - cmake -GNinja -DBUILD_TESTING=ON -DCMAKE_BUILD_TYPE=Release ../Chapter10/
customer
    - cmake --build .
```

Quick tip: Enhance your coding experience with the **AI Code Explainer** and **Quick Copy** features. Open this book in the next-gen Packt Reader. Click the **Copy** button

(1) to quickly copy code into your coding environment, or click the **Explain** button

(2) to get the AI assistant to explain a block of code to you.

```
function calculate(a, b) {
  return {sum: a + b};
};
```

Copy Explain
1 2

The next-gen Packt Reader is included for free with the purchase of this book. Scan the QR code OR go to `https://packtpub.com/unlock`, then use the search bar to find this book by name. Double-check the edition shown to make sure you get the right one.

Repeated steps can be de-duplicated and reused by using YAML format capabilities such as anchors (&) and aliases (*) to optimize GitLab CI/CD configuration files. In the example, `job_before_script` refers to the `before_script` keyword executed before the `build` stage.

If we want CI to bring value beyond simply compiling the code, we need a gating mechanism, which we cover next.

Exploring gating mechanisms

A gating mechanism allows us to discern good code changes from bad ones through automated checks, thus keeping our application safe from modifications that would render it useless. For this to happen, we need, for example, a comprehensive suite of tests. Such a suite allows us to quickly and automatically recognize when a change is problematic.

For individual components, unit tests play the role of a gating mechanism. A CI system can discard any changes that do not pass unit tests or any changes that do not reach a certain code coverage threshold. At the time of building individual components, a CI system may also use integration tests to further ensure that the changes are stable, not only by themselves but also are acting properly together.

Unit tests and integration tests are the most common automated gates. Beyond these, CI platforms can integrate with automated analysis tools that act as additional gates. Some popular tools are Codacy, Checkmarx, Coverity Scan, Codecov, Code Intelligence, CAST Software, DeepSource, Kiuwan, SonarQube, Snyk, and Veracode. For example, the GitLab and GitHub CI platforms support integration with Codacy or SonarQube, which support MISRA C++ 2023 guidelines and the latest C++ standards, enforce C++ core guidelines, and detect vulnerabilities stemming from the **OWASP** Top Ten (a list of most critical security risks for web applications, published by the **Open Worldwide Application Security Project**) and **Common Weakness Enumeration** (CWE) Top 25 (a list of the most dangerous software weaknesses, published by MITRE).

Apart from these, there are other tools, such as linters (analyzing source code for errors, vulnerabilities, and stylistic issues to improve code quality), code formatters (automatically formatting source code according to predefined style guidelines and conventions), and static analyzers (examining source code without running it to detect errors, security vulnerabilities, code smells, and deviations from coding standards), which can help achieve the desired standard of your code base in your CI/CD pipeline.

While static analysis can act as a gating mechanism, you can apply linting and formatting to each commit that enters the central repository to make it consistent with the rest of the code base. Ideally, the linting/formatting check will only have to check whether the code has already been formatted, as the formatting step should be done by developers before pushing the code to the repository. When using Git as a version control system, the mechanism of Git Hooks can prevent committing code without running the necessary tools on it.

But automated analysis can only get you so far. It can guarantee the code works according to design. But there's still a difference between code that works correctly and good code. As you've learned from this book so far, code can be considered good if it fulfills several values. Being functionally correct is just one of them. CI and its automated checks cannot replace the need for human judgment. To ensure that code changes are not only correct but also well-designed, maintainable, and aligned with project goals, manual code reviews are required. In the next section, we'll explore how code reviews complement CI/CD.

Reviewing code changes

The main purpose of manual code reviews is to double-check each change introduced to the code to make sure that it is correct, that it fits the application's architecture, and that it follows the project's guidelines and best practices. In practice, reviews help identify problems both at the subsystem level and in the overall architecture.

Code reviews can be used both with CI systems and without them. When used without CI systems, it is often the reviewer's task to test the change manually and verify that it is working as expected. CI reduces this burden by utilizing automated checks, so that reviewers can focus their manual effort on higher-level concerns such as the logical structure of the code.

Automated performance tests may or may not discover potential problems with a given function. Human eyes, on the other hand, can usually spot a sub-optimal design choice. Whether it is the wrong data structure or an algorithm with unnecessarily high computational complexity, a good architect should be able to pinpoint the problem.

But it isn't just the architect's role to perform code reviews. Peer reviews, that is, code reviews performed by peers of the author, also have their place in the development process. Such reviews are valuable because they not only allow colleagues to find bugs in each other's code but also facilitate awareness of what everybody else is doing. This way, when there is an absence in the team (whether because of a long meeting, vacation, or job rotation), another team member can substitute for the missing one. Even if they're not an expert on the topic, every other member at least knows where the interesting code is located, and everyone should be able to remember the last changes to the code. This means both the time when they happened and the scope and content of those changes.

With more people aware of how the insides of your application appear, it is also more probable that they can figure out a correlation between recent changes in one component and a newly discovered bug. Even though every person on your team probably has a different experience, they can pool their resources when everyone knows the code quite thoroughly.

So, code reviews can check whether the change fits within the desired architecture and whether its implementation is correct. We call such a code review an architectural review, or an expert's review.

If necessary, you can also perform a different kind of expert review—a cross-team expert review—when dealing with changes that integrate with external services.

As each interface is a source of potential problems, changes close to the interface level should be treated as especially dangerous. We advise you to supplement the usual peer review with an expert coming from the other side of the interface. For example, if you are writing a producer's code, ask a consumer for a review. This way, you ensure you won't miss some vital use case that you may consider very improbable, but that the other side uses constantly.

Different approaches to a code review

You will most often conduct code reviews asynchronously. This means that the communication between the author of the change under review and the reviewers does not happen in real time. Instead, each of the actors posts their comments and suggestions at any given time. Once there are no more comments, the author reworks the original change and once again puts it under review. This can take as many rounds as necessary until everyone agrees that no further corrections are necessary.

When a change is particularly controversial and an asynchronous code review takes too much time, it is beneficial to conduct a code review synchronously. This means a meeting (in-person or remotely) to resolve any opposing views on the way forward. This will happen in particular when a change contradicts one of the initial decisions due to the new knowledge acquired while implementing the change.

There are some dedicated tools aimed solely at code reviews. More often, you will want to use a tool that is built into your repository server, such as GitHub, Bitbucket, GitLab, Gerrit, Gitea, Forgejo, Gogs, Codeberg, and Codegiant.

All of the preceding offer both Git hosting and code review. Some of them go even further, providing a whole CI/CD pipeline, issue management, documentation wikis, and much more.

Using pull requests (merge requests) for a code review

When you use the combined package of code hosting and code review, the default workflow is to push the changes as a separate branch and then ask the project's owner to merge the changes in a process known as a pull request (or a merge request). Despite the fancy name, the pull request or merge request informs the project owner that you have code that you wish to merge with the main branch. This means that the reviewers should review your changes to make sure everything is in order.

Creating pull requests or merge requests with systems such as GitLab is very easy. First of all, when we push a new branch to the central repository from the command line, we can observe the following message:

```
remote:
remote: To create a merge request for fix-ci-cd, visit:
remote:    https://gitlab.com/hosacpp/continuous-integration/merge_requests/
new?merge_request%5Bsource_branch%5D=fix-ci-cd
remote:
```

If you previously had CI enabled (by adding the `.gitlab-ci.yml` file), you'll also see that the newly pushed branch has been subjected to the CI process. This occurs even before you open a merge request, and it means you can postpone tagging your colleagues until you get information from CI that every automated check has passed.

The two main ways to open a merge request are as follows:

- By following the link mentioned in the push message
- By navigating to merge requests in the GitLab UI and selecting the **Create merge request** button or the **New merge request** button

When you submit the merge request, having completed all the relevant fields, you will see that the status of the CI pipeline is also visible. If the pipeline fails, merging the change wouldn't be possible.

Code reviews help catch structural and logical issues, but it's best to use them in conjunction with repeatable, automated validation. In the next section, we explore how test-driven automation enhances CI by ensuring that every change behaves as expected.

Exploring test-driven automation

CI mainly focuses on the integration part. It means building the code of different subsystems and making sure it works. While tests are not strictly required to achieve this purpose, running CI without them seems like a waste. CI without automated tests makes it easier to introduce subtle bugs into code while giving a false sense of security.

That's one of the reasons why CI often goes hand in hand with continuous testing, which we'll cover in this section.

We'll begin with behavior-driven development, a collaborative approach that guides code creation based on the requirements. Next, we'll learn how to write tests that support quick and reliable feedback in CI. Finally, we'll show how to incorporate continuous testing into your pipeline so that every commit is automatically verified.

Behavior-driven development

So far, we have managed to set up a pipeline that performs continuous building. Each change we make to the code ends up being compiled, but we don't test it any further. Now it's time to introduce the practice of continuous testing. Testing on a low level will also act as a gating mechanism to automatically reject all the changes that do not satisfy requirements.

How can you check whether a given change satisfies requirements? This is best achieved by writing tests based on these requirements. One of the ways to do this is by following **behavior-driven development** (**BDD**). The concept of BDD is to encourage deeper collaboration between the different actors in an Agile project.

Unlike the traditional approach, where tests are written either by developers or the QA team, with BDD, the tests are created collaboratively by the following individuals:

- Developers
- QA engineers
- Business representatives

The most common way to specify tests for BDD is to use the Cucumber framework, which uses plain English phrases to describe the desired behavior of any part of the system. These sentences follow a specific pattern that can then be turned into working code, integrating with the testing framework of choice.

There is official support for C++ in the Cucumber framework, and it's based on CMake, Boost, GTest, and gMock. After specifying the desired behavior in the Cucumber format (which uses a domain-specific language known as Gherkin), we also need to provide the so-called step definitions. Step definitions are the actual code corresponding to the actions described in the Cucumber specification. For example, consider the following behavior expressed in Gherkin:

```
# language: en
Feature: Summing
In order to see how much we earn,
Sum must be able to add two numbers together

Scenario: Regular numbers
  Given I have entered 3 and 2 as parameters
  When I add them
  Then the result should be 5
```

Thus, the requirement is for a simple addition function. We can save it as a `sum.feature` file.

In order to generate valid C++ code with GTest checks, we use the appropriate Cucumber step definitions:

```
#include <gtest/gtest.h>
#include <cucumber-cpp/autodetect.hpp>
```

```
#include "sum.h"

using cucumber::ScenarioScope;

struct SumCtx {
  Sum sum;
  int a;
  int b;
  int result;
};

GIVEN("^I have entered (\\d+) and (\\d+) as parameters$", (const int a, const
int b)) {
    ScenarioScope<SumCtx> context;

    context->a = a;
    context->b = b;
}

WHEN("^I add them") {
    ScenarioScope<SumCtx> context;

    context->result = context->sum.sum(context->a, context->b);
}

THEN("^the result should be (.*)$", (const int expected)) {
    ScenarioScope<SumCtx> context;

    EXPECT_EQ(expected, context->result);
}
```

In this example, the code shows how Cucumber test steps map to GTest checks:

- The `GIVEN` step saves the two numbers we want to add
- The `WHEN` step calls the sum function
- The `THEN` step checks that the result matches the expected value using `EXPECT_EQ`

`ScenarioScope` is just a way to keep the same test data available across all three steps.

When building an application from scratch, it's a good idea to follow the BDD pattern. This book aims to show the best practices you can use in such a greenfield project. But it doesn't mean you can't try our examples in an existing project. CI and CD can be added at any given time during the life cycle of the project. Since it's always a good idea to run your tests as often as possible, using a CI system just for the purpose of continuous testing is almost always a good idea.

If you don't have behavior tests, you shouldn't need to worry. You can add them later and, for the moment, just focus on those tests you already have. Whether they are unit tests or end-to-end tests, anything that helps you assess the state of your application is a good candidate for the gating mechanism.

Writing tests for CI

For CI, it's best to focus on unit tests and, sometimes, integration tests. They work on the lowest possible level, which means they're usually quick to execute and have the smallest requirements.

Ideally, all unit tests should be self-contained (no external dependencies like a working database) and able to run in parallel. This way, when the problem appears on the level where unit tests are able to catch it, the offending code would be flagged in a matter of seconds.

There are some people who say that unit tests only make sense in interpreted languages or languages with dynamic typing, where a simple typo can cause an application to fail and even crash—for example, by using a non-existent function, class method, or variable. The argument goes that C++ already has testing built in by means of the type system and the compiler checking for erroneous code. While it's true that type checking can catch some bugs that would require separate tests in dynamically typed languages, this shouldn't be used as an excuse not to write unit tests. After all, the purpose of unit tests isn't to verify that the code can execute without any problems. We write unit tests to make sure our code not only executes but also fulfills all the business requirements we have.

As an extreme example, take a look at the following two functions. Both of them are syntactically correct, and they use proper typing. However, just by looking at them, you can probably guess which one is correct and which isn't. Unit tests help to catch this kind of misbehavior:

```
int sum(int a, int b) {
 return a + b;
}
```

The preceding function returns the sum of the two arguments provided. The following one returns their difference, which is syntactically correct, but not logically correct:

```
int sum(int a, int b) {
  return a - b;
}
```

Even though the types match and the compiler won't complain, this code wouldn't perform its task. To distinguish useful code from erroneous code, we use tests and assertions.

Continuous testing

Having already established a simple CI pipeline, it is very easy to extend it with testing. Since we are already using CMake and CTest for the building and testing process, all we need to do is add another step to our pipeline that will execute the tests. The test stage in the pipeline will therefore appear as follows. Since the build directory is restored from the cache, the tests are run from this directory without executing the build steps:

```
# contains the same commands as in the previous example
stages:
  - build
  - test # another stage that runs the tests

# contains the same commands as in the previous example
# run unit tests with ctest
test:
  stage: test
  script:
    - cd build
    - ctest .
```

This way, each commit will not only be subjected to the build process, but also to testing. If one of the steps fails, we will be notified which one was the source of the failure, and we will see in the dashboard which steps were successful.

With changes tested and approved, now it's time to deploy them to one of the operating environments.

Managing deployment as code

Deployment as code means handling the deployment process using version-controlled code, rather than relying on manual steps or improvised scripts. This makes deployments more consistent, repeatable, and easy to automate.

"As-code" systems are key enablers of the DevOps methodology: deployment as code, infrastructure as code, platform as code, configuration as code such as **Jenkins Configuration as Code (JCasC)**, and even everything as code, which includes environments as code, data analytics as code, DevOps pipelines as code, and security as code. They provide declarative models for provisioning and managing application stacks. Such systems are consistent, scalable, portable, and auditable.

In this section, we focus on Ansible, a configuration management tool that supports deployment as code. There are many tools to help with deployment. We decided to provide examples with Ansible as this doesn't require any setup on the target machines besides a functional Python installation (which the majority of Unix systems already have anyway). It is very popular in the configuration management space, and it's backed up by a trustworthy open source company (Red Hat).

Ansible alternatives are Puppet, Chef, Salt, Attune, Rudder, CFEngine, Terraform, OpenTofu, **Amazon Web Services (AWS)** CloudFormation, Codeship, Azure DevOps Server, Azure Automation, and the Nix package manager.

In the upcoming subsections, we'll first compare Ansible with traditional shell scripts and show how its declarative model and idempotent behavior simplify deployment. Then, we'll see how Ansible integrates seamlessly with CI/CD pipelines. Then, we'll look at the importance of components in building reusable and testable deployment code.

Using Ansible

Why not use something that's already available, such as Bourne shell script or PowerShell? For simple deployments, shell scripts may be a better approach. But as our deployment process becomes more complex, it is much harder to handle every possible initial state using the shell's conditional statements.

Dealing with differences between initial states is something Ansible is especially good at. Unlike traditional shell scripts, which use the imperative form (move this file, edit that file, run a particular command), Ansible playbooks, as they are called, use the declarative form (make sure the file is available in this path, make sure the file contains specified lines, make sure the program is running, make sure the program completes successfully).

This declarative approach also helps to achieve idempotence. Idempotence is a feature of a function that means applying the function several times over will have exactly the same results as a single application. If the first run of an Ansible playbook introduces some changes to the configuration, each subsequent execution will detect that no further changes are needed.

In other words, when you invoke Ansible, it will first assess the current state of all the machines you wish to configure:

- If any of them require any changes, Ansible will only run the tasks required to achieve the desired state.
- If there's no need to modify a particular thing, Ansible won't touch it. Only when the desired and actual states differ will you see Ansible taking action to converge the actual state toward the desired one described by the contents of the playbook.

Let's examine how Ansible integrates into the CI/CD pipeline.

How Ansible fits with the CI/CD pipeline

Ansible's idempotence makes it a great target to use in CI/CD pipelines. After all, there's no risk in running the same Ansible playbook multiple times, even if nothing changes between the two runs. If you use Ansible for your deployment code, creating a CD is just a matter of preparing appropriate acceptance tests (such as smoke tests or end-to-end tests).

The declarative approach may require changing the way you think about deployments, but the gains are well worth it. Besides running playbooks, you can also use Ansible to perform one-off commands on remote machines, but we won't cover this use case as it doesn't really help with deployments.

Everything you can do with a shell you can do with Ansible's `shell` module. That's because, in the playbooks, you write tasks specifying which modules they use and their respective parameters. One such module is the aforementioned `shell` module, which simply executes the provided parameters in a shell on a remote machine. But what makes Ansible not only convenient but also cross-platform (at least when different Unix distributions are concerned) is the availability of modules to manipulate common concepts such as user administration, package management, and similar instances.

Using reusable components (roles) and playbooks in Ansible

In addition to the regular modules provided in the standard library, Ansible also supports third-party components to allow for code reuse. You can test such components individually, which also makes your deployment code more robust. Such components are called roles. They contain a set of tasks to make a machine fit to take on a specific role, such as acting as `webserver`, `db`, or `docker`. While some roles prepare the machine to provide particular services, other roles may be more abstract, such as the popular `ansible-hardening` role. This has been created by the OpenStack team and it makes it much harder to break into a machine secured by using this role.

When you start to understand the language Ansible uses, all the playbooks cease to be just scripts. In turn, they will become the documentation of the deployment process. You can either use them verbatim by running Ansible, or you can read the described tasks and perform all the operations manually, for example, on an offline machine.

However, there is one risk related to using Ansible for deployment in your team. Once you start using it, you have to make sure that everyone on the team is able to use it and modify the relevant tasks. DevOps is a practice that the whole team has to follow; it cannot be implemented only partially. When the application's code changes considerably, requiring appropriate changes on the deployment side, the person responsible for changes in the application should also supply the changes in the deployment code. Of course, this is something that your tests can verify, so the gating mechanism can reject the changes that are incomplete.

One noteworthy aspect of Ansible is that it can run both in a push and pull model:

- The push model is when you run Ansible on your own machine or in the CI system. Ansible then connects to the target machine—for example, over an SSH connection—and performs the necessary steps on the target machine.
- In the pull model, the whole process is initiated by the target machine. Ansible's component, `ansible-pull`, runs directly on the target machine and checks the code repository to establish whether there's been any update to the particular branch. After refreshing the local playbook, Ansible performs all the steps as usual. This time, both the controlling component and the actual execution happen on the same machine. Most of the time, you will want to run `ansible-pull` periodically—for example, from within a cron job.

In the next section, we will use Ansible in practice to write the deployment logic.

Building deployment code

In its simplest form, deployment with Ansible may consist of copying a single binary to the target machine and then running that binary. We can achieve this with the following Ansible code:

```
tasks:
  # Each Ansible task is written as a YAML object
  # This uses a copy module
  - name: Copy the binaries to the target machine
    copy:
```

```
      src: our_application
      dest: /opt/app/bin/our_application
    # This tasks invokes the shell module. The text after the `shell:` key
    # will run in a shell on target machine
    - name: start our application in detached mode
      shell: cd /opt/app/bin; nohup ./our_application </dev/null >/dev/null 2>&1
  &
```

Every single task starts with a hyphen. For each of the tasks, you need to specify the module it uses (such as the copy module or the `shell` module), along with its parameters (if applicable). A task may also have a `name` parameter, which makes it easier to reference the task individually.

With the deployment logic in place, let's take the next step and integrate it into a CD pipeline.

Understanding and implementing CD

We have reached the point where we can safely build a CD pipeline using the tools we learned about in this chapter. We already know how CI operates and how it helps to reject changes that are unsuitable for release. The section on test automation presented different ways of making the rejection process more robust. Having smoke tests or end-to-end tests, which we only mentioned briefly, allows us to go beyond CI and to check whether the whole deployed service satisfies requirements. With deployment code, we can not only automate the process of deployment but also prepare a rollback plan when releases fail and the services become unavailable. Fully automated deployment can be dangerously unpredictable and therefore requires strong testing, monitoring, and rollback capabilities.

CD is the automated process that originates when a person pushes a change into the central repository and finishes with the change successfully deployed to the production environment, with all the tests passing. We can therefore say that this is an end-to-end process as the developer's work travels all the way to the customer without manual intervention (following the code review, of course). You may have heard the term GitOps, which relates to such an approach. GitOps uses an infrastructure as code approach to automate IT infrastructure. In a GitOps setup, as all operations are automated, pushing to a specified branch in Git triggers the deployment scripts.

By a funny coincidence, the abbreviation CD can mean both *continuous delivery* and *continuous deployment*. Continuous delivery doesn't go that far. Like continuous deployment, it features a pipeline able to release the final product and test it, but the final product is never automatically delivered to the customers. It can be delivered to the QA first or to the business for internal use. Ideally, the delivered artifact is ready to be deployed in the production environment as soon as the internal clients accept it.

Figure 11.1 presents the scope of continuous integration, continuous delivery, and continuous deployment:

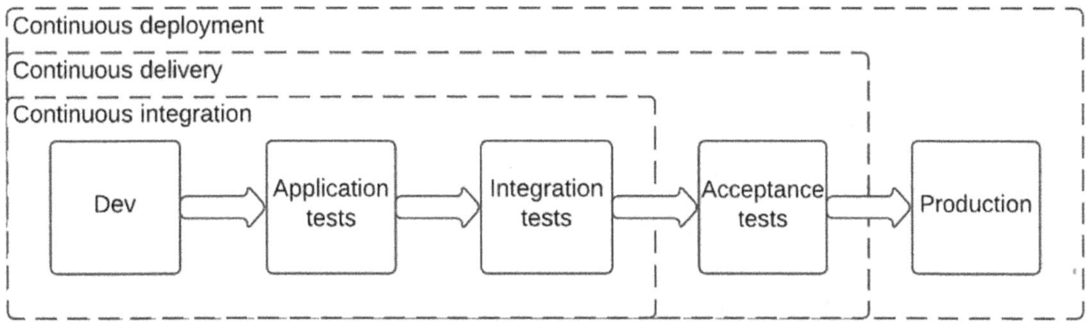

Figure 11.1: Continuous integration versus delivery versus deployment

In this chapter, when we refer to CD, we mean continuous deployment.

Next, we'll build CD pipelines with GitLab and GitHub.

Building an example CD pipeline with GitLab

Let's put all these skills together once again, using the GitLab CI as an example to build our pipeline. Following the testing step, we will add two more steps: one is the package stage, which creates the distributable files, and the other is the deployment stage, which uses Ansible to deploy them.

The package stage includes artifacts' definitions to download them from the dashboard. In the deployment stage, Ansible is invoked. Because the build directory is cached, build artifacts are saved and restored, which reduces execution time by allowing later pipeline stages to skip some steps. Package and deployment stages in the pipeline would then look like the following:

```
# contains the same commands as in the previous example
stages:
  - build
  - test
  - package
  - deploy


# contains the same commands as in the previous example
# package the application and publish the artifacts
package:
  stage: package
  # use CPack for packaging
  script:
    - cd build
    - cpack .
  # save the DEB and RPM package artifacts
  artifacts:
    paths:
```

```
      - build/Customer*.deb
      - build/Customer*.rpm

# deploy using Ansible
deploy:
  stage: deploy
  script:
    - cd build
    - ansible-playbook -i localhost, ansible.yml
```

To see the whole example, go to the repository from the *Technical requirements* section for the original sources. The example in the repository does not include the deploy stage and Ansible scripts, because the deployment configuration is complex and therefore omitted.

Now let's move on to GitHub. On GitHub, we use two workflows: a quick pre-commit workflow that gives fast feedback (in 1–2 minutes) and a longer CI/CD workflow that covers the full pipeline (in 10–20 minutes).

Implementing a pre-commit workflow with GitHub Actions

Here, we will see how our GitLab pipeline is implemented using GitHub tools, but we will start with a simpler configuration.

GitHub Actions is a continuous integration and continuous delivery platform to automate build, test, and deploy workflows. A GitHub workflow runs one or more jobs. Workflows are defined in the `.github/workflows` directory in a repository that can have multiple workflows.

`pre-commit` is a framework for managing Git hooks, which are custom scripts automatically executed every time certain important events occur in a Git repository.

The following code defines the pre-commit workflow. It's saved as `.github/workflows/pre-commit.yml` in the repository. In reality, this script verifies already committed code on the GitHub server and sends notifications to the authors if the code validates some predefined rules:

```
name: pre-commit

on:
  pull_request:
  push:
    branches: [main]

jobs:
  pre-commit:
    runs-on: ubuntu-latest
    steps:
    - uses: actions/checkout@v4
```

```
    - uses: actions/setup-python@v5
      with:
        python-version: '3.13'
    - uses: actions/cache@v4
      with:
        path: ~/.cache/pre-commit
        key: pre-commit|${{ hashFiles('.pre-commit-config.yaml') }}
    - run: pip install pre-commit
    - run: SKIP=no-commit-to-branch pre-commit run --all-files
```

The on keyword triggers a `pre-commit` workflow, and then a `pre-commit` job is executed in a Docker container. The job checks out our Git repo, sets up a Python interpreter, caches the `~/.cache/pre-commit` directory to improve workflow execution time, installs the `pre-commit` Python module, and runs this command to examine a Git commit.

The `hashFiles(path)` function calculates a hash for the set of files. Cached files are restored if the hash matches the value of the previous run.

The `.pre-commit-config.yaml` file in the root of the repository defines the hooks to run:

```
repos:
  - repo: https://github.com/pre-commit/pre-commit-hooks
    rev: v5.0.0
    hooks:
      - id: fix-byte-order-marker
      - id: check-case-conflict
      - id: check-merge-conflict
      - id: check-symlinks
      - id: check-yaml
        exclude: kubernetes
      - id: end-of-file-fixer
        exclude: \.svg$
      - id: mixed-line-ending
      # Prevent direct commits to the following branches
      - id: no-commit-to-branch
        args: [--branch, main]
      - id: trailing-whitespace
  - repo: https://github.com/pre-commit/mirrors-clang-format
    rev: v20.1.6
    hooks:
      - id: clang-format
        args: [--style=llvm, -i]
  - repo: https://github.com/iconmaster5326/cmake-format-pre-commit-hook
    rev: v0.6.13
```

```
    hooks:
      - id: cmake-format
  - repo: https://github.com/hukkin/mdformat
    rev: 0.7.22
  hooks:
    - id: mdformat
      additional_dependencies:
        - mdformat-gfm
        - mdformat-black
```

The names of the hooks are meaningful. You can read their descriptions in the corresponding GitHub repositories.

This script formats C++ and CMake files and returns an error if the formatted files do not match the files in a Git commit. In this case, those files must be formatted before committing them.

Because this workflow only runs lightweight checks, it can provide feedback in just a few minutes.

Implementing the pipeline with GitHub Actions

Here, we will compare how our GitLab pipeline can be implemented using GitHub tools. GitHub and GitLab are popular platforms implemented in significantly different ways. The application pipeline is split into fragments, and each part will be explained separately due to its complexity.

Here's the beginning of the workflow definition:

```
name: customer application
run-name: pipeline for branch ${{ github.ref_name }}

on:
  push:
    branches: [ main ]
  pull_request:
    branches: [ main ]

env:
  BUILD_TYPE: Release

jobs:
  build:
    runs-on: ubuntu-24.04

    steps:
      - uses: actions/checkout@v4
      - uses: actions/setup-python@v5
```

```
        with:
          python-version: '3.13'
          cache: 'pip'
      - run: pip install conan

      - uses: actions/cache@v4
        with:
          path: |
            ~/.conan2
          key: ${{ runner.os }}-${{ hashFiles('./Chapter10/customer/conanfile.
txt') }}

      - name: create default profile
        run: conan profile detect -f
```

This pipeline is executed when the main branch is changed. The `run-name` parameter is an example of string interpolation. The `env` section contains environment variables. Python packages are cached. Caching Conan dependencies is definitely time-saving. The `hashFiles` function calculates a hash of the `./Chapter10/customer/conanfile.txt` file. Previously compiled project dependencies are restored from the cache if the `conanfile.txt` file and the operating system (`runner.os`) are not changed. The last step creates the default Conan profile.

In this fragment, the environment is prepared, Conan installs the project dependencies, and CMake configures the project and builds it:

```
      - name: prepare environment
        uses: ./.github/actions/prepare-environment

      - name: install dependencies
        working-directory: ${{github.workspace}}/build
        run: "conan install ${{github.workspace}}/Chapter10/customer
--build=missing -s:a build_type=${{env.BUILD_TYPE}}
        -s:a compiler=gcc -s:a compiler.version=14 -s:a compiler.cppstd=gnu20
-of ."

      - name: configure
        run: "cmake -GNinja -B ${{github.workspace}}/build -DCMAKE_CXX_
COMPILER=`which g++-14` -DBUILD_TESTING=ON
        -DCMAKE_BUILD_TYPE=${{env.BUILD_TYPE}} ${{github.workspace}}/Chapter10/
customer"

      - name: build
        run: cmake --build ${{github.workspace}}/build --config ${{env.BUILD_
TYPE}}
```

```
      - name: upload build directory
        uses: ./.github/actions/upload-build-dir
```

In the end, the build directory is uploaded as an artifact because the next jobs download this artifact before executing other steps. So, the artifacts can be shared between jobs. Both `./.github/actions/prepare-environment` and `./.github/actions/upload-build-dir` are custom actions. You can use free and paid actions from GitHub Marketplace and publish your own.

After the build is complete, the workflow moves on to testing. The next fragment downloads the build artifact and runs the tests using CTest:

```
  test:
    runs-on: ubuntu-24.04
    needs: build

    steps:
      - uses: actions/checkout@v4

      - name: prepare environment
        uses: ./.github/actions/prepare-environment

      - name: download build directory
        uses: ./.github/actions/download-build-dir

      - name: test
        working-directory: ${{github.workspace}}/build
        run: ctest -C ${{env.BUILD_TYPE}}
```

Here, `./.github/actions/download-build-dir` is also a custom action. GitHub supports the concurrency of workflows and jobs. Therefore, the `test` job needs to wait when the `build` job is completed successfully before downloading the build directory.

Finally, the workflow packages the build into DEB and RPM files and uploads them as artifacts:

```
  pack:
    runs-on: ubuntu-24.04
    needs: test

    steps:
      - uses: actions/checkout@v4

      - name: prepare environment
        uses: ./.github/actions/prepare-environment
```

```
      - name: download build directory
        uses: ./.github/actions/download-build-dir

      - name: pack
        working-directory: ${{github.workspace}}/build
        run: cpack .

      - uses: actions/upload-artifact@v4
        with:
          name: customer packages
          path: |
            build/Customer*.deb
            build/Customer*.rpm
```

The pack needs to wait until the test job is completed successfully before downloading the build directory too, but the job does not need test files. Thereby, the build artifact of the build job is reused here. In fact, the test and pack jobs could be run concurrently, but it makes no sense because publishing malfunctioning programs is useless. The artifacts can be completely overwritten. So, be careful when you use this command. In the end, this job uploads packed DEB and RPM files as artifacts.

Our workflow referenced different custom actions (prepare-environment, upload-build-dir, and download-build-dir). Let's now look at how these actions are defined.

The following code shows the definition of the prepare-environment action, located at .github/actions/prepare-environment/action.yml. This action creates the build directory and installs Ninja:

```
name: prepare environment
description: prepares the environment
runs:
  using: "composite"
  steps:
    - name: prepare environment
      run: |
        mkdir -p ${{github.workspace}}/build
        sudo apt-get install -y ninja-build
      shell: bash
```

In our scenario, CMake generates build.ninja files. The metadata filename must be either action.yml or action.yaml. The shell parameter is a requirement for custom actions. The actions can have inputs and outputs, but they are not necessary in our example.

This is the definition of the `upload-build-dir` action, located at `.github/actions/upload-build-dir/action.yml`. It packs the build directory and uploads it as an artifact. The directory is archived with `tar` to preserve file permissions:

```
name: upload-build-dir
description: packs build directory with the tar command to preserve file
permissions and uploads the archive
runs:
  using: "composite"
  steps:
    - name: tar build directory
      run: tar -C ${{github.workspace}}/build -cvf build-dir.tar .
      shell: bash

    - uses: actions/upload-artifact@v4
      with:
        name: build-dir
        path: build-dir.tar
        retention-days: 1
```

Packing TAR archives is an official workaround to prevent permission loss because ZIP files do not keep file permissions, including the execute permission. The retention period on GitHub is from 1 day to 90 days (about 3 months) for public repositories and from 1 day to 400 days (about 1 year) for private repositories. The default value is 90 days.

Finally, here is the definition of `download-build-dir`, located at `.github/actions/download-build-dir/action.yml`:

```
name: download-build-dir
description: downloads the archive and unpacks build directory with the tar
command to preserve file permissions
runs:
  using: "composite"
  steps:
    - uses: actions/download-artifact@v4
      with:
        name: build-dir

    - name: create build directory
      run: mkdir -p ${{github.workspace}}/build
      shell: bash

    - name: unpack build directory
      run: |
```

```
    tar -xf build-dir.tar -C ${{github.workspace}}/build
  shell: bash
```

This custom action downloads the build artifact and unpacks it to the build directory.

GitHub provides code scanning to find security vulnerabilities and errors. You can run jobs against multiple environments—Linux, macOS, and Windows—on both AMD64 and ARM64 processor architectures, and on self-hosted runners.

To see the whole example, go to the repository from the *Technical requirements* section for the original sources.

Until now, we've focused on deploying just the application onto an existing system. In the next section, we'll take that idea further by learning how to deploy the entire system as one unit.

Using immutable infrastructure

What's the difference between deploying an application onto a running system and deploying the system itself? We will come to know about this in the following sections.

What is immutable infrastructure?

Previously, we focused on how to make your application's code deployable on the target infrastructure. The CI system created software packages (such as containers), and those packages were then deployed by the CD process. Each time the pipeline ran, the infrastructure stayed the same, but the software differed.

However, if you are using cloud computing, you can treat infrastructure just like any other artifact. Instead of deploying a container, you can deploy an entire **virtual machine** (**VM**), for example, as an AWS EC2 or Google Compute Engine instance. You can build such a VM image upfront as yet another element of your CI process. This way, versioned VM images, as well as the code required to deploy them, become your artifacts.

There are two tools, both authored by HashiCorp, that deal with precisely this scenario. Packer helps to create VM images in a repeatable way, storing all the instructions as code, usually in the form of a JSON file. Terraform is an infrastructure as code tool, which means it's used to provision all the necessary infrastructure resources. We will use the output from Packer as input for Terraform. This way, Terraform will create an entire system consisting of the following:

- Instance groups
- Load balancers
- Virtual private clouds
- Other cloud elements while using the VMs containing our own code

The title of this section may confuse you. Why is it called **immutable infrastructure** when we are clearly advocating changing the entire infrastructure after every commit? The concept of immutability may be clearer to you if you've studied functional languages.

A mutable object is one whose state we can alter. In infrastructure, this is pretty easy to understand: you can log in to the VM and download a more recent version of the code. The state is no longer the same as it was prior to your intervention.

An immutable object is one whose state we cannot alter. It means we have no means of logging in to the machines and changing things. Once we deploy a VM from an image, it stays like that until we destroy it. This may sound inflexible, but in fact, it solves a few problems of software maintenance.

Benefits and practical considerations of immutable infrastructure

First of all, immutable infrastructure makes the concept of configuration drift obsolete. There is no configuration management, so there can also be no drift.

The upgrade is much safer as well because we cannot end up in a half-baked state—the state that's neither the previous version nor the next version, but something in between. The deployment process provides binary information: either the machine is created and operational, or it isn't. There's no other way.

However, for this approach to work without affecting uptime, you also need the following:

- Load balancing to distribute traffic
- Some degree of redundancy, so that at least one instance is available at any given time

After all, the upgrade process consists of taking down an entire instance. You cannot rely on this machine's address or anything that's particular to that one machine. Instead, you need to have at least a second one that will handle the workload while you replace the other one with the more recent version. When you finish upgrading the one machine, you can repeat the same process with another one. This way, you will have two upgraded instances without losing the service. Such a strategy is known as the rolling upgrade.

As you can realize from the process, immutable infrastructure works best when dealing with stateless services. When your service has some form of persistence, things become tougher to implement properly. In that case, you usually must split the persistence level into a separate object, for example, an **NFS (Network File System)** or **SMB (Server Message Block)** volume containing all the application data. Such volumes can be shared across all the machines in an instance group, and each new machine that comes up can access the common state left by the previous running applications.

Building instance images with Packer

Considering our example application is already stateless, we can proceed with building an immutable infrastructure on top of it. Packer, which generates VM images as its output, requires us to decide on the format and the builder we would like to use.

In this example, let's focus on AWS, while keeping in mind that a similar approach will also work with other supported providers. A simple Packer template may look like this:

```
{
  "variables": {
    "aws_access_key": "",
```

```
    "aws_secret_key": ""
  },
  "builders": [{
    "type": "amazon-ebs",
    "access_key": "{{user `aws_access_key`}}",
    "secret_key": "{{user `aws_secret_key`}}",
    "region": "eu-central-1",
    "source_ami": "ami-0265dc4673f9d6a35",
    "instance_type": "t2.micro",
    "ssh_username": "admin",
    "ami_name": "Project's Base Image {{timestamp}}"
  }],
  "provisioners": [{
    "type": "shell",
    "inline": [
      "sudo apt-get update",
      "sudo apt-get install -y nginx"
    ]
  }]
}
```

The preceding code will build an image for AWS using the **Elastic Block Store (EBS)** builder. The image will reside in the `eu-central-1` region and will be based on the AMI specified in `source_ami`, which is an Ubuntu Noble Numbat image. We want the builder to be a `t2.micro` instance (that's a VM size in AWS). To prepare our image, we run the two `apt-get` commands.

We can also reuse the previously defined Ansible code and, instead of using Packer to provision our application, we can substitute Ansible as the provisioner. Our code will appear as follows:

```
{
  "variables": {
    "aws_access_key": "",
    "aws_secret_key": ""
  },
  "builders": [{
    "type": "amazon-ebs",
    "access_key": "{{user `aws_access_key`}}",
    "secret_key": "{{user `aws_secret_key`}}",
    "region": "eu-central-1",
    "source_ami": "ami-0f1026b68319bad6c",
    "instance_type": "t2.micro",
    "ssh_username": "admin",
    "ami_name": "Project's Base Image {{timestamp}}"
```

```
  }],
  "provisioners": [{
    "type": "ansible",
    "playbook_file": "./provision.yml",
    "user": "admin",
    "host_alias": "baseimage"
  }],
  "post-processors": [{
    "type": "manifest",
    "output": "manifest.json",
    "strip_path": true
  }]
}
```

The changes are in the `provisioners` block, where we've replaced shell commands with an Ansible playbook, and in the addition of a new block, `post-processors`. The post-processor is here to produce the results of the build in a machine-readable format. Once Packer finishes building the desired artifact, it returns its ID and also saves it in `manifest.json`. For AWS, this would mean an AMI ID that we can then feed to Terraform.

Orchestrating the infrastructure with Terraform

Creating an image with Packer is only the first step. After that, we would like to deploy the image to use it. We can build an AWS EC2 instance based on the image from our Packer template using Terraform.

The terraform configuration block defines the behavior of Terraform itself when applying your configuration. In our case, the configuration requires an AWS provider:

```
terraform {
  required_providers {
    aws = {
      source = "hashicorp/aws"
      version = "~> 5.0"
    }
  }
}
```

Terraform supports input, output, and local variables. In our configuration, this feature is used to specify the path to a public SSH key and the other deployment settings:

```
# Input variable pointing to an SSH key we want to associate with the
# newly created machine
variable "public_key_path" {
  description = <<DESCRIPTION
Path to the SSH public key to be used for authentication.
```

```
Ensure this keypair is added to your local SSH agent so provisioners can
connect.
Example: ~/.ssh/terraform.pub
DESCRIPTION

  default = "~/.ssh/id_rsa.pub"
}

# Input variable with a name to attach to the SSH key
variable "aws_key_name" {
  description = "Desired name of AWS key pair"
  default = "terraformer"
}

# An ID from our previous Packer run that points to the custom base image
variable "packer_ami" {
}

variable "env" {
  default = "development"
}

variable "region" {
}
```

Using these input variables, we can configure the provider and infrastructure objects:

```
# Configure the AWS provider
provider "aws" {
  region  = var.region
}

# Create a new AWS key pair containing the public key set as the input
# variable
resource "aws_key_pair" "deployer" {
  key_name = var.aws_key_name

  public_key = file(var.public_key_path)
}

# Create a VM instance from the custom base image that uses the previously
created key
```

```
# The VM size is t2.xlarge, it uses a persistent storage volume of 60GiB,
# and is tagged for easier filtering
resource "aws_instance" "project" {
  ami = var.packer_ami

  instance_type = "t2.xlarge"

  key_name = aws_key_pair.deployer.key_name

  root_block_device {
    volume_type = "gp2"
    volume_size = 60
  }

  tags = {
    Provider = "terraform"
    Env = var.env
    Name = "main-instance"
  }
}
```

This creates a key pair and an EC2 instance using this key pair. The EC2 instance is based on an AMI provided as a variable. When calling Terraform, we will set this variable to point to the image generated by Packer.

Vagrant is another tool of HashiCorp that implements the infrastructure as code approach, but it is mainly focused on managing development environments.

Of particular interest is OpenTofu, an open source Terraform fork created as a response to HashiCorp's license change from the **Mozilla Public License** (**MPL**) to the **Business Source License** (**BSL**). The code bases will only diverge further, and the OpenTofu documentation provides a migration guide. That's like the Valkey project, which is an open source fork of Redis 7.2.4., created after a licensing change.

Summary

In this chapter, we learned how implementing CI at the beginning of the project can help you save time in the long run. It can also reduce work in progress, especially when paired with CD. We presented useful tools that can help you implement both processes.

We showed how GitLab CI and GitHub Actions allow us to write pipelines in YAML files. We discussed the importance of code review and explained the differences between the various forms of code review. We introduced Ansible, which assists in configuration management and the creation of deployment code. Finally, we tried Packer and Terraform to move our focus from creating applications to creating systems.

The knowledge is not unique to the C++ language. You can use it in projects written in any language using any technology. The important thing that you should keep in mind is this: all applications require testing. A compiler or a static analyzer is not enough to validate your software. As an architect, you would also have to consider not only your project (the application itself), but also the product (the system your application will work in). Delivering working code is no longer sufficient. Understanding the infrastructure and the process of deployment is crucial as they are the new building blocks of modern systems.

The next chapter is focused on the security of the software. We will cover the source code itself, the operating system level, and the possible interactions with external services as well as with end users.

Questions

1. In what ways does CI save time during development?
2. Do you require separate tools to implement CI and CD?
3. When does it make sense to perform a code review in a meeting?
4. What tools can you use to assess the quality of your code during CI?
5. Who participates in specifying the BDD scenarios?
6. When would you consider using immutable infrastructure? When would you rule it out?
7. How would you characterize the differences between Ansible, Packer, and Terraform?

Further reading

- Rafal Leszko, *Continuous Delivery with Docker and Jenkins: Create Secure Applications by Building Complete CI/CD Pipelines*, Third Edition, Packt Publishing: `https://www.packtpub.com/en-us/product/continuous-delivery-with-docker-and-jenkins-3rd-edition-9781803245300`
- Christopher Cowell, Nicholas Lotz, and Chris Timberlake, *Automating DevOps with GitLab CI/CD Pipelines: Build Efficient CI/CD Pipelines to Verify, Secure, and Deploy Your Code Using Real-Life Examples*, Packt Publishing: `https://www.packtpub.com/en-us/product/automating-devops-with-gitlab-cicd-pipelines-9781803242934`
- GitLab Docs, *Use CI/CD to Build Your Application*: `https://docs.gitlab.com/ee/topics/build_your_application.html`
- Eric Chapman, *Mastering GitHub Actions: Advance Your Automation Skills with the Latest Techniques for Software Integration and Deployment*, Packt Publishing: `https://www.packtpub.com/en-us/product/mastering-github-actions-9781805123309`
- Michael Kaufmann, *GitHub Actions Cookbook: A Practical Guide to Automating Repetitive Tasks and Streamlining Your Development Process*, Packt Publishing: `https://www.packtpub.com/en-us/product/github-actions-cookbook-9781835469149`
- GitHub Docs, *How-tos for GitHub Actions*: `https://docs.github.com/en/actions/how-tos`
- pre-commit, *Supported Hooks*: `https://pre-commit.com/hooks.html`
- HashiCorp, *Terraform Language Documentation*: `https://developer.hashicorp.com/terraform/language`

- HashiCorp, *AWS Provider*: `https://registry.terraform.io/providers/hashicorp/aws/latest/docs`

12

Security in Code and Deployment

In the previous chapter, we discussed how to build and deploy applications efficiently using **continuous integration/continuous deployment** (CI/CD). Now, we turn our attention to security, ensuring that the code, dependencies, and environments involved in deployment are robust and resilient. This chapter describes how to assess the security of the code base, including both the internally developed software as well as third-party modules. It will also show how to improve existing software at the code, dependency, and operating system levels. Keep in mind, though, that following every step outlined within this chapter won't necessarily protect you against all possible problems. Our aim is to show you some possible dangers and the ways to deal with them. Given this, you should always be conscious of the security of your system and make audits a routine event.

The following topics will be covered in this chapter:

- Security-conscious design
- Checking whether the dependencies are secure
- Hardening your code
- Hardening your environment

Technical requirements

Some of the examples used in this chapter require the compilers with the minimal versions of the following:

- GCC 14+
- Clang 19+

The code present in the chapter has been placed on GitHub at `https://github.com/PacktPublishing/Software-Architecture-with-Cpp-2E/tree/main/Chapter12`.

Security-conscious design

Before the internet became ubiquitous, software authors weren't too concerned about the security of their designs. After all, if the user presented malformed data, the user could crash their own computer at most. In order to use software vulnerabilities to access protected data, the attacker had to obtain physical access to the machines holding the data.

Even in software that was designed to be used within networks, security was often an afterthought. Take the **HyperText Transfer Protocol** (HTTP) as an example. Even though it allows the password protection of some assets, all of the data is transferred in plain text. This means everyone on the same network can eavesdrop on the data being transferred.

However, today, we should embrace security right from the first stages of design and keep it in mind at every stage of software development, operations, and maintenance. Most of the software we produce every day is meant to, in one way or another, connect with other existing systems.

By omitting security measures, we open up not only ourselves but also our partners to potential attacks, data leaks, and, eventually, lawsuits. For example, failure to protect personal data can result in a fine of several million US dollars.

Regulations such as the **General Data Protection Regulation** (GDPR) in the EU and UK, the **California Consumer Privacy Act** (CCPA) and **California Privacy Rights Act** (CPRA) in California, the **Personal Information Protection Law** (PIPL) in China, and the **Act on the Protection of Personal Information** (APPI) in Japan mandate the protection of personal data. A good practice is to anonymize the data and keep as little personal data as possible to avoid data breaches.

In this section, we'll explore several strategies for designing secure systems. We'll begin by learning how to build interfaces that are both intuitive and difficult to misuse. From there, we'll look at how C++ can help you automate resource management and address common pitfalls of concurrent programming. We'll also briefly touch upon the C++ Core Guidelines, look into defensive programming principles, and review the most common software vulnerabilities developers should be aware of.

Making interfaces easy to use and hard to misuse

How can we design architecture for security? The best way to do this is to think like a potential attacker. There are many ways in which you can break a box open, but usually, you will look for weak points where different elements connect. In the case of a box, this may be between the lid and the bottom of the box.

In software architecture, connections between elements are called **interfaces**. Since their main role is to interact with the external world, they are the most vulnerable part of the entire system. Making sure your interfaces are protected, intuitive, and robust will solve the most obvious ways in which your software can be broken.

To design interfaces in a way that would be both easy to use and hard to misuse, consider the following exercise. Imagine you are a customer of your interface. You want to implement an e-commerce store that uses your payment gateway, or maybe you want to implement a VR application that connects with the Customer API of the example system we've used throughout this book.

As a general rule regarding interface design, avoid the following traits:

- Too many parameters in a function/method
- Ambiguous names of parameters
- Using output parameters for providing results
- Parameters depending on other parameters

Why are these traits considered problematic?

- The first one makes it hard to memorize not only the meaning but also the order of the parameters. This can lead to errors in usage, which, in turn, may lead to crashes and security issues.
- The second trait has similar consequences to the first one. By making it less intuitive to use your interface, you make it easier for the user to make mistakes.
- The third trait is a variant of the second one but with an added twist. Not only does the user have to remember which parameters are input and which are output, but it is also necessary for the user to remember how the output should be treated. Who manages the creation and deletion of the resources? How is this achieved? What is the memory management model behind it? The output parameters are not more efficient than copy elision.

  With modern C++, it's easier than ever to return a value that contains all of the necessary data. With pairs, tuples, and vectors, there is no excuse to use the output parameters. Besides all of this, returning the value helps embrace the practice of not modifying the state of an object. This, in turn, reduces concurrency-related problems.

- Finally, the last trait introduces unnecessary cognitive load, which, as in the previous examples, can result in mistakes and eventually failures. Such code is also harder to test and maintain, as each change introduced has to take into account all the possible combinations already available. Failure to properly handle any combination is a potential threat to the system.

Let's understand this with the help of an example. Coming back to the first rule—avoiding too many parameters—it is very easy to confuse even two parameters when they have the same type, let alone too many parameters.

Consider the `qsort` function from the C standard library. It implements the quicksort algorithm for arrays of arbitrary objects using a user-provided comparison function. This sorting function implements generic programming in C because this language lacks support for generic types, also known as **parametric polymorphism**. In contrast, C++ templates implement generic programming through **monomorphization**, where the compiler converts generic (parametric) code into specific versions for each type used in the program.

The comparison function must return a negative value if its first argument is less than its second, zero if it is equal, and a positive value if it is greater:

```
#include <iostream>
// C Standard General Utilities Library
#include <cstdlib>
// C style cast
```

```
int comp(const void* a, const void* b) {
  return *(int*)a - *(int*)b;
}
```

The sorting result will clearly bewilder you if you accidentally mix up the second and third arguments, which have the same type:

```
int arr[] = {5, 4, 3, 2, 1};
int n = sizeof(arr) / sizeof(arr[0]);

// https://en.cppreference.com/w/c/algorithm/qsort
// void qsort(void* ptr, size_t number, size_t width,
//            int (*comp)(const void*, const void*));

// correct order: 1 2 3 4 5
// qsort(arr, n, sizeof(int), comp);

// oops, it can be on x86-64: 5 65540 0 2 196608
// the array looks like a mangled mess
qsort(arr, sizeof(int), n, comp);

for (int i = 0; i < n; ++i) {
  std::cout << arr[i] << ' ';
}
```

In the example, by swapping the number of elements and element size in bytes in the array, the `qsort` function sorts not 5 elements of 4 bytes each (`sizeof(int)` on Intel and AMD 64-bit processors), but 4 elements of 5 bytes each. Consequently, the `comp` function, when comparing two values, casts the `const void*` pointers to the `int*` type before dereferencing them, which causes even more chaos, since the memory areas overlap.

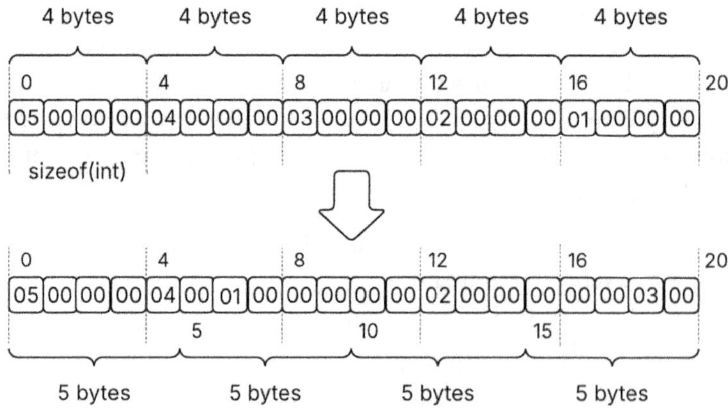

Figure 12.1: The 1-D array memory layout (little-endian byte order)

The position of an array element in memory is calculated using pointer arithmetic (by performing arithmetic operations such as addition, subtraction, increment, and decrement on pointer variables): `pointer = array + index * size`, since `array[i]` is equivalent to `*(array + i)`.

Unlike `qsort`, the templated `std::sort` function from the C++ standard library is more type-safe because it operates on typed array elements rather than the unsafe `void*` pointers. In `qsort`, pointers to the array elements being compared are cast to a specific type in the comparison function. Thus, the compiler cannot prevent type conversion errors in any way since type information is lost.

In this situation, a strong typedef could help, guaranteeing that two types are distinct even if they have the same underlying implementation, since a typedef does not create a new type. C++ does not support such types natively, but they are emulated with user-defined conversion functions.

In this implementation, two classes wrap values of the `size_t` type, but the classes themselves are incompatible:

```
template <typename T> class strong_typedef {
public:
  explicit strong_typedef(T val) : value_(val) {}

  explicit operator T() const noexcept { return value_; }

private:
  T value_;
};

class number : public strong_typedef<size_t> {
public:
  explicit number(size_t val) : strong_typedef(val) {}
};

class width : public strong_typedef<size_t> {
public:
  explicit width(size_t val) : strong_typedef(val) {}
};

void safe_qsort(void *ptr, const number& number, const width& width,
                int (*comp)(const void *, const void *)) {
  qsort(ptr, static_cast<size_t>(number), static_cast<size_t>(width), comp);
}
```

In this safe implementation, the `number` and `width` parameters cannot be swapped due to type incompatibility, resulting in a compile-time error:

```
int arr[] = {5, 4, 3, 2, 1};
constexpr int n = sizeof(arr) / sizeof(arr[0]);

// compile error: no known conversion from 'width' to 'number'
// safe_qsort(arr, width{sizeof(int)}, number{n}, comp);
safe_qsort(arr, number{n}, width{sizeof(int)}, comp);

for (int i : arr) {
  std::cout << i << ' ';
}
```

The concept of strong typedefs, also known as opaque typedefs and phantom types, enhances type safety. They are strong types for strong interfaces. There are C++ libraries that implement this concept: `type_safe`, `mp_units`, `NamedType`, and `strong_type`. The Boost library also implements this concept by providing the `BOOST_STRONG_TYPEDEF` macro.

The preceding rules apply to the external part of the interfaces, with which consumers interact. However, you should also apply similar measures to the internal part by validating the inputs, making sure that the values are correct and sensible, and preventing unwanted use of the services the interface provides.

Enabling automatic resource management

System instability may also result from memory leaks, race conditions, data races, and deadlocks. All of these symptoms are manifestations of poor resource management. Even though resource management is a complex task, there is a mechanism that can help you reduce the number of problems—automatic resource management.

In this context, a **resource** is something you gain access to via the operating system, such as dynamically allocated memory, open files, sockets, processes, or threads, and you have to make sure you use it correctly. All of these resources require specific actions to be taken when you acquire them and when you release them. Some of them also require specific actions during their lifetime. Failure to release such resources at the right time leads to leaks. Since the resources are usually finite, in the long run, leaks will turn to unexpected behavior when no new resources can be created.

Resource management is so important in C++ because, unlike many other high-level languages, there is no garbage collection in C++, and the software developers are responsible for the life cycle of the resources. Understanding this life cycle helps create secure and stable systems.

Nevertheless, while C++ does not have a built-in garbage collector, implementations certainly exist using C++ libraries such as **bdwgc** (which stands for **Boehm–Demers–Weiser Garbage Collector**), also known as `bdw-gc`, `boehm-gc`, or `libgc` (a replacement for the C `malloc` function or C++ `new` operator), and memory-safe implementations of C and C++ such as experimental Fil-C and TrapC.

Memory protection in Fil-C is achieved by using InvisiCap pointers, which track bounds and types of the pointed-to memory. Its garbage collection is handled by **Fil's Unbelievable Garbage Collector (FUGC)**, which controls all memory allocation and deallocation operations. This implementation is powerful enough to run memory-safe versions of tools and libraries such as CMake, CPython, Perl, Wayland, and musl. But Fil-C is currently 1.5x slower than normal C in good cases, and about 4x slower in the worst cases.

However, garbage collection comes with a cost. One of its drawbacks that affects application execution is called **garbage collection pause** (**GC pause**), a temporary suspension of the execution of an application while its garbage collector works to free up memory, which can quickly lead to scalability problems in multi-threaded applications. Unpredictable stalls may impact performance. This makes garbage-collected systems less suitable for some **real-time applications** (**RTAs**), transaction processing, or interactive programs. So, garbage collection libraries in C++ are not universally adopted.

In contrast to these garbage collection systems, the Qt library provides a built-in approach to automatic memory management. It emulates garbage collection for child and parent classes derived from the `QObject` class. This library provides automatic memory management without having to deal with pointers. As a result, when the parent object (including the application itself) is destroyed, all its children are automatically destroyed as well.

Coming back to resource management, the most common idiom of resource management is **resource acquisition is initialization** (**RAII**). Although it originated in C++, it has also been used in other languages, such as Ada, Rust, and Vala. This idiom uses the object's constructor and destructor to allocate and free up resources, respectively. This way, we can guarantee that the resource in use will be deterministically released when the object that holds it goes out of scope.

Some examples of standard library utilities provided by C++ that support RAII are the smart pointers such as `std::unique_ptr` and `std::shared_ptr`, **mutex** (short for **mutual exclusion**) wrappers such as `std::lock_guard`, `std::unique_lock`, and `std::shared_lock`, and files such as `std::ifstream` and `std::ofstream`. Smart pointers automatically manage memory, ensuring that dynamically allocated objects are properly freed when they go out of scope. This behavior follows the RAII principle.

The **Guidelines Support Library** (**GSL**), which we'll discuss at length shortly, also implements a particularly useful utility for automated resource management. By using the `gsl::finally()` function in our code, we create a `gsl::final_action()` object with some code attached to it. This code will be executed when the object's destructor is called. This means the code will be executed both upon a successful return from the function as well as when the stack unwinding happens during an exception.

This approach shouldn't be used too often, as it is generally a better idea to design your classes with RAII in mind. But if you're interfacing with a third-party module that does not follow RAII principles and you want to ensure the safety of your wrapper, `finally()` can help you get there.

As an example, consider that we have a payment operator that allows only a single concurrent login per account. If we don't want to block the user from making future payments, we should always log out as soon as we finish processing the transaction. This is not a problem when we are on a happy path, and everything goes according to our design. But in the event of an exception, we also want to be safe and release the resources. Here's how we could do it using `gsl::finally()`:

```
TransactionStatus processTransaction(AccountName account, ServiceToken token,
Amount amount)
{
  payment::login(account, token);
  auto scope_guard = gsl::finally([] { payment::logout(); });
  payment::process(amount); // We assume this can lead to exception

  return TransactionStatus::TransactionSuccessful;
}
```

Regardless of what happens during the call to `payment::process()`, we can at least guarantee that we log the user out as soon as we go out of `processTransaction()`'s scope.

We can conclude this section by noting that using RAII makes you think more about resource management during the class design phase, when you have full control of the code, and think less about what happens later when you (or other parties) use the interface and your intentions may no longer be as clear.

Dealing with the drawbacks of concurrency

Concurrency is the alternating execution of multiple tasks or processes, giving the illusion of simultaneity by rapidly switching between them, even on a single processor core. This is suitable for multitasking operating systems where tasks can be interrupted and resumed. So, concurrency is the ability of a system to manage multiple tasks and ensure their coordination.

Furthermore, concurrency can be preemptive, where an external scheduler, typically the operating system, interrupts the current task and switches to another, ensuring fair use of CPU resources and responsiveness, and cooperative, where individual tasks voluntarily yield CPU control to other tasks.

It is noteworthy that concurrency is not the same as parallelism, which refers to the real simultaneous execution of multiple tasks across multiple processor cores. This is suitable for tasks that can be distributed and executed simultaneously to reduce execution time.

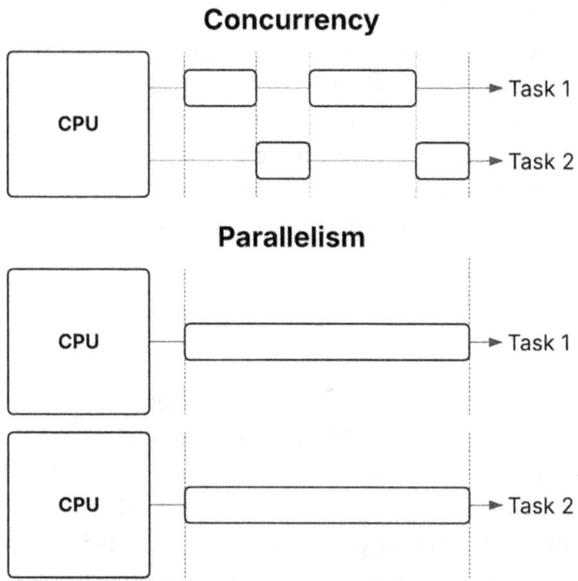

Figure 12.2: Concurrency versus parallelism

While concurrency improves performance and resource utilization, it also makes your code much harder to design and debug. This is because, unlike a traditional single-threaded flow that lacks concurrency, the timing of operations cannot be determined upfront. In a strictly sequential single-threaded code, you either write to the resource or read from it, but you always know the order of the operations and can, therefore, predict the state of the object.

With concurrency, several threads or processes can be either reading from an object or modifying it at the same time. If the modifications aren't atomic, we can reach one of the variants of the common update problem. Consider the following code:

```
TransactionStatus chargeTheAccount(AccountNumber accountNumber, Amount amount)
{
  Amount accountBalance = getAccountBalance(accountNumber);
  if (accountBalance > amount)
  {
    setAccountBalance(accountNumber, accountBalance - amount);
    return TransactionStatus::TransactionSuccessful;
  }

  return TransactionStatus::InsufficientFunds;
}
```

When calling the chargeTheAccount function from a non-concurrent code, everything will end up well. Our program will check the account balance and deduct funds if possible. The concurrent execution, however, can lead to a negative balance. This is because two threads can, one after another, call getAccountBalance(), which will return the same amount, such as 20. After performing that call, both threads check whether the current balance is higher than the required amount. Finally, after the check, they modify the account balance. Supposing both transactions are for the amount of 10, each thread will set the balance to be *20 – 10 = 10*. After *both* operations, the account has a balance of 10, even though it should be 0!

To mitigate a similar class of problems, we can use solutions such as mutexes and critical sections, atomic operations provided by the CPU, or concurrency-safe data structures.

Mutexes, critical sections, and other similar concurrency design patterns prevent more than one thread from modifying (or reading) the data. These programming objects act as locking mechanisms, ensuring that only one thread can access a shared resource or critical section of code at any given time. Even though they are useful when designing concurrent applications, there is a trade-off associated with them. They effectively make parts of your code single-threaded. This is because code guarded by mutexes allows only a single thread to execute it; all of the others have to wait until the mutex is released. And since we introduced waiting, we can make our code less performant even though our original aim was to make it more performant. Non-blocking algorithms allow threads to access shared state (or otherwise collaborate or communicate) without blocking the participating threads. These algorithms generally rely on atomic **read–modify–write** (RMW) primitives, such as **compare-and-swap** (CAS), provided by the hardware.

Atomic operations mean using a single indivisible CPU instruction to get the desired effect. The term can mean any high-level operation that transforms into a single CPU instruction. They are particularly interesting when that single instruction achieves *more* than would be normally possible. For example, CAS is an instruction that compares the current value at a memory location with an expected value and modifies the contents of this location to the new value only if the current value matches the expected value. Since C++11, there's a <std::atomic> header available that contains several atomic data types and operations. CAS, for instance, is implemented as a compare_and_exchange_* set of functions.

Schematically, this instruction can be represented as follows:

```
int compare_and_swap(int *lock, int expected, int new_value)
{
  int original_value = *lock;
  if (*lock == expected)
  {
    *lock = new_value;
  }
  return original_value;
}
```

Finally, concurrency-safe data structures (also known as concurrent data structures) provide safe abstractions for managing shared data state without requiring some sort of synchronization in user code.

For instance, C++26 proposes hazard pointers as a memory reclamation technique for safely reclaiming memory in lock-free programming without garbage collection. The Boost.Lockfree (`https://www.boost.org/doc/libs/1_86_0/doc/html/lockfree.html`) library provides concurrent queues and stacks for use with multiple producers and multiple consumers. `libcds` (`https://github.com/khizmax/libcds`) also offers ordered lists, sets, and maps, but it hasn't been updated in a few years as of the time of writing this book.

Lock-free data structures are used in multithreaded applications to provide thread safety without using locks, which prevents deadlocks and improves scalability on multi-core systems. They are used in high-load systems where maximum performance and low latency are required, such as message queues, caches, database management systems, and real-time systems for inter-process communication.

However, it is no secret that lock-free algorithms and data structures significantly complicate the project. This is confirmed by the C++ Core Guidelines (a set of guidelines, rules, and best practices for writing code in C++), which note that following the lock-free principle makes code difficult to implement and even more difficult to debug. It's virtually impossible to detect all the bugs, which typically only surface in production. The Core Guidelines also state that lock-free programming relying on atomic operations such as CAS is error-prone and requires expert-level knowledge of language features, machine architecture, and data structures.

Useful rules to keep in mind when designing concurrent processing are as follows:

- Consider whether you need concurrency in the first place.
- Pass data by value rather than by pointer or reference. This prevents modifications of the value when other threads are reading it.

If the size of the data makes it impractical to share by value, use `shared_ptr`. This way, it's easier to avoid resource leaks.

Secure coding guidelines and GSL

The Standard C++ Foundation released a set of guidelines to document the best practices for building C++ systems—C++ Core Guidelines. It is a Markdown document released on GitHub under `https://github.com/isocpp/CppCoreGuidelines`. It is an evolving document without a release schedule (unlike the C++ standard itself). The guidelines are aimed at modern C++, which basically means code bases that implement at least C++11 features.

Many of the rules presented in the guidelines cover the topics that we present in this chapter. For example, there are rules related to interface design, resource management, and concurrency. The editors of the guidelines are Bjarne Stroustrup and Herb Sutter, both respected members of the C++ community.

We won't go into detail describing the guidelines. We encourage you to read them yourself. This book is inspired by many of the rules presented there, and we follow them in our examples. You will find a valuable article by Herb Sutter on C++ security listed in the *Further reading* section.

To ease the use of these rules in various code bases, Microsoft released the **Guidelines Support Library** (GSL) as an open source project hosted on `https://github.com/microsoft/GSL`. It is a header-only library that you can include in your project to use the defined types. You can either include the whole GSL or selectively use only some of the types you plan on using.

What's also interesting about the library is the fact that it uses CMake for building, Travis for continuous integration, and Catch2 for unit testing–tools we've covered/mentioned in *Chapter 7, Building and Packaging*, *Chapter 11, Continuous Integration and Continuous Deployment*, and *Chapter 10, Writing Testable Code*, respectively. Travis is a continuous integration service used for testing and building software projects hosted on GitHub, Assembla, Bitbucket, and GitLab.

Defensive coding and validating everything

In *Chapter 10, Writing Testable Code*, we mentioned the method of defensive programming. Even though this method is not strictly a security feature, it happens to help with creating a robust interface. Such interfaces, in turn, increase the overall security of your system.

As a good heuristic, you can treat all the external data as unsafe. What we mean by external data is every input coming to the system via some interface (either a programming interface or a user interface). To denote this, you can go as far as prefixing the appropriate types as `Unsafe`, as follows:

```
RegistrationResult registerUser(UnsafeUsername username, PasswordHash
passwordHash)
{
  SafeUsername safeUsername = username.sanitize();
  try
  {
    std::unique_ptr<User> user = std::make_unique<User>(safeUsername,
passwordHash);
    CommitResult result = user->commit();
    if (result == CommitResult::CommitSuccessful)
    {
      return RegistrationResult::RegistrationSuccessful;
    }
    else
    {
      return RegistrationResult::RegistrationUnsuccessful;
    }
  }
  catch (UserExistsException _)
  {
```

```
        return RegistrationResult::UserExists;
    }
}
```

After converting `UnsafeUsername` to `SafeUsername` using the `sanitize()` function, the input becomes trustworthy for further processing. Sanitizing consists of removing any unsafe characters from user inputs or encoding them to prevent harmful input.

Also, if you have already read the C++ Core Guidelines, you will know that you should generally avoid using the C API directly. Some of the functions in the C API can be unsafe if not used defensively. It is much better to instead use respective concepts from C++ that ensure better type safety as well as protection (for example, against buffer overflow).

Another facet of defensive programming is the intelligent reuse of the existing code. Each time you try to implement some technique, check whether a reliable solution already exists. Writing a sorting algorithm yourself may be a fun challenge to do when you're learning a new programming language, but for production code, it's much better to use the sorting algorithms available in the standard library. The same goes for password hashing. No doubt you can find some clever way to calculate the password hashes and store them in a database, but it is generally wiser to go with the tried and true (and don't forget peer-reviewed!) `bcrypt` algorithm. Keep in mind that intelligent code reuse assumes that you check and audit the third-party solutions with the same due diligence as you would your own code. We will dive deeper into this topic in the next section, *Checking whether the dependencies are secure*.

It's worth noting that defensive programming shouldn't turn into paranoid programming. Checking user input is a sane thing to do, but checking whether a just-initialized variable is still equal to the original is like going too far. Your focus should be on controlling the integrity of your data, your algorithms, and your third-party solutions, not on verifying the correctness of your compiler or language features.

In the given context, it's a good idea from both a security and readability point of view to use `Expects()` and `Ensures()` as presented in C++ Core Guidelines and to distinguish between unsafe and safe data through typing and conversions.

One noteworthy case of defensive programming appears in the Drogon framework, which is used for examples in this book. This framework supports **C++ Server Pages** (**CSP**), a server-side scripting technology, similar to technologies such as ASP.NET Web Pages, **Java Server Pages** (**JSP**), PHP, and Jinja templates in Python. CSP is designed for dynamically generating HTML on the server by embedding C++ code directly in HTML template files using special CSP tags. This technology is nothing new and has been around for at least 20 years. For example, the POCO C++ libraries introduced a CSP implementation long before Drogon.

The special markup symbols used by Drogon's CSP to embed C++ code into HTML pages are <%inc ... %> to include C++ files, <%c++ ... %> to place arbitrary C++ code, <%view ... %> to include sub-views, <%layout ... %> to name the layout, `{% ... %}` to output internal variable values of the views or C++ expressions, `[[ ... ]]` to output external variable values passed to the views by Drogon controllers, and the `@@` and `$$` data variables for view data rendering.

Because CSP allows C++ code to be embedded directly into views on the server side, potential targets for hackers include system calls, file functions, files included in page templates, and dynamic view directories if CSP is used, especially with **dynamic view loading** (DVL)—a programming technique used by the Drogon framework to dynamically recompile and reload views as shared libraries during application runtime.

Statically compiled views are inherently safer because malicious C++ code cannot be injected into them dynamically, but they cannot be updated without recompiling the applications. An alternative to CSP may be template engines such as Mustache and Inja, inspired by Jinja for Python.

In addition to the client side, hackers can attack the server side through CSP because Drogon supports compilation of views during the application runtime, which means views can be compiled and reloaded as shared libraries while the application is running. This DVL feature is mostly meant for development convenience but poses a security risk if enabled in production environments. Of course, this depends on the structure of a CSP page and the special markup symbols on the page. If input data in requests is not properly filtered, attackers can inject malicious code—such as **server-side include** (SSI) injection and **remote code execution** (RCE)—into dynamic CSP views by executing their code via the markup symbols.

Escape special HTML characters, such as < and >, before rendering HTML pages to avoid injected malicious client-side scripts (JavaScript), HTML tags, and attributes if your web server does not render such HTML characters intentionally.

Let's look at a simple example to show how CSP works in practice. The following CSP view, named `greet.csp`, greets users by name. The Drogon framework converts this code into a C++ class using the `drogon_ctl` command, which automates the creation of various objects such as views, controllers, filters, models, and projects. The generated view class that dynamically creates this HTML document is in the build directory. The CSP source file looks like this:

```
<!DOCTYPE html>
<html>
```

The following block presents regular C++ code, except for the @@ markup symbol, where the view gets the `name` parameter passed from the view controller:

```
<%c++
    auto name=@@.get<std::string>("name");
    bool isNameEmpty = name == "";
    if (isNameEmpty) name = "anonymous";
    auto message = "Hello, " + name + "!";
%>
```

This code sets the name of the HTML page using the C++ `name` variable:

```
<head>
    <meta charset="UTF-8">
    <title>[[ name ]]</title>
</head>
```

It then displays the greeting message, defined by the C++ `message` variable, in the body of the HTML document:

```
<body>
    <%c++ $$<<message; %>
```

If the `name` parameter is not specified, the users are prompted to provide it:

```
    <%c++
    if (isNameEmpty)
    {
        $$ << "<br>You can revisit the this page, but append ?name=<i>your_
name</i> to change the name";
    }
    %>
</body>
</html>
```

The view controller gets the optional URL query parameter `name` and passes this parameter to the `greet` view defined previously:

```
// omitted code
...
void ViewController::asyncHandleHttpRequest(
    const HttpRequestPtr &request,
    std::function<void(const HttpResponsePtr &)> &&callback) {
  auto name = request->getOptionalParameter<std::string>("name");
  HttpViewData data;
  if (name) {
    data["name"] = HttpViewData::htmlTranslate (name.value());
  }
  const auto viewResponse = HttpResponse::newHttpViewResponse("greet", data);
  callback(viewResponse);
}
```

The `drogon::HttpViewData::htmlTranslate` function escapes several reserved HTML characters—less than sign (<), greater than sign (>), ampersand, and quotation mark—using their entity names (`<`, `>`, `&`, and `"`, respectively) to display these characters on an HTML page. Hence, they are processed as plain text, but not as HTML code. This escaping is necessary to prevent **cross-site scripting** (**XSS**) attacks, which inject malicious client-side scripts into web pages viewed by users, and correctly display content containing characters that may have special meaning in HTML, such as when displaying "less than" and "greater than" signs instead of HTML tags.

The application using the `greet` view presented previously will be hacked and even defaced without HTML escaping. For instance, if the view controller doesn't escape HTML characters, then executing such a request containing "vicious" JavaScript code will lead to an XSS attack on the application:

```
http://localhost:8080/customer/v4?name=%3Cscript%3Edocument.body.innerHTML%20
=%20%27Hey%20%3Cb%3EArnold%3C/b%3E,%20like%20a%20surgeon,%20Hey%27;%3C/
script%3E
```

Instead of the expected greeting, you'll see this HTML page, as the contents of the `document.body.innerHTML` property have been completely replaced. Of course, in a real situation, it may be much more difficult to notice such attacks:

```
Hey Arnold, like a surgeon, Hey!
```

If the characters in the request had been escaped, the JavaScript code in the request would not have been executed, and the browser would have rendered the code as plain text instead:

```
Hello, <script>document.body.innerHTML = 'Hey <b>Arnold</b>, like a surgeon,
Hey';</script>!
```

In this case, the potentially dangerous script is displayed, and no unwanted modification to the page occurs.

The most common vulnerabilities

To check whether your code is safe against the most common vulnerabilities, you should first learn about these vulnerabilities. After all, defense is only possible when you know what the offense looks like. The **Open Web Application Security Project (OWASP)** catalogs the 10 most common vulnerabilities and publishes them at `https://owasp.org/www-project-top-ten/`. At the time of writing this book, those vulnerabilities are as follows:

- **Injection**: Commonly known as SQL injection. It is not limited to SQL; this vulnerability occurs when untrusted data is passed directly to an interpreter (such as a SQL database, NoSQL database, shell, or `eval` function). The attacker may this way gain access to parts of the system that should be protected.
- **Broken authentication:** If authentication is improperly implemented, attackers may use flaws to either compromise secret data or impersonate other users.
- **Sensitive data exposure:** The lack of encryption and proper access rights may lead to sensitive data being exposed publicly.
- **XML external entities (XXE)**: Some XML processors may disclose the contents of the server's filesystem or allow for remote code execution.
- **Broken access control:** When access control is not enforced properly, attackers may gain access to files or data that should be restricted.
- **Security misconfiguration**: Using insecure defaults and improper care with configuration are the most common sources of vulnerabilities.

- **XSS**: Including and executing untrusted external data, especially with JavaScript, that allows control of the user's web browser.
- **Insecure deserialization:** Some flawed parsers may fall prey to denial of service attacks or RCE.
- **Using components with known vulnerabilities:** A lot of the code in modern applications comes as third-party components. These components should be regularly audited and updated, as known security flaws in a single dependency can result in your entire application and data being compromised. Fortunately, there are tools that help automate this.
- **Insufficient logging and monitoring**: If your system is under attack and your logging and monitoring are not very thorough, the attacker may obtain deeper access and still remain unnoticed.

We won't go into detail regarding each of the vulnerabilities mentioned. In the previous example involving CSP in Drogon, we already saw how defensive programming techniques can prevent some of the most common web vulnerabilities—XSS, SSI, and RCE. What we want to highlight here is that you can prevent injection, XXE, and insecure deserialization by following the defensive programming techniques we mentioned before. By treating all external data as unsafe, you can first sanitize it by removing all the unsafe content before you start the actual processing.

Regarding insufficient logging and monitoring, we will go into detail on logging and monitoring in *Chapter 17, Observability*.

While discussing security-conscious design practices in this section, we came across the importance of auditing third-party solutions. In the next section, we'll explore this topic in more detail.

Checking whether the dependencies are secure

In the early days of computers, all programs were monoliths without any external dependencies. However, ever since the dawn of operating systems, any non-trivial software is rarely free from dependencies. Those dependencies can come in two forms—external and internal:

- **External** dependencies are those that should be present in the environment in which we run our application. Examples can include the aforementioned operating systems, dynamically linked libraries, and other applications (such as a database).
- **Internal** dependencies are modules we want to reuse, so this will usually mean static libraries or header-only libraries.

Both kinds of dependencies provide potential security risks. Each line of code increases the risk of vulnerability, as it could be the entry point for a vulnerability. The more dependencies the code includes, the higher the chance your system may be susceptible to attack. In the following sections, we'll see how to check whether your software is indeed susceptible to known vulnerabilities.

Using the CVE list

A good place to check for known security issues within third-party software components is the **Common Vulnerabilities and Exposures** (CVE) list available at `https://cve.mitre.org/`. The list is constantly updated by several institutions known as **CVE Numbering Authorities** (CNAs). These institutions include vendors and projects, vulnerability researchers, national and industry **computer emergency response teams** (CERTs), and bug bounty programs.

The website also presents a search engine. With this, you can use several methods to learn about the vulnerabilities:

- You can enter the vulnerability number. These are prefixed with CVE, with examples including CVE-2014-6271, the infamous ShellShock, and CVE-2017-5715, also known as Spectre.
- You can enter the vulnerability name, such as the previously mentioned ShellShock or Spectre.
- You can enter the name of the software you want to audit, such as Bash or Boost.

For each search result, you can see the description as well as a list of references to other bug trackers and related resources. The description usually lists versions affected by the vulnerability, so you can check whether the version you are planning to use has already been patched.

Using automated scanners

There are tools that can help you audit your list of dependencies. One such tool is OWASP Dependency-Check (`https://owasp.org/www-project-dependency-check/`). Although it only supports Java and .NET officially, it has experimental support for Python, Ruby, Node.js, and C++ (when used with CMake or `autoconf`). Besides working as a standalone tool, it has integrations for CI/CD software such as Jenkins, SonarQube, and CircleCI.

Another tool that allows checking dependencies for known vulnerabilities is Snyk. This is a commercial product with several levels of support. It also does more than the OWASP Dependency-Check, as Snyk can also audit container images and license compliance issues. It also offers more integrations with third-party solutions.

Automated dependency upgrade management

Monitoring your dependencies for vulnerabilities is only the first step in making sure your project is secure. After that, you need to act and update the compromised dependencies. Typically, this is done manually, but as you might have expected, there are also automated solutions for that.

Tools such as Snyk and Renovate scan your source code repositories and issue pull requests whenever there are security-related updates available. Other than that, these tools support different package managers and can scan Docker images for known vulnerabilities.

However, automated dependency management is not free from risks. It requires mature test support, as switching dependency versions without tests may lead to instabilities and bugs. One protection against problems related to dependency upgrades is using wrappers to interface with third-party code. Such wrappers may have their own suite of tests that instantly tell us when an interface is broken during an upgrade.

In the next sections, we'll explore how to strengthen your code and the execution environment to further reduce risk.

Hardening your code

You can reduce the number of common security vulnerabilities in your own code by using modern C++ constructions as opposed to older C equivalents. Yet, there are always cases when even more secure abstractions prove to be vulnerable as well. It is not enough to choose the more secure implementation and decide you've done your best. Most of the time, there are ways to further harden your code.

But what is code hardening? It is the process of reducing the system's surface of vulnerability. Often, this means turning off the features you won't be using and aiming for a simpler system over a complicated one. It may also mean using tools to increase the robustness of the already available functions.

Such tools may include kernel patches, firewalls, and **intrusion detection systems** (**IDSs**) at the operating system level. At the application level, they may include various buffer overrun and underflow protection mechanisms, the use of containers and **virtual machines** (**VMs**) for privilege separation and process isolation, and the enforcement of encrypted communication and storage.

In this section, we'll focus on some examples from the application level, while the next section will focus on the operating system level.

Security-oriented memory allocator

To protect your application from heap-related attacks, such as heap overflow (`https://cwe.mitre.org/data/definitions/122.html`), use after free (`https://cwe.mitre.org/data/definitions/416.html`), or double free (`https://cwe.mitre.org/data/definitions/415.html`), you may consider replacing your standard memory allocator with a security-oriented version. Three projects that may be of interest are as follows:

- **FreeGuard**, available at `https://github.com/UTSASRG/FreeGuard` and described in a paper at `https://arxiv.org/abs/1709.02746`.
- **hardened_malloc** from the GrapheneOS project, available at `https://github.com/GrapheneOS/hardened_malloc`.
- **Scudo**, currently the default allocator in Fuchsia and Android, available at `https://source.android.com/docs/security/test/scudo`. *Scudo* is Italian for *shield* (like *escudo* in Spanish), reflecting its security-oriented design.

FreeGuard was released in 2017, and it hasn't seen much change since then, other than sporadic bug fixes. `hardened_malloc`, on the other hand, is actively developed. Both allocators are designed to act as drop-in replacements for the standard `malloc()` function. You can use them without modifying your application, simply by setting the `LD_PRELOAD` environment variable or adding the library to the `/etc/preload.so` configuration file.

While FreeGuard targets Linux with the Clang compiler on 64-bit x86 systems, `hardened_malloc` aims at broader compatibility, though at the moment it supports mostly Android's Bionic, `musl`, and `glibc`. `hardened_malloc` is also based on OpenBSD `malloc` implementation, with OpenBSD being the security-focused project itself.

Scudo is a user-mode allocator developed by Google. Based on the LLVM Sanitizers' Combined allocator, it is designed to protect programs against heap-based vulnerabilities, such as heap-based buffer overflow, use after free, and double free, while maintaining performance. The allocator has a low code and memory footprint, making it suitable for use on mobile devices and embedded systems.

Alternatively, instead of replacing the memory allocator, you can replace the collections you use with their safer equivalents. The SaferCPlusPlus (`https://duneroadrunner.github.io/SaferCPlusPlus/`) project provides substitutes for `std::vector<>`, `std::array<>`, and `std::string`, which can be used as drop-in replacements in the existing code. The project also includes substitutes for basic types that guard against issues such as uninitialized use or sign mismatch, as well as concurrent data types and safer pointers and references.

Automated checks

There are certain automated tools that can be especially helpful to ensure the security of the system you are building. In this section, we'll look at some useful options, starting with compiler warnings and followed by static and dynamic analysis.

Compiler warnings

While not necessarily a tool in itself, compiler warnings can be used and tweaked to enhance the output achieved from the one tool every C++ developer uses: the C++ compiler.

Since modern compilers can do some deeper checks than those required by the standard, it is advised to take advantage of this possibility. When using a compiler such as GCC or Clang, the recommended setting involves `-Wall` and `-Wextra` flags, which enable a broad set of diagnostics and result in warnings when your code doesn't follow the diagnostics. If you want to be really strict, you can also enable `-Werror`, which will treat all the warnings as errors and prevent the compilation of code that doesn't pass the enhanced diagnostics. If you want to keep strictly to the standards, there are the `-pedantic` and `-pedantic-errors` flags, which will look for conformance against the standards. For MSVC, the commonly recommended switches are `/W4`, which enables a high level of warnings suitable for finding potential errors without excessive verbosity, and `/WX`, which forces the compiler to treat all compiler warnings as errors.

When using CMake for building, you can use the following function to enable these flags during compilation:

```
add_library(customer ${SOURCES_GO_HERE})
target_include_directories(customer PUBLIC include)
target_compile_options(customer PRIVATE
    $<$<OR:$<CXX_COMPILER_ID:Clang>,$<CXX_COMPILER_ID:AppleClang>,$<CXX_
COMPILER_ID:GNU>>:-Wall;-Wextra;-pedantic;-Werror>
    $<$<CXX_COMPILER_ID:MSVC>:/W4;/WX>)
```

This way, the compilation will fail unless you fix all the warnings reported by the compiler.

You can also find suggested settings for toolchain hardening in articles from OWASP (`https://cheatsheetseries.owasp.org/cheatsheets/C-Based_Toolchain_Hardening_Cheat_Sheet.html`), Red Hat (`https://developers.redhat.com/blog/2018/03/21/compiler-and-linker-flags-gcc/`), and OpenSSF (`https://openssf.org/blog/2023/11/29/strengthening-the-fort-openssf-releases-compiler-options-hardening-guide-for-c-and-c/`).

Static analysis

In this section, we'll look at two ways to apply static analysis in C++: by using dedicated tools and by relying on compiler-supported checks.

Using static application security testing tools

Static application security testing (SAST) tools are a class of tools that can help make your code more secure. They are a variant of static analysis tools, only focused on security aspects.

SAST tools integrate well into CI/CD pipelines as they simply read your source code without executing it. The output is usually suitable for CI/CD as well since it highlights problems found in particular places in the source code.

However, static analysis may miss many types of problems that cannot be found automatically or cannot be found solely with static analysis. These tools are also oblivious to issues related to configuration, as configuration files aren't represented in the source code itself.

Examples of C++ SAST tools include the following open source solutions:

- **Cppcheck** (`https://cppcheck.sourceforge.io/`), which is a general-purpose static analysis tool focused on the low number of false positives
- **Flawfinder** (`https://dwheeler.com/flawfinder/`), which doesn't seem to be actively maintained
- **LGTM** (`https://lgtm.com/help/lgtm/about-lgtm`), which supports several different languages and features, and automated analysis of pull requests
- **SonarQube** (`https://www.sonarqube.org/`), which has great CI/CD integration and language coverage, and offers a commercial version as well

There are also commercial solutions available:

- **Checkmarx SAST** (`https://www.checkmarx.com/products/static-application-security-testing/`), which promises zero configuration and broad language coverage
- **CodeSonar** (`https://codesecure.com/our-products/codesonar/`), which focuses on in-depth analysis and finding the most flaws
- **Klocwork** (`https://www.perforce.com/products/klocwork`), which focuses on accuracy
- **OpenText Fortify** (`https://www.opentext.com/products/fortify-static-code-analyzer`), with broad language support and integration of other tools by the same manufacturer
- **Parasoft C/C++test** (`https://www.parasoft.com/products/parasoft-c-ctest/`), which is an integrated solution for static and dynamic analysis, unit testing, tracing, and more

- **Polyspace Bug Finder from MathWorks** (`https://www.mathworks.com/ products/polyspace-bug-finder.html`), with the integration of Simulink models
- **Veracode Static Analysis** (`https://www.veracode.com/products/binary-static-analysis-sast`), which is a SaaS solution for static analysis
- **Black Duck** (`https://www.blackduck.com/static-analysis-tools-sast.html`), which also focuses on eliminating false positives

Eliminating dangling references in C++ with lifetime bounds

Modern C++ compilers can detect dangling references to objects that have already been destroyed. Modern tools can easily detect such errors at runtime (e.g., using a sanitizer), but it's even better if the compiler reports them right away.

A few C++ compilers (Clang and Visual Studio) support lifetime-bound annotation as a compiler extension that enables compile-time detection of dangling references. The `[[lifetimebound]]` attribute of a function parameter or implicit object parameter specifies that objects referenced by the parameter can also be referenced by the return value of the annotated function (or, for a constructor parameter, by the value of the constructed object). While this attribute cannot prevent all dangling references, when applied judiciously to the appropriate functions and constructors, it can significantly reduce the risk of such issues.

The special `__has_cpp_attribute` operator, introduced in C++11 for feature testing, checks whether a given C++ attribute is supported:

```
#ifndef __has_cpp_attribute
#define lifetime_bound
#elif __has_cpp_attribute(clang::lifetimebound)
#define lifetime_bound [[clang::lifetimebound]]
#elif __has_cpp_attribute(msvc::lifetimebound)
#define lifetime_bound [[msvc::lifetimebound]]
#elif __has_cpp_attribute(lifetimebound)
#define lifetime_bound [[lifetimebound]]
#else
#define lifetime_bound
#endif

using namespace std::literals;
```

The following example defines a function that takes as input a reference to a default value and returns it if the key is not found in the associative container:

```
template <typename T, typename U>
const U &get_or_default(const std::map<T, U> &m lifetime_bound, const T &key,
                        const U &default_value lifetime_bound) {
  if (auto iter = m.find(key); iter != m.end())
```

```
    return iter->second;
  return default_value;
}
```

In the following code, the C++ `""s` user-defined literal, which creates an `std::string` instance from a string literal, is used to create temporary string objects:

```
int main() {
  const std::map<std::string, std::string> m;

  // warning: temporary bound to local reference 'val1' will be destroyed at
the
  // end of the full-expression
  const std::string &val1 = get_or_default(m, "vault"s, "11"s);
  std::cout << val1 << std::endl;

  // no warning
  const auto def_val = "13"s;
  const std::string &val2 = get_or_default(m, "vault"s, def_val);
  std::cout << val2 << std::endl;

  return 0;
}
```

C++ compilers that support lifetime bounds will warn where the `get_or_default` function returns a reference to a destroyed temporary object. In the preceding code, the first call to the function results in undefined behavior due to the dangling reference.

Dynamic analysis

Just like static analysis is performed on the source code, dynamic analysis is performed on the resulting binaries. The *dynamic* in the name refers to the observation of the code in action, processing the actual data. When focused on security, this class of tools can also be called **dynamic application security testing (DAST)**.

Their main advantage over their SAST counterparts is that they can find many flows that cannot be seen from the source code analysis point of view. This, of course, introduces the drawback that you have to run your application in order to perform the analysis. And as we know, running an application can be both time- and memory-consuming.

DAST tools usually focus on web-related vulnerabilities such as XSS, SQL (and other) injection, or disclosed sensitive information. In the following subsections, we'll explore one general-purpose tool—Valgrind—and two other dynamic solutions—sanitizers and fuzz testing.

Valgrind and Application Verifier

Valgrind is mostly known as a memory leak debugging tool. It is, in fact, an instrumentation framework that helps to build dynamic analysis tools not necessarily related to memory problems. Besides detecting memory errors, Valgrind's suite of tools currently consists of a thread error detector, a cache and branch prediction profiler, and a heap profiler. It's supported on various platforms on Unix-like operating systems (including Android).

Essentially, Valgrind acts as a VM: it translates the binary into a simpler form called **intermediate representation**. Instead of running the program on an actual processor, it gets executed under this VM, so each call can be analyzed and validated.

If you develop on Windows, you can use **Application Verifier** (**AppVerifier**) instead of Valgrind. AppVerifier can help you detect stability and security issues. It can monitor running applications and user-mode drivers to look for memory issues such as leaks and heap corruption, threading and locking issues, invalid use of handles, and more.

Sanitizers

Sanitizers are dynamic testing tools that are based on compile-time instrumentation of code. They can help with the overall stability and security of the system, as well as avoid undefined behavior. At `https://github.com/google/sanitizers`, you can find implementations for LLVM (which Clang is based on) and GCC. They address problems with memory access, memory leaks, data races and deadlocks, uninitialized memory use, and undefined behavior.

Here's a list of some notable sanitizers:

- **AddressSanitizer** (**ASan**) protects your code against issues related to memory addressing, such as global buffer overflow, use after free, or stack use after return. Even though it's one of the fastest solutions of its kind, it can still double the runtime. It's best to use it when running tests and doing development, but turn it off in production builds. You can turn it on for your builds by adding the `-fsanitize=address` flag in Clang.
- **AddressSanitizerLeakSanitizer** (**LSan**) integrates with ASan to find memory leaks. It is enabled by default on x86-64 Linux and x86-64 macOS. It requires setting an environment variable, `ASAN_OPTIONS=detect_leaks=1`. LSan performs leak detection at the end of the process. LSan can also be used as a standalone library without ASan, but this mode is much less tested.
- **ThreadSanitizer** (**TSan**) detects problems with concurrency, such as data races and deadlocks. You can enable it with the `-fsanitize=thread` flag in Clang.
- **MemorySanitizer** (**MSan**) focuses on bugs related to access to uninitialized memory. Like Valgrind, it checks memory access dynamically, but it does so through compiler instrumentation. MSan supports 64-bit x86, ARM, PowerPC, and MIPS platforms. You can enable it with the `-fsanitize=memory -fPIE -pie` flag in Clang. The `-fPIE` and `-pie` flags also enable **position-independent executables** (**PIEs**), which are related to **address space layout randomization** (**ASLR**). This way, the compiler produces **position-independent code** (**PIC**), a relocatable object code that can be placed in any area of memory. As a result, both the PIE binary and its shared libraries are loaded at arbitrary addresses each time the application is executed, making it harder for attackers to predict and exploit memory addresses.

- **Hardware-assisted AddressSanitizer** (**HWASan**) is similar to the regular ASan. The main difference is the use of hardware assistance when possible. This feature is, for now, available only on 64-bit ARM architectures.
- **UndefinedBehaviorSanitizer** (**UBSan**) looks for other possible causes of undefined behavior, such as integer overflow, division by zero, or improper bit shift operations. You can enable it with the `-fsanitize=undefined` flag in Clang.

Even though sanitizers can help you uncover many potential problems, they are only as good as the tests that you run against them. When using the sanitizers, keep in mind to keep the code coverage of your tests high, because otherwise, you may get a false sense of security.

Fuzz testing

A subcategory of DAST tools, fuzz testing checks the behavior of your application when confronted with invalid, unexpected, random, or maliciously formed data. Such checks can be especially useful when used against the interfaces that cross the trust boundary (such as end user file upload forms or inputs).

Some interesting tools from this category include the following:

- **Peach Fuzzer**: `https://peachtech.gitlab.io/peach-fuzzer-community/`
- **PortSwigger Burp**: `https://portswigger.net/burp`
- **Zed Attack Proxy** (**ZAP**) by Checkmarx: `https://www.zaproxy.org/`
- **Google's ClusterFuzz**: `https://github.com/google/clusterfuzz` (and OSS- Fuzz: `https://github.com/google/oss-fuzz`)

Process isolation and sandboxing

If you want to run unverified software in your own environment, you may want to isolate it from the rest of your system. This can be achieved using VMs, operating system and application containers, or micro VMs such as Firecracker (`https://firecracker-microvm.github.io/`) used by AWS Lambda, ZeroVM (`https://www.zerovm.org/`), `crosvm` (`https://github.com/google/crosvm`), a **virtual machine monitor** (**VMM**) used to run Linux/Android guests on ChromeOS devices, and Hyperlight (`https://github.com/hyperlight-dev/hyperlight`). This way, the crashes, leaks, and security problems of one application won't propagate to the entire system, rendering it either useless or compromised. As each process will have its own sandbox, the worst-case scenario would be the loss of only one service.

Distrobox and **Toolbx** are tools for running various Linux distributions as containers while maintaining tight integration with the host system. They are useful for testing software across different distributions, isolating applications, or running software incompatible with the host system. These tools provide seamless access to the user's home directory, Wayland, and X11 sockets for running graphical applications, as well as network connectivity (including Avahi), making them convenient tools for developers and system administrators.

For C and C++ code, specialized sandboxing frameworks are also available, such as **Sandboxed API** (**SAPI**; `https://github.com/google/sandboxed-api`), an open source project used by Google's own Chrome and Chromium web browsers, and RLBox (`https://rlbox.dev/`), a C++ framework for sandboxing third-party C libraries within the same process.

Even though VMs and containers can be a part of the process isolation strategy, don't confuse them with microservices, which often use similar building blocks. Microservices are an architectural design pattern, and they don't inherently guarantee better security.

Another way to isolate code is through **WebAssembly (Wasm)**. Wasm modules are executed within a sandboxed environment, separated from the host runtime using fault isolation techniques. One of the most prominent examples of using Wasm in SaaS applications is Figma, whose renderer is written in C++.

Wasm is a binary instruction format and VM that provides near-native performance to web browser applications and allows developers to create high-performance web applications in any language.

Based on this technology, WebVM (`https://webvm.io/`) is a serverless virtual Linux environment running entirely in a web browser. It is powered by CheerpX (`https://cheerpx.io/`), a virtualization engine that implements Linux system calls.

Cheerp (`https://cheerp.io/`) is a C++ and C compiler that compiles C/C++ into efficient Wasm and JavaScript. It is based on and integrated with the LLVM/Clang platform. In addition, the company Learning Technologies (`https://labs.leaningtech.com/`) also develops CheerpJ (`https://cheerpj.com`), a **Java Virtual Machine (JVM)** that runs Java applications and applets directly in a web browser by compiling them into Wasm.

Cheerp supports browser APIs such as **Document Object Model (DOM)** manipulation and WebGL, a low-level 3D graphics API based on OpenGL ES. This compiler integrates quite easily with build systems such as Make, Autoconf, and CMake on Linux, macOS, and Windows because this toolchain includes `clang` (C compiler) and `clang++` (C++ compiler). At the time of writing, the project is in development, but there has been no release since 2023.

Although the Clang compiler also supports compiling C++ to Wasm, this may be a thorny path, requiring deeper knowledge of low-level Wasm features such as the memory model, integration with JavaScript, and browser APIs.

Cheerp simplifies this process. It is designed to complement or replace JavaScript as a web programming language while offering lightweight bidirectional interoperability between C++ and any external JavaScript/DOM. At runtime, Cheerp manipulates the DOM using the same JavaScript APIs as regular JavaScript.

Memory in Wasm is a linear, untyped, zero-based array of bytes for data exchange with JavaScript. Wasm (currently) does not provide automatic memory management mechanisms, so memory allocators and garbage collection must be implemented.

In Cheerp, C++ functions compiled to Wasm are marked with the `[[cheerp::wasm]]` attribute. The attribute resides in the linear memory and operates on regular C++ types (such as integers, floats, structs, and pointers to structs):

```
#include <algorithm>
#include <string>
```

```
#include <cheerp/client.h>
#include <cheerp/clientlib.h>

[[cheerp::wasm]]
std::string transformStr(std::string str) {
  std::reverse(str.begin(), str.end());
  return str;
}
```

The following function creates two DOM elements and sets up event handling using the DOM APIs exposed by the browser:

```
[[cheerp::genericjs]]
void configureUI() {
  using namespace client;
  console.log("configure UI");

  HTMLElement *body = document.get_body();

  auto inputBox =
      static_cast<HTMLInputElement *>(document.createElement("input"));
  inputBox->setAttribute("type", "text");
  inputBox->setAttribute("value", "Input anything in here");
  inputBox->setAttribute("style", "width:200px");

  HTMLElement *textDisplay = document.createElement("h1");
```

The `input` event in the DOM fires whenever the value of an input field changes. In the event handler, the text from the `inputBox` HTML element is immediately copied to the `textDisplay` HTML section heading element.

`client::String` is a wrapper around `DOMString/JSString` and can only exist in the `[[cheerp::genericjs]]` code. Therefore, such an object cannot be passed directly as a parameter to a Wasm function or returned from a Wasm function. Cheerp prohibits the use of the wrapper objects by value because they are "handles" to objects living in the JavaScript heap. If you violate this rule, you will get this error:

```
Types defined in the client namespace can only be used through pointers and
references.
```

Thus, `client::String` is converted to a C++ string before being passed to the Wasm function, and then the result is converted back to `client::String`:

```
auto mirrorText = [textDisplay, inputBox]() -> void {
    const String *text = inputBox->get_value();
```

```
    // no Unicode support
    const auto &jsStr =
        String(transformStr(static_cast<std::string>(*text)).c_str());
    textDisplay->set_textContent(jsStr);
  };

  mirrorText();

  inputBox->addEventListener("input", cheerp::Callback(mirrorText));

  body->appendChild(textDisplay);
  body->appendChild(inputBox);
}
```

When targeting the browser, you should avoid using `main` and use `webMain` instead, as the function is specifically designed to run a program from the browser. This function must initialize the program, set up event handlers, and return control to the browser as quickly as possible. Otherwise, the main thread will lock up, and the browser tab might freeze because the browser processes user events and paints in the main thread. The nature of JavaScript as a web scripting language requires that the event loop never be blocked. After returning, the browser notifies the events the function registered handlers for. The program outlives `webMain` while a normal C++ program terminates when the `main` function returns:

```
[[cheerp::genericjs]]
void webMain() {
  using namespace client;
  console.log("web main");

  configureUI();
}
```

The following Cheerp attributes can be applied to C++ functions, classes, or structs to specify their compilation target: `[[cheerp::genericjs]]` for compiling to JavaScript, `[[cheerp::wasm]]` for compiling to Wasm, and `[[cheerp::jsexport]]` for exposing to JavaScript.

Cheerp does not support POSIX threads, so threading is implemented using web workers (JavaScript scripts that run in the background without affecting page performance).

Now, we need an HTML file to run the program:

```
<!doctype html>
<html lang="en">
<head>
    <meta charset="utf-8" />
    <title>Modifying the DOM</title>
```

```
    <script src="app.js" defer></script>
  </head>
  <body></body>
</html>
```

In a web browser, the running application looks like this:

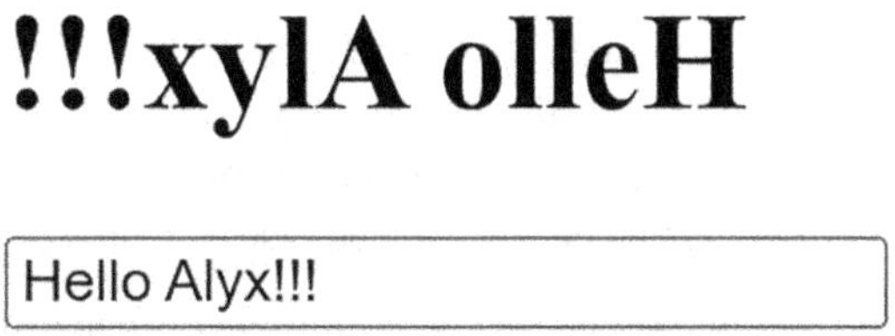

!!!xylA olleH

Hello Alyx!!!

Figure 12.3: A native C++ application compiled with Cheerp running in the browser

For comparison, Emscripten runs code that was not written for the web on the web. For achieving this, Emscripten emulates an entire POSIX operating system. This allows, for example, porting applications using the SDL library to Emscripten. This library provides low-level access to audio, keyboard, mouse, joystick, and graphics hardware, including extensions for WebGPU intended to supersede WebGL. Emscripten and Cheerp are complete compiler toolchains for Wasm.

The absence of server-side logic in such deployments has the advantage of deploying the entire application as static content using static site hosting platforms such as Netlify, Vercel, DigitalOcean, Cloudflare Pages, Surge, Heroku, GitLab Pages, and GitHub Pages, or your own hardware, thus ensuring fast downloads and high uptime for free. However, servers may still be required for the system to work properly.

At the kernel level, sandboxing concepts appear in technologies such as **Extended Berkeley Packet Filter (eBPF)**. eBPF runs in kernel space, while Wasm runs in user space. eBPF is a Linux kernel feature to run sandboxed programs in a privileged context, such as the operating system kernel. Like Wasm programs, eBPF programs are compiled into bytecode because eBPF is also a VM. In C and C++, eBPF programs are implemented with the `libbpf` library maintained as part of the upstream Linux kernel.

Contrary to popular belief, eBPF doesn't always improve performance. Sometimes, it can even slow down the application and its neighbors.

Hardening your environment

Even if you take the necessary precautions to ensure that your dependencies and code are free from known vulnerabilities, there still exists an area that can compromise your security strategy: the execution environment. All applications need an execution environment, and this can mean either a container, a VM, or an operating system. Sometimes, this can also mean the underlying infrastructure.

It's not enough to make your application hardened to the maximum when the operating system it runs on has open access. This way, instead of targeting your application, the attacker can gain unauthorized access to the data directly from the system or infrastructure level.

This section will focus on some techniques of hardening that you can apply at the lowest level of execution. We'll begin with understanding the security implications of linking strategies. These strategies are not environment hardening techniques per se, but they play a crucial role in defining the attack surface of the execution environment and can significantly influence the overall system security.

Linking strategies and their security implications

Linking is the process that occurs after compilation when the code you've written is brought together with its various dependencies (such as the standard library). Linking can occur at build time (static linking), at load time (when the operating system executes the binary), or at runtime, as is the case with plugins and other dynamic dependencies. The last two use cases are only possible with dynamic linking.

So, what is the difference between dynamic and static linking? With static linking, the contents of all the dependencies are copied to the resulting binary. When the program is loaded, the operating system places this single binary in the memory and executes it. Static linking is performed by programs called **linkers** as the last step of the build process.

Figure 12.4 shows the difference between static and dynamic linking:

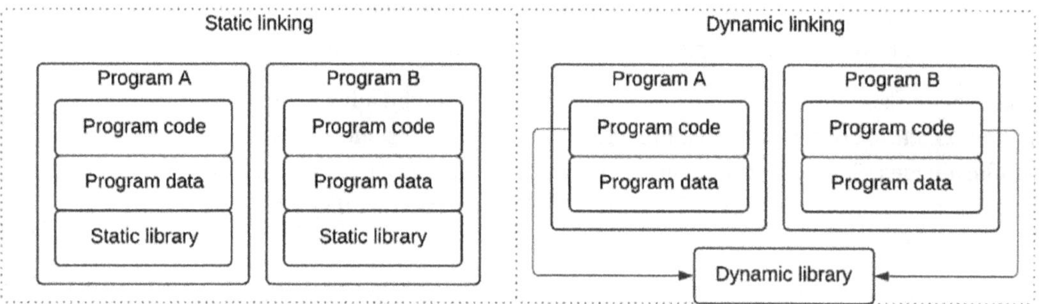

Figure 12.4: Static versus dynamic linking

Because each executable has to contain all the dependencies, statically linked programs tend to be big. This has its upside as well; since everything needed to execute the problem is already available in a single place, the execution can be faster, and it always takes the same amount of time to load the program into memory. However, any changes in the dependencies require recompilation and relinking; there is no way to upgrade one dependency without changing the resulting binary.

In dynamic linking, the resulting binary contains the code you've written, but instead of the contents of the dependencies, there are only references to the actual libraries that need to be loaded separately. During load time, it is the task of the dynamic loader to find the appropriate libraries and load them into memory alongside your binary. When several applications are running simultaneously and each of them is using similar dependencies (such as a JSON parsing library or JPEG processing library), the dynamically linked binaries will result in lower memory usage. This is due to the fact that only a single copy of a given library can be loaded into memory. In contrast, with statically linked binaries, the same libraries would be loaded over and over again as part of the resulting binaries. When you need to upgrade one of your dependencies, you can do so without touching any other component of your system. The next time your application is loaded into memory, it will reference the newly upgraded component automatically.

However, dynamic linking also has security implications. It is easier to gain unauthorized access to dynamically linked applications. This can be achieved by substituting a compromised dynamic library in place of a regular one or by preloading unauthorized libraries into each newly executed process.

A secure deployment strategy is to combine static linking with containers (explained in detail in *Chapter 16, Containers*), creating small, secure, sandboxed execution environments. You may even go further and use such containers with microkernel-based VMs to reduce the attack surface considerably.

Address space layout randomization

ASLR is a technique used to prevent memory-based exploits. It works by replacing the standard memory layout of the program and data with a randomized one. This means an attacker cannot reliably jump to a particular function that would otherwise be present on a system without ASLR.

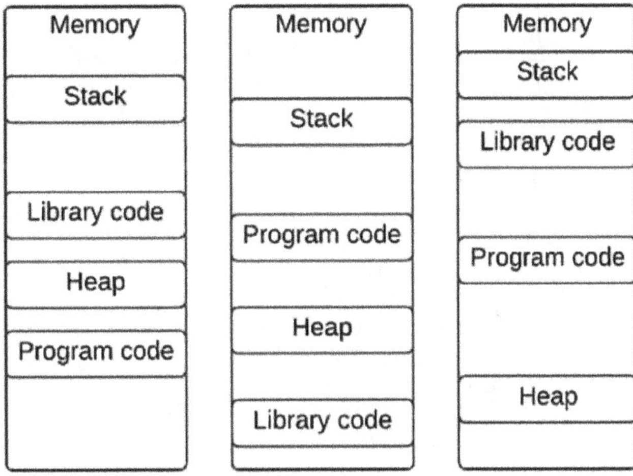

Figure 12.5: ASLR

This technique can be made even more effective when combined with **no-execute** (NX) bit support. The NX bit marks certain pages in the memory, such as the heap and stack, as containing only data that cannot be executed. This ensures that even if malicious code enters these pages, it cannot be executed. NX bit support has been implemented in most mainstream operating systems and can be used whenever hardware supports it.

DevSecOps

To deliver software increments on a predictable basis, it is best to embrace the DevOps philosophy. In short, DevOps means breaking the traditional model by encouraging communication between businesses, software development, software operations, quality assurance, and clients. DevSecOps is a form of DevOps that also emphasizes the need to design with security in mind at each step of the process.

This means that the application you are building has observability built in from the beginning, leverages CI/CD pipelines, and is scanned for vulnerabilities on a regular basis. DevSecOps gives developers a voice in the design of the underlying infrastructure, and it gives operations experts a voice in the design of the software packages that make up the application. Since every increment represents a working system (albeit not fully functional), security audits are performed regularly and therefore take less time than normal. This results in faster and more secure releases and allows for quicker reactions to security incidents.

We've used the term *DevOps* (and *DevSecOps*) several times within this book. This topic deserves some additional space, in our opinion. DevOps is an approach to building software products that breaks with traditional silo-based development.

In the waterfall model, teams operated on single aspects of work independently of each other. The development team would write code, QA would test and validate the code, and security and compliance would come after that. Eventually, the operations team would take care of maintenance. The teams rarely communicated, and even then, it was usually a very formal process.

Knowledge about particular fields of expertise was only available to the teams responsible for a given piece of the workflow. Developers knew very little about QA and next to nothing about operations. While this setup was very convenient, the modern landscape requires more agility than the waterfall model can provide.

That's why a new model of working was proposed, one that encourages more collaboration, better communication, and lots of knowledge sharing between different stakeholders of a software product. While DevOps refers to bringing together developers and operations, what it means is bringing everyone closer.

Developers start working with QA and security even before they write the first lines of code. Operations engineers are more familiar with the code base. Businesses can easily track the progress of a given ticket and, in some cases, can even do a deployment preview in a self-service manner.

DevOps has become synonymous with using tools such as Terraform, OpenTofu, or Kubernetes. But DevOps is by no means the same as using any specific tools. Your organization can follow the DevOps principles without using these tools, and it can use these tools while not practicing DevOps.

One of the principles of DevOps is that it encourages improved information flow among the product's stakeholders. With that, it's possible to fulfill another principle: reduce wasteful activities that don't bring value to the end product.

When you're building modern systems, it is worth doing so using modern methodology. Migrating an existing organization to DevOps may require a massive mindset shift, so it is not always possible. It's worth pursuing when starting a greenfield project that you have control over.

Summary

In this chapter, we discussed different aspects of a secure system. Since security is a complex topic, you cannot approach it only from the angle of an application. All applications nowadays function in some environment, and it is important to either control this environment and shape it according to your requirements or to shield yourself from the environment by sandboxing and isolating the code.

Having read this chapter, you are now ready to search for the vulnerabilities in your dependencies and in your own code. You know how to design systems for increased security and what tools to use in order to find possible flaws. Maintaining security is a constant process, but a good design can reduce the work further down the road.

The next chapter will deal with scalability and the various challenges that we may face when growing our system.

Questions

1. Why is security important in modern systems?
2. What are some challenges of concurrency?
3. What are the C++ Core Guidelines?
4. What's the difference between secure coding and defensive coding?
5. How can you check whether your software contains known vulnerabilities?
6. What's the difference between static and dynamic analysis?
7. What's the difference between static and dynamic linking?
8. How can you use the compiler to fix security problems?
9. How can you implement security awareness in your CI pipeline?

Further reading

- Lester Nichols, *Cybersecurity Architect's Handbook: An End-to-End Guide to Implementing and Maintaining Robust Security Architecture*, Packt Publishing: `https://www.packtpub.com/en-us/product/cybersecurity-architects-handbook-9781803239897`
- Diana Kelley and Ed Moyle, *Practical Cybersecurity Architecture: A Guide to Creating and Implementing Robust Designs for Cybersecurity Architects*, Packt Publishing: `https://www.packtpub.com/en-us/product/practical-cybersecurity-architecture-9781837630288`
- Donald A. Tevault, *Mastering Linux Security and Hardening: A Practical Guide to Protecting Your Linux System from Cyber Attacks*, Packt Publishing: `https://www.packtpub.com/en-us/product/mastering-linux-security-and-hardening-9781837632626`
- Mark Dunkerley and Matt Tumbarello, *Mastering Windows Security and Hardening: Secure and Protect Your Windows Environment from Cyber Threats Using Zero-Trust Security Principles*, Packt Publishing: `https://www.packtpub.com/en-us/product/mastering-windows-security-and-hardening-9781803248745`

- Ivan Murashko, *Clang Compiler Frontend: Get to Grips with the Internals of a C/C++ Compiler Frontend and Create Your Own Tools*, Packt Publishing: `https://www.packtpub.com/en-us/product/clang-compiler-frontend-9781837635238`
- libc++ documentation, *Hardening Modes*: `https://libcxx.llvm.org/Hardening.html`
- Microsoft, *Security Best Practices for C++*: `https://learn.microsoft.com/en-us/cpp/security/security-best-practices-for-cpp`
- Google, *Code Sandboxing*: `https://developers.google.com/code-sandboxing`
- Cheerp.io, *WebAssembly Memory Model*: `https://cheerp.io/docs/reference/sections/wasm/memory-model`
- Pixel Free Studio blog, *How to Compile C/C++ to WebAssembly for the Web* (Blog): `https://blog.pixelfreestudio.com/how-to-compile-c-c-to-webassembly-for-the-web/`
- Rick Battagline, *Hands-On Game Development with WebAssembly: Learn WebAssembly C++ Programming by Building a Retro Space Game*, Packt Publishing: `https://www.packtpub.com/en-us/product/hands-on-game-development-with-webassembly-9781838646837`
- Mohammed Billoo, *Embedded Linux Essentials Handbook: Build Embedded Linux Systems and Real-World Apps with Yocto, Buildroot, and RPi*, Packt Publishing: `https://www.packtpub.com/en-us/product/embedded-linux-essentials-handbook-9781835461563`
- Herb Sutter, *C++ Safety, in Context* (Blog), Sutter's Mill: `https://herbsutter.com/2024/03/11/safety-in-context/`
- ISO C++ Foundation, *C++ Core Guidelines: Pro: Profiles*: `https://isocpp.github.io/CppCoreGuidelines/CppCoreGuidelines#pro-profiles`
- ISO C++ Foundation, *C++ Core Guidelines: CP.free: Lock-Free Programming*: `https://isocpp.github.io/CppCoreGuidelines/CppCoreGuidelines#SScp-free`
- Drogon Framework, *ENG-06 View: Drogon's CSP*, GitHub wiki: `https://github.com/drogonframework/drogon/wiki/ENG-06-View#drogons-csp`
- Drogon Framework, *ENG-12 drog on_ctl Command*, GitHub wiki: `https://github.com/drogonframework/drogon/wiki/ENG-12-drogon_ctl-Command`
- Dan Trebledj, *Abusing Server-Side Rendering in Drogon* (Blog), TrebledJ's Pages: `https://trebledj.me/posts/abusing-server-side-rendering-in-drogon/`
- Fil-C Project, *Fil's Unbelievable Garbage Collector* (FUGC): `https://fil-c.org/fugc`
- Hans-J. Boehm, Alan J. Demers, and Mark Weiser, *A Garbage Collector for C and C++* (Boehm–Demers–Weiser Garbage Collector): `https://www.hboehm.info/gc/`

13

Performance

After ensuring the security of a system's code, dependencies, and environment, we now turn to another critical quality attribute in modern software systems—performance. The most common reasons to choose C++ as a key programming language for a project are its high performance, fine-grained control over system resources, and object-oriented features. Moreover, C++ applications have a small memory footprint and are energy efficient. These features make C++ highly competitive with other performance-oriented languages such as C, Rust, Ada, Go, C#, or Java.

This chapter focuses on increasing the performance of C++ software through performance measurement and practical coding techniques. We'll start by exploring tools for measuring performance. We'll then show you a few techniques for increasing single-threaded compute speed. Next, we'll discuss how to make use of parallel computing. After that, we'll show how you can use C++20's coroutines for non-preemptive multitasking. Finally, we'll discuss how to implement efficient algorithms.

The following topics will be covered in this chapter:

- Measuring performance
- Helping the compiler generate performant code
- Parallelizing computations
- Using coroutines
- Implementing efficient algorithms

First, let's specify what you'll need to run the examples in this chapter.

Technical requirements

To replicate the examples from this chapter, you should install the following:

- CMake 3.28+
- A compiler that supports C++23 (GCC 14+ is recommended)

The source code snippets from the chapter can be found at `https://github.com/PacktPublishing/Software-Architecture-with-Cpp-2E/tree/main/Chapter13`.

Measuring performance

To effectively improve the performance of your code, you must start by measuring how it performs. Without knowing where the actual bottlenecks are, you will end up optimizing the wrong places, losing time, and being surprised and frustrated that your hard work gave little to no gains. In this section, we'll show how to properly measure performance using benchmarks, how to successfully profile your code, and how to gain insights into performance in distributed systems. But first, we'll look at how to prepare your environment for accurate and repeatable performance measurements, followed by an overview of the three approaches mentioned.

Preparing for accurate and repeatable performance measurements

For accurate and repeatable measurements, you might want to put your machine into performance mode instead of the usual default power-saving one. Power-saving modes extend battery life by reducing processor performance and inevitably affect the accuracy of measurements. If you require low latency from your system, you might want to disable power saving permanently both on the machines you benchmark on and in your production environment. Many times, this may mean entering UEFI or BIOS (depending on the firmware) to configure servers properly. Note that this may not be possible if you use a public cloud provider.

If you have root/admin permissions on your machine, the OS can often steer some of the settings too. For instance, you can force your CPU to run at its maximum frequency on a Linux system by running the following:

```
sudo cpupower frequency-set --governor performance
```

Moreover, to obtain meaningful results, you might want to perform measurements on a system that as closely resembles your production environment as possible. Hardware-related configuration aspects such as the different speeds of RAM, the number of CPU caches, and the microarchitecture of your CPUs can also skew your results and lead you to incorrect conclusions. The same goes for the hard drive setup and even the network topology and hardware used. The software you build on also plays a crucial role: from the firmware used, through the OS and kernel, all the way up the software stack to your dependencies. It's best to have a second environment that's identical to your production one and governed using the same tools and scripts.

Now that we have a solid environment for taking measurements, let's see what tools we can use to perform these measurements.

Leveraging different types of measuring tools

There are several ways to measure performance, each focusing on a different scope. Let's go through them one by one.

Benchmarks are typically used to measure execution speed in prepared tests. Usually, they produce results in terms of either the execution time or another performance metric, such as orders processed per second. There are several types of benchmarks:

- **Microbenchmarks**, which you can use to measure the execution of a small code fragment. We'll cover them in the next section.
- **Simulations**, which are synthetic tests on a larger scale with artificial data. They can be useful if you don't have access to the target data or your target hardware—for instance, when you are planning to check the performance of hardware that you're working on, but it doesn't exist yet, or when you plan to handle incoming traffic, but can only assume what the traffic will be like.
- **Replays**, which can be a very accurate way of measuring performance under a real-life workload. The idea is to record all the requests or workloads coming into the production system, often with timestamps. Such dumps can then later be "replayed" into the benchmarked system, respecting the time differences between them, to check how it performs. Such benchmarks can be great to see how potential changes to code or the environment can influence the latency and throughput of your system.
- **Industry-standard benchmarks**, which are a good way to see how our product performs compared to its competitors. Examples of such benchmarks include Super Pi for CPUs, 3DMark for graphics cards, and ResNet-50 for artificial intelligence processors.

Aside from benchmarking, another type of tool that is invaluable when it comes to measuring performance is profilers. Instead of just giving you overall performance metrics, profilers allow you to examine what your code is doing and look for bottlenecks. They're useful for catching unexpected things that slow your system down. We'll cover them in the *Performance profiling* section.

Another way to grasp your system's performance is tracing. Tracing is essentially a way to log your system's behavior during execution. By monitoring how long it takes for a request to complete various steps of processing (such as being handled by different types of microservices), you can gain insight into what parts of your system need to improve their performance, or how well your system deals with accepted and rejected requests. We'll cover this topic in more detail in the *Tracing* section.

Next, we focus on microbenchmarks, as they help us evaluate the performance impact of low-level architectural decisions in C++.

Using microbenchmarks

Microbenchmarks are used to measure how fast a "micro" fragment of code can perform. If you're wondering how to implement a given functionality or how fast different third-party libraries deal with the same task, then they're the perfect tool for the job. While they're not representative of a realistic environment, they're well suited to perform such small experiments.

Let's show how to run such experiments using one of the most commonly used frameworks to create microbenchmarks in C++: Google Benchmark.

Setting up Google Benchmark

Let's start by introducing the library into our code by using Conan. Put the following in `conanfile.py`:

```
from conan import ConanFile

class Pkg(ConanFile):
    settings = "os", "arch", "compiler", "build_type"
    generators = "CMakeDeps"

    def requirements(self):
        self.requires("benchmark/1.9.4")

    def build_requirements(self):
        pass
```

We're going to use the CMakeDeps generator as it's the recommended CMake generator in Conan 2.0. It relies on CMake's `find_package` feature to use the packages installed by our dependency manager. To install the dependencies in their release versions, run the following:

```
cd <build_directory>
conan install .. --build=missing -s build_type=Release -of .
```

Using the library from your `CMakeLists.txt` file is also pretty straightforward, as shown next:

```
list(APPEND CMAKE_PREFIX_PATH "${CMAKE_BINARY_DIR}")
find_package(benchmark REQUIRED)
```

Then, we add our build directory to `CMAKE_PREFIX_PATH` so that CMake can find the config and/or target files produced by Conan. Next, we just use them to find our dependency.

As we're going to create several microbenchmarks, we could use a CMake function to help us with defining them:

```
function(add_benchmark NAME SOURCE)
  add_executable(${NAME} ${SOURCE})
  target_compile_features(${NAME} PRIVATE cxx_std_20)
  target_link_libraries(${NAME} PRIVATE benchmark::benchmark)
endfunction()
```

The function will be able to create single-translation-unit microbenchmarks, each using C++20 and linked to the Google Benchmark library. Let's now use this function to create our first microbenchmark:

```
add_benchmark(microbenchmark_1 microbenchmarking/main_1.cpp)
```

Now we're ready to put some code in our source file.

Writing your first microbenchmark

We'll try to benchmark how much faster a lookup is when it's done using bisection in a sorted vector, as compared to scanning it linearly. Let's start with code that will create the sorted vector:

```
using namespace std::ranges;

template <typename T>
auto make_sorted_vector(std::size_t size) {
  auto sorted = std::vector<T>{};
  sorted.reserve(size);

  auto sorted_view = views::iota(T{0}) | views::take(size);
  std::ranges::copy(sorted_view, std::back_inserter(sorted));
  return sorted;
}
```

Our vector will contain size elements with all the numbers from 0 to size - 1 in ascending order. Let's now specify the element we're looking for and the container size:

```
constexpr auto MAX_HAYSTACK_SIZE = std::size_t{10'000'000};
constexpr auto NEEDLE = 2137;
```

Now we'll benchmark how long it takes to find `NEEDLE` in the sorted "haystack." The simple linear search can be implemented as follows:

```
void linear_search_in_sorted_vector(benchmark::State &state) {
  auto haystack = make_sorted_vector(MAX_HAYSTACK_SIZE);
  for (auto _ : state) {
    benchmark::DoNotOptimize(find(haystack, NEEDLE));
  }
}
```

Here, we can see the first use of Google Benchmark. Each microbenchmark should accept `State` as an argument. This special type does the following:

- Contains information about the iterations performed and the time spent on the measured computation
- Counts the bytes processed if wanted
- Can return other state information, such as the need to run further (through the `KeepRunning()` member function)
- Can be used to pause and resume the timing of an iteration (through the `PauseTiming()` and `ResumeTiming()` member functions, respectively)

The code in our loop will be measured, making as many iterations as desired, based on the total allowed time to run this particular benchmark. The creation of our haystack is outside the loop and won't be measured.

Inside the loop, there's a sink helper named `DoNotOptimize`. Its purpose is to prevent the compiler from eliminating computations it deems unnecessary. In our case, it will mark the result of `std::find` as necessary, so the actual code to find the needle is not optimized away.

Using tools such as `objdump` or sites such as Compiler Explorer (Godbolt) and Quick Bench allows you to peek if the code you want to run wasn't optimized out. Quick Bench has the additional advantage of running your benchmarks in the cloud and sharing their results online.

Back to our task at hand, we have a microbenchmark for the linear search, so let's now time the binary search in another microbenchmark:

```
void binary_search_in_sorted_vector(benchmark::State &state) {
  auto haystack = make_sorted_vector<int>(MAX_HAYSTACK_SIZE);
  for (auto _ : state) {
    benchmark::DoNotOptimize(lower_bound(haystack, NEEDLE));
  }
}
```

Our new benchmark is pretty similar. It only differs in the function used: `lower_bound` will perform a binary search. Note that, similar to our base example, we don't even check whether the iterator returned points to a valid element in the vector, or to its end. In the case of `lower_bound`, we could check if the element under the iterator is the one we're looking for.

Now that we have the microbenchmark functions, let's create actual benchmarks out of them by adding the following:

```
BENCHMARK(binary_search_in_sorted_vector);
BENCHMARK(linear_search_in_sorted_vector);
```

If the default benchmark settings are okay with you, that's all you need to pass. As the last step, let's add a `main()` function:

```
BENCHMARK_MAIN();
```

Simple as that! Alternatively, you can link our program with `benchmark_main` instead of defining your own `main()` with `BENCHMARK_MAIN()`. Using Google Benchmark's `main()` function has the advantage of providing us with some default options. If you compile our benchmark and run it passing `--help` as a parameter, you'll see the following:

```
benchmark [--benchmark_list_tests={true|false}]
          [--benchmark_filter=<regex>]
          [--benchmark_min_time=<min_time>]
          [--benchmark_min_warmup_time=<min_warmup_time>]
          [--benchmark_repetitions=<num_repetitions>]
```

```
            [--benchmark_dry_run={true|false}]
            [--benchmark_enable_random_interleaving={true|false}]
            [--benchmark_report_aggregates_only={true|false}]
            [--benchmark_display_aggregates_only={true|false}]
            [--benchmark_format=<console|json|csv>]
            [--benchmark_out=<filename>]
            [--benchmark_out_format=<json|console|csv>]
            [--benchmark_color={auto|true|false}]
            [--benchmark_counters_tabular={true|false}]
            [--benchmark_context=<key>=<value>,...]
            [--benchmark_time_unit={ns|us|ms|s}]
            [--v=<verbosity>]
```

This is a nice set of features to use. For example, when designing experiments, you can use the `benchmark_format` switch to get a CSV output for easier plotting on a chart.

Let's now see our benchmark in action by running the compiled executable with no command-line arguments. A possible output from running `./microbenchmark_1` is as follows:

```
2025-01-31T18:27:16+01:00
Running ./benchmark_1
Run on (20 X 2022.06 MHz CPU s)
CPU Caches:
  L1 Data 48 KiB (x10)
  L1 Instruction 32 KiB (x10)
  L2 Unified 1280 KiB (x10)
  L3 Unified 24576 KiB (x1)
Load Average: 2.18, 2.55, 2.42
-------------------------------------------------------------------------
Benchmark                        Time        CPU  Iterations
-------------------------------------------------------------------------
binary_search_in_sorted_vector      24.2 ns             24.2 ns      28711079
linear_search_in_sorted_vector       471 ns              471 ns       1477557
```

Starting with some data about the running environment (the time of benchmarking, the executable name, the server's CPUs, and the current load), we get to the results of each benchmark we defined. For each benchmark, we get the average wall time (the actual time the code was running from start to finish) per iteration, the average CPU time per iteration, and the number of iterations that the benchmark harness ran for us. By default, the longer a single iteration, the fewer iterations it will go through. Running more iterations ensures you get more stable results.

Reusing microbenchmark logic via argument capture

If we were to test more ways of dealing with our problem at hand, we could look for a way to reuse the benchmark code and just pass it to the function used to perform the lookup. Google Benchmark has a feature that we could use for that. The framework lets us pass any arguments we want to the benchmark by adding them as additional parameters to the function signature.

Let's see how a unified signature of our benchmark could look:

```
void search_in_sorted_vector(benchmark::State &state, auto finder) {
  auto haystack = make_sorted_vector<int>(MAX_HAYSTACK_SIZE);
  for (auto _ : state) {
    benchmark::DoNotOptimize(finder(haystack, NEEDLE));
  }
}
```

You will notice the new `finder` parameter to the function, which is used in the spot where we previously called either `find` or `lower_bound`. We can now make our two microbenchmarks using a different macro than we did last time:

```
BENCHMARK_CAPTURE(search_in_sorted_vector, binary, lower_bound);
BENCHMARK_CAPTURE(search_in_sorted_vector, linear, find);
```

The `BENCHMARK_CAPTURE` macro accepts the function, a name suffix, and an arbitrary number of parameters. If we wanted more, we could just pass them here. Our benchmark function could be a regular function or a template–both are supported.

Let's now see what we get when running the code:

```
-------------------------------------------------------------------
Benchmark                            Time            CPU   Iterations
-------------------------------------------------------------------
search_in_sorted_vector/binary      24.4 ns         24.4 ns    28365179
search_in_sorted_vector/linear       441 ns          441 ns     1597863
```

As you can see, the arguments passed to the functions are not part of the name, but the function name and our suffix are.

Let's now see how we can further customize our benchmarks.

Varying input sizes using microbenchmark arguments

A common need when designing experiments like ours is to check them on different sizes of arguments. Such needs can be addressed in Google Benchmark in a number of ways. The simplest is to just add a call to `Args()` on the object returned by the `BENCHMARK` macros. This way, we can pass a single set of values to use in a given microbenchmark. To use the passed value, we'd need to change our benchmark function as follows:

```
void search_in_sorted_vector(benchmark::State &state, auto finder) {
  const auto haystack = make_sorted_vector<int>(state.range(0));
  constexpr auto needle = 2137;
  for (auto _ : state) {
    benchmark::DoNotOptimize(finder(haystack, needle));
  }
}
```

The call to `state.range(0)` will read the 0-th argument passed. An arbitrary number can be supported. In our case, it's used to parameterize the haystack size.

What if we wanted to pass a range of value sets instead? This way, we could see how changing the size influences the performance more easily. To achieve this, instead of calling `Args()`, we could call `Range()` on the benchmark:

```
constexpr auto MIN_HAYSTACK_SIZE = std::size_t{1'000};
constexpr auto MAX_HAYSTACK_SIZE = std::size_t{10'000'000};

BENCHMARK_CAPTURE(search_in_sorted_vector, binary, lower_bound)
    ->RangeMultiplier(10)
    ->Range(MIN_HAYSTACK_SIZE, MAX_HAYSTACK_SIZE);
BENCHMARK_CAPTURE(search_in_sorted_vector, linear, find)
    ->RangeMultiplier(10)
    ->Range(MIN_HAYSTACK_SIZE, MAX_HAYSTACK_SIZE);
```

We specify the range boundaries using a predefined minimum and maximum. We then tell the benchmark harness to create the ranges by multiplying by 10 instead of the default value. When we run such benchmarks, we could get the following results:

```
---------------------------------------------------------------------
Benchmark                                       Time        CPU     Iterations
---------------------------------------------------------------------
search_in_sorted_vector/binary/1000             6.25 ns          6.24 ns
110876712
search_in_sorted_vector/binary/10000            11.7 ns          11.7 ns
59759090
search_in_sorted_vector/binary/100000           14.0 ns          14.0 ns
49900767
search_in_sorted_vector/binary/1000000          17.7 ns          17.7 ns
39763768
search_in_sorted_vector/binary/10000000         24.2 ns          24.2 ns
28917491
search_in_sorted_vector/linear/1000              210 ns           210 ns
3327907
```

```
search_in_sorted_vector/linear/10000             437 ns          437 ns
1600476
search_in_sorted_vector/linear/100000            437 ns          437 ns
1602461
search_in_sorted_vector/linear/1000000           441 ns          441 ns
1601974
search_in_sorted_vector/linear/10000000          437 ns          437 ns
1601447
```

You might be wondering why the linear search doesn't show us linear growth. That's because we look for a constant value of the needle that can be spotted at a constant position. If the haystack contains our needle, we need the same number of operations to find it regardless of the haystack size, so the execution time stops growing (but can still be subject to small fluctuations).

Why not play with the needle position as well?

While passing fixed values with `Args()` or `Range()` is useful, sometimes we want more flexibility in controlling the inputs. Generating both the haystack sizes and needle positions might be the easiest when done in a simple function. Google Benchmark allows such scenarios for generating arguments programmatically.

We'll start by rewriting our benchmark function to use two parameters in each iteration:

```
void search_in_sorted_vector(benchmark::State &state, auto finder) {
  const auto needle = state.range(0);
  const auto haystack = make_sorted_vector<int>(state.range(1));
  for (auto _ : state) {
    benchmark::DoNotOptimize(finder(haystack, needle));
  }
}
```

As you can see, `state.range(0)` will mark our needle position, while `state.range(1)` will be the haystack size. This means we need to pass two values each time, and this function generates them:

```
void generate_sizes(benchmark::internal::Benchmark *b) {
  for (long haystack = MIN_HAYSTACK_SIZE; haystack <= MAX_HAYSTACK_SIZE;
       haystack *= 100) {
    for (auto needle :
         {haystack / 8, haystack / 2, haystack - 1, haystack + 1}) {
      b->Args({needle, haystack});
    }
  }
}
```

Instead of using `Range()` and `RangeMultiplier()`, we write a loop to generate the haystack sizes, this time increasing them by 100 each time. When it comes to the needles, we use three positions in proportionate positions of the haystack and one that falls outside of it. We call `Args` on each loop iteration, passing both the generated values.

Now, let's apply our generator function to our benchmarks:

```
BENCHMARK_CAPTURE(search_in_sorted_vector, binary, lower_bound)-
>Apply(generate_sizes);
BENCHMARK_CAPTURE(search_in_sorted_vector, linear, find)->Apply(generate_
sizes);
```

Using such functions makes it easy to pass the same generator to many benchmarks. Possible results of such benchmarks are as follows:

```
--------------------------------------------------------------------------
Benchmark                                          Time      CPU  Iterations
--------------------------------------------------------------------------
...
search_in_sorted_vector/binary/1250000/10000000        24.2 ns         24.2 ns
29021816
search_in_sorted_vector/binary/5000000/10000000        24.1 ns         24.1 ns
29127297
search_in_sorted_vector/binary/9999999/10000000        24.1 ns         24.1 ns
29109150
search_in_sorted_vector/binary/10000001/10000000       24.1 ns         24.1 ns
29127571
...
search_in_sorted_vector/linear/1250000/10000000      255229 ns       255119 ns
2755
search_in_sorted_vector/linear/5000000/10000000     1207806 ns      1207357 ns
601
search_in_sorted_vector/linear/9999999/10000000     2857079 ns      2856264 ns
248
search_in_sorted_vector/linear/10000001/10000000    2847455 ns      2846680 ns
246
// et cetera
```

Now we have a pretty well-defined experiment for performing the searches. As an exercise, run the experiment on your own machine to see the complete results and try to draw some conclusions from the results.

For comparison, the same benchmarks will be implemented using the Catch2 and nanobench frameworks.

Benchmarking with Catch2

Catch2 is a test framework described in *Chapter 10, Writing Testable Code*. The linear and binary searches with this framework can be implemented as follows:

```
TEST_CASE("binary_search_in_sorted_vector", "[benchmark]") {
  BENCHMARK_ADVANCED("lower_bound")(Catch::Benchmark::Chronometer meter) {
    auto haystack = make_sorted_vector(MAX_HAYSTACK_SIZE);
    meter.measure([&] { return lower_bound(haystack, NEEDLE); });
  };
}

TEST_CASE("linear_search_in_sorted_vector", "[benchmark]") {
  BENCHMARK_ADVANCED("find")(Catch::Benchmark::Chronometer meter {
  auto haystack = make_sorted_vector(MAX_HAYSTACK_SIZE);
  meter.measure([&] { return find(haystack, NEEDLE); }); }; }
}
```

`BENCHMARK_ADVANCED` blocks are invoked twice, once during estimation and once during execution to subtract the execution time of the code under test from the total test execution time. The measured code is obviously called in the `measure()` function. The `return` statement is important to avoid optimizing away the benchmarked code by the compiler.

Unlike Google Benchmark, there are no macros such as `BENCHMARK_CAPTURE` available in Catch2. Therefore, the linear and binary search benchmarks just use a common function. The same functionality can be implemented through other means:

```
void search_in_sorted_vector(Catch::Benchmark::Chronometer &meter, auto finder)
{
  auto haystack = make_sorted_vector(MAX_HAYSTACK_SIZE);
  meter.measure([&] { return finder(haystack, NEEDLE); });
}

TEST_CASE("binary_search_in_sorted_vector", "[benchmark]") {
  BENCHMARK_ADVANCED("lower_bound")(Catch::Benchmark::Chronometer meter) {
    search_in_sorted_vector(meter, lower_bound);
  };
}

TEST_CASE("linear_search_in_sorted_vector", "[benchmark]") {
  BENCHMARK_ADVANCED("find")(Catch::Benchmark::Chronometer meter) {
    search_in_sorted_vector(meter, find);
  };
}
```

Data-driven testing in Catch2 is implemented with data generators, and this framework supports custom generators:

```
Catch::Generators::GeneratorWrapper<size_t> size_generator() {
  struct Generator final : Catch::Generators::IGenerator<size_t> {
    size_t cur{MIN_HAYSTACK_SIZE}, end{MAX_HAYSTACK_SIZE}, multiplier{10};

    const size_t& get() const override { return cur; }

    bool next() override {
      cur *= multiplier;
      return cur < end;
    }
  };

  return Catch::Generators::GeneratorWrapper<size_t>{
      Catch::Detail::make_unique<Generator>()};
}

TEST_CASE("binary_search_in_sorted_vector", "[benchmark]") {
  const auto size = GENERATE(size_generator());

  search_in_sorted_vector("lower_bound", size, lower_bound);
}

TEST_CASE("linear_search_in_sorted_vector", "[benchmark]") {
  const auto size = GENERATE(size_generator());

  search_in_sorted_vector("find", size, find);
}
```

Reusing benchmarks with different parameters in Catch2 is possible with the `BENCHMARK` macro too:

```
void search_in_sorted_vector(const std::string &benchmarkName, std::size_t
size,
                             int needle, auto finder) {
  auto haystack = make_sorted_vector<int>(size);

  BENCHMARK(std::format("{}/{}/{}", benchmarkName, needle, size)) {
    return finder(haystack, needle);
  };
}
```

```
void generate_sizes(const std::string &benchmarkName, auto finder) {
  for (std::size_t haystack = MIN_HAYSTACK_SIZE; haystack <= MAX_HAYSTACK_SIZE;
       haystack *= 100) {
    for (auto needle :
         {haystack / 8, haystack / 2, haystack - 1, haystack + 1}) {
      search_in_sorted_vector(benchmarkName, haystack, needle, finder);
    }
  }
}

TEST_CASE("binary_search_in_sorted_vector", "[benchmark]") {
  generate_sizes("lower_bound", lower_bound);
}

TEST_CASE("linear_search_in_sorted_vector", "[benchmark]") {
  generate_sizes("find", find);
}
```

Catch2 is a good choice if you already use Catch2 for testing. It provides decent benchmarking capabilities and reduces the need for extra dependencies.

Benchmarking with nanobench

nanobench (used via the `ankerl::nanobench` namespace) is a lightweight, single-header platform-independent library for C++11/14/17/20, intended to be wrapped and run in another test framework. This framework calculates the asymptotic complexity (Big O) from multiple runs of benchmarks and can generate reports in various formats (Mustache, CSV, HTML Box Plots, JSON, or pyperf).

The linear and binary searches with nanobench and doctest (a test framework described in the previous chapter) can be implemented as follows:

```
TEST_CASE("binary_search_in_sorted_vector") {
  ankerl::nanobench::Bench().run("binary_search_in_sorted_vector", [&]() {
    auto haystack = make_sorted_vector(MAX_HAYSTACK_SIZE);
    ankerl::nanobench::doNotOptimizeAway(lower_bound(haystack, NEEDLE));
  });
}

TEST_CASE("linear_search_in_sorted_vector") {
  ankerl::nanobench::Bench().run("linear_search_in_sorted_vector", [&]() {
    auto haystack = make_sorted_vector(MAX_HAYSTACK_SIZE);
    ankerl::nanobench::doNotOptimizeAway(find(haystack, NEEDLE));
  });
}
```

nanobench does not have macros such as `BENCHMARK_CAPTURE`, but the same functionality as with Google Benchmark can be implemented through other means:

```
void search_in_sorted_vector(const std::string &benchmarkName, auto finder){
    ankerl::nanobench::Bench().run(benchmarkName, [&]() {
    auto haystack = make_sorted_vector(MAX_HAYSTACK_SIZE);
    ankerl::nanobench::doNotOptimizeAway(finder(haystack, NEEDLE));
  });
}

TEST_CASE("binary_search_in_sorted_vector") {
  search_in_sorted_vector("binary_search_in_sorted_vector", lower_bound);
}

TEST_CASE("linear_search_in_sorted_vector") {
  search_in_sorted_vector("linear_search_in_sorted_vector", find);
}
```

Running nanobench benchmarks with varying input parameters is straightforward:

```
void search_in_sorted_vector(const std::string &benchmarkName, auto finder) {
  for (std::size_t s = MIN_HAYSTACK_SIZE; s <= MAX_HAYSTACK_SIZE; s *= 10)
  {
        ankerl::nanobench::Bench().run(
        std::format("{}/{}", benchmarkName, s), [&]() {
        auto haystack = make_sorted_vector<int>(s);
        constexpr auto needle = 2137;
        ankerl::nanobench::doNotOptimizeAway(finder(haystack, needle));
      });
  }
}

TEST_CASE("binary_search_in_sorted_vector") {
  search_in_sorted_vector("binary_search_in_sorted_vector", lower_bound);
}

TEST_CASE("linear_search_in_sorted_vector") {
  search_in_sorted_vector("linear_search_in_sorted_vector", find);
}
```

To measure asymptotic complexity, all benchmarks must run on the same bench object:

```
void search_in_sorted_vector(ankerl::nanobench::Bench &bench,
                              const std::string &benchmarkName,
                              const std::size_t size, int needle, auto finder) {
    bench.complexityN(size).run(
    std::format("{}/{}/{}", benchmarkName, needle, size), [&]() {
    auto haystack = make_sorted_vector<int>(size);
    ankerl::nanobench::doNotOptimizeAway(finder(haystack, needle));
  });
}

void generate_sizes(ankerl::nanobench::Bench &bench,
                    const std::string &benchmarkName, auto finder) {
  for (std::size_t haystack = MIN_HAYSTACK_SIZE; haystack <=
       MAX_HAYSTACK_SIZE; haystack *= 100) {
       for (auto needle :
         {haystack / 8, haystack / 2, haystack - 1, haystack + 1}) {
          search_in_sorted_vector(bench, benchmarkName, haystack, needle,
                                  finder);
        }
  }
}

TEST_CASE("binary_search_in_sorted_vector") {
  ankerl::nanobench::Bench bench;
  generate_sizes(bench, "binary_search_in_sorted_vector", lower_bound);
  std::cout << bench.complexityBigO() << std::endl;
}

TEST_CASE("linear_search_in_sorted_vector") {
  ankerl::nanobench::Bench bench;
  generate_sizes(bench, "linear_search_in_sorted_vector", find);
  std::cout << bench.complexityBigO() << std::endl;
}
```

The purpose of this section and the previous one was to show how to implement benchmarks with similar functionalities without using Google Benchmark. You may already be using Catch2, for example, and introducing another benchmark framework could add complexity to your project.

Alternatively, if for some reason the frameworks described in this chapter do not suit you, consider benchmark frameworks such as hyperfine, Celero, nonius, picobench, sltbench, plf::nanotimer, or microbench.

Choosing what to microbenchmark and optimize

Running such experiments can be educative and even addictive. However, keep in mind that microbenchmarks shouldn't be the only type of performance testing in your project. As Donald Knuth famously said in his paper *Structured Programming with go to Statements* (1974):

> *We should forget about small efficiencies, say about 97% of the time: premature optimization is the root of all evil*

This means that you should microbenchmark only code that matters, especially code on your hot path. Larger benchmarks, along with tracing and profiling, can be used to see where and when to optimize instead of guessing and optimizing prematurely. First, understand how your software executes.

There's one more point we want to make regarding the preceding quote. It doesn't mean you should allow premature *pessimization*. Poor choice of data structures or algorithms, or even small inefficiencies that spread through all of your code, can sometimes influence the overall performance of your system. For instance, performing unnecessary dynamic allocations, although it might not look that bad at first, can lead to heap fragmentation over time and cause you serious trouble if your app should run for long periods of time. Overuse of node-based containers can lead to more cache misses too. Long story short, if it's not a big effort to write efficient code instead of less efficient code, go for it.

Now that we've covered how to approach performance improvement with care, let's now learn what to do to maintain consistent performance over time, especially in performance-sensitive parts of the code base.

Creating performance tests using benchmarks

Like having unit tests for precise testing and functional tests for larger-scale testing of your code's correctness, you can use microbenchmarks and larger benchmarks to test your code's performance.

If you have tight constraints on the execution time for certain code paths, having a test that ensures the limit is met can be very useful. Even if you don't have such specific constraints, you might be interested in monitoring how the performance changes across code changes. If, after a change, your code runs slower than before by a certain threshold, the test could be marked as failed.

Although also a useful tool, remember that such tests are prone to the boiling frog effect: performance that degrades slowly over time can go unnoticed, so be sure to monitor the execution times occasionally. When introducing performance tests to your CI, be sure to always run them in the same environment for stable results.

Let's now discuss the next type of tools in our performance shed.

Performance profiling

While benchmarks and tracing can give you specific measurements and overviews for a given scope, profilers can help you analyze where those performance numbers came from. They are an essential tool if you need to gain insight into your performance and improve it.

Choosing the type of performance profiler to use

There are two types of performance profilers available: instrumentation and sampling profilers.

Instrumentation profilers work by adding additional instructions into a program's source code or compiled binary, to track specific events. These profilers, such as Callgrind (a Valgrind tool suite for Linux, Android, FreeBSD, Solaris, Illumos, and macOS), introduce lots of overhead because they need to, well, insert extra code (instrument) to record the exact timing and frequency of every function call. This way, the results they produce contain detailed data, including the behavior of even the smallest functions, but the execution times they report can be skewed by the profiling overhead.

They also have the drawback of not always catching **input/output** (**I/O**) slowness and jitters. They slow down the execution, so while they can tell you how often you call a particular function, they won't tell you if the slowness is due to waiting on a disk read to finish.

Due to the flaws of instrumentation profilers, it's generally better to use sampling profilers, which take a statistical approach to probe the call stacks periodically rather than recording every call. Such profilers are lightweight and very effective in identifying performance bottlenecks, since a small number of functions account for the majority of execution time.

Two tools worth mentioning are the open source `perf` for profiling on Linux systems and Intel's proprietary tool called VTune (free for open source projects). Although they can sometimes miss key events due to the nature of sampling, they should usually give you a much better view of where your code spends time.

If you decide to use perf, you should know that you can use it by invoking `perf stat`, which gives you a quick overview of statistics such as CPU cache usage. For a more detailed analysis, you can use `perf record -g` to capture results and `perf report -g` to analyze them.

If you don't use Linux or these tools are not enough for your purposes, then consider these sampling profilers: gprof (Linux/Unix), Very Sleepy (Windows), Superluminal (Windows, Xbox One, PlayStation and C++, Rust, .NET), AMD uProf CPU profiler (Windows, Linux, and FreeBSD), and Linaro MAP (Linaro Forge).

Please watch Hubert Matthews's and Chandler Carruth's videos, which show tools' possibilities and how to use them for a solid overview of `perf` and some other tools. Both are linked in the *Further reading* section.

Instrumentation profilers require direct integration into the C++ code base, while sampling profilers, although commonly used, often operate as external tools. Therefore, let's see the former in a bit more detail.

One example of an instrumentation profiler is Tracy, a hybrid profiler that combines both manual instrumentation (frame-based profiling) and automatic sampling (statistical profiling) to analyze performance. It is highly relevant in a C++ context, especially for performance-critical applications such as games, real-time systems, or high-performance computing. This profiler integrates directly into the C++ code and offers fine-grained profiling in real time. It also supports other programming languages such as C, Lua, Python, and Fortran, and has third-party bindings for Rust, Zig, C#, OCaml, Odin, and so on.

Tracy is designed for frame-oriented applications to detect bottlenecks delaying frames. It has a comprehensive guide and runs on major platforms such as Linux, macOS, Windows, Android, iOS, FreeBSD, QNX, Fuchsia, and WSL.

It supports a wide range of features, such as CPU and **graphics processing unit** (**GPU**) profiling (OpenGL, Vulkan, Direct3D, Metal, OpenCL), memory allocation tracking, lock contention analysis, context switch monitoring, frame capture, zone-based statistical information collection, trace comparison, and source-to-assembly code mapping.

The list of features is quite extensive and therefore of great interest. But the project is under active development, so its protocols may be incompatible.

To use Tracy, add this library to `conanfile.py`:

```
from conan import ConanFile

class Pkg(ConanFile):
    settings = "os", "arch", "compiler", "build_type"
    generators = "CMakeDeps"
    default_options = {"tracy/*:no_exit": True}

    def requirements(self):
        self.requires("benchmark/1.9.4")
        self.requires("nanobench/4.3.11")
        self.requires("doctest/2.4.12")
        self.requires("catch2/3.10.0")
        self.requires("tracy/0.12.2")

    def build_requirements(self):
        pass
```

If the `TRACY_NO_EXIT` option is enabled, programs do not terminate and wait for profiling traces to be sent to the Tracy server.

To show the use of Tracy in practice, a Morse code decoder is used here as an example. We start by defining the mapping between Morse code and English letters:

```
#include <cassert>
#include <string>
#include <tracy/Tracy.hpp>
#include <unordered_map>

using namespace std;

const unordered_map<string, string> morse_code{
    {".-", "A"}, {"-...", "B"}, {"-.-.", "C"}, {"-..", "D"},
    {".", "E"}, {"..-.", "F"}, {"--.", "G"}, {"....", "H"},
    {"..", "I"}, {".---", "J"}, {"-.-", "K"}, {".-..", "L"},
    {"--", "M"}, {"-.", "N"}, {"---", "O"}, {".--.", "P"},
    {"--.-", "Q"}, {".-.", "R"}, {"...", "S"}, {"-", "T"},
    {"..-", "U"}, {"...-", "V"}, {".--", "W"}, {"-..-", "X"},
    {"-.--", "Y"}, {"--..", "Z"}, {"-----", "0"}, {".----", "1"},
    {"..---", "2"}, {"...--", "3"}, {"....-", "4"}, {".....", "5"},
    {"-....", "6"}, {"--...", "7"}, {"---..", "8"}, {"----.", "9"},
    {".-.-.-", "."}, {"--..--", ","}, {"..--..", "?"}, {".----.", "'"},
    {"-.-.--", "!"}, {"-..-.", "/"}, {"-.--.", "("}, {"-.--.-", ")"},
    {".-...", "&"}, {"---...", ":"}, {"-.-.-.", ";"}, {"-...-", "="},
    {".-.-.", "+"}, {"-....-", "-"}, {"..--.-", "_"},        {".-..-.", "\""},
    {"...-..-", "$"}, {".--.-.", "@"}, {"...---...", "SOS"}};
```

ZoneScoped and ZoneScopedN are macros from the Tracy library to mark measured scopes. They record function names, source file names, and locations. The first macro assigns names to scopes automatically based on function names, and the second macro allows using any names. The list of macros is not limited to just these two:

```
std::string decode_morse(const std::string &morse_msg) {
  std::string decoded, seq;
  bool is_space{false};

  ZoneScoped; // the scope name is decode_morse
  for (const auto c : morse_msg) {
    ZoneScopedN("decode-loop");
    if (c == '.' || c == '-') {
      ZoneScopedN("dot-dash");
      if (is_space && !decoded.empty()) decoded += ' ';
      seq += c;
      is_space = false;
    } else if (c == ' ') {
      ZoneScopedN("space");
      if (!seq.empty()) {
        decoded += morse_code.at(seq);
        seq.clear();
      } else {
        is_space = true;
      }
    }
  }

  if (!seq.empty()) {
    decoded += morse_code.at(seq);
  }

  return decoded;
}

int main() {
  ZoneScoped; // the scope name is main
  assert(decode_morse("-.-- --- -....- .-- .- -.-- -....- -.-- ---") = "YO-WAY-
YO");

  return 0;
}
```

The Tracy profiler GUI (see *Figure 13.1*) and its accompanying guide are published with every release. You can install Tracy from package managers on Ubuntu, Debian, Arch, Gentoo, and FreeBSD. On macOS and Linux, the tool is also available via Homebrew. Alternatively, you can build the profiler from source, which won't require much effort. The profiler as a server may not be compatible with the client library due to a protocol mismatch between the server and the client, so use the same versions in this case. The following figure shows all the program scopes and even the scope binding to the source code:

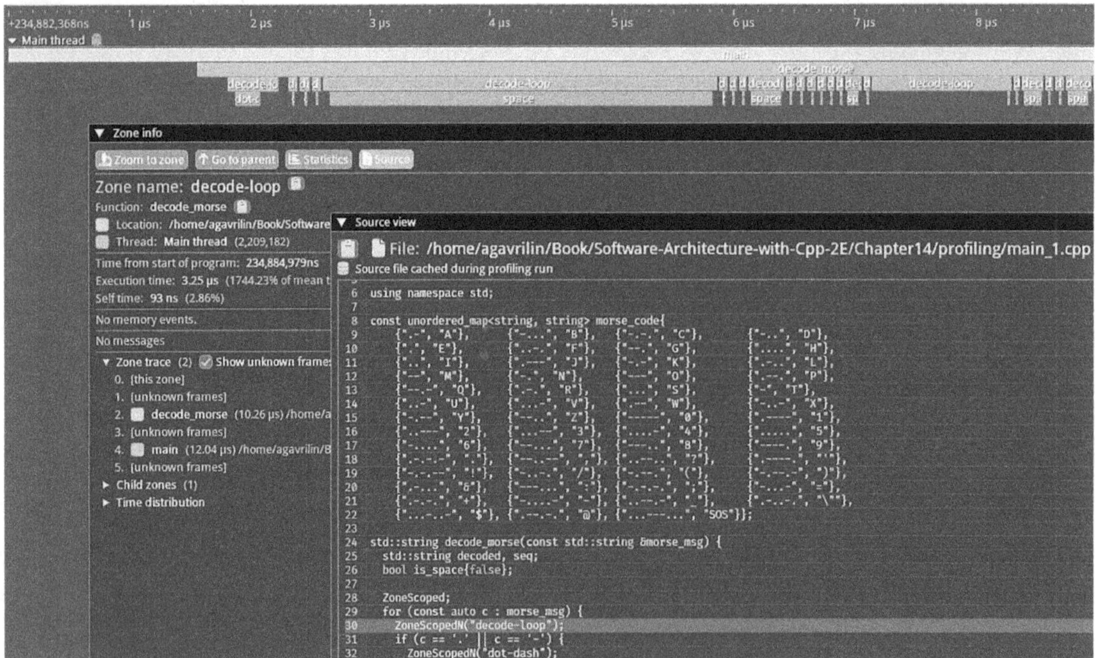

Figure 13.1: An overview of the Tracy profiler GUI (shown partially and lightened)

🔍**Quick tip:** Need to see a high-resolution version of this image? Open this book in the next-gen Packt Reader or view it in the PDF/ePub copy.

The next-gen Packt Reader and a **free PDF/ePub copy** of this book are included with your purchase. Scan the QR code OR visit `https://packtpub.com/unlock`, then use the search bar to find this book by name. Double-check the edition shown to make sure you get the right one.

In case Tracy doesn't suit your needs, consider these instrumentation profiling libraries: gperftools (Linux, macOS, FreeBSD, Windows), Optick (formerly Brofiler; Linux, Windows, macOS), Perfetto (Android, Linux, CrOS, macOS, Windows), easy_profiler (Linux, macOS, FreeBSD, Windows, QNX, Android), Palanteer (Linux, Windows), Coz: Causal Profiling (Linux), Spall, microprofile (OpenGL, D3D11, D3D12, Vulkan), MicroProfiler (Linux, Windows) or DTrace (Solaris, Illumos, macOS, FreeBSD, OpenBSD, NetBSD, Linux, Windows, as well as embedded systems).

It also makes sense to use built-in IDE performance tools such as Windows Performance Toolkit in Visual Studio IDE, Apple Instruments in Xcode (macOS), Performance Analyzer in Qt Creator, and CPU profiler in CLion (based on `perf` and DTrace).

For profiling compilation, there are several options: CMake, since 3.18, supports profiling with the `--profiling-format=google-trace` and `--profiling-output=path` flags; ninjatracing converts `.ninja_log` files to Chrome's `about:tracing` format; Clang Build Analyzer.

Preparing the environment and processing the results

When analyzing profiling results, you may often want to perform some preparation, cleanup, and processing. For instance, if your code mostly spends time spinning around, you might want to filter that out. Before even starting the profiler, be sure to compile or download as many debug symbols as you can for your code, your dependencies, even the OS libraries, and kernel. Also, it's essential you disable frame pointer optimizations. On GCC and Clang, you can do so by passing the `-fno-omit-frame-pointer` flag. It won't affect performance much but will give you much more data about the execution of your code.

When it comes to post-processing of the results, when using perf, it's usually a good idea to create flame graphs from the results. Brendan Gregg's tool from the *Further reading* section is great for that. Flame graphs are a simple and effective tool to see where the execution takes too much time, as the width of each item on the graph corresponds to the resource usage. You can have flame graphs for CPU usage, as well as for resources such as memory usage, allocations, and page faults, or the time spent when the code is not executing, such as staying blocked during system calls, on mutexes, I/O operations, and the like. There are also ways to perform diffs on the generated flame graphs.

Analyzing the results

Keep in mind that not all performance issues will show up on profiling output, and not all can be found using profilers. Therefore, developing a strong understanding of your hardware environment and of the execution model of your software is recommended.

For example, with some experience, you'll be able to see that you could benefit from setting affinity to your threads or changing which threads execute on specific NUMA nodes. **Non-uniform memory access (NUMA)** is a computer system architecture in which memory access time depends on its location relative to the processor.

Moreover, it might not always be that obvious to see that you've forgotten to disable power-saving features or would benefit from enabling or disabling hyper-threading. Sometimes you might see the **Single Instruction Multiple Data** (**SIMD**) registers of your CPU being used in your program, but the code still doesn't run at its full speed: you might be using **Streaming SIMD Extensions** (**SSE**) instructions instead of **Advanced Vector Extensions** (**AVX**), AVX instead of AVX2, or AVX2 instead of AVX512. Knowing what specific instructions your CPU is capable of running can be crucial when you analyze the profiling results.

If you do not have full control over the environment in which your application runs, you can rely on telemetry and observability frameworks to monitor real-world performance. Refer to *Chapter 17, Observability*, and *Chapter 18, Cloud-Native Design*, for more information.

Solving performance issues also requires a bit of experience. On the other hand, sometimes experience can lead you to false assumptions. For instance, in many cases, using dynamic polymorphism will hurt your performance, but there are cases where it is harmless for your code. Before jumping to conclusions, it might be worth profiling the code and gaining knowledge about the various ways a compiler can optimize code and the limits of those techniques.

Talking specifically about virtualization, it's often beneficial to mark your classes of virtual member functions as `final` when you don't want other types to inherit and override them. This tends to help the compilers in lots of cases.

Compilers can also optimize much better if they "see" what type the object is: if you create a type in scope and call its virtual member function, the compiler should be able to deduce which function should be called. GCC tends to devirtualize better than other compilers. For more information on this, you can refer to Arthur O'Dwyer's blog post from the *Further reading* section.

As with other types of tools presented in this section, try not to rely only on your profiler. Improvements in profiling results are not a guarantee that your system has gotten faster. A better-looking profile can still not tell you the whole story, and the better performance of one component doesn't necessarily mean the whole system's performance improved. This is where our last type of tool can come in use.

Tracing

The last technique we'll discuss in this section is particularly valuable for distributed systems. When looking at the overall system, often deployed in the cloud, profiling your software on a single machine won't tell you the whole story. In such cases, your best bet would be to trace the requests and responses flowing through your system.

Tracing is a way to log the execution path of your code. It's often used when a request (and sometimes its response) must flow through many parts of your system. Usually, such messages are traced along the route, with timestamps added at observation points of execution, which is essential for understanding and debugging microservices and complex distributed systems.

A common addition to timestamps is the use of correlation and trace IDs. Very often the trace ID is used as the correlation ID, which can be a source of confusion, but they are not the same thing. A trace ID identifies a single distributed trace, which represents the complete path of a single request across multiple services. On the other hand, a correlation ID links related traces or log entries belonging to the same process.

Basically, they're unique identifiers that get assigned to each message. Their purpose is to correlate the logs and traces produced by different components of your system (like different microservices) during the processing of the same incoming request, and sometimes for the events it caused, too. Such IDs should be passed with the message everywhere it goes, for example, by adding them to HTTP headers. Even when the original request is gone, you could add its unique ID to each of the responses produced.

By using correlation and trace IDs, you can track how messages for a given request propagate through the system and how long it took for different parts of your system to process them.

Often, in addition to timestamps and trace IDs, you'll want tracing to capture additional data along the way, such as the thread that was used to perform the computation, the type and count of responses produced for a given request, or the names of the machines involved.

Tools such as OpenTelemetry can help you add this level of tracing support to your systems with minimal effort. What's interesting is that tracing can be used to debug CI/CD pipelines to find performance bottlenecks; for instance, there is an OpenTelemetry plugin for Jenkins to troubleshoot Jenkins performance with distributed tracing of HTTP requests.

Next, we tackle a different subject and learn how we can write compiler-friendly code for faster execution.

Helping the compiler generate performant code

This section focuses on writing faster single-threaded code by helping the compiler generate optimized instructions. There are many things that can help your compiler generate efficient code for you. Some boil down to steering it properly, and others require writing your code in a compiler-friendly way.

It's also important to know what you need to do on your critical path and to design it efficiently. For instance, try to avoid virtual dispatch there (unless you can prove it's being devirtualized), and try not to allocate new memory on it. Often, the clever design of code to avoid locking (or at least using lock-free algorithms) is helpful. Generally speaking, everything that can worsen your performance should be kept outside your hot path. Having both your **instruction cache (I-cache)** and **data cache (D-cache)** hot is really going to pay off. Even attributes such as `[[likely]]` and `[[unlikely]]` that hint to the compiler which branch it should expect to be executed can sometimes have an impact unless compilers ignore these attributes.

The following subsections explore several approaches to help the compiler produce faster code.

Optimizing whole programs

An interesting way to improve the performance of many C++ projects is to optimize a program by enabling **link-time optimization (LTO)**, since the linker sees the entire program rather than its individual translation units (module files) during regular compilation. During the regular compilation phase, your compiler doesn't know how the code will get linked with other object files or libraries. Many opportunities to optimize executables arise only at the linking stage, when your tools can see the bigger picture of how the parts of your program interact with each other.

By enabling LTO, you can sometimes grab a significant improvement in performance with very little cost. In CMake projects, you can enable LTO by setting either the global `CMAKE_INTERPROCEDURAL_OPTIMIZATION` flag or by setting the `INTERPROCEDURAL_OPTIMIZATION` property on your targets.

One drawback of using LTO is that it makes the building process longer—sometimes a lot longer. To mitigate this cost for developers, you may want to only enable this optimization for builds that undergo performance testing or are meant to be released.

Optimizing based on real-world usage patterns

Another way to optimize your executable file is to apply **profile-guided optimization** (**PGO**), also known as **profile-directed feedback** (**PDF**) or **feedback-directed optimization** (**FDO**). This compiler optimization technique is advantageous because the compiler doesn't make assumptions when choosing optimization methods but instead relies on real data collected during program execution.

You need to compile your code with additional flags that cause the executable to gather special profiling information during runtime. Then, you should run the program under the expected production load. It is important to keep in mind that test runs of the program should be carried out according to the most typical scenarios so that the statistics are representative; otherwise, the program performance may even degrade.

In the next phase, you can use the gathered data to compile the executable again, this time passing a different flag that instructs the compiler to use the gathered data to generate code better suited for your performance profiling metrics.

This way, you'll end up with a binary that's prepared and tuned to your specific workload.

Writing cache-friendly code

Both LTO and PGO can be of use, but there's one more important thing that you need to keep in mind when working on performant systems: cache friendliness.

This is because modern processors rely heavily on cache memory, which is smaller and faster than main memory (RAM). So, frequently accessed instructions and data are loaded into caches. When your program keeps active data within cache lines, you minimize cache misses, leading to speedup.

A common strategy for improving cache efficiency is using flat data structures instead of node-based ones means that you need to perform less pointer chasing at runtime, which helps your performance. Using data that's contiguous in memory, regardless of whether you're reading it forward or backward, means your CPU's memory prefetcher can load it before it's used, which can often make a huge difference. Node-based data structures and the mentioned pointer chasing cause random memory access patterns that can "confuse" the prefetcher and make it impossible for it to prefetch correct data.

These considerations translate directly into container performance in real-world applications. If you want to see some performance results, please refer to *C++ Containers Benchmark*, linked in the *Further reading* section. It compares various usage scenarios of `std::vector`, `std::list`, `std::deque`, and `plf::colony`. If you don't know the last one, it's an interesting "bag"-type container with great fast insertion and deletion of large data.

When choosing from associative containers, you'll most often want to use "flat" implementations instead of node-based ones (separate chaining). This means that instead of using `std::unordered_map` and `std::unordered_set`, you might want to try out ones such as `tsl::hopscotch_map`, Abseil's `flat_hash_map` and `flat_hash_set`, or C++23's `std::flat_map` and `std::flat_set`. A flat hash map is highly efficient because its elements are stored directly in the slot array, providing excellent D-cache performance, but such maps often do not guarantee pointer stability after insertions or deletions, which means that pointers to its elements can potentially become invalid due to re-hashing operations.

In addition, techniques such as putting colder instructions (such as exception handling code) in a non-inline function can help to increase the hotness of your I-cache. This way, by placing rarely used code in separate, non-inline functions, the main, frequently used code paths remain smaller, fit better in the I-cache, and thus maintain a higher *hotness* or hit rate, reducing the number of I-cache misses (additional loading processor instructions), which can improve the program performance.

To better understand why these techniques matter, let's take a quick look at how CPU caches work and why they're so critical for performance.

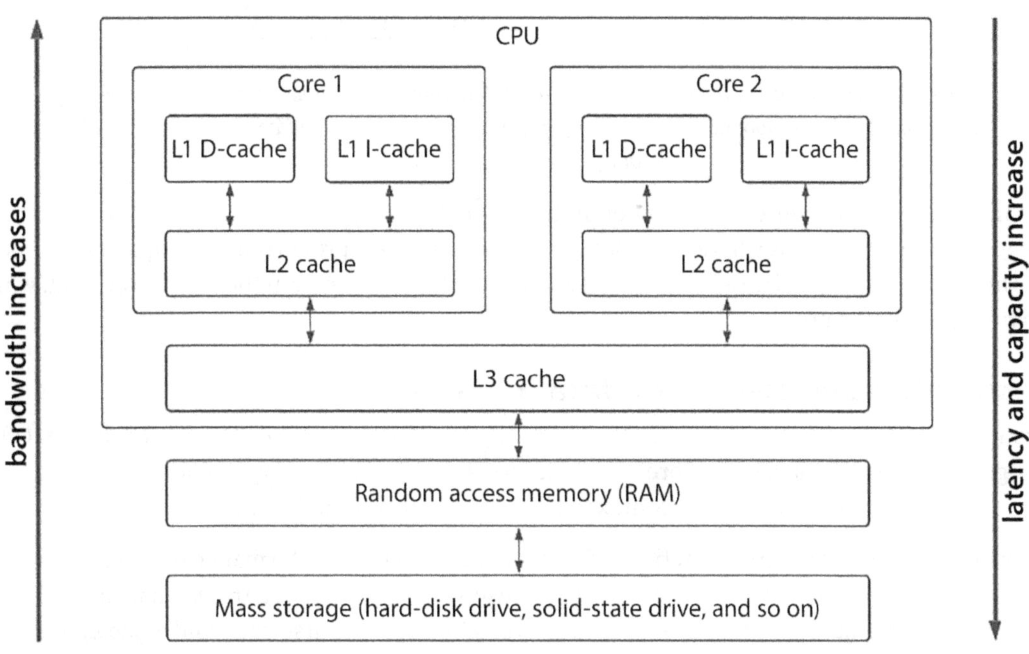

Figure 13.2: CPU caches, main memory (or random-access memory (RAM)), and data storage

Processor caches have hierarchical levels: L1, L2, L3, and rarely even L4. The L1 cache is the smallest and fastest cache located inside the CPU, and often split into I-cache and D-cache. The L2 cache is larger and slightly slower than L1 and can be on-chip or off-chip. The L3 cache is the largest and slowest of the three, shared among all cores. **Static RAM (SRAM)** is much more expensive than **dynamic RAM (DRAM)**, since static memory does not require regeneration, unlike dynamic memory. The L4 cache is currently uncommon and is generally implemented as **embedded DRAM (eDRAM)**, which can be accessed by both the CPU and GPU.

Understanding this cache hierarchy is crucial when writing performance-critical C++ code. This is because the closer your data and instructions are to the L1 or L2 caches, the faster your program can run. Designing data structures and access patterns with this in mind is beneficial.

We have discussed main memory and caches, but it's also helpful to understand the broader computer memory hierarchy, which influences how data and instructions are stored and accessed:

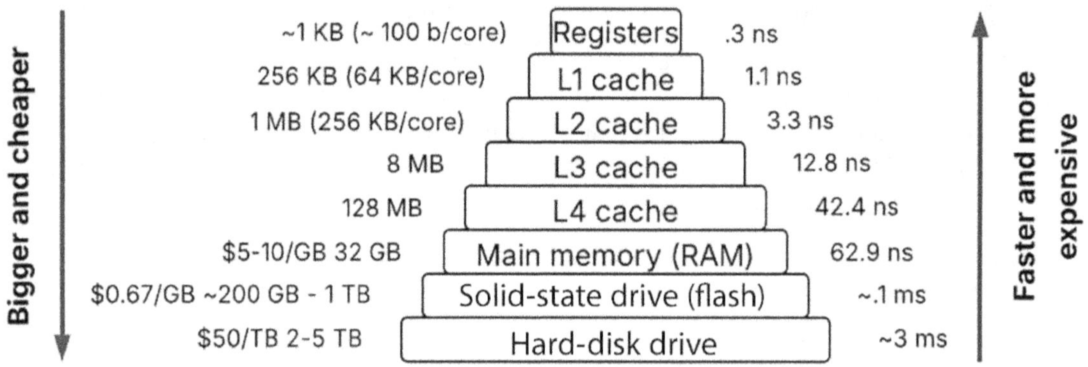

Figure 13.3: The computer memory hierarchy (adapted from lecture slides titled Caches & Memory by Hakim Weatherspoon, Cornell University: https://www.cs.cornell.edu/courses/cs3410/2019sp/schedule/slides/12-caches-pre.pdf)

As can be seen in the figure, in computer architecture, the memory hierarchy separates computer storage into different levels where the cost of memory is inversely proportional to capacity and speed. This hierarchy helps speed up access to large and relatively slow storage at the next lower level, which lies further from the processor.

Designing your code with data in mind

If you want to help your caches, another technique that can be helpful is data-oriented design. Often, it's a good idea to store data used more often close to each other in memory. Colder data can often be placed in another struct and just be connected with hotter data by an ID or a pointer.

For example, in-memory representations of graph nodes affect the performance of graph algorithms when it comes to the choice of data structures to use: edge list, edge set array, adjacency list, adjacency matrix, or adjacency array. Adjacent lists, typically storing sparse data, and adjacent matrices, typically storing dense data, are better suited for fast lookups and dense graph traversal, while edge lists are efficient and memory-friendly for computations. Adjacency matrices are often implemented using a vector of vectors (nested dynamic arrays), which is inefficient due to multiple memory allocations. Fortunately, C++23 introduced `std::mdspan`, a lightweight non-owning representation of a multidimensional array. This class maps a multidimensional index to an element of a single contiguous vector storing the matrix elements, which improves cache locality and reduces memory fragmentation without the overhead of nested containers.

Another approach is to prefer using "objects of arrays" over the "arrays of objects" approach. This means, instead of writing your code in an object-oriented manner, split your object's data members across a few arrays, each containing data for multiple objects. In other words, take the following code:

```
struct Widget {
    Foo foo;
    Bar bar;
    Baz baz;
};

auto widgets = std::vector<Widget>{};
```

Consider replacing it with the following:

```
struct Widgets {
    std::vector<Foo> foos;
    std::vector<Bar> bars;
    std::vector<Baz> bazs;
};
```

This way, when processing a specific set of data points against some objects, the D-cache hotness increases, and so does the performance, because subsequent array elements after the current one are partially loaded into the D-cache during sequential processing. If you don't know whether this will yield more performance from your code, measure.

Sometimes, even reordering members of your types can give you better performance. This is because data alignment of your data structures in memory affects how efficiently they can be stored and accessed. If performance matters, usually it's a good idea to order them so that the compiler doesn't need to insert too much padding between the members. Thanks to that, the size of your data type can be smaller, so many such subsequent objects can fit into one cache line (data block) containing the actual data fetched from the main memory.

Consider the following example (assuming x86_64 architecture):

```
struct TwoSizesAndTwoChars {
    std::size_t first_size;
    char first_char;
    std::size_t second_size;
    char second_char;
};
static_assert(sizeof(TwoSizesAndTwoChars) == 32);
```

Despite the sizes being 8 bytes each and chars being just 1 byte each, we end up with 32 bytes in total! That's because `second_size` must start on an 8-byte aligned address, so after `first_char`, we get 7 bytes of padding. The same goes for `second_char`, as types need to be aligned with respect to their largest data type member.

Can we do better? Let's try switching the order of our members:

```
struct TwoSizesAndTwoChars {
    std::size_t first_size;
    std::size_t second_size;
    char first_char;
    char second_char;
};
static_assert(sizeof(TwoSizesAndTwoChars) == 24);
```

By simply putting the biggest members first, we were able to cut the size of our structure by 8 bytes—a 25% reduction. Not bad for such a trivial change. If your goal is to pack many such structs in a contiguous block of memory and iterate through them, you could see a big performance boost from that code fragment.

Figure 13.4 visually compares the memory layout of the `TwoSizesAndTwoChars` struct before and after reordering its members:

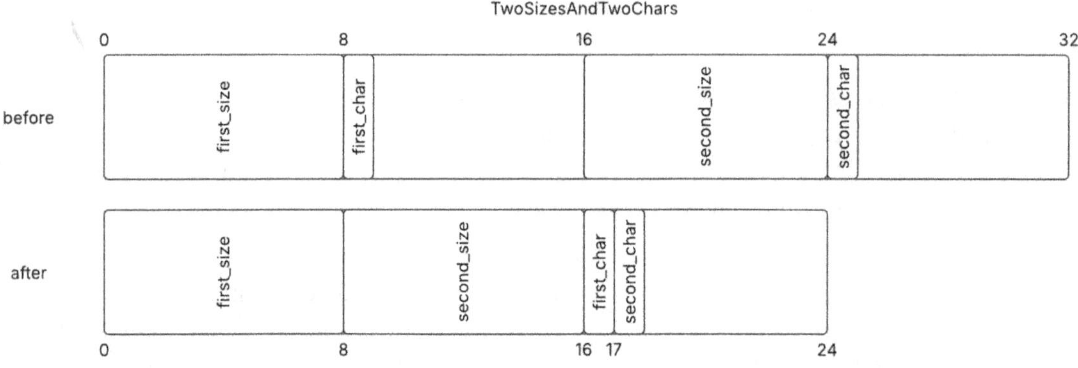

Figure 13.4: Data structure alignment of TwoSizesAndTwoChars in computer memory

In this way, a larger volume of contiguous data is loaded into the processor D-cache. Let's now talk about another way to improve your performance.

Parallelizing computations

In this section, we'll discuss a few ways to parallelize computations, where large tasks are broken into smaller independent sub-tasks and executed simultaneously on multiple processors or cores. Before we start, let's say a few words on how to estimate the maximum possible gains you can have from parallelizing your code. There are three laws that can help us here.

The first is Amdahl's law (see *Figure 13.5*). It states that if we want to speed up our program by throwing more cores at it, then the part of our code that must remain sequential (cannot be parallelized) will limit our scalability. For instance, if 90% of your code is parallelizable, then even with infinite cores, you can still get only up to a 10x speedup. Even if we cut down the time to execute that 90% to zero, the 10% of the code will always remain there.

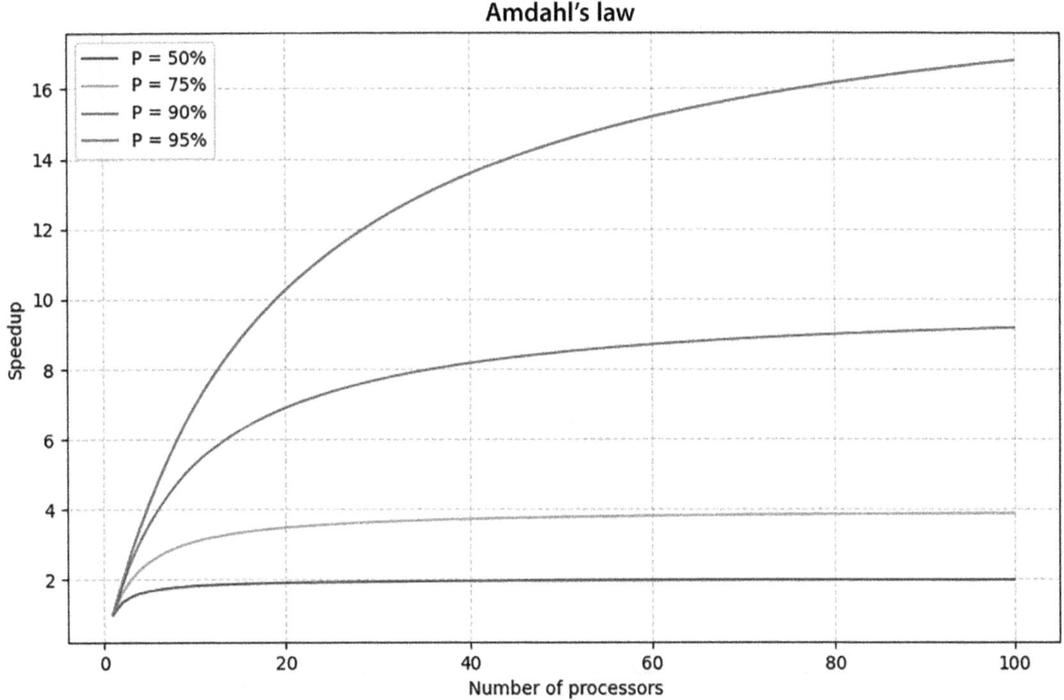

Figure 13.5: Amdahl's law demonstrating the theoretical maximum speedup

The Amdahl law formula for maximum program execution speedup when parallelized is `S(p, n) = 1/(1 - p + p/n)`, where `S(p, n)` is the expected speedup, `p` is the portion of the program executed sequentially, and `n` is the number of processors or computers. The law shows that the maximum speedup is limited by the portion of the program executed sequentially.

The second law is Gustafson's law (see *Figure 13.6*). It states that every large-enough task can be efficiently parallelized. This means that by increasing the size of the problem, we can obtain better parallelization (assuming we have free computing resources to use). In other words, sometimes it's better to add more capabilities to run in the same time frame instead of trying to reduce the execution time of existing code. If doubling the number of cores reduces a task's execution time by half, continuing to double the cores will eventually yield diminishing returns. At that point, it may be more effective to allocate that processing power elsewhere.

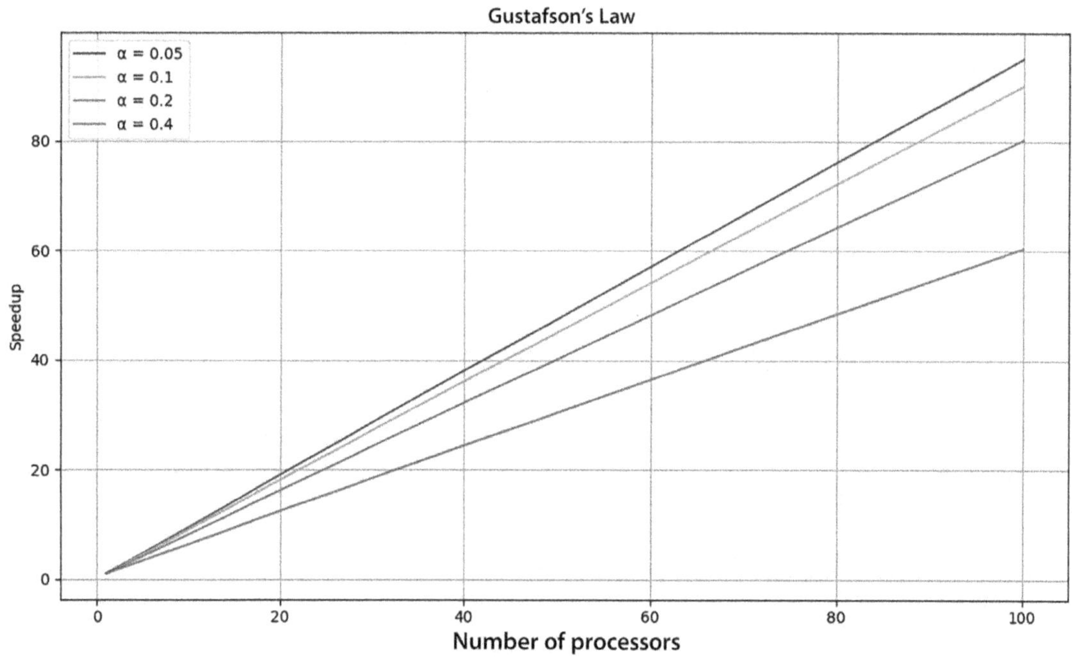

Figure 13.6: Gustafson's law showing the theoretical speedup in the execution time due to parallel computing

The formula for Gustafson's law, which describes the speedup of parallel computing, is `S(α, n) = n - α(n - 1)`, where `S(α, n)` is the overall speedup, `n` is the number of processors, and `α` represents the proportion of a computation that is inherently sequential (cannot be parallelized). This law suggests that by increasing the number of processors and the size of the task, you can achieve greater speedups than Amdahl's law predicts.

The third law is Dr. Gunther's **universal scalability law** (USL; see *Figure 13.7*), applied to distributed systems to model and to optimize the scalability of systems, which conceptualizes system scalability as consisting of three distinct system characteristics: concurrency, contention, and coherence. This law adds a more complete description of the system's behavior when the number of resources increases. It considers both the positive and negative effects of parallelization in distributed systems. While Amdahl's law focuses on the limitations of parallelization, USL describes the behavior of systems more realistically.

The formula for USL is `S(α, β, n) = n/(1 + α(n - 1) + βn(n - 1))`, where `S(α, β, n)` is the speedup of the system, `n` is the number of processors or nodes in the system, α is the contention coefficient, β is the coherence coefficient.

Concurrency represents the ideal case, where speedup increases linearly with the number of processors. Contention represents competition among resources; increased competition for the same resources (memory or network) limits performance gains due to waiting or queuing for shared resources. Coherency refers to the increased need for synchronization with an increasing number of processors, which also reduces the efficiency of the system due to the delay for data to become consistent (or coherent) by virtue of point-to-point exchange.

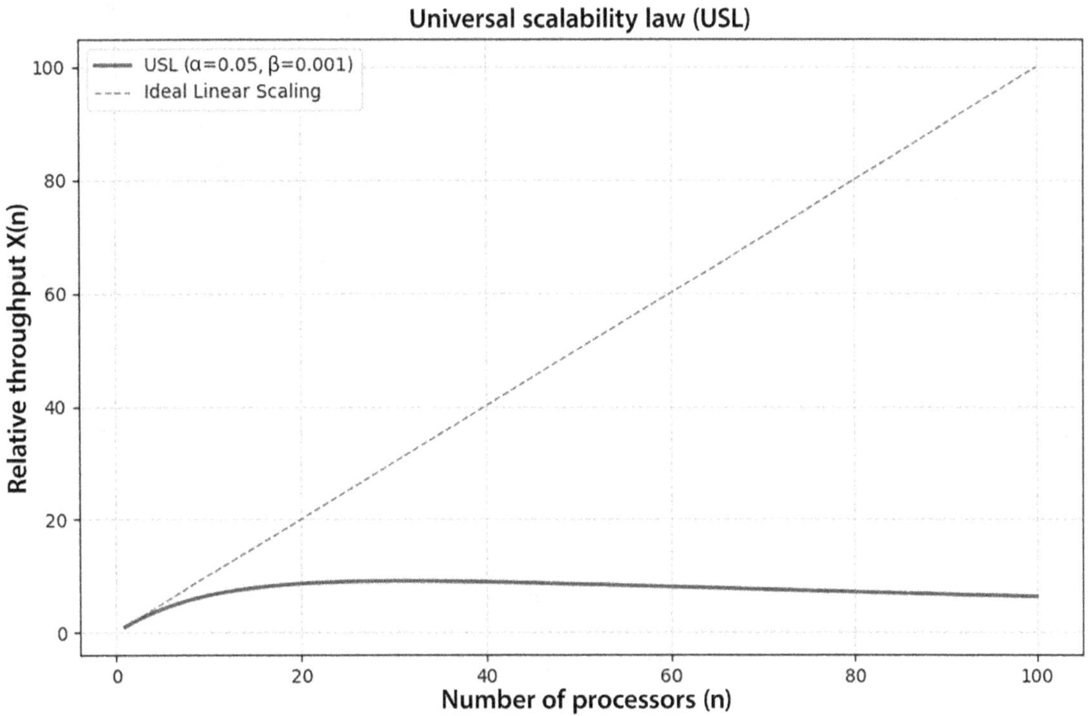

Figure 13.7: Universal scalability law (USL) showing actual (α = 0.05, β = 0.001) versus ideal throughput scaling in parallel systems

Features of USL:

- As `n` tends to infinity and α and β are low, system performance can grow linearly with the number of processors, which is typical for well-scalable systems
- In practice, most often, the growth of performance slows down due to the effect of competition for resources (α), and the acceleration ceases to be linear

When there are too many processors or nodes, the impact of overhead (β) becomes critical, and the system can begin to slow down as resources are spent on coordination rather than on useful work.

In the following subsections, we begin with a discussion on the suitability of using threads versus processes for parallel computations, then explore the standard parallel algorithms and execution policies introduced in C++, touch upon the OpenMP and MPI frameworks, and, finally, introduce some additional tools and frameworks for parallel programming.

Choosing between threads and processes

To parallelize computations efficiently, you also need to understand when to use processes to perform computation and when threads are the better tool for the job.

Parallelism can be achieved even on a single machine, provided it has multiple CPU cores. If your only target is to speed up work, then it's best to start with adding extra threads up to the point where they stop bringing extra benefits, because of CPU saturation. At such a point, scale out by adding more processes on other machines in your network, each with multiple threads too.

Why is it best to start by adding extra threads first to speed up work? Because processes are more heavyweight than threads. Spawning a process and switching between them takes longer than creating and switching between threads. Each process requires its own memory space, while threads within the same process share their memory. Also, inter-process communication is slower than just passing variables between threads. Working with threads is easier than it is with processes, so the development will be faster too.

Processes, however, also have their uses in the scope of a single application. They're great for isolating components that can independently run and crash without taking down the whole application with them. Having separate memory also means one process can't snoop another one's memory, which is great when you need to run third-party code that could turn out to be malicious. Those two reasons are why they're used in web browsers, among other apps. Aside from that, it's possible to run different processes with different OS permissions or privileges, which you can't achieve with multiple threads.

Let's now discuss a simple way to parallelize work in the scope of a single machine.

Using the standard parallel algorithms

If the computations you perform can be parallelized, there are two ways you can use that to your advantage, which we cover in this and the next section. The first one is by replacing your regular calls to standard library algorithms with parallelizable ones. If you're not familiar with parallel algorithms, they were added in C++17 and behave like their sequential versions, but you can pass each of them an execution policy, which determines how the algorithm executes and interacts with the underlying hardware. There are four execution policies, including one introduced in C++20:

- `std::execution::seq`: The sequenced policy for the plain-old execution of an algorithm in a non-parallelized way. This one we know too well.
- `std::execution::par`: A parallel policy that signals that the execution *may* be parallelized, usually using a thread pool under the hood.
- `std::execution::par_unseq`: A parallel policy that signals that the execution *may* be parallelized and vectorized, where a single processor instruction is executed on multiple data elements simultaneously (SIMD).

- `std::execution::unseq`: A C++20 addition to the family. This policy signals that the execution can be vectorized but not parallelized.

If the preceding policies are not enough for you, additional ones may be provided by a standard library implementation. Possible future additions may include ones for CUDA, SyCL, OpenCL, or even artificial intelligence processors.

Let's now see the parallel algorithms in action. As an example, to sort a vector in a parallel way, you can write the following:

```
std::sort(std::execution::par, v.begin(), v.end());
```

That's simple and easy. Although in many cases this will yield better performance, in some cases you might be better off executing the algorithms in the traditional way. Why? Scheduling work on more threads requires additional work and synchronization. Also, depending on the architecture of your app, it may influence the performance of other already existing threads and flush their cores' D-caches. As always, measure first.

Using OpenMP and MPI

Two common ways to implement concurrent and parallel algorithms are the **Open Multi-Processing (OpenMP)** API specification for shared-memory parallel programming and the **Message Passing Interface (MPI)** standard, a standardized means of exchanging data (via messages) between cooperating compute nodes, to implement distributed algorithms in distributed-memory architectures. OpenMP pragmas are an easy way to parallelize many types of computations by just adding a few lines of code, though they are less effective for loops or tasks with complex data dependencies. If you want to distribute your code across multiple nodes in a **high-performance computing (HPC)** cluster, you might want to see what MPI can do for you. Those two can be joined together.

With OpenMP, you can use various pragmas to easily parallelize code. For instance, you can write `#pragma omp parallel for` before a `for` loop to get it executed using parallel threads. The OpenMP library can also do much more, such as executing computations on GPUs and other accelerators.

Integrating MPI into your project introduces greater complexity than just adding an appropriate pragma. Here, you'll need to use the MPI API in your code base to send or receive data between processes (using calls such as `MPI_Send` and `MPI_Recv`) or perform various gather and reduce operations (calling `MPI_Bcast` and `MPI_Reduce`, among other functions in this family). Communication can be done point to point or to all clusters using objects called communicators.

Depending on your algorithm implementation, all MPI processes can execute the same code or different code, depending on their assigned roles. The process will know how it should behave based on its rank—a unique number assigned at the start of the computation that determines the process's role during execution. Speaking of which, to start a process using MPI, you should run it through a wrapper, like so:

```
$ mpirun --hostfile my_hostfile -np 4 program args
```

This command would read hosts from `my_hostfile` one by one, connect to each of them, and run four instances of `program` with the specified arguments.

There are many implementations of MPI. One of the most notable is OpenMPI (don't confuse that with OpenMP). Among some useful features, it offers fault tolerance. After all, it's not uncommon for a node to go down.

So far, we've focused on parallelism using CPU-based approaches, but modern high-performance systems often use accelerators such as GPUs. Let's now take a brief look at platforms and tools that support heterogeneous parallel programming, including both GPU-based solutions and more general frameworks for multi-core and distributed environments.

Other platforms and tools for parallel programming

A popular parallel programming platform from NVIDIA that allows using **general-purpose GPU (GPGPU)** is **Compute Unified Device Architecture** (**CUDA**), which also supports distributed shared memory. To support non-NVIDIA hardware, the ZLUDA library acts as a translation layer that allows running unmodified CUDA applications on other GPUs.

The main CUDA alternative for Intel hardware is Intel's oneAPI initiative, which includes the following:

- **SYCL (pronounced "sickle")**: A royalty-free open standard to program heterogeneous architectures in standard C++
- **DPC++ (Data Parallel C++) compiler**: An implementation of SYCL, designed to reuse code across hardware targets (CPUs and accelerators such as GPUs and FPGAs)
- **OpenCL (Open Computing Language)**: A low-level API for heterogeneous parallel computing
- **oneTBB (oneAPI Threading Building Blocks)**: A C++ template library developed by Intel for simplifying the creation of parallel programs on multi-core processors

The main CUDA alternatives for AMD GPUs are ROCm (originally Radeon Open Compute platform) with its **HIP** (**Heterogeneous-compute Interface for Portability**) tools for porting CUDA code, **OpenCL** (**Open Computing Language**), and the newer, higher-level C++ standard SYCL.

Also worth mentioning is OpenACC, a programming standard that uses preprocessor directives to write parallel code designed for accelerators—primarily GPUs. Its main goal is to simplify the development of parallel applications for accelerators by offloading computations to the graphics processors and parallelizing the code using special compiler directives, rather than low-level programming. This specification supports C, C++, and Fortran.

The last tool we'd like to mention in this section is GNU Parallel, a command-line utility that you might find useful if you want to easily span processes that perform work by spawning parallel processes. It can be used both on a single machine and across a compute cluster.

These tools and platforms are often deployed in distributed memory environments such as HPC clusters.

We'll now discuss one major feature introduced in C++20: coroutines.

Using coroutines

Threads are heavier-weight, OS-level components for concurrent execution, each with its own memory stack. In contrast, coroutines are functions that can suspend and resume execution. They enable cooperative multitasking and allow writing asynchronous code in a very similar manner to how you would write synchronous code.

Compared to writing asynchronous code with `std::async`, coroutines allow writing cleaner code that's easier to understand and maintain. There's no need to write callbacks anymore, and no need to deal with the verbosity of `std::async` with promises and futures. Coroutines, being a more lightweight alternative to threads, are ideal for I/O-bound tasks when thousands of such tasks can run on just a few threads. By suspending without blocking the underlying thread, they achieve greater efficiency and performance in asynchronous operations.

`std::async` based code usually incurs more overhead due to thread switching and waiting. In contrast, coroutines can resume and suspend with minimal cost involved, compared to the overhead of calling functions, which means they can yield better latency and throughput. Also, one of their design goals is to be highly scalable, even to billions of concurrent coroutines.

Figure 13.8 shows how control passes from the caller function to the coroutine and back, showing the points at which the coroutine yields control (`co_yield`) and the caller resumes (`co_await`). Unlike a regular function, a coroutine can suspend and resume multiple times and thus can continue its execution indefinitely:

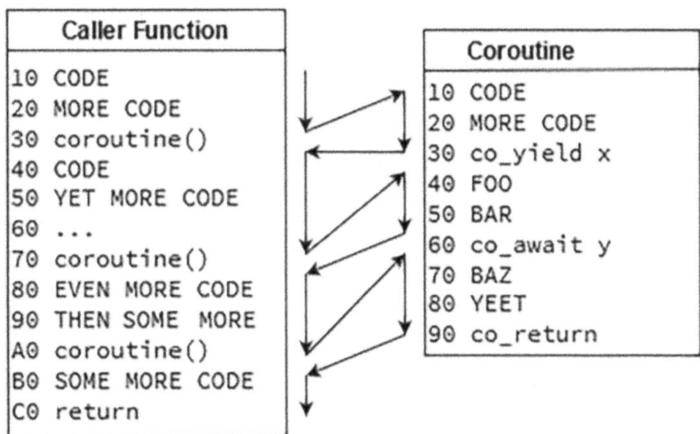

Figure 13.8: Calling and executing coroutines versus regular functions

C++20 coroutines are stackless, which means their state is not stored on the calling thread's stack. This gives them an interesting property: several different threads can pick up the execution of a coroutine. In other words, even though it looks like the coroutine function body would be executed sequentially, parts of it can be executed in different threads. This makes it possible to leave parts of the function to be executed on dedicated threads. For instance, I/O operations can be done in a dedicated I/O thread.

The Drogon web application framework used for the examples in this book also supports coroutines, which help avoid callback hell (nested callbacks) and make asynchronous programming as easy as synchronous programming.

C++23 brought a new standard library component, `std::generator`, which implements a synchronous coroutine generator for ranges. It allows you to write functions that yield values one at a time using `co_yield`. The companion function `std::ranges::elements_of` allows a generator to yield each element of another range. This example implements in-order tree traversal implemented with coroutines and `std::generator`:

```
// partially omitted code
...
struct Node {
  int value{};
  Node *left{nullptr}, *right{nullptr};
};

std::generator<const Node *> in_order(const Node *node) {
  namespace ranges = std::ranges;

  if (node == nullptr)
    co_return;

  if (node->left != nullptr)
    co_yield ranges::elements_of(in_order(node->left));
  co_yield node;
  if (node->right != nullptr)
    co_yield ranges::elements_of(in_order(node->right));
}

void print_tree(
    const Node *node,
    const std::function<std::generator<const Node *>(const Node *node)> &walk)
{
  for (const auto *n : walk(node)) {
    std::cout << n->value << ' ';
  }
  std::cout << std::endl;
}
```

Further, C++26 was expected to introduce stackful coroutines known as fibers to avoid the name clashing with coroutines from C++20. However, this feature is not confirmed in the standard yet, and its inclusion is still speculative at the time of writing. Stackless coroutines require compiler support, but stackful coroutines can be implemented with a library such as Boost.

To check whether a function is a C++ coroutine, you need to look for one of the following keywords in its body:

- `co_await` suspends a coroutine until the value is ready and then returns control to the caller.
- `co_yield` is for returning a value to the caller and suspending the current coroutine. Like Python's `yield` keyword, it is used in generators. It allows generating values lazily.
- `co_return` finishes executing the current coroutine and returns the value (if any) to the caller, which is optional. It's a coroutine equivalent of the `return` keyword; however, unlike regular functions, coroutines do not always require a `co_return` statement because they can be designed to suspend indefinitely.

Whenever a function body has one of those keywords, the function automatically becomes a coroutine. Beyond the implementation details we just learned, there's one more hint that you can use: coroutine return types must satisfy certain requirements; we'll look at a few return types in the next section.

Coroutines are first-class citizens in the C++ world. This means you can get their address, use them as function arguments, return them from functions, and store them in objects.

It is noteworthy that in C++, you could write coroutines even before C++20. This was possible thanks to libraries such as Boost.Coroutine2. A few niche tools, such as Bloomberg's Quantum, were also developed for specific use cases such as stream processing, though they are less well known outside their origin organizations. The latter was even used to implement CoroKafka—an in-house Bloomberg library designed for efficiently dealing with Kafka streams using coroutines.

With the advent of standard C++ coroutines, new libraries, such as libcoro, coost, and Boost.Cobalt, started popping up.

To use these libraries in your project, add them to `conanfile.py`:

```
from conan import ConanFile

class Pkg(ConanFile):
    settings = "os", "arch", "compiler", "build_type"
    generators = "CMakeDeps"
    default_options = {"tracy/*:no_exit": True, "libcoro/*:with_networking":
False}

    def requirements(self):
        self.requires("benchmark/1.9.4")
        self.requires("nanobench/4.3.11")
        self.requires("doctest/2.4.12")
        self.requires("catch2/3.10.0")
        self.requires("tracy/0.12.2")
        # requires Linux for networking
        self.requires("libcoro/0.15.0")
        self.requires("boost/1.88.0")
```

```
        if not self.settings.os == "Windows":
            self.requires("coost/3.0.2")

    def build_requirements(self):
        pass
```

At the time of writing this book, libcoro supports networking only on Linux, and coost is disabled on Windows due to compilation errors.

There are many other popular coroutine-related libraries worth exploring.

High-performance frameworks include Seastar (server-side applications), concurrencpp (tasks, executors, timers and C++20 coroutines), async_simple (an asynchronous component library provided by Alibaba Cloud supporting C++20 stackless coroutines and C++ stackful coroutines, along with numerous asynchronous tools), libunifex (experimental unified executors provided by Meta), Marl (a hybrid thread/fiber task scheduler written in C++11), and Boost.Asio (network and low-level I/O programming).

Less known libraries are asyncio (a C++20 library to write concurrent code using the async/await syntax), Continuable (C++14 asynchronous allocation-aware futures), Boost.fiber (userland threads), libfiber (high performance C/C++ coroutine/fiber library for Linux/FreeBSD/macOS/Windows, supporting select/poll/epoll/kqueue/iouring/iocp/windows GUI), QCoro (C++20 coroutines for Qt5 and Qt6), cppcoro (C++ coroutine abstractions similar to libcoro), coros (a header-only C++23 library designed for task-based parallelism), and asio-grpc (asynchronous gRPC with Asio/unified executors).

Emerging or experimental libraries are liburing4cpp (C++ binding for liburing that uses C++20 coroutines), Coop (C++20 coroutines-based cooperative multitasking), COROIO (high-performance networking library using C++ coroutines), zpp::throwing (using coroutines to implement C++ exceptions for freestanding environments), ZAB (C++20 liburing-backed coroutine executor and event loop framework).

Before going into the implementation details, let's first explore the utilities provided by libcoro.

Distinguishing between libcoro utilities

It's hard to write coroutine-based code from scratch. C++20 only offers the fundamental utilities for writing coroutines, so we need a set of primitives to use when writing our own coroutines. These are offered by libraries such as libcoro. In this section, we'll showcase the libcoro library and demonstrate how to use it when writing coroutine-based code.

Let's start with an overview of the coroutine types the library offers us:

- `coro::task<>`: For scheduling work to be executed later—it starts executing when it's `co_awaited` for or `co_yielded`.
- `coro::generator<>`: Produces a sequence of values lazily and synchronously. It's effectively a `std::range`: it has a `begin()` returning an iterator and an `end()` returning a sentinel.

- `coro::ring_buffer<>`: A statically sized ring buffer where producers and consumers of the ring buffer are suspended and resumed in a **last-in-first-out** (**LIFO**) manner.

You should use the return type of a coroutine based on its intended behavior. Usually, if your coroutine returns a generator type (such as `coro::generator<T>`), you'd want to return values using `co_yield` (like in Python generators) and consume the values synchronously. In your tasks, however, usually, you'll want to schedule work with `co_await` asynchronously.

The library offers many more programming abstractions than just the preceding coroutine types. It also provides the following types:

- **Awaitables** types that you can `co_await` on, such as coroutine-flavored `coro::event` and synchronization primitives: `coro::mutex`, `coro::shared_mutex`, `coro::latch`, and `coro::semaphore`
- **Schedulers**—objects allowing you to schedule work through them, such as `coro::thread_pool` and `coro::io_scheduler`
- **I/O and networking utilities**, allowing you to read from and write to network sockets: `coro::net::dns::resolver` (for async DNS), `coro::net::tcp::client`, `coro::net::tcp::server`, `coro::net::tls::client` (OpenSSL), `coro::net::tls::server` (OpenSSL), `coro::net::udp::peer`
- **Meta-functions and concepts**, such as `awaitable_traits`, `awaitable`, `awaiter`, `const_buffer`, `mutable_buffer`, `executor`, `promise`, and `range_of`, which help build generic coroutine-based components

Aside from the preceding utilities, libcoro offers us functions—utilities for using other classes and steering execution—such as the following:

- `sync_wait`: Blocks until the passed awaitable completes
- `when_all`: Returns an awaitable that completes when all the passed awaitables complete

Before we start using those utilities together, let's say a few more words about awaitables.

Looking under the hood of awaitables and coroutines

Besides what libcoro offers, the standard library offers two more trivial awaitables defined in the `<courotine>` header: `std::suspend_never` and `std::suspend_always`. These indicate whether an `await` expression should suspend the coroutine or not, and they do not produce values.

Looking at their implementation can help us understand how to create our own awaitables when needed:

```
struct suspend_never {
    constexpr bool await_ready() const noexcept { return true; }
    constexpr void await_suspend(coroutine_handle<>) const noexcept {}
    constexpr void await_resume() const noexcept {}
};

struct suspend_always {
```

```
    constexpr bool await_ready() const noexcept { return false; }
    constexpr void await_suspend(coroutine_handle<>) const noexcept {}
    constexpr void await_resume() const noexcept {}
};
```

When using the `co_await` operator, the compiler implicitly calls the awaiter's `await_ready()`method. If it says the awaiter is ready by returning `true`, `await_resume()` will get called. The return type (if any) of `await_resume()` should be the type the awaiter is actually producing. If the awaiter was not ready, the program will instead execute `await_suspend()`. After it's done, we have three cases:

- `await_suspend` returns `void`: The execution will always suspend afterwards
- `await_suspend` returns `bool`: The execution will suspend or not depending on the returned value
- `await_suspend` returns `std::coroutine_handle<PromiseType>`: Another coroutine will get resumed

There's much more going on with coroutines under the hood. Even though coroutines don't use the `return` keyword, the compiler will generate code under the hood to manage control flow and coroutine state. When using keywords such as `co_yield`, the compiler will rewrite them as calls to the appropriate member functions of helper types. For instance, a call to `co_yield x` is equivalent to `co_await promise.yield_value(x)`. If you want to learn more about what's happening exactly and write your own coroutine types, refer to the *Your First Coroutine* article from the *Further reading* section.

Okay, let's now use all this knowledge to write our own coroutines. We'll create a simple application that mimics doing meaningful work. It will use a thread pool to fill a vector with some numbers.

A practical example using libcoro

First, let's define the build target in our CMake file. Our CMake target will look as follows:

```
add_executable(coroutines_1 coroutines/main_1.cpp)
target_link_libraries(coroutines_1 PRIVATE libcoro::libcoro)
target_compile_features(coroutines_1 PRIVATE cxx_std_23)
```

Next, we start our implementation by defining some constants and a `main` function:

```
inline constexpr auto WORK_ITEMS = 5;

int main() {
  auto thread_pool = coro::thread_pool::make_shared({.thread_count = 3});
```

We want to produce five items using three pooled threads. libcoro's thread pool is a neat way to schedule work. By default, it creates as many threads as your machine has CPU cores. Moving onward, we need to specify our work:

```
  std::println("Thread {}: preparing work", std::this_thread::get_id());
  auto work = do_routine_work(thread_pool);
```

```
std::println("Thread {}: starting work",  std::this_thread::get_id());
const auto ints = coro::sync_wait(work);
```

We'll sprinkle our code with log messages so you can better see what's going on in which thread. This will help us better understand how coroutines work. We create work by calling a coroutine named `do_routine_work`. It returns the coroutine, which we run using the `sync_wait` blocking function. A coroutine won't start executing until it is awaited. This means that our actual work will start inside this function call.

Once we have our results, let's log them:

```
std::print("Thread {}: work done.\nProduced ints are: ",
           std::this_thread::get_id());
for (auto i : ints) {
  std::print("{}, ", i);
}
std::println();
```

No voodoo magic here. Let's define our `do_routine_work` coroutine:

```
coro::task<std::vector<int>>
do_routine_work(std::shared_ptr<coro::thread_pool> thread_pool) {
  auto mutex = coro::mutex{};
  auto ints = std::vector<int>{};
  ints.reserve(WORK_ITEMS);
```

It returns a task, which produces some integers. Because we're going to use the thread pool, let's use libcoro's `async_mutex` to synchronize the threads. Let's now start using the pool:

```
  std::println("Thread {}: passing execution to the pool",
               std::this_thread::get_id());
  co_await thread_pool->schedule();
```

You might be surprised that the `schedule()` call doesn't pass in any callable to execute. In the case of a coroutine, this call suspends the current coroutine and hands control back to its caller. This means that the thread running it will now wait for the coroutine to finish (somewhere in the `sync_wait` call).

In the meantime, a thread from our pool will resume the suspended coroutine and simply continue to execute its body. Here's the next part of the coroutine:

```
  std::println("Thread {}: running first pooled job",
               std::this_thread::get_id());

  std::vector<coro::task<>> tasks;
  tasks.reserve(WORK_ITEMS);
```

```
for (int i = 0; i < WORK_ITEMS; ++i) {
  tasks.emplace_back(fill_number(i, ints, thread_pool, mutex));
}

co_await coro::when_all(std::move(tasks));

co_return ints;
```

We create a vector of tasks to execute. Each task fills one number in `ints` under the mutex. The `schedule_on` call ensures that each filling coroutine uses a separate thread from our pool. We wait for all the results. At this point, our tasks start executing. Finally, as our coroutine is a task, we use `co_return` to return the final result.

Don't forget to use `co_return` to return the produced value. If we removed the `co_return ints;` line from our example, we would simply return a default constructed vector. The program would run, happily print the empty vector, and exit with code 0.

Our last step is to implement the coroutine that will produce a number:

```
std::random_device rd;
std::mt19937 gen(rd());
std::uniform_int_distribution<> distrib(0, 800);

coro::task<> fill_number(int i, std::vector<int> &ints,
                         std::shared_ptr<coro::thread_pool> thread_pool,
                         coro::mutex &mutex) {
co_await thread_pool->schedule();

std::println("Thread {}: producing {}",  std::this_thread::get_id(), i);
std::this_thread::sleep_for(std::chrono::milliseconds(distrib(gen)));
```

This one is a task that doesn't return any value. Instead, it will add a number to our vector. Its hard work begins by dozing off for several milliseconds. After the wake-up, the coroutine continues with more productive endeavors—it acquires a lock and appends a number to the shared vector:

```
{
  // remember to co_await!
  auto lock = co_await mutex.scoped_lock();
  ints.emplace_back(i);
}
```

The coroutine will lock the mutex using `co_await`. In our case, locking is just an await expression. Once the mutex is acquired, the coroutine will add a number to our vector—the same number it was called with.

Remember to use `co_await`. If you forget and your awaitable allows that (perhaps because it's okay to not consume each awaitable), then you might skip some essential computations. In our example, this could mean not locking a mutex.

Let's finish the coroutine's implementation now:

```
std::println("Thread {}: produced {}",  std::this_thread::get_id(), i);
co_return;
```

Just a simple status print and a `co_return` to mark the coroutine as complete are needed. Once it returns, the coroutine frame can be destroyed, freeing the memory occupied by it.

That's all. Let's now run our code and see what happens:

```
Thread 140471890347840: preparing work
Thread 140471890347840: starting work
Thread 140471890347840: passing execution to the pool
Thread 140471890282240: running first pooled job
Thread 140471890282240: producing 4
Thread 140471881828096: producing 1
Thread 140471873373952: producing 0
Thread 140471890282240: produced 4
Thread 140471890282240: producing 3
Thread 140471890282240: produced 3
Thread 140471890282240: producing 2
Thread 140471881828096: produced 1
Thread 140471873373952: produced 0
Thread 140471890282240: produced 2
Thread 140471890347840: work done.
Produced ints are: 4, 3, 1, 0, 2,
```

Our main thread fired up the work on the pool and then waited for the results. Then, our three threads from the pool began producing numbers. The last task scheduled was actually the first one that ran, producing the number 4. This is because it was the one that continued executing `do_routine_work` all the time: first, it scheduled all other tasks on the pool, then started performing the first task when `when_all` was called. Later, the execution continued with the first free thread taking the next task scheduled on the pool until the whole vector was filled. Finally, the execution returned to our main thread.

A practical example using coost

coost is a high-performance, cross-platform library supporting Go-style coroutines rather than C++20 coroutines, which makes this library curious.

One of the standout features of coost is its ability to efficiently handle a large number of coroutines with minimal memory overhead. Unlike standard C++ coroutines, which require more stack space, coost implements a lightweight, Go-style coroutine model that is optimized for scalability and concurrency. According to the coost authors, *"Coroutines in the same thread share several stacks (the default size is 1 MB), and the memory usage is low. Test on Linux shows that 10 millions [sic] of coroutines only take 2.8 G[B] of memory (for reference only)"* (`https://coostdocs.github.io/en/co/concurrency/coroutine/basic/`).

Apart from coroutines, other core features offered by coost include logging and JSON libraries, memory operations, unit test and benchmark frameworks, network programming utilities such as socket API, TCP, HTTP, RPC, and other components compatible with IPv6, and SSL support.

Just like in the previous example, we'll use randomly generated sleep durations to simulate work. We'll begin by declaring the number of work items and initializing the random generator:

```
inline constexpr auto WORK_ITEMS = 5;

std::random_device rd;
std::mt19937 gen(rd());
std::uniform_int_distribution<> distrib(0, 800);
```

The `DEF_main` macro defines the main function running in a coroutine. This macro also parses the command-line arguments:

```
co::mutex g_m;

DEF_main(argc, argv) {
  std::println("Thread {} co_thread {} co_sched {}: preparing work",
               std::this_thread::get_id(), co::thread_id(), co::sched_id());
```

The `co::wait_group` class is a waiting group that waits for the exit of coroutines or threads. The internal counter of the `wg` object increases by `WORK_ITEMS`, and this group will wait for the exit of 5 coroutines:

```
  co::wait_group wg;
  wg.add(WORK_ITEMS);

  std::vector<int> ints;

  std::println("Thread {} co_thread {} co_sched {}: starting work",
               std::this_thread::get_id(), co::thread_id(),
               co::sched_id());
```

Here, the program creates and runs coroutines by using the go function:

```
for (int i = 0; i < WORK_ITEMS; ++i) {
     go([wg, i, &ints]() {
     std::println( "Thread {} co_thread {} co_routing {} co_sched {}:
```

```
                producing {}",
    std::this_thread::get_id(), co::thread_id(), co::coroutine_id(),
    co::sched_id(), i);
```

Each coroutine waits for some time, acquires the vector with `co::mutex_guard` to add a value, then releases it and exits:

```
      std::this_thread::sleep_for(std::chrono::milliseconds(distrib(gen)));

      {
        co::mutex_guard g(g_m);
        ints.emplace_back(i);
      }

      std::println(
          "Thread {} co_thread {} co_routing {} co_sched {}: produced {}",
          std::this_thread::get_id(), co::thread_id(), co::coroutine_id(),
          co::sched_id(), i);
      wg.done();
    });
  }
```

The wait group, `wg`, waits for all the coroutines to finish. Then, the program prints numbers randomly added to the vector:

```
  wg.wait();
  std::print(
    "Thread {} co_thread {} co_sched {}: work done.\nProduced ints are: ",
    std::this_thread::get_id(), co::thread_id(), co::sched_id());
    for (auto i : ints) {
        std::print("{}, ", i);
    }
  std::println();
  return 0;
}
```

Based on this example, we can say that although coost does not use C++20 coroutines, its alternative coroutine model can still be convenient.

A practical example using Boost.Cobalt

Boost.Cobalt is a coroutine-based library built on top of Boost.Asio. It provides coroutines of different types: `promise` to return a single result, `task` (a lazy version of the promise), and `generator` to yield multiple values. For synchronization, it provides functions such as `race` to wait for one coroutine out of a set, `join` to wait for a set of coroutines, and `gather` (similar to `join` except for catching exceptions). It also offers utilities, such as `channel` to send values between coroutines and `with` (an async RAII helper).

In this example, we again populate a vector with values, but using C++20 coroutines. Boost.Cobalt does not have mutexes but supports routine synchronization using channels. A channel is limited to one value, which is equivalent to an exclusive capture of the resource by a mutex. When a value is written to the channel, the lock is acquired, and when the value is read, the lock is released.

Just like in the previous example, the sleep durations are randomized. However, the delay is implemented with Boost.Asio's asynchronous timer: `async_wait()` does not block but instead suspends the coroutine until the timer expires, in line with Asio's asynchronous model. The `fill_number` function is a coroutine returning nothing. It produces a number and appends it to a shared vector, using a single-value channel to synchronize access:

```
cobalt::task<void> fill_number(int i, std::vector<int> &ints,
                               cobalt::channel<void> &mutex) {
  std::println("Thread {}: producing {}", std::this_thread::get_id(), i);
  asio::steady_timer timer{cobalt::this_thread::get_executor(),
                           std::chrono::milliseconds(distrib(gen))};
  co_await timer.async_wait(cobalt::use_op);

  {
    // remember to co_await!
    co_await mutex.write();
    ints.emplace_back(i);
    co_await mutex.read();
  }

  std::println("Thread {}: produced {}", std::this_thread::get_id(), i);
  co_return;
}
```

The `do_routine_work` function is also a coroutine. It collects all numbers into a vector. The `mutex` channel accepts only one value. Therefore, it behaves as a mutex:

```
cobalt::task<std::vector<int>> do_routine_work() {
  cobalt::channel<void> mutex{1, cobalt::this_thread::get_executor()};

  auto ints = std::vector<int>{};
  ints.reserve(WORK_ITEMS);

  std::println("Thread {}: passing execution to the pool",
               std::this_thread::get_id());

  std::println("Thread {}: running first pooled job",
               std::this_thread::get_id());
```

The function creates a vector of coroutines:

```
std::vector<cobalt::task<void>> tasks;
  tasks.reserve(WORK_ITEMS);

  for (int i = 0; i < WORK_ITEMS; ++i) {
    tasks.emplace_back(fill_number(i, ints, mutex));
  }
```

Then, the `cobalt::gather` function waits for the exits of all these coroutines, gathers results (if any), and returns the vector of results:

```
  co_await cobalt::gather(std::move(tasks));
  co_return ints;
}
```

The `co_main` function defines an implicit `main` function and runs asynchronous code:

```
cobalt::main co_main(int argc, char *argv[]) {
  auto executor = co_await cobalt::this_coro::executor;

  std::println("Thread {}: preparing work", std::this_thread::get_id());
```

The `do_routine_work` task is run synchronously by calling `run`. Then, the program prints numbers randomly added to the vector:

```
  auto work = do_routine_work();

  std::println("Thread {}: starting work", std::this_thread::get_id());
  const auto ints = run(std::move(work));

  std::print("Thread {}: work done.\nProduced ints are: ",
             std::this_thread::get_id());
  for (auto i : ints) {
    std::print("{}, ", i);
  }
  std::println();

  co_return 0;
}
```

This concludes our brief set of examples demonstrating coroutine implementations using different libraries. coost is, to some extent, an experiment in transferring Go language practices to C++, whereas libcoro focuses more on asynchronous operations and Boost.Cobalt focuses more on task-based parallelism.

Implementing efficient algorithms

No program can be effective without implementing effective algorithms and programming techniques.

> *Reviewing the old as a means of realizing the new—such a person can be considered a teacher.*
>
> *- Confucius, 551–479 BC*

Simply put, everything new is well-forgotten old. The same applies to algorithm design, where established techniques such as iteration and recursion inspire optimizations such as tail-recursion. In this section, we'll implement iterative, recursive, and tail-recursive (a form of recursion optimization) functions to benchmark their performance and draw some conclusions.

The following code shows the iterative implementation, which has nothing unusual:

```
namespace iteration {
uint64_t factorial(uint32_t n) {
  uint64_t res = 1;
  for (auto i = 1; i <= n; ++i) {
    res *= i;
  }
  return res;
}

uint64_t fibonacci(uint32_t n) {
  uint64_t b = 0, a = 1, res = 0;
  for (auto i = 2; i <= n; ++i) {
    res = b + a;
    b = a;
    a = res;
  }
  return res;
}
} // namespace iteration
```

Recursive functions are often used to break down complex problems into simpler subproblems, solving the problems from top to down and implementing the divide-and-conquer principle. This approach helps keep the focus on the current context by storing the current context on the stack, which is later restored when the nested function call returns.

The following code shows the recursive implementation:

```
namespace recursion {
uint64_t factorial(uint32_t n) {
  if (n == 0) {
    return 1;
  }
  return n * factorial(n - 1);
}

uint64_t fibonacci(uint32_t n) {
  if (n < 2) {
    return n;
  }

  return fibonacci(n - 2) + fibonacci(n - 1);
}
} // namespace recursion
```

It is worth noting here that the recursive `fibonacci` function is called multiple times, recalculating the same values. In this case, it is advisable to apply memoization, which is an optimization technique to store already calculated values in a cache so that they can be reused when the same inputs occur again.

An alternative to memoization is tabulation, a bottom-up approach in which a table is filled with solutions to smaller subproblems and used to compute solutions to larger problems. This method is common in iterative problem-solving for dynamic programming.

Another optimization technique related to recursion is tail-call elimination, which can significantly improve performance for deeply recursive functions. The `musttail` attribute is placed on a `return` statement to guarantee tail-call elimination and prevent stack overflow. Unfortunately, not all C++ compilers implement this functionality, or they implement it differently. That's why this macro works for Clang and GCC, but not MSVC:

```
#ifndef __has_cpp_attribute
#define musttail
#elif __has_cpp_attribute(clang::musttail)
#define musttail [[clang::musttail]]
#elif __has_cpp_attribute(musttail)
#define musttail [[musttail]]
#else
#define musttail
#endif
```

In comparison with C++ compilers, WebAssembly explicitly defines the return instructions `return_call` (the tail-call version) and `return` without any interpretations.

The following code shows the tail-recursive implementation. The inner anonymous namespace has a private scope, so the internal details of the outer namespace are hidden:

```
namespace tail_recursion {
namespace { // anonymous namespace
uint64_t factorial(uint32_t n, uint64_t a) {
  if (n == 1) {
    return a;
  }
  musttail return factorial(n - 1, a * n);
}

uint64_t fibonacci(uint32_t n, uint64_t a, uint64_t b) {
  if (n == 0) {
    return a;
  }
  if (n == 1) {
    return b;
  }
  musttail return fibonacci(n - 1, b, a + b);
}
} // anonymous namespace

uint64_t factorial(uint32_t n) { return factorial(n, 1); }

uint64_t fibonacci(uint32_t n) { return fibonacci(n, 0, 1); }
} // namespace tail_recursion
```

The disadvantage of normal recursive calls is that they heavily use the call stack, which affects performance. Tail-recursion performance is higher because compilers can optimize it into an iterative loop, eliminating the overhead of creating a new stack frame for each call. This optimization also prevents stack overflow errors.

Such optimized functions simply terminate without returning to the point of call—except for the topmost function, which returns control to the calling function—since their last statement is a `return`. They literally have no place to go and nothing to do after passing control to other functions as their stack frames are demolished and execution is finished. Tail calls are subroutine calls that are executed as the last action in a function.

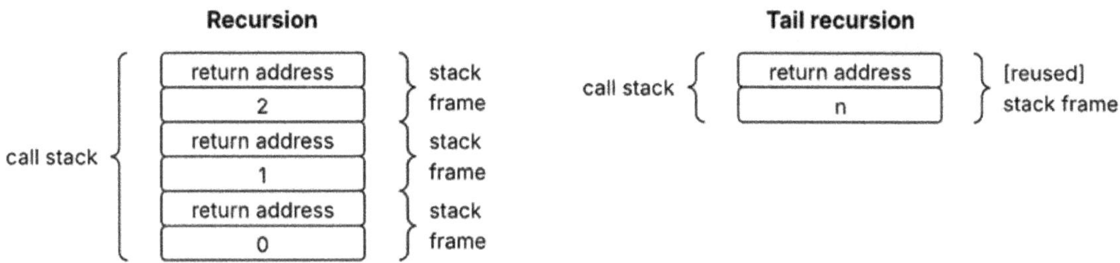

Figure 13.9: Recursion versus tail recursion

In the case of `factorial`, the difference in the execution of functions is not particularly noticeable, although the resulting values overflow the integer type:

```
void BM_test(benchmark::State &state, auto func) {
  const auto n = state.range(0);
  for (auto _ : state) {
    benchmark::DoNotOptimize(func(n));
  }
}

namespace {

constexpr auto MIN_FACTORIAL = 32768;
constexpr auto MAX_FACTORIAL = 65536;

BENCHMARK_CAPTURE(BM_test, iteration::factorial, iteration::factorial)
    ->RangeMultiplier(2)
    ->Range(MIN_FACTORIAL, MAX_FACTORIAL);
BENCHMARK_CAPTURE(BM_test, recursion::factorial, recursion::factorial)
    ->RangeMultiplier(2)
    ->Range(MIN_FACTORIAL, MAX_FACTORIAL);
BENCHMARK_CAPTURE(BM_test, tail_recursion::factorial, tail_
recursion::factorial)
    ->RangeMultiplier(2)
    ->Range(MIN_FACTORIAL, MAX_FACTORIAL);
```

In the case of the Fibonacci sequence, you probably run out of patience waiting for the recursive implementation to complete, so the test range is kept small:

```
constexpr auto MIN_FIBONACCI = 16;
constexpr auto MAX_FIBONACCI = 32;

BENCHMARK_CAPTURE(BM_test, iteration::fibonacci, iteration::fibonacci)
    ->RangeMultiplier(2)
```

```
    ->Range(MIN_FIBONACCI, MAX_FIBONACCI);
BENCHMARK_CAPTURE(BM_test, recursion::fibonacci, recursion::fibonacci)
    ->RangeMultiplier(2)
    ->Range(MIN_FIBONACCI, MAX_FIBONACCI);
BENCHMARK_CAPTURE(BM_test, tail_recursion::fibonacci, tail_
recursion::fibonacci)
    ->RangeMultiplier(2)
    ->Range(MIN_FIBONACCI, MAX_FIBONACCI);

} // namespace

BENCHMARK_MAIN();
```

Well, it's hammer time to measure and analyze the results:

```
--------------------------------------------------------------------------
Benchmark                                          Time             CPU
Iterations
--------------------------------------------------------------------------
BM_test/iteration::factorial/32768             20131 ns        20128 ns
34818
BM_test/iteration::factorial/65536             40311 ns        40303 ns
17279
BM_test/recursion::factorial/32768             20024 ns        20022 ns
34923
BM_test/recursion::factorial/65536             39842 ns        39838 ns
17503
BM_test/tail_recursion::factorial/32768        20047 ns        20037 ns
35243
BM_test/tail_recursion::factorial/65536        39629 ns        39624 ns
17613
BM_test/iteration::fibonacci/16                 2.85 ns         2.85 ns
246077490
BM_test/iteration::fibonacci/32                 6.74 ns         6.74 ns
103553893
BM_test/recursion::fibonacci/16                  814 ns          813 ns
861534
BM_test/recursion::fibonacci/32              2389913 ns      2389778 ns
292
BM_test/tail_recursion::fibonacci/16            3.40 ns         3.40 ns
181188049
BM_test/tail_recursion::fibonacci/32            6.94 ns         6.94 ns
100046816
```

The performance of the iterative and tail-recursive implementations is comparable, but the recursive `fibonacci` function is horrific. Although the running time of the factorial implementations is approximately the same due to the simplicity of the computations, the recursive implementation may lead to stack overflow for large values.

The next approach is used quite rarely and is generally not recommended, except perhaps in specific cases such as implementing virtual machines that interpret bytecode to avoid the overhead of C/C++ `switch` statements in performance-oriented code. Computed goto is a non-standard feature supported by many popular C and C++ compilers. Basically, this feature allows using labels as values by storing the address of the label in a variable and jumping to the label, which is different from calling a function on a pointer since there is no return. This is a very low-level solution, reminiscent of the implementation of jumps by addresses in assembly language.

The goto statement allows jumping to any part of a program, but it can make program logic complex and tangled. In most C++ programs, the goto statement can be replaced by using the `break` and `continue` statements. In general, the goto statement is stigmatized in structured programming. Perhaps the most widespread use of this statement was in BASIC implementations such as ZX Spectrum BASIC and Commodore BASIC in the 1980s.

The following virtual machine implementation is based on the `switch` statement. The interpreter fetches the next instruction from the instruction array and executes it. In this simplified implementation, the `OP_HALT` operation is mandatory, or otherwise execution would never halt. Here, the `switch` operator selects which condition to execute:

```
enum class op_code {
  OP_HALT = 0x00,
  OP_INC = 0x01,
  OP_DEC = 0x02,
  OP_MUL2 = 0x03,
  OP_DIV2 = 0x04,
  OP_REM2 = 0x05,
  OP_NEG = 0x06,
  OP_SENTINEL = OP_NEG
};

namespace switch_vm {
int64_t bytecode_interpreter(const op_code *bytecode, int64_t init_val) {
  int64_t val = init_val;
  std::size_t pc = 0;

  while (true) {
    switch (bytecode[pc++]) {
    case op_code::OP_HALT:
      return val;
```

```
    case op_code::OP_INC:
      ++val;
      break;
    case op_code::OP_DEC:
      --val;
      break;
    case op_code::OP_MUL2:
      val *= 2;
      break;
    case op_code::OP_DIV2:
      val /= 2;
      break;
    case op_code::OP_REM2:
      val %= 2;
      break;
    case op_code::OP_NEG:
      val = -val;
      break;
    default:
      return val;
    }
  }
}
} // namespace switch_vm
```

This virtual machine implementation is based on computed gotos. In this version also, the interpreter fetches the next instruction from the instruction array and executes it. But here the unconditional execution immediately goes to the next instruction. In this simplified implementation, the potential danger is that one of the instructions might not be implemented, leaving the goto statement with nowhere to go, which results in a runtime error:

```
namespace computed_goto_vm {
int64_t bytecode_interpreter(const op_code *bytecode, int64_t init_val) {
  static void *dispatch[] = {&&TARGET_HALT, &&TARGET_INC,  &&TARGET_DEC,
                             &&TARGET_MUL2, &&TARGET_DIV2, &&TARGET_REM2,
                             &&TARGET_NEG};

#define DISPATCH() goto *dispatch_table[std::to_underlying(bytecode[pc++])];

  int64_t val = init_val;
  std::size_t pc = 0;
```

```
  DISPATCH()

 TARGET_HALT: { return val; }
 TARGET_INC: {
  ++val;
  DISPATCH()
 }

 TARGET_DEC: {
  --val;
  DISPATCH()
 }

 TARGET_MUL2: {
  val *= 2;
  DISPATCH()
 }

 TARGET_DIV2: {
  val /= 2;
  DISPATCH()
 }

 TARGET_REM2: {
  val %= 2;
  DISPATCH()
 }

 TARGET_NEG: {
  val = -val;
  DISPATCH()
 }
 }
} // namespace computed_goto_vm
```

This C++ implementation is somewhat safer than C implementations because the operation codes are typed. The C++23 `std::to_underlying` function converts the enumeration to its underlying integer type, which is then used to select the address of a label from the dispatch table because enumeration constants contain indices of operation codes in the table.

Great Scott! It's time to benchmark these virtual machines. This test compares both virtual machines with the same randomized test data. Casting integers to non-existent `enum class` values results in unspecified or undefined behavior. To some extent, this is protected by the `OP_SENTINEL` code, which is the last in the list of contiguous operation codes. The virtual machines are written with some assumptions to demonstrate the approaches without overloading the implementation with technical details:

```
TEST_CASE("virtual_machine", "[benchmark]") {
  std::random_device rd;
  std::mt19937 gen(rd());
  std::uniform_int_distribution<> distrib(
      0, static_cast<int>(op_code::OP_SENTINEL));

  constexpr auto SIZE = 1 << 24;
  auto bytecode = std::unique_ptr<op_code[]>(new op_code[SIZE]);
  std::generate_n(bytecode.get(), SIZE, [&distrib, &gen]() {
    return static_cast<op_code>(distrib(gen));
  });
  bytecode[SIZE - 1] = op_code::OP_HALT;

  BENCHMARK_ADVANCED("switch_vm")(Catch::Benchmark::Chronometer meter) {
    meter.measure(
        [&] { return switch_vm::bytecode_interpreter(bytecode.get(), 0); });
  };

  BENCHMARK_ADVANCED("computed_goto_vm")(Catch::Benchmark::Chronometer meter) {
    meter.measure([&] {
      return computed_goto_vm::bytecode_interpreter(bytecode.get(), 0);
    });
  };
}
```

The results of this test speak louder than any words. The implementation based on computed `gotos` is 23% faster than the implementation with one large `switch`:

```
benchmark name                  samples       iterations    est run time
                                mean          low mean      high mean
                                std dev       low std dev   high std dev
-------------------------------------------------------------------------------
switch_vm                       100           6181          618.1 us
                                1.8159 ns     1.80829 ns    1.84087 ns
                                0.0623443 ns  0.0187728 ns  0.136989 ns
```

```
computed_goto_vm                   100           7913           791.3 us
                                   1.4094 ns     1.40561 ns     1.41721 ns
                                   0.0266696 ns  0.0147317 ns   0.0439994 ns
```

These demonstrated techniques have a practical basis. CPython's first bytecode interpreter (virtual machine) introduced in 1991 was based on the `switch/case` dispatch. It takes the next instruction, looks at its opcode, and jumps to the appropriate `case` block. Simple, reliable, stable... and slow! The second interpreter introduced in 2008 is based on computed gotos and does not rely on `switch/case` optimization by the compiler but instead converts a large `switch` into a table of opcodes. The computed-goto interpreter can also become a source of problems if the interpreter function is massive, since such code is difficult to maintain. Consequently, the third interpreter released in 2025 is a tail-call interpreter. In some scenarios this implementation is faster; in others it is slower compared to the standard interpreter. The 2025 interpreter builds on principles first discussed by Guy Steele in 1977, and the decision to implement the interpreter this way is justified by the fact that his work argued that tail calls are equivalent to goto in most scenarios.

Summary

In this chapter, we explored ways to achieve better performance with our code. We began by understanding how to set up a reliable environment for accurate performance measurements. Then, we discussed how to write microbenchmarks using Google Benchmark, Catch2, and nanobench. Moreover, we covered profiling and saw how to observe runtime behavior using tools and libraries such as Tracy. We also learned how (and why) to implement distributed tracing in complex systems. Along the way, we explored techniques for writing more performant code. We also discussed parallelizing our computations using both standard library utilities and external solutions. Then, we introduced coroutines. You now know what C++20 and C++23 bring, and what the upcoming C++26 could bring, to the coroutine table, as well as how libraries such as libcoro, coost, and Boost.Cobalt help build coroutine-based programs. You've also learned how to write your own coroutines. Finally, we looked at code optimization techniques and how implementation choices impact virtual machine performance.

The most important lesson from this chapter is: when it comes to performance, measure first and optimize later. This will help you maximize the impact of your work.

That's it for performance—the last of the quality attributes we wanted to discuss in our book. In the next chapter, we'll start moving into the world of services and the cloud.

Questions

1. What can we learn from the performance results from this chapter's microbenchmarks and profiling?
2. Is how we traverse a multi-dimensional array important for performance? Why/why not?
3. In our coroutines example, why can't we create our thread pool inside the `do_routine_work` function with libcoro?
4. How can we rework our coroutine example so it uses a generator instead of just tasks?

Further reading

- Arthur O'Dwyer, *When Can the C++ Compiler Devirtualize a Call?* (Blog): `https://quuxplusone.github.io/blog/2021/02/15/devirtualization/`
- Chandler Carruth, *Tuning C++: Benchmarks, and CPUs, and Compilers! Oh My!* (YouTube video), CppCon 2015: `https://www.youtube.com/watch?v=nXaxk27zwlk`
- Hubert Matthews, *Optimising a Small Real-World C++ Application* (YouTube video), ACCU 2019: `https://www.youtube.com/watch?v=fDlE93hs_-U`
- Perf Wiki, *perf: Linux Profiling with Performance Counters*: `https://perf.wiki.kernel.org/index.php/Tutorial`
- Brendan Gregg, *CPU Flame Graphs*: `http://www.brendangregg.com/FlameGraphs/cpuflamegraphs.html`
- Baptiste Wicht, *C++ Containers Benchmark: vector, list, deque, plf::colony* (Blog): `https://baptiste-wicht.com/posts/2017/05/cpp-containers-benchmark-vector-list-deque-plf-colony.html`
- Dawid Pilarski, *Your First Coroutine* (Blog), Panic Software: `https://blog.panicsoftware.com/your-first-coroutine`
- Google, *Google Benchmark User Guide*, GitHub: `https://github.com/google/benchmark/blob/main/docs/user_guide.md`
- Catch2, *Authoring Benchmarks*, GitHub: `https://github.com/catchorg/Catch2/blob/devel/docs/benchmarks.md`
- Catch2, *Data Generators*, GitHub: `https://github.com/catchorg/Catch2/blob/devel/docs/generators.md`
- nanobench, *Test Set/Comparison*: `https://nanobench.ankerl.com/comparison.html`
- Drogon Wiki, *Coroutines*, GitHub: `https://github.com/drogonframework/drogon/wiki/ENG-17-Coroutines`
- Drogon Wiki, *Understanding Drogon's Threading Model,* GitHub: `https://github.com/drogonframework/drogon/wiki/ENG-FAQ-1-Understanding-drogon-threading-model`
- Documents for coost, *Introduction,* GitHub: `https://coostdocs.github.io/en/about/co/`
- Documents for coost, *Basic Concepts of Coroutine,* GitHub: `https://coostdocs.github.io/en/co/concurrency/coroutine/basic/`
- Boost, *Documentation boost.cobalt*: `https://www.boost.org/doc/libs/master/libs/cobalt/doc/html/index.html`
- Tracy, *Tracy Profiler*, GitHub: `https://github.com/wolfpld/tracy/releases`
- Tracy official site: `https://tracy.nereid.pl/`
- `Chris Lott`, *C is the Greenest Programming Language,* Hackaday: `https://hackaday.com/2021/11/18/c-is-the-greenest-programming-language/`
- Jim Ledin, *Modern Computer Architecture and Organization: Learn x86, ARM, and RISC-V Architectures and the Design of Smartphones, PCs, and Cloud Servers,* Second Edition, Packt Publishing: `https://www.packtpub.com/en-pl/product/modern-computer-architecture-and-organization-second-edition-9781803234519`

- Paulo Motta, *GPU Programming with C++ and CUDA: Uncover Effective Techniques for Writing Efficient GPU-Parallel C++ Applications*, Packt Publishing: `https://www.packtpub.com/en-us/product/gpu-programming-with-c-and-cuda-9781805128823`
- Alibaba Cloud Community, *The Mechanism behind Measuring Cache Access Latency* (Blog): `https://www.alibabacloud.com/blog/the-mechanism-behind-measuring-cache-access-latency_599384`
- Eli Bendersky, *Computed goto for Efficient Dispatch Tables*, Eli Bendersky's Website: `https://eli.thegreenplace.net/2012/07/12/computed-goto-for-efficient-dispatch-tables`

Part 4

Cloud-Native Design Principles

This part focuses on the modern architectural style that originated with distributed systems and within cloud environments. It shows concepts including service-oriented architecture, microservices, containers, messaging systems, and observability practices.

This part contains the following chapters:

14

Architecture of Distributed Systems

A very common architecture for distributed systems is **service-oriented architecture** (SOA), which organizes applications into loosely coupled services communicating over a network. It's not a new invention, as this architectural style is almost as old as computer networking, with architectural implementations ranging from **enterprise service bus** (ESB) to cloud-native microservices.

In this chapter, we focus on SOA and microservices as one of its implementations. Given the popularity of microservices, we would like to cover them in depth. When discussing architecture, you will probably at some point hear, "Should we use microservices for that?". This chapter will equip you with the principles, patterns, and techniques needed to plan a migration to microservices or to design a new application that utilizes them.

If your applications include web, mobile, or **Internet of Things** (IoT) interfaces, this chapter will help you understand the architectural principles behind building them with a focus on modularity and maintainability. As most of the current systems work in a client–server (or other network topology) manner, learning about SOA principles will help you design and improve such systems.

The following topics will be covered in this chapter:

- Understanding SOA
- Diving into microservices
- Design considerations for scalable microservices
- Leveraging managed services and cloud providers

Technical requirements

Most of the examples presented in this chapter do not require any specific software. For an **Amazon Web Services** (AWS) API example, you will need the AWS **Software Development Kit** (SDK) for C++, which can be found at `https://aws.amazon.com/sdk-for-cpp/`.

The code presented in the chapter has been placed on GitHub at `https://github.com/PacktPublishing/Software-Architecture-with-Cpp-2E/tree/main/Chapter14`.

Understanding SOA

SOA is an example of a software design that features loosely coupled components that provide services to each other. The components use a shared communication protocol, usually over a network. In this design, services mean units of functionality that can be accessed outside of the originating component. An example of a component could be a mapping service that provides a map of the area in response to geographical coordinates.

According to the definition, a service has four properties:

- It is a representation of business activity with a defined outcome
- It is self-contained
- It is opaque to its users, which means its internal implementation details are hidden
- It may be composed of other services

Architectural implementations

SOA does not regulate how to approach the service orientation. It's a term that may be applied to many different implementations. There are discussions on whether some approaches should be considered as SOA. We don't want to take part in these discussions; instead, we will highlight some of the approaches that are often mentioned as SOA approaches.

Let's explore some of them.

ESB

ESB is often the first concept that comes to mind when someone says SOA. It's one of the oldest approaches to implementing SOA. While ESBs are primarily implemented in Java and .NET, in this book, dedicated to C++, this topic is present because you might encounter scenarios where C++ services need to interoperate with services written in other languages or run in cross-platform environments.

ESB draws an analogy from computer hardware architectures such as **Peripheral Component Interconnect** (PCI)—a computer bus, a complex central telephone switchboard, or a universal adapter for connecting various electronic devices to achieve modularity. This way, third-party providers can implement modules (such as graphics cards, sound cards, or I/O interfaces) independently of the motherboard manufacturer as long as everyone is adhering to the standards required by the bus. Similarly, an ESB manages message routing, data transformation, and communication protocols to connect disparate enterprise systems, allowing different applications and systems to interact and exchange data without requiring a direct connection, much like a switchboard operator connects calls between different people.

Much like the PCI, the ESB architecture aims to build a standard, general-purpose way to allow for the interaction of loosely coupled services, as shown in *Figure 14.1*. Such services are expected to be developed and deployed independently. It should also be possible to combine heterogeneous services.

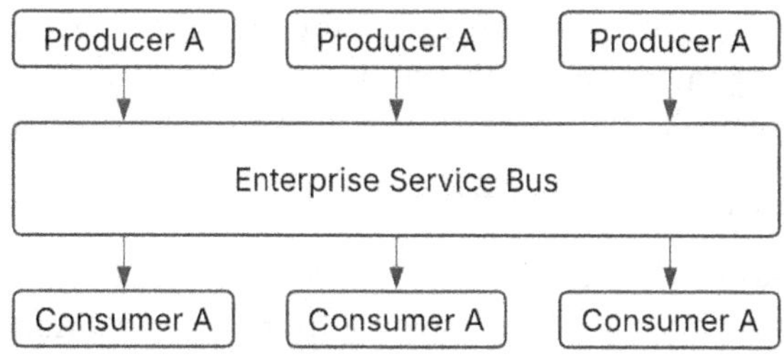

Figure 14.1: ESB

As with SOA itself, an ESB is not defined by any global standard. To implement an ESB, it is necessary to establish an additional component in the system. This component is the bus itself. The communication over ESB is event-driven and often achieved with the means of **message-oriented middleware (MOM)** and message queues, which we'll discuss in *Chapter 15, Interservice Communication*.

The ESB component serves the following roles:

- Controlling the deployment and versioning of services
- Maintaining service redundancy
- Routing messages between services
- Monitoring and controlling the message exchange
- Resolving contention between the components
- Providing common services, such as event handling, encryption, or message queuing
- Enforcing **quality of service (QoS)**

There are both proprietary commercial products as well as open source ones that implement the ESB functionality. The lists that follow may come in handy when integrating C++ systems with ESBs in heterogeneous environments.

Some of the most popular open source products are as follows:

- **Apache Camel:** An open source integration framework that helps in connecting various systems and technologies through predefined enterprise integration patterns
- **Apache ServiceMix:** An open source, enterprise-level distributed integration platform unifying the features and functionality of Apache ActiveMQ (messaging), Camel (integration patterns), CXF (web services), and Karaf (runtime)
- **Apache Synapse:** A lightweight and high-performance ESB powered by a fast and asynchronous mediation engine supporting application and transport layer protocols: REST, HTTP/S, Mail (POP3, IMAP, and SMTP), JMS, TCP, UDP, VFS, SMS, XMPP, and FIX
- **JBoss ESB:** An open source middleware platform developed by Red Hat to connect systems together, especially non-interoperable systems
- **OpenESB:** Runs billions of complex processes around the world, 24/7, for organizations in banking, finance, logistics, and government
- **Red Hat Fuse:** An integration platform based on Apache Camel, Apache CXF, Apache ActiveMQ, Fabric8, Switchyard, and **Open Services Gateway initiative (OSGi)**

- **Spring Integration:** A lightweight framework for adding messaging in Spring-based applications and supporting integration with external systems through declarative adapters using **domain-specific language (DSL)**

The most popular commercial products are the following:

- **IBM Integration Bus (replacing IBM WebSphere ESB):** Enables the transfer of messages between various business applications, ranging from large traditional systems to unmanned devices such as sensors on conveyors.
- **Microsoft Azure Service Bus:** Forms the backbone of messaging in an Azure-based ESB. It supports reliable message queuing and durable publish–subscribe messaging in combination with Azure Logic Apps, Azure Functions, Event Grid, and Event Hubs. Client libraries are available for C#, C++, C, Java, JavaScript, Go, Python, and Rust.
- **Microsoft BizTalk Server:** An integration system that supports data exchange in various formats and protocols, data transformation and execution of business processes, as well as a comprehensive development environment.
- **Oracle Enterprise Service Bus:** A platform for fast and easy implementation of an industrial service bus, specially designed to solve the problems of integration, virtualization, and service management in a complex distributed service infrastructure.
- **SAP Process Integration:** An enterprise integration platform that enables seamless integration between SAP applications and other applications, either within an organization (application to application) or even outside of it (**business to business**, or **B2B**).

As with all the patterns and products that we present in this book, you will have to consider the strengths and weaknesses before deciding to go with a particular architecture. Some of the benefits of introducing ESB are as follows:

- Better scalability of services
- Distributed workload
- Can focus on configuration rather than implementing custom integration in services
- An easier way to design loosely coupled services
- Replaceable services
- Built-in redundancy capability

The disadvantages, on the other hand, mostly revolve around the following:

- A single point of failure—the ESB component's failure means the outage of an entire system
- The configuration is more complex, which impacts maintenance
- Message queuing, message translation, and other services provided by ESB may reduce performance or even become a bottleneck

Web services

Web services are another popular implementation of SOA. By their definition, web services are services offered by one machine to another machine (or operator) where communication occurs over World Wide Web protocols. Even though the **World Wide Web Consortium** (W3C), the governing body concerning the World Wide Web, allows the use of other protocols such as FTP or SMTP, most web services typically use HTTP as transport.

Although it is possible to implement web services using proprietary solutions, most implementations are based on open protocols and standards.

The benefits of web services are as follows:

- Use of popular web standards
- Rich ecosystem of tooling
- Extensibility

Given next are the disadvantages:

- A lot of overhead
- Some implementations are too complex (for example, SOAP/WSDL/UDDI specifications)

Messaging and streaming

We've mentioned message queues and message brokers already when covering the ESB architecture. Other than as part of an ESB implementation, messaging systems may also be standalone architectural elements.

Message queues

Message queues are components used for **interservice communication** (ISC), which we will explore in depth in the next chapter. As the name suggests, they use the queue data structure to pass messages between different processes. Usually, message queues are a part of MOM designs.

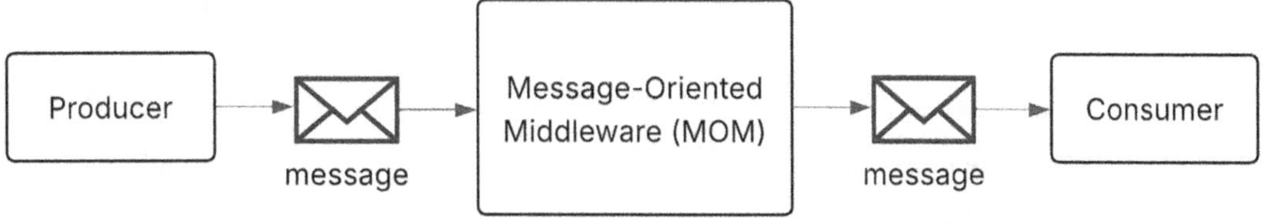

Figure 14.2: MOM architecture

On the lowest level, message queues are available in Unix specifications, both in System V and in POSIX. While they are useful when implementing interprocess communication on a single machine, we would like to focus on message queues that are suitable for distributed computing.

To address the needs of distributed environments, several message queuing standards have emerged. The following list gives a brief overview of commonly used options (if your focus is on grasping the concepts for now, you can skim through the list or skip it; you can always return to it later as a reference):

- **Advanced Message Queuing Protocol (AMQP)**: A binary protocol operating on the application layer of the seven-layer **Open Systems Interconnection (OSI)** model. Popular implementations include Apache Qpid, Apache ActiveMQ, RabbitMQ, Azure Event Hubs, and Azure Service Bus.
- **Streaming Text Oriented Messaging Protocol (STOMP)**: A text-based protocol similar to HTTP (uses verbs such as `CONNECT`, `SEND`, and `SUBSCRIBE`). Popular implementations include Apache ActiveMQ, RabbitMQ, and syslog-ng.
- **Message Queuing Telemetry Transport (MQTT)**: A lightweight protocol aimed at embedded devices. Popular implementations include home automation solutions such as OpenHAB, Adafruit IO, IoT Guru, Node-RED, Home Assistant, Pimatic, AWS IoT, and Azure IoT Hub.

Message brokers

A message broker builds on top of the queuing concept. They manage one or more queues and deal with advanced features such as translation, validation, and routing of messages in a messaging system. Like message queues, they are parts of MOM.

Using message brokers, you can minimize the application's awareness regarding other parts of the system. This leads to designing loosely coupled systems, as message brokers take all the burden related to common operations on messages. It is known as a publish–subscribe design pattern.

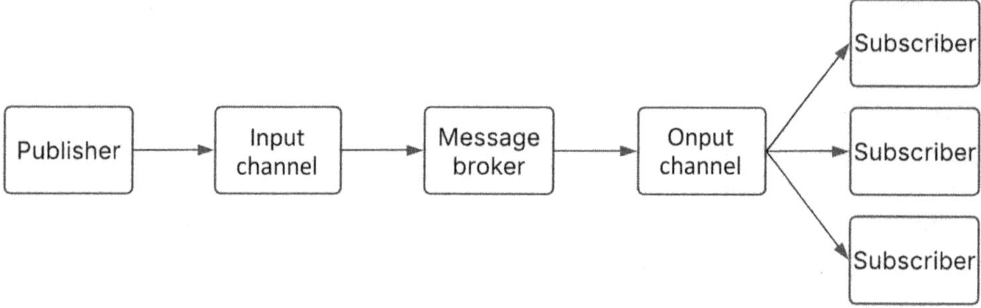

Figure 14.3: Publish–subscribe pattern

Brokers typically manage message queues for receivers but are also able to perform additional functions, such as the following:

- Translating messages from one representation to another
- Validating the message sender, receiver, or contents
- Routing messages to one or more destinations
- Aggregating, decomposing, and recomposing messages in transit
- Retrieving data from external services
- Augmenting and enriching messages through interaction with external services
- Handling and responding to errors and other events
- Providing different routing patterns, such as publish–subscribe

Popular implementations of message brokers are the following. As with the list in the preceding section, if your focus right now is on understanding the concept, you can skim through it or skip it and return to it later as a reference:

- **Apache ActiveMQ**: An open source, multi-protocol, Java-based message broker. It provides client libraries for JavaScript, C, C++, Python, and .NET, and integrates multi-platform applications using the AMQP, STOMP, and MQTT protocols, as well as the **Jakarta Messaging (JMS)** API
- **Apache Kafka**: An open source, distributed, event-streaming platform for processing real-time data, written in Java and Scala, with client libraries for Java, Python, Go, C#/.NET, C, C++, SQL, D, Rust, Perl, Swift, Lua, PHP, Kotlin, and so on
- **Apache Qpid**: An open source messaging system written in C++, Java, Ruby, Perl, Python, and C#, implementing the AMQP protocol and providing transaction management, queuing, distribution, security, management, clustering, federation, and heterogeneous multi-platform support
- **Eclipse Mosquitto MQTT Broker**: An open source broker written in C, enabling communication between clients and IoT devices using the MQTT protocol, with client libraries for C and C++
- **NATS**: An open source messaging system (also called MOM) written in Go, with client libraries for Arduino, C, C++, Elixir, Go, Java, Lua, MicroPython, .NET, Nim, OCaml, Pascal, Python, Rust, and so on
- **RabbitMQ**: A reliable and mature messaging and streaming broker implementing the AMQP protocol, written in Erlang, mainly known for its flexibility, reliability, and easy-to-use nature, with client libraries for .NET, Java, Python, JavaScript, Ruby, PHP, Rust, Swift, Julia, C, C++, Delphi, Erlang, Perl, COBOL, and so on
- **Remote Dictionary Server (Redis) and its forks**: An open source, in-memory, NoSQL key/value store written in C, primarily used as an application cache or quick-response database, with client libraries for C#/.NET, Java, JavaScript, PHP, Go, Python, C, C++, Ruby, Rust, Dart, and Delphi
- **Amazon MQ**: A managed message broker service written in Java for Apache ActiveMQ and RabbitMQ
- **Amazon Kinesis**: A service to collect, store, capture, and process many logs from distributed streams in real time, with client libraries for .NET, Java, PowerShell, Python, C++, Rust, and SAP ABAP
- **Azure Service Bus**: Described in the *ESB* section
- **HiveMQ**: A proven MQTT IoT data streaming platform written in Java for secure, real-time data connectivity, enabling smarter decisions and digital transformation, having client libraries for C#, C++, Java, Python, and more
- **VerneMQ**: A high-performance, low-latency, distributed MQTT broker written in Erlang and designed to handle large numbers of concurrent clients, having client libraries for C, C++, Java, Lua, Python, Ruby, JavaScript, PHP, Arduino, and so on
- **EMQX**: A large-scale, distributed MQTT messaging platform written in Erlang, designed for event streaming and connecting IoT devices, with client libraries for C, C++, .NET, Java, Python, JavaScript, Go, Swift, Rust, and so on
- **Aedes**: An MQTT broker written in JavaScript and run on Node.js (a cross-platform, open source JavaScript runtime environment), enabling efficient communication for IoT applications

- **ejabberd:** An **Extensible Messaging and Presence Protocol** (**XMPP**) server, Jabber server, MQTT broker, and **Session Initiation Protocol** (**SIP**) gateway written in Erlang and built to create real-time services such as massive chat, instant communication, and IoT
- **BlazingMQ**: An open source, distributed message queuing system written in C++, providing durable, fault-tolerant, highly performant, and highly available queues with various message routing strategies, with client libraries for C++, Java, and Python

Cloud computing

Cloud computing is a broad term with a lot of different meanings. Initially, the term *cloud* referred to a layer of abstraction that the architecture shouldn't be too worried about. This could, for example, mean servers and network infrastructure managed by a dedicated operations team.

Later, service providers started applying the term *cloud computing* to their own products that abstracted the underlying infrastructure with all its complexities. Instead of having to configure each piece of infrastructure individually, it was possible to use a simple **API** to set up all the necessary resources.

This shows the transition from an internal architectural concept into an on-demand service model that organizations could rent from third-party providers.

Nowadays, cloud computing has grown to include many novel approaches to application architecture. It may consist of the following:

- Managed services, such as databases, cache layers, and message queues
- Scalable workload orchestration
- Container deployment and orchestration platforms
- Serverless computing platforms

The most important thing to remember when considering cloud adoption is that hosting your application in the cloud requires an architecture designed specifically for the cloud. Most often, it also means architecture designed specifically for the given cloud provider.

This means that choosing a cloud provider is not just a decision about whether one choice is better than another at a given moment in time. It means that the future cost of switching providers may be too big to warrant the move. Migration between providers requires architectural changes, and for a working application, they may outweigh the savings expected from the migration.

There is also another consequence of cloud architecture design. For legacy applications, it means that in order to take advantage of the cloud benefits, the applications would first have to be rearchitected and rewritten. Migration to the cloud is not just a matter of copying binary and configuration files from on-premises hosting to virtual machines managed by a cloud provider. Such an approach would only mean a waste of money, as cloud computing is only cost-effective if your applications are scalable and cloud-aware.

Cloud computing doesn't necessarily mean using external services and leasing machines from third-party providers. There are also solutions such as OpenStack, CloudStack, Proxmox, and MicroCloud that run on-premises, which allow you to leverage the benefits of cloud computing using the servers you already own. Hybrid cloud computing is a way of combining private clouds (on-premises data centers) with public clouds.

Microservices

There is some debate regarding whether microservices are a part of SOA or not. Most of the time, the term *SOA* is pretty much equivalent to the ESB design. Microservices are, in many respects, the opposite of ESB. This leads to opinions that microservices are a distinct pattern from SOA, being the next step in the evolution of software architecture.

We believe that they are, in fact, a modern approach to SOA that aims to eliminate some of the problems featured in ESB. After all, microservices fit within the definition of SOA very well.

Benefits of SOA

Splitting the system's functionality over multiple services has several benefits. First of all, each service can be maintained and deployed separately. This helps the team focus on a given task without the need to understand every possible interaction within the system. It also enables Agile development as tests must only cover a particular service, not the entire system.

The second benefit is that the modularity of the services helps create a distributed system. With a network (usually based on the **Internet Protocol**, or **IP**) as a means of communication, services can be split between different machines to provide scalability, redundancy, and better resource usage.

Implementing new features and maintaining the existing software is a difficult task when there are many producers and many consumers for each service. This is why SOA encourages the use of documented and versioned APIs.

Another way to make it easier for both service producers and consumers to interact is by using established protocols that describe how to pass data and metadata between different services. These protocols may include SOAP, REST, GraphQL, or gRPC.

The use of APIs and standard protocols makes it easy to create new services that provide added value over the existing ones.

Considering we have a service, *A*, that returns our geographical location and another service, *B*, that provides the current temperature for a given location, we can invoke *A* and use its response in a request to *B*. This way, we get the current temperature for the current location without implementing the entire logic on our own.

All the complexity and implementation details of both services are unknown to us, and we treat them as **black boxes**. The maintainers of both services may also introduce new functionality and release new versions of the services without the need to inform us about it.

Testing and experimenting with SOA is also easier than with monolithic applications. A small change in a single place doesn't require the recompilation of an entire code base. It is often possible to invoke services in an ad hoc manner using client tools.

Let's return to our example with the weather and geographical location service. If both services are exposing a REST API, we are able to build a prototype using nothing more than a cURL client to send appropriate requests manually. When we confirm that the response is satisfactory, we may then start writing code that will automate the entire operation and possibly expose the results as another service.

To get the benefits of SOA, we need to remember that all of the services have to be loosely coupled. If services depend on each other's implementation, it means they are no longer loosely coupled and are tightly coupled instead. Ideally, any given service should be replaceable by a different analogous service without impacting the operation of the entire system.

In our weather and location example, this means that reimplementing a location service in a different language (say, switching from Go or Rust to C++) should not affect the downstream consumers of that service as long as they use the established API.

It is possible to still introduce breaking changes in the API by releasing a new API version. A client connecting to version 1.0 would observe the legacy behavior, while clients connecting to 2.0 would benefit from bug fixes, better performance, and other improvements that come at the cost of compatibility.

For services relying on HTTP, API versioning usually occurs at the URI level. So, a version 1.0, 1.1, or 1.2 API can be accessed when calling `https://service.local/v1/customer`, while the version 2.0 API resides at `https://service.local/v2/customer`. An API gateway, HTTP proxy, or a load balancer is then able to route the requests to the appropriate services.

Challenges with SOA

Introducing an abstraction layer always comes at a cost. The same rule applies to SOA. It's easy to see the abstraction costs when looking at ESB, web services, or message queues and brokers. What may be less obvious is that in the case of microservices, additional costs arise from the **remote procedure call** (**RPC**) frameworks they use, because network latency is never zero, and the resource consumption related to service redundancy and duplication of functionality.

Another target of criticism related to SOA is the lack of uniform testing frameworks. Individual teams that develop the services of an application may use tooling unknown to other teams. Other issues related to testing are that the heterogeneous nature and interchangeability of components mean there is a huge set of combinations to test. Some combinations may introduce edge cases that are not typically observed.

Moreover, according to Conway's Law (introduced in *Chapter 2, Architectural Styles*), the architecture of a system tends to mirror the communication structure of the organization that builds it. In an SOA environment, as the knowledge about particular services is mostly concentrated in a single team, this can lead to a lack of knowledge sharing and inconsistent practices, making it much harder to understand how an entire application works.

Further, when the SOA platform is developed during the lifetime of an application, it may introduce the need for all the services to update their version to target the recent platform development. This means that instead of introducing new features, developers would be focused on making sure their application functions correctly after the changes to the platform. In an extreme case, maintenance costs may rise drastically for those services that don't see new releases and are constantly patched to adhere to platform requirements.

In modern software architecture, microservices have emerged as a widely adopted approach because of the advantages they offer. Therefore, we'll discuss them next.

Diving into microservices

While microservices are not tied to any particular programming language or technology, a common choice when implementing microservices has been the Go language. That does not mean that other languages are not suitable for microservices development—quite the contrary. The low computational and memory overhead of C++ makes it an ideal candidate for microservices.

Before going into scaling considerations, we will start with a detailed view of some of the pros and cons of microservices. After that, we'll focus on design patterns that are often associated with microservices.

The benefits of microservices

You may often hear about microservices in superlatives. It is true that they can bring some benefits, and here are some of them.

Modularity

Since the entire application is split into many relatively small modules, it is easier to understand what each microservice does. The natural consequence of this understanding is that it is also easier to test individual microservices. Testing is also aided by the fact that each microservice typically has a limited scope. After all, it's easier to test just the calendar application than to test the entire **personal information management** (PIM) suite.

This modularity, however, comes at some cost. Your teams may have a much better understanding of individual microservices, but at the same time, they may find it harder to grasp how the entire application is composed. While it shouldn't be necessary to learn all the internal details of the microservices that form an application, the sheer number of relationships between components presents a cognitive challenge. It's good practice to use microservices API contracts when using this architectural approach, which is important in managing the complexity of distributed systems. By defining clear and enforceable specifications for how independent services interact, you prevent breaking changes, enable independent deployments, and promote collaboration across teams.

Another consideration is how to organize the code repositories for these services. You need to choose between **monolithic repositories (mono-repos)** and **multiple repositories (multi-repos)** for microservices, which impact the modularization of these services, time and complexity of their development, testing, connections with other services, deployment complexity, and communication between teams.

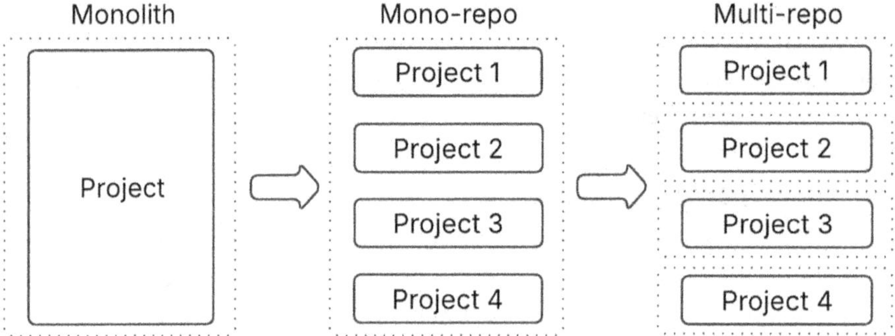

Figure 14.4: Mono-repos and multi-repos

A mono-repo does not mean a monolithic application; it still consists of independently deployable services. It implies having more than one microservice in a source code repository. This approach simplifies dependency management, streamlines CI/CD pipelines, eases refactoring, and facilitates code reuse, but when the code base grows, it complicates versioning and increases project complexity and build times. Also, things could go wrong when participants compete to apply pull requests to a project. This approach often leads to cross-dependencies of microservices.

A multi-repo approach gives each microservice its own repository. This approach eases releases and scales development, but it duplicates code and complicates dependency management and CI/CD pipelines.

The choice depends on various factors, including the project complexity, organizational needs, team structures, and locations.

While repo strategies address backend service organization, frontend architectures can also benefit from a modular approach, such as micro frontends. A micro frontend is an architectural pattern for web development based on the concept of microservices. Instead of a traditional monolithic application, a frontend application is split into smaller and self-contained components.

With WebAssembly, even frontend parts can be written in C++. It is a possibility that makes micro frontends relevant for C++ developers, as both the backend and frontend can be modular and work together in a fragmented architecture. *Figure 14.5* illustrates this evolution.

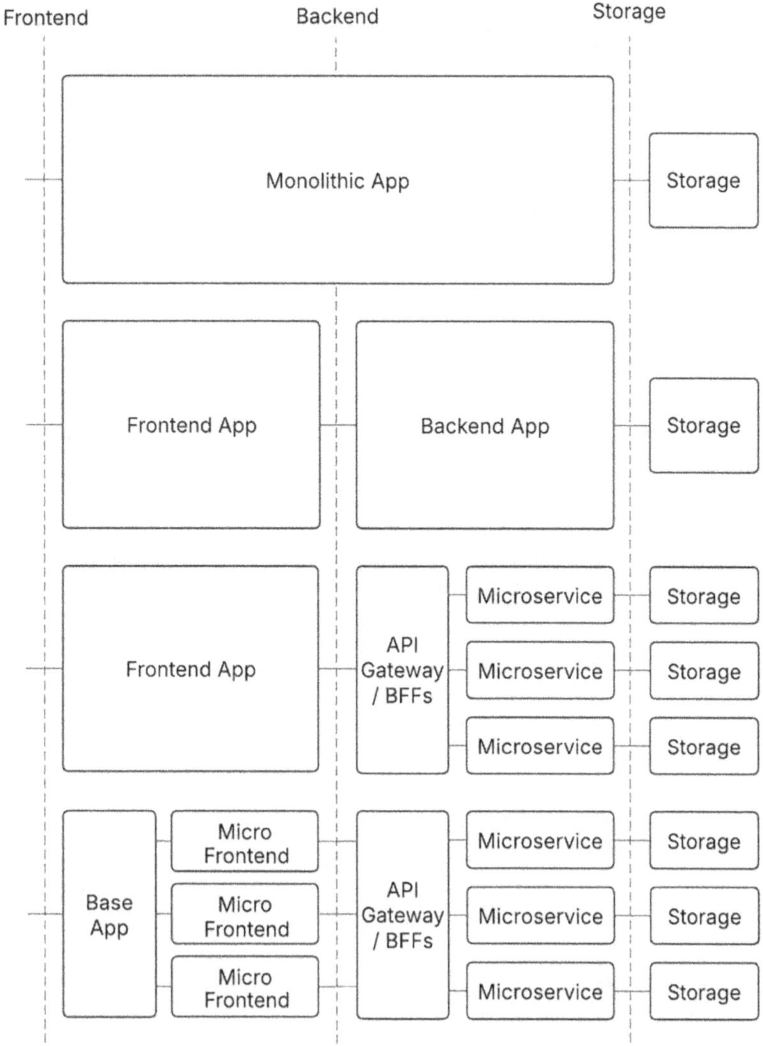

Figure 14.5: Microservices and micro frontends

The figure presents different combinations of frontend, backend, and storage layers to show their evolution from a monolithic architecture through separated frontend/backend to microservices and micro frontends.

Scalability

It is easier to scale applications that are limited in scope. One reason for that is that there are fewer potential bottlenecks.

Scaling smaller pieces of a workflow is also more cost-effective. Imagine a monolithic application responsible for managing a trade fair. Once the system starts showing performance issues, the only way to scale is to bring in a bigger machine for the monolith to run on. This is called **vertical scaling**.

With microservices, the first advantage is that you can scale horizontally, that is, bring in more machines instead of a bigger machine (which is usually cheaper). The second advantage comes from the fact that you only need to scale those parts of the application that are having performance issues. This also contributes to money saved on infrastructure.

Flexibility

Microservices, when properly designed, are less susceptible to vendor lock-in. When you decide you want to switch one of the third-party components, you don't have to do the entire painful migration all at once. Microservices design takes into account that you need to use interfaces, so the only part that requires modification is the interface between your microservice and the third-party component.

Microservices also allow migration in stages, wherein some services could continue using the software from the old provider, while others adopt the new one. This means you can separate the risk of introducing breaking changes in many places at once. What's more, you can combine this with the canary deployment pattern to manage risk with even more granularity.

This flexibility is not just related to services but also to the underlying architecture. It may also mean different databases, different queueing and messaging solutions, or even entirely different cloud platforms. While different cloud platforms typically offer different services and APIs to use them, with a microservices architecture, you can start migrating your workload piece by piece and test it independently on a new platform.

Finally, when rewrites are necessary due to performance issues, scalability, or available dependencies, it is much faster to rewrite a microservice than a monolith.

Integration with legacy systems

Microservices are not necessarily an all-or-nothing approach. If your application is well-tested and migration to microservices may create a lot of risks, there's no pressure to dismantle the working solution altogether.

Instead, you can split only the parts that require further development and introduce them as microservices that the original monolith will use. However, avoid the trap of designing a prematurely designed network of microservices.

By following this approach, you will gain the benefits of the Agile release cycle associated with microservices, while at the same time avoiding creating a new architecture from scratch and basically rebuilding an entire application. If something is already working well, it's better to focus on how to add new features without breaking the good parts. Be careful here, as starting from scratch is often used as an ego boost!

Distributed development

The era of development teams being small and colocated is long gone. Remote work and distributed development are a fact even in traditional office-based companies. Giants such as IBM, Microsoft, and Intel have people from different locations working together on a single project.

Microservices support this trend by allowing for smaller and more agile teams, which makes distributed development much easier. This reduces the need to facilitate communication between a group of 20 or more people and makes it easier to build self-organized teams that require less external management.

Disadvantages of microservices

Even if you think you may need microservices due to their benefits, keep in mind that they also have some serious drawbacks. In short, they are definitely not for everyone. Larger companies can generally offset these drawbacks, but smaller companies often don't have this luxury.

Reliance on a mature DevOps approach

Building and testing microservices should be much faster than performing similar operations on big, monolithic applications. But in order to achieve Agile development, this building and testing would need to be performed much more often.

While it may be sensible to deploy the application manually when you are dealing with a monolith, the same approach will lead to a lot of problems if applied to microservices.

In order to embrace microservices in your development, you must ensure that your team has a DevOps mindset and understands the requirements of both building and running the microservice. It's not enough to simply hand the code to someone else and forget about it.

The DevOps mindset will help your team automate as much as possible. Developing microservices without a CI/CD pipeline is probably one of the worst possible ideas in software architecture. Such an approach will bring all the other disadvantages of microservices without enabling most of the benefits.

Harder to debug

Microservices require introducing observability. Without it, when something breaks, you're never sure where to start looking for the potential root cause because microservices are distributed and can be replicated (having more than one instance). Observability is a way to deduce the state of your application without the need to run a debugger or log to the machines your workload is running on, since the source of the error is likely to be very difficult to determine in a distributed system.

A combination of log aggregation, application metrics, monitoring, and distributed tracing is a prerequisite to managing a microservices-based architecture. This is especially true once you consider that autoscaling and self-healing may even prevent you from accessing individual services if they start crashing.

Additional overhead

Microservices should be lean and agile. And that's usually true. However, microservices-based architecture usually requires additional overhead. The first layer of overhead is related to the additional interfaces used for microservices communication. RPC libraries, API providers, and consumers must be multiplied not only by the number of microservices but also by the number of their replicas. Then there are auxiliary services, such as databases, message queues, and so on. Those services also include observability facilities that usually consist of both storage facilities and individual collectors that gather data.

The costs that you optimize with better scaling may be outweighed by the costs required to run the entire fleet of services that don't bring immediate business value. What's more, it may be hard for you to justify these costs (both in terms of infrastructure and development overhead) to the stakeholders.

Design patterns for microservices

A lot of general design patterns apply to microservices as well. There are also some design patterns that are typically associated with microservices. The patterns presented here are useful for both greenfield projects as well as migration from monolithic applications.

Decomposition patterns

These patterns relate to the ways in which microservices are decomposed. We want to ensure that the architecture is stable and the services are loosely coupled. We also want to make sure that services are cohesive and testable. Finally, we want autonomous teams to fully own one or more services.

Decomposition by business capability

One of the decomposition patterns requires decomposition by business capability. Business capability relates to what a business does in order to produce value. Examples of business capabilities are merchant management and customer management. Business capabilities are often organized in a hierarchy.

The main challenge when applying this pattern is to correctly identify the business capabilities. This requires an understanding of the business itself and may benefit from cooperation with a business analyst.

Decomposition by subdomain

A different decomposition pattern is related to the **domain-driven design** (DDD) approach. To define services, it is necessary to identify DDD subdomains. Just like business capability, identifying subdomains requires knowledge of the business context, which is e-commerce in our example. Examples of subdomains in e-commerce include order fulfillment, payment processing, and product catalog management.

The main difference between the two approaches is that with decomposing by business capability, the focus is more on the organization of the business (its structure), whereas with decomposing by subdomain, the focus is on the problems that the business tries to solve.

Database per service pattern

Storing and handling data is a complex issue in every software architecture. Wrong choices may impact scalability, performance, or maintenance costs. With microservices, there's an added complexity coming from the fact that we want the microservices to be loosely coupled.

This leads to a design pattern where each microservice connects to its own database, so it is independent of any changes introduced by the other services. While this pattern adds some overhead, its additional benefit is that you can optimize the schema and indexes for each microservice individually.

Since databases tend to be pretty huge pieces of infrastructure, this approach may not be feasible, so sharing a database between microservices is an understandable trade-off.

Deployment strategies

With microservices running on multiple hosts, you will probably wonder which is the better way to allocate resources. Let's compare the two possible approaches.

Single service per host

Using this pattern, we allow each host to only serve a particular type of microservice. The main benefit is that you can tweak the machine to better fit the desired workload, and services are well isolated. When you provide extra-large memory or fast storage, you'll be sure that it is used only for the microservice that needs it. The service is also unable to consume more resources than provisioned.

The downside of this approach is that some of the hosts may be underutilized. One possible workaround is to use the smallest possible machines that still satisfy the microservice requirements and scale them when necessary. This workaround, however, does not solve the issue of additional overhead on the host itself.

Multiple services per host

An opposite approach is hosting multiple services per host. This helps to optimize the utilization of the machines, but it also comes with some drawbacks. First of all, different microservices may require different optimizations, so hosting them on a single host will still be impossible. What's more, with this approach, you lose control of the host allocation, so the problems in one microservice may cause outages in a colocated microservice even if the latter would be otherwise unaffected.

Another problem is the dependency conflict between the microservices. When the microservices are not isolated from one another, the deployment must take into account different possible dependencies. This model is also less secure.

Now that some of the important pros, cons, and patterns are known to you, we'll look at design considerations for scaling applications, a few of which apply to both monolithic and microservice architectures. Some of these approaches—those about addressing bottlenecks—not only help scalability but can also ease incremental migration from monoliths to microservices.

Design considerations for scalable microservices

Before we go into specific scalability-related techniques, it's worth noting that opinions differ on whether monoliths or microservices are inherently better at scaling. Some architects believe that monoliths are inherently evil because they don't scale well, are tightly coupled, and are hard to maintain. There are others who claim that the performance benefits coming from monoliths counterbalance their shortcomings. It's a fact that tightly coupled components require much less overhead in terms of networking, processing power, and memory than their loosely coupled counterparts.

As each application has unique business requirements and operates in a unique environment when it comes to stakeholders, there is no universal rule regarding which approach is better suited. Even more confusing is the fact that after the initial migration from monoliths to microservices, some companies started consolidating microservices into macroservices. This was because the burden of maintaining thousands of separate software instances proved to be too big to handle.

The choice of one architecture over another should always come from the business requirements and careful analysis of different alternatives. Putting ideology before pragmatism usually results in a lot of waste within an organization. When a team tries to adhere to a given approach at all costs, without considering different solutions or diverse external opinions, that team is no longer fulfilling its obligations to deliver the right tools for the right job.

If you are developing or maintaining a monolith, you may still benefit from techniques that improve scalability. The approaches in the next section can help you scale both monolithic and microservice-based applications, while also making a monolith easier to migrate to microservices if you choose to do so. However, for simplicity, our discussion will focus on microservices.

Addressing scalability bottlenecks

In both monoliths and microservices, three primary causes of scalability bottlenecks are as follows:

- Memory
- Storage
- Computing

We will look at approaches to address each of these bottlenecks, using techniques that are applicable to both microservices and monoliths.

Outsourcing memory management

One of the ways to help microservices scale is to outsource some of their tasks. One such task that may hinder scaling efforts is memory management and caching data.

For a single monolithic application, storing cached data directly in the process memory is not a problem, as the process will be the only one accessing the cache anyway. But with several replicas of a process, this approach starts to show some problems.

What if one replica has already computed a piece of a workload and stored it in its local cache? The other replica is unaware of this fact and must compute it again. This way, your application wastes both computational time (as the same task must be performed multiple times) and memory (as the results are also stored with each replica separately).

To mitigate such challenges, consider switching to an external in-memory store rather than managing the cache internally within an application. Another benefit of using an external solution is that the life cycle of your cache is no longer tied to the life cycle of your application. You can restart and deploy new versions of your application, and the values already stored in the cache are preserved.

This may also result in shorter startup times as your application no longer needs to perform the computing during startup. Two popular solutions for in-memory cache are Memcached and Redis.

Memcached

Memcached, released in 2003, is the older product of the two. It's a general-purpose, distributed key-value store. The original goal of the project was to offload databases used in web applications by storing the cached values in memory.

Memcached is distributed by design. In its original versions, all cached data was lost when the server restarted. However, since version 1.5.18, Memcached supports a *warm restart* feature. This allows the cache to be reloaded after a *clean shutdown*. This is possible through the use of a RAM disk as a temporary storage space. The main use cases for this system are database query caching, session storage, API response caching, and content caching.

This system uses a simple API that can be operated via Telnet (a network protocol providing access to virtual terminals of remote systems), via `netcat` (often abbreviated to `nc`, a network tool reading and writing data in the network using **Transmission Control Protocol** (**TCP**) and **User Datagram Protocol** (**UDP**)), or by using bindings for many popular programming languages. The official client library for C++ does not exist since the project is written in C, but it's possible to use the C/C++ `libmemcached` library.

Redis

Redis is a newer project than Memcached, with the initial version released in 2009. Since then, Redis has replaced the usage of Memcached in many cases. Just like Memcached, it is a distributed, general-purpose, in-memory, key-value store.

Unlike Memcached, Redis also features optional data durability. While Memcached operates on keys and values being simple strings, Redis also supports other data types, such as the following:

- Lists of strings
- Sets of strings
- Sorted sets of strings
- Hash tables where keys and values are strings
- Geospatial data (since Redis 3.2)
- HyperLogLogs

The design of Redis makes it a great choice for caching session data, caching web pages, and implementing leaderboards. Apart from that, it may also be used for message queueing. The popular distributed task queue library for Python, Celery, uses Redis as one of the possible brokers, along with RabbitMQ and Apache SQS.

Microsoft, Amazon, Google, and Alibaba all offer Redis-based managed services as part of their cloud platforms.

There are many implementations of a Redis client in C++. Interesting ones are `Hiredis` (`https://github.com/redis/hiredis`), `redis-plus-plus` (`https://github.com/sewenew/redis-plus-plus`), the `redis-cpp` library (`https://github.com/tdv/redis-cpp`) written using C++17, and Boost.Redis (`https://github.com/boostorg/redis`).

The following example of `redis-plus-plus` usage illustrates how to set and get some data in the store. First, we connect to a Redis server and store a key-value pair:

```
#include <sw/redis++/redis++.h>
#include <algorithm>
#include <iostream>
```

```
#include <iterator>
using namespace sw::redis;

int main() {
  try {
    auto redis = Redis("tcp://127.0.0.1:6379");
    redis.set("poem", "late goodbye");
    if (const auto val = redis.get("poem")) {
      std::cout << *val << std::endl;
    }
```

If the list is not deleted first, subsequent operations will append new values to the existing ones:

```
    redis.del("students");
```

We then push multiple values into the list:

```
    redis.rpush("students", {"Allison", "John", "Brian", "Andrew",
                "Claire"});
```

Finally, we read from the list and print its content:

```
    std::vector<std::string> vec;
    redis.lrange("students", 0, -1, std::back_inserter(vec));
    std::copy(vec.begin(), vec.end(),
              std::ostream_iterator<std::string>(std::cout, " "));
  } catch (const Error& e) {
    std::cerr << "Error: " << e.what() << std::endl;
  }

  return 0;
}
```

💡**Quick tip:** Enhance your coding experience with the **AI Code Explainer** and **Quick Copy** features. Open this book in the next-gen Packt Reader. Click the **Copy** button

(1) to quickly copy code into your coding environment, or click the **Explain** button

(2) to get the AI assistant to explain a block of code to you.

```
function calculate(a, b) {
  return {sum: a + b};
};
```

Copy (1) Explain (2)

🔒**The next-gen Packt Reader** is included for free with the purchase of this book. Scan the QR code OR go to `https://packtpub.com/unlock`, then use the search bar to find this book by name. Double-check the edition shown to make sure you get the right one.

As you can see, `redis-plus-plus` makes it easy to set both single values and lists.

Which in-memory cache is better?

For most applications, Redis would be a better choice nowadays. It has a large user community and many client libraries, and is thus well-supported. Other than that, it features snapshots, replication, transactions, and the publish–subscribe model. It is possible to embed Lua scripts with Redis, and the support for geospatial data makes it a great choice for geo-enabled web and mobile applications.

Direct alternatives to Redis are forks created after Redis changed its license away from open source: KeyDB (backed by Snapchat), Redict, and Valkey (backed by Aiven, Amazon, ByteDance, Ericsson, Google, NetApp Instaclustr, Oracle, Percona, UpCloud, and kOrdent). The other popular alternatives are ScyllaDB (based on the Seastar framework), Dragonfly (fully compatible with Redis and Memcached APIs), RocksDB (developed and maintained by Meta), GridDB (a NoSQL/SQL database for IoT), RaimaDB (an embedded database for mission-critical applications), Tarantool (an in-memory computing platform), Couchbase (a NoSQL distributed document database), and Aerospike (a real-time, high-performance NoSQL database).

However, if your main goal is to cache the results of database queries in web applications, Memcached is a simpler solution with much less overhead. Its lower overhead means it uses the resources better, as it doesn't have to store type metadata or perform conversions between different types.

Outsourcing storage

Another possible limitation when introducing and scaling microservices is storage. Traditionally, local block devices have been used for storing objects that don't belong to the database (such as static PDF files, documents, or images). Even nowadays, block storage remains very popular, whether through local block devices or network filesystems such as **Network File System** (NFS) or **Server Message Block** (SMB).

While NFS and SMB are the domain of **Network-Attached Storage** (NAS) (a centralized server for storing and sharing files among multiple users), there are also protocols related to a concept operating on a different level: **Storage Area Network** (SAN) (a specialized, high-speed network providing network access to storage devices). Some of the popular ones are **Internet Small Computer Systems Interface** (iSCSI), **Network Block Device** (NBD), **ATA (Advanced Technology Attachment) over Ethernet** (AoE), Fibre Channel Protocol, and Fibre Channel over Ethernet.

A different approach features clustered filesystems designed for distributed computing: GlusterFS, CephFS, or Lustre. All of these, however, operate as block devices exposing the same POSIX file API to the user.

A fresh point of view on storage has been proposed as part of AWS. Amazon **Simple Storage Service** (S3) introduced object storage. An API provides access to objects stored in buckets. This is different from the traditional filesystem, as there is no distinction between files, directories, and inodes; there are only buckets and keys that point to binary objects stored by the service.

Outsourcing computing

One of the principles of microservices is that a process should only be responsible for doing a single piece of the workflow. A natural step while migrating from monoliths to microservices would be to define possible long-running tasks and split them into individual processes.

This is the concept behind task queues. Task queues handle the entire life cycle of managing tasks. Instead of implementing threading or multiprocessing on your own, with task queues, you delegate the task to be performed, which is then asynchronously handled by the task queue. The task may be performed on the same machine as the originating process, but it may also run on a machine with dedicated requirements.

The tasks and their results are asynchronous, so there is no blocking in the main process. Examples of popular task queues in web development are Celery, written in Python, Sidekiq, written in Ruby, BullMQ, written in TypeScript for Node.js, and Machinery, written in Go. All of them can be used with Redis as a broker. Unfortunately, there aren't any similar mature solutions written in C++.

If you are seriously considering taking this route, one possible approach would be to implement a task queue directly in Redis, utilizing its list and set data structures. However, there's a risk of losing unprocessed messages if the Redis server fails because it processes messages primarily in memory.

Another possible approach is to use one of the existing task queues, such as Go Machinery, and invoke them by directly calling Redis. This, however, is not advised, as it depends on the implementation details of the task queue rather than the documented public API.

Yet another approach is to interface the task queue using bindings provided by **Simplified Wrapper and Interface Generator** (**SWIG**) to connect computer programs or libraries written in C or C++ with scripting languages (such as JavaScript, Perl, PHP, Python, Tcl, and Ruby) or non-scripting languages (such as C#, D, Go, Java, Lua, OCaml, Octave, Scilab, and R). However, this method introduces additional complexity, as it requires careful handling of cross-language memory management. Also, debugging becomes harder because errors may propagate across languages.

Scaling microservices

One of the significant benefits attributed to microservices is that they scale more efficiently than monoliths. Given the same hardware infrastructure, you could, in theory, get more performance out of microservices than monoliths.

However, in practice, the benefits are not that straightforward. Microservices and related helpers also provide overhead that, for smaller-scale applications, may be less performant than an optimal monolith.

Remember that even if something looks good "on paper," it doesn't mean it will fly. If you want to base your architectural decisions on scalability or performance, it is better to prepare calculations and experiments. This way, you'll act based on data, not just emotion.

When it comes to scaling, the strategy you choose often depends on your deployment model. We have already covered two deployment strategies earlier in the chapter. We saw what the strategies entail and their pros and cons; we'll now discuss the same strategies in the context of scaling.

Scaling a single service per host deployment

For a single service per host deployment, scaling a microservice requires adding or removing additional machines that host the microservice. If your application is running on a cloud architecture (public or private), many providers offer a concept known as autoscaling groups.

Autoscaling groups define a base virtual machine image that will run on all grouped instances. Whenever a critical threshold is reached (for example, 80% CPU use), a new instance is created and added to the group. Since autoscaling groups run behind a load balancer, the increasing traffic then gets split between both the existing and the new instances, thus reducing the mean load on each one. When the spike in traffic subsides, the scaling controller shuts down the excess machines to keep the costs low.

Different metrics can act as triggers for the scaling event. The CPU load is one of the easiest to use, but it may not be the most accurate one. Other metrics, such as the number of messages in a queue, may better fit your application.

Here's an excerpt from a Terraform configuration for a scaler policy:

```
autoscaling_policy {
    max_replicas = 5
    min_replicas = 3

    cooldown_period = 60

    cpu_utilization {
      target = 0.8
    }
}
```

It means that at any given time, there will be at least three instances running and at most five instances. The scaler will trigger once the CPU load hits at least an 80% average for all the group instances. When that happens, a new instance is spun up. The metrics from the new machine will only be collected after it has been running for at least 60 seconds (the cooldown period).

Scaling multiple services per host deployment

The autoscaling approach just described can also be applied to multiple services per host deployments. However, as you can probably imagine, this isn't the most efficient method in the given scenario. Scaling an entire set of services based only on a reduced throughput of a single one is similar to scaling monoliths.

If you're using the multiple services per host deployment pattern, a better way to scale your microservices is to use an orchestrator. If you don't want to use containers, Nomad is a great choice that works with a lot of different execution drivers. For containerized workloads, either Docker Swarm or Kubernetes will help you. Orchestrators are a topic that we'll come back to in *Chapter 16, Containers*.

Leveraging managed services and cloud providers

SOA may be extended to the current cloud computing trend. While ESB features services usually developed in-house, with cloud computing, it is possible to use the services provided by one or more cloud providers.

While designing an application architecture for cloud computing, you should always consider the managed services (services fully provided and maintained by the cloud provider) before implementing other alternatives. For example, before you decide that you want to host your own PostgreSQL database with selected plugins, make sure you understand the trade-offs and costs when compared to a managed database hosting offered by your provider.

The current cloud landscape provides a lot of services designed to handle popular use cases, such as the following:

- Storage
- Relational databases

- Document (NoSQL) databases
- In-memory cache
- Email
- Message queues
- Container orchestration
- Computer vision
- Natural language processing
- Text-to-speech and speech-to-text
- Telemetry: monitoring, logging, and tracing
- Big data
- Content delivery networks
- Data analytics
- Task management and scheduling
- Identity management
- Key and secret management

Given the huge choice of available third-party services, it is clear how cloud computing naturally aligns with SOA.

Cloud computing as an extension of SOA

Cloud computing is an extension of virtual machine hosting. What differentiates cloud computing providers from traditional **virtual private server** (VPS) providers is two things:

- Cloud computing is available via an API, which makes it a service in itself.
- Besides virtual machine instances, cloud computing offers additional services such as storage, managed databases, programmable networking, and many others. All of them are also available via an API.

Before we explore specific ways to use the cloud provider's API in your application, let's first understand how to access these APIs.

Accessing the cloud API

Accessing cloud computing resources via an API is one of the most important features that distinguishes it from traditional hosting. Using an API means you are able to create and delete instances at will without the intervention of an operator. This way, it becomes very easy to implement features such as load-based autoscaling, advanced deployments (canary releases or blue-green deployments), and automated development and testing environments for an application.

Cloud providers usually expose their APIs as RESTful services. On top of that, they often also provide client libraries for several programming languages. While all three of the most popular providers support C++ as a client library, the support from smaller vendors may vary.

If you're thinking about deploying your C++ application to the cloud and plan on using a cloud API, make sure your provider has released a C++ SDK. It is still possible to use a cloud API without an official SDK, for example, using Boost.Beast or Seastar libraries, but keep in mind that this would require a lot more work to implement.

To access the **cloud SDK**, you will also need access control. Typically, there are two ways your application can be authenticated to use the cloud API.

The first is by providing an API token. The API token should be secret and never stored as part of the version control system or inside a compiled binary. To prevent theft, it should also be encrypted at rest.

One of the ways to pass the API token securely to the application is by means of a security framework such as HashiCorp Vault. This is programmable secret storage with built-in lease time management and key rotation.

The second approach involves being hosted on an instance with appropriate access rights. Many cloud providers allow giving access rights to particular virtual machine instances. This way, an application hosted on such an instance doesn't have to authenticate using a separate token. Access control is then based on the instance from which the cloud API request originates.

This approach is easier to implement since it doesn't have to factor in the need for secret management. The downside is that when the instance becomes compromised, the access rights will be available to all of the applications running there, not just the application you've deployed.

There are several ways you can use the cloud provider's API to feature in your application, which we will now present.

Using cloud provider APIs

In this section, we'll understand the different ways you can interact with the cloud provider's APIs.

Using API calls directly

If your cloud provider offers an API accessible in your language of choice, you can interact with the cloud resources directly from your application.

The following two examples both involve using API calls directly from C++ for the same task—allowing users to upload their own pictures by creating a dedicated storage bucket for each newly registered user. The first relies on AWS's vendor-specific SDK, while the second uses MinIO's vendor-agnostic SDK that works with any S3-compatible service.

Example 1

This example uses the AWS SDK for C++ to create an S3 storage bucket for each newly registered user:

```
#include <aws/core/Aws.h>
#include <aws/core/utils/UUID.h>
#include <aws/s3/S3Client.h>
#include <aws/s3/model/CreateBucketRequest.h>
#include <spdlog/spdlog.h>
#include <string>
```

Each AWS Region represents a separate geographic area, but the buckets created in this example are in the Europe (`eu-central-1`) Region. You must obtain the credentials yourself, which is described on the website (`https://docs.aws.amazon.com`), but is beyond the scope of this book:

```
constexpr auto region = Aws::S3::Model::BucketLocationConstraint::eu_central_1;

bool create_user_bucket(const std::string& username) {
  Aws::S3::Model::CreateBucketRequest request;
```

The `create_user_bucket` function creates a bucket for a given username. S3 bucket names must be between 3 (min) and 63 (max) characters long.

In our example, the name is randomized, so each created bucket is unique:

```
  const Aws::String unique_prefix = Aws::Utils::UUID::RandomUUID();

  const Aws::String bucket_name("games-" + username);
  const Aws::String full_name = unique_prefix + bucket_name;
```

The bucket name and regional settings are set in the requests sent by the Amazon S3 client when creating the buckets:

```
  request.SetBucket(Aws::Utils::StringUtils::ToLower(full_name.c_str()));

  Aws::S3::Model::CreateBucketConfiguration bucket_config;
  bucket_config.SetLocationConstraint(region);
  request.SetCreateBucketConfiguration(bucket_config);

  const Aws::S3::S3Client s3_client;

  if (const auto outcome = s3_client.CreateBucket(request);
      !outcome.IsSuccess()) {
    const auto& err = outcome.GetError();
    spdlog::error("ERROR:  CreateBucket:  {}:  {}", err.GetExceptionName(),
                  err.GetMessage());
    return false;
  }

  return true;
}
```

The username is only semantic here since all created buckets belong to your account:

```
int main() {
  const std::string username = "david-lightman";

  const Aws::SDKOptions options;
  Aws::InitAPI(options);

  if (create_user_bucket(username)) {
    std::cout << "The bucket for " << username << " is ready" << std::endl;
  }

  ShutdownAPI(options);}
}
```

Here, we have a C++ function that creates an Amazon S3 bucket named after the username provided as a parameter. This bucket is configured to reside in a given Region. If the operation fails, we want to get the error message and log it using `spdlog`.

Example 2

The same functionality can be implemented with MinIO (Amazon S3-compatible open source cloud storage). This object storage system supports any Amazon S3-compatible object storage and different credential providers:

```
#include <miniocpp/client.h>
#include <sole.hpp>
#include <spdlog/spdlog.h>
#include <string>
```

In a real application, credentials most likely won't be hardcoded into the program code, but this is a demo. These are taken from the MinIO website:

```
std::string access_key = "Q3AM3UQ867SPQQA43P2F";
std::string secret_key = "zuf+tfteSlswRu7BJ86wekitnifILbZam1KYY3TG";
bool create_user_bucket(const std::string& username) {
```

The `create_user_bucket` function creates a bucket for a given username.

The MinIO playground deployment is at `https://play.min.io:9443`. Our client application connects to this address, and the created buckets are located there:

```
    minio::s3::BaseUrl base_url("play.min.io");
    minio::creds::StaticProvider provider(access_key, secret_key);
    minio::s3::Client client(base_url, &provider);
```

Each created bucket has a **universally unique identifier** (UUID) prefix in its name:

```
    std::string unique_prefix = sole::uuid4().str();
    std::string bucket_name{"petticoat-acres-" + username};
    std::string full_name{unique_prefix + bucket_name};

    minio::s3::MakeBucketArgs args;
    args.bucket = full_name;

    if (const minio::s3::MakeBucketResponse resp =client.MakeBucket(args))
    {
        spdlog::info("{} bucket is created successfully", args.bucket);
    } else {
        spdlog::error("Unable to create bucket {}: {}", args.bucket,
                      resp.Error().String());
        return false;
   }

    return true;
}
```

In this case, the username has no meaning other than being semantically used as a suffix in the bucket names:

```
int main() {
    if (const std::string username = "prayerincpp";
            create_user_bucket(username)) {
        spdlog::info("The bucket for {} is ready", username);
    }

    return 0;
}
```

Many cloud service providers, including Amazon, Google, and Microsoft, provide SDKs to their platforms.

Using API calls through a CLI tool

Some operations don't have to be performed during the runtime of your application. They are typically run during the deployment and, therefore, may be automated in shell scripts, for example. One such use case is invoking a **command-line interface** (CLI) tool to create a new **virtual private cloud** (VPC):

```
gcloud compute networks create database --description "A VPC to access the
database from private instances"
```

We use the `gcloud` CLI tool from Google Cloud Platform to create a network called `database` that will be used to handle traffic from the private instances to the database.

Using third-party tools that interact with the cloud API

Let's look at an example of running HashiCorp Packer to build a virtual machine instance image that is preconfigured with your application:

```
{
   variables : {
     do_api_token : {{env `DIGITALOCEAN_ACCESS_TOKEN`}} ,
     region : fra1 ,
     packages : "customer"
     version : 1.0.3
  },
  builders : [
    {
       type : digitalocean ,
       api_token : {{user `do_api_token`}} ,
       image : ubuntu-25-04-x64 ,
       region : {{user `region`}} ,
       size : 512mb ,
       ssh_username : root
    }
  ],
  provisioners: [
    {
       type : file ,
       source : ./{{user `package`}}-{{user `version`}}.deb ,
       destination : /home/ubuntu/
    },
    {
       type : shell ,
       inline :[
         dpkg -i /home/ubuntu/{{user `package`}}-{{user `version`}}.deb
      ]
    }
  ]
}
```

In the preceding code, we provide the required credentials and region and employ a builder to prepare an instance from the Ubuntu image for us. The instance we are interested in needs to have 512 MB of RAM. Then, we provide the instance first by sending a `.deb` package to it, and then by executing a shell command to install this package.

Using the cloud CLI

The cloud CLI is typically used by human operators to interact with the cloud API. Alternatively, it may be used for scripting or using the cloud API with languages that are officially unsupported.

As an example, the following Bourne shell script creates a resource group in the Microsoft Azure cloud and then creates a virtual machine belonging to that resource group:

```
#!/bin/sh
RESOURCE_GROUP=dominicanfair
VM_NAME=dominic
REGION=germanynorth

az group create --name $RESOURCE_GROUP --location $REGION

az vm create --resource-group $RESOURCE_GROUP --name $VM_NAME --image UbuntuLTS
--ssh-key-values dominic_key.pub
```

When looking for documentation on how to manage cloud resources, you will encounter a lot of examples using the cloud CLI. Even if you wouldn't normally use the CLI, instead preferring a solution such as Terraform or OpenTofu, having the cloud CLI at hand may help you with debugging infrastructure problems.

Using tools that interact with the cloud API

You have already learned about the dangers of vendor lock-in when using products from cloud providers. Typically, each cloud provider will offer its own API and CLI, which differ from those of other providers. There are cases where smaller providers offer abstraction layers that allow accessing their products via an API similar to that of the well-known providers. This approach aims to help with migrating the application from one platform to another.

Such instances are rare, though, and in general, tools used to interact with services from one provider are incompatible with those from another provider. This is a problem not only when you consider migration from one platform to the next. It may also be problematic if you want to host your application on a variety of providers.

For this purpose, there's a new set of tools, collectively known as **infrastructure as code** (IaC) tools, that offer an abstraction layer on top of different providers. These tools are not necessarily limited to cloud providers either. They're usually general-purpose and help to automate many different layers of your application's architecture.

In *Chapter 11, Continuous Integration and Continuous Deployment*, we briefly covered some of them.

Cloud-native tools

While IaC tools focus on automating infrastructure, cloud-native tools allow architects and developers to abstract the infrastructure even more and build, first and foremost, with the cloud in mind. Popular solutions such as Kubernetes and OpenShift are driving this trend, but the landscape consists of a lot of smaller players as well. The last chapter of this book is dedicated to cloud-native design and explores building applications with these tools.

Summary

In this chapter, we examined SOA as a key approach to implementing distributed systems, and explored microservices as one of its modern implementations, along with a quick look at a few others. We also covered the benefits and challenges associated with SOA.

Microservices are a great trend in software architecture. They could be a good fit, provided you make sure you know about the hazards and prepare for them. We discussed their benefits as well as their drawbacks, introduced a range of microservice-specific design patterns, and looked at how to build microservices by outsourcing memory management, storage, or computing. Finally, we explored techniques for scaling microservices.

We saw how managed services and cloud computing extend SOA by offering a wide range of ready-to-use capabilities.

In the next chapter, we will turn to the communication layer of distributed systems and examine ISC patterns and technologies.

Questions

1. What are the properties of a service in SOA?
2. What are some benefits of web services?
3. When are microservices not a good choice?
4. How do microservices help you to use the system's resources better?
5. How can microservices and monoliths coexist (in an evolving system)?
6. Which types of teams benefit the most from microservices?
7. Why is it necessary to have a mature DevOps approach when introducing microservices?
8. What are the deployment strategies for microservices? What are the benefits of each of them?
9. How do cloud platforms differ from traditional hosting?

Further reading

- Gigi Sayfan, *Hands-On Microservices with Kubernetes: Build, Deploy, and Manage Scalable Microservices on Kubernetes*, Packt Publishing: `https://www.packtpub.com/product/hands-on-microservices-with-kubernetes/9781789805468`

- Gigi Sayfan, *Mastering Kubernetes: Dive into Kubernetes and Learn How to Create and Operate World-Class Cloud-Native Systems*, Fourth Edition, Packt Publishing: `https://www.packtpub.com/en-us/product/mastering-kubernetes-9781804614754`
- Gineesh Madapparambath and Russ McKendrick, *The Kubernetes Bible: The Definitive Guide to Deploying and Managing Kubernetes across Cloud and On-Prem Environments*, Second Edition, Packt Publishing: `https://www.packtpub.com/en-us/product/the-kubernetes-bible-9781835468241`
- Anand Rai, *Bootstrapping Service Mesh Implementations with Istio: Build Reliable, Scalable, and Secure Microservices on Kubernetes with Service Mesh*, Packt Publishing: `https://www.packtpub.com/en-us/product/bootstrapping-service-mesh-implementations-with-istio-9781803235967`
- Alessandro Arrichiello and Gianni Salinetti, *Podman for DevOps: Containerization Reimagined with Podman and Its Companion Tools*, Packt Publishing: `https://www.packtpub.com/en-us/product/podman-for-devops-9781803248967`
- Lonneke Dikmans and Ronald van Luttikhuizen, *SOA Made Simple*, Packt Publishing: `https://www.packtpub.com/product/soa-made-simple/9781849684163`
- Martin Fowler, *Microservices—A Definition of This New Architectural Term*: `https://martinfowler.com/articles/microservices.html`
- Chris Richardson, *Microservice Architecture*: `https://microservices.io/`
- *Micro Frontends*: `https://micro-frontends.org/`
- MinIO, *Exascale Object Store for AI Data, Agentic Computing, and Analytics*: `https://min.io/`
- MinIO, *MinIO C++ SDK*: `https://minio-cpp.min.io/`
- MinIO, *Software Development Kits (SDKs)*: `https://miniodocs.cc/developers/minio-drivers`
- TrueNAS, *TrueNAS Apps*: `https://www.truenas.com/apps/`
- Redis, *Connect with Redis Client API Libraries*: `https://redis.io/docs/latest/develop/clients/`
- Luigi Fugaro and Mirko Ortensi, *Redis Stack for Application Modernization: Build Real-Time Multi-Model Applications at Any Scale with Redis*, Packt Publishing: `https://www.packtpub.com/en-us/product/redis-stack-for-application-modernization-9781837637591`
- Redis, *Redis Queue*: `https://redis.io/glossary/redis-queue/`
- Dragonfly, *SDKs*: `https://www.dragonflydb.io/docs/development/sdks`
- Valkey, *Valkey GLIDE*, GitHub: `https://github.com/valkey-io/valkey-glide`
- Chris Richardson, *Pattern: Decompose by Subdomain*: `https://microservices.io/patterns/decomposition/decompose-by-subdomain.html`
- Chris Richardson, *Pattern: Decompose by Business Capability*: `https://microservices.io/patterns/decomposition/decompose-by-business-capability.html`
- AWS, *AWS SDK for C++*: `https://aws.amazon.com/sdk-for-cpp/`
- Azure SDK, *Azure SDK for C++*: `https://azure.github.io/azure-sdk-for-cpp/`
- Google Cloud, *Cloud SDK: Libraries and Command Line Interface*: `https://cloud.google.com/sdk`

- Boost, *Boost.Beast*: https://www.boost.org/doc/libs/1_87_0/libs/beast/doc/html/index.html
- *Seastar*: https://seastar.io/
- *Enterprise Integration Patterns*: https://www.enterpriseintegrationpatterns.com/patterns/messaging/toc.html

15

Interservice Communication

Microservices are so useful because they can be combined in many ways to create new value. That combination depends on effective communication. This means that, most of the time, when we want to use a particular microservice, we must learn how to interact with it. The good news is that while it is possible to implement any communication method in microservices, there are a few popular approaches that most microservices follow.

In a microservices architecture, interservice communication is crucial to ensuring the system's functionality, maintainability, and performance. To effectively manage this communication, a suitable API architecture that supports it is needed. We'll explore the main communication styles supported by such architectures.

The following topics will be covered:

- Introduction to interservice communication
- Interaction styles
- Messaging systems
- Using web services
- Remote procedure calls

Technical requirements

The code present in the chapter has been placed on GitHub at `https://github.com/PacktPublishing/Software-Architecture-with-Cpp-2E/tree/main/Chapter15`.

Introduction to interservice communication

Interservice communication (ISC) is a subset of **inter-process communication** (IPC). So, let's start by looking at IPC first.

IPC refers to a broad set of methods for exchanging data between threads in one or more processes, which can run on the same machine or across multiple machines connected to a network, including localhost. These methods include files, signals, network and local (Unix domain) sockets, semaphores, message queues, message passing, anonymous and named pipes, shared memory, and memory-mapped files (used only for local IPC, not for ISC).

ISC is the exchange of data between independent services, often distributed over a network and interacting via higher-level protocols. Thus, it is implemented in a higher-level, networked context, while IPC covers all mechanisms for exchanging data between processes, including local ones. Therefore, ISC is one of the types of IPC.

Communication between microservices is a key aspect of their successful operation. The correct choice of interaction patterns and protocols ensures the performance and smooth operation of the entire system. Communication over a network is often described in terms of standard models. The **Open Systems Interconnection** (**OSI**) model is a seven-layer conceptual model that describes how systems communicate over a network. The **Transmission Control Protocol/Internet Protocol** (**TCP/IP**) model is a simplified four-layer variant of the OSI model.

While core IPC concepts remain consistent across all **operating systems** (**OSs**), the specific implementation, performance characteristics, and nuances differ. Fortunately, cross-platform higher-level C++ libraries—such as the STL, Boost, Qt, and SDL—largely abstract away platform-specific differences in IPC implementations, greatly facilitating software development on multiple platforms.

With these fundamentals in place, we can now look at how microservices actually interact.

Interaction styles

Microservices can communicate in different interaction styles. In practice, these styles can be expressed as client–server interactions. Importantly, the client–server relationship describes the role a machine plays at a given time, rather than its fundamental identity. The relationship can be classified according to two dimensions: the communication type (synchronous or asynchronous) and the interaction model (one-to-one, one-to-many, many-to-one, or many-to-many).

The communication type determines how the client and server interact in real time. **Synchronous communication** follows a *request–response* model: the client sends a request and waits for a response. In synchronous mode, the client might even be blocked for a long time waiting for the response from the service. **Asynchronous communication** is a *send-and-forget* model: the client sends a message/event and doesn't expect an immediate response. In asynchronous mode, the client continues to work without being blocked while the server is executing the request.

The interaction model describes the number of clients and servers involved in the exchange.

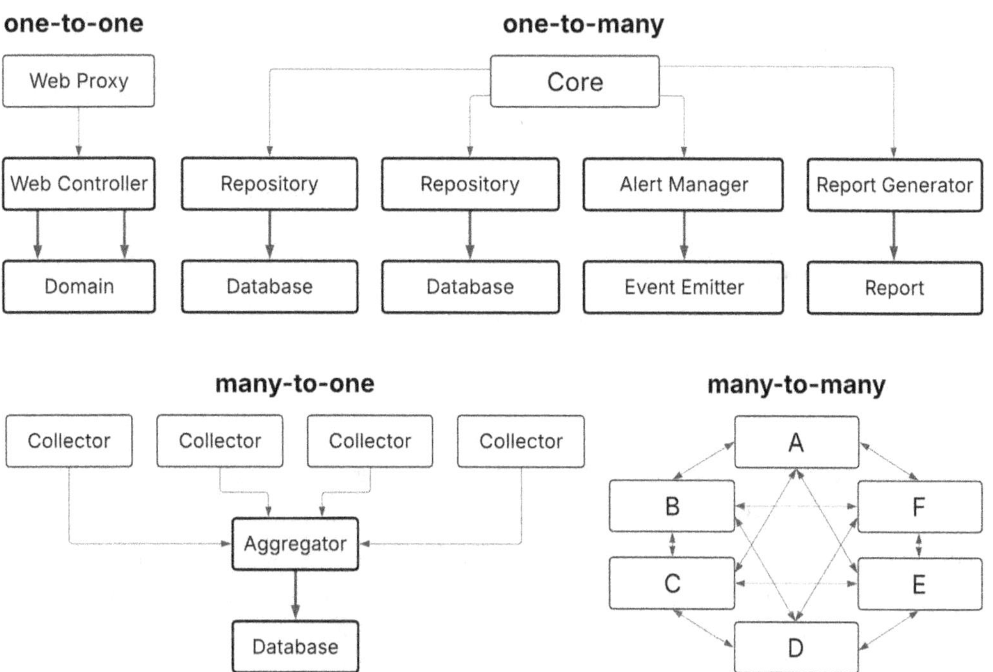

Figure 15.1: Interaction styles

A **one-to-one communication** is a simple interaction in which each service has a unique and direct connection to another service, implying a common, defined contract or interface. This type is useful when two services are highly dependent on each other and need to exchange data in real time. It's worth noting that the functionality of such services directly depends on the functionality and availability of each other, which can lead to tight coupling.

One-to-many communication occurs when one service interacts with multiple services. In such cases, messages are routed and filtered. However, even when the communication system provides delivery guarantees, messages might still get lost or duplicated. This model reduces the tight coupling of services, allowing them to operate independently, making it suitable for scenarios requiring scalability and availability with multiple concurrent client messages.

Many-to-one communication is the direct opposite of one-to-many communication. So, the central service receiving messages must handle a large volume of incoming requests having different formats from many services. This model requires a flexible and extensible architecture and is useful when services need a centralized functionality or data storage. This type of communication facilitates loose connections between services, allowing them to operate independently while maintaining access to shared resources through the central point.

A **many-to-many communication** is a complex interaction in which multiple services interact with multiple services. The reliability and fault tolerance of such a system, including failure detection and recovery, must be considered because the failure of one service can impact the entire system. It is necessary to diligently choose the communication protocols to ensure compatibility and interoperability of services. Efficient communication of services may require performance optimization techniques, including caching and load balancing. This model is useful for complex and dynamic situations.

In many distributed architectures, including microservices, these interaction styles are implemented using messaging, which allows applications or services to exchange discrete messages without requiring a direct or always-available connection. We will explore different messaging systems in the next section.

Messaging systems

Messaging has many different use cases, ranging from IoT and sensor networks to microservices-based distributed applications running in the cloud.

One of the benefits of messaging is that it is a neutral way to connect services implemented using different technologies. When developing a **service-oriented architecture** (**SOA**), each service is typically developed and maintained by a dedicated team. Teams may choose the tools they feel comfortable with. This applies to programming languages, third-party libraries, and build systems.

Maintaining a uniform set of tools may be counterproductive, as different services may have different needs. For example, a kiosk application may require a **graphical user interface** (**GUI**) library, while a hardware controller that is part of the same application will have other requirements, such as dependency on the hardware manufacturer's third-party components. These dependencies may then impose some restrictions that cannot be satisfied for both components simultaneously; for example, a GUI application may require a recent compiler, while the hardware counterpart may be pinned to an older one. Using messaging systems to decouple these components lets them have separate life cycles.

Some use cases for messaging systems include the following:

- Financial operations
- Fleet monitoring
- Logistics capturing
- Processing sensor
- Data order fulfillment
- Task queuing

The following sections focus on the messaging systems designed for low overhead and messaging systems with brokers, both of which can be used for distributed systems. Distributed messaging systems distribute work across many connected points, rather than relying on just one point to handle all messages.

Low-overhead messaging systems

Low-overhead messaging systems are designed for environments with limited resources, such as sensor networks, IoT devices, and embedded systems, where small footprints and low latency are critical. They are less common in large-scale cloud services, but it's still possible to use them in such scenarios by integrating them with other systems.

For instance, the typical RAM sizes on microcontrollers are quite limited. Arduino boards have 2–4 KB, ESP32 has 520 KB, and STM32 devices have 16–192 KB. **Peripheral interface controller** (**PIC**) RAM sizes vary widely but are typically in the range of tens of bytes to tens of kilobytes. Naturally, there can be no talk of megabyte messages processed in the memory of these microcontrollers. Programming such controllers is not so much different from programming early processors, such as the Zilog Z80 (produced from 1976 to 2024).

In contrast, industrial **programmable logic controller** (**PLC**) devices typically have 3–20 MB, whereas typical Linux IoT controllers can have RAM ranging from 32 MB to 4 GB or more, depending on their purpose and complexity. These devices can support more advanced messaging systems but may still benefit from low-overhead messaging systems in resource-sensitive scenarios.

MQTT

MQTT stands for **Message Queuing Telemetry Transport**. It is an open standard under **Organization for the Advancement of Structured Information Standards** (**OASIS**) and **International Organization for Standardization** (**ISO**). MQTT uses the publish–subscribe model usually over TCP/IP, but it can also work with other transport protocols such as QUIC (based on **User Datagram Protocol—UDP**) or Bluetooth.

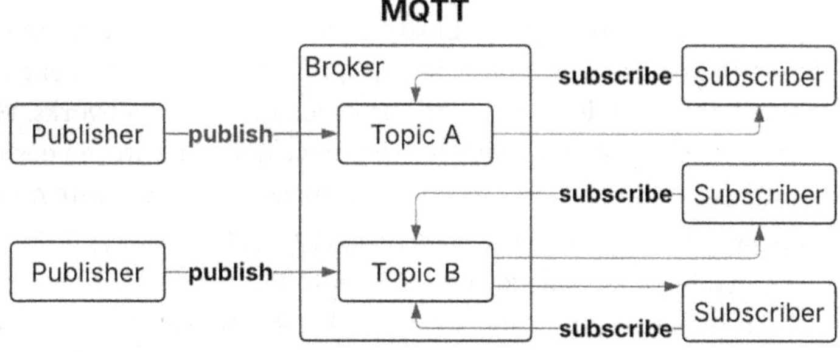

Figure 15.2: MQTT architecture

MQTT is a lightweight messaging protocol designed for constrained devices and low-bandwidth, high-latency, or unreliable networks. There is a separate specification called **MQTT-SN**, which stands for **MQTT for Sensor Networks**. It focuses on battery-powered embedded devices without the TCP/IP stack.

MQTT uses a message broker that receives all the messages from the client and routes those messages to their destinations. It provides **quality of service** (**QoS**) at three levels, each impacting performance and overhead:

- **At most once delivery (no guarantee)**: Messages are sent, but no confirmations are expected. Suitable for high-frequency, non-critical data where message loss is acceptable and minimal latency and low load are important.

- **At least once delivery (acknowledged delivery)**: Duplicate messages may occur (for example, due to an unstable connection). Suitable for important data where some duplication is acceptable.
- **Exactly once delivery (assured delivery)**: No messages are lost or duplicated. Used for uniquely critical one-time data (for example, financial transactions, medical device readings, or security alerts).

The theoretical maximum message size for the MQTT protocol is 256 MB, but in practice, it is often much smaller due to broker and client limitations.

It should be no surprise that MQTT is especially popular with various IoT applications, where high latency and low bandwidth are common. It's supported by openHAB, Node-RED, Pimatic, ThingsBoard, Microsoft Azure IoT Hub, Alibaba Cloud IoT, and Amazon IoT. It's also popular with instant messaging, being used in ejabberd and Facebook Messenger, primarily for mobile applications, where this protocol saves battery consumption. Other use cases include car-sharing platforms, logistics, and transportation.

To place MQTT in context, it is helpful to see it alongside other communication protocols commonly used in IoT systems. Communication protocols are generally grouped by their function and their layer on the OSI or TCP/IP models. Within the IoT protocol stack, communication directions include *sensor to sensor* (the most common protocol is DDS), *sensor to server* (CoAP, MQTT, XMPP, STOMP), and *server to server* (AMQP). These represent different ways devices and systems interact, with choices based on factors such as bandwidth, latency, and device constraints. Common IoT messaging protocols include the following:

- **MQTT**: This collects data from multiple nodes and transmits it to a server. The protocol is based on the publish–subscribe model using an intermediate server called a **broker** that handles message prioritization and broker queuing. MQTT-SN, based on MQTT, is a specialized protocol for sensor networks. MQTT's transport protocol is TCP. Its main characteristics include a lightweight design, suitability for low-bandwidth networks, and reliable message delivery with minimal bandwidth.
- **Constrained Application Protocol (CoAP)**: This is like HTTP but uses short headers, making it suitable for networks with limited bandwidth. This protocol has a client–server architecture and is suitable for transmitting node state information to the server (`GET`, `PUT`, `HEAD`, `POST`, `DELETE`, and `CONNECT` messages). Its transport protocol is UDP. Its main characteristics are suitability for low-power, constrained devices and low-power, interactive networking.
- **Data Distribution Service (DDS)**: This implements a publish–subscribe pattern for real-time data sharing between distributed nodes. This protocol decouples data producers (publishers) from data consumers (subscribers) by using *topics* to categorize data, such as temperature, location, or pressure. DDS ensures reliable delivery with QoS management. Its transport protocol is UDP. It is middleware that facilitates data connectivity and scalable real-time data exchange.

Extensible Messaging and Presence Protocol (**XMPP**): This has long been used on the internet for real-time messaging. Its XML format makes it suitable for IoT networks. This protocol operates on top of publish–subscribe and client–server architectures. It can also be used to address `name@domain.com` type devices in small networks. The standard XMPP protocol uses TCP, but it can be transported over HTTP (BOSH/WebSocket) to bypass network restrictions such as firewalls. Its main characteristics are real-time communication and data exchange, instant feedback, and interactivity.

The IoT protocol stack is built on the TCP/IP model, where each layer (application, transport, internet, and network access) performs a specific function of transmitting data from a device to an application

However, this protocol also has disadvantages:

- Does not support video streaming.
- All communications go through the broker, so its failure can stop the entire system.
- Although the protocol supports **Secure Sockets Layer / Transport Layer Security** (**SSL/TLS**), implementing secure connections requires additional effort. Vulnerabilities can be caused by weak authentication mechanisms (username and password only), unencrypted messages, and incomplete **access control lists** (**ACLs**).
- Using TLS / **Datagram Transport Layer Security** (**DTLS**) for security can put too much of a burden on devices with very limited resources, which may make them unable to work with MQTT.
- On very large networks with many devices, additional optimization may be required to maintain performance.
- The MQTT protocol is not designed to handle large datasets or complex structures.
- Many popular brokers, such as Mosquitto, do not have a built-in web interface, forcing the use of third-party tools for management and monitoring.

The C++ libraries supporting this standard are Eclipse Paho, `mqtt_cpp` (based on C++14 and Boost. Asio), `Boost.MQTT5` (a C++17 MQTT client based on Boost.Asio), `libmosquitto`, `qmqtt`, and Qt MQTT for the cross-platform Qt framework, `pubsubclient`, `arduino-mqtt` for `Arduino`, and `esp-mqtt` and `esp-idf` for ESP32.

The following example shows how to publish and subscribe to MQTT messages using the Eclipse Paho library.

In `publisher.cpp`, the `callback` class handles two events: connection loss and message delivery. These event callbacks are triggered by the MQTT client:

```
// omitted code
...
const std::string SERVER_ADDRESS("tcp://localhost:1883");
const std::string CLIENT_ID("publisher");
const std::string TOPIC("test/topic");
```

```
constexpr int QOS = 1;

class callback final : public mqtt::callback {
public:
  void connection_lost(const std::string &cause) override {
    std::cout << "Connection lost: " << cause << std::endl;
  }

  void delivery_complete(mqtt::delivery_token_ptr token) override {
    std::cout << "Message delivered" << std::endl;
  }
};
```

This asynchronous client sets the event handler, connects to the MQTT server, sends a message to the `test/topic` topic, and terminates after disconnecting from the server:

```
// omitted code
...
mqtt::async_client client(SERVER_ADDRESS, CLIENT_ID);
callback cb;
client.set_callback(cb);

mqtt::connect_options conn_opts;
conn_opts.set_keep_alive_interval(20);
conn_opts.set_clean_session(true);

try {
  client.connect(conn_opts)->wait();
  std::cout << "Connected to MQTT broker" << std::endl;

  std::string payload = "It's a UNIX system!";
  mqtt::message_ptr pub_msg = mqtt::make_message(TOPIC, payload, QOS, false);
  client.publish(pub_msg)->wait();
  std::cout << "Message published: " << payload << std::endl;

  client.disconnect()->wait();
  std::cout << "Disconnected" << std::endl;
} catch (const mqtt::exception &exc) {
  std::cerr << "MQTT Exception: " << exc.what() << std::endl;
  return 1;
}
```

We have now prepared the client with its configuration and event handlers, established a connection, published a message, and cleaned up by disconnecting from the broker.

In `subscriber.cpp`, the `callback` class handles two events: connection loss and message arrival. These event callbacks are triggered by the MQTT client:

```
// omitted code
...
const std::string SERVER_ADDRESS("tcp://localhost:1883");
const std::string CLIENT_ID("subscriber");
const std::string TOPIC("test/topic");
constexpr int QOS = 1;

class callback final : public mqtt::callback {
public:
  void connection_lost(const std::string &cause) override {
    std::cout << "Connection lost: " << cause << std::endl;
  }

  void message_arrived(mqtt::const_message_ptr msg) override {
    std::cout << "Message arrived: " << msg->get_payload_str() << std::endl;
  }

};
```

This asynchronous client sets the event handler, connects to the MQTT server, waits for the messages to the `test/topic` topic, and terminates after disconnecting from the server when the *Enter* key is pressed:

```
// omitted code
...
mqtt::async_client client(SERVER_ADDRESS, CLIENT_ID);
callback cb;
client.set_callback(cb);

mqtt::connect_options conn_opts;
conn_opts.set_keep_alive_interval(20);
conn_opts.set_clean_session(true);

try {
  client.connect(conn_opts)->wait();
  std::cout << "Connected to MQTT broker" << std::endl;

  client.subscribe(TOPIC, QOS)->wait();
```

```
    std::cout << "Subscribed to topic: " << TOPIC << std::endl;

    std::cout << "Press Enter to exit..." << std::endl;
    std::cin.get();

    client.disconnect()->wait();
    std::cout << "Disconnected" << std::endl;
  } catch (const mqtt::exception &exc) {
    std::cerr << "MQTT Exception: " << exc.what() << std::endl;
    return 1;
  }
```

The subscriber now connects to the broker, receives messages published on the subscribed topic, and disconnects when the program ends.

ZeroMQ

ZeroMQ (also known as ØMQ, 0MQ, or zmq) is a brokerless messaging queue. It supports many communication patterns, such as publish–subscribe, request–reply, push–pull, pair, dealer–router, router–dealer, and xpub–xsub (an extended publish–subscribe pattern that enables dynamic discovery of topics). It is independent of any particular transport and can be used with TCP, UDP, **Pragmatic General Multicast** (**PGM**, a reliable multicast transport protocol), **NACK-Oriented Reliable Multicast** (**NORM**, a multicast transport protocol), inproc (direct memory access within a single process), **Generic Security Services Application Programming Interface** (**GSSAPI**), WebSocket, and IPC (inter-process transport passing messages between local processes).

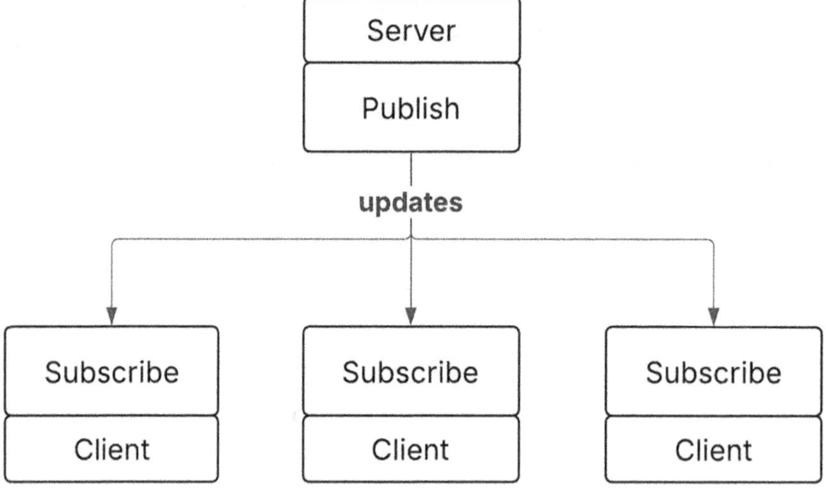

Figure 15.3: ZeroMQ publish–subscribe communication

ZeroMQ, as a messaging system, or "message-oriented middleware," is used in a wide variety of industries, including financial services, game development, embedded systems, academic research, and aerospace. Originally, this system was conceived as an ultra-fast messaging system for stock trading, so extreme optimization was a major focus. Thus, this system is suitable for real-time applications where quick message delivery is essential. Later, the development focus shifted to providing a general system for building distributed applications and supporting arbitrary message patterns, multiple language bindings, and various transport mechanisms. The main idea, contained in the name, is that ZeroMQ is brokerless by design, which reduces centralized administration but transfers responsibilities (routing, persistence, and monitoring) to the application. It is also advocated as providing zero latency, which means no latency is added coming from the presence of a broker. Besides, ZeroMQ is capable of handling messages up to 2^{63}-1 bytes.

The main drawback of ZeroMQ is the lack of built-in message delivery guarantees. Brokerless messaging may not scale as well as brokered messaging because message distribution and load balancing are the responsibility of individual services. Without a central message broker, it is more difficult to monitor and manage message flows and ensure consistent message handling across all services. However, a broker for ZeroMQ does exist and is called Malamute.

The low-level code library of ZeroMQ is written in C, and it has implementations for various popular programming languages, including C++. The most popular implementation for C++ is `libzmq`, which is mainly written in C++98 with some optional C++11 fragments, and the other libraries are `azmq` (which integrates ZeroMQ with Boost.Asio) and `cppzmq` (a header-only library written in C++11).

The following example is based on the `libzmq` library. ZeroMQ provides two ways to send data: the `zmq_send` function for simple messages and the `zmq_msg_send` function for sending multi-part messages. They have corresponding receive functions.

In `publisher.cpp`, the `zmq_send` function returns the number of bytes sent. A discrepancy between the message length and the transmitted data indicates an error:

```
// omitted code
...
void *context = zmq_ctx_new();
void *publisher = zmq_socket(context, ZMQ_PUB);

int rc = zmq_bind(publisher, "tcp://127.0.0.1:5556");
assert(rc == 0);

char msg[] = "Gravity cascades";
size_t msg_size = strlen(msg);

while (true) {
  rc = zmq_send(publisher, msg, msg_size, 0);
  assert(rc == msg_size);
```

It is worth noting that such a loop, without the slightest delay between messages, overloads the processor and network, but this implementation is intentionally simplified and purely educational.

When terminating, publishers should close sockets and destroy ZeroMQ contexts to release system resources:

```
}

zmq_close(publisher);
zmq_ctx_destroy(context);
```

The loop is designed to keep sending the same message endlessly so that subscribers connecting later can still receive the messages.

In `subscriber.cpp`, the `zmq_recv` function receives a message into a buffer and returns the number of bytes read. It truncates the message if it exceeds the buffer length. On the other hand, the `zmq_msg_recv` function allows receiving multipart messages, but the following code uses only `zmq_recv`:

```
// omitted code
...
#define MSG_SIZE 1024

void *context = zmq_ctx_new();
void *subscriber = zmq_socket(context, ZMQ_SUB);

int rc = zmq_connect(subscriber, "tcp://127.0.0.1:5556");
assert(rc == 0);

rc = zmq_setsockopt(subscriber, ZMQ_SUBSCRIBE, "", 0);
assert(rc == 0);

char msg[MSG_SIZE + 1];

while (true) {
  rc = zmq_recv(subscriber, msg, MSG_SIZE, 0);
  assert(rc != -1);
  msg[rc] = '\0'; // important

  printf("%s\n", msg);
}

zmq_close(subscriber);
zmq_ctx_destroy(context);
```

The `zmq_recv` function returns the number of bytes received. Since the message is treated as a null-terminated C string (ASCIIZ), being an array of characters, this value is used to place the terminating null character (`'\0'`) after the received bytes. Otherwise, leftover characters from the stack are displayed on the screen. When terminating, the subscriber should also close sockets and destroy ZeroMQ contexts.

Even though it offers C++ bindings, in terms of program writing style and resource management, `libzmq` is a C library. To some extent, the `cppzmq` and `azmq` libraries hide the C features of this library by wrapping them in C++ classes.

Brokered messaging systems

Popular brokered messaging systems are RabbitMQ and Apache Kafka. Both are mature solutions that are extremely popular in a lot of different designs.

Many articles focus on superiority in a particular area of either RabbitMQ or Apache Kafka. This is a slightly incorrect point of view, as both messaging systems are based on different paradigms.

Apache Kafka focuses on streaming vast amounts of data and storing the stream in persistent memory to allow future replay. RabbitMQ, on the other hand, is often used as a message broker between different microservices or a task queue to handle background jobs. For this reason, routing in RabbitMQ is much more advanced than the one present in Apache Kafka. Although both systems are often used in parallel in projects, each technology has its own strengths.

RabbitMQ and Apache Kafka have distinct message delivery models. While consumers of Apache Kafka pull messages, RabbitMQ pushes messages to consumers.

The scaling concerns could also drive the choice of one message broker over another. The architecture of Apache Kafka allows for easy horizontal scaling, which means adding more machines to the existing pool of workers. RabbitMQ, on the other hand, was designed with vertical scaling in mind, which means adding more resources to the existing machine, rather than adding more machines of similar sizes.

Apache Kafka

Apache Kafka, written in Java, is a distributed event-streaming platform for building real-time data pipelines and streaming applications. High throughput, low latency, scalability, and reliability make it suitable for a wide range of use cases: message queuing, real-time data streaming (for example, processing continuous data from IoT devices), log aggregation, event mining, data integration, big data analytics, **extract, transform, load** (ETL—a data warehousing process), and microservices interoperability. Apache Kafka was originally created by LinkedIn for its own purposes, but is currently widely used in logistics and supply chain, the financial sector, telecommunications, and online commerce.

Apache Kafka has its own protocol based on TCP/IP. The platform can be integrated with other systems via Kafka connectors, in particular Cassandra, FTPS, MQTT, Mongo, MySQL, PostgreSQL, RabbitMQ, and Redis.

Briefly, the architecture of the system can be characterized as follows:

- **Producer**: An application that publishes messages (generating and sending data) to Kafka topics.

- **Consumer:** An application that subscribes to Kafka topics and reads messages (generated by a producer) from partitions, typically in a consumer group. The group shares the workload of processing messages from topic partitions to ensure parallelism.
- **Message:** A data packet required to perform some operation. Messages in Kafka are stored in a commit log, where each record (log) is arranged in a strict sequence. Messages can only be appended to the log, but not deleted or changed. Kafka brokers store messages in topics on the cluster, with each topic divided into partitions. Log retention is not permanent but continues up to a certain threshold or for a certain period (days, weeks, months). This allows data to be processed and analyzed at any time, even after it has been transmitted. The default maximum message size in Apache Kafka is 1 MB, and exceeding this limit is strongly discouraged to prevent brokers from being overwhelmed by large messages. However, in cases where it is absolutely necessary to increase the recommended maximum message size, the producer, consumer, and topic configuration parameters should be modified.
- **Topic:** A named, logical channel for messages of the same or similar content, organized as an immutable, time-ordered sequence of records.
- **Broker:** A dispatcher (node) transmitting messages from the producer to the consumer. Hence, brokers working together form a Kafka cluster.
- **Partition:** A smaller, ordered segment of a topic for scaling and parallel processing across multiple brokers. Partitions are replicated between brokers for fault tolerance.
- **Coordination service:** A distributed service managing Kafka brokers and clusters. The service maintains configuration information, naming, distributed synchronization, fault tolerance, and leader election for partitions. The recommended choice for new Apache Kafka clusters is **Kafka Raft (KRaft)**, whereas previously it was Zookeeper. Raft is a consensus algorithm that allows brokers to elect and follow a leader. The leader handles all read and write operations for the partition, and each partition has its own leader, while followers replicate the leader's data to ensure redundancy and failover.

Figure 15.4 presents the architecture of Apache Kafka:

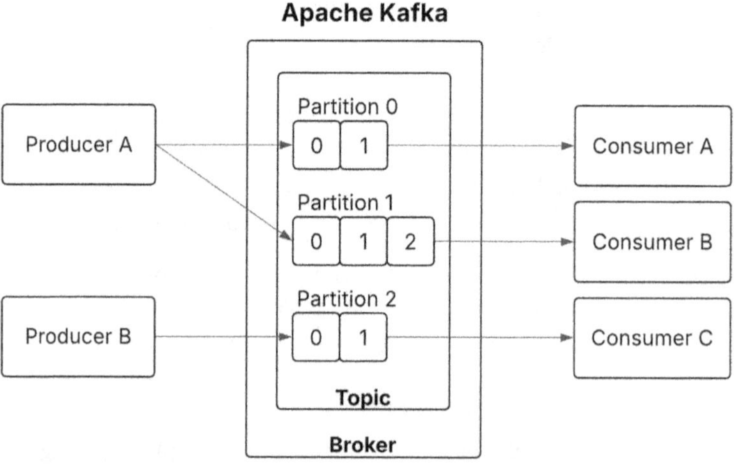

Figure 15.4: Apache Kafka architecture

Kafka has tools that ensure secure operation and data reliability. There are three types of delivery guarantees: at most once, at least once, and exactly once. Moreover, the `read_committed` transaction isolation level in Kafka transactions can prevent consumers from reading messages from ongoing or aborted transactions, which include unfinished or canceled messages.

Setting up Kafka can be complex due to its distributed architecture and configuration requirements. While this solution provides greater scalability and fault tolerance, it requires a deeper understanding of the technology from the service provider. Kafka offers a huge number of configuration parameters that are difficult to understand, even for experienced developers, let alone beginners. For complex message processing patterns, it's better to use a ready-made solution such as RabbitMQ, as Kafka simply doesn't offer this functionality out of the box. Consequently, Apache Kafka is overkill for small and simple projects without real-time data processing requirements.

Popular Kafka GUI tools are Kafbat UI, KafkIO, Aiven Kafka UI, Kafka-UI, AKHQ, Burrow, **Cluster Manager for Apache Kafka** (CMAK), Conduktor, Kafdrop, Kafka IDE, Redpanda Console, and kPow.

C++ client libraries for Apache Kafka include `librdkafka`, `modern-cpp-kafka`, and `cppkafka`.

The following example is based on the `modern-cpp-kafka` library, which depends on the `librdkafka` library.

In `producer.cpp`, the list of active Kafka brokers is specified by the `KAFKA_BROKER_LIST` environment variable. If it is not set, the producer uses a local broker by default. The topic can likewise be specified by the `TOPIC` environment variable:

```
// omitted code
...
using namespace kafka;
using namespace kafka::clients::producer;

// 192.168.0.1:9092,192.168.0.2:9092,192.168.0.3:9092
const char *tmp = std::getenv("KAFKA_BROKER_LIST");
std::string brokers{tmp != nullptr ? tmp : "127.0.0.1:9092"};

tmp = std::getenv("TOPIC");
const Topic topic{tmp != nullptr ? tmp : "test-topic"};
```

Kafka brokers have the `auto.create.topics.enable` property to control automatic topic creation (the full list of properties is much longer, so for more customized settings, you should refer to the Kafka documentation):

```
const Properties props({{"bootstrap.servers", {brokers}},
                        {"auto.create.topics.enable", {"true"}}});
KafkaProducer producer(props);
```

With the producer configured, the code sends a message, calls a delivery callback that prints the delivery status, and then terminates:

```
std::string line{"Ready player three"};
ProducerRecord record(topic, NullKey, Value(line.c_str(), line.size()));

auto deliveryCb = [](const RecordMetadata &metadata, const Error &error) {
  if (!error) {
    std::cout << "Message delivered: " << metadata.toString() << std::endl;
  } else {
    std::cerr << "Message failed to be delivered: " << error.message()
              << std::endl;
  }
};

producer.send(record, deliveryCb);

producer.close();
```

Now that the producer is able to publish messages, the next step is to see how a consumer receives them.

In `consumer.cpp`, the consumer settings are similar to producer settings:

```
// omitted code
...
using namespace kafka;
using namespace kafka::clients::consumer;

// common code
...

KafkaConsumer consumer(props);
```

The consumer subscribes to the topic and polls for records in an infinite outer loop:

```
consumer.subscribe({topic});

while (true) {
  auto records = consumer.poll(std::chrono::milliseconds(100));

  for (const auto &record : records) {
    if (!record.error()) {
      std::cout << "Got a new message..." << std::endl;
      std::cout << "\tTopic    : " << record.topic() << std::endl;
```

```
            std::cout << "\tPartition: " << record.partition() << std::endl;
            std::cout << "\tOffset   : " << record.offset() << std::endl;
            std::cout << "\tTimestamp: " << record.timestamp().toString()
                      << std::endl;
            std::cout << "\tHeaders  : " << toString(record.headers())
                      << std::endl;
            std::cout << "\tKey   [" << record.key().toString() << "]"
                      << std::endl;
            std::cout << "\tValue [" << record.value().toString() << "]"
                      << std::endl;
        } else {
            std::cerr << record.toString() << std::endl;
        }
    }
}

consumer.close();
```

The consumer receives and prints messages until the inner loop exits. This completes the consumer workflow.

RabbitMQ

RabbitMQ, written in Erlang, is a lightweight message broker used for exchanging messages between various systems. RabbitMQ uses the asynchronous **Advanced Message Queuing Protocol** (**AMQP**), but supports other protocols as well, such as MQTT and **Simple Text Oriented Messaging Protocol** (**STOMP**). This means that RabbitMQ is interoperable with other existing solutions based on these supported protocols. If you write an application that uses AMQP to interact with RabbitMQ, it should be possible to migrate it later to use Apache Qpid, Apache ActiveMQ, or managed solutions such as Amazon MQ and Azure Service Bus.

RabbitMQ components are as follows:

- **Publisher:** An application that creates and sends messages to an exchange.
- **Consumer:** An application that receives and processes messages, subscribing to the messages from queues.
- **Queue:** Stores prioritized messages and distributes them to consumers. The default maximum message size in RabbitMQ is 16 MB in versions 4.x and 128 MB in older versions.
- **Binding:** A connection linking an exchange to a queue for routing messages to the specific queue. This rule defines the relation between the exchange and the queue.
- **Exchange:** Routes messages to a queue based on the bindings between the exchange and the queue. There are different types of exchanges:
    - **Direct exchange:** Messages are sent to the queue whose routing key matches the message's routing key.

- **Topic exchange:** Messages are sent to the queue having a routing key matching a pattern. Patterns may consist of numbers, English letters, and the * (matches exactly one word) and # (matches zero or more words) wildcards, with words separated by dots.
- **Fanout exchange:** Messages are sent to all the queues unconditionally.
- **Headers exchange:** Messages are sent to the queue with binding attributes corresponding to the message headers. The `x-match` binding argument specifies whether all or any one of the header attributes must match.

Figure 15.5 presents the architecture of RabbitMQ:

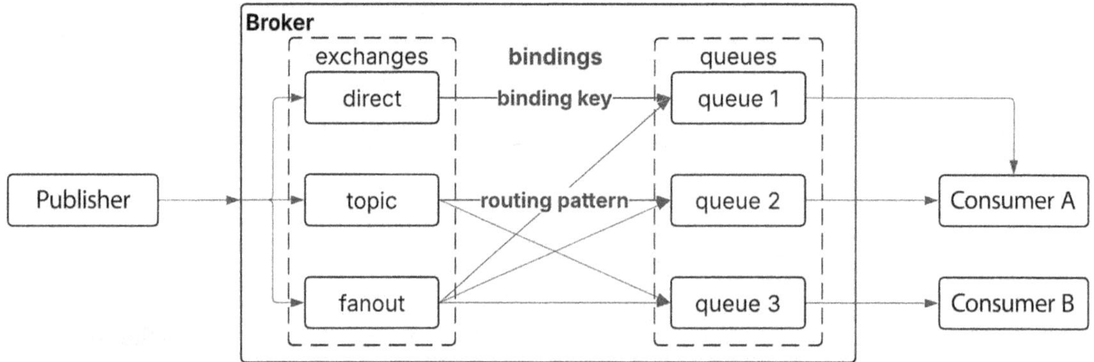

Figure 15.5: RabbitMQ architecture

RabbitMQ can create virtual hosts to isolate messaging environments within the broker. It also supports clustering for high availability and scalability.

The queue length can be limited. By default, RabbitMQ drops or dead-letters messages from the front of the queue (that is, the oldest messages in the queue). However, this behavior can be changed using queue settings so that the broker will discard or dead-letter the most recently published messages. And if publication confirmation is enabled, it will inform the publisher about this event.

With RabbitMQ, you can also specify a **time to live** (**TTL**) argument or policy for messages and queues. This way, the messages and queues will expire automatically. Dead letter exchanges are a way to republish expired messages later if they have not been processed for some reason.

Queues in RabbitMQ are single-threaded, and a single queue can handle up to 50,000 messages. Therefore, for better throughput in a multi-core system, it is advisable to create multiple queues and consumers.

RabbitMQ delivery guarantees are achieved through message durability, consumer acknowledgements, and publisher confirmations. Classic queues do not survive a broker restart because they are not replicated and persisted to disk unless declared *durable*, unlike replicated quorum queues. By default, there are no publisher confirmations from the broker, so if the broker or connection fails, the message is simply lost. Therefore, if that confirmation is not received, the message must be resent.

Furthermore, the broker can delete the message from the queue only after the consumer acknowledges that the message has been delivered, or otherwise it will be redelivered. Using confirmations guarantees *at least once* delivery. Without acknowledgements, messages can be lost during publishing and consuming, and only *at most once* delivery is guaranteed. Transactions are not often used in RabbitMQ due to unclear guarantees and poor performance.

Background processing and long-running processing are the optimal use cases for RabbitMQ, where a message is placed in a queue without immediate processing. RabbitMQ is often used for microservice architecture, where it serves as a means of communication between applications. It is ideal for complex message routing (for example, selective subscription or publication), providing very flexible features. It can be a great choice for sending short-lived messages from one microservice to another. It can be used for sending real-time notifications, task distribution on web servers, IoT device communication, real-time data ingestion and analytics, e-commerce order processing and transactions, gaming applications, search engine indexing, and document processing.

RabbitMQ comes with a built-in user-friendly interface called the management plugin.

C++ client libraries for RabbitMQ are `AMQP-CPP`, `SimpleAmqpClient`, `rmqcpp`, `amqpcpp`, and `hareflow`.

The following example shows how to publish and consume messages using the `AMQP-CPP` and `libevent` libraries. `libevent` is a high-performance event-driven networking library designed for asynchronous communication. It can provide efficient I/O multiplexing, timing event management, and signal processing. The `AMQP-CPP` library also supports the Boost.Asio (a C++ library for network and low-level I/O programming), `libev` (a high-performance C library for asynchronous I/O), and `libuv` (a C library for asynchronous I/O, used in Node.js) libraries.

In `producer.cpp`, event handling and opening the channel are implemented identically for both producer and consumer:

```
// omitted code
...
auto evbase = event_base_new();

AMQP::LibEventHandler handler(evbase);
AMQP::TcpConnection connection(
    &handler, AMQP::Address("amqp://guest:guest@localhost:5672/"));
AMQP::TcpChannel channel(&connection);

channel.onError([&evbase](const char *message) {
  std::cout << "Channel error: " << message << std::endl;
  event_base_loopbreak(evbase);
});
```

The exchange declaration is also identical for both:

```
auto exchange_name = "greet-exchange";
channel.declareExchange(exchange_name, AMQP::ExchangeType::direct);
```

Because AMQP is an asynchronous protocol by its nature, the code follows an **event-driven architecture (EDA)**, where every action happens in response to events. These events require handlers and event callbacks, which initiate the next actions in the workflow:

```
channel.confirmSelect()
    .onSuccess([&]() {
      auto routing_key = "greet-routing";
      channel.publish(exchange_name, routing_key,
                      "Tommy, Chuckie, Phil and Lil");
    })
    .onAck([&](uint64_t delivery_tag, bool multiple) {
      event_base_loopbreak(evbase);
    })
    .onNack([&](uint64_t delivery_tag, bool multiple, bool requeue) {
      event_base_loopbreak(evbase);
    });

event_base_dispatch(evbase);
event_base_free(evbase);
```

Here, the channel handles both successful and error events. Once the channel is successfully opened, it becomes possible to publish a message, which occurs in the corresponding event callback. The `ack` and `nack` events signal the successful processing of a previously sent message by the consumer. This approach allows for complex message processing scenarios, but in our simple example, both events result in the program termination.

The call to `event_base_dispatch(evbase)` starts the `libevent` loop, which waits for AMQP events and dispatches the appropriate callbacks. The loop gets broken inside those callbacks; otherwise, the program would continue running indefinitely. After the loop exits, `event_base_free(evbase)` performs the cleanup before termination.

In `consumer.cpp`, the consumer declares a queue and binds this queue to the exchange:

```
// omitted code
...
// common code
...

auto queue_name = "greet-queue";
channel.declareQueue(queue_name, AMQP::durable);

auto routing_key = "greet-routing";
channel.bindQueue(exchange_name, queue_name, routing_key);
```

The consumer then registers a handler to process incoming messages. It runs continuously and acknowledges that messages have been processed:

```
channel.consume(queue_name)
    .onReceived(
        [&channel](const AMQP::Message &msg, uint64_t tag, bool
                   redelivered) {
                                std::cout << "Received: " << std::string{
                                msg.body(), msg.bodySize()
                                }
                   << std::endl;
         channel.ack(tag);
        });
event_base_dispatch(evbase);
event_base_free(evbase);
```

Messaging is just one way for components to communicate. In many cases, especially when immediate responses are required, web services take center stage. Let's turn our attention to them in the next section.

Using web services

The common characteristic of web services is that they are based on standard web technologies. Most of the time, this will mean HTTP, which is the technology we will focus on. Although it is possible to implement web services based on different protocols, such services are extremely rare and therefore out of our scope.

Tools for working with web services

One of the major benefits of using HTTP as a transport is the wide availability of tools. For the most part, testing and debugging a web service may be performed using nothing more than a web browser. Apart from that, there are a lot of additional programs that may be helpful in automation. These include the following:

- The standard Unix file downloader, `wget`
- The modern HTTP client, `curl`
- Popular open source libraries such as `libcurl`, `curlpp`, `cpr` (C++ HTTP requests library), `cpp-httplib`, and Asio C++ Library
- Testing frameworks such as Appium, Cypress, K6, Locust, Playwright, Puppeteer, Selenium, and Robot Framework
- Browser extensions such as Wappalyzer, Percy, Lighthouse, and Firebug
- HTTP/API clients such as Bruno, Hoppscotch, Insomnia, and Postman
- Dedicated testing software, including SoapUI, Burp Suite, and Katalon Studio
- Packet analyzers such as Wireshark, HTTP Toolkit, and Fiddler

Web API payload formats

Microservices commonly expose APIs. These APIs make it possible to communicate with the microservices. Since the typical manner of communication utilizes computer networking, the most popular form of an API is the web (HTTP) API.

HTTP-based web services work by returning an HTTP response to an HTTP request that uses appropriate HTTP verbs (`GET`, `POST`, `PUT`, `PATCH`, `DELETE`, `HEAD`, `OPTIONS`, `TRACE`, and `CONNECT`). The semantics of how the request and the response should look and what data they should convey differ by style and technology.

Web services are often grouped by payload format: XML-based and JSON-based. JSON-based formats are currently displacing XML-based ones, but it is still common to find services that use XML formats.

Using JSON and XML to transmit data can be incredibly slow and expensive for bandwidth-constrained environments, such as in telecommunications. Data compression is an important way to improve website performance by reducing network bandwidth requirements. For this reason, the HTTP content-encoding algorithms—Gzip, Brotli, Zstandard, and Deflate—compress the payload to reduce its size. The algorithms vary in their compression speed and ratio.

Zstandard is better suited for dynamic content, while Brotli is for static, cacheable content. Gzip, based on Deflate, was designed in the early 1990s for providing high compression at the expense of CPU time on low-bandwidth networks. On high-bandwidth networks, Gzip may slow down applications, although due to its widespread use, this is the most widely supported compression algorithm.

For dealing with data encoded with either JSON or XML, additional tools such as `xmllint`, `xmlstarlet`, `jq`, and `libxml2` may be required.

Data formats such as **Protocol Buffers** (**Protobuf**), MessagePack, **Binary JSON** (BSON), **Universal Binary JSON** (UBJSON), Apache Avro, Apache Parquet, **Concise Binary Object Representation** (CBOR), and **Optimized Row Columnar** (ORC) are faster and more compact alternatives to JSON and XML, helping to optimize data serialization. A proper serialization strategy is important for ISC, EDA, and data storage. It optimizes performance and scalability, especially in distributed applications, and is crucial when working with large datasets or complex data structures that require efficient storage and transmission. Optimized, efficient serialization can be faster than unoptimized serialization plus compression, especially for smaller or less redundant data. However, data serialization is not a complete substitute for data compression.

XML-based web services

The earliest web services that gained traction were primarily based on XML. **XML**, or **eXtensible Markup Language**, was at the time the interchange format of choice in distributed computing and in the web environment. There were several different approaches to designing services with an XML payload. One of the earliest and most influential of these was XML-RPC.

It is possible that you may want to interact with existing XML-based web services that are developed either internally within your organization or externally. However, we advise you to implement new web services using more lightweight methods, such as JSON-based web services, RESTful web services, or gRPC.

XML-RPC and its relationship to SOAP

One of the first standards that emerged was called XML-RPC. The idea behind the project was to provide a **remote procedure call** (RPC) technology that would compete with the then-prevalent **Component Object Model** (COM) and **Common Object Request Broker Architecture** (CORBA). The aim was to use HTTP as a transport protocol and make the format human-readable and human-writable as well as parsable to machines. To achieve that, XML was chosen as the data encoding format.

When using XML-RPC, the client that wants to perform an RPC sends an HTTP request to the server. The request may have multiple parameters. The server answers with a single response. The XML-RPC protocol defines several data types for parameters and results.

Although SOAP features similar data types, it uses XML schema definitions, which make the messages much less readable than those in XML-RPC.

Since XML-RPC is no longer actively maintained, there aren't any modern C++ implementations for the standard. If you want to interact with XML-RPC web services from modern code, the best way could be to use the gSOAP toolkit, which supports XML-RPC and other XML web service standards. Overall, this toolkit is used rarely, especially in modern C++ projects, as SOAP-based services have been largely replaced by REST and other lightweight approaches.

The main criticism of XML-RPC was that it didn't give much value over sending plain XML requests and responses while making the messages significantly larger.

Over time, the standard evolved into SOAP, which formed the basis for the protocol stack of the **World Wide Web Consortium** (W3C).

SOAP

The original abbreviation of **SOAP** stood for **Simple Object Access Protocol**. The abbreviation was dropped in version 1.2 of the standard.

SOAP consists of three parts:

- **The SOAP envelope**, defining the message's structure and processing rules
- **The SOAP header** rules defining application-specific data types (optional)
- **The SOAP body**, which carries RPCs and responses

Here's an example SOAP message using HTTP as transport:

```
POST /FindMerchants HTTP/1.1
Host: www.domifair.org
Content-Type: application/soap+xml; charset=utf-8
Content-Length: 345
SOAPAction: "http://www.w3.org/2003/05/soap-envelope"

<?xml version="1.0"?>
<soap:Envelope xmlns:soap="http://www.w3.org/2003/05/soap-envelope">
 <soap:Header>
```

```
    </soap:Header>
    <soap:Body xmlns:m="https://www.domifair.org">
        <m:FindMerchants>
            <m:Lat>54.350989</m:Lat>
            <m:Long>18.6548168</m:Long>
            <m:Distance>200</m:Distance>
        </m:FindMerchants>
    </soap:Body>
</soap:Envelope>
```

The example uses standard HTTP headers and the `POST` method to call a remote procedure to find merchants within a certain distance of a given geographic location. One header that is unique to SOAP is `SOAPAction`. It points to a **uniform resource identifier** (**URI**) identifying the intent of the action. It is up to the clients to decide how to interpret this URI.

`soap:Header` is optional, so we leave it empty. Together with `soap:Body`, it is contained within `soap:Envelope`. The main procedure call takes place within `soap:Body`. We introduce our own XML namespace that is specific to the hypothetical *St. Dominic's Fair* application. The namespace points to the root of our domain. The procedure we call is `FindMerchants`, and we provide three arguments: latitude, longitude, and distance.

As SOAP was designed to be extensible, transport-neutral, and independent of the programming model, it also led to the creation of other accompanying standards. This means it is usually necessary to learn all the related standards and protocols before using SOAP. Typically, this protocol is used in conjunction with **Web Services Description Language** (**WSDL**).

Learning about the related standards and protocols is not a problem if your application makes extensive use of XML and your development team is familiar with all the terms and specifications. However, if all you want is to expose an API for a third party, a much easier approach would be to build a REST API, as it is much easier to learn for both producers and consumers.

Unfortunately, due to the verbosity of the messages, the size and bandwidth requirements for SOAP services are generally huge. If this is not an issue, then SOAP can have its uses. It allows for both synchronous and asynchronous calls, as well as stateful and stateless operations. If you require rigid, formal means of communication, SOAP can provide it. Just make sure to use version 1.2 of the protocol due to the many improvements it introduces. One of them is the enhanced security of the services. Another is the improved definition of services themselves, which aids interoperability, and the ability to formally define the means of transportation (allowing for the usage of message queues), to name just a few.

SOAP gained popularity as a communication protocol for distributed computing in the mid-2000s, with dozens of implementations available in various programming languages, including Java, C/C++, .NET, Perl, and PHP. The term *web service* became popular at that time thanks to standards such as SOAP and XML-RPC, which enabled machine-to-machine communication over the internet. Within 10 years, SOAP had virtually disappeared as no one was writing new services using the protocol anymore, having been supplanted by REST and JSON.

The most significant drawback of SOAP is that both the request and the response can be practically unreadable due to the large amount of data and the XML format itself. Moreover, JSON parsing is typically faster and less memory-intensive compared to XML parsing because JSON has a simpler structure and can be directly converted to the native data types of most programming languages.

In the following sections, we'll cover a few supporting standards and tools that typically accompany SOAP. To use SOAP effectively, it's important to understand these.

WSDL

WSDL provides a machine-readable description of how services can be called and how messages should be formed. Like the other W3C web services standards, it is encoded in XML.

It is often used with SOAP to define interfaces that the web service offers and how they may be used.

Once you define your API in WSDL, you may (and should!) use automated tooling to help you create code out of it. For C++, one framework with such tools is gSOAP. It comes with a tool named `wsdl2h`, which will generate a header file out of the definition. You can then use another tool, `soapcpp2`, to generate bindings from the interface definition to your implementation.

UDDI

The next step after documenting the web service interfaces is service discovery, which allows applications to find and connect to the services implemented by other parties.

Universal Description, Discovery, and Integration (**UDDI**) is a registry for WSDL files that may be searched manually or automatically. As with the other technologies discussed in this section, UDDI uses an XML format.

UDDI registry may be queried with SOAP messages for automated service discovery. Even though UDDI provided the logical extensions of WSDL, its adoption on the open internet was disappointing. However, it is still possible to find UDDI systems used internally by companies.

SOAP libraries

Two of the most popular libraries for SOAP are **Apache Axis** and **gSOAP**.

Apache Axis is suitable for implementing both SOAP (including WSDL) and REST web services. It's worth noting that the library hasn't seen a new release for over a decade.

gSOAP is a toolkit that allows for creating and interacting with XML-based web services with a focus on SOAP. It handles data binding, SOAP and WSDL support, JSON and RSS parsing, UDDI APIs, and several other related web services standards. Although it doesn't use modern C++ features, it is still actively maintained.

JSON-based web services

JSON stands for **JavaScript Object Notation**. Contrary to what the name suggests, it is not limited to JavaScript. It is language-independent. Parsers and serializers for JSON exist in most programming languages. However, its syntax is derived from JavaScript as it was based on a JavaScript subset.

It is noteworthy that JSON is much more compact than XML.

Supported data types for JSON are the following:

- **Number:** The exact format may vary between implementations; defaults to the double-precision floating-point in JavaScript
- **String:** Unicode-encoded text
- **Boolean:** `true` or `false` values
- **Array:** an ordered list of values, which may be empty
- **Object:** A map with key-value pairs
- `null`: Representing an empty value

The `Packer` configuration presented in *Chapter 11, Continuous Integration and Continuous Deployment*, is an example of a JSON document:

```
{
  "variables": {
    "aws_access_key": "",
    "aws_secret_key": ""
  },
  "builders": [{
    "type": "amazon-ebs",
    "access_key": "{{user `aws_access_key`}}",
    "secret_key": "{{user `aws_secret_key`}}",
    "region": "eu-central-1",
    "source_ami": "ami-0265dc4673f9d6a35",
    "instance_type": "t2.micro",
    "ssh_username": "admin",
    "ami_name": "Project's Base Image {{timestamp}}"
  }],
  "provisioners": [{
    "type": "ansible",
    "playbook_file": "./provision.yml",
    "user": "admin",
    "host_alias": "baseimage"
  }],
  "post-processors": [{
    "type": "manifest",
    "output": "manifest.json",
    "strip_path": true
  }]
}
```

One of the standards using JSON as a format is the JSON-RPC protocol.

JSON-RPC

JSON-RPC is a JSON-encoded RPC protocol similar to XML-RPC and SOAP. Unlike its XML predecessor, it requires little overhead. It is also very simple while maintaining the human-readability of XML-RPC.

This is how our previous example, expressed in a SOAP call, will look with JSON-RPC 2.0:

```
{
  "jsonrpc": "2.0",
  "method": "FindMerchants",
  "params": {
    "lat": "54.350989",
    "long": "18.6548168",
    "distance": 200
  },
  "id": 1
}
```

This JSON document still requires proper HTTP headers, but even with the headers, it is still considerably smaller than the XML counterpart. The only metadata present is the file with the JSON-RPC version and the request ID. The `method` and `params` fields are pretty much self-explanatory. The same can't always be said about SOAP.

However, even though the protocol is lightweight, easy to implement, and easy to use, it hasn't seen widespread adoption when compared to both SOAP and REST web services. It was released much later than SOAP and around the same time that REST services started to get popular. While REST quickly rose to success (possibly due to its flexibility), JSON-RPC failed to get similar traction.

C++ implementations of JSON-RPC include `jsonrpc-cpp-lib`, `jsonrpc2` (a C++23 header-only library), `jsonrpcpp`, `libjson-rpc-cpp`, and `json-rpc-cxx`. `json-rpc-cxx` is a modern reimplementation of `libjson-rpc-cpp`. The JSON-RPC protocol is simple and can be implemented, for example, using a more popular library such as `nlohmann/json` (JSON for modern C++).

For instance, Sony uses the JSON-RPC protocol over the REST API as a lightweight protocol for making RPCs over a network to enable communication and control of its devices, such as BRAVIA professional displays and cameras.

Web API design approaches

Two widely used approaches to build HTTP APIs are **Representational State Transfer** (**REST**) and **GraphQL**; we cover both in this section. While REST is an architectural style, Graph QL is a query-language-based API paradigm.

REST

REST is currently the most popular API architecture for web services and microservice-based systems due to its simplicity and ease of use, scalability, flexibility, caching support, and compatibility with various technologies. Services that conform to this architectural style are often called RESTful services.

The main difference between REST and SOAP or JSON-RPC is that REST is based almost entirely on HTTP and URI semantics.

Roy Fielding, the creator of REST, described the REST approach back in 2000 in his dissertation titled *Architectural Styles and the Design of Network-based Software Architectures*:

> *The name "Representational State Transfer" is intended to evoke an image of how a well-designed Web application behaves: a network of web pages (a virtual state-machine), where the user progresses through the application by selecting links (state transitions), resulting in the next page (representing the next state of the application) being transferred to the user and rendered for their use.*

REST is an API architectural style defining a set of constraints for implementing web services. These constraints are as follows:

- **Client–server architecture**: It enforces a clear separation between the client and the server. The client requests data, and the server provides it. This separation improves system scalability and allows clients to operate independently of server logic.
- **Statelessness**: Neither the client nor the server needs to store the state related to their communication.
- **Cacheability**: Responses should be defined as cacheable or non-cacheable to take advantage of standard web caching, which is achieved using the `Cache-Control` and `ETag` (entity tag) HTTP headers. This improves scalability and performance by reducing server load and accelerating data fetching.
- **Layered system**: The architecture can include multiple layers, such as load balancers, proxy servers, and authentication systems, where each layer performs its own function and is independent of the others. It increases the system's reliability and flexibility.
- **Uniform interface**: It simplifies and decouples the architecture, allowing each part to evolve independently. It consists of four sub-constraints:
    - **Resource identification (in requests)**: Each resource has a unique, consistent URI. URIs should be simple and predictable. They should represent nouns (resources), not verbs (actions).
    - **Manipulation of resources through representations:** A representation is the current or desired state of a resource and is used to perform actions on the resource. Standardized HTTP methods ensure consistent and predictable communication.
    - **Self-descriptive messages:** The request and response must contain all the information necessary for their processing.

    - **Hypermedia as the Engine of Application State (HATEOAS)**: This guides clients to discover actions via hypermedia links provided by the server. It allows clients to dynamically locate and interact with resources on the server without having prior knowledge of all possible URLs and actions. The server provides (in responses) not only data but also links to related resources and possible actions, which increases the loose coupling and flexibility of the API.
- **Code on demand (optional)**: It sends executable code (for example, JavaScript and WebAssembly) to the client for execution.

REST APIs must be hypertext-driven, but Fielding explained that simply calling a service over HTTP does not make it RESTful. Nevertheless, HATEOAS isn't always implemented due to its complexity, which can slow down development, especially in simple APIs where clients can safely use hardcoded routes. Developers often prefer faster, non-HATEOAS methods where navigation is not an issue.

Due to reliance on web standards, RESTful web services can reuse existing components such as proxies, load balancers, and the cache. Thanks to the low overhead, such services are also very performant and efficient.

REST uses HTTP as the transport protocol with URIs representing resources and HTTP verbs used to manipulate the resources or invoke operations. There is no standard regarding how each HTTP method should behave, but the semantics most often agreed on are the following:

- `POST`: Create a new resource
- `GET`: Retrieve an existing resource
- `PATCH`: Update an existing resource
- `DELETE`: Delete an existing resource
- `PUT`: Replace an existing resource

Because REST is resource-oriented, its URL design differs from RPC-style APIs. In REST, HTTP requests target *resources* rather than *actions*. A **uniform resource locator** (**URL**) points to a resource, and the HTTP method indicates what to do with this resource, making the verbs in a URL meaningless and not RESTful.

A resource can be any entity accessed via a REST API, for example, a user, a product, an order, a document, a ticket, an image, or a calculation result. One resource can represent multiple items. A group of resources is called a collection. Resources can also be nested within other resources. In some cases, a resource is a singleton and has no parent collection.

An example of a collection is `items`, and `123` is the ID of a resource in that collection:

```
https://localhost:8080/api/items/123
```

Although the REST architectural style doesn't impose strict restrictions on the format of transferred data, certain standards have emerged in practice. REST APIs can use a variety of formats, such as XML, YAML, and even plain text. However, JSON is the undisputed leader due to its simplicity and easy-to-read syntax, understandable by both humans and machines.

Just like with XML-based web services, RESTful services can be described in both a machine- and human-readable way. There are a few competing standards available for this, with OpenAPI being the most popular. (It is noteworthy that OpenAPI describes HTTP APIs, not only REST.)

Currently, some of the most performant C++ frameworks for implementing HTTP APIs in C++ are Lithium, Drogon, `ffead-cpp`, `userver`, and Cutelyst (built on top of Qt). These frameworks perform well in the TechEmpower Web Framework Benchmarks.

Often, the REST API is used as a proxy to records in a database. **CRUD** (**create, read, update, and delete**) operations frequently map to REST operations, but the concepts are not identical. Due to the similarities between REST and CRUD, it is easy to confuse them and mistake one for the other. REST and CRUD can work together because CRUD functions can exist in the REST architecture.

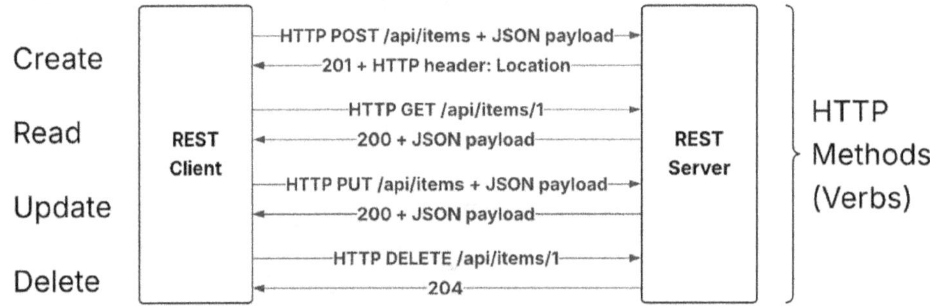

Figure 15.6: CRUD operations and REST

The figure shows the relationship between CRUD functions and the REST endpoints at the API level. However, the following implementation provides a simple RESTful controller that exposes the full set of CRUD operations for the `items` resource—create, read, update, and delete.

The read operation (`GET`) returns either all records from the collection or just one by its ID:

```
// omitted code
...
using namespace drogon;

class ItemsController final : public HttpController<ItemsController> {
public:
  METHOD_LIST_BEGIN
  // list of items
  ADD_METHOD_TO(ItemsController::getItems, "/api/items", Get);
  // create new item
  ADD_METHOD_TO(ItemsController::createItem, "/api/items", Post);
  // view an item
  ADD_METHOD_TO(ItemsController::getItemById, "/api/items/{1}", Get);
  // update an item
  ADD_METHOD_TO(ItemsController::updateItem, "/api/items/{1}", Put);
```

```
// delete an item
ADD_METHOD_TO(ItemsController::deleteItem, "/api/items/{1}", Delete);
METHOD_LIST_END
```

This implementation is simplified. In practice, REST APIs typically provide filtering, sorting, and pagination of requested data. Pagination is the process of breaking large amounts of data into smaller, more manageable chunks for paginated data queries. This improves usability and performance by preventing a single page from becoming overwhelmed with too much content and reducing server load.

The `getItems` method locks the repository by applying a scoped `std::lock_guard` until the function finishes because the data can be modified by a competing request to the web server. The HTTP code `200 (OK)` is returned by default:

```
void getItems(const HttpRequestPtr &,
              std::function<void(const HttpResponsePtr &)> &&callback) {
  Json::Value array(Json::arrayValue);
  std::lock_guard lock(storage_mutex_);

  for (const auto &[id, name] : items_) {
    Json::Value item;
    item["id"] = id;
    item["name"] = name;
    array.append(item);
  }

  auto resp = HttpResponse::newHttpJsonResponse(array);
  callback(resp);
}
```

The `createItem` method locks the repository only when the entry is being made and emplaced in the storage. REST APIs typically return HTTP status code `201 (Created)` and either the absolute or relative location of the created entry in the collection:

```
void createItem(const HttpRequestPtr &req,
                std::function<void(const HttpResponsePtr &)> &&callback) {
  auto json = req->getJsonObject();

  if (!json || !json->isMember("name")) {
    auto resp = HttpResponse::newHttpResponse();
    resp->setStatusCode(k400BadRequest);
    resp->setBody("No name");
    callback(resp);
    return;
```

```
    }

    int id;
    auto name = (*json)["name"].asString();
    {
      std::lock_guard lock(storage_mutex_);

      items_.emplace(id = ++next_id_, name);
    }

    Json::Value result;
    result["id"] = id;
    result["name"] = name;

    auto resp = HttpResponse::newHttpJsonResponse(result);
    resp->setStatusCode(k201Created);
    resp->addHeader("Location", "/api/items/" + std::to_string(id));
    callback(resp);
  }
```

The `getItemById` method locks the repository only when searching for an entry in the storage:

```
  void getItemById(const HttpRequestPtr &,
                   std::function<void(const HttpResponsePtr &)> &&callback,
                   int id) {
    auto item = [this, id]() -> std::optional<std::pair<int, std::string>> {
      std::lock_guard lock(storage_mutex_);

      if (const auto it = items_.find(id); it != items_.end()) {
        return {{it->first, it->second}};
      }
      return std::nullopt;
    }();

    if (!item.has_value()) {
      auto resp = HttpResponse::newHttpResponse();
      resp->setStatusCode(k404NotFound);
      callback(resp);
      return;
    }

    Json::Value json;
```

```
    json["id"] = item->first;
    json["name"] = item->second;

    auto resp = HttpResponse::newHttpJsonResponse(json);
    callback(resp);
  }
```

The `updateItem` method locks the repository only when updating an existing entry in the repository:

```
  void updateItem(const HttpRequestPtr &req,
                  std::function<void(const HttpResponsePtr &)> &&callback,
                  int id) {
    auto json = req->getJsonObject();
    if (!json || !json->isMember("name")) {
      auto resp = HttpResponse::newHttpResponse();
      resp->setStatusCode(k400BadRequest);
      resp->setBody("No name");
      callback(resp);
      return;
    }

    auto item = [this, id,
                 json]() -> std::optional<std::pair<int, std::string>> {
      std::lock_guard lock(storage_mutex_);

      if (const auto it = items_.find(id); it != items_.end()) {
        it->second = (*json)["name"].asString();
        return {{it->first, it->second}};
      }
      return std::nullopt;
    }();

    if (!item.has_value()) {
      auto resp = HttpResponse::newHttpResponse();
      resp->setStatusCode(k404NotFound);
      callback(resp);
      return;
    }

    Json::Value result;
    result["id"] = item->first;
    result["name"] = item->second;
```

```
    auto resp = HttpResponse::newHttpJsonResponse(result);
    callback(resp);
  }
```

The `deleteItem` method locks the repository only when deleting an entry in the repository. The function returns HTTP code `204 (No Content)` because the entry no longer exists and there is nothing to return:

```
  void deleteItem(const HttpRequestPtr &,
                  std::function<void(const HttpResponsePtr &)> &&callback,
                  int id) {
    auto item = [this, id]() -> std::optional<int> {
      std::lock_guard lock(storage_mutex_);

      if (const auto it = items_.find(id); it != items_.end()) {
        items_.erase(it);
        return {it->first};
      }
      return std::nullopt;
    }();

    auto resp = HttpResponse::newHttpResponse();
    if (!item.has_value()) {
      resp->setStatusCode(k404NotFound);
      callback(resp);
      return;
    }

    resp->setStatusCode(k204NoContent);
    callback(resp);
  }

private:
  std::unordered_map<int, std::string> items_;
  int next_id_ = 0;
  std::mutex storage_mutex_;
};
```

Of course, REST APIs can also use other HTTP status codes indicating success, request redirection, client, and server errors.

HATEOAS

Although providing a binary interface, such as a *gRPC-based* one, can give you great performance, in many cases, you'll still want to have the simplicity of a RESTful interface. HATEOAS can be a useful principle to implement if you want an intuitive REST-based API.

Metaphorically, HATEOAS can be described as follows: "Web services are people too, and they also want to follow links, just like real people do, using HTTP/HTML." In other words, it's a kind of hypertext for REST clients. The key to understanding HATEOAS is surprisingly simple: every response received contains a reference to the next request.

> *When I say hypertext, I mean the simultaneous presentation of information and controls such that the information becomes the affordance through which the user (or automaton) obtains choices and selects actions. Hypermedia is just an expansion on what text means to include temporal anchors within a media stream; most researchers have dropped the distinction.*
>
> *– Roy Fielding, REST APIs Must Be Hypertext-Driven, 2008*

Just as you would open a web page and navigate based on the hypermedia shown, you can write your services with HATEOAS to achieve the same thing. This promotes the decoupling of server and client code and allows a client to quickly know what requests are valid to send, which is often not the case with binary APIs. The discovery is dynamic and based on the hypermedia provided.

If a REST client must hardcode all resource URLs, it is tightly coupled to your service's implementation. However, if the server returns URLs for the available actions, the client is loosely coupled. In this case, there is no strict dependency on the URI structure, as it is specified in and used from the response.

If you take a typical RESTful service, when executing an operation, you get JSON with data such as an object's state. With HATEOAS, aside from that, you would get a list of links (URLs) showing you the valid operations you can run on said object. These links (hypermedia) are the engine of the application. In other words, the available actions are determined by the state of the resources. While the term *hypermedia* may sound strange in this context, it basically means linking to the resources, including text, images, and video.

For example, suppose we have a REST method that allows us to add an item by using the `PUT` method. With HATEOAS, we can not only return the created object, but we can also add a return parameter that links to the resource created. If we use JSON for serialization, this could take the following form:

```
{
    "itemId": 8,
    "name": "Sękacz",
    "locationId": 5,
    "links": [
        {
            "href": "item/8",
            "rel": "items",
```

```
            "type": "GET"
        }
    ]
}
```

When developing a RESTful service, you must specify how to return both the data and links that match the request. **Hypertext Application Language (HAL)** is one convention for defining hypermedia links within JSON or XML code.

There is no universally accepted method of serializing HATEOAS hypermedia. On the one hand, it makes it easier to implement regardless of the server implementation. On the other hand, the client needs to know how to parse the response to find the relevant traversal data.

One of the benefits of HATEOAS is that it makes it possible to implement the API changes on the server side without necessarily breaking the client code. When one of the endpoints gets renamed, the new endpoint is referenced in subsequent responses, so the client is informed where to direct further requests.

The same mechanism may provide features such as paging or make it easy to discover methods available for a given object. Getting back to our item example, here's a possible response we could receive after making a `GET` request:

```
{
    "itemId": 8,
    "name": "Sękacz",
    "locationId": 5,
    "stock": 8,
    "links": [
        {
            "href": "item/8",
            "rel": "items",
            "type" : "GET"
        },
        {
            "href": "item/8",
            "rel": "items",
            "type" : "POST"
        },
        {
            "href": "item/8/increaseStock",
            "rel": "increaseStock",
            "type" : "POST"
        },
        {
```

```
            "href": "item/8/decreaseStock",
            "rel": "decreaseStock",
            "type" : "POST"
        }
    ]
}
```

Here, we have links to two methods responsible for modifying the stock.

If the stock is no longer available, the response changes accordingly (note that one of the methods is no longer advertised):

```
{
    "itemId": 8,
    "name": "Sękacz",
    "locationId": 5,
    "stock": 0,
    "links": [
        {
            "href": "items/8",
            "rel": "items",
            "type" : "GET"
        },
        {
            "href": "items/8",
            "rel": "items",
            "type" : "POST"
        },
        {
            "href": "items/8/increaseStock",
            "rel": "increaseStock",
            "type" : "POST"
        }
    ]
}
```

Adding traversable hypermedia would be much easier to consume if it were always presented in the same format. However, the freedom of expression here makes it harder to write clients unaware of the server's implementation. Even so, HATEOAS remains a core constraint of the REST application architecture.

GraphQL

The **QL** in the name stands for **Query Language**. Rather than relying on the server to serialize and present the necessary data, in GraphQL, clients query and manipulate the data directly because it allows clients to define the structure of responses. This solves the problem of over-fetching or under-fetching data, which is typical for REST.

Apart from this reversal of responsibility, GraphQL also features mechanisms that make it easier to work with data: strong typing, static validation, introspection, and schemas are all parts of the specification.

Figure 15.7 shows the difference between GraphQL and REST:

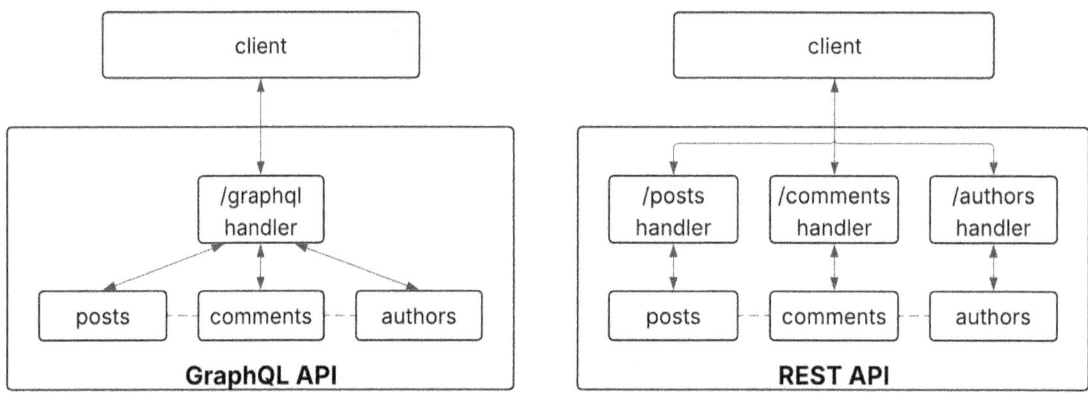

Figure 15.7: GraphQL versus REST

The main difference between GraphQL and REST API is that when using GraphQL, a client can get all the data with just one request, even if the data is located in different sources, whereas when using REST API, several requests must be made to process the data from the responses. GraphQL uses a single URL endpoint and is suitable for large, complex, and interrelated data sources. REST uses multiple endpoints to define resources and is well-suited for simple data sources where resources are well-defined.

GraphQL was originally developed as an internal Facebook project around 2012. This influenced the design because GraphQL is best suited to a graph data model, which aligns with the structure of the social network itself. Query languages used to manage graph data (such as **GQL—Graph Query Language**) define how to retrieve data modeled as a graph, defining the data manipulation capabilities of graph **database management systems** (**DBMSs**). GraphQL can return such a complex data graph with a single network request.

GraphQL requires declarations of schemas that define data types and relations between them. It allows the server to validate a client request, as all schemas are strongly typed.

Data operations in GraphQL are implemented through different types of requests:

- **Query**: Read-only data retrieval
- **Mutation**: Creating and changing data

- **Subscriptions:** Receiving real-time backend updates from the server, which is typical for online exchanges and online games, most commonly over WebSocket (a network protocol providing a persistent bidirectional connection between the client and the server)

However, the REST API remains the *golden mean*: it is simpler and more flexible than SOAP, and more standardized in terms of HTTP usage and caching than GraphQL.

GraphQL has its own disadvantages:

- **Steep learning curve:** Developers must master **Schema Definition Language** (SDL), resolvers, and over-query protection mechanisms.
- **Increased server load:** Complex nested queries may require multiple round-trips to data sources. Without limiting the depth and complexity of a request, it is easy to overload the server.
- **Security risks:** Developers must implement protection against **distributed denial of service (DDoS)**, field-level authorization, authentication, and auditing. GraphQL doesn't manage data access by default. All access checks must be implemented in resolvers, which complicates maintenance and increases the risk of errors.
- **Resolver reliability:** Errors or delays in one resolver can affect the entire chain of fields in the request. A resolver is a function responsible for populating a single field in the schema with data.
- **Complexity in caching:** Standard HTTP caching is less effective, but custom caching can be difficult to configure. For implementing caching, it is necessary to use additional solutions: proxies, custom cache keys, or client libraries. Since all GraphQL queries are sent to a single HTTP endpoint, it is impossible to use URL-level caching, as in REST.
- **Monitoring difficulty:** Due to the implementation via POST/HTTP, it is necessary to analyze specific requests to understand what exactly does not work properly.
- **Versioning complexity:** In REST, it is enough to add a new URL and disable the old one later, whereas GraphQL is built around the philosophy of schema evolution, which requires more careful planning.
- **N+1 problem:** This occurs when retrieving related data requires making many additional database queries (instead of one or two), which can severely impact performance—for example, when a list additionally requests related resources for each item in the list. Such an application will work fine on localhost, but it will become a disaster if the application and its database are deployed on different servers, since network lag is never zero. In *Chapter 4, Architectural and System Design Patterns*, there is a link to a cautionary story called *How millisecond delays may kill database performance*.

There are implementations of GraphQL available for a lot of languages, including C++. One of the popular schema-service generators for C++ is `cppgraphqlgen` from Microsoft. There are also many tools that help with development and debugging throughout the GraphQL workflow. What's interesting is that you can use GraphQL to query the database directly thanks to products such as Hasura or PostGraphile, which add the GraphQL API on top of a Postgres database.

GUI tools for GraphQL include GraphiQL, GraphQL Voyager, Apollo Studio, Insomnia, Altair, and Postman.

Let's now look at a minimal end-to-end example of a GraphQL API.

First, we'll define a schema. `schema.graphql` is a GraphQL schema written in SDL. It defines the GraphQL API by specifying the available data types, as well as the operations and their arguments, including a `Query` type with the `name` field of a non-null `String` type (`String!`):

```
schema {
  query: Query
}

type Query {
  name: String!
}
```

Next, `query.graphql` defines a request sent to the API and written in the GraphQL query language, where `query` is the operation type (a GraphQL query), `GetName` is the name of the operation, and `name` is the field of the `Query` type being requested:

```
query GetName {
  name
}
```

The server and client are based on the Drogon framework and `cppgraphqlgen`, with the `rapidjson` library used for JSON handling. The `cppgraphqlgen` library can use custom JSON libraries, but this requires defining the appropriate classes and their methods as described in its manual.

The `schemagen` and `clientgen` library utilities can generate server and client types, respectively, based on schemas and queries such as those presented previously. `schemagen` requires only a schema definition, but `clientgen` additionally requires a request document.

The server implementation includes the `GraphQLController` class, which is an HTTP controller that exposes a single GraphQL endpoint. In GraphQL, everything flows through a single entry point, which, in this example, is the `/graphql` HTTP endpoint, defined in `GraphQLController.h`:

```
// omitted code
...
class GraphQLController : public drogon::HttpController<GraphQLController> {
public:
  METHOD_LIST_BEGIN
  ADD_METHOD_TO(GraphQLController::handleGraphQL, "/graphql",
                drogon::Post);
  METHOD_LIST_END

  void handleGraphQL(
      const drogon::HttpRequestPtr &req,
      std::function<void(const drogon::HttpResponsePtr &)> &&callback);
```

```
};
```

Here, `GraphQLController` registers a single `POST` handler at `/graphql`. All GraphQL requests are sent to this endpoint and handled by `handleGraphQL`.

The implementation from `GraphQLController.cpp` uses types generated by `cppgraphqlgen` from the earlier `schema.graphql` and `query.graphql` files, and provides a simple server-side implementation of the `Query` type:

```
// omitted code
...
// generated types
#include "QueryObject.h"
#include "ServiceSchema.h"
```

The `QueryImpl` class is a server-side implementation of the `Query` type specified in `schema.graphql`. The `getName` method provides the value for the `name` field defined in the schema:

```
class QueryImpl {
public:
  static std::string getName() { return "Jack Mower, Tina and Umagon"; }
};

void GraphQLController::handleGraphQL(
    const drogon::HttpRequestPtr &req,
    std::function<void(const drogon::HttpResponsePtr &)> &&callback) {
  auto jsonBody = req->getJsonObject();
  if (!jsonBody) {
    auto resp =
        drogon::HttpResponse::newHttpJsonResponse(Json::Value("Invalid JSON"));
    resp->setStatusCode(drogon::k400BadRequest);
    callback(resp);
    return;
  }
```

Request parameters of the GraphQL query are extracted from the request in JSON format:

```
  std::string query = (*jsonBody)["query"].asString();
  std::string operationName = jsonBody->get("operationName", "").asString();

  auto queryImpl = std::make_shared<QueryImpl>();
  graphql::greet::Operations operations(queryImpl);

  auto ast = graphql::peg::parseString(query);
```

```
    graphql::service::RequestResolveParams params{ast};
    params.operationName = operationName;
```

The operations object resolves the query by calling the getName function of the queryImpl class. It is an object of the generated class:

```
    auto result = operations.resolve(std::move(params)).get();
```

After this, the result is converted to JSON format and sent to the client:

```
    std::string jsonString = graphql::response::toJSON(std::move(result));

    Json::Value jsonResult;
    Json::CharReaderBuilder builder;
    std::istringstream iss(jsonString);
    Json::String errs;
    Json::parseFromStream(builder, iss, &jsonResult, &errs);

    auto resp = drogon::HttpResponse::newHttpJsonResponse(jsonResult);
    callback(resp);
  }
```

The client implementation is much simpler than that of the server.

The following code shows the client application's main file (main.cpp), which initializes the HTTP client and sends a GraphQL request:

```
  // omitted code
  ...
  // generated types
  #include "ServiceClient.h"

  int main() {
    auto client = HttpClient::newHttpClient("http://localhost:8080");
```

The JSON query includes the GetName operation specified in query.graphql. The GetRequestText and GetOperationName functions are generated automatically:

```
    Json::Value requestBody;
    requestBody["query"] =
        graphql::client::query::GetName::  GetRequestText();
    requestBody["operationName"] =
        graphql::client::query::GetName::GetOperationName();

    auto req = HttpRequest::newHttpJsonRequest(requestBody);
```

```
    req->setMethod(Post);
    req->setPath("/graphql");
    req->addHeader("Content-Type", "application/json");
```

The client sends a request and processes its response inside the callback:

```
    client->sendRequest(req, [](
            ReqResult result, const HttpResponsePtr &resp
    ) {
      if (result == ReqResult::Ok && resp) {
        auto jsonResponse = resp->getJsonObject();
        graphql::response::Value gqlResponse(graphql::response::Type::Map);
        auto data = (*jsonResponse)["data"];
        auto parsedResponse =
        graphql::response::parseJSON(data.toStyledString());
```

The `parseResponse` function is also generated. It converts the JSON response into strongly typed C++ objects that correspond to the fields defined in `query.graphql`:

```
        auto response = graphql::client::query::GetName:: parseResponse(
            std::move(parsedResponse));
```

The `name` field is specified in `query.graphql`, but its type is defined in `schema.graphql`:

```
        std::cout << "Name: " << response.name << std::endl;
      } else {
        std::cerr << "Request failed" << std::endl;
      }

      app().quit();
    });

    app().run();

    return 0;
  }
```

This completes the example. The client sends a GraphQL request, the server resolves it using the auto-generated GraphQL types, and the response is returned to the client as a strongly typed C++ object.

API description languages

API description languages are also called API specification formats. These provide a structured and machine-readable way to describe an API and can serve as executable contracts between teams.

Contract-driven development uses API specifications such as OpenAPI, AsyncAPI, gRPC proto files, GraphQL, and WSDL as executable contracts. Without going into detail, this approach includes negotiating contracts before development, facilitating parallel development, and accelerating the speed and quality of testing.

OpenAPI and AsyncAPI follow the API-first design, which is based on the principle that when designing an API, a document is created first before writing code. In this workflow, the OpenAPI and AsyncAPI documents are the API contracts.

Creating the API design in the beginning has several advantages. Many errors are discovered at the design stage. Moreover, documentation provides an understanding of how to use your API. Further, the development of the API client and server, as well as testing, can be carried out in parallel, which speeds up development. This requires a well-thought-out set of examples and a clear API description. An API specification simplifies the creation of test cases, which ensures higher overall software quality. Besides, API tests can also be created based on specifications.

OpenAPI and AsyncAPI are useful not only for contract-driven development, but also for contract testing, which sits between unit testing and integration testing in the testing pyramid.

OpenAPI

OpenAPI is a specification overseen by the OpenAPI Initiative, part of the Linux Foundation. It used to be known as the Swagger Specification, as it used to be a part of the Swagger framework.

The specification is language-agnostic. It uses JSON or YAML input to generate documentation of methods, parameters, and models. By doing so, OpenAPI helps to keep the documentation and source code up to date. There is a wide selection of tools compatible with OpenAPI, such as code generators, editors, user interfaces, and mock servers.

OpenAPI generators follow the OpenAPI specifications when generating server stubs, API client libraries (SDK generation), and documentation. They support various programming languages, in particular C++, C#, Go, Java, JavaScript, PHP, Python, Rust, and Swift. A big plus is that IDEs such as Clion and Visual Studio (via plugins) support code generation based on OpenAPI specifications. Unfortunately, the code generators for C++ are somewhat outdated and require upgrading.

The online OpenAPI editor is available here: `https://editor.swagger.io/`.

To illustrate how an API is defined using OpenAPI, consider the following minimal YAML specification of a greeting service for a simple echo-style HTTP server:

```
openapi: 3.0.4
info:
  title: Greet API
  version: 2.0.0
paths:
```

```
/customer/v1:
  get:
    operationId: greet
    summary: Greet customers
    parameters:
      - name: name
        in: query
        description: Customer name
        schema:
          type: string
    responses:
      '200':
        description: OK
        content:
          application/json:
            schema:
              type: object
              properties:
                status:
                  type: integer
                response:
                  type: string
              example:
                status: 200
                response: Hi, Scott
      '400':
        description: Bad Request
        content:
          application/json:
            schema:
              type: object
              properties:
                status:
                  type: integer
                response:
                  type: string
              example:
                status: 400
                response: No name
```

The first two fields (openapi and info) are metadata describing the document. The paths field contains all the possible paths that correspond to the resources and methods of the REST interface. In the preceding example, we are only documenting a single path (/customer/v1) and a single method (GET). This method takes name as an optional parameter. We provide two possible response codes: 200 (OK) and 400 (Bad Request). Both responses contain bodies formatted as JSON documents. The value associated with the example key is the example payload of a response.

Swagger UI is a web application used to visualize an OpenAPI specification in an interactive user interface, send requests to the server, and receive responses. This web application can be integrated with a web service as static files on the server or through a **content delivery network** (CDN) such as global UNPKG, because Swagger UI is a JavaScript application.

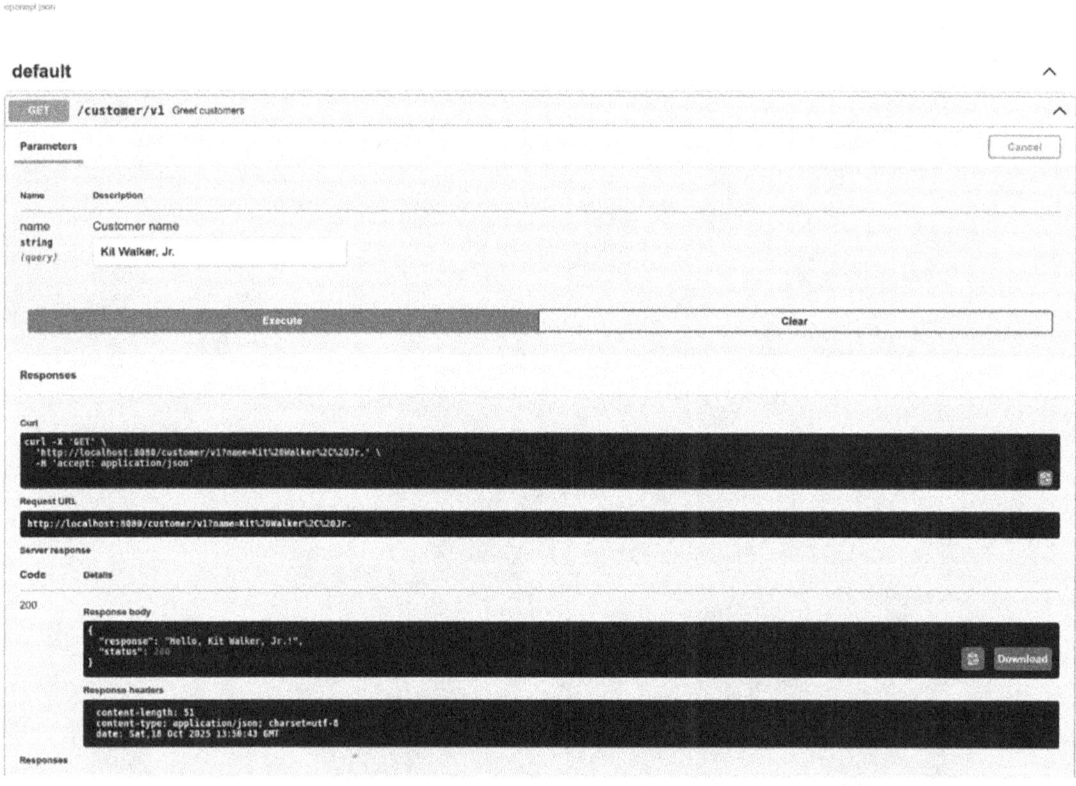

Figure 15.8: An overview of the Swagger UI interface

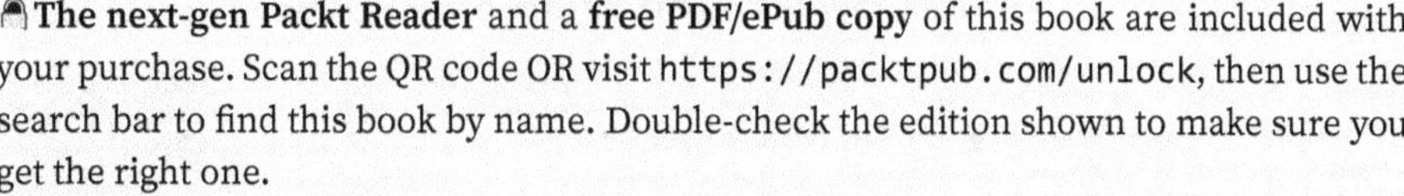

🔍**Quick tip:** Need to see a high-resolution version of this image? Open this book in the next-gen Packt Reader or view it in the PDF/ePub copy.

The next-gen Packt Reader and a **free PDF/ePub copy** of this book are included with your purchase. Scan the QR code OR visit `https://packtpub.com/unlock`, then use the search bar to find this book by name. Double-check the edition shown to make sure you get the right one.

One of the most popular tools for testing HTTP APIs is Postman. This tool supports configuring HTTP requests (`GET`, `POST`, `PUT`, `DELETE`, and other methods), including headers and parameters; managing authentication and authorization settings; defining variables and environments; adding JavaScript scripts; organizing and grouping API requests into collections; creating manual and automated tests; and generating documentation. It is also extensible with the Postman API and supports different APIs (REST, SOAP, GraphQL).

Postman integrates easily into CI/CD using Newman, a command-line collection runner for running Postman tests.

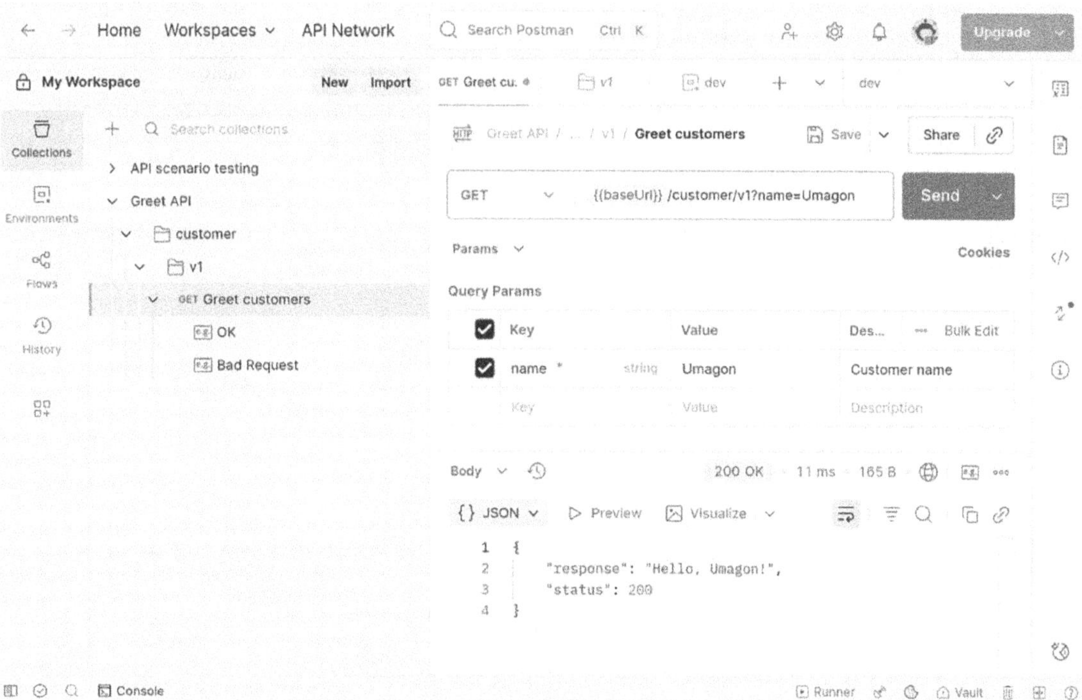

Figure 15.9: An overview of the Postman interface

Postman supports OpenAPI specifications. It can also interpret example responses from the specification, such as `200 (OK)` and `400 (Bad Request)`. It also generates code, but not in C++. Server code is generated only for Go, Node.js, Java, and Python, and client libraries are generated for programming languages such as C#, C, Go, Java, JavaScript, PHP, Python, and Swift.

Postman's competitors include Bruno, Insomnia, Hoppscotch, RapidAPI, Scalar, and Thunder Client, all of which support OpenAPI. HTTPie is another competitor, but it does not support this specification.

AsyncAPI

AsyncAPI started as an adaptation of the OpenAPI specification, with the goal of achieving maximum compatibility with OpenAPI, so that users could reuse common component definitions. In general, synchronous APIs can be defined using the OpenAPI standard, and asynchronous APIs can be defined using the AsyncAPI standard, which handles asynchronous messaging patterns commonly found in microservices architectures, IoT systems, and real-time applications.

Despite this connection to OpenAPI, AsyncAPI is a protocol-agnostic specification for describing message-driven APIs that work over a variety of protocols, for example, AMQP, MQTT, WebSocket, Kafka, STOMP, HTTP, and Mercure.

This specification standardizes the description of interfaces between various services and applications, simplifying development, integration, and documentation. AsyncAPI is an initiative aimed at improving the current state of EDAs. The long-term goal is to make working with EDAs as easy as working with HTTP APIs, in terms of documentation, code generation, and more.

The online editor is available here: `https://studio.asyncapi.com/`. Currently, AsyncAPI generators do not generate server and client stubs for C++. However, the advantage is that AsyncAPI specifications are supported by the new Swagger editor located here: `https://editor-next.swagger.io/`. Note that this web editor generates a static HTML version of the specification, not an interactive documentation, without the ability to send test requests to the servers specified in the specification. By default, the editor uses the server on which it is running.

The greeting API from the previous example would look like this when documented using AsyncAPI in `asyncapi.yaml`:

```
asyncapi: 3.0.0
info:
  title: Greet API
  version: 2.0.0
  description: HTTP API to greet customers
  contact:
    name: API Support
    url: 'https://www.example.com/support'
    email: support@example.com
  license:
    name: MIT
    url: 'https://mit-license.org/'
```

```
  tags:
    - name: greet-api
defaultContentType: application/json
```

The `info` fields provide key metadata such as API name, version, description, contact information, and license.

The `servers` fields describe a set of servers that define the endpoints or message brokers to which applications can connect:

```
servers:
  development:
    host: localhost:8080
    protocol: http
    protocolVersion: '1.1'
    tags:
      - name: 'env:dev'
        description: Development environment
      - name: 'kind:local'
        description: This server is local
      - name: 'visibility:private'
        description: This resource is private
```

The `channels` fields define a list of channels with which the application communicates, where channels refer to the paths along which messages are transmitted:

```
channels:
  customerGreeting:
    address: /customer/v1
    messages:
      greetRequest:
        $ref: '#/components/messages/GreetRequest'
      greetResponse:
        $ref: '#/components/messages/GreetResponse'
      greetError:
        $ref: '#/components/messages/GreetError'
    bindings:
      http:
        method: GET
```

The `operations` fields comprehensively describe all operations performed by the application. For HTTP, AsyncAPI describes interactions using operations such as `send` (sending a request) and `receive` (waiting for a response):

```
operations:
  greet:
    action: send
    channel:
      $ref: '#/channels/customerGreeting'
    messages:
      - $ref: '#/channels/customerGreeting/messages/greetRequest'
    reply:
      channel:
        $ref: '#/channels/customerGreeting'
      messages:
        - $ref: '#/channels/customerGreeting/messages/greetResponse'
        - $ref: '#/channels/customerGreeting/messages/greetError'
```

The `components` fields define components referenced by various parts of the document. This helps improve the readability of the specification and facilitates the reuse of common components:

```
components:
  messages:
    GreetRequest:
      payload:
        type: object
        properties:
          name:
            type: string
            description: Customer name
    GreetResponse:
      payload:
        type: object
        properties:
          status:
            type: integer
          response:
            type: string
        example:
          status: 200
          response: Hi, Ramona
      bindings:
        http:
```

```
          statusCode: 200
      GreetError:
        payload:
          type: object
          properties:
            status:
              type: integer
            response:
              type: string
          example:
            status: 400
            response: No name
        bindings:
          http:
            statusCode: 400
```

Of course, this specification describes a very simple HTTP echo server.

It can also be an implementation of the asynchronous reply-response pattern, where the client sends a request and does not wait for an immediate response because the server processes the request in the background and returns the response later.

One solution for receiving delayed responses can be HTTP polling. HTTP polling is a client-server communication technique where the client repeatedly requests updates from the server. It can be implemented as "short polling," where the client sends requests at fixed intervals, and the server responds immediately with specific status codes or an empty response, and "long polling," where the client sends a request, and the server holds the connection open until new data is available. Unlike the traditional approach, where the client is blocked until a response is received, the client can perform other tasks while the server processes the request.

Alternatives to HTTP polling are **Server-Sent Events** (**SSE**) (unidirectional communication where the server pushes real-time updates to the client over a persistent (keep-alive) HTTP connection) and WebSocket (a persistent, full-duplex communication over a single TCP connection, enabling real-time client-server interaction).

Remote procedure calls

While web APIs such as REST allow easy debugging and great interoperability, there's a lot of overhead related to data translation and using HTTP for transport.

This overhead may be too much for some microservices, which is the reason for lightweight RPCs.

In this section, we'll cover both HTTP-based RPC (gRPC) and non-HTTP RPC (for example, Thrift).

Apache Thrift

Apache Thrift, originally developed at Facebook, is an **interface definition language** (**IDL**) and binary communication protocol. It is used as an RPC method for creating distributed, scalable, high-performance, and fault-tolerant systems built in various programming languages, in particular C++, C#, Delphi, Go, Java, JavaScript, Python, and Swift, for seamless cross-platform communication. Thus, this cross-language framework is designed to simplify the integration of systems written in different programming languages.

It supports several data serialization formats, including JSON, compact formats, and binary, ensuring efficient data transfer and bidirectional communication between client and server. Compared to gRPC, Thrift supports a wider range of serialization formats and transport mechanisms. For instance, when using Kafka, published messages can be efficiently serialized and deserialized utilizing Apache Thrift. Data structures defined in the Thrift IDL can be complex, and depending on the programming language, Apache Thrift offers several transport methods: network and Unix domain sockets, pipes, files, and memory.

Thrift's application areas include distributed systems, microservices, and message-oriented middleware. It is also supported in embedded Linux ecosystems such as Zephyr RTOS and OpenEmbedded—the latter being an open source build framework and cross-compilation environment for creating custom Linux distributions for embedded devices.

While Apache Thrift hasn't gained as much popularity as gRPC in recent years, this framework still has a strong community and long-term support from the Apache Foundation.

Instructions to install the Thrift C++ library are here: `https://thrift.apache.org/lib/cpp.html`.

Let's now see a practical implementation.

First, we define our service in `service.thrift`. The `thrift` command generates server and client classes based on specifications written in the Thrift IDL:

```
namespace cpp Service

service Service {
  string sayHello(1: string name)
}
```

Here is the server implementation in `server.cpp`:

```
// omitted code
...
// generated types
#include "gen-cpp/Service.h"

using namespace apache::thrift;
using namespace apache::thrift::protocol;
using namespace apache::thrift::transport;
```

```
using namespace apache::thrift::server;

using namespace Service;
```

The `ServiceHandler` class implements the `sayHello` pure virtual function of the abstract `ServiceIf` class:

```
class ServiceHandler final : public ServiceIf {
public:
  void sayHello(std::string &_return, const std::string &name) {
    std::cout << name << std::endl;
    _return = "Trust me " + name;
  }
};
```

In the IDL specification, `sayHello` returns a value, but in the generated class, this value is provided through the `_return` reference.

An object of the `ServiceHandler` class, which inherits from `ServiceIf`, is passed to the constructor of the generated `ServiceProcessor` class to set up the server:

```
int main() {
  std::shared_ptr<ServiceHandler> handler(new ServiceHandler());
  std::shared_ptr<TProcessor> processor(new ServiceProcessor(handler));
  std::shared_ptr<TServerTransport> serverTransport(
      new TServerSocket(9090));
  std::shared_ptr<TTransportFactory> transportFactory(
      new TBufferedTransportFactory());
  std::shared_ptr<TProtocolFactory> protocolFactory(
      new TBinaryProtocolFactory());

  TSimpleServer server(processor, serverTransport, transportFactory,
                       protocolFactory);
  server.serve();

  return 0;
}
```

This sets up and starts the Thrift server, which listens for incoming requests on port `9090` and dispatches them to the `ServiceHandler` implementation.

Here comes the client implementation in `client.cpp`:

```
// omitted code
...
// generated types
```

```
#include "gen-cpp/Service.h"

using namespace apache::thrift;
using namespace apache::thrift::protocol;
using namespace apache::thrift::transport;

using namespace Service;

int main() {
  std::shared_ptr<TTransport> socket(new TSocket("localhost", 9090));
  std::shared_ptr<TTransport> transport(new TBufferedTransport(socket));
  std::shared_ptr<TProtocol> protocol(new TBinaryProtocol(transport));
```

The `ServiceClient` class is generated by the Thrift compiler. Any value assigned to the `return_` variable before calling the `sayHello` function is not transmitted to the server, since this variable is only for `return` values:

```
  ServiceClient client(protocol);

  try {
    transport->open();

    std::string return_;
    client.sayHello(return_, "I'm an engineer");

    transport->close();

    std::cout << return_ << std::endl;
  } catch (TException &ex) {
    std::cerr << "Error: " << ex.what() << std::endl;
  }

  return 0;
}
```

This completes the example, where the client sends a request to the Thrift server, which processes it using `ServiceHandler`, and the response is returned to the client.

RPC with RabbitMQ

RabbitMQ uses the request–reply pattern to implement RPC, which allows clients to send requests to the server, and the server to respond to these requests. Every message in RabbitMQ has the `correlation_id` property, which is used to correlate RPC responses with requests.

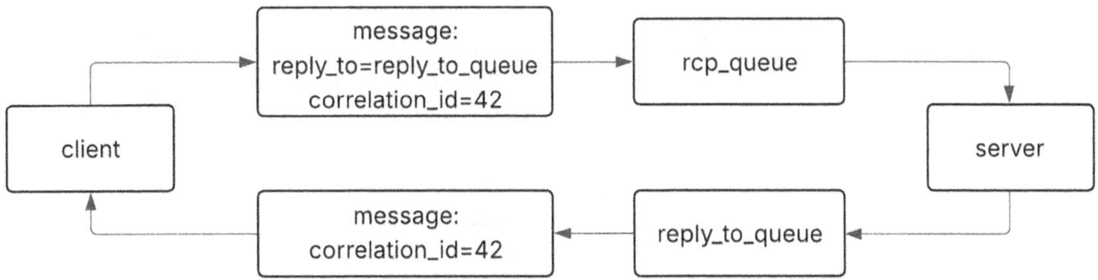

Figure 15.10: The request-reply pattern in RabbitMQ

First, the client sends a request as a message to the server queue to execute a remote procedure, specifying a unique request identifier in the message using the `correlation_id` property. Then, the server processes the request and sends a response message to the client queue, setting the same identifier in the `correlation_id` property, but as a response identifier. Finally, the client receives the response when the response identifier matches the request identifier.

gRPC

gRPC is a modern framework for building fast and efficient services. It is rapidly gaining popularity due to its speed, ease of use, and support for multiple languages, including C++, C#, Dart, Go, Java, Python, and Swift. This technology enables the creation of faster, more reliable, and more scalable applications, making it particularly attractive for microservice architectures and distributed systems capable of handling large volumes of traffic and real-time streaming data.

Unlike REST, gRPC is originally designed for developing high-performance systems running in distributed data centers. gRPC messages are always smaller than equivalent JSON messages due to Protobuf's binary serialization, making gRPC more suitable for network-constrained environments. Also, gRPC can be used for communication between applications on the same computer due to its support for IPC transports such as Unix domain sockets and named pipes.

As its name suggests, gRPC is an RPC system that was initially developed by Google. gRPC uses HTTP/2 as its transport protocol and Protobuf as the default IDL for interoperability between multiple programming languages and for data serialization. Alternatives such as FlatBuffers and Bebop can be used, but Protobuf is the common choice. Anyway, all these are binary data serialization formats.

gRPC can be used both synchronously and in an asynchronous manner and allows creating both simple services and streaming ones, which are especially useful for chats, online games, and monitoring systems.

It's worth noting that REST, GraphQL, and gRPC are not mutually exclusive technologies, as they can be combined in hybrid APIs to leverage the strengths of each approach. The choice depends on the specific project requirements for performance, platform support, request complexity, and application architecture features. REST is simple and versatile, GraphQL is optimal for complex and detailed APIs, and gRPC is ideal for high-load distributed systems and microservices. For instance, gRPC-Gateway exposes both gRPC and RESTful APIs. It uses Protobuf service definitions to generate a reverse proxy that translates RESTful calls into gRPC+Protobuf calls and sends the calls over HTTP/2 to the gRPC service.

gRPC is supported across different platforms (such as Android and macOS) and on mobile (Android and iOS); for browsers, use **gRPC-Web**. The fact that gRPC is supported by Android and iOS implies that mobile apps can use gRPC internally—you don't have to provide an additional server to translate the traffic from your mobile applications. In networking, **gRPC Network Management Interface** (**gNMI**), **gRPC Network Operations Interface** (**gNOI**), and **Routing Information Base Interface** (**gRIBI**) define services for managing network devices.

The difference between REST and gRPC-Web is illustrated in *Figure 15.11*:

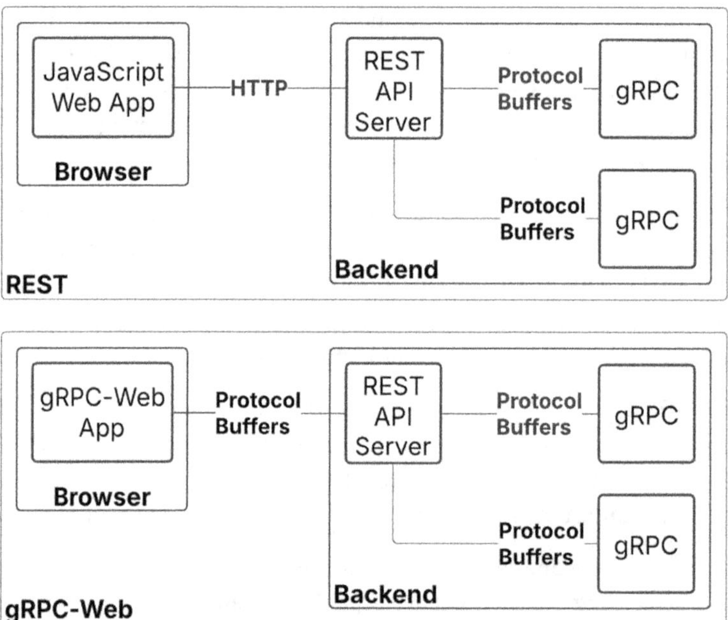

Figure 15.11: REST versus gRPC-Web

gRPC-Web is a JavaScript client library that enables web applications to communicate directly with gRPC backend services, without requiring an HTTP server to act as an intermediary. Before gRPC-Web, a REST API server was required specifically to translate HTTP REST commands into ProtoBuf.

APIs evolve, so all gRPC implementations follow semantic versioning, which takes the form *Major.Minor.Patch*, distinguishing incompatible (major) changes from backward-compatible (minor) updates and small bug fixes (patches). This allows programmers to understand what changes have occurred and organize software releases.

In addition to the project itself, gRPC is supported by C++ libraries such as Qt, `asio-grpc`, and `userver`, and tools such as Postman, Bruno, Insomnia, Kreya, and gRPC UI.

Let's now look at a practical gRPC example of a simple greeting service defined using Protobuf and implemented with a synchronous gRPC server and client in C++.

Since we decided to use Protobuf, our `Greeter` service definition can look like this in `service.proto`:

```
syntax = "proto3";

service Greeter {
 rpc Greet(GreetRequest) returns (GreetResponse);
}

message GreetRequest {
 string name = 1;
}

message GreetResponse {
 string reply = 1;
}
```

Using the `protoc` compiler, you can generate data access code from this definition. In this example, generated assets include the `Greeter::Service`, `GreetRequest`, `GreetResponse`, and `Greeter::Stub` classes, and the `Greeter::NewStub` function—all based on the `service.proto` specification.

Next, assuming we want to have a synchronous server for `Greeter`, we can create the service in `async_server.cpp` in the following way:

```
class GreeterImpl : public Greeter::Service {
  Status Greet(ServerContext *context, const GreetRequest *request,
               GreetResponse *reply) override {
    auto name = request->name();
    if (name.empty()) {
      return Status(StatusCode::INVALID_ARGUMENT, "name is empty");
    }
    reply->set_reply("Get over here! " + name);
    return Status::OK;
  }
};
```

Then, we must build and run the server for it:

```
int main() {
  std::string address("localhost:50000");
  GreeterImpl service;
  ServerBuilder builder;

  builder.AddListeningPort(address, grpc::InsecureServerCredentials());
  builder.RegisterService(&service);

  auto server(builder.BuildAndStart());
  server->Wait();
}
```

Let's now look at a client to consume this service. For this, we have the following code in `async_client.cpp`:

```
#include <grpcpp/grpcpp.h>

#include <string>

#include "service.grpc.pb.h"

using grpc::ClientContext;
using grpc::Status;

int main() {
  std::string address("localhost:50000");
  auto channel =
      grpc::CreateChannel(address, grpc::InsecureChannelCredentials());
  auto stub = Greeter::NewStub(channel);

  GreetRequest request;
  request.set_name("Neosapien");

  GreetResponse reply;
  ClientContext context;
  Status status = stub->Greet(&context, request, &reply);

  if (status.ok()) {
    std::cout << reply.reply() << '\n';
  } else {
    std::cerr << "Error: " << status.error_code() << '\n';
```

```
    }
  }
```

This was a simple, synchronous example. To make it work asynchronously, you'll need to add tags and `CompletionQueue`, as described on gRPC's website (`https://grpc.io/docs/languages/cpp/async/`), or use the `asio-grpc` library.

Summary

In this chapter, we examined how microservices communicate. We began with an introduction to ISC and then covered different interaction styles, with a focus on client–server interactions. Then, we explored low-overhead messaging systems (MQTT and ZeroMQ) and brokered messaging systems (Apache Kafka and RabbitMQ). After that, we saw different ways to use web services: web API payload formats (XML-based and JSON-based), web API design approaches (REST and GraphQL), and tools to debug and describe these services (OpenAPI and AsyncAPI). Finally, we discussed both HTTP-based and non-HTTP RPCs: Apache Thrift, gRPC, and RabbitMQ.

Microservices are especially popular in combination with containers, which are the subject of the next chapter.

Questions

1. What is the scope of different interaction types?
2. What are some of the use cases for message queues?
3. What are some of the benefits of choosing JSON over XML?
4. How does REST build on web standards?
5. Why might REST not be the best choice for connecting microservices?

Further reading

- Sigismondo Boschi and Gabriele Santomaggio, *RabbitMQ Cookbook*, Packt Publishing: `https://www.packtpub.com/en-us/product/rabbitmq-cookbook-9781849516518`
- Dilip Sundarraj, *Kafka for Developers - Data Contracts Using Schema Registry: Build a Kafka Producer/Consumer Application that Uses AVRO Data Format and Confluent Schema Registry*, Packt Publishing: `https://www.packtpub.com/en-us/product/kafka-for-developers-data-contracts-using-schema-registry-9781837633487`
- Perry Lea, *IoT and Edge Computing for Architects: Implementing Edge and IoT Systems from Sensors to Clouds with Communication Systems, Analytics, and Security*, Second Edition, Packt Publishing: `https://www.packtpub.com/en-us/product/iot-and-edge-computing-for-architects-9781839218873`
- Dhairya Parikh, *Raspberry Pi and MQTT Essentials: A Complete Guide to Helping You Build Innovative Full-Scale Prototype Projects Using Raspberry Pi and MQTT Protocol*, Packt Publishing: `https://www.packtpub.com/en-us/product/raspberry-pi-and-mqtt-essentials-9781803238395`

- Praveenkumar Bouna, *The Ultimate Swagger Tools Course: Build OpenAPI with Ease: Be a Part of the Swagger Tutorial for Simplified API Design, Documentation, Development, and Testing*, Packt Publishing: `https://www.packtpub.com/en-us/product/the-ultimate-swagger-tools-course-build-openapi-with-ease-9781803242743` and `https://swagger.io/docs/`, `https://www.asyncapi.com/docs`
- Andrzej Jarzyna and Samir Amzani, *RESTful API Design Patterns and Best Practices: Master REST API Design with Real-World Patterns, Lifecycle Management, and OpenAPI Practices*, Packt Publishing: `https://www.packtpub.com/en-us/product/restful-api-design-patterns-and-best-practices-9781835885291`
- Dave Westerveld, *API Testing and Development with Postman: API Creation, Testing, Debugging, and Management Made Easy*, Second Edition, Packt Publishing: `https://www.packtpub.com/en-us/product/api-testing-and-development-with-postman-9781804616000`
- Artur Czemiel, *GraphQL Best Practices: Gain Hands-On Experience with Schema Design, Security, and Error Handling*, Packt Publishing: `https://www.packtpub.com/en-us/product/graphql-best-practices-9781835462522`
- Joshua B. Humphries, David Konsumer, David Muto, Robert Ross, and Carles Sistare: *Practical gRPC: Build Highly-Connected Systems with a Framework That Can Run on Any Platform*, Packt Publishing: `https://www.packtpub.com/en-us/product/practical-grpc-9781839212666`
- Krzysztof Rakowski, *Learning Apache Thrift: Make Applications Cross-Communicate Using Apache Thrift!*, Packt Publishing: `https://www.packtpub.com/en-us/product/learning-apache-thrift-9781785888670`
- Confluent Developer, *Getting Started with Apache Kafka and C/C++*: `https://developer.confluent.io/get-started/c/`
- RabbitMQ, *RabbitMQ Tutorials*: `https://www.rabbitmq.com/tutorials`
- HiveMQ, *MQTT Tutorial: An Easy Guide to Getting Started with MQTT* (Blog): `https://www.hivemq.com/blog/how-to-get-started-with-mqtt/`
- *ØMQ - The Guide*: `https://zguide.zeromq.org/`
- HashiCorp, *Packer Documentation*: `https://developer.hashicorp.com/packer/docs`
- Talking IoT, *Understanding the IoT Protocol Stack*: `https://talkingiot.io/understanding-the-iot-protocol-stack/`
- NetRom Software, *Alternatives to JSON: Modern Serialization Formats in the Big Data Era*: `https://www.netromsoftware.com/insights/alternatives-to-json/`
- Lokesh Gupta, *HATEOAS Driven REST APIs*, REST API Tutorial: `https://restfulapi.net/hateoas/`
- Roy Fielding, *REST APIs Must Be Hypertext-Driven* (Blog), Untangled: `https://roy.gbiv.com/untangled/2008/rest-apis-must-be-hypertext-driven`
- Roy Fielding, *Architectural Styles and the Design of Network-based Software Architectures*: `https://roy.gbiv.com/pubs/dissertation/top.htm`
- REST API Tutorial, *REST API URI Naming Conventions and Best Practices*: `https://restfulapi.net/resource-naming/`

- REST API tutorial, *REST API Response Pagination, Sorting and Filtering*: https://restfulapi.net/api-pagination-sorting-filtering/
- Zuplo, *How to Choose the Right REST API Naming Conventions*: https://zuplo.com/learning-center/how-to-choose-the-right-rest-api-naming-conventions
- Hayk Simonyan, *REST API Basics & Best Practices Explained*: https://hayksimonyan.substack.com/p/rest-api-basics-and-best-practices
- Specmatic, *Contract Driven Development*: https://docs.specmatic.io/contract_driven_development.html
- SBB, *API Principles*, GitHub: https://schweizerischebundesbahnen.github.io/api-principles/
- gRPC Ecosystem, *A Curated List of Useful Resources for gRPC*, GitHub: https://github.com/grpc-ecosystem/awesome-grpc
- ECE 252: Systems Programming and Concurrency, *Event-Driven I/O with libevent* (Lecture slides), GitHub: https://github.com/smajidzahedi/ece252/blob/master/lectures/out/L28-slides.pdf
- Confluent, *Introduction to Apache Kafka*: https://docs.confluent.io/kafka/introduction.html
- Rabbit MQ, *AMQP 0-9-1 Model Explained*: https://www.rabbitmq.com/tutorials/amqp-concepts
- Rabbit MQ, *Reliability Guide*: https://www.rabbitmq.com/docs/reliability
- GraphQL, *GraphQL Best Practices*: https://graphql.org/learn/best-practices/
- REST API tutorial, *Caching REST API Response*: https://restfulapi.net/caching/
- Paul Wilton, *GraphQL and Graph Databases* (Blog), DataGraphs: https://datagraphs.com/blog/graphql-and-graph-databases

16

Containers

In the previous chapters, we explored SOA and microservices and how those services interact through interservice communication mechanisms. The next consideration is how to package and deploy these services in a consistent way across heterogeneous environments.

Transitioning from development to production has always been a painful process. It involves a lot of documentation, hand-offs, installation, and configuration. Since every programming language produces software that behaves slightly differently, the deployment of heterogeneous applications is always difficult.

Some of these problems have been mitigated by containers. With containers, the installation and configuration are mostly standardized, and distribution also now follows established practices. This makes containers a great choice for organizations that want to increase the cooperation between development and operations.

The following topics will be covered in this chapter:

- Reintroducing containers
- Building container images
- Practical runtime considerations for containers
- Understanding container orchestration

Technical requirements

The examples listed in this chapter require the following:

- **Docker 27.2+**: A software platform for developing, delivering, and running containerized applications
- **manifest-tool 2.1.9+**: A utility for viewing or pushing multi-platform container image references located in a container registry
- **Ansible 11.1+**: A tool for automating application deployment, machine configuration management, and infrastructure orchestration

- **ansible-bender 0.10+**: A tool that uses Ansible playbooks to build container images
- **Buildah 1.38+**: A daemonless and rootless image builder tool complementary to Podman
- **Podman 5.3+**: A daemonless and rootless container engine to run, manage, and interact with containers
- **Skopeo 1.17+**: A tool complementing Podman and Buildah to manipulate, inspect, sign, and transfer container images and image repositories
- **runc 1.2+ (made by Docker in Golang) or crun 1.19+ (made by Red Hat in C)**: Container runtimes that can be used interchangeably as both implement the **Open Container Initiative** (**OCI**) runtime specification
- **CMake 3.28+**: An open source, cross-platform, software development tool designed to build, test, and package software via compiler-independent instructions

The code present in the chapter has been placed on GitHub at `https://github.com/PacktPublishing/Software-Architecture-with-Cpp-2E/tree/main/Chapter16`.

Reintroducing containers

Containers are generating a lot of interest in the software world. One might think they are a brand-new technology. However, that is not the case. Before the rise of Docker and Kubernetes, the dominating players in the industry, there were already solutions such as **Linux Containers** (**LXC**) that offered a lot of similar features.

We can trace the origins of separating one execution environment from another to the **chroot** (short for **change root**) mechanism available in Unix systems since 1979. Similar concepts were also used in FreeBSD jails and Solaris zones.

The main task of the container is to isolate one execution environment from another. This isolated environment can have its own configuration, different applications, and even different user accounts than the host environment.

Even though the containers are isolated from the host, they usually share the same operating system kernel as the host. This is the main differentiator from virtualized environments. Virtual machines have dedicated virtual resources, which means they are separated at the hardware level. Containers are separated at the process level, which means there is less overhead to run them.

The ability to package and run an environment that is already optimized and configured for running your application is a strong advantage of containers. Without containers, the build and deploy process usually consists of several steps:

1. The application is built
2. The example configuration files are provided
3. Installation scripts and associated documentation are prepared
4. The application is packaged for a target operating system (such as Debian, Red Hat, Arch, or Gentoo)

5. The packages are deployed to the target platform
6. Installation scripts prepare the basis for the application to run
7. The configuration has to be tweaked to fit the existing system

When you switch to containers, there is less of a need for a robust installation script. The application will only target a single well-known operating system—the one present in the container. The same goes for configuration: instead of preparing many configurable options, the application is pre-configured for the target operating system and distributed alongside it. The deployment process consists only of unpacking the container image and running the application process inside it because container images deliver packaged software, including development environments with preinstalled dependencies and tools such as compilers and debuggers. In essence, a container image is a snapshot of filesystem changes, not of the in-memory state of running processes.

Containers quickly became very popular, resolving several vexing development problems at once, especially when developing in environment-sensitive languages such as C++. As an illustration, if development is carried out on several computers (such as home, work, and laptop), then it is necessary to constantly maintain the same settings, library versions, and other environment parameters everywhere, which is not always possible. As a result, the working environments and compiled executables differ on all these computers. But containers provide isolated and reproducible build environments, so the same container image can be used by both developers on workstations and CI/CD servers, eliminating the *"it works on my machine, but not on CI/CD!"* problem. However, reproducible builds (byte-for-byte identical executables given the same sources) are not always possible in containers due to external dependencies either mounted or delivered into running containers from the host or servers.

What is especially irritating is when the whole setup process of development environments repeats over and over again. At times, your environment may even suddenly break. Fortunately, development containers come into play, which can be used as full-featured development environments.

Finally, while containers and microservices are often thought to be the same thing, they are not. Moreover, containers may mean application containers or operating system containers, and only application containers fit well with microservices. The following sections will tell you why. We'll describe the different container types that you can encounter, show you how they relate to microservices, and explain when it's best to use them (and when to avoid them).

Exploring the container types

Of the container types mentioned so far, operating system containers—isolated virtual environments that share the host operating system's kernel—have been around for decades. Examples include LXC, **Open Virtuozzo (OpenVZ)**, FreeBSD jails, DragonFly BSD virtual kernels, and Solaris zones. These are fundamentally different from the application container trend led by Docker, Podman, and Kubernetes. These modern platforms follow the model of application containers, which, instead of focusing on recreating an entire operating system with services such as syslog and cron, focus on running a single process within a container—just the application.

Figure 16.1 compares application containers, operating system containers, and virtual machines:

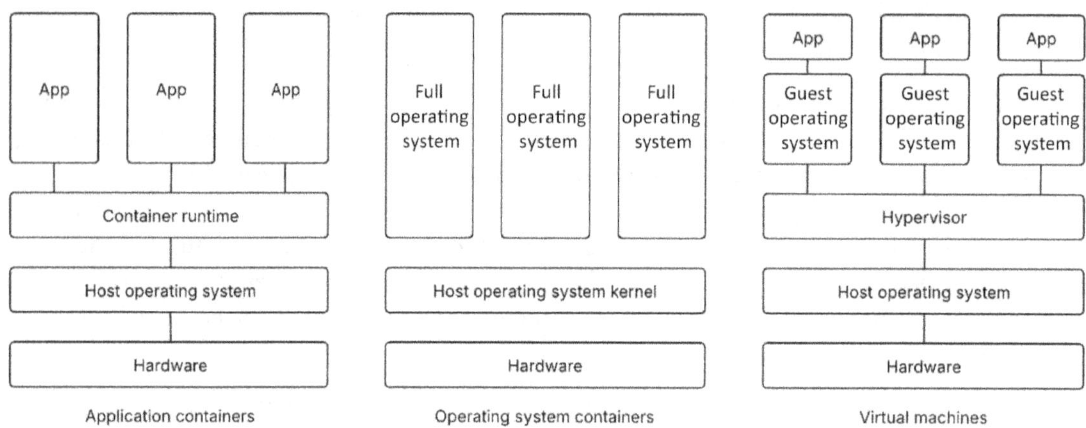

Figure 16.1: Containers and virtual machines

An application container contains only the application and its dependencies, isolating them from the host operating system. An operating system container, or system container, shares the host operating system kernel but provides user-space isolation. A virtual machine is a virtual computer that uses the dedicated resources of a real computer (processor, disk, and adapter). A hypervisor is software that manages the physical resources of a single server platform and distributes them among multiple virtual machines. Application containers are lightweight and fast, while operating system containers and virtual machines provide more complete isolation but require more resources.

Coming back to the idea that application containers are built to run a single process, let's look at why this matters in practice. Although we can also run multiple processes in a Docker container using wrapper scripts, Bash job controls, or process managers such as supervisord, it is not recommended. This is because it violates the principle of the separation of concerns; introduces technical challenges, especially around proper signal handling, health checks, and logging; and violates design principles of container-based applications, which are meant to be packaged into isolated units with their dependencies (libraries, binaries, and configuration files). Moreover, when logs of different processes in a container are mixed, it is hard to identify the source. Also, a single-process container scales more efficiently and independently because multiple processes within the container do not compete for CPU and memory, degrading performance. This also reduces the impact of failures, since failures are limited to a given single-process faulty container, while maintaining system stability. Thus, a failure in one service does not cascade to the entire system and makes it easier to identify and troubleshoot failures.

In application containers, proprietary solutions replace the usual operating system-level services. These solutions provide a unified way to manage the applications within a container. For example, instead of using syslog to handle logs, the standard output of the main process (PID 1) is considered as the application log. Instead of using an init system such as SysVinit, OpenRC, procd, Finit, Dinit, or systemd, the application container's life cycle is handled by the container runtime. This design has its limitations: when that main process crashes, child processes may be left orphans or zombies.

Since Docker is, at the moment, the dominant solution for application containers, we mostly use it as an example throughout this book. In this chapter, we will explain how to use Docker to build, deploy, run, and manage application containers.

To make the picture complete, we will also present viable alternatives, as they may be better suited to your needs. Since the project and specification are open source, these alternatives are compatible with Docker and can be used as replacements.

But first, let's understand why the success of application containers is closely tied to the rise of microservices.

Unless otherwise noted, whenever we use the word *containers* from now on, it relates to *application containers*.

The parallel rise of microservices and containers

The success of application containers, which many people associate with Docker, coincided with the rise of microservices. It is no surprise since microservices and application containers fit together naturally, and both align closely with the **Twelve-Factor App methodology** (the best practices drafted by developers at Heroku, a Platform-as-a-Service company, to enable portable and resilient applications deployed to the web):

- **Code base:** A deployed service has exactly one code base tracked in version control (such as Git, Mercurial, or Subversion) and used for many deployments.
- **Dependencies:** All dependencies are explicitly declared and isolated, with no implicit dependency on system tools or libraries (for example, `pip` and `virtualenv` in Python, Gemfile and `bundle exec` in Ruby, or Docker containers in general).
- **Config:** Configuration that varies between deployments (staging, production, development, and other environments) is stored in the environment, which requires strict separation of configuration from code.
- **Backing services:** Backing services (such as data storage, web services, caching systems, messaging/queuing systems, monitoring tools, and email services) are treated as attached resources. Connections should be transparent and not require changes to the code, and there's no distinction between local and third-party services.
- **Build, release, and run:** The build, release, and run stages are strictly separated in CI/CD pipelines.
- **Processes:** Applications execute as one or more stateless, shared-nothing processes, where each process can be scaled independently and has no persistent state, with persistent data stored on a backing service.
- **Port binding:** Completely self-contained services are exposed via port binding and do not rely on external runtime injection of the services into the execution environment.

- **Concurrency:** Concurrency is achieved by scaling the application as a pool of one or more stateless processes, where each process is assigned a type to handle different workloads (process formation).
- **Disposability:** Processes are disposable, which ensures minimized startup time, graceful shutdown, and robustness against sudden death (crash-only design), which is crucial for scaling and resilience.
- **Dev/prod parity:** The maximum similarity of development, staging, and production environments, especially backing services, should be ensured.
- **Logs:** Applications should produce logs as event streams, typically written unbuffered to **standard output (stdout)** for centralized collection and monitoring.
- **Admin processes:** One-off administrative tasks, such as database migrations or batch jobs, are stored in source control and packaged with the application to avoid synchronization issues in the environments, which must be identical.

Without application containers, there was no easy and unified way to package, deploy, and maintain microservices. Even though individual companies developed some solutions to fix these problems, none were popular enough to approach being an industry standard.

Conversely, without microservices, the application containers were pretty limited in scope. The software architecture focused on building entire systems explicitly configured for the given set of services. Replacing one service with another required a change to the architecture.

When brought together, application containers and microservices became a powerful combination. Application containers provided a standard way for the distribution of microservices, and each microservice comes packaged with its own configuration and environment, so operations such as autoscaling and self-healing no longer require knowledge about an underlying application.

Looking at C++, it is a good choice for compute-intensive microservices with small memory footprints, where performance and memory footprint are crucial. These qualities make C++ better suited for binary services (e.g., with the gRPC protocol used in telecommunications and other fields), which require compact and fast data handling, than for textual services exposing RESTful APIs.

Binary data is valuable in telecommunications and networking as it enables efficient, low-bandwidth communications, produces compact data representations, and enables faster processing with strong interoperability. An example is the standard format **Abstract Syntax Notation One** (**ASN.1**), introduced in 1984, which is used in telecommunications protocols such as UMTS, GPRS, EDGE, LTE, 5G, and likely 6G.

In addition to telecommunications, other areas of demand for C++ include the gaming industry, the automotive industry and autonomous vehicle communication, industrial **Internet of Things** (**IoT**) applications, aerospace and defense, smart city infrastructure, finance, and banking, where containerized applications are used.

It must be noted that developers often prefer programming languages that simplify coding, such as C#, Java, Python, JavaScript, Go, Nim, and Zig. This is why C++ has adopted microservice architectures more slowly, partly because C++ programmers traditionally prefer to run all the components in the same process. Nevertheless, C++ remains relevant for microservices wherever performance and resource efficiency are essential.

Lastly, it's worth noting that you can still use microservices without application containers and you can use application containers without hosting microservices in them. For instance, even though neither PostgreSQL databases nor Nginx web servers were designed as microservices, they are typically used in application containers.

Choosing when to use containers

There are several benefits to the container approach. Operating system containers and application containers also have some different use cases in which their strengths lie. Here, we'll focus on application containers.

The benefits of containers

When compared to virtual machines, containers—the other popular way of isolating environments—require less overhead during runtime. This is because unlike virtual machines, there is no need to run a separate version of an operating system kernel and use the hardware or software virtualization techniques. Moreover, application containers also do not run other operating system services that are typically found in virtual machines, such as syslog, cron, or init. Another advantage of application containers is that they offer smaller images as they do not usually have to carry an entire operating system copy. In extreme examples, an application container can consist of a single statically linked binary. From the operating system's perspective, the containers are simply processes, like any other application, running directly on the host.

At this point, you may wonder, why bother with containers at all if there is just a single binary inside? The answer is that containers offer a unified and standardized way to build and run applications. As containers have to follow specific conventions, it is easier to orchestrate them than regular binaries, which can have different expectations regarding logging, configuration, opening ports, and so on.

Another thing that containers provide is a built-in means of isolation. Each container has its own namespace for processes, user accounts, and other resources. This means that the process (or processes) from one container has no notion of the processes on the host or in the other containers. The sandboxing can go even further as you can assign memory and a CPU quota to your containers with the same standard user interface (whether it is Docker, Kubernetes, or something else) by managing resources efficiently with **control groups (cgroups)**.

As most modern container technologies are built on Linux kernel features, it is useful to understand how Linux implements isolation:

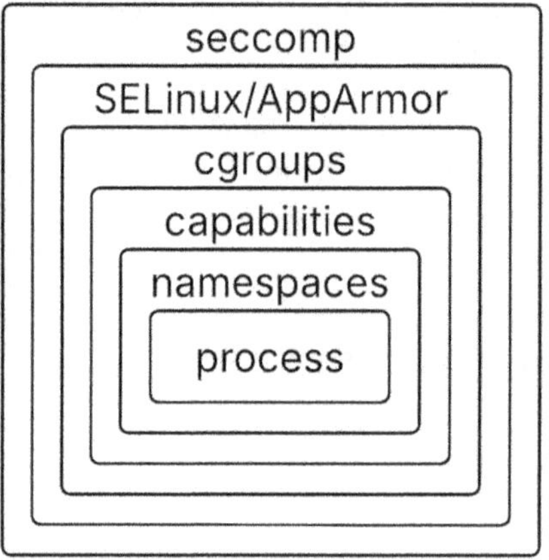

At the core of Linux kernel mechanisms are Linux namespaces, which create isolated environments for processes and resources allocated to them, thereby containerizing them. This includes mounted file systems, network interfaces, IP addresses and routes, host and domain names, inter-process communication, user, group, and process IDs, and system time. These are a fundamental technology for running containers. These independent, self-contained environments ensure security, provide more efficient resource management, and prevent conflicts between applications.

Linux namespaces are used in conjunction with cgroups to limit and meter the resources used by processes: processor time (CPU), memory, input/output (I/O), and network bandwidth. They organize processes into hierarchical groups and distribute system resources along the hierarchy.

To further enhance security, Linux has the capabilities to grant permissions in a more granular way. These capabilities allow specific permissions, restricting the groups of privileged system operations that a process and its children are allowed to perform.

Container isolation is reinforced by additional kernel security features, such as **Security-Enhanced Linux** (**SELinux**), **Application Armor** (**AppArmor**), and TOMOYO, which enforce mandatory access control policies. Furthermore, tools such as **seccomp** (**secure computing mode**) and grsecurity (a set of patches for the Linux kernel) further enhance a system's overall security by filtering system calls and applying kernel-level protections.

Finally, standardized runtime also means higher portability. Once a container is built, you can typically run it on different operating systems without modifications. This also means what runs in production is very close, or identical, to what runs in development. Issue reproduction is more effortless and so is debugging.

The disadvantages of containers

Since there is a lot of pressure nowadays to move workloads to containers, you want to understand all the risks associated with such migration as an architect. The benefits are touted everywhere, but the drawbacks are often less visible.

The main obstacle to container adoption is that not all applications can be easily migrated to containers. This is especially true for application containers, which are designed with microservices in mind. If your application is not based on microservices architecture, putting it into containers may introduce more problems than it would solve.

If your application already scales well, uses TCP/IP-based **inter-process communication** (**IPC**), and is mostly stateless, the move to containers should not be challenging. Otherwise, each of these aspects would pose a challenge and prompt a rethink of the existing design.

Another problem associated with containers is persistent storage. Ideally, containers should have no persistent storage of their own. This makes it possible to take advantage of fast startups, easy scaling, and flexible scheduling. The problem is that applications providing business value cannot exist without persistent storage.

This drawback is usually mitigated by making most containers stateless and relying on an external non-containerized component to store the data and the state. Such an external component can be either a traditional self-hosted database or a managed database from a cloud provider. Going in either direction requires you to reconsider the architecture and modify it accordingly.

Also, application containers follow specific conventions, so the application must be modified to follow these conventions. For some applications, it will be a low-effort task. For others, such as multiprocess components using in-memory IPC, it will be complicated. Linux containers can use host IPC, **graphics processing unit** (**GPU**) devices, or networking, but only if explicitly allowed, which further increases deployment complexity.

Further, while containers promise portability, they are not equally portable in all operating systems. Windows containers, which require Hyper-V (hypervisor) isolation, exist, but they are less attractive than Linux containers due to performance issues, security and isolation weaknesses compared to Linux counterparts, and the dominance of Linux in server environments and cloud platforms. Even though Windows containers provide isolation for Windows applications and are supported by Microsoft, their use remains niche, especially when compared to the widely used Linux containers.

Windows container hosts also include more built-in services and utilities, even if most services and utilities are not necessary for Docker hosting, which increases the security attack vector. Moreover, Windows container base images require licensing under the container operating system image **End-User License Agreement** (**EULA**). The Windows ecosystem provides far fewer OCI-compliant public images than Linux, making image discovery and reuse more difficult.

It is easier to enjoy the application containers' benefits if you are building a new application from scratch and can base your design on this technology. Moving an existing application to application containers, especially if it is complicated, will require a lot more work and possibly also a revamp of the entire architecture. In such a case, we advise you to consider all the benefits and disadvantages extra carefully. Making a wrong decision may harm your product's lead time, availability, and budget.

Building container images

Application containers are the focus of this section. While operating system containers mostly follow system programming principles, application containers bring new challenges and patterns. However, they also provide specialized build tools to deal with those challenges.

The primary tool we will consider is Docker, as it's the current de facto standard for building and running application containers.

Figure 16.2 shows Docker architecture:

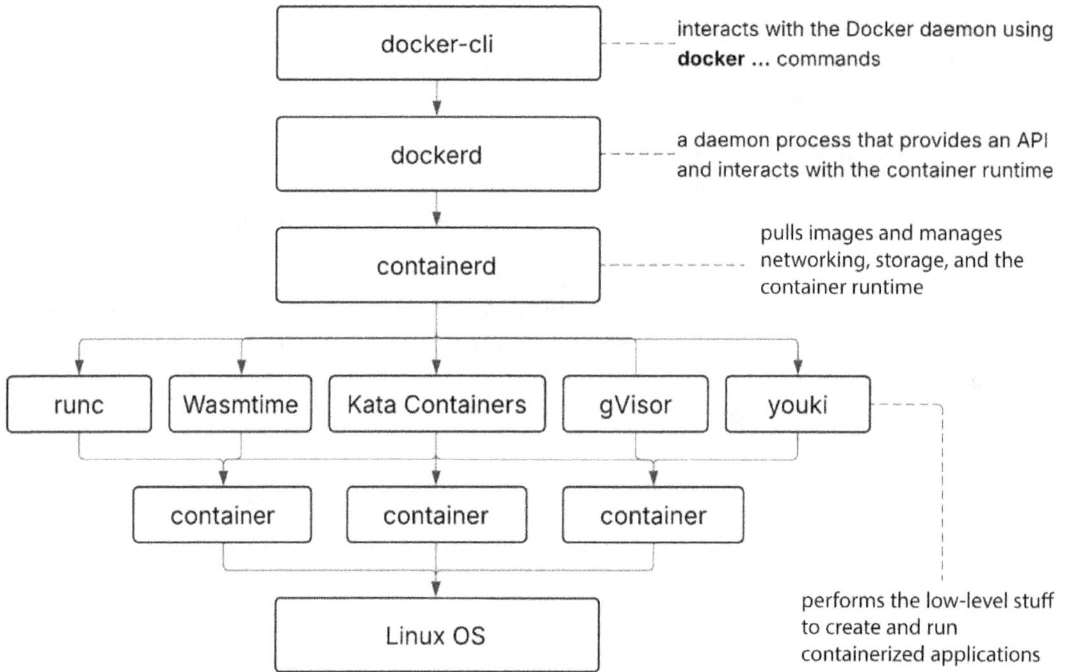

Figure 16.2: Docker architecture

The Docker stack (written in Go) consists of the following:

- **docker-cli:** A CLI tool managing various aspects of the container ecosystem
- **dockerd:** A daemon process interacting with the high-level container runtime
- **containerd:** A high-level container runtime interacting with the low-level container runtimes:
    - **runc:** A lightweight, portable container runtime used by default
    - **Wasmtime:** A WebAssembly runtime (written in Rust)
    - **GVisor (runsc):** A sandbox compatible with most Linux kernel system calls and providing a security level similar to virtualization

- **Kata Containers:** Runs containers in an isolated, lightweight virtual machine for greater security (written in Rust)

We will also present some alternative approaches to building application containers.

Container images explained

Before we describe how to build container images, it is vital to understand the distinction between containers and container images. There is often confusion between the terms, especially during informal conversations.

The difference between a container and a container image is the same as between a running process and an executable file:

- **Container images are static:** They're composed of layers where each layer is a snapshot of a particular filesystem's changes and associated metadata. The metadata describes, among other things, what environmental variables are set during runtime or which program to run when the container is created from the image.
- **Containers are dynamic:** They are the running instances created from the container image. We can create containers from the container images and we can also create container images by snapshotting a running container. The container image build process consists, in fact, of creating several containers, executing commands inside them, and snapshotting them after the command finishes.

To distinguish between the data introduced by the container image and the data generated during runtime, Docker uses union mount filesystems to create different filesystem layers. These layers are also present in the container images. Typically, each build step of the container image corresponds to a new layer in the resulting container image.

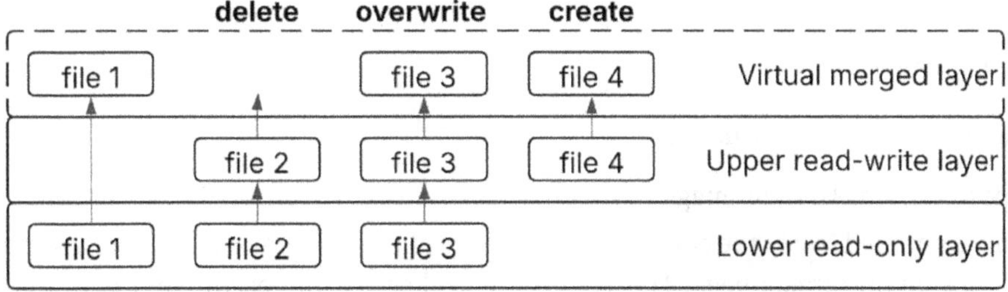

Figure 16.3: Docker Union File System (UFS)

Docker has a **Union File System** (**UFS**) to manage layers. This filesystem creates a single, consistent filesystem by stacking multiple filesystems on top of each other, where each filesystem has its own properties, and permissions can hide and override files of underlying filesystems but not change them. Underlying layers of the **boot filesystem** (**bootfs**) and container images are open for reading only (read-only), since only the top container layer is open for reading and writing (read-write). In turn, the container's file changes can also be committed to form the basis for another container image.

Also, on top of the container layer, Docker can mount files, directories, and persistent volumes, which are designed to store data outside containers so that they can be backed up or shared. But containerized applications are isolated by default, so they must communicate with the outside world using network protocols by exposing open ports inside the container and mapping them to host ports.

Building container images with Dockerfiles

The most common way to build an application container image using Docker is by writing a Dockerfile. A Dockerfile is a text file that uses an imperative language to describe the operations required to produce the resulting image. Some of the operations create new filesystem layers; others operate on metadata.

We will not go into every detail of Dockerfiles; instead, we will focus on different approaches to containerizing a C++ application: one that uses a standard base image, which has build tools installed, and another for builds from scratch. For this, we need to introduce some syntax and concepts related to Dockerfiles.

Ubuntu **Long-Term Support** (**LTS**) versions are supported for a long time with security updates and bug fixes, making them ideal for servers, businesses, and users who value stability and reliability over time. LTS releases undergo rigorous testing, providing a more stable and predictable environment than interim releases, which are only supported for nine months. However, using LTS versions is not always possible or desirable due to outdated software versions. The examples in this chapter are based on Ubuntu 25.10 (Questing Quokka) because its default versions of the provided C++ compilers make the examples simpler and less complex.

Here is an example of a very simple Dockerfile:

```
FROM ubuntu:questing
RUN apt update && apt install -y build-essential gcc
CMD ["/usr/bin/gcc"]
```

The steps we take are the following:

1. Import the base Ubuntu image.
2. Run a command inside the container. The results of the command will create a new filesystem layer inside the target image. This means the packages installed with `apt` will be available in all the containers based on this image.
3. Set the runtime metadata. When creating a container based on this image, we want to run `GCC` as the default process.

Thus, typically, we can divide a Dockerfile into three parts:

- Importing the base image (the `FROM` instruction)
- Performing operations within the container that will result in a container image (the `RUN` instruction)
- Metadata used during runtime (the `CMD` command)

The latter two parts may well be interleaved, and each of them may comprise one or more instructions. It is also possible to omit any of the later parts as only the base image is mandatory. This does not mean you cannot start with an empty filesystem. There is a special base image named `scratch` exactly for this purpose. Adding a single statically linked binary to an otherwise empty filesystem could look like the following:

```
FROM scratch
COPY customer /bin/customer
CMD ["/bin/customer"]
```

The container images built with the scratch approach have the smallest sizes. However, this approach has its trade-offs. It's impossible to get into the container shell because there's obviously no shell. In fact, there's only a single static binary and nothing more. As a result, you cannot attach to the container for debugging. Nevertheless, this is the most secure option because it prevents anyone from attaching the terminal to the running container. In contrast, many base images, such as Ubuntu, Debian, Manjaro (`manjarolinux/base`), and Fedora, provide shells by default, which makes them easier to work with interactively but also increases the image size.

Further, because containers built from scratch often rely on statically linked binaries, it's worth noting that compiling static binaries can result in certain functions of the standard **GNU C Library (glibc)** not working, but this is not a problem unless those functions are used. The advantage of using static binaries is that the assembly of container images is simplified with static binaries, as there is no need to copy shared libraries into the built image.

To build an image from a Dockerfile, you will use the `docker build` command. It takes one required argument—the directory containing the build context, which means the Dockerfile itself and other files you want to copy inside the container. To build a Dockerfile from the current directory, use `docker build`. Remember to include a `.dockerignore` file to exclude unnecessary files and directories from the build context to reduce build time.

This will build an anonymous image, which is not very useful. Most of the time, you want to use named images so they can be easily referred to. There is a convention to follow when naming container images and that's what we'll cover in the next section.

Naming and distributing images

Each container image in Docker has a distinctive name consisting of three elements: the name of the registry, the name of the image, and a tag. Container registries are object repositories holding container images. The default container registry for Docker is `docker.io`. When pulling an image from this registry, we may omit the registry name.

Our previous example with `ubuntu:questing` has the full name of `docker.io/ubuntu:questing`. In this example, `ubuntu` is the name of the image, while `questing` is a tag that represents a particular version of an image.

To assign a name when building an image, you need to pass the `-t` argument to the `docker build` command. For example, to build an image named `tradefair/merchant:v2.0.3`, you would use `docker build -t tradefair/merchant:v2.0.3..`

Once built, you will be interested in storing and sharing images through container registries. It is possible to host your private registry and keep your images there or use a managed solution. Popular managed container registries include the following: Amazon **Elastic Container Registry** (**ECR**), **Azure Container Registry** (**ACR**), Docker Hub container registry, GitHub Packages registry, GitLab Container Registry, **Google Artifact Registry** (**GAR**), Harbor container registry, JFrog Container Registry, Red Hat Quay, and Sonatype Nexus Repository OSS.

Docker Hub is still the most popular one, though some public images are migrating to quay.io. Both are general-purpose and allow the storage of public and private images. GitHub, GitLab, or cloud providers will be mainly attractive to you if you are already using their ecosystems. Using the same platform as your CI/CD pipelines or deployment targets reduces the number of individual services you need.

If none of the solutions appeal to you, hosting your own local registry is also very easy and requires you to run a single container.

Compiled applications and containers

When building container images, the most obvious approach is to install all the dependencies first, copy the source files, and then compile the application as one of the container build steps. The major benefit is that we can accurately control the toolchain's contents and configuration and therefore have a portable way to build an application. However, the downside is too big to ignore: the resulting container image contains a lot of unnecessary files. After all, we will need neither source code nor the toolchain during runtime. Due to the way layered filesystems work, it is impossible to remove the files after being introduced in a previous layer because file changes are recorded. For this reason, it is common to perform multiple actions in a single Dockerfile instruction to reduce the volume of layers and committed file changes. What is more, the source code in the container may prove to be a security risk if an attacker manages to break into the container. A Dockerfile following this approach might look like this:

```
FROM ubuntu:questing

RUN apt update && DEBIAN_FRONTEND=noninteractive apt install -y build-essential
gcc cmake git python3-pip python3-venv && \
    python3 -mvenv /opt/venv && . /opt/venv/bin/activate && pip3 install conan
&& conan profile detect

ADD . /root/src
WORKDIR /root/src

RUN mkdir -p build && cd build && . /opt/venv/bin/activate &&
    conan install .. --build=missing -s:a build_type=Release -s:a compiler.
cppstd=gnu20 -of . && \
    cmake .. -DCMAKE_BUILD_TYPE=Release && cmake --build . && cmake --install .

CMD ["/usr/local/bin/customer"]
```

Another obvious approach is building the application on the host machine and only copying the resulting binaries inside the container image. This requires fewer changes to the current build process when one is already established. The main drawback is that you have to match the same set of libraries, operating system, and processor architecture on your build machines as you do in your containers. If you're running, for example, Ubuntu 25.10 as your host operating system, your containers will have to be based on Ubuntu 25.10 as well, or compile statically linked executable files. Otherwise, you risk incompatibilities. With this approach, it is also necessary to configure the toolchain independently of the container. A corresponding Dockerfile might look like this:

```
FROM ubuntu:questing
COPY customer /bin/customer
CMD ["/bin/customer"]
```

This minimal image contains only the binary, with no toolchain or source code. Don't forget to copy or install shared libraries if they are linked; otherwise, executable files will not run. Distroless container images are a way to create secure and lightweight images that contain only applications and their runtime dependencies.

A slightly more advanced approach is to have a multi-stage build. With multi-stage builds, one stage may be dedicated to setting up the toolchain and compiling the project, while another stage copies the resulting binaries to their target container image.

Unlike a single-stage build, which runs one temporary container to which the commands are applied, a multi-stage build uses multiple temporary containers. When the next stage starts, only files from the base image exist in the currently running container. This is the reason why stages copy any additional files from previous stages or reinstall dependencies, and a stage can copy files from many previous stages or external images.

This approach has several benefits over the previous solutions. First of all, the Dockerfiles now control both the toolchain and the runtime environment, so every step of the build is thoroughly documented. Second, it is possible to use the image with the toolchain to ensure compatibility between development and the CI/CD pipeline. This also makes it easier to distribute upgrades and fixes to the toolchain itself. The major downside is that the containerized toolchain may not be as comfortable to use as a native one. Also, build tools are not particularly well suited to application containers, which require that there is one process running per container. This may lead to unexpected behavior whenever some of the processes crash or are forcefully stopped.

A multi-stage version of the preceding example would look like this:

```
FROM ubuntu:questing AS builder

RUN apt update && DEBIAN_FRONTEND=noninteractive apt install -y build-essential
gcc cmake ninja-build git python3-pip python3-venv

RUN python3 -m venv /opt/venv
ENV PATH="/opt/venv/bin:$PATH"
RUN pip3 install conan==2.* && conan profile detect

ADD . /root/src
WORKDIR /root/src

RUN mkdir -p build && cd build && \
    conan install .. --build=missing -s:a build_type=Release -s:a compiler.
cppstd=gnu20 -of . && \
    cmake .. -G Ninja -DCMAKE_BUILD_TYPE=Release && cmake --build . && cmake
--install .

FROM ubuntu:questing

COPY --from=builder /root/src/build/bin/customer /bin/customer

CMD ["/bin/customer"]
```

The first stage, starting at the first `FROM` command, sets up the builder, adds the sources, and builds the binaries. Then, the second stage, starting at the second `FROM` command, copies the resulting binary from the previous stage without copying the toolchain or the sources.

This significantly reduces the size of the final Docker image. For example, in the assembly of container images, a single-stage build version with compilers and development libraries produces an image of about 3.57 GB in size due to undeleted auxiliary files. For comparison, the multi-stage build version produces an image of only 137 MB in size, because all the auxiliary files are simply discarded. Both these versions include 77 MB of the base Ubuntu image, because base layers remain in the Docker image history. Although the size of the scratch version can be as small as approximately 17 MB, this approach is often impractical for complex applications. In this case, you must prepare and copy absolutely all their dependencies into the image being built yourself.

Obviously, the larger the container image size, the more disk space it takes up in the Docker registry and the longer it takes to download the image from the server. Furthermore, Docker images are stored by being packed in the registry and unpacked during download. Thus, such images may take up disk space without doing anything useful at all, but deleting all the auxiliary files is not always possible, preferable, or necessary. As an illustration, Python Docker images are huge (over 3 GB), but that's only because these images provide modules for every need, like a Swiss Army knife with many features.

Additionally, each layer is assigned a unique identifier, known as a hash or digest, which is calculated based on the layer's content, including metadata, configuration, and files. This is a cryptographic fingerprint that ensures both the integrity of the layer and deduplication, preventing layers from being downloaded twice from the repository. Thus, changing even a small file results in the creation of a new layer. Therefore, periodically prune unused Docker objects and dangling images that are not tagged and not used by any container.

During a build, Docker applies Dockerfile instructions to a running container and then commits file changes. In a multi-stage build, this process is repeated across multiple containers (one for each stage), with files copied from one container to another. This approach also simplifies the Dockerfile instructions, since explicit removal of auxiliary files is not required at all.

The `dive` tool (`wagoodman/dive`) will help you dive into exploring each layer in a Docker image and layer contents, and discovering ways to shrink the sizes of your Docker/OCI images.

Targeting multiple architectures

Application containers with Docker are typically used on x86_64 (also known as AMD64) machines. If you are only targeting this platform, you have nothing to worry about. However, if you are developing IoT, embedded, or edge applications, you may be interested in multi-architecture images.

Since Docker is available on many different CPU architectures, there are several ways to approach image management on multiple platforms.

One way to handle images built for different targets is by using the image tags to describe a particular platform. Instead of `merchant:v2.0.3`, we could have `merchant:v2.0.3-aarch64`. Although this approach may seem to be the easiest to implement, it is, in fact, a bit problematic.

Not only do you have to change the build process to include the architecture in the tagging process, but when pulling the images to run them, you will also have to take care to manually append the expected suffix everywhere. If you are using an orchestrator, you won't be able to share the manifests between the different platforms in a straightforward way, as the tags will be platform-specific.

A better way that doesn't require modifying the deployment step is to use `manifest-tool` (`https://github.com/estesp/manifest-tool`). The build process at first looks like the one suggested previously. Images are built separately on all the supported architectures and pushed to the registry with a platform suffix in their tags. After all the images are pushed, `manifest-tool` merges the images to provide a single multi-architecture one. This way, each supported platform is able to use the exact same tag.

An example configuration for `manifest-tool` is provided here:

```
image: tradefair/merchant:v2.0.3
manifests:
  - image: tradefair/merchant:v2.0.3-amd64
    platform:
      architecture: amd64
      os: linux
  - image: tradefair/merchant:v2.0.3-arm64
    platform:
      architecture: arm64
      os: linux
  - image: tradefair/merchant:v2.0.3-riscv64
    platform:
      architecture: riscv64
      os: linux
```

Here, we have three supported platforms, each with its respective suffix (`tradefair/merchant:v2.0.3-amd64`, `tradefair/merchant:v2.0.3-arm64`, and `tradefair/merchant:v2.0.3-riscv64`). `manifest-tool` combines the images built for each platform and produces a `tradefair/merchant:v2.0.3` image that we can use everywhere.

Another possibility is to use Docker manifests or Docker's built-in feature called buildx. Docker buildx uses BuildKit, an advanced container image build engine developed. buildx is included by default in Docker Desktop for Windows and macOS, while on Linux, it usually needs to be enabled manually. With buildx, you can attach several builder instances, each of which targets a required architecture. What's interesting is that you don't need to have native machines to run the builds; you can also use the **Quick EMUlator** (**QEMU**), Bochs, FEX, or Box64 emulation to run x86 Docker images on ARM, for example, or use cross-compilation in a multi-stage build. Although it is much more powerful than the previous approach, buildx is also more complex.

Example code to prepare the build environment and build a multi-platform image may look like the following:

```
# create two build contexts running on different machines
docker context create \
    --docker host=ssh://docker-user@host1.domifair.org \
    --description="Remote engine amd64" \
    node-amd64
docker context create \
    --docker host=ssh://docker-user@host2.domifair.org \
    --description="Remote engine arm64" \
    node-arm64

# use the contexts
docker buildx create --use --name mybuild node-amd64
docker buildx create --append --name mybuild node-arm64

# build an image
docker buildx build --platform linux/amd64,linux/arm64 .
```

As you can see, this may be a little confusing if you're used to the regular `docker build` command.

Alternative tools to build application containers

Building container images with Docker requires the Docker daemon to be running. The Docker daemon requires root privileges, which may pose security problems in some setups. Even though the Docker client that does the building may be run by an unprivileged user, it is not always feasible to install the Docker daemon in the build environment.

To address these challenges, alternative tools have been developed that can build container images.

Buildah

Buildah is an alternative tool to build container images that can be configured to run without root access. It is complemented by Podman and optionally Skopeo.

Podman runs, manages, and interacts with containers. It is designed to be daemonless and rootless. This container management tool interacts with the OCI runtime `runc` by default (written in Go) and optionally `crun` (written in C). These tools can be used as replacements for the traditional Docker workflow.

Skopeo manipulates, inspects, signs, and transfers container images and image repositories.

These tools ultimately depend on Linux kernel mechanisms to provide process isolation and security. A Linux container runs in a lightweight virtual environment isolated from the host system with Linux namespaces, cgroups, and kernel security features such as SELinux and seccomp.

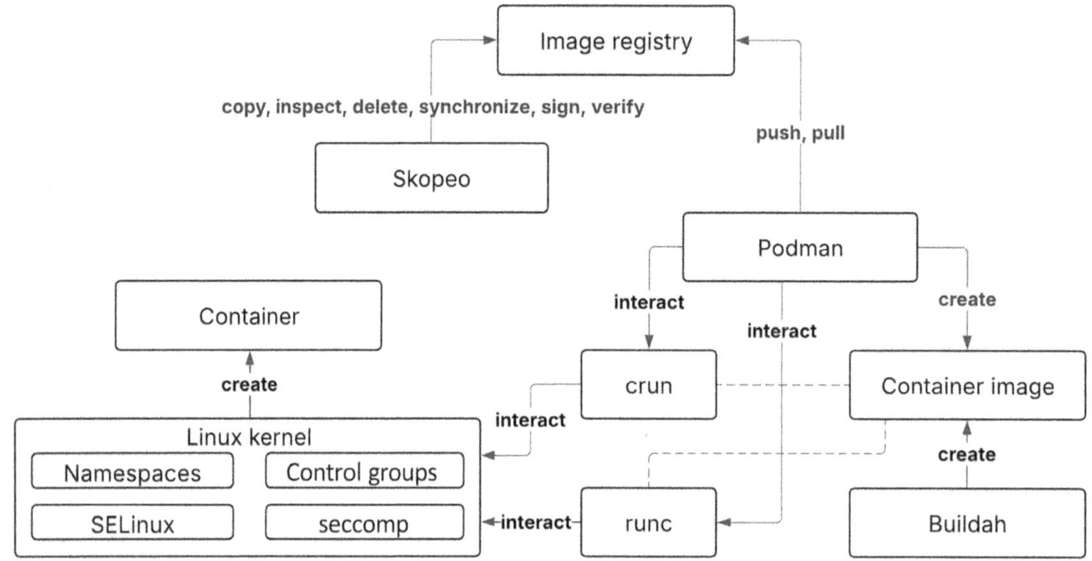

Figure 16.4: Buildah, Podman, and Skopeo

Buildah can work with standard Dockerfiles, which we discussed earlier, but it also presents its own CLI that you can use in shell scripts or other automation workflows you find more intuitive. One of the previous Dockerfiles rewritten as a shell script using the Buildah interface will look like this:

```
#!/bin/sh

ctr=$(buildah from ubuntu:questing)

buildah run $ctr -- /bin/sh -c 'apt update && apt install -y build-essential
gcc'

buildah config --cmd '/usr/bin/gcc' "$ctr"

buildah commit "$ctr" tradefair-gcc

buildah rm "$ctr"
```

One interesting feature of Buildah is that it allows you to mount the container image filesystem into your host filesystem. This way, you can use your host's commands to interact with the contents of the image. If you have software you don't want (or can't use due to licensing restrictions) within the container, it's still possible to invoke it outside of the container when using Buildah.

However, this tool lacks a built-in registry for storing container images, does not support the Docker Compose format, and does not have the same level of integration with other tools and services as Docker, which integrates with Kubernetes, for instance.

ansible-bender

`ansible-bender` uses Ansible playbooks and Buildah to build container images. All of the configuration, including base images and metadata, is passed as a variable within the playbook.

Here is our previous example converted to Ansible syntax:

```
---
- name: Container image with ansible-bender
  hosts: all
  vars:
    ansible_bender:
      base_image: python:3

      target_image:
        name: tradefair-gcc
        cmd: /usr/bin/gcc
  tasks:
  - name: Install Apt packages
    apt:
      pkg:
        - build-essential
        - gcc
```

As you can see, the `ansible_bender` variable is responsible for all the configuration specific to containers, and the listed tasks are executed inside the container built from the specified `base_image`.

One thing to note is that Ansible requires a Python interpreter to be present in the base image. Since official Ubuntu images do not include Python by default, we had to change the `ubuntu:questing` used in previous examples to `python:3`.

This tool abstracts away the details of container image building by using Buildah. Of course, container images can be built without `ansible-bender`, since Ansible already provides a set of modules for running Docker containers, building images, setting up networks, and much more.

There are also other tools to build container images. For example, you can use Nix to create a filesystem image and then put it inside the image using the Dockerfile's `COPY` instruction. In fact, you can prepare a filesystem image by any other means and then import it as a base container image using `docker import`.

Choose whichever solution fits your needs. Keep in mind that building with a Dockerfile using `docker build` is the most popular approach, hence it is the best-documented one and the best supported. Buildah offers more flexibility and allows you to fit container image creation more naturally into your build process. Finally, `ansible-bender` may be a good solution if you're already heavily invested in Ansible and you want to reuse already-available modules.

Integrating containers with CMake

In this section, we'll demonstrate how to create a Docker image as part of a CMake-based build process. While CMake is not inherently designed to work with Docker, it can be extended to generate and build container images as part of the workflow.

Configuring the Dockerfile with CMake

First and foremost, we'll need a Dockerfile. We'll generate it from a CMake input file using the following command:

```
configure_file(${CMAKE_CURRENT_SOURCE_DIR}/Dockerfile.in
               ${PROJECT_BINARY_DIR}/Dockerfile @ONLY)
```

Note that we're using `PROJECT_BINARY_DIR` to ensure we do not overwrite any Dockerfiles created by other projects in the source tree if our project is part of a bigger one.

Our `Dockerfile.in` file will look as follows:

```
FROM ubuntu:questing
ADD Customer-@PROJECT_VERSION@-Linux.deb .

RUN apt update && \
    apt -y --no-install-recommends install ./Customer-@PROJECT_VERSION@-Linux.
deb && \
    apt autoremove -y && apt clean && \
    rm -r /var/lib/apt/lists/* Customer-@PROJECT_VERSION@-Linux.deb

ENTRYPOINT ["/usr/bin/customer"]
EXPOSE 8080
```

First, we specify that we'll take the latest Ubuntu image, install our DEB package on it, along with its dependencies, and then tidy up. It's important to update the package manager cache in the same step as installing the package to avoid issues with stale caches due to how layers in Docker work. Cleanup is also performed as part of the same `RUN` command (in the same layer) so that the layer size is smaller. After installing the package, we make our image run the `customer` microservice when it is started. Finally, we tell Docker to expose the port that it will be listening on.

Now, let's return to our `CMakeLists.txt` file.

Building container images with CMake

For CMake-based projects, it is possible to include a build step responsible for building the containers. For that, we need to tell CMake to find the Docker executable and issue a warning if it is not found. We can do this using the following:

```
find_program(Docker_EXECUTABLE docker)
 if(NOT Docker_EXECUTABLE)
   message(WARNING "Docker not found")
 endif()
```

To illustrate how Docker can be integrated into a CMake build, let's revisit one of the examples from *Chapter 7, Building and Packaging*. There, we built a binary and a Conan package for the customer application. Now, we want to package this application as a Debian archive and build a Debian container image that includes this package.

To create our DEB package, we need a helper target. Let's use CMake's `add_custom_target` functionality for this:

```
add_custom_target(
   customer-deb
   COMMENT "Creating Customer DEB package"
   COMMAND ${CMAKE_CPACK_COMMAND} -G DEB
   WORKING_DIRECTORY ${PROJECT_BINARY_DIR}
   VERBATIM)
 add_dependencies(customer-deb libcustomer)
```

Our target invokes CPack to create just the one package that's interesting for us and omit the rest. We want the package to be created in the same directory as the Dockerfile for convenience. The `VERBATIM` keyword is recommended as it ensures that CMake will escape problematic characters. If it's not specified, the behavior of your scripts may vary across different platforms.

The `add_dependencies` call will make sure that before CMake builds the `customer-deb` target, `libcustomer` is already built. As we now have our helper target, let's use it when creating the container image:

```
add_custom_target(
   docker
   COMMENT "Preparing Docker image"
   COMMAND ${Docker_EXECUTABLE} build ${PROJECT_BINARY_DIR}
           -t tradefair/customer:${PROJECT_VERSION}
           -t tradefair/customer:latest
   VERBATIM)
add_dependencies(docker customer-deb)
```

As you can see, we invoke the Docker executable we found earlier in the directory, containing our Dockerfile and DEB package, to create an image. We also tell Docker to tag our image both as the latest and with the version of our project. Finally, we ensure the DEB package will be built when we invoke our Docker target.

Building the image is as simple as running `make docker` if `make` is the generator you chose. If you prefer the full CMake command (for example, to create generator-agnostic scripts), the invocation is `cmake --build . --target docker`. The size of the resulting Docker image is 252 MB. Define the service in `compose.yaml` and run it with `docker compose up`:

```
services:
  customer:
    image: tradefair/customer:latest
    ports:
      - "8080:8080"
```

Enter `http://localhost:8080/customer/v1?name=your_name` in a browser to see the application running.

So far, we have focused on building container images and packaging applications inside them. In practice, architects must also consider how these containers behave at runtime. We'll look at some of these considerations in the next section.

Practical runtime considerations for containers

One of the practical runtime advantages of containers is their flexibility in testing and deployment environments. Containers fit very well with CI/CD pipelines. Since they mostly require no further dependencies other than the container runtime itself, they can be easily tested. Worker machines don't have to be provisioned to fulfill the testing needs, so adding more nodes is much easier. What is more, all of them are general-purpose so that they may act as both builders and test runners, as in the GitLab and GitHub CI/CD pipelines from *Chapter 11, Continuous Integration and Continuous Deployment*, run on Ubuntu Docker images, and even deployment executors without any prior configuration.

Traditionally, integration testing is a complex process, as it requires deploying and configuring necessary services such as databases, message brokers, and web servers. However, by using containers, you can can combine the simplicity of unit tests with the reliability of integration tests that work with real dependencies. One of the popular libraries that uses this approach is Testcontainers. This testing library allows writing tests with real dependencies instead of mocked services by using disposable Docker containers. It supports many programming languages such as C++, C#, Go, Java, JavaScript, PHP, Python, Ruby, Rust, and Swift. However, at the time of writing, native C++ support is in the early stages of development.

Another great benefit of using containers in CI/CD is the fact that they are isolated from one another. This means multiple copies running on the same machine should not interfere. That is true unless the tests require some resources from the host operating system, such as port forwarding or volume mounting. Therefore, it's best to design tests so that such resources are not necessary (or at least avoid conflicts by, for example, randomizing port numbers).

Beyond testing in CI/CD pipelines, there are also other runtime considerations—such as the choice of system libraries inside containers and the availability of alternative container runtimes—that can significantly affect how applications are built and deployed.

Runtime libraries inside containers

The choice of containers may influence the choice of a toolchain and, therefore, the C++ language features available to the application. Since containers are typically Linux-based, the system compiler available is usually GNU GCC with the widely supported glibc as a standard library of the GNU/ Linux operating system. However, some Linux distributions popular with containers, such as Alpine and BusyBox, are based on different standard C libraries, musl and uClibc.

musl is a lightweight, compact library focused on strict POSIX compliance, static linking, and security through simplicity, but it can cause compatibility issues with certain software or during compilation. uClibc is a small standard C library for embedded Linux systems and mobile phones, widely used in low-cost embedded systems and IoT devices.

If you are targeting such a distribution, make sure the code you'll be using, whether developed in-house or from third-party providers, is compatible with musl or uClibc. The main advantage is smaller container images.

For example, a Python image built for Debian Bookworm is around 365 MB, the slimmed-down Debian version is around 43 MB, while the Alpine version is only around 12 MB. BusyBox images are even smaller: 740 KB (uClibc) and 840 KB (musl). Smaller images mean less wasted bandwidth (for uploads and downloads) and quicker updates.

However, if you decide to use either musl or uClibc with Python, on the contrary, it can increase the build time and the sizes of Docker images since the compiled packages for these libraries are usually not published.

Alpine may also introduce some unwanted traits, such as longer build times, obscure bugs, or reduced performance. If you want to use it to reduce the size, run proper tests to make sure the application behaves without problems.

To reduce your images' size even more, you may consider ditching the underlying operating system altogether. What we mean by operating system here is all the userland tools ordinarily present in a container, such as a shell, package manager, and shared libraries. After all, if your application is the only thing that's going to be running, everything else is unnecessary.

It is typical for Go or Rust applications to provide a static build for this purpose. While this might not be as straightforward in C++, it is worth considering and can be easily implemented. For instance, you need to pass the `CMAKE_EXE_LINKER_FLAGS`, `BUILD_SHARED_LIBS`, and `CMAKE_FIND_LIBRARY_SUFFIXES` options to CMake like so:

```
rm -rf ./build/ && mkdir build && cd build
cmake .. -G Ninja -DCMAKE_BUILD_TYPE=Release -DCMAKE_EXE_LINKER_FLAGS="-static"
-DBUILD_SHARED_LIBS=OFF -DCMAKE_FIND_LIBRARY_SUFFIXES=".a"
cmake --build .
```

There are a few drawbacks related to decreasing the image size as well. First of all, if you decide to go with Alpine, BusyBox, or Void Linux, keep in mind that it is not as popular as, say, Ubuntu, Debian, Arch, or Fedora. Although it is often the platform of choice for container developers, it's very unusual for any other purpose.

This means that there might be new compatibility problems, mostly stemming from the fact that it's not based on the de facto standard glibc implementation. If you rely on third-party components, the provider may not offer support for this platform.

If you decide to go down the single statically linked binary inside the container image route, there are also some challenges to consider. First of all, you are discouraged from statically linking glibc as it uses dynamic loading (`dlopen`) internally for services such as **Name Service Switch** (**NSS**) and iconv. If your software relies on DNS resolving or character set conversion, you'll have to provide a copy of glibc and the relevant libraries anyway.

Another point to consider is that shell and package managers are often used for debugging containers that misbehave. When one of your containers is acting strangely, you may start another process inside the container and figure out what is happening inside by using standard Unix tools such as `ps`, `ls`, or `cat`. To run such an application inside the container, it has to be present in the container image first.

The **GNU Debugger** (**GDB**) and **LLVM Project** (**LLDB**) are capable of remotely debugging applications, including in Linux containers, but they necessitate `gdb-server` and `lldb-server`, respectively, on the targets. Also, IDEs such as CLion IDE, Qt Creator, Visual Studio, and Visual Studio Code support remote debugging equipped with these debugging tools.

Alternative container runtimes

Docker is the most popular way of building and running containers, but since container runtimes follow open standards, there are also alternative runtimes that you may use. The main replacement for Docker that offers a similar user experience is Podman. Together with Buildah, described in the previous section, these tools can replace Docker entirely.

The added benefit is that they *don't require an additional daemon running on a host machine, as Docker does*. Both also have support for rootless operations, which makes them a better fit for security-critical operations. Podman accepts all the commands you would expect the Docker CLI to take, so you can simply use it as an alias this way, and it also has support for FreeBSD, NetBSD, and OpenBSD. Since version 14.2, FreeBSD also includes OCI-compatible images, and Podman runs them on both AMD64 and ARM64 systems.

Another approach to containers that aims to provide better security is the **Kata Containers** initiative. Kata Containers uses lightweight virtual machines to leverage the hardware virtualization required for an additional level of isolation between the containers and the host operating system.

CRI-O and containerd are also popular runtimes used in Kubernetes clusters.

Till now, we've looked at containers running in isolation. However, modern architectures usually involve several containers running together. This is where container orchestration comes in.

Understanding container orchestration

Some of the containers' benefits only become apparent when you are using a container orchestrator to manage them. An orchestrator keeps track of all the nodes that will be running your workload, and it also monitors the health and status of the containers spread across these computing nodes, or worker machines, which are virtual or physical.

More advanced features, for example, high availability, require the proper setup of the orchestrator, which typically means dedicating at least three machines for the control plane and another three machines for worker nodes. The autoscaling of nodes, in addition to the autoscaling of containers, also requires the orchestrator to have a driver able to control the underlying infrastructure (for example, by using the cloud provider's API).

Here, we will give you an overview of some of the most popular orchestrators that you can choose from.

Although the presented orchestrators differ in their features and operating principles, they operate on similar objects (services, containers, and batch jobs). What they have in common is that you typically write a configuration file that declaratively describes the required resources, and then you apply this configuration using a dedicated CLI tool. To illustrate the differences between the tools, we provide an example configuration specifying a web application introduced before (the merchant service) and a popular web server, Nginx, to act as a proxy.

Self-hosted solutions

Whether you are running your application on-premises, in a private cloud, or in a public cloud, you may want to have tight control over the orchestrator of your choice. The following is a collection of self-hosted container orchestration solutions. Keep in mind that most of them are also available as managed services. However, going with a self-hosted option helps you prevent vendor lock-in, which may be desirable for your organization.

Kubernetes

Kubernetes is probably the best-known orchestrator of all the ones that we mention here. It is prevalent, which means there is a lot of documentation and community support if you decide to implement it.

Kubernetes uses the same application container format as Docker, but this is basically where the similarities end. It is impossible to use standard Docker tools to interact with Kubernetes clusters and resources directly. Instead, there is a new set of tools and concepts to learn when using Kubernetes.

While with Docker, the container is the main object you will operate on, with Kubernetes, the smallest piece of the runtime is called a Pod. A Pod may consist of one or more containers that share storage volumes, networking resources, and a single cluster-private IP address. Containers within a Pod can communicate with each other over `localhost`, while all Pods in a cluster can communicate directly without **Network Address Translation** (NAT). Pods in themselves are rarely of interest as Kubernetes also has higher-order concepts such as ReplicationControllers, DeploymentControllers, and DaemonSets. Their role is to keep track of the Pods and ensure the desired number of replicas is running on the nodes.

The networking model in Kubernetes is also very different from Docker's. With Docker, you can forward ports from a container to make it accessible from different machines. With Kubernetes, if you want to access a Pod, you typically create a Service resource, which may act as a load balancer to handle the traffic to the Pods that form the service's backend. Services may be used for Pod-to-Pod communication, but they may also be exposed to the internet. Internally, Kubernetes resources perform service discovery using DNS names.

Kubernetes is declarative and eventually consistent. This means that instead of directly creating and allocating resources, you only must provide the description of the desired end state and Kubernetes will do the work required to bring the cluster to the desired state. Resources are often described using YAML.

Kubernetes is built on the concept of labels and selectors. Labels are key–value pair properties attached to each Kubernetes object. These labels identify, organize, and associate resources, and selectors select those resources based on these labels.

Since Kubernetes is highly extensible, there are a lot of associated projects developed under the **Cloud Native Computing Foundation** (CNCF), which turn Kubernetes into a provider-agnostic cloud development platform.

Here's how the resource definition looks in the Kubernetes `merchant.yaml` manifest using YAML, but JSON is also supported. The templates in the Kubernetes manifest define Pods. Kubernetes services provide access to Kubernetes deployments and route traffic to Pods. These two blocks define the frontend server:

```
apiVersion: apps/v1
kind: Deployment
metadata:
  labels:
    app: tradefair-front
  name: tradefair-front
spec:
  selector:
    matchLabels:
      app: tradefair-front
  template:
    metadata:
      labels:
        app: tradefair-front
    spec:
      containers:
        - name: webserver
          imagePullPolicy: Always
          image: nginx
          ports:
```

```
          - name: http
            containerPort: 80
            protocol: TCP
        restartPolicy: Always
---
apiVersion: v1
kind: Service
metadata:
  labels:
    app: tradefair-front
  name: tradefair-front
spec:
  ports:
    - port: 80
      protocol: TCP
      targetPort: 80
  selector:
    app: tradefair-front
  type: ClusterIP
```

These two blocks define the backend server:

```
---
apiVersion: apps/v1
kind: Deployment
metadata:
  labels:
    app: tradefair-merchant
  name: merchant
spec:
  selector:
    matchLabels:
      app: tradefair-merchant
  replicas: 3
  template:
    metadata:
      labels:
        app: tradefair-merchant
    spec:
      containers:
        - name: merchant
          imagePullPolicy: Always
```

```
          image: tradefair/merchant:v2.0.3
          ports:
            - name: http
              containerPort: 8000
              protocol: TCP
      restartPolicy: Always
---
apiVersion: v1
kind: Service
metadata:
  labels:
    app: tradefair-merchant
  name: merchant
spec:
  ports:
    - port: 80
      protocol: TCP
      targetPort: 8000
  selector:
    app: tradefair-merchant
    type: ClusterIP
```

To apply this configuration and orchestrate the containers, use the following:

```
kubectl apply -f merchant.yaml.
```

Kubernetes is covered in more detail in the next chapter.

Docker Swarm

Docker Engine, required to build and run Docker containers, comes pre-installed with its own orchestrator. This orchestrator is Docker Swarm, and its main feature is high compatibility with existing Docker tools by using the Docker API.

Docker Swarm uses the concept of Services to manage health checks and autoscaling. It supports rolling upgrades of the services natively. Services are able to publish their ports, which will then be served by Swarm's load balancer. It supports storing configs as objects for runtime customization and has basic secret management built in.

Docker Swarm is much simpler and less extensible than Kubernetes. This could be an advantage if you do not want to learn all the details of Kubernetes. However, the main disadvantage is a lack of popularity, which means it is harder to find relevant material about Docker Swarm.

One of the benefits of using Docker Swarm is that you don't have to learn new commands. If you're already used to Docker and Docker Compose, Swarm works with the same resources. It allows specific options that extend Docker to handle deployments.

Two services orchestrated with Swarm would look like this (`compose.yaml`):

```
services:
  web:
    image: nginx
    ports:
      - "80:80"
    depends_on:
      - merchant
  merchant:
    image: tradefair/merchant:v2.0.3
    deploy:
      replicas: 3
    ports:
      - "8000"
```

To apply the configuration, run the following:

```
docker stack deploy --compose-file compose.yml tradefair.
```

Nomad

Nomad is different from the previous two solutions, as it is not focused solely on containers. It is a general-purpose orchestrator with support for Docker, Podman, QEMU Virtual Machines, isolated fork/exec, and several other task drivers. Nomad is a solution worth learning about if you want to gain some of the advantages of orchestration without migrating your application to containers.

Developed by HashiCorp, Nomad is relatively easy to set up, and it integrates well with other HashiCorp products, such as Consul for service discovery and Vault for secret management. Like Docker and Kubernetes, Nomad clients can run locally and connect to the server responsible for managing your cluster.

There are three job types available in Nomad:

- **Service:** A long-lived task that should not exit without manual intervention (for example, a web server or a database).
- **Batch:** A short-lived task that can complete within as little as a few minutes. If the batch job returns an exit code indicating an error, it is either restarted or rescheduled according to configuration.
- **System:** A task that is necessary to run on every node in the cluster (for example, logging agent).

Compared to other orchestrators, Nomad is relatively easy to install and maintain. It is also extensible when it comes to task drivers or device plugins (used to access dedicated hardware such as GPUs or **Field-Programmable Gate Arrays (FPGAs)**). Its downsides are weaker community support and fewer third-party integrations when compared to Kubernetes. However, Nomad does not require you to redesign the application's architecture to access the provided benefits, which is often the case with Kubernetes.

To configure the two services with Nomad, we need two configuration files since a job file contains exactly one job declaration specified in **HashiCorp Configuration Language** (HCL).

The first one is `nginx.nomad`, defining the frontend service scheduled in the data center and grouping tasks managed together as a single unit:

```
job "web" {
  datacenters = ["dc1"]
  type = "service"
  group "nginx" {
    task "nginx" {
      driver = "docker"
      config {
        image = "nginx"
        port_map {
          http = 80
        }
      }
      resources {
        network {
          port "http" {
              static = 80
          }
        }
      }
      service {
        name = "nginx"
        tags = [ "tradefair-front", "web", "nginx" ]
        port = "http"
        check {
          type = "tcp"
          interval = "10s"
          timeout = "2s"
        }
      }
    }
  }
}
```

The second defines the merchant service, so it's called `merchant.nomad`:

```
job "merchant" {
  datacenters = ["dc1"]
  type = "service"
  group "merchant" {
    count = 3
    task "merchant" {
      driver = "docker"
      config {
        image = "tradefair/merchant:v2.0.3"
        port_map {
          http = 8000
        }
      }
      resources {
        network {
          port "http" {
              static = 8000
          }
        }
      }
      service {
        name = "merchant"
        tags = [ "tradefair-front", "merchant" ]
        port = "http"
```

Nomad supports different health check probes—`grpc`, `http`, `script`, and `tcp`:

```
        check {
          type = "tcp"
          interval = "10s"
          timeout = "2s"
        }
      }
    }
  }
}
```

To apply the configuration, run the following:

```
nomad job run merchant.nomad && nomad job run nginx.nomad.
```

OpenShift

OpenShift is Red Hat's commercial container platform built on Kubernetes. It includes a lot of additional components that are useful in the everyday operations of Kubernetes clusters. You get a container registry; CI/CD pipelines based on the Tekton framework; OpenTelemetry for logging, monitoring, and tracing; a service mesh based on Istio, Envoy, and Kiali (a console for Istio); Windows container orchestration; sandboxed containers based on Kata containers (a container runtime for building lightweight virtual machines that seamlessly plug into the containers ecosystem); and serverless applications based on Knative. It also supports virtualization technologies such as **Kernel-based Virtual Machine** (**KVM**), Xen, and Microsoft Hyper-V, and GitOps through Argo CD. However, it is not fully compatible with Kubernetes, so it shouldn't be thought of as a drop-in replacement.

OpenShift runs on **Red Hat Enterprise Linux CoreOS** (**RHCOS**), provides many pre-created app templates, and supports multiple programming languages (such as C++, C#, Go, Java, and Python) and accelerator hardware such as GPUs, **Tensor Processing Units** (**TPUs**), and FPGAs. You can use it on-premises, within Red Hat Cloud, on one of the supported public cloud providers (including AWS, Google Cloud, IBM Cloud, Microsoft Azure, Oracle Cloud, or Alibaba Cloud), or as a hybrid cloud.

There is also an open source community-supported project called **Origin Community Distribution of Kubernetes** (**OKD**), which forms the basis of Red Hat's OpenShift. If you do not require commercial support and other benefits of OpenShift, you may still use OKD for your Kubernetes workflow.

Managed services

As previously mentioned, some of the aforementioned orchestrators are also available as managed services. Kubernetes, for instance, is available as a managed solution in multiple public cloud providers. This section will show you some of the different approaches to container orchestration, which are not based on any of the solutions mentioned previously.

AWS ECS

Before Kubernetes released its 1.0 version, AWS proposed its own container orchestration technology called **Elastic Container Service** (**ECS**). ECS provides an orchestrator that monitors, scales, and restarts your services when needed.

To run containers in ECS, you need to provide the Amazon **Elastic Compute Cloud** (**EC2**) instances on which the workload will run. You are not billed for the orchestrator's use, but you are billed for all the AWS services that you typically use (the underlying EC2 instances, for example, or an Amazon **Relational Database Service** (**RDS**) database).

One of the significant benefits of ECS is its excellent integration with the rest of the AWS ecosystem. If you are already familiar with AWS services and invested in the platform, you will have less trouble understanding and managing ECS.

If you do not require many of the Kubernetes advanced features and its extensions, ECS may be a better choice as it's more straightforward and more comfortable to learn, but this service is proprietary. Thus, migrating to another service provider requires more time and effort than with Kubernetes due to vendor lock-in.

AWS Fargate

Another managed orchestrator offered by AWS is Fargate. Unlike ECS, it does not require you to provision and pay for the underlying EC2 instances. The only components you are focused on are the containers, the network interfaces attached to them, and AWS **Identity and Access Management (IAM)** permissions.

Fargate requires the least amount of maintenance compared to other solutions and is the easiest to learn. Autoscaling and load-balancing are available out of the box thanks to the existing AWS products in this space.

The main downside here is the premium that you pay for hosting your services when compared to ECS. A straight cost comparison is not possible as ECS requires paying for the EC2 instances, while Fargate requires paying for the memory and CPU usage independently. This lack of direct control over your cluster may easily lead to high costs once your services start to autoscale.

Azure Service Fabric

The problem with all of the preceding solutions is that they mostly target Docker containers, which are first and foremost Linux-centric. Azure Service Fabric, on the other hand, is a Windows-first product backed by Microsoft. It enables running legacy Windows apps without modifications, which may help you migrate your application if it relies on such services.

As with Kubernetes, Azure Service Fabric is not just a container orchestrator but also a platform on top of which you can build your applications. One of the building blocks happens to be containers, so it works fine as an orchestrator.

With the introduction of Azure Kubernetes Service, the managed Kubernetes platform in the Azure cloud, there is less need for using Service Fabric.

Summary

When you are an architect of modern software, you must consider modern technologies. Taking them into account doesn't mean following the trends blindly; it means being able to objectively assess whether a particular proposition makes sense in your case or not.

Both microservices, presented in the previous chapters, and containers, presented in this chapter, are worth considering and understanding. Are they worth implementing as well? It depends heavily on what type of product you are designing. If you've read this far, you are ready to make the decision for yourself.

In this chapter, we compared operating system and application containers with virtual machines and examined how application containers relate to microservices and the Twelve-Factor App methodology. We then discussed the advantages and disadvantages of containers, the Linux mechanisms used for process containerization, and the industries where C++ remains particularly relevant. Finally, we explored container design, building container images, and running them across different processor architectures and container runtimes, as well as the choice between self-hosted and managed container orchestration solutions.

The next chapter is dedicated to observability—a crucial capability for identifying the root cause of issues when multiple containers and microservices are used in a distributed system.

Questions

1. How do application containers differ from operating system containers?
2. What are some early examples of sandboxing environments in Unix systems?
3. Why are containers a good fit for microservices?
4. What are the main differences between containers and virtual machines?
5. When are application containers a bad choice?
6. What are some tools to build multi-platform container images?
7. Besides Docker, what are some other container runtimes?
8. What are some popular orchestrators?

Further reading

- Richard Bullington-McGuire, Andrew K. Dennis, and Michael Schwartz, *Docker for Developers: Develop and Run Your Application with Docker Containers Using DevOps Tools for Continuous Delivery*, Packt Publishing: `https://www.packtpub.com/product/docker-for-developers/9781789536058`
- Emmanouil Gkatziouras, *A Developer's Essential Guide to Docker Compose: Simplify the Development and Orchestration of Multi-Container Applications*, Packt Publishing: `https://www.packtpub.com/en-us/product/a-developers-essential-guide-to-docker-compose-9781801813815`
- Gabriel N. Schenker, *The Ultimate Docker Container Book: Build, Test, Ship, and Run Containers with Docker and Kubernetes*, Third Edition, Packt Publishing: `https://www.packtpub.com/en-us/product/the-ultimate-docker-container-book-9781804613184`
- Alessandro Arrichiello and Gianni Salinetti, *Podman for DevOps: Containerization Reimagined with Podman and Its Companion Tools*, Packt Publishing: `https://www.packtpub.com/en-us/product/podman-for-devops-9781803248967`
- Docker Docs, *Run Multiple Processes in a Container*: `https://docs.docker.com/engine/containers/multi-service_container/`
- Docker Docs, *Docker Compose Quickstart*: `https://docs.docker.com/compose/gettingstarted/`
- Docker Docs, *How Compose Works*: `https://docs.docker.com/compose/intro/compose-application-model/`
- Docker Docs, *Compose Build Specification*: `https://docs.docker.com/reference/compose-file/build/`
- Jeremie Drouet, *Multi-Arch Build and Images, the Simple Way* (Blog), Docker: `https://www.docker.com/blog/multi-arch-build-and-images-the-simple-way/`
- Docker Docs, *Multi-Platform Builds*: `https://docs.docker.com/build/building/multi-platform/`
- Docker Docs, *Multi-Stage Builds*: `https://docs.docker.com/build/building/multi-stage/`

- GoogleContainerTools, *Distroless,* GitHub: `https://github.com/GoogleContainerTools/distroless`
- Microsoft, *Development Containers,* containers.dev: `https://containers.dev/overview`
- Adam Wiggins, *The Twelve-Factor App,* 12factor.net: `https://12factor.net/`
- Marcio Morales, *Running Windows Containers on AWS: A Complete Guide to Successfully Running Windows Containers on Amazon ECS, EKS, and AWS Fargate,* Packt Publishing: `https://www.packtpub.com/en-us/product/running-windows-containers-on-aws-9781804617199`
- Testcontainers Native, *Testcontainers for C/C++/Swift and Other Native Projects,* GitHub: `https://testcontainers.github.io/testcontainers-native/`

17

Observability

In the last few chapters, we explored microservices as one of the key architectural styles in distributed systems, saw how these services communicate with each other, and then looked at containers as an efficient way to package and deploy them.

In this chapter, we cover another challenge that surfaces when we use multiple containers and microservices in a distributed system: quickly identifying the root cause of issues. If you've ever tried debugging and monitoring microservices-based distributed systems, you've probably encountered situations where this became a real headache. Observability helps counter this issue.

Observability is a measure of the extent to which the internal state of a system is inferred from its external outputs, using real-time metrics, logs, and traces to guarantee resilience. These signals help detect and analyze performance bottlenecks, identify and debug issues across multiple microservices, ensure system reliability and uptime, and improve response times and user experience. In short, observability is crucial to designing resilient distributed systems; without it, you risk losing the ability to debug your applications.

This chapter focuses on exploring key approaches to achieving observability. We describe here several open source solutions that you might find useful when designing your system.

Moreover, we'll often use the terms *application*, *service*, and *microservice* somewhat interchangeably. While an application may be a complete system, with a microservice forming one part of it, in our small-scale examples, a single service effectively represents the whole application.

The following topics will be covered in this chapter:

- Logging
- Monitoring
- Tracing

Technical requirements

The code present in the chapter has been placed on GitHub at `https://github.com/PacktPublishing/Software-Architecture-with-Cpp-2E/tree/main/Chapter17`.

Logging

Logging is a topic that should be familiar to you, even if you've never designed microservices. Logs (or log files) store the information about the events happening in a system. The system may mean your application, the operating system your application runs on, or the cloud platform you use for deployment. Each of these components may provide logs.

Logs are stored as separate files because they provide a permanent record of all the events taking place. When the system becomes unresponsive, we want to query the logs and figure out the possible root cause of the outage.

This means that logs also provide **audit logging** (also called **audit trailing**). Because the events are recorded in chronological order, we are able to understand the state of the system by examining the recorded historical state.

To help with debugging, logs are usually human-readable. Binary formats also exist, but such formats are rather rare when using files to store the logs.

Logging with microservices

This approach to logging itself doesn't differ much from the traditional approach. The main difference is in where the logs go and how they are consumed. Rather than using text files to store the logs locally, microservices usually print logs to `stdout`, avoiding the need to keep logs in a running container. As a result, the application is decoupled from the logging agent and routing mechanism, leaving that responsibility to the container orchestrator or execution environment. This makes the application simpler and more portable, since it only needs to produce logs rather than manage them. A unified logging layer is then used to retrieve the logs and process them. To implement this, you need a logging library that you can configure to suit your needs.

Logging in C++ with spdlog

One of the most popular and fast logging libraries for C++ is `spdlog`, which supports different platforms: Linux, macOS, Windows, Solaris, AIX, and Android. It's built using C++11 and can be used either as a header-only library or as a static library (which reduces compile time).

Some interesting features of `spdlog` include the following:

- Feature-rich formatting
- Multiple sinks:
  - Rotating log files
  - Daily log files
  - Colored console logging
  - syslog (system log)
  - Windows event log
  - Windows debugger (`OutputDebugString(..)`)
  - Log to Qt widgets
  - Custom sinks (implemented as a single function)

- Single- and multi-threaded loggers
- Synchronous and asynchronous logging
- Filtering by log level at compile time and runtime
- Support for loading log levels from command-line arguments or environment variables
- Backtrace support—storing debug messages in a ring buffer and displaying them on demand

Among its features, log rotation is an automated process of renaming, compressing, and archiving log files on a schedule (such as daily or weekly) or when they exceed a certain size. Syslog is a standard network protocol and system for collecting, sending, and storing system event logs for Unix-like systems.

When it comes to synchronous and asynchronous logging, the library's creator recommends using the regular synchronous logging mechanism unless there is a specific need for asynchronous logging. The asynchronous mode isolates the application from unexpected load spikes caused by factors such as slow disk I/O or network latency.

One feature that might be missing from `spdlog` is the direct support for Logstash or Fluentd. If you want to use one of these aggregators, it is still possible to configure `spdlog` with file sink output and use Filebeat or Fluent Bit to forward the file contents to the appropriate aggregator.

The sinks of `spdlog` have `_mt` (multi-threaded) or `_st` (single-threaded) suffixes indicating the thread safety. Although single-threaded sinks cannot be used from multiple threads simultaneously, they are faster because no mutex locking is employed, which incurs some overhead.

The following example demonstrates how logging appears using `spdlog::sinks::stdout_sink_st`, a single-threaded sink synchronously sending log messages to the standard output stream (`stdout`) in `responder.h`:

```
// the implementation is partially omitted
...
template <typename Responder> void handle_get(
    const drogon::HttpRequestPtr &request, Responder &responder,
    std::function<void(const drogon::HttpResponsePtr &)> &&callback) {
  const auto sink = std::make_shared<spdlog::sinks::stdout_sink_st>();
  const auto logger = std::make_shared<spdlog::logger>("responder", sink);
```

The `SPDLOG_LOGGER_INFO` and `SPDLOG_LOGGER_ERROR` macros, corresponding to the info and error logging levels, wrap the `SPDLOG_LOGGER_CALL` macro. In turn, this macro wraps an object of class `spdlog::source_loc`, which stores information about the current file, line, and function at the location of the macro (C++20 introduces the `std::source_location` class for the same purpose):

```
  SPDLOG_LOGGER_INFO(logger, "get optional parameter 'name'");
  auto name = request->getOptionalParameter<std::string>("name");

  if (!name) {
    const auto err = "missing value for 'name'";
```

```
        SPDLOG_LOGGER_ERROR(logger, err);
        responder.respond(drogon::k400BadRequest, Json::Value(err),
                          std::move(callback));
        return;
    }

    SPDLOG_LOGGER_INFO(logger, "return response to '{0}'", name.value());

    const auto [code, response] = responder.prepare_response(name.value());
    responder.respond(code, response, std::move(callback));
}
```

This produces the following terminal output, with log messages corresponding to the placement of the macros in the application:

```
[2025-09-14 12:17:34.599] [main] [info] [main.cpp:22] handling HTTP request to
/customer/v1
[2025-09-14 12:17:34.599] [responder] [info] [responder.h:27] get optional
parameter 'name'
[2025-09-14 12:17:34.599] [responder] [error] [responder.h:33] missing value
for 'name'
[2025-09-14 12:18:02.067] [main] [info] [main.cpp:22] handling HTTP request to
/customer/v1
[2025-09-14 12:18:02.067] [responder] [info] [responder.h:27] get optional
parameter 'name'
[2025-09-14 12:18:02.068] [responder] [info] [responder.h:39] return response
to 'Motoko'
```

The other popular C++ logging libraries are log4cplus (C++23), Plog, Quill, loguru, Abseil Logging, and Boost.Log, and less popular ones are g3log, Log4Qt, reckless, lwlog, and Blackhole.

We just saw application-level logging using `spdlog`, where each service writes its own logs. In real-world distributed systems, these logs must be collected, standardized, and analyzed across many services and hosts. This is where the following three layers come into the picture: unified logging, log aggregation, and log visualization.

Unified logging

Most of the time, we won't be able to control all of the microservices that we use. Some of them will use one logging library, while others will use a different one. On top of that, the formats will be entirely different, and so will their rotation policies. To make things worse, you often need to correlate application events with operating system events. This is where the unified logging layer comes into play.

One of the purposes of the unified logging layer is to collect logs from different sources. Unified logging layer tools provide many integrations and understand different logging formats and transports (such as file, HTTP, and TCP).

This layer is also capable of filtering the logs. We may want filtering to satisfy compliance, anonymize the personal details of our customers, or protect the implementation details of our services.

To make it easier to query the logs at a later time, the layer can also perform translation between formats. Even if the different services that you use store the logs in JSON, CSV, and the Apache format, the unified logging layer solution is able to translate them all to JSON to give them structure.

The final task of the unified logging layer is forwarding the logs to their next destination. Depending on the complexity of the system, the next destination may be a storage facility or another filtering, translation, or forwarding facility.

Here are some popular components that let you build the unified logging layer.

Logstash

Logstash is one of the most popular unified logging layer solutions. Currently, it is owned by Elastic, the company behind Elasticsearch. If you've heard of the ELK stack (now known as the Elastic Stack), Logstash is the *L* in the acronym.

Logstash was written in Ruby and has been ported to JRuby. This, unfortunately, means that it is rather resource-intensive. For this reason, it is not advisable to run Logstash on each machine. Rather, it is meant to be used mainly as a log forwarder, with lightweight Filebeat deployed to each machine to handle log collection.

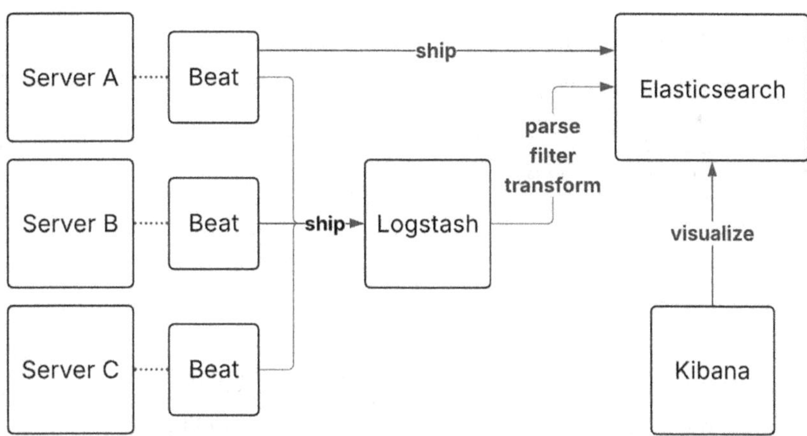

Figure 17.1: The Elastic stack: Elasticsearch, Logstash, and Kibana (ELK)

In the figure, we can see that Logstash collects logs from various sources, including Beats (data shippers for Elasticsearch), and forwards the logs to the centralized logging platform.

Filebeat

Filebeat is part of the Beats platform, a family of lightweight data shippers collecting and sending operational data (such as logs, metrics, and network packets) from servers and other systems to Elasticsearch or Logstash for processing and visualization. Unlike Logstash, these data shippers may be used directly with the application.

Elastic provides these data shippers:

- **Auditbeat:** Audits the activities of users and processes on the systems
- **Filebeat:** Forwards log files and journals to centralize log data
- **Heartbeat:** Periodically checks the status of services to determine their availability
- **Metricbeat:** Periodically collects metrics from the operating system and services running on the server
- **Packetbeat:** Captures network traffic between application servers and analyzes network packets in real time
- **Winlogbeat:** Ships Windows event logs

Filebeat can act as a lightweight alternative to Logstash in simpler setups. However, in a usual setup, Filebeat handles log shipping at scale, whereas a centralized Logstash installation performs all the heavy lifting, including translation, filtering, and forwarding.

Fluentd

Fluentd is the main competitor of Logstash. It is also the tool of choice of some cloud providers.

Thanks to its modular, plugin-based approach, you can find plugins for data sources (such as Ruby applications, Docker containers, SNMP, or MQTT protocols), data outputs (such as Elastic Stack, SQL Database, Sentry, Datadog, or Slack), and several other kinds of filters and middleware.

Figure 17.2 shows how Fluentd can be used as a Docker logging driver:

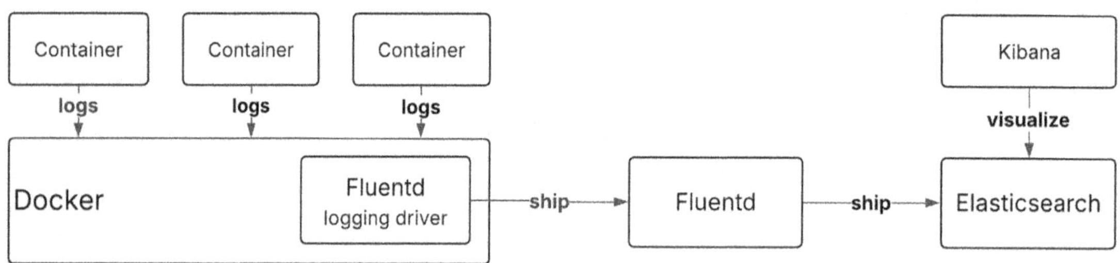

Figure 17.2: Docker with Fluentd as a logging driver

In the figure, the Fluentd logging driver sends container logs to the Fluentd collector, which sends them to the centralized logging platform.

Fluentd is generally lighter on resources than Logstash, but it is still not a perfect solution for running at scale. For lightweight log forwarding, Fluentd is often paired with Fluent Bit, which plays a role like Filebeat in the Logstash ecosystem.

Fluent Bit

Fluent Bit is written in C and provides a faster and lighter solution that plugs into Fluentd. As a log processor and forwarder, it also features many integrations for inputs and outputs.

Besides log collection, Fluent Bit can also export system-level metrics such as CPU, disk, network, and process statistics on Linux and Windows systems. It might be used together with Fluentd, or it can forward directly to Elasticsearch or InfluxDB (a time-series database), as shown in *Figure 17.3*.

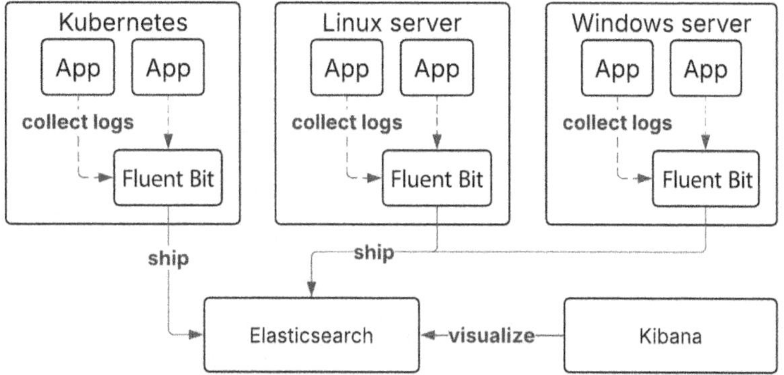

Figure 17.3: Fluent Bit monitoring Kubernetes, Linux, and Windows servers

Fluent Bit collects logs from multiple environments (Kubernetes, Linux, and Windows) and sends them to the centralized logging platform.

Vector

While Logstash and Fluentd are stable, mature, and tried solutions, there are also newer alternatives in the unified logging layer space.

One of them is Vector, developed by Datadog, which aims to handle all of the observability data in a single tool. Vector is a high-performance observability data pipeline for collecting, transforming, and routing logs and metrics. This is also reflected in the choice of technology. Vector uses Rust for the engine, Lua for scripting, and **VRL** (**Vector Remap Language**), a powerful custom scripting transformation language for processing observability data (logs, metrics, traces).

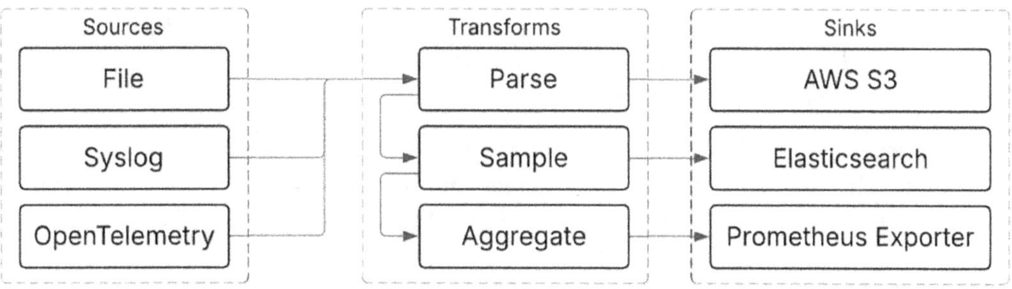

Figure 17.4: Vector data pipeline showing the processing of log events

Vector takes raw logs and standardizes them into a unified log event format. As log events pass through the pipeline, they undergo various transformations. The logs are then sent to multiple destinations for subsequent storage and analysis.

Being a newer tool, Vector's ecosystem of integrations and community support is still growing compared to established alternatives such as Fluentd or Logstash. Writing custom plugins for Vector can be challenging. Although the tool is under active maintenance, some bugs and operational issues may still exist due to its relatively recent development.

Log aggregation

Log aggregation solves another problem that arises from the large volume of data: how to store and access the logs. While the unified logging layer makes logs available even in the event of a machine outage, it is the task of log aggregation to help us quickly find the information that we are looking for.

Instead of storing the logs locally, the logs are aggregated and forwarded to a central facility. This way, the logs are available even if the service itself is down. Storing logs in a centralized manner also helps correlate data coming from different microservices.

Also, log aggregation systems often provide features such as a centralized **exception tracking** system, which helps manage exceptions in microservices.

The two possible products that allow storing, indexing, and querying huge amounts of data are Elasticsearch and Loki.

Elasticsearch

Elasticsearch and its fork OpenSearch are popular solutions for self-hosted log aggregation. This is the *E* in the (former) ELK Stack. It features a great search engine based on Apache Lucene, optimized for storing, indexing, and querying large volumes of log data.

Elasticsearch has a lot of integrations and has great support both from the community and as a commercial service. Some cloud providers offer Elasticsearch as a managed service, which makes it easier to introduce Elasticsearch in your application. Other than that, Elastic, the company that makes Elasticsearch, offers a hosted solution that is not tied to any particular cloud provider.

Loki

The focus area for Loki is horizontal scalability and high availability. It's built from the ground up as a cloud-native solution inspired by Prometheus, which we cover in the next section.

While Loki should be a stable solution, it is not as popular as Elasticsearch, which means some integrations might be missing, and the documentation and community support won't be on the same level as for Elasticsearch. Both Fluentd and Vector have plugins that support Loki for log aggregation.

Log visualization

The last piece of the logging stack we want to consider is log visualization. This helps us to query and analyze the logs. It presents the data in an accessible way so it can be inspected by all the interested parties, such as operators, developers, QA, or business teams.

Log visualization tools allow us to create dashboards that make it even easier to read the data we are interested in. With that, we are able to explore the events, search for correlations, and find outlying data from a simple user interface.

There are two major products dedicated to log visualization.

Kibana

Kibana is the final element of the ELK Stack. It provides a simpler query language on top of Elasticsearch. Even though you can query and visualize different types of data with Kibana, it is mostly focused on logs.

Grafana

Grafana is another data visualization tool. It was mostly focused on time-series data such as performance metrics. However, with the introduction of Loki, it can also be used for log analysis.

One of its strengths is that it's built with pluggable backends in mind, so it's easy to switch the storage to fit your needs.

Figure 17.5 shows the key components of the Grafana stack and how they work together to collect, store, and visualize observability data:

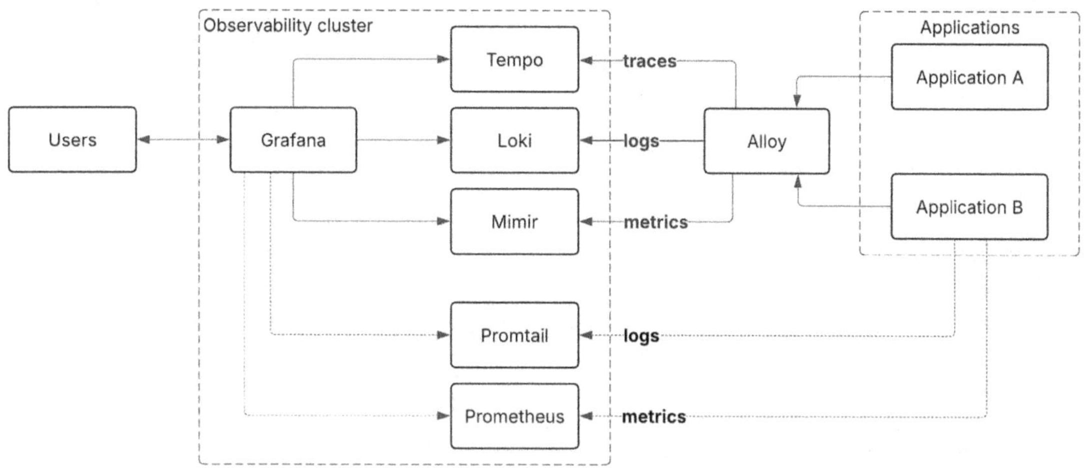

Figure 17.5: The Grafana stack

Clearly, a microservice can support multiple monitoring systems simultaneously, but in general, it makes sense to limit the number of connected tools. Grafana recommends migrating from deprecated Promtail and Prometheus to Alloy (an OpenTelemetry Collector), although Prometheus remains popular and actively used. Note that, here, we focus on demonstrating the OpenTelemetry Collector's integration with Prometheus and Loki rather than showcasing the full range of OpenTelemetry capabilities.

The Grafana stack includes many products—in particular, the following:

- **Grafana:** A visualization and dashboarding platform
- **Loki:** A horizontally scalable, highly available, multi-tenant log aggregation system
- **Mimir:** A horizontally scalable, highly available, multi-tenant **time series database** (**TSDB**) for long-term storage for Prometheus
- **Tempo:** A high-scale distributed tracing backend

- **Promtail:** An agent shipping the contents of local logs to a private Grafana Loki instance or Grafana Cloud
- **Prometheus:** A monitoring and alerting system collecting metrics from applications and infrastructure in real time, storing them in a time-series database for analysis and visualization
- **Alloy:** An OpenTelemetry Collector with built-in Prometheus pipelines and support for metrics, logs, traces, and performance profiles (such as Go pprof profiles or eBPF profiles)

Figure 17.6 shows how application logs collected by Loki are visualized in Grafana:

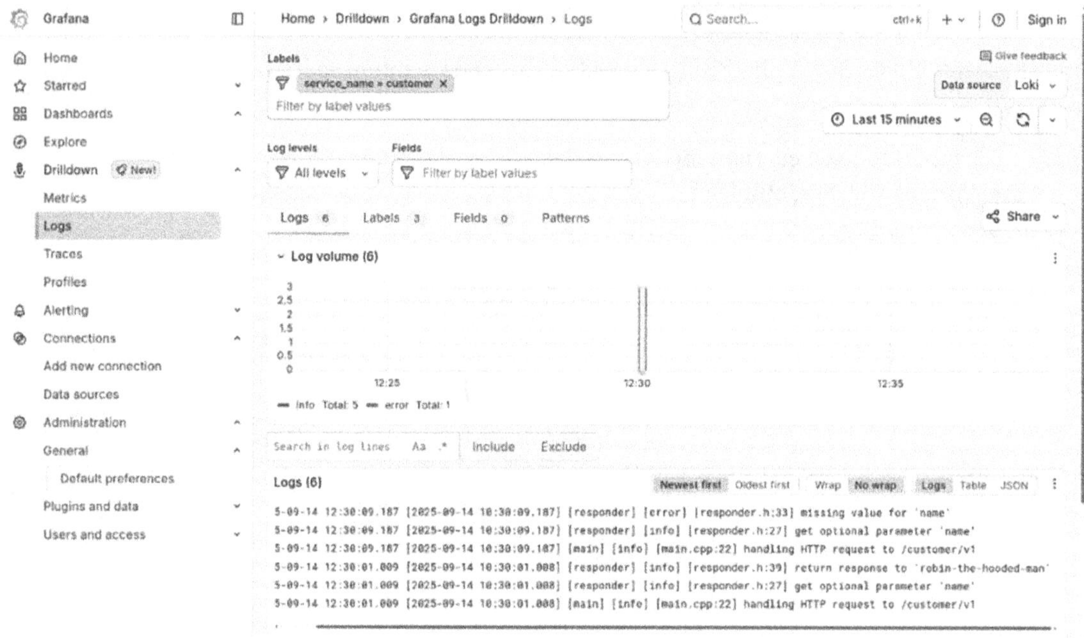

Figure 17.6: An overview of log messages of the application on the Grafana Logs Drilldown dashboard

The dashboard acts as a log analysis tool as it allows logs to be filtered and searched.

While logs give us detailed event-level insights, to make informed decisions at scale, we also need an overview of system health. This is where monitoring comes into the picture.

Monitoring

To make decisions based on data, you need some data to act on. Monitoring is the process of systematically collecting and analyzing data, such as application performance metrics, to understand, manage, and improve the health and behavior of the system. When paired with alerting, monitoring metrics and health checks help us understand when our system behaves as expected and when an incident happens.

Collecting application metrics helps to understand the application behavior as used by the actual users, and not in synthetic tests. Metrics are numerical measurements reported over time, such as CPU/memory load, requests per second, or service response time. They are stored as time series and used to evaluate the effectiveness of the system and generate alerts.

The three types of metrics that would interest us the most are as follows:

- **Availability**, which lets us know which of our resources are up and running, and which of them have crashed or become unresponsive
- **Resource utilization** gives us insight into how the workload fits into the system
- **Performance**, which shows us where and how to improve service quality

The two common models of monitoring are push and pull. In the former, each monitored object (a machine, an application, or a network device) pushes data to the central point. In the latter, the objects present the data at the configured endpoints, and the monitoring agent scrapes the data periodically. Prometheus uses both approaches: push for short-lived batch jobs and pull for long-lived services.

The pull model makes it easier to scale. This way, multiple objects won't clog the monitoring agent connection. Instead, multiple agents may collect the data whenever ready, thus better utilizing the available resources.

Two monitoring solutions that feature C++ client libraries are Prometheus and InfluxDB. By default, InfluxDB uses the push model. Besides monitoring, it is also popular in areas such as the Internet of Things, sensor networks, and home automation. Prometheus focuses on collecting and storing time-series data.

Both Prometheus and InfluxDB are typically used with Grafana for visualizing data and managing dashboards. Both have alerting built in, but they can also integrate with the external alerting system through Grafana.

Now, let's implement application metrics in C++ using Prometheus.

Implementing application metrics

The official C++ client library of Prometheus, `prometheus-cpp`, provides standard metric types. Metrics are exposed according to the OpenMetrics specification, which has become the standard interface. In addition, the Drogon framework has its own metrics exporter for seamless integration.

In the example we cover in this section, we'll dig beyond Drogon macros and component auto-creation so that you understand this framework better.

Drogon's middleware uses the onion model, where callbacks are intended to enter the inner layer (`nextCb`) and return to the upper layer (`mcb`) of the onion.

The following example implements a Prometheus middleware, `PromStat`, using Drogon, which intercepts HTTP requests and measures their count and duration:

```
// not auto created
class PromStat final : public HttpMiddleware<PromStat, false> {
 public:
  void invoke(const HttpRequestPtr &req, MiddlewareNextCallback &&nextCb,
              MiddlewareCallback &&mcb) override;
};
```

This middleware provides two metrics: `http_requests_total` and `http_request_duration_seconds`. The following implementation in `promstat.cpp` shows how these metrics are recorded for each HTTP request:

```
void PromStat::invoke(const HttpRequestPtr &req,
                      MiddlewareNextCallback &&nextCb,
                      MiddlewareCallback &&mcb) {
  std::string path{req->matchedPathPattern()};
  auto method = req->methodString();
  const auto promExporter = app().getPlugin<plugin::PromExporter>();
```

Before collecting data, it is necessary to check that the plugin is properly configured. The `http_requests_total` metric tracks the number of calls made to a particular HTTP endpoint specified by the `method` and `path` parameters:

```
  if (promExporter) {
    const auto collector =
        promExporter->getCollector<monitoring::Counter>("http_requests_total");
    if (collector) {
      collector->metric({method, path})->increment();
    }
  }
```

Next, the initial timestamp is captured to measure the request's processing duration:

```
  const auto start = trantor::Date::date();
```

After this, the next callback (`nextCb`) in the middleware chain is called, which reaches the endpoint handler:

```
  nextCb([mcb = std::move(mcb), &promExporter, start, method,
          path](const HttpResponsePtr &resp) {
```

Then, as control returns from the called functions, the `http_request_duration_seconds` metric is updated to record how long the request took to execute:

```
    if (promExporter) {
      const auto collector = promExporter->getCollector<monitoring::Histogram>(
          "http_request_duration_seconds");
      if (collector) {
        static const std::vector<double> boundaries{0.0001, 0.001, 0.01, 0.1,
                                                    0.5,    1,     2,    3};
```

The duration of the request execution is the difference between the current timestamp at this point and the initial timestamp:

```
        const auto end = trantor::Date::date();
        const auto duration =
            end.microSecondsSinceEpoch() - start.microSecondsSinceEpoch();
```

This difference is collected in the `http_request_duration_seconds` histogram metric:

```
        // The parameters 1h and 6 specify the lifetime of the metric (1 hour)
and the number of rotating time buckets
        collector->metric({method, path}, boundaries, 1h, 6)
            ->observe(static_cast<double>(duration) / 1000000);
      }
    }
```

Finally, control returns to the upper layer of the middleware with the response:

```
    mcb(resp);
  });
}
```

The Drogon framework divides histogram metrics into equal time intervals, placing values into buckets, and rotates these buckets, removing expired values exceeding the maximum age.

The corresponding Drogon configuration file enables the Prometheus exporter and its `/metrics` HTTP endpoint. As you can see, this plugin collects the counter and histogram metrics implemented in the middleware. Prometheus also supports the other metric types, such as gauge and summary.

The configuration file looks as follows:

```
{
  // the other application settings, including port listeners
  ...
  "plugins": [
    {
```

```
        "name": "drogon::plugin::PromExporter",
        "config": {
          "path": "/metrics",
          "collectors":[
            {
              "name": "http_requests_total",
              "help": "The total number of http requests",
              "type": "counter",
              "labels": ["method", "path"]
            },
            {
              "name": "http_request_duration_seconds",
              "help": "The processing time of http requests, in seconds",
              "type": "histogram",
              "labels": ["method", "path"]
            }
          ]
        }
      }
    ]
  }
```

In this multi-stage build, the application is compiled in a temporary container:

```
FROM ubuntu:questing AS builder

RUN apt update && DEBIAN_FRONTEND=noninteractive apt install -y build-essential
gcc cmake ninja-build python3-pip python3-venv

RUN python3 -m venv /opt/venv
ENV PATH="/opt/venv/bin:$PATH"
RUN pip3 install conan==2.* && conan profile detect

ADD . /root/src
WORKDIR /root/src

RUN mkdir -p build && cd build && \
    conan install .. --build=missing -s:a build_type=Release -s:a compiler.
cppstd=gnu20 -of . && \
    cmake .. -G Ninja -DCMAKE_BUILD_TYPE=Release && cmake --build . && cmake
--install .
```

Then, the executable and configuration files are copied from the builder to the final container image. The configuration file is copied from the build container since it is already there, along with the source code. The `EXPOSE` keyword in a Dockerfile is a means of documenting that an application promises to listen on the specified network port:

```
FROM ubuntu:questing

RUN apt update && apt install -y curl && apt clean

COPY --from=builder /root/src/build/bin/customer /bin/customer
COPY --from=builder /root/src/build/bin/config.json /bin/config.json

EXPOSE 8080

CMD ["/bin/customer"]

WORKDIR /bin
```

The time for uniting these components has come. Drogon macros normally hide the `registerHandler` method of the application, which in this case calls the `invoke()` method of the registered `PromStat` middleware. As an implementation of the Decorator design pattern, the middleware extends the functionality of the handler and can be attached by name and as an object. The following code in `main.cpp` demonstrates this, where `spdlog::sinks::stdout_sink_mt` is a multi-threaded sink:

```
// the implementation is partially omitted
...
const auto logger = spdlog::stdout_logger_mt("main");

app()
    .loadConfigFile("config.json")
    // not auto created
    .registerMiddleware(std::make_shared<PromStat>())
    .registerHandler(
        "/customer/v1",

[&logger, &get_responder](
            const HttpRequestPtr &request,
           std::function<void(const HttpResponsePtr &)> &&callback) {
          SPDLOG_LOGGER_INFO(logger, "handling HTTP request to {}",
                             request->path());

          handle_get(request, get_responder, std::move(callback));
        },
        {Get, "PromStat"})
```

Through this example, you've seen how to implement application metrics in Drogon and integrate them with Prometheus.

Figure 17.7 shows how application metrics collected by Prometheus are visualized in Grafana:

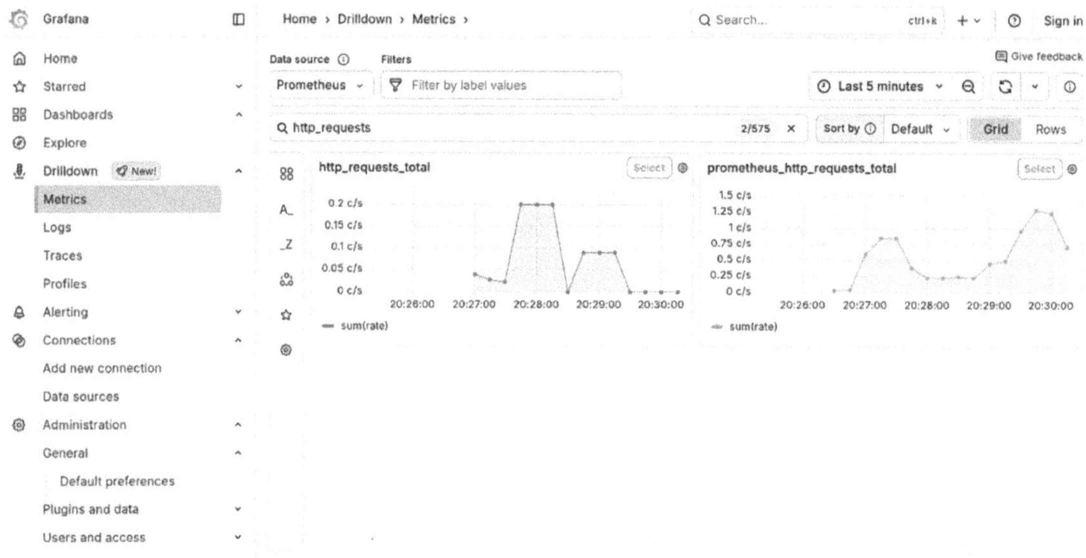

Figure 17.7: An overview of application metrics visualized on the Grafana Drilldown Metrics dashboard

This dashboard acts as a metric analysis tool, allowing metrics to be filtered and searched.

A key part of the Prometheus monitoring system is Alertmanager, which sends notifications based on threshold breaches in metrics to various notification channels (such as email and Slack). Grafana can be connected to this alert system to provide a unified monitoring experience. (Beyond logs and metrics, Grafana's observability platform collects and analyzes profiling data and traces.)

Beyond metrics and alerts, a fundamental part of monitoring in distributed systems is checking service health, which we'll explore next.

Monitoring health checks

Since microservices are often targets of automation, they need to have the ability to communicate their internal state. Even if the process is present in the system, it doesn't mean the application is operational. The same goes for an open network port; the application may be listening, but it is not yet able to respond. Health check APIs provide a way for external services to determine whether the application is ready to process the workload. Self-healing and autoscaling use health checks to determine when an intervention is needed. The base premise is that a given endpoint (such as `/health`) returns an HTTP code `200` when the application behaves as expected and a different code (or does not return at all) if any problem is found.

Kubernetes goes further and granulates probes with three main types: liveness for determining when to restart a container, readiness for determining when a container is ready to accept traffic, and startup probes to verify whether the application within a container is started. If an application is unresponsive for a certain timeout period, Kubernetes terminates the container and starts a new one, assuming the application is faulty. Therefore, health checks must respond very quickly; otherwise, Kubernetes will enter an endless loop of restarting the containers containing the application.

Kubernetes probes use several protocols to check the health of containers: HTTP, HTTPS (secure, encrypted version of HTTP), TCP (a quick check that the application is listening on a specific TCP port), command (any arbitrary command), and gRPC (a high-performance RPC framework for inter-service communication).

The following code registers a health check endpoint of the web application in `main.cpp`:

```
// the implementation is partially omitted
...
app()
    ...
    .registerHandler(
        // combines liveness and readiness health checks due to the simplicity
        "/health",
        [](const HttpRequestPtr &,
            std::function<void(const HttpResponsePtr &)> &&callback) {
          const auto resp =
              HttpResponse::newHttpResponse(k200OK, CT_TEXT_PLAIN);
          resp->setBody("OK");
          callback(resp);
        },
        {Get})
    run();
```

Next, we explore tracing, which helps not only to investigate performance issues but also to gain better insight into the application behavior under real-world traffic.

Tracing

While logging collects pieces of information from a single point, tracing is concerned with the entire life cycle of a single transaction, starting at the point where it originates from a user action. Distributed tracing extends the idea of tracing across multiple services and machines.

Information captured by tracing may include function calls, their parameters, their size, and execution time. Each trace also has a unique trace identifier (trace ID) assigned to individual requests, which is used for tracking requests as they traverse through various services in a distributed system to provide visibility into complete request paths.

Each trace is composed of spans. Hierarchical spans in traces are used to construct and visualize a dependency graph between services in a distributed system. This is based on context propagation, transferring request metadata such as trace IDs, span IDs, and user data between different services, layers, or threads in a distributed application.

It is important to note that although a trace ID can be used as a correlation ID, they are not the same thing. A correlation ID is a unique identifier used to track all log records for a particular request as it moves within a single service or system.

Therefore, when implementing tracing, it is necessary to use a tracing solution that integrates with all the possible elements of the system: frontend applications, backend applications, and databases. This way, requests can be followed end to end, making it also possible to pinpoint performance bottlenecks, troubleshoot errors, and understand the interactions between services.

The following diagram is an overview of a single trace:

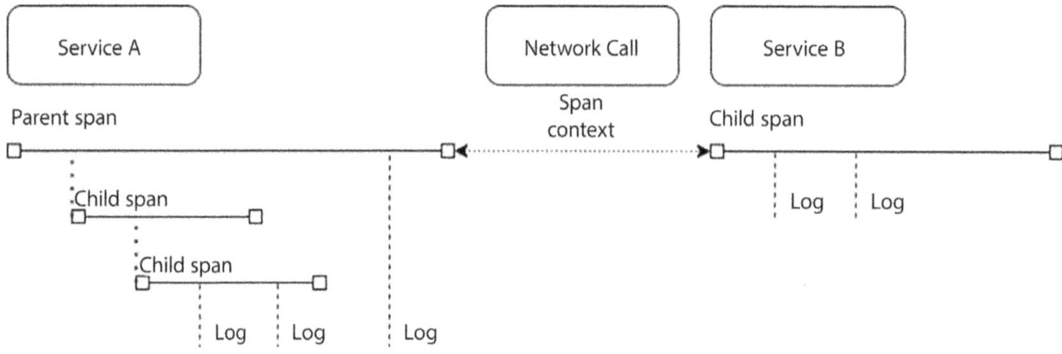

Figure 17.8: Single trace

- In the figure, we see two services communicating over a network. In *Service A*, we have one parent span that contains a child span and a single log. Child spans usually correspond to deeper function calls. A log represents the smallest piece of information. Each of them is timed and may contain additional information.
- The network call to *Service B* preserves the span context. Even though *Service B* is executed in a different process on another machine, all the information can be later reassembled as the trace ID is preserved.

In the following subsections, we'll look at some of the most notable open source standards and tools that have been developed to implement distributed tracing.

Jaeger and OpenTracing

One of the early standards in distributed tracing was OpenTracing, supported by the authors of Jaeger. The OpenTracing project was archived in 2022 in favor of OpenTelemetry. In 2023, the Jaeger agent was deprecated, but the Jaeger backend is still maintained. The OpenTelemetry observability framework supports the Jaeger backend and is the recommended strategy to connect the backend.

OpenTracing and the agent are still in use in multiple production environments because migration to other software takes time and usually does not happen instantly due to project dependencies and already deployed infrastructure. Thus, the further information provided is mostly for reference only.

Jaeger is a tracer built for cloud-native applications. It addresses the problems of monitoring distributed transactions and propagating the tracing context. It is useful for the following purposes:

- Performance or latency optimization
- Performing a root cause analysis
- Analyzing the inter-service dependencies

OpenTracing is an open standard presenting an API that is vendor-neutral. This means that when your application is instrumented using OpenTracing, you avoid vendor lock-in to one particular vendor. If, at some point, you decide to switch from Jaeger to Zipkin, DataDog, or any other compatible tracer, you don't have to modify the entire instrumentation code.

There are many client libraries compatible with OpenTracing. You can also find many resources, including tutorials and articles that explain how to implement the API. OpenTracing officially supports the following languages: Go, JavaScript, Java, Python, Ruby, PHP, Objective-C, C++, and C#. There are also unofficial libraries available, and specific applications such as NGINX and Envoy can export OpenTracing data as well.

Jaeger also accepts samples in Zipkin format. What it means is that you don't have to rewrite the instrumentation from one format to another if you (or any of your dependencies) already use Zipkin. We will cover Zipkin in the next section.

Jaeger backend scales well. You can run it as a single binary or a single application container if you want to evaluate it. You may configure Jaeger for production use to use its own backend or a supported external one, such as Elasticsearch, Cassandra, or Kafka.

Jaeger is a **Cloud Native Computing Foundation** (CNCF) graduated project. This means it reached a similar level of maturity to Kubernetes, Prometheus, and Fluentd.

Zipkin

Zipkin is an older project, which also means it is well-established and stable. Usually, more senior projects are also better supported. Nonetheless, this system is significantly less popular than OpenTelemetry, which is considered the modern standard for distributed tracing.

Zipkin includes support for the (now deprecated) OpenTracing API, but it may not be at the same maturity and support level as the native Jaeger protocol. As we mentioned earlier, it is also possible to configure Jaeger to collect traces in Zipkin format. This means the two are, at least to some point, interchangeable. The project is hosted under the Apache Software Foundation but is not considered a CNCF project. One drawback is that Zipkin doesn't have a supported C++ implementation. There are unofficial libraries, but they don't seem to be well supported.

OpenTelemetry

OpenTelemetry, a merger of OpenTracing and OpenCensus, is a CNCF project and the industry standard for collecting and transmitting telemetry data, including logs, metrics, and traces, called signals in the project terminology, which provides a comprehensive view of the system state. In practice, tracing was the first widely adopted use case, which is why OpenTelemetry is often discussed in tracing contexts.

While OpenTelemetry collects more than just traces, the framework can associate traces with logs by storing the current trace ID and span ID in a log record. OpenTelemetry also introduces a special signal type called baggage to pass contextual information between signals. This observability framework is 100% free and open source.

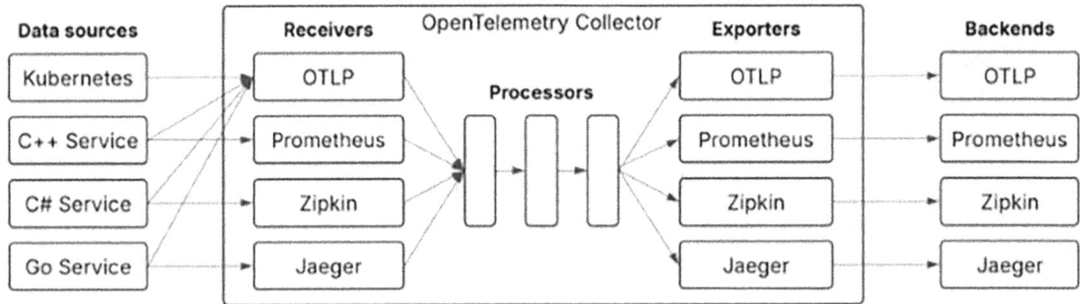

Figure 17.9: OpenTelemetry architecture

A key component of OpenTelemetry is the OpenTelemetry Collector, which collects, processes, and transmits telemetry data from various data sources to monitoring and analysis systems. Receivers gather telemetry data, processors filter, transform, and enrich it, and exporters send the processed data to various backends. Pipelines define the paths that data follows in the Collector, from reception to processing (or modification) and finally to export. Communication uses the **OpenTelemetry Protocol (OTLP)**, which supports two transport options: gRPC and HTTP, both pull and push models for collecting metrics.

This framework provides SDKs for a wide range of languages, including C++, C#/.NET, Go, Java, JavaScript, PHP, Python, and Swift, but automatic instrumentation is available only for .NET, Go, Python, Java, JavaScript, and PHP.

Automated instrumentation involves using libraries or agents to automatically collect and send telemetry data without requiring changes to application code. Manual instrumentation involves adding specific code snippets to application code to capture and send telemetry data. This way, you can collect custom metrics specific to your applications.

Many libraries and frameworks already support OpenTelemetry or are supported through the OpenTelemetry instrumentation—in particular, Boost.Log, Log4cxx, and `spdlog`.

Furthermore, OpenTelemetry integrates with eBPF, a Linux kernel technology enabling engineers to embed programming code directly into an operating system kernel via sandbox and pre-compilation without modifying the kernel source code or loading a kernel module. This allows the collection of low-level telemetry from the Linux kernel and high-level telemetry from cloud and Kubernetes environments, providing deep insights into application behavior.

By bypassing instrumentation points within the application, eBPF provides a more complete picture of system operation, especially in complex distributed environments such as Kubernetes. For example, in Kubernetes, eBPF can be used to monitor network traffic between Pods, analyze application performance, and detect resource leaks.

Integrated observability solutions

If you don't want to build the observability layer on your own, there are some popular commercial solutions that you might consider. They all operate in a Software-as-a-Service model. We won't go into a detailed comparison here, as their offerings may change drastically after the writing of this book. These services are as follows: Uptrace, Datadog, New Relic, Dynatrace, Splunk, Grafana, Elastic, Lightstep, Honeycomb, Better Stack, Logz.io, Coralogix, Sumo Logic, and SigNoz.

Summary

In this chapter, we explored observability in microservices, focusing on the three pillars of telemetry—logs, traces, and metrics. We began with logging, discussing logging in the context of microservices. Next, we examined monitoring, where metrics and health checks are continuously collected to track system performance. When combined with alerting mechanisms, these enable automated detection of anomalies and incidents. We also looked at a hands-on example of implementing Prometheus application metrics in C++ using the Drogon framework, demonstrating how these concepts come together in practice. Finally, we turned to tracing, which provides a higher-level view of how requests flow across microservices. Together, log aggregation, distributed tracing, application metrics, and health-check APIs form the core observability patterns in modern cloud-native systems.

The next chapter is dedicated to cloud-native design—a very interesting but also complex topic that ties in SOA, CI/CD, microservices, containers, and cloud services. As it turns out, the great performance of C++ is a welcome feature for some of the cloud-native building blocks.

Questions

1. How do observability, monitoring, logging, and tracing differ?
2. What is a unified logging layer?
3. What is the difference between pull and push models for collecting application metrics?

Further reading

- Rob Chapman and Peter Holmes, *Observability with Grafana: Monitor, Control, and Visualize Your Kubernetes and Cloud Platforms Using the LGTM Stack*, Packt Publishing: `https://www.packtpub.com/en-us/product/observability-with-grafana-9781803249643`
- Malcolm Orr and Yang-Xin Cao, *Mastering Elastic Kubernetes Service on AWS: Deploy and Manage EKS Clusters to Support Cloud-Native Applications in AWS*, Packt Publishing: `https://www.packtpub.com/en-us/product/mastering-elastic-kubernetes-service-on-aws-9781803234823`

- Drogon Framework, *Middleware and Filter*, GitHub Wiki: `https://github.com/drogonframework/drogon/wiki/ENG-05-Middleware-and-Filter`
- Drogon Framework, *Controller Introduction*, GitHub Wiki: `https://github.com/drogonframework/drogon/wiki/ENG-04-0-Controller-Introduction`
- Drogon Framework, *Configuration File*, GitHub Wiki: `https://github.com/drogonframework/drogon/wiki/ENG-11-Configuration-File`
- Prometheus, *Metric Types*: `https://prometheus.io/docs/concepts/metric_types/`
- Gabi Melman, *spdlog Wiki*, GitHub: `https://github.com/gabime/spdlog/wiki/`
- Drogon Framework, *Understanding Drogon's Threading Model*, GitHub Wiki: `https://github.com/drogonframework/drogon/wiki/ENG-FAQ-1-Understanding-drogon-threading-model`
- Kubernetes, *Configure Liveness, Readiness and Startup Probes*: `https://kubernetes.io/docs/tasks/configure-pod-container/configure-liveness-readiness-startup-probes/`
- Elastic, *Beats*: `https://www.elastic.co/docs/reference/beats`
- LibHunt, *Awesome C++: A Curated List of Awesome C/C++ Frameworks, Libraries, Resources, and Shiny Things*: `https://cpp.libhunt.com/`

18

Cloud-Native Design

As the name suggests, **cloud-native design** describes the application's architecture built, first and foremost, to operate in the cloud. It is not defined by a single technology or language but rather takes advantage of all that the modern cloud platforms offer.

This may mean a combination of using **Platform as a Service** (**PaaS**) whenever necessary, multi-cloud deployments, edge computing, **Function as a Service** (**FaaS**), static file hosting, microservices, and managed services. It transcends the boundaries of traditional operating systems. Instead of targeting the POSIX API and Unix-like operating systems, cloud-native developers build on higher-level concepts using libraries and frameworks such as Pulumi and platforms such as Kubernetes, Docker Swarm, Cloud Foundry, and OpenStack.

Although cloud-native development is often associated with languages such as C#, Go, Java, JavaScript (Node.js), or Python, C++ remains a powerful contender for building high-performance, scalable cloud applications. Its proximity to hardware enables unmatched performance and efficient use of resources. Moreover, C++ is compatible with a wide range of libraries and frameworks, making it suitable for applications that must run across different cloud providers, operating systems, and hardware environments.

That said, C++ requires a deep understanding of systems programming. Writing and maintaining code in C++ can be time-consuming compared to higher-level languages such as Python or TypeScript, and it may not have as many cloud-based tools and libraries as languages such as Go, Java, or C#. Nevertheless, Kubernetes fully supports C++ applications, enabling them to run in any cloud environment.

In this chapter, we'll go over some of the core building blocks (such as Kubernetes, service discovery, and service mesh) and design patterns (such as declarative configuration, observability, and GitOps) that define cloud-native architecture. Observability is especially vital for cloud-native distributed systems and remotely operated embedded devices, and this chapter shows how to instrument applications using OpenTelemetry, introduced in the previous chapter.

The following topics will be covered in this chapter:

- Understanding cloud-native
- Using Kubernetes to orchestrate cloud-native workloads
- Observability in cloud-native distributed systems
- Connecting services with a service mesh
- Going GitOps

By the end of the chapter, you'll have a good understanding of how modern cloud-native trends in software architecture can be used in your applications.

Technical requirements

The examples in this chapter require Docker 27.2 and Kubernetes 1.32.

The code present in the chapter has been placed on GitHub at `https://github.com/PacktPublishing/Software-Architecture-with-Cpp-2E/tree/main/Chapter18`.

Understanding cloud-native

While it is possible to migrate an existing application to run in the cloud, such a migration won't make the application cloud-native. It would be running in the cloud, but the architectural choices would still be based on the on-premises model.

In contrast, cloud-native applications are distributed by nature, loosely coupled, and scalable. They're not tied to any particular physical infrastructure and don't require the developers to even think about specific infrastructure. Such applications are usually web-centric.

In this section, we'll look at the **Cloud Native Computing Foundation** (**CNCF**), the organization that maintains many of the tools and frameworks we rely on. We'll also explore the concept of treating the cloud as an operating system, and then examine some key mechanisms that support cloud-native systems: load balancing, reverse proxies, and service discovery.

Cloud Native Computing Foundation

One proponent of cloud-native design is the CNCF, which hosts the Kubernetes project. The CNCF is home to various technologies, making it easier to build cloud-native applications independent of the cloud vendor. Examples of CNCF-hosted and ecosystem technologies include the following:

- **Fluentd**, **Jaeger**, **Prometheus**, and **OpenTelemetry** for observability
- **CoreDNS** and **etcd** for coordination and service discovery
- **Kubernetes**, **KubeEdge**, and **wasmCloud** for scheduling and orchestration

- **Argo** and **Flux** for continuous delivery and **OpenKruise** for application automation
- **Dapr**, **Helm**, and **KubeVela** for application definition and deployment, and **Buildpacks** for image building
- **Falco**, **Open Policy Agent**, **Kubescape**, and **Kyverno** for security and compliance

Cloud-native applications are typically built with application containers, often running on top of the Kubernetes platform. However, this is not a requirement, and it's entirely possible to use many of the CNCF frameworks outside Kubernetes and containers.

In cloud-native design, instead of treating servers or virtual machines as the foundation, we view the cloud itself as the operating system. This concept is explored in the next section.

Cloud as an operating system

The main trait of cloud-native design is to treat the various cloud resources as the building blocks of your application. Individual **virtual machines (VMs)** are seldom used in cloud-native design. Instead of targeting a given operating system running on some instances, with a cloud-native approach, you target either the cloud API directly (for example, with FaaS) or some intermediary solution such as Kubernetes. In this sense, the cloud becomes your operating system, as the POSIX API no longer limits you.

Moreover, as containers changed the approach to building and distributing software, it is now possible to free yourself from thinking about the underlying hardware infrastructure. At the same time, your software is not working in isolation, so it's still necessary to connect different services, monitor them, control their life cycle, store data, or pass the secrets. This is something that Kubernetes provides, and it's one of the reasons why it became so popular.

As you can probably imagine, cloud-native applications are web- and mobile-first. Desktop applications can also benefit from having some cloud-native components, but it's a less common use case.

It's still possible to use hardware and other low-level access in cloud-native applications. If your workload requires the use of either GPU or FPGA, this should not prevent you from going cloud-native.

What's more, cloud-native applications can be built on-premises if you want access to custom hardware unavailable elsewhere. Thus, the term is not limited to the public cloud, but rather to the way of thinking about different resources.

Let's now shift from the overall concept of treating the cloud as an operating system to the practical mechanisms that keep distributed applications reliable. Here, load balancing, reverse proxy, and service discovery emerge as three key building blocks.

Load balancing

Load balancing is an essential part of distributed and cloud-native applications. It not only spreads the incoming requests across a cluster of services, which is essential for scaling, but it can also help improve the responsiveness and availability of the applications. A smart load balancer can gather metrics to react to patterns in incoming traffic, monitor the state of the servers in its cluster, and forward requests to the less loaded and faster responding nodes, avoiding the currently unhealthy ones.

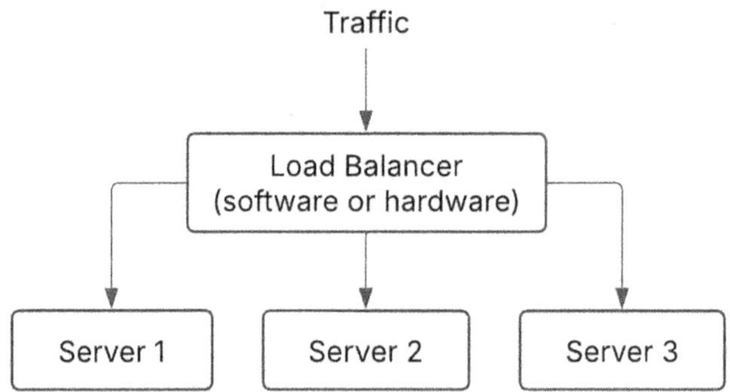

Figure 18.1: Load balancing

Load balancing brings more throughput and less downtime. By forwarding requests to many servers, a single point of failure is eliminated, especially if multiple load balancers are used, for example, in an active–passive scheme.

Load balancers can be used anywhere in your architecture: you can balance the requests coming from the web, requests made by web servers to other services, requests to cache or database servers, and whatever else suits your requirements.

There are a few things to remember when introducing load balancing. One of them is session persistence—make sure all requests from the same customer go to the same server to maintain session-specific state, so the carefully chosen pink stilettos won't disappear from their basket in your e-commerce site. Sessions can get tricky with load balancing: take extra care to not mix sessions, so customers won't suddenly start being logged into each other's profiles; countless companies stumbled upon this error before, especially when adding caching into the mix. It's a great idea to combine caching with load balancing; just make sure it is done the right way.

While load balancers are often used to distribute traffic across multiple servers, sometimes all you need is a simpler solution. In such cases, a reverse proxy can be placed in front of your server as an alternative.

Reverse and forward proxies

If you want to deploy just one instance of your server, it might be a good idea to add another service in front of it instead of the load balancer—a reverse proxy. While a forward proxy usually acts on behalf of the client sending some requests, a reverse proxy acts on behalf of the servers handling those requests, hence the name.

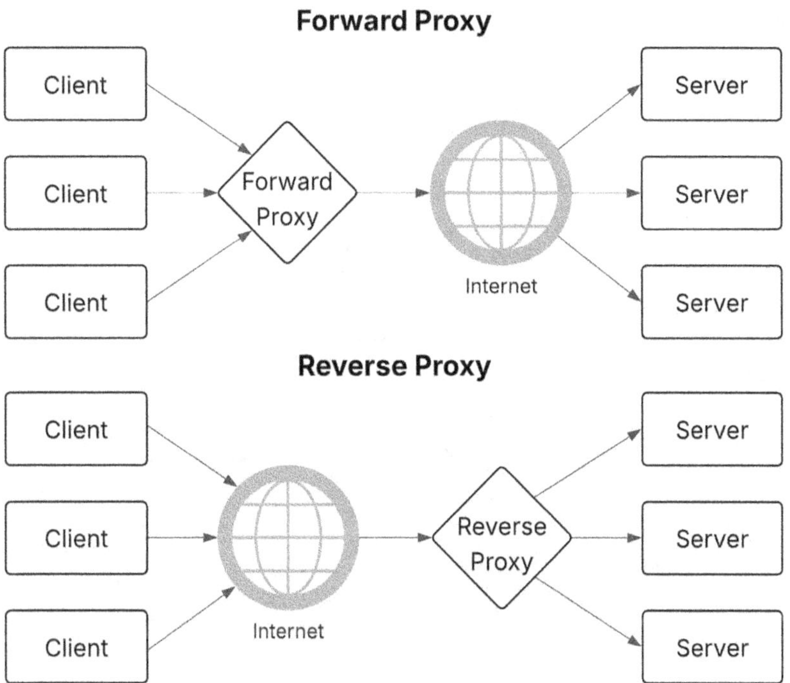

Figure 18.2: Forward versus reverse proxies

There are several reasons and uses for a reverse proxy:

- **Security**: The address of your server is now hidden, and the server can be protected by the proxy's **distributed denial of service** (**DDoS**) prevention capabilities.
- **Flexibility and scalability**: You can modify the infrastructure hidden behind the proxy in any way you want and when you want.
- **Caching**: Why bother the server if the proxy can deliver the same answer directly from its cache?
- **Compression**: Compressing data will reduce the bandwidth needed, which may be especially useful for mobile users with poor connectivity. It can also lower your networking costs (but will likely cost you compute power).
- **Secure Sockets Layer** (**SSL**) **termination**: Reduce the backend server's load by taking its burden to encrypt and decrypt network traffic.

Popular reverse proxies include NGINX, Traefik, HAProxy, Varnish, and Caddy. Popular forward proxies include Squid, Privoxy, and Tinyproxy. Envoy, NGINX, and Apache can be configured in both forward and reverse proxy (also known as gateway) modes. Reverse proxies often also provide load balancing capabilities and A/B testing (split testing). One of their capabilities is service discovery. Let's see how it can be helpful.

Service discovery

As the name suggests, **service discovery** (**SD**) allows for automatically detecting instances of specific services in a computer network. Instead of hardcoding a domain name or IP where the service should be hosted, the caller must only be pointed to a service registry. Using this approach, your architecture gets a lot more flexible, as now all the services you use can be easily found. If you design a microservice-based architecture, introducing SD really goes a long way.

There are several approaches to SD. In client-side SD, the caller contacts the SD instance directly. Each service instance has a registry client, which registers and deregisters the instance, handles heartbeats, and others. While quite straightforward, in this approach, each client has to implement the SD logic. Netflix Eureka is an example of a service registry commonly used in this approach.

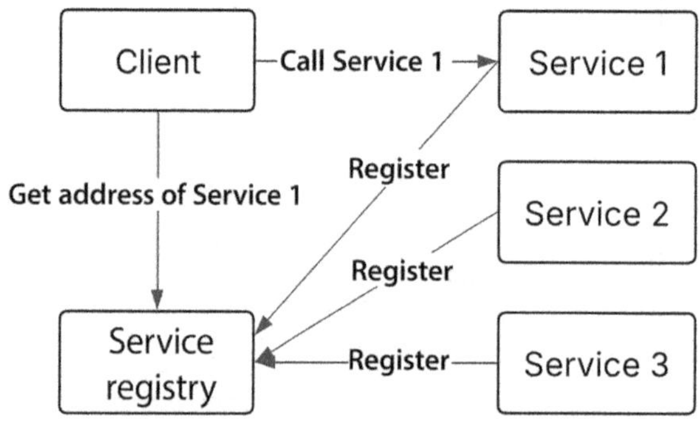

Figure 18.3: Client-side service discovery

An alternative is to use server-side SD. Here, a service registry is still present, along with the registry clients in each service instance. The callers, however, don't contact it directly. Instead, they connect to a load balancer (for example, AWS Elastic Load Balancing, Azure Load Balancer, or Google Cloud Load Balancing), which, in turn, either calls a service registry or uses the built-in service registry before dispatching the client calls to specific instances.

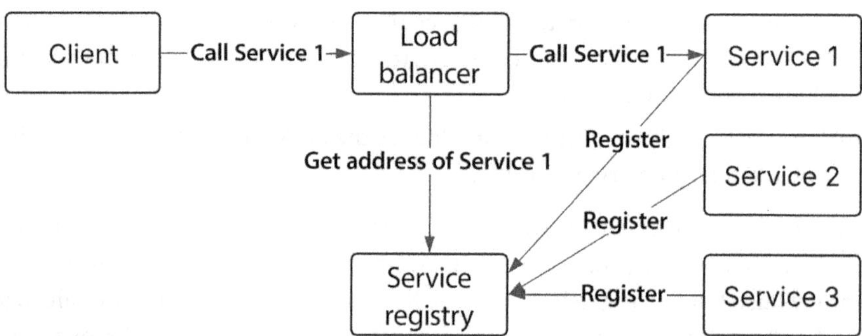

Figure 18.4: Server-side service discovery

This approach is often implemented through cloud load balancing, also known as **Load Balancer as a Service** (**LBaaS**), which abstracts the complexity of provisioning load balancers. In addition to cloud-provider load balancers, tools such as NGINX and Consul can also provide server-side discovery capabilities.

Client-side discovery often offers more control over load balancing but complicates the client implementation. On the other hand, server-side discovery simplifies the client implementation but can introduce latency and a single point of failure. The choice depends on factors such as system complexity, desired level of control, and latency sensitivity.

SD is also inextricably linked to service registration. In self-registration, services interact with the service registry directly by adding themselves to the registry when they start and deleting themselves when they shut down. In third-party registration, the service registry registers all the microservices by polling the deployment environment or subscribing to events.

SD in C++ is implemented, for instance, in the Eclipse `iceoryx` library. This is an open source, **inter-process communication** (IPC) middleware used in the automotive industry and **Internet of Things** (IoT) across operating systems (Linux, macOS, QNX, FreeBSD, and Windows).

In Kubernetes, SD is usually provided by CoreDNS, which implements DNS SD and DNS resolution (translating domain names into their IP addresses through DNS lookup). By default, Kubernetes automatically assigns names to Services in the format `<service-name>.<namespace>.svc.cluster.local` and Pods in the format `<pod-name>.<namespace>.pod.cluster.local`, where `namespace` is a Kubernetes namespace. The default domain name used in Kubernetes for internal SD is `cluster.local`.

We now know how to find and use our services efficiently, so let's learn how best to deploy them.

Using Kubernetes to orchestrate cloud-native workloads

Some concepts of Kubernetes were introduced in *Chapter 16, Containers*. We will briefly revisit them here to provide continuity. Kubernetes is an extensible open source platform for automating and managing container applications. It is sometimes referred to as K8s since it starts with *K*, ends with *s*, and there are eight letters in the middle.

Its design is based on Borg, a system used internally by Google. Kubernetes was initially codenamed Project Seven after *Seven of Nine*, a friendly *Star Trek* character who was once a former Borg drone. Some of the features present in Kubernetes are as follows:

- Autoscaling of applications
- Configurable networking
- Batch job execution
- Unified upgrading of applications
- The ability to run highly available applications on top of it
- The declarative configuration

Kubernetes is flexible and can be deployed in many environments. The more complex the infrastructure and architecture, the more benefits Kubernetes has:

- Scales to large clusters and balances workloads efficiently
- Automatically replicates Pods during failures, restarts failed containers, and balances the load
- Makes it easy to define **infrastructure as code** (IaC) and launch new applications with just one command, `kubectl`

- Abstracts the infrastructure level
- Supports service meshes for provisioning and balancing Pods

However, Kubernetes is a fairly complex platform that only experienced professionals can properly understand. Hiring such specialists is expensive, and waiting for your own team to figure out all the intricacies takes a long time. Using Kubernetes makes sense when its scalability and fault tolerance benefits are critical to a product; otherwise, the complexity may outweigh the benefits.

For fully utilizing the system, knowledge of command-line utilities is essential—most notably, `kubectl`. On the other hand, well-designed, well-thought-out graphical and text interfaces can perform most common tasks and open up additional capabilities when operating the system. Such interfaces for Kubernetes are classic Kubernetes Dashboard, Portainer (a universal, user-friendly GUI management platform for Docker, Docker Swarm, Kubernetes, and Podman), k9s (Kubernetes CLI), Headlamp (Kubernetes UI), and Kubernetes IDEs: Monokle, K8Studio, Lens, and Freelens.

Kubernetes also has both built-in and third-party debugging tools such as Telepresence (a local development environment for a remote Kubernetes cluster), Traceloop (a system call tracing and observability tool), and Inspektor Gadget (a set of tools and framework for data collection and system inspection on Kubernetes clusters and Linux hosts using the Linux kernel technology **Extended Berkeley Packet Filter** (**eBPF**)).

Before exploring deployment choices, let's first look at the typical structure of a Kubernetes cluster.

Kubernetes structure

It is possible to run Kubernetes on a single machine using tools such as MicroK8s, minikube, kind, k3d, K3s, k0s, or KubeFire, as well as applications such as Docker Desktop, Rancher Desktop, or Podman Desktop. These setups are useful for development and testing, but they are not recommended for use in production, as single-machine clusters have limited functionality and no failover mechanisms.

A typical size for a Kubernetes cluster is six machines or more. Three of the machines then form the control plane. The other three are worker nodes.

Figure 18.5 illustrates the components of the control plane and worker nodes. For simplicity, it shows a single control plane node and two worker nodes:

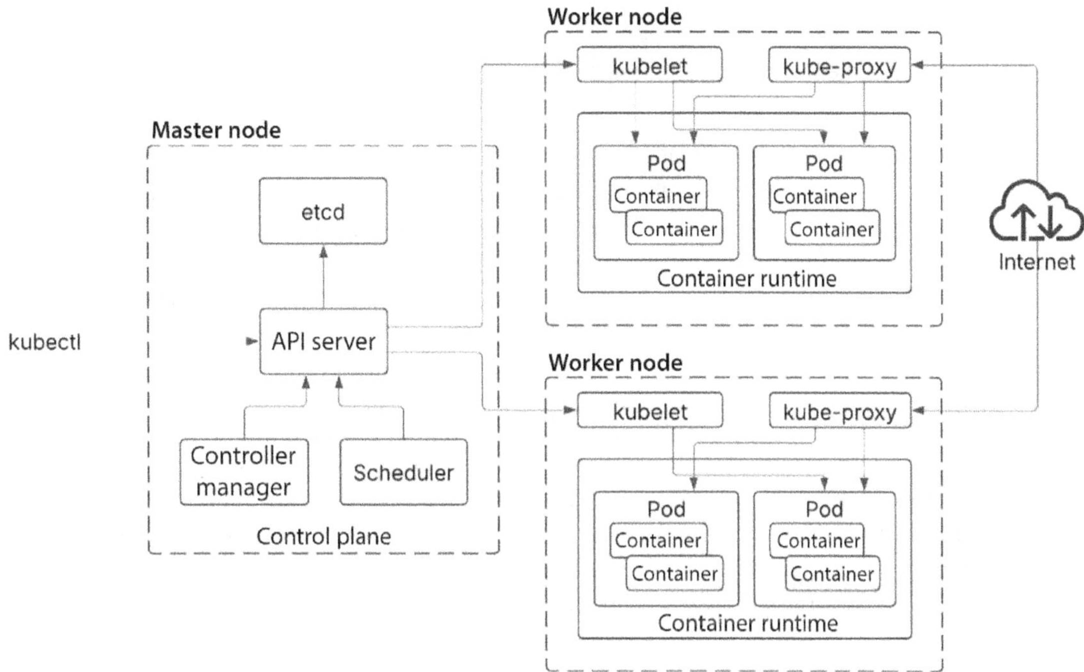

Figure 18.5: Kubernetes components

The minimum requirement of three control plane nodes comes from the fact that this is the minimum number to provide high availability. A single-master configuration is only used for workloads that can tolerate cluster downtime due to a master node failure, but mission-critical production workloads require a multi-master cluster. It is possible to have the control plane nodes also available as worker nodes, although this is not encouraged. This can negatively impact cluster performance, increase latency, and compromise the high availability of the cluster.

Control plane

In Kubernetes, you rarely interact with individual worker nodes directly. Instead, all the API requests go to the control plane. The control plane then decides on the actions to take based on the requests, and then it communicates the instructions to the worker nodes.

You can interact with the control plane in several ways:

- Using the `kubectl` CLI
- Using a web dashboard
- Using the Kubernetes API from inside an application other than `kubectl`

Control plane nodes usually run several important components:

- **API server**: The entry point for all cluster requests.
- **Scheduler**: Decides where to place workloads.
- **etcd**: A distributed key-value store that holds the configuration data, state data, and metadata.
- **Additional components to handle the specific needs**: For example, Kubernetes clusters deployed in a public cloud, such as Canonical Kubernetes and Google Cloud Platform, run cloud controllers on control plane nodes. The cloud controller interacts with the cloud provider's API to replace the failed machines, provision load balancers, or assign external IP addresses.

Worker nodes

As the name suggests, worker nodes are the machines that run application workloads. They can be physical servers that you host on-premises, VMs hosted privately, or VMs from your cloud provider.

Kubernetes worker nodes support both Linux and Windows operating systems. However, worker nodes running macOS are only integrated through virtualization, such as using `macOS-vz-Kubelet`, a virtual kubelet running directly on macOS, allowing Kubernetes to directly manage native macOS workloads.

Every worker node in a cluster runs at least the following three programs:

- A container runtime (for example, containerd, CRI-O, Docker Engine, **Mirantis Container Runtime** (**MCR**), gVisor, or Kata Containers) that allows the machine to handle the application containers
- A kubelet, which is responsible for receiving requests from the control plane and managing the individual containers based on those requests
- A kube-proxy, which is responsible for networking and load balancing on the node level

We'll now look at different ways to deploy Kubernetes in your organization. Choosing one over the other requires you to analyze additional costs and benefits related to them.

Possible approaches to deploying Kubernetes

One of the ways to deploy Kubernetes is to deploy it directly onto bare-metal servers hosted on-premises, for instance, by using the `kubeadm` setup tool provided by Kubernetes. One of the benefits of this approach is that this may be cheaper for large-scale applications than what the cloud providers offer. However, there's one major drawback: you will require an operator to provide the additional nodes whenever necessary.

To mitigate this issue, you can run a virtualization appliance such as OpenStack or Xen Orchestra (Web UI for XCP-ng or XenServer) on top of your bare-metal servers. This makes it possible to use the Kubernetes built-in cloud controller to provision the necessary resources automatically. You still have the same control over the costs, but there's less manual work. Virtualization adds some overhead, but in most cases, this should be a fair trade-off.

If you are not interested in hosting the servers yourself, you can deploy Kubernetes to run on top of VMs from a cloud provider. This approach gives you more flexibility than bare metal. Moreover, by choosing this route, you can use some of the existing templates for optimal setup.

There are Terraform and Ansible modules available to build a cluster on popular cloud platforms. However, the management overhead gets added, as you are responsible for operating and upgrading the cluster.

Finally, there are the managed services available from the major cloud players. You only have to pay for the worker nodes in some of them, while the control plane is free of charge.

Why would you choose self-hosted Kubernetes over the managed services when operating in a public cloud? One of the reasons may be a specific version of Kubernetes that you require. Cloud providers are typically a bit slow when it comes to introducing updates.

To simplify deployment and management in either case, you can rely on automation tools such as Charmed Kubernetes (a curated set of tools for Kubernetes deployment), **Kubernetes Operations (kOps**; a tool for automated installation and management), Kubespray (a tool for the automated deployment), Crossplane (a framework for building cloud native control planes), and Cozystack (a free PaaS platform and framework for building clouds). Cozystack also provides container-native virtualization to run VMs within containers managed and hosted through KubeVirt, making it possible to migrate legacy applications or hybrid workloads into a Kubernetes environment.

Understanding the Kubernetes concepts

Kubernetes introduces some concepts that may sound unfamiliar or be confusing if you hear them for the first time. When you learn their purpose, it should be easier to grasp what makes Kubernetes special. Here are some of the most common Kubernetes objects:

- A **container**, specifically, an application container, is a method of distributing and running a single application. It contains the code and configuration necessary to run the unmodified application anywhere.
- A **Pod** is a basic Kubernetes building block. It is atomic and consists of one or more containers. All the containers inside the Pod share the same network interfaces, volumes (such as persistent storage or secrets), and resources (CPU and memory). They can communicate with one another using `localhost`.
- A **Deployment** is a higher-level object that manages Pods and their life cycle. It typically manages a set of Pod replicas, allows for rolling upgrades, and manages rollbacks in case of failure. This is what makes it easy to scale and manage the life cycle of Kubernetes applications.
- A **DaemonSet** is a controller similar to a Deployment in that it manages where the Pods are distributed. While Deployments are concerned with keeping a given number of replicas, DaemonSets spread the Pods across all worker nodes. The primary use case is to run a system-level Service, such as a monitoring or logging agent, on each node.
- **Jobs** are designed for one-off tasks. Pods in Deployments restart automatically when the containers inside them terminate. They are suitable for all the always-on Services that listen on network ports for requests. However, Deployments are unsuited for batch jobs, such as thumbnail generation, which you want to run only when required. Jobs create one or more Pods and watch them until they complete a given task. When a specific number of successful Pods terminate, the job is considered complete.

- **CronJobs**, as the name suggests, are the jobs that are run periodically within the cluster.
- **Services** represent a particular function performed within a cluster. They have a network endpoint associated with them (which is usually load-balanced). Services may be performed by one or more Pods. The life cycle of Services is independent of the life cycles of the many Pods. Since Pods are transient, they may be created and destroyed at any time. Services abstract individual Pods to allow for high availability. Services have their own IP addresses and DNS names for ease of use.

Managing Kubernetes declaratively

We've covered the differences between declarative and imperative approaches earlier in *Chapter 11, Continuous Integration and Continuous Deployment*. Kubernetes takes the declarative approach. Instead of giving instructions regarding the steps that need to be taken, you provide the resources that describe your cluster's desired state. It is up to the control plane to allocate internal resources so that they fulfill your needs.

It is possible to add the resources using the command line directly. This can be quick for testing, but in most cases, you'll want to have a record of the resources you created. Thus, most people work with manifest files, which provide a coded description of the resources required. Manifests are typically YAML files, but it is also possible to use JSON.

Here's an example YAML manifest that defines a single Pod:

```
apiVersion: v1
kind: Pod
metadata:
  name: simple-server
  labels:
    app: tradefair-front
spec:
  containers:
    - name: webserver
      image: nginx
      ports:
        - name: http
          containerPort: 80
          protocol: TCP
```

The first line is mandatory, and it states which API version will be used in the manifest, as some resources are only available in specific API groups. This information tells Kubernetes how to interpret the resource definition.

The second line describes what resource we are creating. Next, there is metadata and the specification of the resource.

A name is mandatory in `metadata` as this is the way to distinguish one resource from another. If we wanted to create another Pod with the same name, we would get an error stating that such a resource already exists. The label is optional and useful when writing selectors. For example, if we wanted to create a Service that allows connection to the Pod, we would use a selector matching the `app` label with a value equal to `tradefair-front`.

The specification is also the mandatory part, as it describes the actual content of the resource. In our example, we list one container named `webserver` using an image, `nginx`, from Docker Hub. Since we want to connect to the NGINX web server from the outside, we also expose the container port `80` on which the server is listening. The name in the port description is optional.

While Pods are the most basic unit in Kubernetes, you rarely manage them directly in real-world deployments. Instead, you often use Deployments, which manage identical Pods and ensure that the desired number of them are running at all times.

This Deployment manages our `customer` application:

```
apiVersion: v1
kind: Deployment
metadata:
  name: customer-deployment
  labels:
    app: customer
```

Next, in the `spec` section, we define replicas and selectors. Kubernetes replicas are clones that allow Kubernetes to run multiple identical Pods simultaneously, enabling self-healing (if one Pod fails, Kubernetes recreates it). Kubernetes uses selectors to flexibly select objects based on their labels:

```
spec:
  replicas: 3
  selector:
    matchLabels:
      app: customer
  template:
    metadata:
      labels:
        app: customer
```

Inside the `template` section of the Deployment, we define the containers to run. When `imagePullPolicy` is set to `Never`, the kubelet will only use the version of the image that is already cached (available) locally on that node. This mode can be used, for example, for development, since local container images are not pushed to any container registry. Such images have nowhere to pull from except by being built locally. The other image pull policy options are `IfNotPresent` and `Always`:

```
    spec:
      containers:
```

```
    - name: customer
      image: customer:latest
      imagePullPolicy: Never
      ports:
        - name: http
          protocol: TCP
          containerPort: 8080
```

Kubernetes also supports probes to monitor application health. A readiness probe determines when an application is ready to receive traffic, while a liveness check determines when an application is malfunctioning and requires a restart. Therefore, health checks must be quick to prevent Kubernetes from getting stuck in a loop of constantly restarting Pods. In the simplest case, an application can have a single quick health check endpoint. The default timeout is one second:

```
      readinessProbe:
        httpGet:
          path: /health
          port: http
      livenessProbe:
        httpGet:
          path: /health
          port: http
```

The OpenTelemetry Collector can be configured by using environment variables. `OTEL_EXPORTER_OTLP_INSECURE` is an environment variable used by OpenTelemetry to enable client transport security for the exporter's gRPC connection when sending telemetry data (traces, metrics, and logs). You should almost never set `OTEL_EXPORTER_OTLP_INSECURE=true` in a production environment. Unencrypted data transmission over a network (especially the internet) makes it vulnerable to interception. Always use a secure connection for any external or production receivers:

```
      env:
        - name: OTEL_EXPORTER_OTLP_ENDPOINT
          value: http://aspire-dashboard-otlp-clusterip:8080
        - name: OTEL_SERVICE_NAME
          value: customer
        - name: OTEL_EXPORTER_OTLP_INSECURE
          value: "true"
```

In our setup, telemetry is sent to the Aspire dashboard, which is written in C# and is a free, open source OpenTelemetry dashboard for debugging and monitoring distributed applications using telemetry data according to the OpenTelemetry standard, providing a real-time overview of services, their logs, traces, and metrics in a single interface.

Let's now look at how Kubernetes enhances security and isolation at the container and Pod level. A good practice for improving the security of Pods is to configure security contexts according to the principle of least privilege, which advocates providing any entity only the minimum level of access or permissions necessary to perform its intended function.

Thus, Kubernetes and Docker support mounting the container filesystem as read-only, which hardens containerized workloads by minimizing the attack surface of the overall application. A read-only root filesystem helps enforce an immutable infrastructure strategy because the container only needs to write data on the mounted volume within the known directories. An immutable root filesystem can also prevent malicious binaries from writing to the host system and ensure that an attacker cannot manipulate the executables of your container.

However, the application may need to record its state somewhere. This can be an ephemeral volume, and Kubernetes offers several types of ephemeral volumes. For instance, the `emptyDir` volume is ephemeral because all the data is deleted permanently when a Pod is removed from a node. Logs can also be ingested into the observability pipeline using `emptyDir` as a semi-permanent storage volume because not all applications stream logs to standard output (`stdout`), but follow the more traditional way of storing them on disk:

```
      securityContext:
         readOnlyRootFilesystem: true
       volumeMounts:
         - mountPath: /var/run
           name: tmpfs
   volumes:
     - name: tmpfs
       emptyDir: {}
```

Other best practices for Pod security include running containers as non-root users (`securityContext.runAsNonRoot` and `securityContext.runAsUser`), forbidding privilege escalation (`securityContext.allowPrivilegeEscalation`), and disabling the automatic mounting of the ServiceAccount token (`automountServiceAccountToken`).

In addition, containers are increasingly being used to manage peripheral devices in IoT or 5G networks, where maintaining runtime security is crucial. The runtime security can be enhanced with the help of KubeArmor (a cloud-native runtime security enforcement engine leveraging eBPF and Linux Security Modules), K8TLS (pronounced *cattles*; assesses server port security by detecting its **Transport Layer Security (TLS)** and certificate configuration), and ThreatMapper (a **cloud-native application protection platform (CNAPP)** for IDEs, CI/CD pipelines, and clusters).

Moving on to Kubernetes Services, their type determines whether a Service is accessible externally or internally. By default, Kubernetes creates a `ClusterIP` Service, meaning the service is accessible within the cluster only.

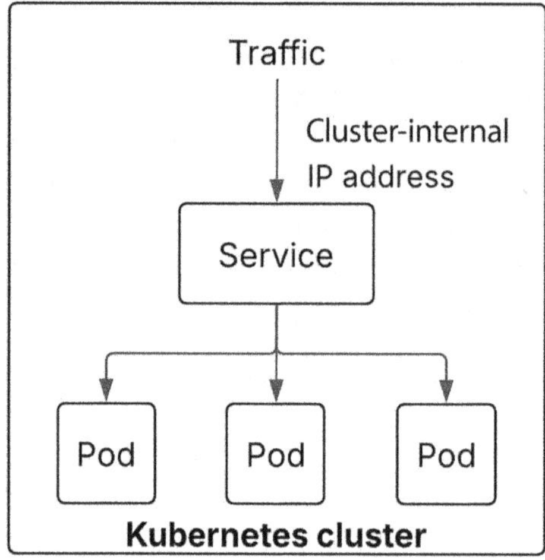

Figure 18.6: ClusterIP Service in Kubernetes

`NodePort` is the simplest way to route external traffic to a Service. The Service can be accessed via `NodeIP:NodePort`. It exposes Pods to a port on each cluster node. Kubernetes allocates a port in the range `30000-32767` (by default) and binds it to the Service. In this example, our Service listens on the node port `30000`:

```
---
apiVersion: v1
kind: Service
metadata:
  name: customer
spec:
  type: NodePort
  selector:
    app: customer
  ports:
    - name: http
      protocol: TCP
      port: 8080
      targetPort: 8080
      nodePort: 30000
```

The resulting setup is illustrated in *Figure 18.7*:

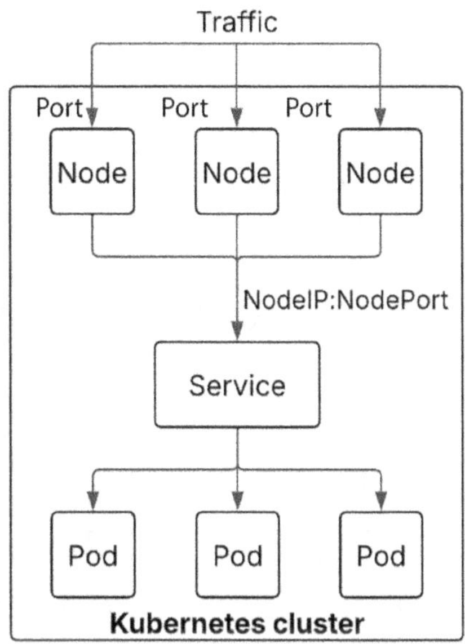

Figure 18.7: NodePort Service in Kubernetes

`LoadBalancer` Services provide access to applications in a cluster through a load balancer created in the cloud infrastructure. This type of Service automatically assigns an external IP address to the application and distributes incoming traffic across multiple application Pods, providing high availability, fault tolerance, and scalability. However, it relies on native cloud provider solutions. This Kubernetes Service is defined for NGINX Ingress Controller in MicroK8s (a lightweight Kubernetes distribution):

```
---
apiVersion: v1
kind: Service
metadata:
  name: ingress
  namespace: ingress
spec:
  selector:
    name: customer-ingress-microk8s
  type: LoadBalancer
  ports:
    - name: http
      protocol: TCP
      port: 8080
      targetPort: 8080
```

Figure 18.8 illustrates this concept:

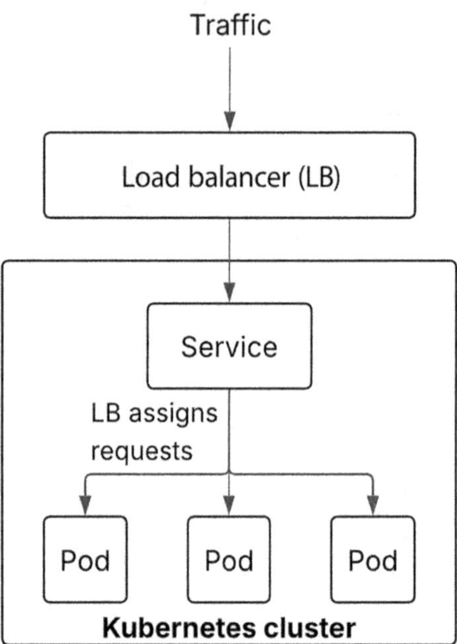

Figure 18.8: Load balancer Service in Kubernetes

`Ingress` is a Kubernetes resource that manages external access to Services within a cluster and acts as an intelligent router. In the following configuration, all HTTP traffic goes through the `customer` Service listening on port `8080`:

```
---
apiVersion: networking.k8s.io/v1
kind: Ingress
metadata:
  name: customer-ingress
spec:
  ingressClassName: nginx
  rules:
    - host: customer.local
      http:
        paths:
          - path: /
            pathType: Prefix
            backend:
              service:
                name: customer
                port:
                  number: 8080
```

Figure 18.9 shows how `Ingress` routes traffic to Services within the cluster:

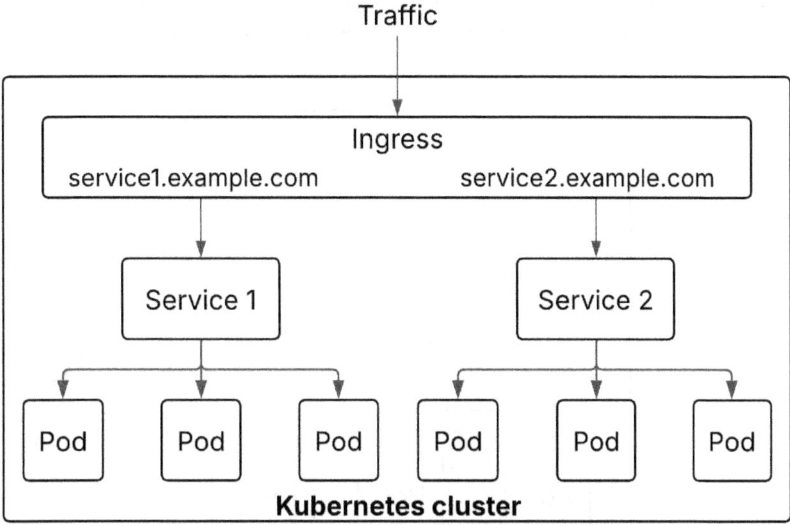

Figure 18.9: Ingress controller in Kubernetes

An `ExternalName` Service defines DNS **Canonical Name** (**CNAME**) records for servers located outside the Kubernetes cluster:

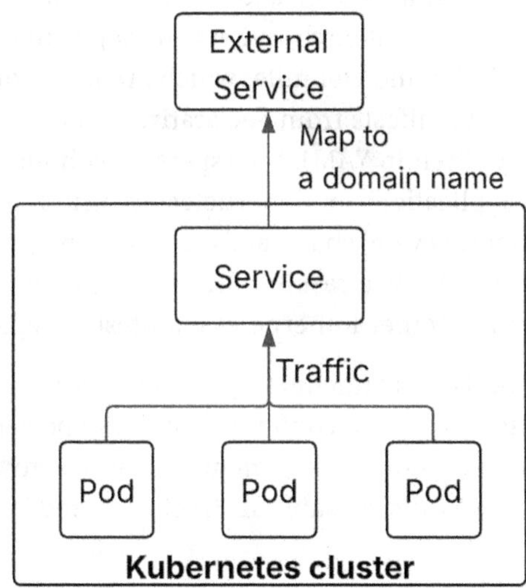

Figure 18.10: ExternalName Service in Kubernetes

A headless Service does not have a cluster IP address and instead provides DNS records for each individual Pod matching the specified selectors. In this way, applications directly access each Pod without going through load balancing, which is useful for distributed systems such as databases or message processing systems requiring direct access to specific instances.

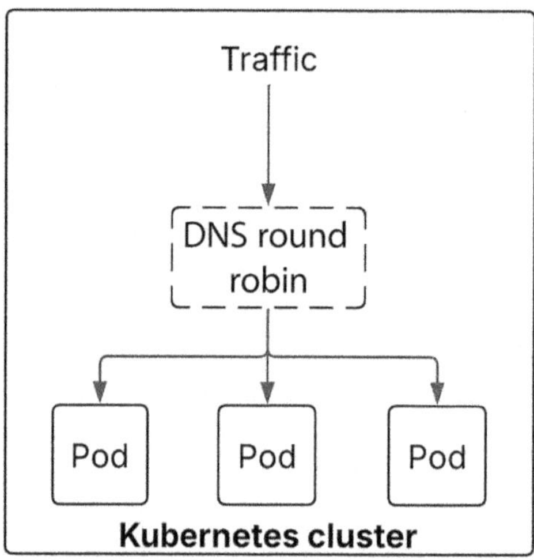

Figure 18.11: Headless Service in Kubernetes

Further, as deployments grow, using static Kubernetes manifests quickly becomes cumbersome if you constantly need to adapt them to different environments or deployments. Consequently, generative tools quickly emerged, notably Helm and Helmfile, which are based on the Go template engine, to dynamically produce Kubernetes manifests from declarative specifications. Helm organizes applications into charts (Helm charts written in YAML interspersed with instructions for the Go template engine) and deploys packaged applications on Kubernetes. In turn, Helmfile wraps Helm charts in a declarative specification to combine several charts and create a managed, comprehensive deployment artifact in a Kubernetes environment. As a result of this paradigm, it is usually enough to change a few parameters instead of writing another Kubernetes manifest to deploy an application.

Alternatives to these tools may be Skaffold (facilitating continuous development), Kustomize (customizing Kubernetes objects), Grafana Tanka (a configuration utility powered by the Jsonnet language), Kapitan (generic templated configuration management), cdk8s (a software development framework for defining Kubernetes applications and reusable abstractions), and Helmwave (a tool for deploying Helm charts).

Finally, client libraries for interacting with the Kubernetes REST API exist, but they are not widely used. In the case of statically typed languages, this is most likely because they require recompilation of the program, making any configuration changes opaque. It is usually impossible to tell exactly which Kubernetes manifest is being applied without having the program's source code or even disassembling it.

Kubernetes networking

Kubernetes allows for pluggable network architectures through the **container network interface** (CNI), a framework for configuring network interfaces in Linux containers. Several CNI plugins—such as Cilium, Calico, Flannel, Weave Net, AWS VPC, Azure CNI, GKE, and Terway—exist that may be used depending on requirements.

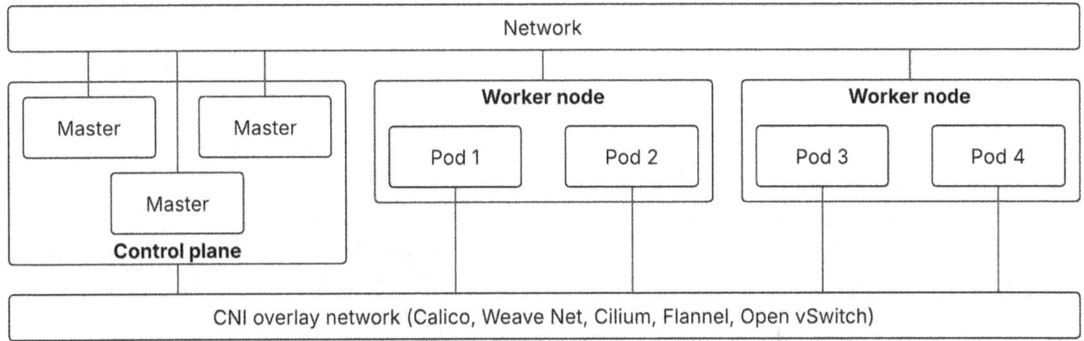

Figure 18.12: Kubernetes networking

Whichever plugin you select, some concepts are universal. The following are the typical networking scenarios.

Container-to-container communication

A single Pod may host several different containers. Since the network interface is tied to the Pod and not to the containers, each container operates in the same Linux network namespace. This means various containers may address one another using Linux loopback networking. These are virtual network interfaces designed to send network data within the system itself, for example, to the address `127.0.0.1` (`localhost`).

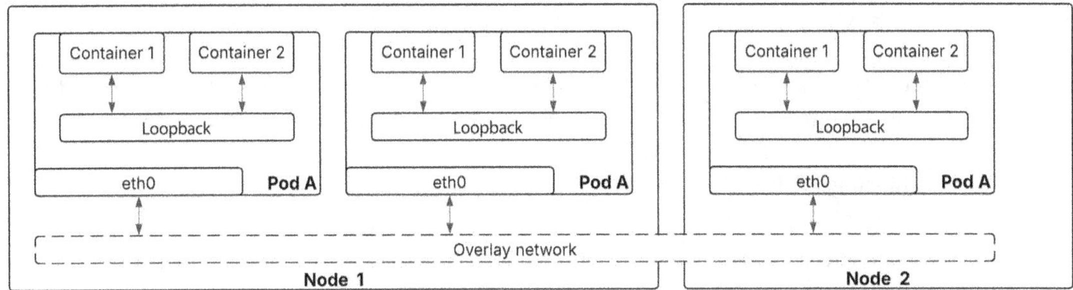

Figure 18.13: Kubernetes container-to-container communication and the overlay network that enables Pod-to-Pod communication across nodes

Strictly speaking, containers aren't isolated boxes. They are normal processes executed using two features of the Linux kernel called namespaces and **control groups** (**cgroups**), which provide process isolation and resource management. These Linux features are described in *Chapter 16, Containers*.

Linux namespaces are a kernel feature that isolates system resources, such as process ID, networking, and filesystems, to separate groups of processes at the operating system level running within a single Linux host. So, between containers, the `IPC` namespace provides a layer for inter-process communication, the `UTS` namespace provides a layer for using the same hostname, and the `network` namespace provides a layer for using the same network stack. Hence, containers in the same Pod can communicate with each other via `localhost`.

Due to the shared port space, containers in the same Pod cannot be bound to the same port numbers, while containers in other Pods have their own network interfaces and port spaces, eliminating port conflicts between different Pods.

Digging into the networking in more technical detail, a network socket is addressed by combining an IP address and a port number in the form of `IP:port`, known as a unique *socket address*. In the case of the Pod, this is an internal *unique* IP address `127.0.0.1`. The `localhost` IPv4 range contains 16,777,216 IP addresses in the `127.0.0.0/8` (CIDR notation) address range that are reserved for loopback, meaning that it routes traffic back to the local machine, but not to other machines. Although any address in this block can be used for loopback, the standard and most used address is `127.0.0.1`. In fact, multiple such identical but isolated virtual loopback network interfaces are created in the namespaces, taking process containerization in Linux to a whole new level.

Pod-to-Pod communication

Each Pod is assigned a unique, internal IP address that is valid only within the cluster. The address does not persist once the Pod has been deleted. One Pod can connect to another's exposed ports when it knows the other's address, as they share the same flat network. Pod networking is handled by a kubelet using CNI. You can think of Pods as VMs that host containers within this communication model.

Pod-to-Pod isolation is not provided by default. Kubernetes namespaces provide a mechanism for organizing and scoping resources, but they do not inherently prevent Pods in one namespace from communicating with Pods in another. They divide resources within a cluster into logical units, for example, development and production environments. By default, Kubernetes resources are created in the default namespace, called `default`. For achieving Pod isolation, other resources, such as network policies, are configured.

Pod-to-Service communication

Pod-to-Service communication is the most popular use case for communication within the cluster. Each Service has an individual IP address and a DNS name assigned to it, making it discoverable by other Pods. Service networking is handled by kube-proxy, which balances traffic load and routes client requests to the appropriate modules based on the Service selector. Unlike Pods, Services are not created or assigned to individual nodes, but they are cluster-wide.

External-to-internal communication

External traffic typically comes to the cluster via the means of load balancers. These are either tied to or handled by specific Services or ingress controllers. When the externally exposed Services handle the traffic, it behaves like Pod-to-Service communication. With the ingress controller, you have additional features available that allow for routing, observability, or advanced load balancing. Ingress routes can be host-based or path-based.

What to consider before adopting Kubernetes

Introducing Kubernetes within an organization requires some investment. There are many benefits provided by Kubernetes, such as auto-scalability, automation, and deployment scenarios. However, these benefits may not justify the necessary investment.

This investment concerns several areas:

- **Infrastructure costs:** The costs associated with running the control plane and the worker nodes may be relatively high. Additionally, the costs may rise if you want to use various Kubernetes expansions, such as GitOps or a service mesh (described later). They also require additional resources to run and add more overhead on top of your application's regular services. Apart from the nodes themselves, you should also factor in other costs. Some of the Kubernetes features work best when deployed to a supported cloud provider. This means that in order to benefit from those features, you'd have to go down one of the following routes:
    - Move your workload to the specifically supported cloud
    - Implement your own drivers for a cloud provider of your choice
    - Migrate your on-premises infrastructure to a virtualized API-enabled environment, such as VMware vSphere or OpenStack
- **Operations costs:** The Kubernetes cluster and associated Services require maintenance. Even though you get less maintenance for your applications, this benefit is slightly offset by the cost of keeping the cluster running.
- **Education costs:** Your entire product team has to learn new concepts. Even if you have a dedicated platform team that will provide developers with easy-to-use tools, developers would still require a basic understanding of how the work they do influences the entire system and which API they should use.

Before you decide on introducing Kubernetes, consider whether you can afford the initial investment it requires.

Observability in cloud-native distributed systems

Distributed systems, such as those in cloud-native architectures, pose some unique challenges. The sheer number of different services working at any given time makes it very inconvenient to investigate how well the components perform.

In monolithic systems, logging and performance monitoring are usually enough. However, in a distributed system, distributed tracing becomes essential, as it allows you to follow a request as it moves across services, tracking its life cycle. Moreover, with a distributed system, even logging requires careful design. Different components produce different log formats. Those logs must be stored somewhere. Keeping them together with a service that delivers them will make it challenging to get the big picture in an outage case. Besides, since microservices may be short-lived, you will want to decouple the life cycle of logs from the life cycle of a service that provides them or a machine that hosts the service.

In *Chapter 17, Observability*, we described how a unified logging layer helps manage the logs. We also explored different specialized tools for logging, monitoring, and tracing. However, managing logs, metrics, and traces across different tools can be fragmented. This is where OpenTelemetry helps—by standardizing how observability data is gathered and exported, while still allowing you to choose the different tools meant for logging, monitoring, and tracing.

Instrumenting an application with OpenTelemetry

The OpenTelemetry Operator (a Kubernetes Operator) automates the deployment and management of the OpenTelemetry Collector, which gathers telemetry data from applications. It also automatically instruments applications to collect telemetry data without manually changing code. A Kubernetes Operator is a custom controller that extends the Kubernetes API with application-specific knowledge and automates the deployment or management of highly complex applications and their components.

However, the OpenTelemetry Operator does not support the injection and configuration of automatic instrumentation for C++ services. Thus, C++ applications implement manual instrumentation using the `opentelemetry-cpp` library, which provides metric, logger, and tracer providers.

Here's an example from `metrics.cpp`. The OpenTelemetry Collector supports both **OpenTelemetry Protocol** (**OTLP**) HTTP and gRPC exporters for sending telemetry data. The example initializes only the gRPC exporter, which is configured automatically:

```
// omitted code
...
namespace otlp_metrics {
void init_metrics() {
  const otlp_exporter::OtlpGrpcMetricExporterOptions exporter_options;
  auto exporter =
  otlp_exporter::OtlpGrpcMetricExporterFactory::Create(exporter_options);

  const
  metrics_sdk::PeriodicExportingMetricReaderOptions reader_options;

  std::unique_ptr<metrics_sdk::MetricReader> reader{
      new metrics_sdk::PeriodicExportingMetricReader(std::move(exporter),
                                                     reader_options)};
  const auto provider =
```

```
    std::static_pointer_cast<metrics_api::MeterProvider>(
        std::make_shared<metrics_sdk::MeterProvider>()
    );
    const auto p =
    std::static_pointer_cast<metrics_sdk::MeterProvider>(provider);
    p->AddMetricReader(std::move(reader));
    metrics_api::Provider::SetMeterProvider(provider);
  }
```

The primary OpenTelemetry metric types used for numeric measurements over time are counters, gauges, and histograms. The counters can be either of the integral type, `uint64_t`, or of the floating-point type, `double`:

```
  opentelemetry::nostd::unique_ptr<metrics_api::Counter<uint64_t>>
  init_uint64_counter(const std::string &name) {
    const auto provider = metrics_api::Provider::GetMeterProvider();
    const opentelemetry::nostd::shared_ptr<metrics_api::Meter> meter =
        provider->GetMeter(name);
    return meter->CreateUInt64Counter(name + "_counter");
  }
  } // namespace otlp_metrics
```

Next, we see an example from `logger.cpp` that initializes the OpenTelemetry logger. This enables OpenTelemetry logs to be sent to the terminal and collector simultaneously, which is also useful for debugging when the collector is not available:

```
  // omitted code
  ...
  namespace otlp_logger {
  void init_logger() {
    const otlp_exporter::OtlpGrpcLogRecordExporterOptions logger_options;
    auto exporter =
    otlp_exporter::OtlpGrpcLogRecordExporterFactory::Create(logger_options);

    auto processor =
    logs_sdk::SimpleLogRecordProcessorFactory::Create(std::move(exporter));
    std::vector<std::unique_ptr<logs_sdk::LogRecordProcessor>> processors;
    processors.push_back(std::move(processor));

    auto context =
    logs_sdk::LoggerContextFactory::Create(std::move(processors));
    const std::shared_ptr<logs_api::LoggerProvider> provider =
        logs_sdk::LoggerProviderFactory::Create(std::move(context));
        logs_api::Provider::SetLoggerProvider(provider);
  }
```

To record log entries, a `logger` instance must first be obtained from the OpenTelemetry provider, as shown here:

```
opentelemetry::nostd::shared_ptr<logs_api::Logger> get_logger(
const std::string &name
) {
  const auto provider = logs_api::Provider::GetLoggerProvider();
  return provider->GetLogger(name + "_logger");
}
} // namespace otlp_logger
```

Let's now look at an example from `tracer.cpp`. The implementation of an OpenTelemetry tracer provider is not much different from metrics and logs:

```
namespace otlp_tracer {
void init_tracer() {
  auto exporter =
      opentelemetry::exporter::otlp::OtlpGrpcExporterFactory::Create();

  auto processor =
      trace_sdk::SimpleSpanProcessorFactory::Create(std::move(exporter));

  const std::shared_ptr<opentelemetry::trace::TracerProvider> provider =
      trace_sdk::TracerProviderFactory::Create(std::move(processor));

  trace_api::Provider::SetTracerProvider(provider);

  context::propagation::GlobalTextMapPropagator::SetGlobalPropagator(

opentelemetry::nostd::shared_ptr<context::propagation::TextMapPropagator>(
          new trace_api::propagation::HttpTraceContext()
));
}

opentelemetry::nostd::shared_ptr<trace_api::Tracer>
get_tracer(const std::string &name) {
  const auto provider = trace_api::Provider::GetTracerProvider();
  return provider->GetTracer(name + "_tracer");
}
```

The preceding code initializes both tracer provider and propagator. In real-world systems, context propagation is critical: it carries request-specific metadata across services so that spans can be correlated into a single trace.

The OpenTelemetry library has the `HttpTextMapCarrier` template class for reading and writing trace context through HTTP headers. But it is incompatible with the Drogon framework because these two use different internal conventions for the headers: OpenTelemetry stores them in a capitalized form (for example, `TraceParent` and `TraceState`), while Drogon uses lowercase (`traceparent`, `tracestate`).

To resolve this issue, the following `HttpTextMapCarrier` class acts as an adapter for the Drogon framework for propagating HTTP request headers:

```
class HttpTextMapCarrier final :
public context::propagation::TextMapCarrier {
public:
  explicit HttpTextMapCarrier(const drogon::SafeStringMap<std::string>
  &headers): headers_(headers) {}

  [[nodiscard]] opentelemetry::nostd::string_view
  Get(const opentelemetry::nostd::string_view key) const noexcept override {
    if (const std::string key_ = key.data(); headers_.contains(key_)) {
      return headers_.at(key_);
    }
    return "";
  }

  void Set(const opentelemetry::nostd::string_view,
           const opentelemetry::nostd::string_view) noexcept override {
    // not required for server
  }

  const drogon::SafeStringMap<std::string> &headers_;
};
```

Once the adapter is in place, the trace context is created by extracting the parent context from the propagated HTTP request headers. The current context is then created based on this extracted parent context. The `Extract` method for servers is paired with the `Inject` method for clients to propagate the context along with the request over a network connection:

```
opentelemetry::nostd::shared_ptr<trace_api::Span> get_http_request_span(
    const drogon::HttpRequestPtr &request,
    const opentelemetry::nostd::shared_ptr<trace_api::Tracer> &tracer,
    const std::string &name) {
  trace_api::StartSpanOptions options;
  options.kind = trace_api::SpanKind::kServer;

  const HttpTextMapCarrier carrier{request->headers()};
  const auto propagator =
```

```
        context::propagation::GlobalTextMapPropagator::GetGlobalPropagator();

    // extract context from HTTP headers
    auto current_ctx = context::RuntimeContext::GetCurrent();
    const auto new_context = propagator->Extract(carrier, current_ctx);
    options.parent = trace_api::GetSpan(new_context)->GetContext();
```

The terms *client* and *server* refer only to roles within a specific interaction. A service can act as a client when it sends a request and as a server when it receives one. This concept confuses many people.

Each trace and span has corresponding identifiers: `trace_id` and `span_id`. When the first span is created, the OpenTelemetry library generates these identifiers, stores them in memory, and then exports them to the external system. Each new span is linked to a trace and, if present, to a parent span, forming a complete chain.

The trace context is conveyed using two standardized HTTP headers defined by the W3C Trace Context specification:

- `traceparent`: A mandatory header containing the protocol version, `trace_id`, and `span_id` of the parent
- `tracestate`: An optional header carrying additional vendor-specific information

The `traceparent` header has a specific format. Here's what it looks like: `00-95c05e0080dd609cf8434c32053fbea1-00077415d33cdca4-01`.

The `traceparent` header consists of four parts separated by hyphens, as explained:

- **Version** (`00`): The format version
- **Trace ID** (`95c05e0080dd609cf8434c32053fbea1`): A 32-character hex string uniquely identifying the entire trace
- **Parent span ID** (`00077415d33cdca4`): A 16-character hex string identifying the immediate parent span
- **Trace flags** (`01`): A single byte holding trace options

OpenTelemetry defines semantic conventions, also called semantic attributes, to provide common names for different kinds of operations and data. Semantic conventions involve following a standardized, common naming scheme across the entire code base, libraries, and platforms for traces, metrics, logs, profiles, and resources. Here's how a span is started with the parent context extracted from HTTP headers, using semantic attributes to describe the request:

```
    // start span with parent context extracted from HTTP headers
    auto span = tracer->StartSpan(
        name,
        {{semconv::http::kHttpRequestMethod, request->method()},
         {semconv::url::kUrlPath, request->path()},
         {semconv::url::kUrlQuery, request->query()},
         {semconv::network::kNetworkLocalAddress, request->getLocalAddr().
```

```
toIp()},
        {semconv::network::kNetworkLocalPort,
         std::to_string(request->getLocalAddr().toPort())},
        {semconv::network::kNetworkPeerAddress, request->getPeerAddr().toIp()},
        {semconv::network::kNetworkPeerPort,
         std::to_string(request->getPeerAddr().toPort())}},
       options);
```

In addition to these semantic attributes, OpenTelemetry traces can include custom attributes. Unlike context propagation, which only handles the necessary HTTP headers, span attributes can preserve all the headers:

```
  for (const auto &[key, value] : request->headers()) {
    span->SetAttribute("http.header." + key, value);
  }

  return span;
}
} // namespace otlp_tracer
```

Once tracing is instrumented, the next step is configuring how the telemetry data is exported. The exporters can be configured either by setting properties explicitly or with environment variables. The most important environment variables are as follows:

- `OTEL_EXPORTER_OTLP_ENDPOINT`: A base endpoint URL for any signal type, for example, `http://otel.collector:4317/`
- `OTEL_SERVICE_NAME`: The name of our application

Metrics, logs, and spans can be added to instrumented functions once the meter, logger, and tracer are set up. The `std::source_location::current()` function returns an object with values representing the call location that is used to attribute the log record. A span is started in the `get_http_request_span` function and then marked as active using the `WithActiveSpan` function called in the current scope. The following code in `main.cpp` demonstrates this:

```
const auto tracer = otlp_tracer::get_tracer("http-server");
auto span = otlp_tracer::get_http_request_span(
     request, tracer, "customer/handle_get/outer");
auto scope = opentelemetry::nostd::shared_ptr<trace_api::Tracer>::element_
type::WithActiveSpan(span);

const auto location = std::source_location::current();
const auto ctx = span->GetContext();
logger->Info("handling HTTP request to " + request->path(),
             common::MakeAttributes({{"file", location.file_name()},
                                      {"line", location.line()}}),
```

```
            ctx.trace_id(), ctx.span_id(), ctx.trace_flags(),
            std::chrono::system_clock::now());

span->AddEvent("Processing request");
handle_get(request, get_responder, std::move(callback));
span->End();
```

The logging functions used here are variadic function templates, which accept arguments of different types: `std::string_view`, `SpanContext`, `SpanId`, `TraceId`, `TraceFlags`, `SystemTimestamp`, `std::chrono::system_clock::time_point`, `KeyValueIterable`, and `std::span<std::pair<std::string_view, AttributeValue>>`. The `AttributeValue` class is a variant type, acting as a common class for types such as `bool`, `int32_t`, `uint32_t`, `int64_t`, `uint64_t`, `double`, and `const char *`.

OpenTelemetry log records can have attributes, which are used for analytics and filtering log records. In the screenshot, the **file** and **line** attributes correspond to the C++ file from which the log entry is sent to the collector. Additional attributes include the recording time and the current trace context, which correspond to the **Timestamp** and **Trace** columns:

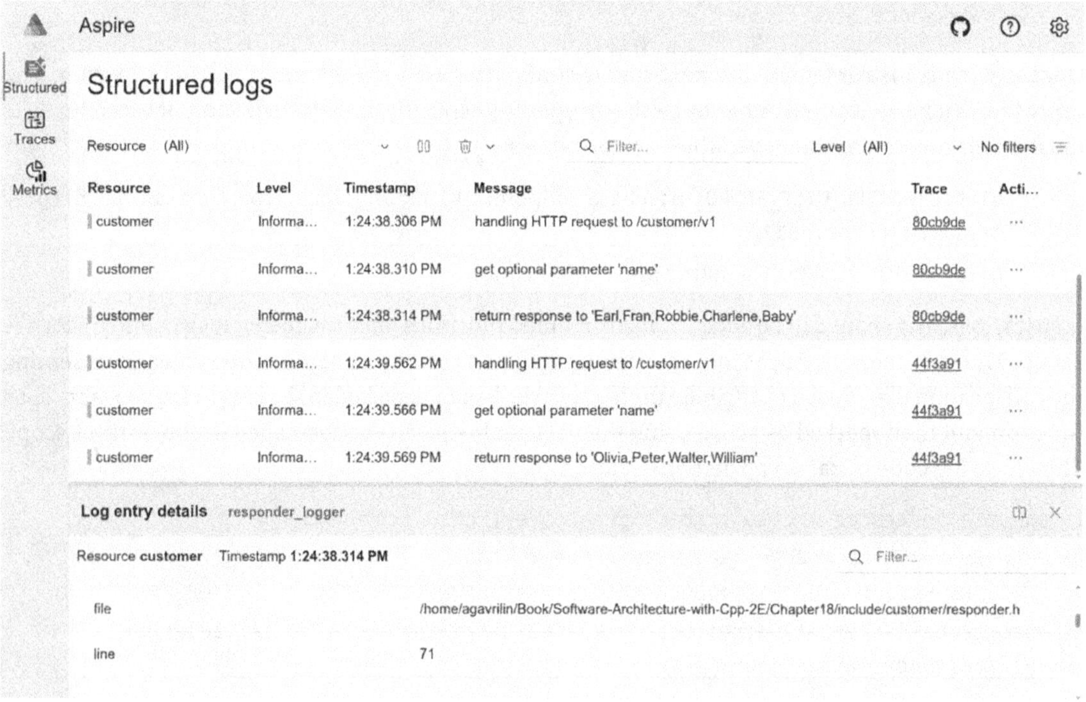

Figure 18.14: OpenTelemetry logs of the application on the Aspire dashboard

🔍**Quick tip:** Need to see a high-resolution version of this image? Open this book in the next-gen Packt Reader or view it in the PDF/ePub copy.

The next-gen Packt Reader and a **free PDF/ePub copy** of this book are included with your purchase. Scan the QR code OR visit `https://packtpub.com/unlock`, then use the search bar to find this book by name. Double-check the edition shown to make sure you get the right one.

The next screenshot shows a few trace attributes, although the list is quite big:

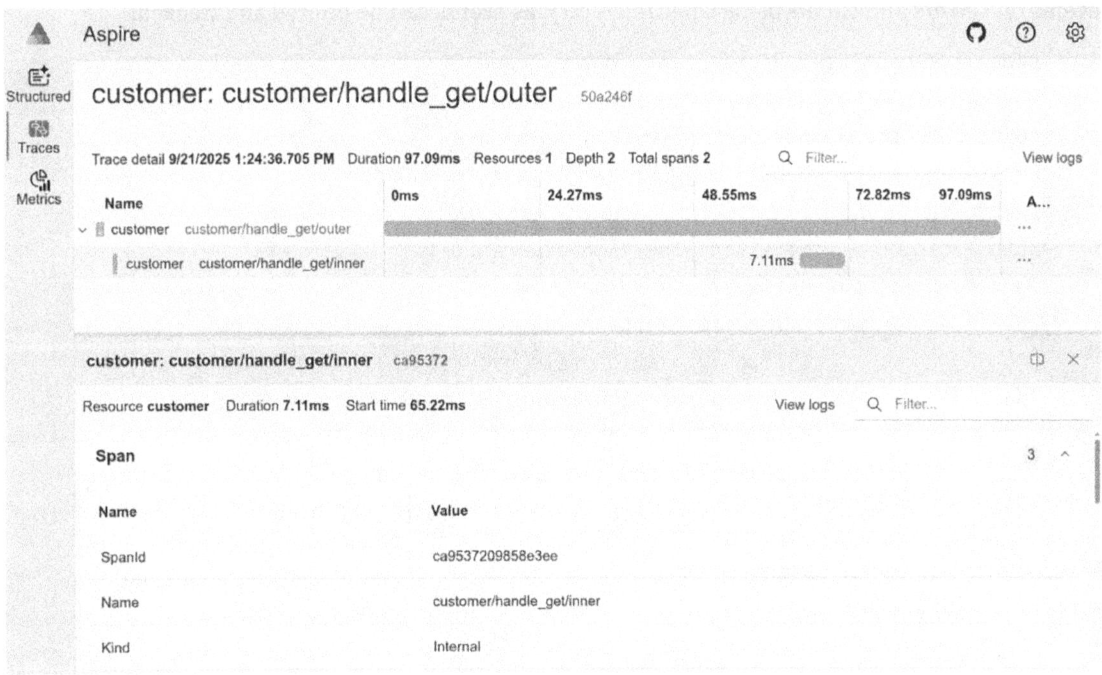

Figure 18.15: OpenTelemetry traces of the application on the Aspire dashboard

In more complex scenarios, traces often contain nested spans, which are implied by the presence of a parent span ID, where child spans represent sub-operations. This is how it appears in `responder.h`:

```
// omitted code
...
template <typename Responder>
void handle_get(
    const drogon::HttpRequestPtr &request, Responder &responder,
    std::function<void(const drogon::HttpResponsePtr &)> &&callback) {
    auto span = otlp_tracer::get_tracer("http-server")
                ->StartSpan("customer/handle_get/inner");
    auto scope = opentelemetry::nostd::shared_
ptr<opentelemetry::trace::Tracer>::element_type::WithActiveSpan(span);
```

After the span is active, the current context can be associated with log entries that are needed to analyze events on servers and clients using OpenTelemetry, as events can be filtered and tracked:

```
  span->AddEvent("get optional parameter 'name'");

  const auto ctx = span->GetContext();
  const auto logger = otlp_logger::get_logger("responder");

  auto location = std::source_location::current();
  logger->Info("get optional parameter 'name'",
               common::MakeAttributes(
                   {{"file", location.file_name()},
                    {"line", location.line()}}),
               ctx.trace_id(), ctx.span_id(), ctx.trace_flags(),
               std::chrono::system_clock::now());
  auto name = request->getOptionalParameter<std::string>("name");
```

Make sure to end started spans:

```
  if (!name) {
    const auto err = "missing value for 'name'";
    span->AddEvent(err);
    span->SetStatus(opentelemetry::trace::StatusCode::kError)

    location = std::source_location::current();
    logger->Error(err,
                  common::MakeAttributes({{"file", location.file_name()},
                                          {"line", location.line()}}),
                  ctx.trace_id(), ctx.span_id(), ctx.trace_flags(),
                  std::chrono::system_clock::now());
```

```
    responder.respond(drogon::k400BadRequest, Json::Value(err),
                      std::move(callback));
    span->End();
    return;
  }
```

Finally, let's look at how metrics appear in practice. The `handle_get` counter associated with the `name` URL query parameter counts successful calls to the `handle_get` function:

```
const auto counter = otlp_metrics::init_uint64_counter("handle_get");
const std::map<std::string, std::string> labels =
{{"name", name.value()}};
const auto attributes = common::KeyValueIterableView{labels};
counter->Add(1, attributes);
```

OpenTelemetry metrics are attributed, which makes it possible to filter and analyze metrics by dimension. In the following example, the `handle_get` counter values are differentiated by the `name` URL query parameter:

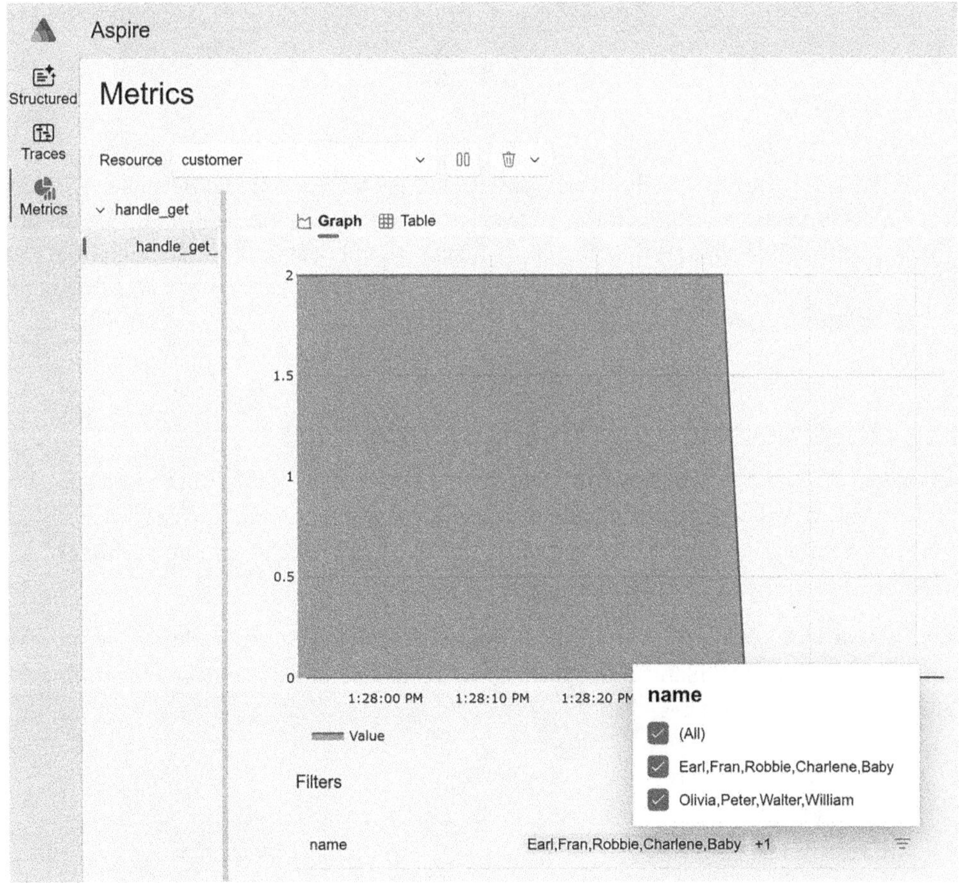

Figure 18.16: OpenTelemetry metrics of the application on the Aspire dashboard

OpenTelemetry signals (traces, metrics, logs, and baggage) can be enriched by adding attributes of different types:

```
    span->AddEvent("return response");
    location = std::source_location::current();
    logger->Info("return response to '" + name.value() + "'",
                 common::MakeAttributes(
                     {{"file", location.file_name()},
                      {"line", location.line()}}),
                 ctx.trace_id(), ctx.span_id(), ctx.trace_flags(),
                 std::chrono::system_clock::now());

    const auto [code, response] = responder.prepare_response(name.value());
    responder.respond(code, response, std::move(callback));

    span->SetStatus(opentelemetry::trace::StatusCode::kOk);
    span->End();
}
```

With manual instrumentation in place, a C++ application can now emit consistent telemetry data through OpenTelemetry.

Cloud-native observability tools such as OpenTelemetry provide rich telemetry data, which paves the way for the creation of testing frameworks such as Testkube. This is a test orchestration and execution framework for cloud-native applications that simplifies testing Kubernetes applications, integrates with multiple platforms and tools, and utilizes multiple testing frameworks.

Connecting services with a service mesh

Microservices and cloud-native design come with their own set of problems. Communication between different services, observability, debugging, rate limiting, authentication, access control, and A/B testing may be challenging even with a limited number of services. When the number of services rises, so does the complexity of the aforementioned requirements.

That's where a service mesh enters the fray. In essence, a service mesh trades off some resources (necessary to run the control plane and sidecars) for an automated and centrally controlled solution to the aforementioned challenges.

Introducing a service mesh

Traditionally, all of the aforementioned requirements used to be coded within each application itself. As it turns out, many of these requirements are shared across many different applications. When your application consists of many services, adding new features to all of them starts to be costly. With a service mesh, you may control these features from a single point instead. A service mesh abstracts these features into a dedicated infrastructure layer, providing security, reliability, traffic management, and observability without requiring changes to the application code.

Since a containerized workflow already abstracts some of the runtime and some networking, a service mesh takes the abstraction to another level. This way, the application within a container is only aware of what happens at the application level of the OSI networking model, while the service mesh handles lower levels. While we often explain this using the theoretical and more detailed seven-layer OSI model, the four-layer TCP/IP model is more practical and simpler, being the technical foundation of the internet.

	OSI Model	Protocols in Each Layer	TCP/IP Model
7	Application	DNS, DHCP, FTP, HTTP, IMAP, POP3, SMTP, SNMP, LDAP, RTP, RTSP, SSH, SIP, Telnet	Application
6	Presentation	JPEG, MPEG, TIFF, SSL, TLS	
5	Session	NFS, SMB, NetBIOS, RPC, P2P, SCP, RAP, PPTP	
4	Transport	TCP, UDP	Transport
3	Network	IPv4, IPv6, ARP, ICMP, IGMP, IPSec, IPX, RIP	Internet
2	Data Link	ARP, ATM, CDP, FDDI, HDLC, MPLS, PPP, STP	Network Access
1	Physical	Ethernet, Bluetooth, DSL, ISDN, Wi-Fi, RS-232, RJ45, USB	

Figure 18.17: OSI model versus TCP/IP model

Setting up a service mesh allows you to have fine-grained control over network traffic and gives you better insights into this traffic. The dependencies become visible, as does the flow, shape, and amount of traffic.

Not only is the flow of traffic handled by the service mesh, but other popular patterns, such as circuit breaking, rate limiting, or retries, don't have to be implemented by each application and configured separately. This is also a feature that can be outsourced to the service mesh. Similarly, A/B testing or canary deployments are the use cases that a service mesh is able to fulfill.

One of the benefits of the service mesh, as previously mentioned, is greater control. Its architecture typically consists of a manageable edge proxy for external traffic and internal proxies usually deployed as sidecars along each microservice. This way, the networking policies can be written as code and stored alongside all the other configurations in a single place. Rather than having to switch on mutual SSL/TLS encryption for two of the services you want to connect, you only must enable the feature once in your service mesh configuration.

However, a service mesh increases CPU and memory load and adds latency. If your services require maximum performance, it's better to optimize communication directly, without intermediary proxies. If you have a monolith and are just transitioning to a microservices architecture, don't immediately implement a service mesh. Start with an API gateway such as Tyk, Kong, KrakenD, Gravitee, Apache APISIX, or Express Gateway. Implement logging and monitoring—and only then evaluate whether you need a mesh. Setting up a service mesh requires knowledge and skill. Incorrect configuration can create vulnerabilities, increase debugging difficulties, and impede scaling.

Next, we'll cover some of the service mesh solutions.

Service mesh solutions

All of the solutions described here are self-hosted.

Istio

Istio is a powerful collection of service mesh tools written in Go and C++. It allows you to connect microservices through the deployment of Envoy proxies as sidecar containers. Because Envoy is programmable, the Istio control plane's configuration changes are communicated to all the proxies, which then reconfigure themselves accordingly.

Figure 18.18 shows this sidecar architecture; each service instance is paired with an Envoy proxy (the data plane), while the control plane manages configuration, SD, and certificates:

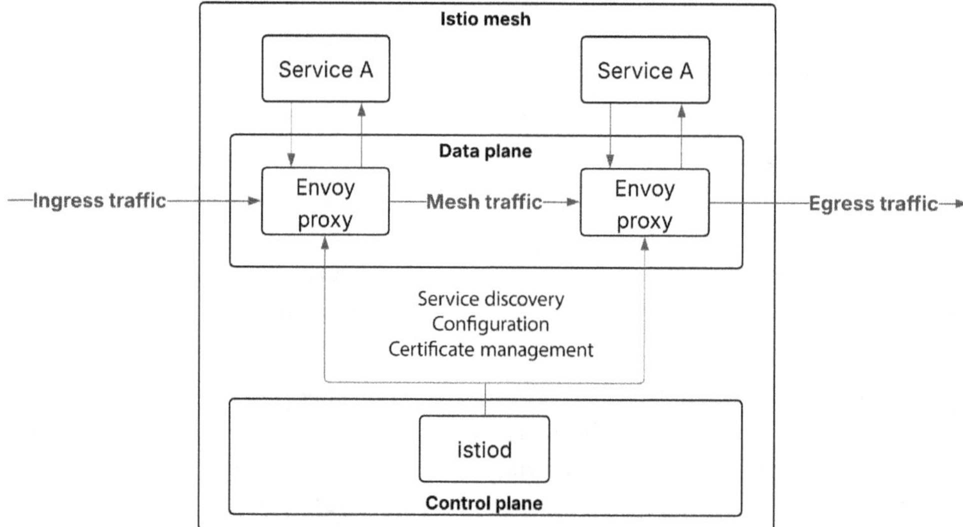

Figure 18.18: Istio service mesh architecture in sidecar mode

The Envoy proxies are, among other things, responsible for handling encryption and authentication. With Istio, enabling **mutual TLS (mTLS)** between your services requires a single switch in the configuration for the majority of the time. If you don't want mTLS between all your services, you can selectively enable it for specific services while allowing unencrypted traffic between everything else.

Istio also helps with observability. First of all, the Envoy proxies export proxy-level metrics compatible with Prometheus and OpenTelemetry. There are also service-level metrics and control plane metrics exported by Istio. Next, there are distributed traces that describe the traffic flow within the mesh. Istio can serve the traces to different backends: Zipkin, Jaeger, Lightstep, and Datadog. Finally, there are Envoy access logs, which show every call in a format similar to NGINX.

It's possible to visualize your mesh using Kiali, the console for Istio service mesh. This way, you can configure, validate, and troubleshoot your mesh, and visualize a graph of your services, including information such as whether the encryption is enabled, what the size of the flow between different services is, or what the health check status of each of them is.

Envoy is at the core of Istio. The service proxy acts much like NGINX or HAProxy. The main difference is that it can be reconfigured on the fly. This happens programmatically via an API and does not require the configuration file to be changed, and the daemon to then be reloaded. Also, Envoy can be extended with WebAssembly, a sandboxing technology. Two notable aspects of Envoy are its performance and popularity.

The authors of Istio claim that this service mesh should be compatible with different technologies. At the time of writing, the best documented, best integrated, and best tested is the integration with Kubernetes. Other supported environments are on-premises, general-purpose clouds, and Nomad with Consul.

If you work in an industry concerned with compliance, such as **Payment Card Industry Data Security Standard** (**PCI DSS**) for financial institutions, then Istio can help in these aspects through automated policy enforcement, robust service-to-service authentication, and comprehensive traffic encryption.

Istio shouldn't be used if you're managing a small, simple application or a small Kubernetes cluster, where Istio's additional overhead and complexity may outweigh its benefits. It also shouldn't be used unless you have a team capable of handling its complex setup and maintenance, or unless you require the advanced traffic management and telemetry capabilities it provides.

Using Istio makes sense if a unified service mesh plane is required across geo-distributed regions and clouds, unified access control and security policies are essential, and unified traffic management (routing, retries, timeouts) is required for microservices across different clusters. However, if your infrastructure does not require redundant network connectivity or security is addressed through other means, Istio may be an overkill solution.

Linkerd

Before Istio became synonymous with a service mesh, this field was represented by Linkerd. The original Linkerd project was designed to be platform-agnostic and targeted the Java VM. This meant that it was resource-heavy and often sluggish. The newer version, called Linkerd2, was written in Go and Rust to address these issues. Linkerd2, as opposed to the original Linkerd, is only focused on Kubernetes. Linkerd2 also integrates with OpenTelemetry for observability.

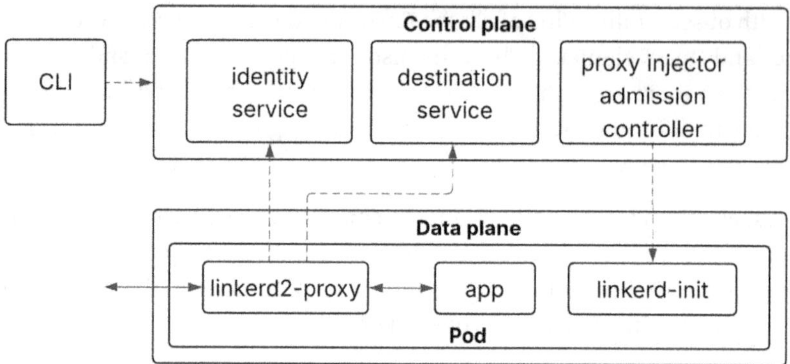

Figure 18.19: Linkerd service mesh architecture

Linkerd2 services are clearly defined by their functional domains and even named plainly. The control plane consists of three services: identity, destination, and proxy injector. The identity service provides secure service identification by using cryptographic authentication via TLS. The destination service configures data plane proxies for routing traffic, along with other behavioral configurations such as per-route metrics, retries, and timeouts. The proxy injector service automatically injects a proxy container into each Pod created.

The data plane consists of sidecar proxies that intercept all network traffic between services, automatically encrypt connections, manage retries and timeouts, and provide metrics.

The `linkerd-init` container runs iptables, a utility that configures the Linux kernel firewall, to automatically forward all incoming and outgoing TCP traffic through a proxy server.

Linkerd2 uses its own proxy, named `linkerd2-proxy`, written in Rust instead of relying on an existing project such as Envoy, which has more community support and standardization. If you need broader industry support or a proxy with a more developed ecosystem, you should choose a different tool. An attractive feature of Linkerd2 is that the company that developed it also offers paid support.

Consul service mesh

An addition to the service mesh space is the Consul service mesh written in Go. This is a product from HashiCorp, a well-established cloud company known for tools such as Terraform, Vault, Packer, Nomad, and Consul.

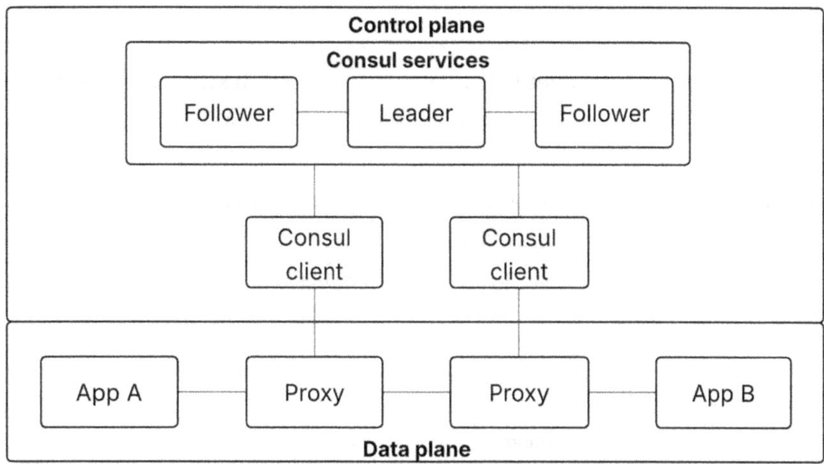

Figure 18.20: Consul service mesh architecture

Consul's architecture is hierarchical, but the same Consul agent service performs different roles. Agents in the control plane can run in either server mode or client mode.

In the server mode, one leader maintains the cluster's state, processes all client requests, and replicates changes to follower agents. If the leader fails, the followers conduct an election to establish a new leader, using the Raft consensus algorithm to ensure data consistency and prevent data loss. Moreover, server agents store service registry entries and respond to DNS/HTTP API queries, thus providing and implementing SD.

In the client mode, the agents run on nodes, interact with server nodes to perform most operations, and maintain their own small states. They lack voting rights and cannot become a cluster leader. Their responsibility is to register local services with the server cluster, report node and service health status to the cluster, and relay DNS/RPC requests to servers.

Sidecar proxies in the data plane transparently handle incoming and outgoing service connections.

Just like the other solutions, Consul features mTLS and traffic management. It's advertised as a multi-cloud, multi-data center, and multi-region mesh. This service mesh integrates with different platforms, data plane products, and observability providers. At the time of writing, the reality is a bit more modest as the main supported environments and runtimes are Kubernetes, Nomad, and VMs. The Envoy proxy should be used for production deployments, and the built-in L4 proxy for testing and development.

If you are considering using Nomad for your application, then the Consul service mesh may be a great choice and a good fit, as both are HashiCorp products.

The Consul service mesh shouldn't be used if your system is small and doesn't require complex network security or traffic management. It is also not recommended for simple applications where the required functionality is already implemented at the code level, or if your infrastructure is not prepared for the increased complexity of implementing a proxy server and control plane.

Going GitOps

The last topic that we would like to cover in this chapter is GitOps. It's an extension of the well-known **continuous integration/continuous deployment** (CI/CD) pattern. Maybe an *extension* is not a good description.

While CI/CD systems usually aim to be very flexible, GitOps seeks to minimize the number of possible integrations. The two main constants are Git and Kubernetes. Git is used for version control, release management, and environment separation. Kubernetes is used as a standardized and programmable deployment platform.

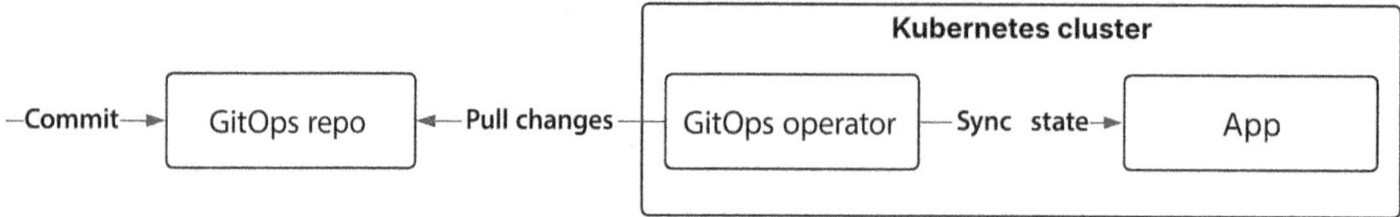

Figure 18.21: GitOps

GitOps is an approach to infrastructure and application management based on using Git as a single source of truth and continuously synchronizing from it. This enables the automation of deployment and system state management using continuous integration and delivery tools.

GitOps uses declarative configurations to simplify application state management. A Git repository contains a declaratively described state of the application expected in a particular environment. The process of continuous synchronization is necessary to ensure that the environment continues to maintain the desired state. Observability plays a key role here, allowing you to verify in real time that everything in the application is working properly.

This way, the CI/CD pipeline becomes almost transparent. It's the opposite approach to that of imperative code, handling all the stages of the build. To allow such a level of abstraction, you will typically need the following:

- IaC to allow the automated deployment of all the necessary environments
- A Git workflow with feature branches and pull requests or merge requests
- A declarative workflow configuration, which is already available in Kubernetes

The principles of GitOps

Since GitOps builds on the established CI/CD pattern, it may not be very clear how it differs. Here are some of the GitOps principles that differentiate this approach from general-purpose CI/CD.

Declarative description

The main difference between a classical CI/CD system and GitOps lies in the mode of operation. Most CI/CD systems are imperative: they consist of a sequence of steps to be taken in order for a pipeline to succeed.

Even the pipeline's notion is imperative as it implies an object that has an entry, a set of connections, and a sink. Some of the steps may be performed in parallel, but a process has to stop and wait for the dependent step to finish whenever there is a dependency.

In GitOps, the configuration is declarative. The entire state of your system—the applications, their configuration, monitoring, and dashboards—is all treated as code, giving it the same features as regular application code.

System state versioned in Git

Since the state of your system is written in code, you derive some benefits from that fact. Features such as easier auditing, code reviews, and version control are now applicable not just to the application code. The consequence is that in the case that anything goes wrong, reverting to a working state requires a single `git revert` command.

You can use the power of Git's signed commits and **Secure Shell** (**SSH**) and **GNU Privacy Guard** (**GPG**) keys to give control over different environments. By adding a gating mechanism that makes sure only the commits meeting required standards can be pushed to the repository, you also eliminate many accidental errors that may result from running commands manually using `ssh` or `kubectl`.

Auditability

Everything that you store in your version control systems becomes auditable. Before introducing a new code, you perform a code review. When you notice a bug, you can revert the change that introduced it or get back to the last working version. Your repository becomes the single point of truth regarding your entire system.

It's already useful when applied to the application code. However, extending the ability to audit configuration, helper services, metrics, dashboards, and even deployment strategies makes it even more powerful. You no longer have to ask yourself why a configuration ended up in production. All you have to do is check the Git log.

Integrated with established components

Most CI/CD tools introduce proprietary configuration syntax. For example, Jenkins uses Jenkins DSL, and each of the popular SaaS solutions uses YAML. But the YAML files are incompatible with each other. You can't switch from Travis to CircleCI or from CircleCI to GitLab CI without rewriting your pipelines.

This has two drawbacks. One is the obvious vendor lock-in. The other is the need to learn the configuration syntax to use the given tool. Even if most of your pipeline is already defined elsewhere (shell scripts, Dockerfiles, or Kubernetes manifests), you still need to write some glue code to instruct the CI/CD tool to use it.

It's different with GitOps. Here, you don't write explicit instructions or use proprietary syntax. Instead, you reuse other common standards, such as Helm or Kustomize. There's less to learn, and the migration process is much more comfortable. Also, GitOps tools usually integrate well with other components from the CNCF ecosystem, so you can get your deployment metrics stored in Prometheus and auditable with Grafana.

Configuration drift prevention

Configuration drift happens when a given system's current state differs from the desired state as described in the repository. Multiple causes can contribute to the configuration drift.

For example, let's consider a **configuration management** (**CM**) tool with a VM-based workload. All of the VMs start in the same state. As the CM runs for the first time, it brings the machines to the desired state. But if an auto-update agent is running on those machines by default, this agent may update some of the packages on its own, without considering the desired state from the CM. Moreover, as network connectivity may be fragile, some of the machines may update to a newer version of a package, while others won't.

One of the updated packages may be incompatible with the pinned package that your application requires in extreme cases. Such a situation will break the entire CM workflow and leave your machine in an unusable state.

With GitOps, an agent is always running inside your system that keeps track of the current state and the desired state of the system. If the current state suddenly differs from the desired one, an agent may fix it or issue an alert regarding configuration drift.

Preventing configuration drift adds another layer of self-healing to your system. If you're running Kubernetes, you already have self-healing on the Pod level. Whenever a Pod fails, another one is recreated in its place. If you are using a programmable infrastructure underneath (such as a cloud provider or OpenStack on-premises), you also have self-healing capabilities for your nodes. With GitOps, you get self-healing for workloads and their configuration.

The benefits of GitOps

As you can imagine, the described features of GitOps afford several benefits. Here are some of them.

Increased productivity

CI/CD pipelines already automate a lot of usual tasks. They reduce lead time by helping get more frequent deployments. GitOps adds a feedback loop that prevents configuration drift and allows self-healing. This means that your team can ship features quickly and worry less about introducing potential problems, as they are easy to revert. This, in turn, means that the development throughput increases and you can introduce new features faster and with more confidence.

Better developer experience

With GitOps, developers don't have to worry about building containers or using `kubectl` to control the cluster. Deploying new features requires just the use of Git, which is already a familiar tool in most environments.

This also means that onboarding is quicker since new hires don't have to learn a lot of new tools in order to be productive. GitOps uses standard and consistent components, so introducing changes to the operations side should not impact developers.

Higher stability and reliability

Using Git to store the state of your system means you have access to an audit log. This log contains a description of all the changes introduced. If your task tracking system integrates with Git (which is a good practice), you can typically tell which business feature is related to the system's change.

With GitOps, there is less need to allow manual access to the nodes or the entire cluster, which reduces the chance of accidental errors originating from running an invalid command. Those random errors that get into the system are easily fixed by using Git's powerful revert feature.

Recovery from a severe disaster (such as losing the entire control plane) is also a lot easier. All it requires is setting up a new, clean cluster, installing a GitOps operator (a Kubernetes Operator) there, and pointing it to the repository with your configuration. After a short while, you have an exact replica of your previous production system, all without manual intervention.

Improved security

A reduced need to give access to the cluster and nodes means improved security. This lowers the risk of lost or stolen keys. You avoid a situation where someone retains access to your production environment even though this person is no longer working on the team (or in the company).

When it comes to access to the system, the single point of truth is handled by the Git repository. Even if a malicious actor decides to introduce a backdoor into your system, the change required will undergo a code review. Impersonating another developer is also more challenging when your repository uses GPG-signed commits with strong verification.

So far, we've mainly covered the benefits from the development and operations point of view. But GitOps also benefits the business. It affords business observability in the system—something that was hard to achieve before.

It's easy to track the features present in each release as they are all stored in Git. Since Git commits a link to the task tracker, business people can get preview links to see how the application looks in various development stages.

It also gives clarity that allows the following common questions to be answered:

- What's running in production?
- Which tickets have been resolved with the last release?
- Which change might be responsible for service degradations?

The answers may even be presented in a friendly dashboard. Naturally, the dashboard itself can be stored in Git as well.

GitOps tools

The GitOps space is a new and growing one, but there are already tools that can be considered stable and mature. Here are some of the most popular ones.

FluxCD

FluxCD is an opinionated GitOps operator for Kubernetes. Selected integrations provide core functionality. It uses Helm charts and Kustomize to describe the resources. Its integration with Prometheus adds observability to the deployment process. To help with maintenance, FluxCD features a CLI.

ArgoCD

Unlike FluxCD, it offers a broader choice of tools to use. This might be useful if you're already using Jsonnet for your configuration. Like FluxCD, it integrates with Prometheus and features a CLI.

Jenkins X

Contrary to what the name might suggest, Jenkins X doesn't have much in common with the well-known Jenkins CI system. It is backed by the same company, but the entire concepts of Jenkins and Jenkins X are totally different.

While the other two tools are purposefully small and self-contained, Jenkins X is a complex solution with many integrations and a broader scope. It supports the triggering of custom build tasks, making it look like a bridge between a classic CI/CD system and GitOps.

Summary

Congratulations on reaching the end of the book! Using modern C++ is not limited to understanding the recently added language features. Your applications will run in production. As an architect, it's also your choice to make sure the runtime environment matches requirements. In the few previous chapters, we described some popular trends in distributed applications. We hope this knowledge will help you decide which one is the best fit for your product.

Going cloud-native brings a lot of benefits and can automate a good chunk of your workflow. Switching custom-made tools to industry standards makes your software more resilient and easier to update. In this chapter, we have covered the pros, cons, and use cases of popular cloud-native solutions.

Some technologies, such as distributed telemetry with OpenTelemetry, bring immediate benefits to most projects. Others, such as Istio, Linkerd, or Kubernetes, perform best in large-scale operations. After reading this chapter, you should have sufficient knowledge to decide whether introducing cloud-native design into your application is worth the cost.

Our broader goal in writing this book was to help you make informed decisions regarding the design of your applications and systems. There are a lot of things we haven't even touched on in this book, as they were extensive and out of the scope of the book. Either we had too little experience with the given topic, or we thought that it was too niche. Nevertheless, even though this book couldn't cover everything, our intent was to provide a solid foundation and spark your curiosity so that you can continue exploring and let your own experience take these ideas further.

Questions

1. What's the difference between running your applications in the cloud and making them cloud-native?
2. How can you run cloud-native applications on-premises?
3. What's the minimal highly available cluster size for Kubernetes?
4. Which Kubernetes object represents a microservice that allows network connections?
5. Why is logging not sufficient in distributed systems?
6. How does a service mesh help with building secure systems?
7. How does GitOps increase productivity?

Further reading

- Marc Boorshtein and Scott Surovich, *Kubernetes – An Enterprise Guide: Master Containerized Application Deployments, Integrate Enterprise Systems, and Achieve Scalability*, Third Edition, Packt Publishing: `https://www.packtpub.com/en-us/product/kubernetes-an-enterprise-guide-9781835081754`
- George Hantzaras, *The Platform Engineering Playbook: A Practical Guide to Implementing and Scaling DevOps with Cloud Native Internal Developer Platforms*, Packt Publishing: `https://www.packtpub.com/en-us/product/the-platform-engineering-playbook-9781837632695`
- Anand Rai, *Bootstrapping Service Mesh Implementations with Istio: Build Reliable, Scalable, and Secure Microservices on Kubernetes with Service Mesh*, Packt Publishing: `https://www.packtpub.com/en-us/product/bootstrapping-service-mesh-implementations-with-istio-9781803235967`
- LM Academy, *Helm Masterclass – From Beginner to Advanced: Elevate Your Kubernetes Package Management Skills with Helm*, Packt Publishing: `https://www.packtpub.com/en-us/product/helm-masterclass-from-beginner-to-advanced-9781837025374`
- CNCF, *CNCF Landscape*: `https://landscape.cncf.io/`
- Kubernetes, *Kubernetes Components*: `https://kubernetes.io/docs/concepts/overview/components/`
- Kubernetes, *Creating a Cluster with kubeadm*: `https://kubernetes.io/docs/setup/production-environment/tools/kubeadm/create-cluster-kubeadm/`
- Kubernetes, *Operator Pattern*: `https://kubernetes.io/docs/concepts/extend-kubernetes/operator/`
- Kubernetes, *Ingress Controllers*: `https://kubernetes.io/docs/concepts/services-networking/ingress-controllers/`
- Kubernetes at Home, *Introduction*: `https://k8sh.net/`
- Ingress-Nginx Controller, *Basic Usage - Host Based Routing*, GitHub: `https://kubernetes.github.io/ingress-nginx/user-guide/basic-usage/`
- Zesty, *cgroups in Kubernetes*: `https://zesty.co/finops-glossary/cgroups-in-kubernetes/`
- Zesty, *Kube-proxy in Kubernetes*: `https://zesty.co/finops-glossary/kubernetes-kube-proxy/`

- F5, *Kubernetes Networking 101*: `https://www.f5.com/company/blog/nginx/kubernetes-networking-101`
- Cloud Native Now, *Understanding Kubernetes Networking Architecture*: `https://cloudnativenow.com/topics/cloudnativenetworking/understanding-kubernetes-networking-architecture/`
- Helm, Helm Documentation: `https://helm.sh/docs/`
- Helmfile, Helmfile Documentation: `https://helmfile.readthedocs.io/en/latest/`
- ArtifactHUB, *Find, Install and Publish Cloud Native Packages*: `https://artifacthub.io/`
- ChartMuseum, *Host Your Own Helm Chart Repository*: `https://chartmuseum.com/`
- OpenTelemetry, *Collector Architecture*: `https://opentelemetry.io/docs/collector/architecture/`
- OpenTelemetry, *C++ Instrumentation*: `https://opentelemetry.io/docs/languages/cpp/instrumentation/`
- OpenTelemetry, *General SDK Configuration*: `https://opentelemetry.io/docs/languages/sdk-configuration/general/`
- OpenTelemetry, *Services*: `https://opentelemetry.io/docs/demo/services/`
- OpenTelemetry, *OpenTelemetry eBPF Instrumentation*: `https://opentelemetry.io/docs/zero-code/obi/`
- W3C, *Trace Context*: `https://www.w3.org/TR/trace-context/`

19

Unlock Your Book's Exclusive Benefits

Your copy of this book comes with the following exclusive benefits:

Next-gen Packt Reader

AI assistant (beta)

DRM-free PDF/ePub downloads

Use the following guide to unlock them if you haven't already. The process takes just a few minutes and needs to be done only once.

How to unlock these benefits in three easy steps

Step 1

Have your purchase invoice for this book ready, as you'll need it in *Step 3*. If you received a physical invoice, scan it on your phone and have it ready as either a PDF, JPG, or PNG.

For more help on finding your invoice, visit `https://www.packtpub.com/unlock-benefits/help`.

Note: Did you buy this book directly from Packt? You don't need an invoice. After completing *Step 2*, you can jump straight to your exclusive content.

Step 2

Scan this QR code or go to `https://packtpub.com/unlock`.

On the page that opens (which will look similar to *Figure 19.1* if you're on desktop), search for this book by name. Make sure you select the correct edition.

<packt> Search... Subscription

Explore Products Best Sellers New Releases Books Videos Audiobooks Learning Hub Newsletter Hub Free Learning

Discover and unlock your book's exclusive benefits

Bought a Packt book? Your purchase may come with free bonus benefits designed to maximise your learning. Discover and unlock them here

Discover Benefits Sign Up/In Upload Invoice

Need Help?

1. Discover your book's exclusive benefits

Search by title or ISBN

CONTINUE TO STEP 2

2. Login or sign up for free

3. Upload your invoice and unlock

Figure 19.1: Packt unlock landing page on desktop

Step 3

Once you've selected your book, sign in to your Packt account or create a new one for free. Once you're logged in, upload your invoice. It can be in PDF, PNG, or JPG format and must be no larger than 10 MB. Follow the rest of the instructions on the screen to complete the process.

Need help?

If you get stuck and need help, visit `https://www.packtpub.com/unlock-benefits/help` for a detailed FAQ on how to find your invoices and more. The following QR code will take you to the help page directly:

Note: If you are still facing issues, reach out to `customercare@packt.com`.

Assessments

Chapter 1

1. Why care about software architecture?
    - Architecture allows you to achieve and maintain the requisite qualities of software. Being mindful and caring about it prevents a project from having accidental architecture, thereby losing quality, and also prevents software decay.
2. Should the architect be the ultimate decision-maker in an Agile team?
    - No. Agile is about empowering the whole team. An architect brings their experience and knowledge to the table, but if a decision has to be accepted by the whole team, the team should own it, not just the architect. Considering the needs of stakeholders is also of great importance here.
3. How is the **single responsibility principle** (**SRP**) related to cohesion?
    - Following the SRP leads to better cohesion. If a component has multiple responsibilities, it usually becomes less cohesive. In such instances, it's best to just refactor it into multiple components, each having a single responsibility. This way, we increase cohesiveness, so the code becomes easier to understand, develop, and maintain.
4. In what phases of a project's lifetime can it benefit from having an architect?
    - An architect can bring value to a project from its inception until the time it goes into maintenance. The most value can be achieved during the early phases of the project's development, as this is where key decisions about how it should look will be taken. However, this doesn't mean that architects cannot be valuable during development. They can keep the project on the right course and on track. By aiding decisions and overseeing the project, they ensure that the code doesn't end up with accidental architecture and is not subject to software decay.
5. What's the benefit of following the SRP?
    - Code that follows the SRP is easier to understand and maintain. This also means that it has fewer bugs.

Chapter 2

1. What are the traits of a RESTful service?
    - Obviously, the use of REST APIs.
    - Statelessness: Each request contains all the data required for its processing. Remember, this doesn't mean that RESTful services cannot use databases—quite the opposite.
    - Using optional cookies or tokens on the client side instead of keeping sessions on the server side.
2. What toolkit can you use to aid you in creating a resilient distributed architecture?
    - Chaos Mesh, Chaos Monkey, Gremlin, Harness Chaos Engineering, LitmusChaos.
3. Should you use centralized storage for your microservices? Why/why not?
    - Microservices should use decentralized storage. Each microservice should choose the storage type that suits it best, as this leads to increased efficiency and scalability.
4. When should you write a stateful service instead of a stateless one?
    - Only when it's not reasonable to have a stateless one and you won't need to scale. For instance, when the client and service have to keep their state in sync or when the state to send would be enormous.
5. How does a broker differ from a mediator?
    - A mediator "mediates" between services, so it needs to know how to process each request. A broker only knows where to send each request, so it's a lightweight component. It can be used to create a **publisher–subscriber** (**pub–sub**) architecture.
6. What is the difference between an *N*-tier and an *N*-layer architecture?
    - Layers are logical and specify how you organize your code. Tiers are physical and specify how you run your code. Each tier has to be separated from others, by being run either in a different process or even on a different machine.
7. How should you approach replacing a monolith with a microservice-based architecture?
    - Incrementally. Carve small microservices out of the monolith. You can use the strangler pattern described in *Chapter 4, Architectural and System Design Patterns*, to help you with this.

Chapter 3

1. What are quality attributes?
    - Traits, or qualities, that a system may have. Often called *ilities*, as many of them have this postfix in their names—for instance, portability.

2. What sources should be used when gathering requirements?
    - The context of your system, existing documentation, and the system's stakeholders.
3. How can you tell whether a requirement is architecturally significant?
    - **Architecturally significant requirements** (**ASRs**) often require a separate software component, impact a large part of the system, are hard to achieve, and/or force you to make trade-offs.
4. How should you document graphically the functional requirements various parties may have regarding your system?
    - By preparing a use case diagram.
5. When is development view documentation useful?
    - In cases where you're developing a large system with many modules and need to communicate global constraints and common design choices to all the software teams.
6. How can you automatically check whether your code's API documentation is out of date?
    - Doxygen has built-in checks, including warnings about mismatches between the function signatures and their parameters in comments.
7. How can you indicate on a diagram that a given process is handled by different components of the system?
    - Use one of the UML interaction diagrams for this purpose. Sequence diagrams are a good choice, although communication diagrams can be fine in certain scenarios as well.

Chapter 4

1. What is event sourcing?
    - This is an architectural pattern that relies on keeping track of events that change the state of the system instead of keeping track of the state **per se**. It brings benefits such as lower latency, free audit logs, and debuggability.
2. What are the common practical consequences of the CAP and PACELC theorems?
    - As network partitions happen, if you want a distributed system, you'll need to choose between consistency, availability, and latency. In cases of partitions, you can return stale data, return an error, or risk timeouts.
3. What can you use Netflix's Chaos Monkey for?
    - It can help you prepare for unexpected downtime of your services.
4. Where can caching be applied?
    - Either on your client's side, in front of web servers, databases, or applications, or on a host near your potential client, depending on your needs.

5. How do you prevent your app from going down when a whole data center does?
   - By deploying the application across **geographical nodes (geodes)** in multiple regions.
6. Why use an API gateway?
   - To simplify client code, as it doesn't need to hardcode the addresses of your service instances.
7. How can Envoy help you achieve various architectural goals?
   - It aids your system's fault tolerance by providing backpressure, circuit breaking, automatic retries, and outlier detection
   - It aids deployability by allowing canary releases and blue-green deployments
   - It also offers load balancing, tracing, monitoring, and metrics

Chapter 5

1. How can you ensure that each file of your code that's open will be closed when no longer in use?
   - By using the RAII idiom—for instance, by using `std::fstream` (input/output file stream) classes, which automatically close files when they go out of scope.
2. When should you use raw pointers (not encapsulated in smart pointers) in C++ code?
   - The use of smart pointers does not conflict with the use of raw pointers as long as the latter *use* objects rather than *own* them. *Don't allow multiple smart pointers to own the same resource*. Raw pointers should be used in small blocks of code with limited scope, helper functions, and loops. This could also be either a third-party library or performance-critical code.
3. What is a deduction guide?
   - A way of telling the compiler what parameters it should deduce for a template. They can be implicit or user-defined.
4. When should you use `std::optional` and `gsl::not_null`?
   - The former is for cases where we want to pass the contained value around. The latter just passes the pointer to it. Also, the former can be empty, while the latter will always point to an object.
5. When should you use `std::optional` and `std::expected`?
   - `std::expected` allows acting upon detailed error information, giving more control over the execution than `std::optional`.

6. When should you use `const`, `constexpr`, `consteval`, and `constinit`?

    - The `const` keyword declares a variable as constant. The `constexpr` keyword declares that a variable or function is a constant expression and can be evaluated at compile time whenever possible. `Constexpr` variables are implicitly `const`. The `consteval` keyword enforces constant evaluation and marks immediate functions that must be evaluated at compile time, and any call to such a function results in a compile-time constant expression. The `constinit` keyword enforces constant initialization that guarantees that a static or thread-local variable is initialized before any dynamic initialization happens, thus preventing the static initialization order fiasco, but the variables themselves may not be `const`.

7. How are range algorithms different than views?

    - Algorithms are eager, while views are lazy. Algorithms also allow the use of projections.

8. How can you constrain your type by doing more than just specifying the concept's name when you're defining a function?

    - By using a `requires` clause.

Chapter 6

1. What are the rules of three, five, and zero?

    - The rules of three, five, and zero in C++ are guidelines for resource management in C++ classes. The rule of three (pre-C++11) states that if a class implements a destructor, a copy constructor, or a copy assignment operator, then it will most likely explicitly define all three. This is crucial when the class directly manages a resource, since copy operations can result in double-free errors or memory leaks without implementing all three member functions. The rule of five (since C++11) extends the rule of three by including a move constructor and move assignment operator. It allows classes to benefit from move semantics by avoiding unnecessary copying. The rule of zero is the opposite and suggests that if a class doesn't manage resources directly, then it probably doesn't need any of these functions at all and shouldn't implement any of them. So, such a class delegates resource ownership to other classes.

2. When do we use niebloids versus hidden friends?

    - Niebloids "disable" ADL, while hidden friends rely on it to be found. The former can therefore speed up compilation (fewer overloads to consider), while the latter can help you implement customization points.

3. How can array interfaces be improved to be more production-ready?

    - `begin` and `end`, along with their constant and reverse equivalents, should be added so the array can be used like a proper container. Traits such as `value_type`, `pointer`, and `iterator` can be useful for reusing the array type in generic code. Sprinkling the members with `constexpr` and `noexcept` could aid safety and performance. A `const` overload of `operator[]` would also help.

4. What are fold expressions?

    - Expressions that fold, or reduce, a parameter pack over a binary functor. In other words, statements that apply a given operation to all the passed variadic template arguments so that a single value (or `void`) is produced.

5. When shouldn't you use static polymorphism?

    - When you need to provide the consumers of your code with a way to add more types at runtime.

6. What facilities does C++ have for placing objects in a pre-allocated buffer? What are the reasons for this?

    - Memory arenas and the placement new operator. Memory arenas help with performance, memory locality, and simplified memory management. The placement new operator is used as an optimization to avoid reallocating memory every time you need a new instance.

7. How can we save on one more allocation in the winking out example?

    - By avoiding the resizing of the vector when adding elements.

Chapter 7

1. What's the difference between installing and exporting your targets in CMake?

    - Exporting means the targets will be available for other projects that try to find your package, even if your code is not installed. CMake's package registry can be used to store data about the locations of the exported targets. The binaries never leave the build directory. Installation requires copying the targets somewhere and, if it's not a system directory, setting up paths to the config files or the targets themselves.

2. How do you make your template code compile faster?

    - By following the Rule of Chiel.

3. How can we ensure we force a specific C++ standard in CMake?

    - By calling `set_target_properties(our_target PROPERTIES CXX_STANDARD our_required_cxx_standard CXX_STANDARD_REQUIRED YES CXX_EXTENSIONS NO)`.

4. How would you build documentation in CMake and ship it along with your DEB and RPM packages?

    - By creating a target to generate the documentation, as described in *Chapter 3, Functional and Nonfunctional Requirements*, installing it to `CMAKE_INSTALL_DOCDIR`, and then making sure the path is not specified in the `CPACK_RPM_EXCLUDE_FROM_AUTO_FILELIST` variable.

Chapter 8

1. How do you use multiple compilers with Conan?

    - Use Conan profiles.

2. What would you do if you'd like to compile your Conan dependencies with the pre-C++11 GCC ABI?

    - Set `compiler.libcxx` to `libstdc++` instead of `libstdc++11`.

3. What is the purpose of using `conanfile.txt` and `conanfile.py`?

    - The `conanfile.txt` file is a simplified version of the more flexible `conanfile.py`. While the former is suitable for basic dependency management and consumption, the latter is aimed at creating packages and expressing conditional requirements.

4. Which approach is used in Conan to test packages?

    - Conan tests packages using a dedicated `test_package` folder and a `test()` method within its `conanfile.py`.

5. Why is the `exports_sources` attribute or `export_sources` method declared in `conanfile.py`?

    - It declares the set of files that should be exported together with the recipe and will be available to generate the package.

Chapter 9

1. What flaws do header files have, and how do modules resolve them?

    - The flaws of header files are slow compilation, ODR violations, macro conflicts, and name conflicts because the order of inclusion matters, and they have weak encapsulation. Modules improve dependency management and encapsulation, provide clearly defined interfaces, reduce compilation times, and make large projects easier to manage.

2. What approaches to code organization do modules support?

    - C++ organizes modules into logical units. They consist of public module interface units and private module implementation units. Module decomposition is achieved using module partitions and submodules.

3. How is `import X` different than `import <X>`?

    - The latter allows macros from the imported `<x>` header to be visible.

Chapter 10

1. What is the base layer of the testing pyramid?
    - Unit tests.
2. What kinds of non-functional tests are there?
    - Performance, endurance, security, availability, integrity, and usability.
3. What is the name of the famous method for root cause analysis?
    - 5 whys
4. Is it possible to test the compile-time code in C++?
    - Yes, for example, using `static_assert`.
5. What should you use when you're writing unit tests for code with external dependencies?
    - Test doubles such as mocks, spies, dummies, fakes, and stubs.
6. What is the role of unit tests in continuous integration/continuous deployment?
    - They are the basis of a gating mechanism and act as an early warning feature.
7. What are some tools that allow you to test infrastructure code?
    - Serverspec, Testinfra, Goss.
8. Is it a good idea to access the class's private attributes and methods in a unit test?
    - You should design classes in such a way that you never have to access their private attributes directly.

Chapter 11

1. In what ways does continuous integration save time during development?
    - It allows you to catch bugs earlier and fix them before they enter production.
2. Do you require separate tools to implement continuous integration and continuous deployment?
    - The pipelines are usually written using a single tool; multiple tools are used for actual testing and deployment.
3. When does it make sense to perform a code review in a meeting?
    - When an asynchronous code review is taking too long.
4. What tools can you use to assess the quality of your code during continuous integration?
    - Tests, static analysis.
5. Who participates in specifying behavior-driven development scenarios?
    - Developers, QA, and the business.

6. When would you consider using immutable infrastructure? When would you rule it out?
    - It is best used with stateless services or services that can outsource storage using a database or network storage. It is not suitable for stateful services.
7. How would you characterize the differences between Ansible, Packer, and Terraform?
    - Ansible is designed for the configuration management of existing **virtual machines (VMs)**, Packer is for building cloud VM images, and Terraform is for building the cloud infrastructure (such as networks, VMs, and load balancers).

Chapter 12

1. Why is security important in modern systems?
    - Modern systems are typically connected to a network and are therefore potentially vulnerable to external attacks.
2. What are some challenges of concurrency?
    - Code is harder to design and to debug. Update problems may arise.
3. What are the C++ Core Guidelines?
    - Best practices that document how to build C++ systems.
4. What's the difference between secure coding and defensive coding?
    - Secure coding offers robustness to end users, whereas defensive coding offers robustness to interface consumers.
5. How can you check whether your software contains known vulnerabilities?
    - By using a CVE database or an automated scanner such as OWASP Dependency-Check or Snyk.
6. What's the difference between static and dynamic analysis?
    - Static analysis is performed on source code without executing it. Dynamic analysis requires execution.
7. What's the difference between static and dynamic linking?
    - With static linking, the executable contains all the code necessary to run the application. With dynamic linking, some parts of the code (the dynamic libraries) are shared between different executables.
8. How can you use the compiler to fix security problems?
    - Modern compilers include sanitizers that check for certain flaws.
9. How can you implement security awareness in your continuous integration pipeline?
    - By using automated tools that scan for vulnerabilities and perform all kinds of static and dynamic analysis.

Chapter 13

1. What can we learn from the performance results from this chapter's microbenchmarks and profiling?

    - The fact that a binary search is a lot faster than a linear search, even if the number of elements to check is not that high. This means that computational complexity (aka the Big O) matters. Probably on your machine, even the longest search on the biggest dataset for a binary search was still faster than the shortest one for a linear search!
    - Depending on your cache sizes, you may have also noticed how increasing the required memory caused slowdowns when the data could no longer fit in specific cache levels.

2. Is how we traverse a multi-dimensional array important for performance? Why/why not?

    - It's crucial, as we may access the data linearly in memory, which the CPU prefetcher would like and reward us with better performance, or jump through the memory, hindering our performance.

3. In our coroutines example, why can't we create our thread pool inside the `do_routine_work` function with libcoro?

    - Because of lifetime issues.

4. How can we rework our coroutine example so it uses a generator instead of just tasks?

    - The body of the generator would need to use `co_yield`. Also, the threads from our pool would need to synchronize, probably using an atomic.

Chapter 14

1. What are the properties of a service in service-oriented architecture?

    - It is a representation of business activity with a defined outcome
    - It is self-contained
    - It is opaque to its users
    - It may be composed of other services

2. What are some benefits of web services?

    - They are easy to debug using common tools, they work well with firewalls, and they may take advantage of existing infrastructure, such as load balancing, caching, and CDNs.

3. When are microservices not a good choice?

    - When the cost of RPC and redundancy outweighs the benefits.

4. How do microservices help you to use the system's resources better?

    - It is easier to scale just the resources that are lacking instead of entire systems.

5. How can microservices and monoliths coexist (in an evolving system)?
   - New features may be developed as microservices, while some features may be split and outsourced from the monolith.
6. Which types of teams benefit the most from microservices?
   - Cross-functional autonomous teams following DevOps principles.
7. Why is it necessary to have a mature DevOps approach when introducing microservices?
   - Testing and deploying lots of microservices is almost impossible to handle manually by separate teams.
8. What are the deployment strategies for microservices? What are the benefits of each of them?
   - **Single service per host:** easier to tweak the machines to the workload
   - **Multiple services per host:** better utilization of resources
9. How do cloud platforms differ from traditional hosting?
   - Cloud platforms offer easy-to-use APIs, meaning the resources can be managed programmatically.

Chapter 15

1. What is the scope of different interaction types?
   - The client–server relationship can be classified according to two dimensions: the communication type (synchronous, asynchronous) and the interaction model (one-to-one, one-to-many, many-to-one, many-to-many).
2. What are some of the use cases for message queues?
   - IPC, transactional services, and IoT.
3. What are some of the benefits of choosing JSON over XML?
   - JSON requires lower overhead, is gaining in popularity over XML, and is generally easier to read by a human.
4. How does REST build on web standards?
   - It uses HTTP verbs and URLs as its building blocks.
5. Why might REST not be the best choice for connecting microservices?
   - It may provide bigger overhead compared to gRPC, for example.

Chapter 16

1. How do application containers differ from operating system containers?
    - Application containers are designed to host a single process, while operating system containers usually run all the processes typically available in a Unix system.
2. What are some early examples of sandboxing environments in Unix systems?
    - chroot, BSD Jails, and Solaris Zones.
3. Why are containers a good fit for microservices?
    - They offer a unified interface to run applications regardless of the underlying technology.
4. What are the main differences between containers and VMs?
    - Containers are more lightweight as they don't require a hypervisor, a copy of an operating system kernel, or auxiliary processes, such as an init system or syslog.
5. When are application containers a bad choice?
    - When you want to put a multi-process application in a single container.
6. What are some tools to build multi-platform container images?
    - `manifest-tool` and `docker buildx`.
7. Besides Docker, what are some other container runtimes?
    - Podman, containerd, runc, Wasmtime, gVisor (runsc), Kata Containers, and CRI-O.
8. What are some popular orchestrators?
    - Kubernetes, OpenShift, Docker Swarm, and Nomad.

Chapter 17

1. How do observability, monitoring, logging, and tracing differ?
    - Observability is the ability to understand the internal state of a system from its external outputs, combining real-time metrics, logs, and traces to guarantee resilience. Monitoring tracks predefined metrics to understand, manage, and improve the health and behavior of the system. Logging records specific events happening in a system for debugging. Tracing tracks the full journey of a single request across multiple services to diagnose performance bottlenecks and dependencies, and for debugging.
2. What is a unified logging layer?
    - It is a configurable facility for collecting, processing, and storing logs.

3. What is the difference between pull and push models for collecting application metrics?

    - In the push model, applications actively send (push) their metrics to a central collector. In the pull model, a central monitoring service actively scrapes (pulls) metrics by periodically polling application endpoints. The push model is designed for short-lived batch jobs, while the pull model is designed for long-lived services.

Chapter 18

1. What's the difference between running your applications in the cloud and making them cloud-native?

    - Cloud-native design encompasses modern technologies such as containers and serverless functions that break the dependency on VMs.

2. How can you run cloud-native applications on-premises?

    - It's possible with solutions such as OpenStack.

3. What's the minimum **highly available** (HA) cluster size for Kubernetes?

    - The minimum HA cluster requires three nodes in the control plane and three worker nodes.

4. Which Kubernetes object represents a microservice that allows network connections?

    - Service.

5. Why is logging not sufficient in distributed systems?

    - Gathering logs and looking for correlations between them in distributed systems is problematic, because each service logs independently. As a result, it is hard to trace the path of a request. Distributed tracing is better suited for this purpose.

6. How does a service mesh help with building secure systems?

    - A service mesh abstracts connectivity between different systems, which allows encryption and auditing to be applied.

7. How does GitOps increase productivity?

    - It uses a familiar tool, Git, to handle continuous integration and continuous deployment without the need to write dedicated pipelines.

packtpub.com

Subscribe to our online digital library for full access to over 7,000 books and videos, as well as industry leading tools to help you plan your personal development and advance your career. For more information, please visit our website.

Why subscribe?

- Spend less time learning and more time coding with practical eBooks and Videos from over 4,000 industry professionals
- Improve your learning with Skill Plans built especially for you
- Get a free eBook or video every month
- Fully searchable for easy access to vital information
- Copy and paste, print, and bookmark content

At www.packtpub.com, you can also read a collection of free technical articles, sign up for a range of free newsletters, and receive exclusive discounts and offers on Packt books and eBooks.

Other Books You May Enjoy

If you enjoyed this book, you may be interested in these other books by Packt:

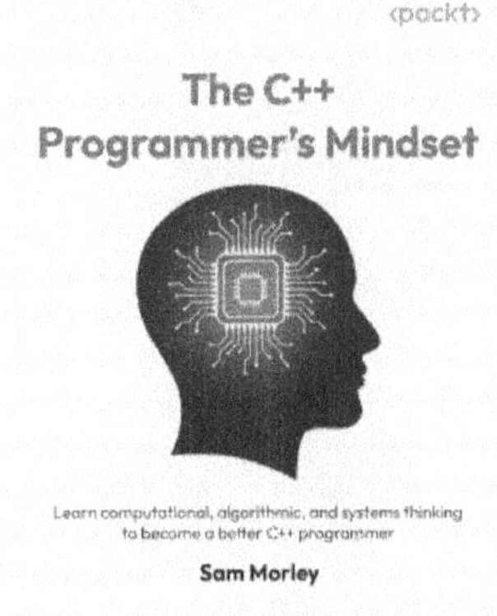

The C++ Programmer's Mindset

Sam Morley

ISBN: 9781835888438

- Apply computational thinking to complex C++ problems
- Break problems into components using abstraction
- Use algorithms and data structures effectively in C++
- Design modular and reusable C++ code
- Analyze and improve algorithmic performance
- Parse, transform, and interpret data in multiple formats
- Scale up with concurrency, GPUs, and profiling tools

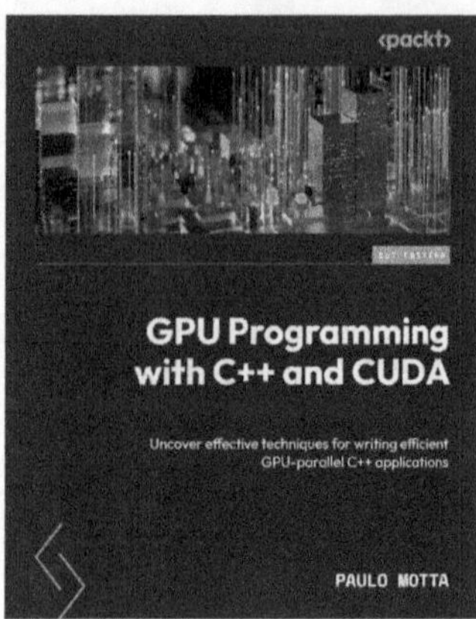

GPU Programming with C++ and CUDA

Paulo Motta

ISBN: 9781805128823

- Manage GPU devices and accelerate your applications
- Apply parallelism effectively using CUDA and C++
- Choose between existing libraries and custom GPU solutions
- Package GPU code into libraries for use with Python
- Explore advanced topics such as CUDA streams
- Implement optimization strategies for resource-efficient execution

Packt is searching for authors like you

If you're interested in becoming an author for Packt, please visit `authors.packt.com` and apply today. We have worked with thousands of developers and tech professionals, just like you, to help them share their insight with the global tech community. You can make a general application, apply for a specific hot topic that we are recruiting an author for, or submit your own idea.

Share your thoughts

Now you've finished *Software Architecture with C++*, we'd love to hear your thoughts! Scan the QR code below to go straight to the Amazon review page for this book and share your feedback or leave a review on the site that you purchased it from.

`https://packt.link/r/1803243015`

Your review is important to us and the tech community and will help us make sure we're delivering excellent quality content.

Subscribe to Deep Engineering

Join thousands of developers and architects who want to understand how software is changing, deepen their expertise, and build systems that last.

Deep Engineering is a weekly expert-led newsletter for experienced practitioners, featuring original analysis, technical interviews, and curated insights on architecture, system design, and modern programming practice.

Scan the QR or visit the link to subscribe for free.

https://packt.link/deep-engineering-newsletter

Index

Symbols

A

D

E

F

N

Q

R

S

T

U

V

W

X

Z

www.ingramcontent.com/pod-product-compliance
Lightning Source LLC
Chambersburg PA
CBHW081208220326
41598CB00037B/6716